THE SAGA OF
AMERICAN SOCIETY

Mr. and Mrs. Charles (Elizabeth Heyward) Manigault (1795–1877) and children
Charles Heyward Manigault on dog—Louis by mother's knee

Painted by Ferdinando Cavalleri in Rome in 1831

This painting is owned by the estate of Manigault Jenkins and is in the Gibbs Memorial Art
Gallery of the Carolina Art Association, Charleston, S. C.

The Saga of American Society

A Record of Social Aspiration

1607-1937

By

Dixon Wecter

NEW YORK
CHARLES SCRIBNER'S SONS

PREFACE

To dismiss Society as vanity of vanities or as a *chronique scandaleuse* is to throw away a rich segment of human experience, moulded of wisdom and folly, graciousness and snobbery. Until a Marcel Proust rises in America and refines gross fact into great art, it may not be entirely useless to gather some of these widely scattered materials along the march of our national history. Every city, town, and village in the United States has its record of social aspiration. Necessarily a book of this kind is selective, seeking to represent by certain communities and families a social pattern which is endlessly repeated.

Most of the books, magazine articles, newspaper files, and historical manuscripts which the author has used are acknowledged in footnotes and in the Note on Bibliography. But with all its shortcomings this book would have been far more imperfect without the generous help of those whose knowledge supplements the printed word. For information, advice, and other kindnesses received while he was engaged in writing it, the author wishes heartily to thank the following persons: Mr. James Truslow Adams, Miss Dorothy Arms, Mr. Lucius Beebe, Professor Samuel Flagg Bemis, Mr. Theodore Bolton, Mrs. Gerald Mark Borden, Mr. Henry Collins Brown, Mrs. O. M. Bullock, Mrs. Harvey H. Bundy, Mr. Marquis Childs, Miss Marian Cruger Coffin, Mr. Frank Crowninshield, Professor S. Foster Damon, Mrs. Vanderbilt Davis, Mr. Donald Downs, Mr. Fairfax Downey, Mrs. Alfred V. du Pont, Mr. William Esty, Doctor Max Farrand, Miss E. M. Fitzsimons, Mrs. John Farquhar Fulton, Professor Ralph H. Gabriel, Doctor W. A. R. Goodwin, Mr. Austin K. Gray, Mr. A. Whitney Griswold, Mr. Frank Gray Griswold, Mr. Norman Hapgood, Mr. Du Bose Heyward, Mr. Will Irwin, Professor Howard Mumford Jones, Doctor and Mrs. S. Fosdick Jones, Reverend Ronald A. Knox, Mrs. Nicholas Longworth, Mr. G. Andrews Moriarty, Professor Samuel Eliot Morison, Mrs. P. Randolph Morris, Mr. O. F. Morshead, Professor Wallace Notestein, Mrs. James H. Oliver, Mr. Norman Holmes Pearson, Mr. John Marshall Phillips, Miss Josephine Pinckney, Mr. Joseph Verner Reed, Reverend T. Lawrason Riggs, Sir Humphrey Rolleston, Mrs. Archibald

Preface

Roosevelt, Miss Anna Wells Rutledge, Mr. George Dudley Seymour, Mrs. Grant Simmons, Mrs. Charles Sperry, Mr. Francis B. Stewart, Mrs. Edrington Symes, Mr. R. P. Tolman, Mr. Arthur Train, Miss Constance Turner, Mrs. Cornelius Vanderbilt, Mrs. De Forest Van Slyck, Mr. George Henry Warren, Mrs. Frances B. Wayne, Mr. Thornton Wilder, Professor James Southall Wilson, Mr. Owen Wister, Mrs. Charles R. Wood, Miss Helen Worden, Mr. John S. Wurts, and Mrs. Christopher B. Wyatt. To early discussions of the subject with Miss Benicia Batione, Mrs. Charles Mac-Allister Willcox, Mrs. Charles Sperry, and Mr. Peter H. Holme the author owes much; to Professor Chauncey Brewster Tinker he is indebted for whatever he once learned about methods of research. To Mrs. Walker Van Riper, Mrs. George Cranmer, Mrs. Andrew Anderson, Mrs. Frederick McFarlane, Mrs. Verner Z. Reed, and other generous friends in the West whose solicitude sought him out in darker days, the author wishes most gratefully to acknowledge a kindness without which the writing of this book would have been impossible.

Special mention is due Mr. Charles Dana Gibson for generously allowing us to include a number of his Society cartoons which originally appeared in *Life*.

Mr. Charles Scribner has helpfully criticized several chapters in manuscript, and Mr. J. H. Chapin has been most resourceful in respect to the illustrations. To Mr. Maxwell E. Perkins a debt for wise counsel and encouragement is so great that it can be fully appreciated only by those other and better authors who have shared such good fortune.   D. W.

CONTENTS

ILLUSTRATIONS

Illustrations

Illustrations

Illustrations

Illustrations

THE SAGA OF
AMERICAN SOCIETY

CHAPTER ONE

THE PAGEANT AND FAIRY TALE

MORE than half a century ago the Swiss philosopher Amiel suggested that the splendor of Society, which in his day was called "high life," was a form of poetry. Haunted by dim memories of an age of gold, of Arcadia or Utopia, the human heart hungers for "the pageant and fairy tale" of dwelling in palaces and castles, surrounded with paintings and jewels, and having at one's call the slaves and horses and ships of kings. Those who are rich attempt to live out this dream. Those who are not stand admiringly—as near as the police will allow—to carriage entrances of opera-houses, the marquees of great doorways, and the steps of fashionable churches in June. Others read the newspapers. But one and all conspire to pay homage to the *beau ideal*—even the Communists today who throng the Winter Palace of the Tsar, and gaze with open mouth at the fallen glories of the Hermitage.

In America the fantasy of riches and aristocracy is less naïve and respectful now than when Amiel's Journal was published. The millionaire is no longer the awesome hero he was in Horatio Alger's time, and bankers' sons in the more democratic day-schools have lately been known to prevaricate—in the manner of prosperous bootleggers' children of another decade—concerning their fathers' profession. Moreover the spectacle of Hollywood nowadays can supply more glitter than a Society which has grown a trifle weary of its past magnificence and also a little timorous of its future. Hollywood's strings of pearls are longer, its Cattleyas rarer, its Hispano-Suizas newer, and its divorces bigger and better. And to some extent it has stolen the show—for that, in this era of specialization, has become the cinema's particular business. The little stenographer and the soda-clerk now thrill to what Amiel calls the sense of poetry through the medium of celluloid—where every one is eternally young and handsome, every Jack has his Jill, and the hawthorn blows white in the wood.

Yet for the multitude life among the social rich has not really lost its savor. The inflection alone has changed. Makers of metal beds, cheap cold-cream, and cigarets are hard-headed realists—not sentimentalists trying to bolster the tottering prestige of Park Avenue. And editors of tabloids well know that John Pierpont Morgan, John Jacob Astor VI, Doris Duke Cromwell, Mrs. Reginald Vanderbilt, and Barbara von Haugwitz-Reventlow, along with the kings of Europe reigning or cashiered, at times allure the public more powerfully than all the cinema stars together. Aside from the fact of their greater financial resources, they stir in the commonalty a special curiosity which puppets of amusement cannot evoke. For several of them at any rate still attempt to maintain private lives, and these are the best quarry. A hedge is always a challenge, and flight provocative of pursuit. Today then in the United States public attitude toward the rich and the socially august—popularly regarded as identical—is one of inquisitiveness rather than reverence. It is not unlike the attitude toward prize-fighters, Olympic athletes, and quintuplets—equal testaments to the prodigality of luck and Nature.

One would like to think with Henry Dwight Sedgwick, threnodist for the vanishing cult of gentlemen, that "the women in a suburban train, reading of clubmen and social leaders" are groping at the bottom of a ladder of spiritual aspiration which leads upward to hero-worship, religious veneration, and even the Platonic idea of absolute beauty. This was the attractive theory of Matthew Arnold, who held that "the refinement of an aristocracy may be precious and educative to a raw nation" too prone to order its life according to the narrow vulgarisms of the middle class. Americans before Mr. Sedgwick have voiced the same hope. During the first growth of industrialism Cooper wrote in *The Redskins* that "a landed gentry is precisely what is most needed for the higher order of civilization, including manners, tastes, and the minor principles, and is the very class which if reasonably maintained and properly regarded, would do the most good at the least risk of any social caste known." James Russell Lowell praised the enrichment of life and art through hereditary wealth in Boston, most stable perhaps of all social and financial coteries. The late Major Henry Lee Higginson in giving to Harvard College the grounds now known as Soldiers Field, conceded that democracy and socialism having got fast hold of the world would dominate the future, and therefore called upon those with social background, knowledge, and cultivation faithfully to help the new masters of the world rule "more wisely and more humanely than the kings and nobles have done. Our chance is *now*—before the country is full and the struggle for bread becomes intense. I would have the gentlemen of this country lead the new men, who are trying to become gentlemen, in their gifts and in their efforts to promote education." These are wise and generous though belated words which make a victory of defeat, and suggest perhaps a way in which Jerusalem may yet be builded here amid these dark Satanic mills.

The late years of economic tension have demonstrated to everybody certain painful weaknesses in the fabric of American life. We have attended too much to wealth and bluff indiscriminate philanthropy, and too little to the quieter obligations of an aristocracy. Today the cry for social justice has become fully articulate. The age of the predatory capitalist is gone; subtle changes in the spiritual climate have made him almost as much an anachronism as the brontosaurus. Though in the future great wealth will be accumulated, most probably it will be scattered after one generation thanks to death and taxes—which are now seen to be not only equally inevitable but synchronous. Even if by some calamity we should fall beneath the whip of a dictator in a red, black, or brown shirt, none but the most purblind idealists would expect to see the erasure of all distinctions: unquestionably there will be storm-troopers, friends of the Party or of the Masses who form their snug little oligarchy, or 'Stakhanovists' entitled to wear silk shirts because they can screw ten instead of nine thousand bolts a day in a belt of tractors. Absolute equality is like the physicist's absolute zero, or the mathematician's theoretical point, line, and circle—a convenience in speculation.

The classic plutocrat today is no more than a bogey in the Marxist nursery. In fact he has been so harassed by levies, laws, codes, public criticisms, and gruelling committees of investigation that a lover of paradox might forecast the day when a hard-bitten plutocracy, driven to its burrows, would revolt and assert the claims of human brotherhood against a pampered, effete proletariat. The distaste of the American rich for politics—noted as early as De Tocqueville and as late as Bryce[1]—has finally

[1]Of the American aristocracy Alexis De Tocqueville wrote in 1835: "As they cannot occupy in public a position equivalent to what they hold in private life, they abandon the former, and give themselves up to the latter; and they constitute a private society in the state, which has its own tastes and pleasures." Lord Bryce in his chapter "Why the Best Men do not go into Politics," *The American Commonwealth* (New York and London, 1912), vol. II, pp. 69 ff., noted "a certain apathy among the luxurious classes and fastidious minds, who find themselves of no more account than the

drawn a heavy penalty by leaving them at the mercy of a democratic electorate. This plight of the millionaire from a purely economic viewpoint is not likely to draw many tears from the impartial, who cannot regard the discharge of a second gardener or the reduction of sixteen cylinders to twelve as an essentially tragic privation. Or even the vague fear of barricades and the *jacquerie* discussed over highballs in the bar of the Philadelphia Club. Last year at the Newport Flower Show America's last great hostess—who, like the readers of the tabloids, still believes in Society—remarked to friends with a certain ethereal complacency, "Isn't it terrible? —And you know, *our* heads will be the first to fall!"

But much more serious losses would now follow the complete cancellation of that margin of sumptuary grace and leisure which America has managed to attain. Its aristocracy is on the whole not a very well seasoned one; the behavior of the rich and conspicuous in so-called Society has often been cheap, snobbish, and absurd, as the following chapters from its

ordinary voter, and are disgusted by the superficial vulgarities of public life." Among the seven reasons which Bryce saw for this disinclination, the last deserves special notice—the fact that in the United States political ambition is "wholly disjoined from social success," whereas "the fascination which politics have for many people in England is largely a social fascination." Although a senator or cabinet officer in Washington is given some measure of rank in Society—as reflected by his ex officio inclusion in *The Social Register*—a congressman, governor, or mayor gains virtually nothing in a social way from his position. The relative dullness and social stagnation of Washington in contrast to London or Paris is also observed by Bryce. Small wonder, he concludes, that the best brains and executive ability go into business and commerce, where the financial and social prizes are greater—leaving government to the mediocre and the professional politician. Of course there were exceptions like William C. Whitney, Theodore Roosevelt, Henry Cabot Lodge in Bryce's own day; latterly with Cuttings, Bacons, Vanderbilts, more Roosevelts and Lodges, and a few keenly interested laymen like Vincent Astor, exceptions appear to be multiplying. The recent gift of $2,000,000 from Lucius N. Littauer to establish a Graduate School of Public Administration at Harvard may help the new rapprochement between politics and the college-bred. As chairman of an advisory committee appointed by Harvard, President Dodds of Princeton in a report published January 27, 1937 recommended the plan warmly, and implied—perhaps not without irony—that certain brain-trusters might profitably return to college for further instruction. Yet a complete about-face, in conformity with the British and our own post-Revolutionary tradition, has certainly not been achieved. The history of American divorcement between politics and aristocracy—which includes the malodorous career of Aaron Burr, the spoils system of Andrew Jackson, the dominion of Tammany Hall, and the social repercussions of the Civil War—can be indicated only briefly in the present book. In regard to the period 1800–1840 and to a single state, the subject has received scholarly analysis in Dixon Ryan Fox, *The Decline of Aristocracy in the Politics of New York* (Columbia Press, 1919).

history may indicate. Yet its destruction, root and branch, would do little good and much irreparable harm. The distribution of a few dollars per capita and the conversion of a fleet of steam yachts into proletarian picnic-boats would hardly compensate for the annihilation, among some members of that aristocracy, of gentle manners, beautiful speech, and the connoisseurship of gracious living. Mr. Edward F. Hutton, with the arrogance of the newly rich, and Mr. Michael Gold, with the desperation of the eternally poor, are both equally blind to the ancient Hellenic wisdom of Santayana's words: "You individually can't raise the lowest level of human life, but you may raise the highest level." Beyond the clamors of class selfishness to the right and the left, two problems demand solution. The law-maker must learn to forego the axe when only the pruning-hook is needed, to employ control rather than the confiscation which would leave a denuded plain. And the rich must learn the new alchemy of turning gold into something better.

At the outset one might notice the difference between Plutocracy, Society, and Aristocracy in America. A generation ago Henry Clews, a lower middle-class Englishman of scanty education who became a successful broker in Wall Street and a noted host in Newport, expressed the viewpoint of the old school: "The modern nobility spring from success in business. The *personelle* [*sic*] of the English nobility makes a sorry showing beside that of young George Gould, the young Vanderbilts and others of our wealthy Americans." This was the day of Coal Barons, Merchant Princes, Tin-Plate Kings, and Monarchs of Finance. Bigness was synonymous with greatness, and expensiveness with worth. Although dynasties were often short—"three generations from shirtsleeves to shirtsleeves," as Oliver Wendell Holmes remarked—they sought to be as gloriously baroque as the brief reign of Heliogabalus. A château by Hunt, a box at the Metropolitan and a pair of opera-glasses made by Lemaire, a C-spring carriage and a pair of spanking bays to drive through Central Park, and a yacht with rosewood panelling and marble pilasters in the saloon were the dream of every ambitious young accountant and bond-salesman. To own them was to belong to Society. Even though one might have his moments of doubt—and surely William Black exaggerated in thinking that "the American young man spends five-sixths of his waking time in asking himself if he is a gentleman"—one gained assurance from the newspapers, and from the swarms of British, French, Hungarian, and

The Saga of American Society

Italian noblemen who had suddenly decided that daughters of railway manipulators, meat-packers, department-store owners, and patent-medicine maufacturers made the best of all possible brides.[2] It became a pious American belief that money could buy everything, whether an exit from prison or an entry into Society.

In retrospect this invasion of new wealth from 1880 to the Great War seems uncommonly crass—and as a matter of fact only those social groups which held out against it or assimilated it slowly and reluctantly, like Philadelphia, Boston, and Baltimore, or were too impoverished to invite assault, like Richmond and Charleston, can today claim even a vestige of solidarity. Cities with less traditional ballast, like Chicago, Cincinnati, and San Francisco, keeled over before the blast; as for the social cultivation of new communities which took their growth during the Age of Gold, like Los Angeles, Kansas City, and Fort Worth, one can only say as Renan did of the leading families of Bonapartist Society that "their ignorance gives one a rough idea of the infinite." Society in the metropolis and commercial focus of America, and therefore most attractive of all cities to the parvenu, New York, passed through the degeneration which more slowly has befallen the Faubourg St. Germain and Mayfair. It is the immemorial cycle which Nature recapitulates as faithfully as the life-history of butterfly or spider. A group of families with a common background and racial origin becomes cohesive, and fortifies itself by the joint sharing of sports and social activities, by friendships and intermarriage. Rough and piratical grandfathers had seized its real estate, laid out its railroads, and provided for its trust-funds. The second and third generation, relieved from counting-house and shop, now begin to travel, buy books and pictures, learn about horses and wine, and cultivate the art of charm. Epicures themselves rather than creators, they stimulate artisans and artists because they love and can pay for the performance of music and drama, and wish to surround themselves with beautiful colors and fabrics. In an astonishing way that Lamarck might have explained better than Darwin, they come in time to look like the hawk-nosed, high-domed, blue-blooded portraits of other people's ancestors which they used

[2]Alexander Mackay, a canny British journalist in the United States during 1846–47, wrote: "The Americans are almost universally known to be a sensitive people. . . . As a nation they feel themselves to be in the position of an individual whose permanent place in society has not yet been ascertained."

6

to buy. Now they sit for their own pictures, and begin to feel like Medicis. With their inheritance of the best land in the city they build regal houses with Cerberean butlers at the door, and drive about the city in black and chromium motor-cars bearing the lowest possible license-numbers. Everything about them proves that their grandfathers were in upon the Ground Floor, which also generally means the Foot of the Ladder. By this time their habits of life have become so enticing and their minority so conspicuous that emigrants from the gold and oil fields with dollars and no grandfathers begin to regard them with envy. The more exclusive their reputation, the more avid to join them do outsiders grow. The siege is almost certainly foredoomed to end in surrender, because the paths of ingress are so devious. If other ways fail, some impoverished defender on the inside is sure to play Ganelon and throw a key over the wall, or else the wooden horse of Charity is unwarily hauled into the sacred precincts. Once the citadel is overwhelmed and the aggressors have held a victory barbecue, they either tire of their conquest and move to fresh battle-fields or else rebuild against future comers the breaches which they themselves made, and the cycle is repeated. Thus, time out of mind, all socially exclusive groups have invited their own ruin.

What then is the relation between wealth and aristocracy? If any one is so vulgar as to believe they are synonymous let him go to Charleston, South Carolina, the home of the stranded gentry, and then travel on to Palm Beach where every prospect pleases. Yet as has been pointed out with great truth, social distinctions sooner or later disappear when they have lost all economic bulwarks. Privacy, leisure, cultivation, and beauty —things vital as bread and meat to the aristocratic life—are increasingly expensive in this modern world. The center of gravity must therefore always remain among the well-to-do, though possessing this equilibrium the true aristocracy will readily extend its privileges to those whose charm, gentleness, consideration for others, and good manners have persisted in the face of poverty. They bear the symbols of its freemasonry, and are admitted without having to show their bank-books at the door. The self-assured aristocrat—who can most readily be distinguished from the arrivist by the nonchalance with which he invites the world in general to go to hell—has passed beyond the servility of regarding wealth as the measure of success. Rich enough to take it for granted, or else poor enough to ignore it, he under no circumstances crooks the knee.

The Saga of American Society

At this point one begins to see the difference in texture between the stout garment of aristocracy and that fringe of its gold braid called Society. Society is the overt manifestation of caste. It is active, conspicuous, articulate, specialized. Many people of birth and breeding as well as fortune prefer to live quietly, not a little bored with the social game of ceaseless entertaining, sponsorship, and snubbing—which they are glad enough to leave to their more restless cousins, to lavish spenders, and to flashy newcomers who have done so much to bring the word Society into disrepute. To the old aristocrat notoriety is a type of social nudism, and a number of ultra-conservative families today from New York to San Francisco pay a mild sort of blackmail to keep their names out of the press, travel under assumed names, and with mortal fear and hatred flee the photographers, reporters, and kidnappers whom they lump together. Society however generally delights in publicity and novelty, though in recent years it has learned in self-defense to affect some protective coloration along with the old guard. Another earmark of Society is the extreme seriousness with which it takes itself. The seasoned aristocrat accepts social life as a passing amusement, a decorative puppet-show, an escape from work or boredom; the *nouveau* regards it as an end in itself. He never bivouacs upon the level earth, content to eat and drink and watch the stars come out, but thinks of human existence as an inclined plane upon which going upward is the only alternative to slipping back. *Ad astra per aspera* is his motto.[3] Several of America's most brilliant social leaders have risen by a career which is a blend of the national success-story with dazzling fantasy—an Alice in Wonderland written with the pen of Elbert Hubbard. Lessing observed that

> The iron pot longs to be lifted up
> By tongs of silver from the kitchen fire
> That it may think itself an urn.

From an early day the pecuniary cost of such competitive aspiration has been terrific. Harriet Martineau, that British spinster who brought her

[3] In reviewing Ward McAllister's *Society as I Have Found It* in 1890 the New York *Times* observed respecting the social leader: "The first requisite for success, as in so many other things, is intense moral earnestness. No suspicion that he is making a continental laughing stock of himself must disturb his mind or interfere with the singleness of his devotion."

The Pageant and Fairy Tale

keen eyes and ear-trumpet to bear upon the American scene from 1834 to 1836, tells of a New York hostess who staged a magnificent ball; a few days later she asked Miss Martineau if she disapproved of such extravagance, and added boastfully, "Oh, but we all live beyond our incomes."[4] It was America which invented felicity on the instalment plan. Society in the United States has never really lived down its essentially mercantile origins—to which it lapses atavistically even today by its eagerness to endorse almost every commodity under heaven, to model and wear clothes which are less fashions than advertisements, and to join hands seasonally for Velvet and Rayon Balls.

Society is therefore much less defensible than aristocracy, though the two are constantly becoming confused. In the following pages more will be said about Society than generic aristocracy, in accord with the principle that happy is the country which has no history—though the theme will be the building of any and all exclusive minorities in the midst of this the world's greatest professed democracy. That political democracy may cohabit with social exclusiveness should cause little surprise; somewhat cynically Saki wrote a quarter century ago: "Government by democracy means government of the mentally unfit by the mentally mediocre tempered by the saving grace of snobbery." The absence of an hereditary governing class has had the effect of removing all bounds from social ambition. If every boy can be President, then surely every girl can sit in Marble House at Newport. In this sense Society is more characteristic of America at large than is aristocracy; it is the symbol of a chiefly feminine achievement as impressive in its way as the Brooklyn Bridge and the transcontinental railway. But the traditional aristocrat is born not made, as Doctor Holmes knew when he answered an anxious mother's inquiries by predicating that "a child's education should begin at least

[4] With great wisdom Miss Martineau added that aristocracy in the United States "must remain otherwise too insignificant to be dangerous. It cannot choose its own members, or keep its gentility from contamination; for it must be perpetuated, not by hereditary transmission, but by accessions from below. Grocers grow rich, and mechanics become governors of States; and happily there is no law, no reason, nor desire that it should be otherwise. This little cloud will always overhang the republic, like the perpetual vapour which hovers above Niagara, thrown up by the force and regularity of the movement below. Some observers may be sorry that the heaven is never to be quite clear: but none will dread the little cloud. It would be about as reasonable to fear that the white vapour should drown the cataract from whence it issues as that the conventional aristocracy of America should swamp the republic." *Society in America* (London, 1837), vol. III, pp. 36–7.

one hundred years before he was born."[5] That at any rate is beyond purchase or enterprise, and though the social leader may raise a plucked eyebrow at the world in general she cannot escape a certain malaise in the presence of a rare old vintage aristocrat.

For we do have a few of them, and to the parvenu as well as to the democrat and the socialist, their complacency is maddening. Although they do not by any means make up the complete roster of New York Junior Assembly, the Philadelphia Assembly, the Somerset Club of Boston, the Union and Knickerbocker Clubs, and a score of similar groups scattered through the country, they are the sheet-anchor of our social ark. They belong to those organizations which are our nearest equivalent to the Order of the Garter, of which Lord Melbourne said there was "no damned nonsense of merit about it." They represent Pure Being, the *ens reale* of St. Thomas Aquinas.

Some years ago a great lady of Charleston was being regaled by her grandchildren concerning the sights they had seen in Paris. They dwelt in particular upon their visit to the Louvre, and the knot of people who were always found in rapt contemplation before Whistler's *Mother*. The old lady listened attentively, and when they paused for breath she inquired with all imaginable sweetness, "But why? After all, she was only a MacNeill of North Carolina."

[5]Descendant of Anne Bradstreet the poetess, great-grandson of Dorothy Quincy, cousin of Wendell Phillips, and son of a well-known Cambridge clergyman, Holmes also wrote in *The Autocrat of the Breakfast Table:* "I go (always, other things being equal) for the man who inherits family traditions and the cumulative humanities of at least four or five generations." He asked himself, "What do I mean by a man of family? Four or five generations of gentlemen and gentlewomen; among them a member of His Majesty's Council for the Province, a Governor or so, one or two Doctors of Divinity, a member of Congress, not later than the time of long boots with tassels," and so forth. Doctor Holmes could have found no finer justification for his requirement than the career of his late distinguished son, Justice of the Supreme Court.

CHAPTER TWO

PLANTER, PURITAN, AND PATROON

No one is more incurably romantic than a democrat, and we in America have fostered the legendary glamor of a Virginia peopled exclusively by Cavaliers fleeing the axe of Cromwell's headsman with their pockets stuffed with crested silver and a family portrait or two under their arm, a New York colonized by lordly patroons stepping off *The Little Sea-Mew* straight from Amsterdam with Indians genuflecting on the shore, and a Plymouth Rock on which was kindled the blaze of religious liberty to illuminate the world. Refreshing is the story told by Cotton Mather in his *Magnalia* of a Massachusetts clergyman preaching to a congregation in the northeast region who exhorted them to continue "a religious people from this consideration that otherwise they would contradict the main end of planting this wilderness; whereupon a well-known person, there in the assembly, cryed out, Sir, you are mistaken, you think you are preaching to the people at the Bay; our main end was to catch fish."

Idealists have often forgotten the fact that trade and the hope of better fortune were the mainspring of immigration to America during the seventeenth and eighteenth centuries, when first the Puritan shopkeeper, and later the Whig merchant, were in flower in England. Their social ambitions as well as their commercial enterprise were infused into the New World. Almost without exception the permanent settlers in America—F. F. V.s, *Mayflower* passengers, Knickerbockers, and Quakers—were drawn from the middle and lower classes, from the aggressive, the dissenter, the ne'er-do-well, the underprivileged, and the maladjusted. The aristocrat whose birth and heritage gave him a stake in the old order had no reason for uprooting himself; if indeed he visited these coasts—as did George Percy, brother of the Duke of Northumberland, Lord De La Warr, four Lord Baltimores, and a score of others—he came for riches, adventure, or a term of exile as colonial governor. As has often been said, "Dukes don't emigrate." A true picture of the origins of Colonial Society

11

The Saga of American Society

must begin, then, by expunging the pious frauds of romance and amateur genealogy.

A glance is also necessary at the social system which the Colonies inherited in a modified form from England. Voltaire compared the English people to their own ale—"froth at the top and dregs at the bottom, but sound and bright and strong in the middle." He might have added that there has always been a constant stirring by which the froth, as he calls it, is maintained. While the *haute noblesse* of France before the fateful days of 1789 was a frozen class, a sacred band whose blood was thought to be bluer than that of the estates below them, the British peerage has never arrogated to itself such magnificent isolation. The children of dukes, marquises, earls, viscounts, and barons are commoners, and so remain all their lives with the exception of the eldest son, who upon the death of his father becomes a peer.[1] Only these peers, the heads of families, can sit in the House of Lords, and even they have never claimed exemption from taxes and other privileges held by the old Continental aristocracies. And more important, there has been steady inter-marriage between peers and middle-class women, especially the daughters of able, aggressive, newly rich stock, and also the mingling of a nobleman's younger sons and daughters with untitled families. This "circulation of gentle blood throughout England" added to the frank practice of creating new peers out of the self-made—whether they be strong of sinew, as in the Wars of the Roses, or long of purse, as in the days of civic-minded brewers, journalists, and automobile makers—has been a greater boon to eugenics and economics than to the College of Heralds[2]. Only three of the more than 450 hereditary peerages now existing date from the thirteenth century, while more than two-thirds of the present House of Lords are grandsons or great-grandsons of commoners.

Such traditional British compromise and flexibility in respect to social classes is the first fact to be reckoned with among American colonists of

---

[1] The eldest son of an earl, a marquis, or a duke is known socially by the title of his father's next peerage; but this courtesy title is always recognized as such by any public or legal document, which refers to him as, for example, 'John Smith, Esq., commonly known as Viscount Blackacre.'

[2] The so-called venality of the peerage is no new thing. James I, that canny Scot, in 1610 instituted the order of baronets, each of whom was to pay £1080 for the policing of Ireland. His son Charles I insisted upon thrusting the honors of knighthood upon the well-to-do, whether they liked it or not, in order to collect the fees.

Planter, Puritan, and Patroon

the seventeenth century. Since the Middle Ages the English country gentleman had customarily left his landed estates to the eldest son, sent the second to Cambridge or Oxford to be bred to the Church, law, or medicine, apprenticed the third to a local surgeon or apothecary, and given the fourth a chance to go to London and learn the trade of weaver, goldsmith, watchmaker, or the like. Thus a strong bond unknown to Continental aristocracies developed between the gentry and the commercial classes—the ground-work for that later sneer, spread by a self-made American, Sam Adams, but mistakenly assigned to Napoleon's authorship, about "a nation of shop-keepers." These families in trade, though not technically "gentlemen" since they owned no landed estates nor belonged to the learned professions, often kept their coats of arms and a vague tradition of having come down in the world, even after generations of separation from the parent stock.[3] Hence a number of middle-class immigrants to Virginia and New England brought with

[3]To avoid misconception it should be added that the antiquity of one's social place is, according to conservative English standards of measurement, more trustworthy than merely the rank alone. Certain Anglo-Saxon or Norman families who for centuries have been anchored to the same modest freehold with its kitchen-garden and orchard consider themselves immeasurably superior to Lord Beaverbrook, the newspaper-man, or Lord Nuffield of Oxford ("where Morris Motors are made"). In fact most of them take pride in having escaped such dubious honors. Regarding the social structure from which early American colonies sprang, one might cite this resumé by William Harrison in Elizabethan times, in his notes to *Holinshed's Chronicles* (1577). He describes the way one might achieve higher status and coat-armor: "We in England diuide our people commonlie into foure sorts, as gentlemen, citizens or burgesses, yeomen [and those?] which are artificers, or laborers. Of gentlemen the first or cheefe (next the king) be the princes, dukes, marquesses, earls, viscounts, and barons: and these be called gentlemen of the greater sort, or (as our common vsage of speech is) lords and noblemen: and next vnto them be knights, esquiers and, last of all they that are simplie called gentlemen; so that in effect our gentlemen are diuided into their conditions, whereof in this chaptter I will make particular rehearsall. . . . Who soeuer studieth the laws of the realme, who so abideth in the vniuersitie giuing his mind to his booke, or professeth physicke and the liberall sciences or beside his seruice in the roome of a capteine in the warres, of good counsell giuen at home, whereby his common-wealth is benefitted, can liue without manuell labour, and thereto is able and will beare the port, charge and countenance of a gentleman, he shall for monie haue a cote and armes bestowed vpon him by heralds (who in the charter of the same doo of custom pretend antiquitie and seruice, and manie other gaie things), and thereunto being made so good cheape be called master, which is the title that men giue to esquiers and gentlemen, and reputed for a gentleman euer after." It appears then that the College of Heralds (which a short time later granted a coat of arms to newly-prosperous Will Shakespeare, the Stratford butcher's son) was, like later genealogists, inclined to bestow upon forged pedigrees a benign wink.

them coats of arms and a memory of distant relatives in the peerage—of whom they were all the more proud for being themselves the sons of woolen drapers, merchants, skinners, mercers, and maltsters.

Hotten's, *The Original Lists of Persons of Quality, Emigrants, Religious Exiles, Political Rebels, Serving Men Sold for a Term of Years, Apprentices, Children Stolen, Maidens Pressed, and Others who went from Great Britain to the American Plantations, 1600–1700*, and similar works compiled from such passenger-lists as can be got together, show the overwhelmingly lower and middle-class status of these early arrivals. Despite a sprinkling of royal governors drawn from the peerage, who almost invariably went home as soon as their term was finished, an occasional nobleman who added America to the Grand Tour, and at rare intervals a lady of high birth married to a commoner, the Colonies are fairly described by James Truslow Adams as the social cake with the icing left off. Instead of the multiple layers of British society from plowman to prince, there were only two classes in America: indentured servants or slaves, and freemen. Among the freemen certain distinctions were felt by those of English origin—in regard to breeding, learning, seniority of residence, political influence, and public service—but they were ill-defined, vague, and constantly in need of revision. In general, however, what has been called the "vacuum in the accustomed social structure" was quickly filled by the ambitious, assertive, and able.[4] Since the Norman Conquest the climber had never had so magnificent an opportunity.

In the beginning, land was the criterion of power and social position, and the wise colonist—like the first two Colonel Byrds of Westover, Kiliaen Van Rensselaer from remote Amsterdam, Thomas Smith in the Carolinas, and in New England Gurdon Saltonstall, Paul Dudley, Addington Davenport, and the Stoddards—hungered and thirsted after more acres. In those early days the necessary simplicity of life and the less potent power of gold in the midst of a wilderness hampered any other display of pomp and circumstance than that marked by the surveyor's chain. Great landowners were the familiars and favorites of

---

[4]In *Provincial Society: 1690–1763* (New York, 1927), pp. 56–57. Mr. Adams concludes: "There never was an aristocracy, speaking strictly, in the colonies and perhaps never more than a few score at most of genuine aristocrats permanently domiciled there. . . . The fact, however, that the entire population of the colonies, English or foreign and practically without a single exception, were from the middle or lower classes was a social fact of great importance."

royal governors, who not only helped to enlarge their holdings, and flattered their social vanity, but also recommended to the King their appointment as members of the Council in each colony. Rather too often, as in the case of those extravagant grants to Captain Frederick Philipse, Nicholas Bayard, Robert Livingston, Philip Schuyler, and Colonel William Smith made by governors of New York with an amiable weakness for bribery, like Fletcher and Cornbury, the whole procedure recalls the vigorous words of a later self-made citizen of the same State, Commodore Vanderbilt: "Law! What do I care about law? Hain't I got the power?"

Gradually in the course of the eighteenth century, after most of the desirable land had been claimed and cities firmly planted, the mercantile class began its irresistible rise to dominance. The Amorys, Faneuils, Hancocks, and Boylstons of Boston; the Wartons of Newport and the Browns of Providence; the Crugers, Waltons, and Lows of New York; the Willings, Morrises, Pembertons, and Whartons of Philadelphia—these merchants, traders, and shippers were the second growth of plutocracy in America, the heralds of that New World equivalent for the ancient aristocrat, the successful business man. It was a type one stage further removed from the English country gentry, a departing path which later followed the track of steamship owners, railroad magnates, steel and iron manufacturers, down to our most recent fortunes in oil, automobiles, chain-stores, and patent medicines. Yet the absence of a recognized social order or an hereditary peerage with its theory that "by their roots ye shall know them," has caused such distinctions as do exist, or are imagined, to be taken seriously and self-consciously. This fact is borne out in the history of all the Colonies.

First in point of time was the settlement of Virginia. The London Company, formed to colonize "that part of America commonly called Virginia," was sponsored by a modest roll of knights, gentlemen, merchants, and adventurers. Its first expedition, sent out in 1607, with 35 "gentlemen" listed out of 105 men, gained social luster from the presence of the younger brother of the Duke of Northumberland, who for a while was governor, but returned to England after five years. On the second voyage, numbering 33 "gentlemen" out of 120 persons, came Francis West, brother of Lord De La Warr, and with him the first evidences of European court pomp—a gilt crown and gorgeous robe for Powhatan, who thus learned what a monarch should really look like, and whose daughter Pocahontas—having found that a princess was not supposed to turn cartwheels naked before the astonished soldiery—became a Christian, married John Rolfe, was presented at Court, died of smallpox at Gravesend, but left her royal blood as a heritage to Randolphs, Morrises, Guys, Bollings, Elbridges, and Robertsons.

Of the 295 men who founded Jamestown, 92 were classified on contemporary records as "gentlemen." Most of these courtiers had at first some hope of finding gold and precious stones, under the assumption that what had befallen the Conquistadors in Peru and Mexico might happen to them, and seem to have brought with them the panoply of aristocracy. Captain John Smith tells us that those who came as "laborers" were really footmen in attendance upon their masters; and it is well to remember that the First Supply of 1608 included a perfumer and six tailors. Yet these gallants met not only cruel disappointment but frequently death itself from disease, famine, and redskins; aside from the descendants of John Rolfe, a man of petty rank, there is not a single American family today which stems from the first settlers of Jamestown.

In 1609 the London Company had been supplanted by the Virginia Company, with the more impressive backing from overseas of eight great English earls and a dozen miscellaneous peers. Lord De La Warr himself arrived in 1610 with the title of "Lord-Governor and Captain-General, by land and sea, of the Colony of Virginia," and ruled with seigniorial majesty until he was taken ill, and went home after six months. Soon the Virginia Company discovered that the colonists who throve most contentedly as tobacco planters were those recruited from the middle class, with some mixture from below. As Sir William Berkeley, crustiest of Tories, was to remark in 1651, hundreds of examples showed that no man in Virginia, however lowly his origin, was denied the opportunity to rise in the social and economic scale.[5] Of the forty-four burgesses in the Assembly of 1629—the only elective body in the Colony—seven had been

[5] Berkeley, Governor of Virginia from 1641 to 1677 save for a brief and unpopular Puritan interregnum, wrote home shortly after the Restoration: "I thank God there are no free schools and printing, and I hope we shall not have these hundred years." A significant revolt against him and the aristocrats he favored, like Philip Ludwell and Robert Beverley, occurred in 1676 under Bacon's leadership of the 'rag, tag and bobtayle.' Like later democratic movements it was essentially the buckskins of the frontier against gentry of town and tidewater.

listed as servants in the muster-roll of only five years before; in the Assembly of 1632 there were at least six former indentured servants, while thirty years later we find that 43 per cent of the House of Burgesses had had their way paid to Virginia as bondsmen. In fact, many snobs in England were coming by hearsay to regard Virginia as an aristocracy of ex-footmen and of jail-birds with new plumage.[6] In Aphra Behn's comedy, *The Widow Ranter, or The History of Bacon in Virginia*, acted in 1690, a character exclaims: "This country wants nothing but to be peopled with a well-born race to make it one of the best colonies in the world; but for want of a governor we are ruled by a council, some of whom have been perhaps transported criminals, who having acquired great estates are now become Your Honour and Right Worshipful, and possess all places of authority." Similarly Defoe's Moll Flanders, pickpocket and harlot who was sent to Virginia instead of being hanged at Tyburn, quotes this opinion in 1722: "Hence, child, says she, many a Newgate-bird becomes a great man, and we have . . . several justices of the peace, officers of the trained band, and magistrates of the towns they live in, that have been burnt in the hand." It was a slander that died hard, and caused Doctor Johnson with his stout, seasoned prejudices to remark to Boswell in 1775: "Sir, they are a race of convicts, and ought to be thankful for anything we allow them short of hanging." It was a notion as absurd as the cisatlantic theory that all First Families sprang from belted earls.

Lord Bryce tells the story of the captain of a ferry-boat plying between Maryland and Virginia who was asked for a "lift" by a threadbare Virginian. The captain asked whether he belonged to one of the F. F. V. "No, I can't exactly say that," he replied; "rather to one of the second families." "Jump on board," invited the captain; "I never met one of your sort before." The so-called First Families may be roughly divided into three groups: those having fairly close connections with the British peerage, those of more distant relationship or of sound county families, and finally those of lower middle class, plebeian, or unknown origin. To appraise all the old Virginia strains would be tedious to any save the

---

[6]As a commentary on the democratic bias of politics, Lieutenant-Governor William Gooch of Virginia writes to his brother, August 5, 1735: "The Elections are just ended, and a great many of the old Members dropt, Gentlemen here having no influence over the meaner People, who are vastly the Majority of Electors." (Unpublished MS., permission Williamsburg Department of Research.)

confirmed genealogist. A selection however may be representative.

In the first class belong a few families like Wyatt, Throckmorton, and Peyton, founded by younger brothers of baronets, lowest of hereditary titled orders. In general they have produced gentlemen farmers, vestry-men, sheriffs, soldiers, and in recent times lawyers and stock-brokers, but have played no commanding part in the New World. The present head of the Throckmorton family is a New York colonel who makes a prac-tice of rallying enthusiastically around genealogical groups like the Sov-ereign Colonial Society of Americans of Royal Descent, Descendants of the Barons of the Magna Charta, and Descendants of Knights of the Most Noble Order of the Garter. This recalls Mr. Walter Lippmann's remark: "There are no people who cling so ardently to a family tree as do those who have come down in the world."

The Fairfaxes of Greenway Court, Virginia, can claim the honor of being the one family of long domicile in America which has held an undisputed place in the British peerage. Descended from Richard Fair-fax, a Yorkshireman of the early thirteenth century, the first Baron Fair-fax of Cameron was so created in 1627. The third Baron became Com-mander-in-chief of the Parliamentary Army and victor over Prince Rupert. The fifth Baron, who succeeded to the title in 1688, married the daughter and heir of Lord Colepeper, owner of a large estate in Virginia, and their eldest son came to settle at Greenway Court. Though he died without issue, other Fairfaxes married into the Cary, the Carlyle, and the Herbert families, and the title—with a segment of the original estate of 5,000,000 acres—was kept in Fairfax County, Virginia, near Mount Vernon. Incidentally, George Washington's half-brother Laurence married Anne Fairfax. Whether, after Revolutionary times, the eldest male of the family chose to style himself Lord or Mr. Fairfax was a matter of taste; the ninth Baron, for example, never assumed his title till he went to England to claim an inheritance. His son, Charles S. Fairfax, tenth Baron, was clerk of the Supreme Court of California in the days of the gold rush, but no greater public distinction has ever come to the family. The eleventh Baron, Doctor John Contée Fairfax, was a physician; his son, the present Lord Fairfax, became a British citizen, had his title confirmed by the House of Lords in 1908, and now lives in Essex. Among the members of this family on the distaff side who have been well known in Society should be mentioned Constance Cary, Mrs. Burton Harrison, a New York hostess of forty years ago, a conservative of the Gilded Age, and writer of books of fiction and etiquette. Her son, Fairfax Harrison, is president of the Southern Railway. Mr. and Mrs. Guy Fairfax Cary, who belong to the old guard of Newport, now keep the name under social notice.

Among early Virginia families of the second class, owning more distant connections with nobility, one sees that social osmosis so typical of England. Thomas and Philip Ludwell, who came to play a distinguished part in the social and official life of the Tidewater, were sons of a mercer, who however had married a niece of Lord Cottington, noted diplomat in the reign of Charles II. Thomas Fitzhugh appears to have been the grandson of a maltster, but distantly related to the baronial house of that name. The noted Bland family sprang from Adam Bland, a member of the skinners' guild of London, but had blood-ties with a baronetcy of recent creation. Miles Cary, remotely connected with Robert Cary, Lord Hunsdon, was the son of a woolen draper of Bristol. Of course there were others whose pedigree was less sullied by trade, such as Colonel Richard Lee, from a Shropshire family of gentlefolk which occasionally had received the honors of knighthood; John Page, scion of good Middlesex gentry; and the two sons of the Reverend Lawrence Washington, whose brother Sir William had married a half-sister of George Villiers, Duke of Buckingham. William Randolph sprang from a reputable though by no means outstanding Sussex family; not until they acquired land along the Lower James River, filled public offices, and in the person of Sir John Randolph received the only accolade of knighthood ever given to a Virginian, did the Randolphs become the grandees of Turkey Island and Tuckahoe—progenitors of Edmund Randolph, called in Washington's day "the first gentleman of Virginia," of Thomas Jefferson, John Marshall, John Randolph of Roanoke, and Robert E. Lee.

These last families, which, if measured by the old English criterion of public service in war and peace, have been the ducal clans of Virginia, did not arrive with the first waves of immigration, but during the years 1641–1660—as refugees from the ascendancy of Oliver Cromwell, Praise-God Barebones, Put-Thy-Trust-in-Christ-and-Flee-Fornication Williams, and that tribe. For the first and last time in the annals of English migration to America, the fugitive was a loyalist to Church and Crown.[7] Contrary to popular opinion, these exiles were few in number, but upon the social life of tidewater Virginia they stamped clearly their superscription.[8] Superior as a class to the earlier settlers in birth and breeding, they brought more courtly manners, together with the ideal of English country life with its handsome houses, fast horses, and open-handed cheer, and the equally British belief that public offices should be held by the gentry. Usually they had salvaged enough gold and silver to buy good estates in the new homeland, and thus without apprenticeship to poverty take up the thread of their old life. Also, according to Governor Nicholson, they married most of the heiresses and desirable widows of the Colony.[9] They apparently traced the pattern of society in Virginia, which—amplified and enriched by their slave-holding sons and grandsons—became the great aristocratic legend of America.

Among Parvenus—the third class of more frankly mercantile origins, who under prosperity were quick to learn and often outshone their teachers—should be mentioned Isaac Allerton, the son of a merchant tailor, William Byrd, the son of a humble goldsmith in London (explained by the Southern genealogists as *"goldsmith:* an old expression for banker"), and John Carter who arrived about 1649, of origins unknown despite spurious claims of the family tree. The prominence of the Carter family begins in the next century with Robert ("King") Carter, so nicknamed from his proud, imperious bearing, the owner of 300,000 acres and

[7]Though Royalist refugees who took sanctuary in Virginia were frequently men of social position and means, one must guard against the assumption that a Cavalier was *ipso facto* an aristocrat and a Roundhead one of the *canaille*—a heresy to be pointed out hereafter.

[8]Professor T. J. Wertenbaker, of Virginia and now at Princeton University, observes: "The widespread belief that during the years from 1645 to 1660 Virginia was the refuge of large numbers of English Cavaliers is entirely without foundation in fact." *The First Americans: 1607–1690* (New York, 1927), p. 306.

[9]Francis Nicholson, recalled from his governorship in 1704, seems to have had a strong anti-aristocratic bias; he once told the common people that "the gentlemen imposed upon them," and informed the servant population that they had all been kidnapped and brought overseas, and hence had a lawful action against their masters. Of his successors, the one most sympathetic to aristocracy was the celebrated Colonel Alexander Spotswood, appointed governor in 1710—whose mansion was famous for its brilliant receptions, balls, and dinners, and who in 1716 in a spirit of chivalric adventure and fun organized a company of young knights errant, later dubbed "the Knights of the Golden Horseshoe," to explore the Blue Ridge Mountains.

1000 negro slaves, an iron-works and a flour-mill—who studied law and music, and collected a library of 1500 volumes, and about 1725–32 built Nomini Hall, of brick covered with mortar, pure white from the exterior, with a ballroom thirty feet long, which became the social capital of Westmoreland County.

Although Virginia Society was something like a truncated pyramid, with no class above that of the country squire, such discriminations as existed were treated very tenderly. As early as 1623 a law had been passed exempting "persons of quality" from the whipping usually inflicted for certain offences, since they were "not fit to undergo corporal punishment"; instead a fine was generally levied. The respect accorded to leading citizens is shown in the case of Humphrey Chamberlaine, a stranger of good birth, who in 1685 unluckily got into a quarrel with the first Colonel Byrd and drew his sword; he was clapped into jail by the horrified sheriff, and when he sought to escape a heavy fine on the ground that he was a newcomer, was rebuked by the justices, who declared that "no stranger, especially an English gentleman, would be insensible of ye respect and reverence due to so honorable a person" as the Colonel. Even of course, if he were only a goldsmith's son who had risen to the zenith within twenty years. If a man had two titles he was generally given the benefit of both: thus in the records of Lower Norfolk County we find such combinations as "Lieutenant Thomas Willoughby, gentleman." The ranking title in Virginia was that of "Esquire," reserved exclusively for members of the Council, the provincial equivalent of the House of Lords, while the governor, secretary, auditor, and treasurer were addressed also as "Honorable." "Mr." and "Gent." were not only claimed tenaciously during life, but were customarily carved upon tombstones. Here there was no such attempt, however, as in New England to regulate clothes as social badges or impose fines upon those who tried to dress beyond that station in life to which it had pleased God to call them; John Pory writes: "Our cow-keeper in Jamestown on Sundays goes accoutred in fresh flaming silk, and the wife of one in England that had professed the black art, not of a scholar, but of a collier of Croyden, wears her rough beaver hat with a fair pearl hatband and a silken suit thereto correspondent."

Till well after 1700 it may safely be said that there was not a gentleman of leisure in Virginia or in fact the whole of North America, unless, as Mr. Adams observes, "he were a jailbird or a redskin."[10] But in the course of the next quarter century several important events took place which gave the planter of Virginia, Maryland, and the Carolinas that relief from toil, or the personal supervision of it, which meant cultivation of the arts of living and social intercourse, as well as an increasing snobbishness of class. First was the introduction of slavery by "the Saints of New England," as the second Colonel Byrd ironically called them in 1736, who "import so many Negroes hither that I fear the Colony will some time or other be Confirmed by the name of New Guinea." Slavery placed a stigma hitherto unknown upon working with the hands, and also drove a sharp cleavage between even the modest owner of one or two slaves, and the farmer or mechanic who did everything for himself.[11] The poor white, that plague of the Southern aristocracy, was thus created; if a commoner had spirit he usually packed his tools and moved beyond the mountains toward the frontier—which, steadily advancing westward, for more than a century took up the slack of an underprivileged and disgruntled demos. Furthermore, hardships in Central Europe which followed the Thirty Years' War sent throngs of lower and middle class Germans to America, along with boatloads of poor Irish fleeing famine, smallpox epidemics, the sheep rot, and the evils of absentee landlordism which were emptying the Deserted Village. Although for religious reasons they gravitated to Maryland and Pennsylvania, yet throughout all the middle colonies they helped create a tenant farmer class removed by an infinite social chasm from masters like Dulany and Carroll.

The quarter-century from 1740 to 1765 saw the greatest florescence of luxury which this land had ever known—silks, jewels, gold and silver plate, French and Spanish wines, portrait-painting, carriages from London, horse-racing for high stakes, fox-hunts, concerts, balls and plays in the theatres at Williamsburg and Charleston—a social manifestation so widespread and competitive that it can be compared only to the Gilded Age three decades before the Great War. People of means felt no need

[10]*The Epic of America* (Boston, 1931), p. 37. He cites a contemporary report from Maryland which remarks that "the Son works as well as the Servant, so that before they eat their bread they are commonly taught how to earn it."

[11]One instance out of many is the remark of the Duke de la Rochefoucauld, visiting America in 1796, that in Virginia the taste for reading and study is greater among men of the upper class (*la première classe*) than anywhere else in America. But, he adds, the ignorance of the common people there is also unparalleled.

to affect that later republican simplicity which became fashionable and perhaps expedient, after revolutions in America and France. The deluge had not yet come. It was a movement begun, generally speaking, by a second-generation aristocracy, poised midway between their frugal fathers and reckless heirs to follow—those prodigals who, like Henry Vassall of Cambridge and the third William Byrd of Westover, often completed the return to impoverishment thanks to the bottle and the gaming-table.

Meanwhile the mould of fashion was indisputably the Virginian or the Carolinian, celebrated not only for elegance in dress, speech, dining, and sport, but also for that graceful lotus-eating in a land where the abundance of nature had made hard work seem almost an act of ingratitude. Félix de Beaujour in the course of his travels later observed: "A Bostonian would seek his fortune in the bottom of hell, but a Virginian would not go four steps for it." Furthermore, sectional snobbery was already in the air: Virginians begin to bring home tidings that the ladies of Philadelphia are "homely, hard favored, and sour," and another citizen of the Old Dominion calls the Scotch-Irish "a spurious race of mortals," while farther south dwellers in Charleston were already coming to despise the tar-heels of their sister-colony. The late President Alderman of the University of Virginia voiced an immemorial attitude when he pleasantly observed, "I come from North Carolina, that lowly valley between twin-peaks of conceit." Long before the initials F. F. V. were popularized early in the nineteenth century, the family pride for which they stood was proverbial. The type seems to have changed little up to the Civil War; and in 1853 in a book by Joseph G. Baldwin we find this timeless sketch of the Virginian:

How far back he traced his lineage I do not remember, but he had the best blood of both worlds in his veins; sired high up on the paternal side by some Prince or Duke, and dammed on his mother's side by one or two Pocahontases. . . . The Virginian is a magnanimous man. He never throws up to a Yankee the fact of his birthplace. He feels on the subject as a man of delicacy feels in alluding to a rope in the presence of a person, one of whose brothers "stood upon nothing and kicked at the United States," or to a female indiscretion, where there has been some scandal concerning the family. So far do they carry this refinement, that I have known one of my countrymen, on occasion of a Bostonian owning where he was born, generously protest that he had never heard of it before.

But he adds that the Virginian excels in all the social arts—in getting up a good dinner, a picnic, or a fish fry, in promoting horse-races and fox-hunts, in mixing juleps or an apple toddy with nutmeg on top, and also in the strategy of "filling up of the chinks of conversation with small fugitive observations, the supplying the hooks and eyes that kept the discourse together." Unlike most of his compatriots, who knew nothing but trade and commerce, the Virginian had a fund of social small-talk.

America, without the cult of the Virginia planter in the eighteenth century, would have been appreciably more gray and barren. For one thing, with all his vanities he had taste. Frequently he had gone to Eton, Winchester, Oxford, Cambridge, or the Middle Temple for his schooling; he often had had his fling as a gay young buck in London— the London of the Chevalier de Grammont in the Restoration, or the coffee-house wits in the days of Queen Anne—and perhaps he had taken in Paris and Rome on the Grand Tour. Then he had come home with trunkfuls of books, silk shirts, and claret-colored waistcoats of the newest cut, to a social round which comprised hunting his own pack of hounds, playing cricket in the green meadows along the Potomac, ogling young ladies in the boxes of the theatre at Williamsburg, or dancing with them at the winter Assemblies. The bonds with the Mother Country had always been very close. In 1661 the Virginia Assembly moved to improve postal service from England, whence letters, pamphlets, books, and all the diet of social and intellectual curiosity were drawn; a little later a regular packet line was established, and continued till 1782, between Falmouth and the Southern ports. Commerce and social intercourse followed the same sea-lanes. The Reverend Hugh Jones in 1724, in *The Present State of Virginia,* observed: "The habits, life, customs, computations, etc., of the Virginians are much the same as about London, which they esteem their home." Yet to suppose that Virginia rivalled or excelled the highest sumptuary standards of England—as fiction writers have sometimes led us to assume—is another pleasant embellishment of fact. At best it was a provincial imitation of country life lived at Chatsworth or Blenheim in that most extravagant period of English society when, as Horace Walpole tells us, an income of £20,000 a year barely sufficed to keep up appearances. The Virginia planter might challenge comparison in luxury and sophistication with a squire of the Midlands, but he could scarcely vie with a duke. Yet this aspiration, such as it was, dotted the plantations with fine old houses, mostly in the Georgian style, dating from about 1720 to the mid-century: Upper and Lower Brandon, Sabine Hall, Nomini Hall, Mount Airy, Rosewell, and Ampthill.

Best preserved is Shirley, ancient seat of the Hill and Carter family, and still in their possession. Its present chatelaine, Mrs. James H. Oliver, born Marian Carter, is a gracious aristocratic old lady with a twinkling eye and rich vein of humor, who has here entertained a half-dozen of the more acceptable Presidents of the United States and to whom Lady Astor is always prompt to pay her respects upon setting foot in Virginia. Although Mrs. Oliver was compelled to sell a Peale portrait of Washington to Mr. Rockefeller for Williamsburg—carefully providing that it should never leave the Old Dominion—she has continued to maintain Shirley in the style to which it has been accustomed since its foundation in 1650. Its fine old staircase, its portraits of King Carter in scarlet and long vanished belles in silk ball-gowns and young heirs in Roman togas, its splendid plate with the hallmark of silversmiths in the time of George II, its candles in hurricane-glasses, its dovecote and weeping willow, its gnarled poplars and generous lawns to the James River, represent a tradition so fragrant to romantic nostrils. The kitchen is of course some fifty paces from the house—since, no matter what the hazard of cold dishes, the gentry of Virginia believed that cooking had no business under the same roof with eating. Shirley's only concession to modernity is the presence of a Frigidaire behind a Japanese screen in its gracious dining-hall.

The daily life of a guest at Shirley in 1833—substantially unchanged since the mid-eighteenth century—is thus described by Henry Barnard, a visiting Yale undergraduate. Upon waking, one finds that a servant has built the fire, brushed shoes and clothes, and now stands ready for further orders—for every visitor has an appointed black servant for his exclusive benefit. At eight o'clock one breakfasts with the family, on a table bare except for doilies under the plates, drinking first coffee and then tea, and eating cold ham "of the real Virginia flavor" with hot breads. Until one o'clock the guest rides or reads; then the gentlemen congregate to drink grog and the ladies to chat. Dinner is served at three. Mrs. Carter ladles soup at one end of the table, while her husband carves a saddle of mutton at the other. Black boys hand round dishes of ham, beef, turkey, duck, eggs and greens, sweet potatoes, and hominy. After a round of champagne the upper cloth is removed, and upon the damask beneath plum pudding, tarts, ice cream, and brandied peaches are served. "When you have eaten this, off goes the second table cloth, and then upon the bare mahogany table is set the figs, raisins, and almonds, and before Mr. Carter is set two or three bottles of wine—Madeira, Port, and a sweet wine for the ladies—he fills his glass and pushes them on." After a toast to the ladies and the drinking of two glasses, the ladies themselves retire for an hour of music and chit-chat, while "the gentlemen begin to circulate the bottle pretty briskly." Through the twilight the dinner-guests drive home, while those remaining sit down to a rubber of whist, with a light supper and a night-cap to follow.

The evolution of the Byrds, most famous of tidewater magnificos, is symbolic of Virginia society over a span of several generations. The first William Byrd, born in 1652, had the good luck to possess a maternal uncle who upon dying childless left him some property in the New World. Young Byrd arrived in 1671, just as social life was beginning to crystallize after the Cavalier migration. He advanced rapidly as a shrewd merchant, dealing in tobacco, rum, and indentured servants. In 1673 he married the daughter of a Royalist officer who had close social connections with Governor Berkeley. Proving himself a sharp trader with the Indians, William Byrd was also addicted to life's little economies, sending his old wig to London to be made over and his battered sword to be exchanged for a new one. His son, the second William Byrd, succeeded to the estate in 1704. At his mother's desire he had been sent to school in England, and became the first great American Anglophile. He counted among his friends the Duke of Argyle, the Marquis of Halifax, the Earl of Orrery, Lord Oxford, Lord Egmont, and Lady Betty Cromwell, whose portraits he had painted and brought over to hang on the walls of Westover—perhaps, as a cynic might comment, like the hunter home from the hill. If tradition be trusted, however, he did not always love a lord above all else: his daughter Evelyn, sent to London in 1717 for her education and presentation to Society, became the fashionable toast, and

King Powhatan's daughter, Pocahontas

Robert (King) Carter, 1663–1732

From a portrait at Shirley

Shirley, Virginia

All three reproduced from "Some Colonial Mansions." Henry T. Coates & Co., Philadelphia, Pa.

William Byrd

From a portrait by Sheppard after the original at Brandon

Evelyn Byrd

In 1717 she went to London for her education

From "Some Colonial Mansions." Henry T. Coates & Co.

Westover, Virginia

The river front

was courted by the Earl of Peterborough. According to legend, Byrd objected to the character of the noble lord and recalled Evelyn, who died at Westover of a broken heart. A witty letter-writer, Fellow of the Royal Society, and thrice-appointed agent from Virginia to the British Crown, the second Colonel Byrd had none of his father's haggling parsimony. But he did inherit a land-hunger which he gratified by increasing the estate from 23,231 acres to 179,440. He also loved grandiose schemes, like his profitless venture in iron-mining. He built the second and more lordly Westover and furnished it in the best Georgian taste. A certain architectural pride is seen in his remark in *The History of the Dividing Line* about the plantations on Albemarle Sound, where "a Citizen is counted Extravagant, if he has Ambition enough to aspire to a Brick-chimney." His portrait shows a haughty, high-bred face and something of that distinguished style which led his adoring descendants to call him "the Black Swan." The third Colonel William Byrd completed the transformation from Industrious Apprentice to Rake's Progress, the orbit typical of any new aristocracy not effectually safeguarded by entail and tradition. A fine gentleman and a brave soldier, he had neither business sense nor control over his appetites. Being a wastrel at cards and a con-noisseur of horses, he came dangerously near selling Westover and did indeed mortgage the silver plate and 159 slaves. Before his suicide on New Year's Day, 1777 he passed through stormy vicissitudes with two wives, pert and frivolous Elizabeth Carter who had a passion for London gowns and lutestring petticoats, and met a mysterious end ascribed to a fall from an upstairs window, and secondly Mary Willing of Philadel-phia, whose alacrity in claiming the new widower led to the unkind nickname of "Willing Molly" by which old Virginians still call her. Though today the Byrds of Virginia possess Upper Brandon, the grander Westover across the James has long been relinquished. With its mag-nificent avenue of tulip trees, its massive stone gates, and its unparalleled prospect of the broad river, Westover is now owned by Mr. Richard Crane, heir of the manufacturer of plumbing fixtures and former Min-ister to Czecho-Slovakia. Although a replica of Evelyn Byrd's celebrated picture hangs over the fireplace in the library, the interior of Westover has almost wholly lost its former appearance, being equipped throughout with excellent bathrooms and Czecho-Slovakian *objets d'art*.

From the late eighteenth century to the Civil War the tidewater planter continued to cherish those qualities for which he gained early renown—social grace, urbanity, a nodding acquaintance with Horace and Blackstone, a dash of hot temper which sometimes led to the duelling field,[12] and a reckless hospitality[13]—though all the while he was losing money through the suicidal economics of the plantation system. The Civil War merely dealt him an heroic *coup de grâce*. Yet while it lasted his had been an attractive life.

The social milieu of old Virginia is gone beyond recall, though the architectural reconstruction of its gay and worldly capital, Williamsburg, has been possible through the munificence of Mr. John D. Rockefeller, Jr., and the astonishing skill of the historians, archivists, builders, and landscape architects whom he has assembled. The Governor's Palace on the green—a tribute to the grandeur of Governor Spotswood which first roused democratic disapproval—once more lifts its stately cupola to

[12]The mores of duelling had a slow growth in early Virginia—another proof that the code of the English aristocracy was not brought over ready-made, but rather was worked out independently under a ripening society. Only five or six duels are recorded during the whole Colonial period, but after the Revolution there is a steady crescendo, as Wertenbaker points out, *Patrician and Plebeian in Virginia* (Charlottesville, 1910), pp. 76–9. Most zealous patrons of the duel were the young bloods of Charleston and New Orleans. Dodd, *The Cotton Kingdom* (New Haven, 1919), p. 21, observes: "An affair of honor, a duel which always followed the slightest insult among men of family, was attractive to men who were just climbing to the higher rungs of the social ladder."

[13]The impoverishment in old age of Thomas Jefferson, so typical of his class, is illuminated by the testimony of his overseer regarding hospitality to wayfarers, especially to those Virginians travelling to the Hot Springs via Monticello: "I have often sent a wagon-load of hay up to the stable, and the next morning there would not be enough left to make a bird's nest. I have killed a fine beef, and it would all be eaten up in a day or two." In time the cult of Southern hospitality became a patriotic duty, though often in sparsely settled tracts a pleasure as well. Probably the most persuasive host on record is that described by an early writer on Georgia: "I have often been told of the gentleman and his wife, who, being asked to dine at a residence on St. Simon, found that during the meal a boat had been sent to Darien, fifteen miles distant, for their luggage, and that so much pleased were host, hostess, and guests with one another, that their stay was prolonged until two children had been born to the visiting couple." Q. in Calhoun, *Social History of the American Family* (Cleveland, 1917–19), vol. II, p. 336. In South Carolina, according to Doctor Ramsay, innkeepers complained bitterly that they could not make a living because to any traveller of decent appearance, with or without letters of introduction, every front door on the great plantations swung open. The actor-manager Bernard in 1798 tells of planters who captured guests at the point of a gun in the olden times, but adds that "as immigrants began to pour into the woods the planter had seldom to lift his rifle to his shoulder in demanding their society, but, on the contrary, he probably soon obtained those who required some such gesticulation to be got rid of."

the sky and shelters a richly tiled ante-chamber, great dining-hall that outstripped the best efforts of the planter gentry, wallpaper in the Chinese taste imported from London, and library of classics bound in vellum. The only building in America for which plans were undoubtedly drawn by the great Sir Christopher Wrenn once more graces the yard of William and Mary College. So keen is Mr. Rockefeller's quest for fidelity that, some five years ago, when Wrenn Hall was almost completed along the lines of a rough contemporary sketch, the discovery of a better and more revealing design in the Bodleian Library, Oxford, which showed the back as well as front of the original, caused him cheerfully to order most of the new building torn down and accurately rebuilt at an added cost of $50,000. The reconstruction in the Machine Age of this once aristocratic capital has not been without humor. The Williamsburg A. & P. store has been compelled to give up its red facade in favor of a chaste white with archaic script; while to the exasperation of Mr. Rockefeller's staff neon signs glitter occasionally through the early Colonial dusk and have promptly to be suppressed.

Both the Maryland and the Carolina planter came surprisingly close to having nobility thrust upon them. In founding the former colony, George Calvert first Lord Baltimore obtained a charter from Charles I which stipulated that his family could grant not only land to their settlers in Maryland, but honors as well, and could "adorn them with whatever titles and dignities they shall appoint." Although the Calverts always looked upon themselves as feudal lords, the planters as their barons, and the laboring class as their tenantry, they never actually erected a New World peerage—partly no doubt because the Assembly showed from early times of what democratic mettle it was made, and talked back to the Lord Proprietor himself. Families of prevailingly middle-class origin who became the landed aristocracy of Maryland were Tilghmans, Burwells, Lloyds, Goldsboroughs, Blakes, Ridgelys, Lowndes, and others. Greatest aristocrat of Revolutionary times was Charles Carroll of Carrollton, great-grandson on his mother's side of a maid of honor to Queen Henrietta Maria and on his father's descended from Irish landed gentry, the Ely O'Carrolls. In post-Revolutionary days Lord Brougham wrote: "Charles Carroll's family was settled in Maryland ever since the reign of James II, and had during that period been possessed of the same ample property, the largest in the Union. It stood, therefore, at the head of the aristocracy of the country." Educated in France chiefly because of his Catholic heritage, at home in the best society of Britain and the Continent, and worth the then immense fortune of $2,000,000, Charles Carroll enthusiastically threw his diplomatic gifts and his great prestige upon the side of the American Revolution largely, it is believed, for the sake of religious independence. With a blend of Old World manners and great personal simplicity, he never aspired to social preëminence or any exhibition of his wealth. Three granddaughters became the Duchess of Leeds, the Marchioness of Wellesley, and the Baroness Stafford; Charles Carroll's son and heir married Harriet Chew, daughter of the Chief Justice of Pennsylvania. Their descendants—though lacking the princely fortune of the first Charles Carroll, broken up save for the old Doughoregan Manor by the laws against entail—have always been known to Society in Maryland, Pennsylvania, and New York City, though they have never possessed outstanding personality or gifts for dominant social and political leadership.

When in 1663 Charles II granted South Virginia—henceforth the Carolinas—to eight noble Proprietaries, one of the most enterprising, Lord Ashley, invited the philosopher John Locke to draw up the Fundamental Constitutions which, "in order to avoid a too numerous democracy," should create a "nobility" on the basis of land ownership wholly divorced from birth and breeding. Land cost a penny an acre, and any one able to buy 12,000 acres became a "baron"; if he could afford 24,000 he might call himself by the Hispano-Indian title "cacique," while the ownership of 48,000 acres gave him the top rank of "landgrave." In practice no grants seem to have gone much beyond 12,000 acres, but thanks to a marked-down sale of titles everybody who held a fairly large grant could dub himself Landgrave Morton or Landgrave Smith.

The largest of these grants was probably that given to Sir Robert Montgomery in 1717—so impressive indeed that he was called Margrave and his domain the Margravate of Azilia; in 1732 it became Oglethorpe's colony for debtors called Georgia. But the most famous landgrave was Thomas Smith, who became governor in 1695; his son the second landgrave built legendary Yeamans Hall on the Cooper River—now converted into a country club where Northern bankers shoot ducks in the rice fields, play golf, and drink excellent "corn" on the broad verandah, to the almost total oblivion of the local aristocracy. The Smiths, it may be noted, lost their holdings generations ago and sank to the level of obscure and down-at-heels gentry, though the last heir currently styles himself "Landgrave" Smith. Locke had revived this old Palatinate title so that no New World noble, however broad his acres, could ever be confused socially with *bona fide* peers like the English Proprietaries themselves. As a matter of fact the early landgraves and caciques were rather commonplace British merchants, tradesmen, and factors. The future aristocracy of South Carolina did not begin to arrive until the governorship of Sir John Yeamans from Barbadoes; in his train during the closing years of the seventeenth century came planters from the West Indies—rich, slave-holding, Church of England men who settled along Goose Creek. They were joined by a well-born and thrifty company of Huguenots, uprooted by the Revocation of the Edict of Nantes in 1685, who brought to Charleston such famous names as Huger (pronounced "U. G."), Ravenel, Manigault, Prioleau, St. Julien, Laurens, and Legaré (pronounced "Legree," as spelled by Harriet Beecher Stowe, who may have heard the name of Charleston's rich slave-owner James Legaré).

The names of their Low Country plantations are filled with English nostalgia or Gallic poetry—Runnymede, Rice Hope, Silk Hope, The Blessing, Chantilly, Cedar Grove, Sea Cloud, Mexico, The Haze, Brook Green, Ophir, Hanover, Hobcaw, Kensington, Snug-it-is, Belvidere, Pimlico, Twickenham, Laurel Hill. Surrounded by gardens of camellias, azaleas, and magnolias, and ponds of water lilies and yellow lotus, embowered in hoary live-oaks dripping Spanish moss, these plantations were the outposts of another graceful provincial Society. Some of them fell a prey to slowly encroaching poverty when steam transportation brought the rice of China many leagues nearer, and caused the old fields to be abandoned to rushes and swamp-birds, while Sea-Island cotton became the new staple of Carolina. Others survived to be burned by Sherman in his vindictive march to the sea; for few planters had the resourcefulness of Doctor John Drayton, who saved Drayton Hall by quartering Negro smallpox patients there and spreading the report before the advancing troops.[14] Sherman's name is still anathema in South Carolina, and it is said that several years ago the pre-nuptial round of parties for a Charleston bride was cancelled when one of her bridesmaids was discovered to be

---

[14]Yet in writing his memoirs Sherman paused to praise the architectural beauty of the plantations which he fired.

a distant relative of Sherman. Some years ago Mrs. Randolph, granddaughter of Abraham Lincoln, bought an imposing old Charleston house, but she has never chosen to occupy it. Today the big plantation manors, renovated and rebuilt, have been largely captured by mercantile fortunes from the North—Hartfords, Kresses, Huttons, and Coes. In general their presence is regarded as a mixed blessing.

Colonial Society in South Carolina was not unlike that of Virginia, with one important difference—its nearer approximation to the pattern of English life because of its even sharper focus upon a social London, the city of Charleston, which drew the aristocracy away from the marsh lands and the "country fever" from the tenth of May until November frost fell. After Christmas on the plantation the family often returned to town in January for the gay season—the concerts and balls of the St. Cecilia Society, the Races, and the Jockey Club Ball. Summer then brought darkened shutters and furniture shrouded in dust-cloths—much like the West End of London in August—as the gentry began to flock to the Virginia Hot Springs or Flat Rock. Before the popularity of such resorts they had secluded themselves in their high-ceilinged mansions, embellished with wrought-iron balconies and tall white columns. Their leisurely day was punctuated by the chimes of St. Michael's, in whose walled churchyard their fathers slept—a fate more desirable in a Charlestonian's eyes, we are told, than to be alive in the more barbarous provinces. In the late eighteenth century the Duc de la Rochefoucauld remarked "that from the hour of four in the afternoon the people of Charleston rarely thought of anything but pleasure and amusement," and about the same time Crèvecoeur declared that to North America Charleston was what Lima had long been to the South—the magnificent pleasure capital of a continent. From the duelling, the reckless gambling, the high-bred delirium tremens and courtly debauchery which startled even Parisian visitors, one may perhaps account for La Rochefoucauld's surprised observation that all South Carolina gentlemen over fifty had white hair.[15]

[15]Other visitors of the era like Schoepf and J. F. D. Smith agreed that the town was "the gayest in America." By hearsay Edmund Burke reported that of all American cities Charleston "approached more nearly to the social refinement of a great European capital. "Of a later generation Achille Murat wrote thus in *A Moral and Political Sketch of America* (London, 1833), p. 14: "The society of Charleston is the best I have met with in my travels, whether on this or your side of the Atlantic. In respect to finish, and elegance of manners, it leaves nothing to be desired, and what is of more value with people who, like you and me, attach little importance to mere

Planter, Puritan, and Patroon

Gentlemen were partial to blue—the product of their staple indigo—while their wives and daughters dressed in the latest French mode as they drove on the Battery, or attended concerts and the events of Race Week. Such royal governors as Lord Charles Montagu, son of the Duke of Manchester, or Lord William Campbell of the Argylls who married Sarah Izard, found it difficult to excel the epicurism of dinners given by Middletons, Rutledges, Pinckneys, and Izards: tables set out with satin-fine damask cloths, Nankin or East India china and heavy plate, and a menu devoted to the special cult of turtle and terrapin, washed down with Madeiras ripened carefully in cedar-shingled garrets. At the Assemblies and in private houses there were Olympian suppers—boned turkeys, terrapin stew (called "cooter stew"), intricate desserts of blanc-mange and candied orange-peel, or a "preserve of fowle" (which consisted of a dove put into a partridge, and the partridge into a guinea-hen, the hen into a duck, the duck into a capon, the capon into a goose, and that in turn into a peacock or turkey, and so roasted and cut in transverse section). Little wonder that Lafayette in June 1777 wrote to his wife from Charleston that he had sat five hours at a great dinner given in his honor.

Like Virginia squires, young Carolina planters were often sent to Winchester, Eton, and the Inns of Court for education in that land which even native-born Charlestonians called "home" up to the Revolution.[16] According to a joke current at the end of the century, "they could read Homer and make a speech to explain the Constitution, but couldn't do a sum in vulgar fractions." A few were intimately related to members of the British peerage—like Pierce Butler, cousin of the Duke of Ormond

politeness, it swarms with real talent, and that without the alloy of pedantry." Fredrika Bremer commented from Charleston, June 10, 1850: "In South Carolina the spirit and the links of social life are aristocratic to a degree which I cannot approve of, however much I may like certain people there." The inhabitants were of course proud of Charleston's reputation as the most sophisticated city in America. Hugh S. Legaré, shortly before his death in 1842, wrote from Brussels, where he had entry into the best Continental Society: "I have never, since I could form an opinion on such matters, doubted of the immense superiority of Carolina society over all others on that continent, and now feel it more than ever."

[16]Lord Adam Gordon noted in the decade of 1760: "It is the fashion to Send home all their Children for education, and if it was not owing to the nature of their Estates in this Province, which they keep all in their own hands, and require the immediate overlooking of the Proprietor, I am of opinion the most opulent planters would prefer a home life [*i.e.,* in Britain]. It is in general believed, that they are more attached to the Mother Country, than those Provinces which lie more to the Northward."

The Saga of American Society

and "inordinately vain of it," and Henry Middleton who had married the daughter of the Jacobite Earl of Cromartie. Still, the aristocracy of Charleston was essentially mercantile, even as it is today when Best Families sell real estate, liquor, and fertilizer. For more than two centuries intermarriage between cousins and old clans has been spinning the thread of relationships which at present unites, for example, that patrician little band called the Society for the Preservation of Negro Spirituals.[17] Consanguinity is largely responsible for that gentle spirit of complacence so deeply ingrained in Charleston, where invitations to the St. Cecilia Ball are regularly received by certain inmates of the county poor-farm but never by Mr. Lamont and Mr. Wiggin of New York or Mr. Coe of Long Island. Charleston learned long ago the art of conserving its values, whether by gentle suavity as at present or by some more melodramatic devices known to the past—as on occasion of that misalliance recorded in Revolutionary days when "one young lady wedded the coachman. An old servant stabbed the fellow to death. The unfortunate girl (said to have been weak-minded) and her child fell to a lower social level." Much more typical of old coachmen in Charleston was the proud darkey who drove the Huger carriage in the 1840's in the early days of the South Carolina Railroad. On one occasion after frightening his white folks severely by driving them across the tracks a few yards from an oncoming locomotive, he answered his employer's rebuke by explaining, "Good Lawd, Suh, I thought everybody 'ud know the Huger coach."

Among the geographical snobberies of American history—tidewater despising the frontier, and older centers of population patronizing strug-

---

[17]This Society, which today carries much greater social éclat than the traditional St. Cecilias, was formed in 1923 by some twenty children and grandchildren of slaveholders and is now expanded to fifty. To record and keep alive authentic spirituals and the gestures and inflections which should accompany them, members of the Society invite groups of old-time darkies to a fish-fry or barbecue and get them to sing. At its own social gatherings, the Society takes a few drinks to thaw the Nordic ice, and launches into a rich repertory represented in part by the lyrics in its volume *The Carolina Low-Country* (New York, 1931). Although George Gershwin was a little impatient with renditions of the Society while gathering materials for the music of *Porgy and Bess,* it is generally admitted to sing spirituals better than any other white organization and coincident with the late enthusiasm for folk-music has given excellent concerts for Negro charity in New York, Washington, Boston, Philadelphia, Atlanta, and elsewhere. Miss Alice R. Huger Smith, Miss Josephine Pinckney, Mr. DuBose Heyward, and their friends are its leaders; one who marries a member automatically becomes a member. It is a group representative of the pleasant, informal, highly talented social milieu of present-day Charleston.

gling villages in the West—none had had more tragic consequences than that of the South toward the North. Among social nebulae which helped to roll up the thunder-clouds of civil war it was of great importance. Robert Toombs in 1860 gave tongue to a class sentiment at least as old as the days of the second Colonel Byrd when he said of the Southerners, "We are the gentlemen of this country." On the eve of the War throughout the South editorials on the same theme began to appear as thick as June blackberries; typical is this excerpt from the Muscogee (Georgia), *Herald,* which was copied by the New York *Tribune* of September 10, 1856:

Free society! we sicken at the name. What is it but a conglomeration of greasy mechanics, filthy operatives, small-fisted farmers, and moonstruck theorists? All the northern, and especially the New England states, are devoid of society fitted for well-bred gentlemen. The prevailing class one meets with is that of mechanics struggling to be genteel, and small farmers who do their own drudgery, and yet are hardly fit for association with a southern gentleman's body servant.

Hand in hand with this prejudice went the theory that upper-class Southerners were scions of Old World aristocracy, while Yankees of wealth and power were the grandsons of blue-nosed tailors, runaway 'prentices, and the offscourings of ship-yards. It was a theory cherished more tenaciously than ever after the surrender at Appomattox, the regime of the carpet-bagger, and the long years of proud and pinched gentility that followed. John Fiske was probably the first historian of national standing to point out the truth, which now seems self-evident, that the leading families of New England—Saltonstall, Lowell, Cabot, Dudley, Winthrop, Peabody, and the rest—were recruited from the same essentially middle-class stratum which had produced Randolph, Cary, Cabell, and Lee. Though the former were Puritan and the latter Cavalier, that fact alone meant nothing about their social standing in England—where, on the one hand, masses of the common people adored the Stuarts and died for them on the field of battle, while on the other the King's most implacable enemies were the Earls of Warwick, Bedford, Manchester, and Essex, banded with such ranking gentlemen as Hampden, Pym, and Cromwell. In the three Rolls of Arms published recently by that worthy company of genealogists, the New England Historic Genealogical Society, more than a hundred old families of New England are awarded authentic coats of arms—a traditional though not infallible mark of gentle birth. Whatever differences there were between the social structure of Virginia and Massachusetts sprang not from any essential difference in original rank, but from environment—plantation versus township, slavery as opposed to free labor, rich soil and mild weather against the rock-bound coast and winter storm, sympathy or hostility toward kingship in England, and the choice between sporting parson and Calvinist divine.

Well-descended Bostonians today deprecate the dourness, grimness, and bigotry of their forefathers—but they are intensely proud of them. The essence of Puritanism escapes definition. We are still a little baffled after erudite admirers like the late Stuart Sherman and Percy A. Scholes have done proving that the Puritan was not such a sour fellow after all, after so subtle an alien as George Santayana has analyzed Puritanism as "a natural reaction against nature," a kind of pedantry of the soul, and after a sophisticated wit of our era has defined it as an attitude of mind which finds adultery a greater sin than murder because murder gives pleasure to only one person. The social aspect of Puritanism is, happily, a trifle simpler. In the beginning it attempted, as the late Vernon L. Parrington wrote, to "substitute an aristocracy of the Saints for the landed aristocracy, and refashion society upon ethical rather than economic lines." With the card-playing, horse-racing, fox-hunting round of the planter it had no traffic—and in spite of its recent apologists often looked upon social gaiety in a peculiarly theological light.[18] There are distinctly morbid implications in a social scheme which led one of the leaders of public life in seventeenth century Massachusetts to amuse himself by rearranging the coffins in the family vault and speak of the chore as "an awful yet pleasing Treat."[19]

As in the case of the permanent settlers of Virginia, the first immigrants to arrive in New England—the *Mayflower* group, from which descend Brewsters, Bradfords, Allertons, Standishes, and Winslows in the male

[18]Characteristic is the close of a letter, at the late date of 1780, from Mary Baldwin in Connecticut to her brother Simeon, a leading citizen of Boston: "I think you have doubtless heard that there is a number of the french troops stationed at Lebanon they seem to be the chief topick of discourse I think now in town & I hear since I come home that the Duke is going to have a grand Ball next friday at Lathrops so as to get acquainted with our Norwich Ladys I suppose he has had one at Windham What will be the event of these things I cant say but he Who governs all things will no doubt order all things for the best."

[19]Cf. Wertenbaker, *The First Americans*, p. 281.

line, and on the female side dozens of families on the roster of the May-flower Society—were people of extremely humble origin in comparison with the later arrivals. A congregation of simple folk, born and bred in poverty, living chiefly by manual labor in Nottinghamshire and adjoining counties, who met at Scrooby for prayers and mutual succor, and then moved quietly to Holland where they were scandalized by the worldliness of the Dutch, these Pilgrims arrived at Plymouth in December, 1620. They were under the governorship of William Bradford, a yeoman by birth, and brought up to follow the plough as his forefathers had done. Of the forty-one men who signed the Covenant of the *Mayflower*, eleven bore the title of "Mr." but none that of "Gent." A group of English emigrants more socially insignificant could hardly be imagined; time and sentiment alone have given them the luster they possess.[20] Still, the rudiments of social ambition were already stirring in these earnest bosoms clothed in home-spun. Bradford tells us in regard to the failure of the communistic theory under which the Plymouth Colony was begun: "The aged and graver men to be ranked and equalised in labours, and victuals, cloaths, etc., with the meaner and younger sorte, thought it some indignitie and disrespect unto them. And for mens wives to be commanded to doe servise for other men, as dressing their meate, washing their cloaths, etc., they deemd it a kind of slaverie, neither could many husbands well brooke it." As in all human groups, social distinctions were bound to appear, on the basis of age if no other yardstick were at hand.

The upper middle class did not begin to arrive till after the chartering of the Massachusetts Bay Company in 1629, which began as a trading enterprise but soon undertook to furnish an asylum to the English Puritan gentry as well. With approval of the Earl of Warwick, leadership was assumed by a country squire forty-one years old, John Winthrop, grand-

[20]Andrews, *The Fathers of New England*, p. 19, comments impartially upon the *Mayflower*: "Her people, humble and simple, were without importance in the world of thought, literature, or education. Their intellectual and material poverty, lack of business enterprise, unfavorable situation, and defenceless position in the eyes of the law rendered them almost a negative factor in the later life of New England. . . . The Pilgrim Fathers stand rather as an emblem of virtue than a moulding force in the life of the nation." And J. Franklin Jameson, quoted in Samuel Eliot Morison, *Builders of the Bay Colony*, p. 12: "It is the story of a small and feeble enterprise, glorified by faith and hope and charity, but necessarily and always limited by the slender resources of the humble men who originated it." A carping critic might take exception to the ingredient of charity, which from their narrow and suspicious lives was all too often absent.

son of a London clothier who had worked up from poverty to riches, bought the manor of Groton in Suffolk and so had become a landed gentleman, and enabled his son Adam to buy a coat of arms. In 1630 John Winthrop came over in the *Arbella,* named in honor of Lady Arbella Johnson, daughter of the Puritan Earl of Lincoln; she had married a squire, Isaac Johnson, but shortly after reaching these shores both died and have left no descendants.[21] The *Arbella* brought the first company of authentic blue-bloods to New England. Lady Arbella herself, together with her sister Lady Susan, wife of John Humphrey, Sir Richard Saltonstall and his family, and Simon Bradstreet and his "verse-making wife" Anne, dined in the "great cabin," as befitted people of quality, away from the evicted tenants, artisans, and indentured servants who formed the bulk of those on shipboard, together with horses, cattle, and dogs. We also know that these ladies brought their personal maids, and that one of these maids—being among those injudicious sufferers from sea-sickness who "gave themselves to drink hot waters immoderately"—fainted, and was with difficulty brought to her senses. Two of the names on the *Arbella's* passenger-list which came to figure in the later annals of Brahmin New England are those of Sir Richard Saltonstall and Thomas Dudley. Sir Richard, knighted in 1618, was nephew of a lord mayor of London in Queen Elizabeth's day who belongs in the ancestry of the Norths, later earls of Guilford. Not members of the nobility themselves, the Saltonstalls were sound gentry with Puritan sympathies, though Sir Richard soon found Massachusetts Bay too bigoted for him, and returned home to rebuke the clergy by letter for "your tyranny and persecutions." His son Richard however struck root in the New World, became a prominent citizen of Ipswich where townspeople called him "the Worshipful Mr. Saltonstall," and by his marriage to Muriel Gurdon of Suffolk founded a line of clergymen, colonial governors, lawyers, men of business and public affairs who have been proud of their patrician ancestry, their

---

[21]It might be added that further honor was paid the Lady Arbella, who had come from Boston, England, in the naming of that harbor where they eventually settled. Another early emigrant from Britain related to nobility, Thomas Cammock of Maine, nephew of the Puritan Earl of Warwick, died in 1643 also without issue. Still another, Jeremy Clarke, founder of a family of Newport Quakers who played no important rôle, was a nephew of Richard Weston, first Earl of Portland; cf. G. Andrews Moriarty, "Social Classes among Emigrants," *Commonwealth History of Massachusetts,* ed. Hart, vol. I, p. 53.

Planter, Puritan, and Patroon

wealth, and their orthodoxy in the councils of Massachusetts.[22] The Saltonstalls are the only family to boast eight unbroken generations of Harvard men, from Nathaniel, class of 1659, to the present Leverett Saltonstall, class of 1914, lawyer and Speaker of the Massachusetts House of Representatives. Thomas Dudley, born in 1576, was the son of a Captain Roger Dudley of whom nothing is known save that he was "slain in the wars" and left the child an orphan, to be brought up as a page in the household of the Earl of Northampton. Later he became steward to the Earl of Lincoln and in 1630 joined the expedition to Massachusetts Bay in which the Earl's two daughters were enrolled. Eventually he became deputy-governor and finally governor of the Colony, and from him have descended jurists, lawyers, soldiers, merchants, and clergymen. Dudley was a staunch believer in autocracy as the ideal government, but unlike many of his neighbors held that the State should rule the Church. Yet others of aristocratic tastes who shared his belief, like John Winthrop, Jr., and Henry Vane, son of the great Puritan statesman Sir Henry, followed the example of the elder Saltonstall by returning to England in disgust with this narrow theocracy.

But the dominant personality of them all was Governor Winthrop, with his wealth, his Cambridge education, his stiff-necked piety, and his equally inflexible will. Disapproving of tobacco and of drinking toasts, and renouncing wild-fowl shooting out of season because—being a poor marksman—he was sure it was displeasing to God, he allowed himself only the indulgence of marriages: four, to be exact, and all to women of position and wealth. From 1630 to 1639 he was "The Right Worshipful John Winthrop, Esquire, Governor of the Massachusetts," who with a

[22]Most lordly of the Saltonstalls was Gurdon, born 1666, great-grandson of the patentee of Massachusetts Bay Colony. A stirring preacher, one of the founders of Yale College, and Governor of Connecticut, Gurdon Saltonstall suffered only one recorded lapse from his ponderous dignity. That occurred *ca.* 1708 on his estate adjoining Furnace Pond, Branford. Vexed with the flocks of his neighbors' geese which continually crossed his land going to and from the Pond, he set upon them with a broom and routed the geese in confusion and slaughter. It became known in local history as the Battle of Furnace Pond, and was so regarded as "a cruel and unnecessary war" by Saltonstall's neighbors that in the next election for governor he failed to receive a single vote from East Haven.

Twelve years ago an antiquary of New Haven who cited this amusing episode from Hughes, *History of East Haven*, 1908, in a monograph prepared for the Society for the Preservation of New England Antiquities found that it was entirely deleted by the secretary of that organization, "out of deference to the Saltonstall family" as he wrote privately to the scholar.

sense of pomp ordered the charter of the colony to be carried before him on state occasions in a large leather-covered box—which the ignorant, unimpressed, mistook for a fiddle-case. He also delighted to stage his little progresses accompanied by halberd-bearers. Even after he sank to the level of deputy-governor some one presented him in 1646 with a sedan-chair which had been captured from a Spanish galleon, and in this aristocratic turnout, which was carried by four lackeys, he moved grandly through the cobbled streets of Boston. In the chronicles of etiquette it should be noted that he was the first man in America to own a fork, which had been sent to him in 1633 in a leather case with a knife and a bodkin.[23] His descendants have inherited some of his characteristics including a good business sense; for the past four generations they have usually been drawn to banking, as was Robert (1833–92) who founded the important house of the family in New York finance, or to the law, ably represented by Bronson, born 1863. Since 1762 the strain of the New York Winthrops has been mingled with the equally notable blood of the Stuyvesants.

Governor Winthrop and his powerful henchman, the Reverend John Cotton, believed firmly in an aristocracy of Zion in which the clergy—most of them men of humble birth—should be the ranking class. Winthrop said, regarding democracy, that "among nations it has always been accounted the meanest and worst of all forms of government," and of society in general that "the best part is always the least, and of that part the wiser part is always the lesser." The Reverend Mr. Cotton agreed fully: "Democracy I do not conceive that God did ever ordain as a fit government for either church or commonwealth. If the people be governors, who shall be governed? As for monarchy and aristocracy, they are both clearly approved and directed in the Scriptures. . . . He setteth up theocracy . . . as the best form of government in the commonwealth as in the church." Under this system it was natural that election by God should be the basis of rank and that the names inscribed in the Lamb's Book of Life should be also first in the social register. Accorded the place of honor on all occasions official and social, the clergy ruled with absolute

---

[23]Cf. Earle, *Home Life in Colonial Days*, p. 77. Up to about 1700 the fork was generally ridiculed as a little instrument 'to make hay with our mouths,' but gradually during the eighteenth century gentlefolk adopted it, along with china instead of pewter, and upholstered chairs in place of wood and hard leather seats.

Edmund Randolph
From a painting owned by
Stevens Taylor

Mrs. Ralph Izard
(Alice de Lancey)
From a miniature by
Edward G. Malbone*

John Randolph of Roanoke
From a painting by Gilbert Stuart

Mr. and Mrs. Ralph Izard
From a portrait by John Singleton Copley in the possession of the Museum of Fine Arts, Boston, Mass.

*Reproduced from "The History of the Centennial Celebration of the Inauguration of
George Washington." D. Appleton-Century Co.

Sir Richard Saltonstall

Reproduced by permission of Mrs. R. M. Saltonstall from the painting while at
the Museum of Fine Arts, Boston, Mass., in the Tercentenary
Exhibition of Colonial Portraits

power until 1691 when Massachusetts received a new royal charter, much like that of Virginia, which set up a representative assembly and a franchise based no longer upon church membership but on property. Meanwhile the harsh attitude of Puritan divines as persecutors of Baptists and Quakers cost them ultimately in prestige, as did also their furious witch-hunting. For, to the old Puritan populace, strangling a witch seems to have accomplished what the tragic drama did for ancient Greeks, a catharsis of pity and terror. When finally the delusion was spent, people turned in disgust against the ministers who had egged them on, while a few like the Reverend Cotton Mather chose the humiliation of a public apology. It is little wonder then that Mather in *The Good Old Way* (Boston, 1706) laments that common people no longer regard the clergy as "Angels of God" nor provide for them so generously. Though with the rise of a merchant class the secularizing of New England went forward during the eighteenth century, the old system of divines' rights—a caste so often reënforced, as in the Mather dynasty, by intermarriage—died hard. Thus in 1764 when young John Adams, a budding lawyer, courted and won a minister's daughter descended from the Quincys, his father-in-law took occasion after the ceremony to deliver an "Apology" from the text, "John came neither eating bread nor drinking wine, and ye say: 'He hath a devil.'"

Four social classes are pretty clearly defined in early New England. The first was made up of the ministers, as indicated, plus a sprinkling of gentlemen—Saltonstalls, Dudleys, Bradstreets, Pynchons—who brought with them from England a middling social rank which in Massachusetts Bay became the top. In time these folk admitted to their company the successful merchant, whose fortune in merchandise, timber, ships, fishing, spermaceti, and speculation in land and townships, made him vital to the economic life of New England and, by inevitable logic, soon acceptable socially as well. Rising from obscurity of birth to a place of eminence made possible by brains, thrift, and industry was approved as part of the Divine economy of the universe, a kind of social predestination which it would be impious to challenge. Many were even proud of the distance they had come; John Dunton writes from Boston in 1686 concerning the son of a London brazier: "Mr. Shrimpton has a very stately house there, with a Brass Kettle atop, to shew his Father was not asham'd of his Original." Only two decades after the founding of Boston Edward

The Saga of American Society

Johnson states that "there are many hundreds of laboring men who had not enough to bring them over, yet now worth scores, and some hundreds of pounds." Typical of the success-story in Massachusetts was Sir William Phips, son of a poor settler on the Kennebec River: he got his start as a carpenter in Boston, learned to read and write, saved money, married a rich wife, salvaged a Spanish galleon in the West Indies, sacked Port Royal in Acadia with the unscrupulousness of a pirate, and met virtually the only set-back of his life by a disastrous expedition in 1690 against Quebec. And there was William Pepperrell, a Maine trader in groceries, fish, lumber, and land, who also was knighted and took a flyer in military adventure, with better luck, against the French garrison of Louisbourg, in 1745. Others by thrift and shrewdness founded families which have remained steadily among the Brahmins ever since, like the Sturgis clan descended from one Edward Sturges [sic], a poor Kentishman who in 1646 was "lycensed to keep an ordinary and draw wyne" at Yarmouth on Cape Cod.

The jealousy with which this upper class guarded its preëminence is indicated as early as 1634 when Lord Saye and Sele, Lord Brook, and other Puritans of nobility and quality offered to transport themselves and families to New England if the Colony would create two official ranks: gentlemen, who should sit for life in a colonial House of Lords, and pass on this privilege to their heirs, and freeholders, qualified on the basis of property, who could elect deputies to a House of Commons. The local gentry, seeing their primacy thus threatened, replied evasively through the Reverend John Cotton that although they would be pleased to be ruled by any "noble and generous family with a spirit and gifts fit for government," yet "if God should not delight to furnish some of their posterity with gifts fit for magistracy" it would be sinful "if we should call them forth, when God hath not, to public authority." Seldom has a panicky little band of parvenus pled the doctrine of a Divine vocation to better effect; the noble lords dropped their proposal forthwith.

Below them were artisans and freeholders, who did most of the skilled work—cobbling, weaving, tinkering, farming, fishing. They called each other "Goodman" and "Goodwife," being very particular about the social earmarks which set them apart from the third class of unskilled laborers, wage-earners and journeymen, addressed by their Christian name alone. The fourth class was composed of indentured servants, who seem often to have been very unsatisfactory to their betters: John Winthrop justified his wife for beating their "lubberly" serving-maid, and Cotton Mather made it "an Article of special Supplication before the Lord, that He would send a good Servant into" his household, while President Timothy Dwight of Yale remarked later that the early settlers brought with them "a collection of peasants and servants remarkable for their profligacy." In the course of time a very small fifth class, of Indian and Negro slaves, was added, but in general New England industry was grounded not upon servant or slave labor but upon the small farmer, skilled craftsman, fisherman, and sailor. Unlike the Spaniard who chose exploitation rather than extermination of the red man, and unlike the Southerner who presently came to see the advantages of slave labor, the Yankee attempted to do everything for himself, and as a result never attained that spacious margin of leisure in which Society of the Old World pattern flourished.

Social life in early Massachusetts was simple: a mid-week lecture in church was considered the convivial flood-mark, and among minor indulgences was counted a stroll on Boston Common "where the Gallants a little before sunset walk with their Marmalet Madams . . . till the Nine-a-clock Bell rings them home." But class distinctions were solemnly respected. As in Virginia, gentlemen were exempt from corporal punishment. When in 1631 Mr. Josias Plaistowe was convicted of stealing corn from the Indians, the court ordered his servants flogged, but against him levied only a fine and directed that henceforth he "should be called by the name of Josias, and not Mr. as formerlie." As early as 1638 John Winthrop reports that the court deliberated about passing laws to regulate the increasing sumptuousness of apparel, "but little was done about it; for diverse of the elders' wives, etc., were in some measure partners in this disorder." But in 1651 the Massachusetts General Court expressed its "utter detestation that men and women of meane condition, education, and calling, should take vppon them the garb of gentlemen by wearinge of gold or silver lace, or buttons or poynts at their knees, or walke in great boots, or women of the same ranke to weare silke or tiffany hoods or scarfs." It was decreed that ladies and gentlemen might wear lace, silver and gold thread, slashed sleeves, hat-bands, and elaborate girdles, belts and ruffs—but that goodman and goodwife could not do so. In 1653 two women were arrested at Newbury for wearing silk hoods and scarves, but were released upon proving that their husbands were worth

£200 apiece. In 1676 Connecticut passed a law that any one wearing "gold or silver lace, or gold or silver buttons, silk ribbons or other superfluous trimmings" was to be taxed as possessing £150 of property, but it exempted "such whose quality and estate have been above the ordinary degree though now decayed." Even before this time the records of Connecticut towns show the arrest of at least thirty aspiring women, arraigned before magistrates as "persons of small estate who used to wear silk."

But no kind of social gradation was more jealously guarded than seating in church, according to "dignity, age and estate." There were laborious rules of precedence, such as that "the fore seat in the front gallery shall be equall in dignity with the second seat in the body";[24] at Saco the people were separated into seven classes and seated correspondingly by a vote of the town, while Woburn had a committee of five to seat the whole congregation, while these committee-members were in turn seated by an inner council of two. How these remaining dignitaries seated each other there is no record. At New Haven no seats were allotted to any below the rank of goodman. Even at Deerfield, when massacre by the Indians was imminent at any hour, rules were scrupulously worked out by a committee on church protocol. This is a typical order: "Brother Richard Jackson's wife to sit where Sister Kempster was wont to sit. Ester Sparhawke to sit in the place where Mrs. Upham is removed from. Mr. Day to sit the second seat from the table. Ensign Samuel Greene to sit at the Table. Goody Gates to sit at the end of the Deacon's seat. Goody Wines to sit in the Gallery."[25] People often crowded into pews above their station, were ejected, and sometimes heavily fined. In old Newbury social climbers were fined up to £27 for persistently attempting to sit in the wrong pew.

Quite naturally the same attitude was carried over into other spheres. In the college founded in 1636 and named in honor of the Reverend John Harvard, the son of a butcher, students were listed in the catalogue ac-

---

[24]In some Virginia churches gallery seats were deemed the most dignified; see Earle, *Home Life*, p. 383.

[25]Cited by Earle, *Stage-coach and Tavern Days*, pp. 16–17. John Greenleaf Whittier wrote:

> In the goodly house of worship, where in order due and fit,
> As by public vote directed, classed and ranked the people sit.
> Mistress first and good wife after, clerkly squire before the clown,
> From the brave coat lace-embroidered to the gray coat shading down.

cording to their social rank up to 1773.[26] In 1644 "a great silver salt" had been given to the college, and its position on the table at the commons divided graduates and faculty from undergraduates, whilst among the latter, sons of wealth and eminence outranked commoners, such for example as young John Adams in the mid-eighteenth century, who did well to grade fourteenth in a class of twenty-four. Other badges of social display strike us as even more extraordinary—like the leather fire-buckets which every householder owned in Colonial Boston, and with which he ran upon hearing the tocsin of alarm: these were generally embellished with his family crest and motto, if he had one.[26a]

Thanks to a quatrain of recent years—

> And this is good old Boston,
> The home of the bean and the cod,
> Where the Lowells talk to the Cabots,
> And the Cabots talk only to God—[27]

these two families have achieved such eminence in the popular eye that the makers of Camel cigarettes recently led off a series of expensive testimonials with Mrs. James Russell Lowell and Mrs. Powell M. Cabot. Yet neither family is of first rank either by date of arrival in America or by inherited status from the Old World. With the observation that "even the Hossiers know the truth," the New York *Times* in 1923 quoted the

[26]*Publications of the Colonial Society of Massachusetts,* vol. III, p. 411. Yale likewise listed its students in social order till late in the eighteenth century.

[26a]During the nineteenth century every large American city had several companies of volunteer firemen; keen rivalry and social snobbery often sprang up between them. In New York for example No. 29, recruited from sons of the first families, with its engine-house at Fifth Avenue and Twenty-first Street, was the cynosure of fashion seventy years ago. No. 33 ranked second in the social scale, and upon the outbreak of a large fire their running feud sometimes found expression in fighting over the possession of a choice hydrant. Cf. F. Gray Griswold, *The Horse and Buggy Days* (Privately printed, 1936), pp. 73–4.

[27]According to the New York *Times,* July 6, 1923, "An Immortal Poem," the genesis of this rhyme was a jingle recited by Doctor Bushnell at the 25th anniversary dinner of the Harvard Class of 1880; in its present form it is the revision made by Doctor John C. Bossidy for a Holy Cross Alumni dinner. Professor S. Foster Damon, biographer of Amy Lowell, writes the author that he has always heard the version that "The Lowells speak only to God," but that the late Miss Lowell in quoting it to a correspondent in China modestly reversed the places of Lowells and Cabots. The consensus of opinion, however, seems to place the Cabots face to face with their Maker.

Indianapolis *News's* assertion that the Lowells, clearly outdistanced by Saltonstalls, Winthrops, and Quincys, reached New England in 1639, while the three Cabot brothers did not come till about 1700. One is reminded of that snobbish club at Oxford which blackballed the present Duke of Windsor when he was an undergraduate at Magdalen, on the ground that his family had arrived in England at the comparatively late date of 1066.

Percival Lowle, a respectable merchant of Bristol—who on his mother's side, the Percivals, inherited a pedigree apparently going back to Norman times—came to Massachusetts to better his lot. His children and grandchildren, following the callings of cooper, cordwainer, and preacher, were remarkable chiefly for the size of their families. The first distinguished member of the family occurred in the fifth generation, in the person of the Reverend John Lowell, noted Puritan divine who died in 1767. Wealth was later amassed by Francis Cabot Lowell, mill owner, who died in 1817, and John Lowell the lawyer, who survived him by a score of years and endowed the Lowell Institute with its lectures on religion, science, and art.[28] John Amory Lowell, who graduated from Harvard in 1815, took as his Commencement thesis "Whether Prosperity and Increase of Wealth have a Favorable Influence upon the Manners and Morals of the People"; apparently deciding that they did, he launched into a mercantile career of notable success, married a Lowell-and-Cabot cousin, and further concentrated the family wealth. Henceforth the Lowell tree has grown thick with manufacturers, diplomats, poets, judges, historians, educators, clergymen, and one brilliant soldier, General Charles Russell Lowell, Jr., killed at the age of twenty-nine in the Civil War. James Russell Lowell, first editor of the *Atlantic,* poet, essayist, and U. S. Ambassador to Spain and to England, gave the name international celebrity—which has been augmented within this century by Percival Lowell, astronomer, and Abbott Lawrence Lowell, President Emeritus of Harvard. Best known to the public was Amy Lowell, imagist poet and biographer, who always flouted the minor conventions—from the days when, as a débutante, stout but witty, she danced at the Somerset and the Bachelors' Balls and "was fairly snatched from one partner to another,

[28]His bequest of $250,000 in 1836 was up to that time the largest ever made for an institution of education and culture in America, save the Girard endowment in Philadelphia.

while she joked at the top of her lungs and shouted to other couples as she whirled past,"[29] up to the 1920's when she was the idol of those literary dinners at which everybody waited somewhat breathlessly for her to light the first cigar.[30]

An equally self-willed citizen, Mrs. Jack Gardner, once cancelled her passage on a Boston Cunarder at the last moment, upon learning that there were twenty-eight members of the Cabot family on board. "God," she said, "has too good a chance." George, John, and François Cabot, three brothers from the Isle of Jersey, emigrated to America at the beginning of the eighteenth century. Henry Cabot Lodge, supported by professional genealogists, denied any relationship with John and Sebastian Cabot, those intrepid explorers; it is equally improbable that any connection exists with the Chabot family of France, whose arms they bear: "Or, three Chabots [bull-heads] gules." The pertinacity of that escutcheon is, however, no mean symbol of a family trait. François was a merchant, George a bricklayer who failed in business, but John—most worthy of the later tradition—married an heiress and prospered. The family first struck root in Salem and in Beverly, the latter being the village where the firm of J. & A. Cabot took out letters of marque to board British merchantmen during the Revolution, from which war they emerged rich. Shipowners, magnates in the India and China trade, promoters of cotton mills, bankers, architects, and doctors, the Cabots have never been remarkable for personal distinction, but rather for their shrewd business sense, family solidarity, and ability to marry money. Lacking the intellectual interests and the Bohemian friends of the Lowells, the Cabots have had small share in the academic life of Cambridge—with the present exception of Professor Philip Cabot of the Harvard Business School, who shows even then the characteristic bent. Typical of earlier Cabots was George, born in 1751, who ran away from Harvard to ship as a cabin-boy, learned all about the sea, and entered the mercantile field with much success, and

[29]Damon, *Amy Lowell* (Boston, 1936), p. 104.

[30]On October 16, 1924, in a letter to Archibald MacLeish Miss Lowell wrote that the Lowells were "one of the thirteen families in New England that have a right to their coat of arms." On the other hand, when the Lowell arms were used recently in the decoration of Lowell House at Harvard, Charles Francis Adams protested in public that to his certain knowledge only two New England families were entitled to a coat of arms—Winthrops and Saltonstalls. These statements, like most assumptions of amateur genealogists, are erroneous, as the recent Rolls of the New England Historic Genealogical Society bear witness.

another Cabot of that day thus mentioned in the diary of Nathaniel Ames, Harvard senior in 1761:

May 19. Joseph Cabot rusticated as soon the President said he was rusticated. He took his Hat and went out of the Chap[el] without staying to hear the President's Speech out. After Prayers he bulrags the Tutors at a high rate & leaves Coll[ege] his mother faints at the News.

With the exception of rich, secretive George Cabot, a member of the Hartford Convention in 1814, who according to John Adams had a "close-buttoned ambition . . . to be President of New England," the stirring of political interest among the Cabots was slower than in most of the old clans; its first great product was Henry Cabot Lodge, aristocratic disciple of Alexander Hamilton's philosophy. It reappears today in his grandson and namesake the young Senator. That tissue of intermarriage between old and powerful families of New England—so extensive as to connect all of them, with the rather curious exception that no Saltonstall has ever married a Lowell—seems to find the center of its web in the Cabots. Colonel Henry Lee of Lee, Higginson and Company, who himself married Elizabeth Perkins Cabot, is reported to have said that the Lowells, the Higginsons, and the Jacksons "came up from Newburyport to Boston, social and kindly people inclined to make acquaintances and mingle with the world pleasantly. But they got some Cabot wives who shut them up."

Society in Colonial Boston never wholly lost the artlessness of its earliest phase. The fashionable dinner hour was three o'clock; supper parties came in the early evening, followed by cards. Etiquette demanded that a bride receive her friends daily for four successive weeks after the wedding. Among the most popular social occasions were funerals, to which private invitations as well as public announcements were issued. As a modern critic of Boston, Charles Macomb Flandrau from Minnesota, has observed, funerals are "the only form of social gathering at which absolutely no one, under any circumstances, is ever expected to be either amusing or amused." Yet Boston had already begun to assume a rich magnificence—solid as a silver tankard by Jeremy Dummer or Paul Revere—thanks to its godly prosperity. French nobles in the Revolutionary War were vastly pleased with Boston—like the Comte de Ségur, who found that "democracy has not banished luxury," the Marquis de

Residence of His Excellency John Hancock, Esq., of Boston, Mass.

From "Gardens of Colony and State," by permission of The Garden Club of America

John Hancock

Painted by Copley, Boston Art Museum

Mrs. Abigail (Smith) Adams, 1744–1818,
wife of John Adams

Thomas Handasyd Perkins, 1764–1854

Painted by Gilbert Stuart, 1800

Portrait by Gambadella

From "Gardens of Colony and State," by permission of The Garden Club of America

The first Mrs. Harrison Gray Otis

Mrs. Harrison Gray Otis (Eliza Boardman)

After a painting by Malbone

From a portrait by G. P. A. Healy in the possession
of the Bostonian Society

Both portraits reproduced from "Famous Families of Massachusetts." Courtesy of Little, Brown & Co.

Planter, Puritan, and Patroon

Chastellux who attended the Tuesday Evening Club and was charmed with a certain *"ton* of ease and freedom," and the Prince de Broglie who was enchanted by the good dinners, elegant napery, and plates changed whenever you wished.[31]

Among the grandees of late eighteenth century Boston none excelled Governor John Hancock and Colonel Thomas Handasyd Perkins. The governor, whose purse was longer than his pedigree, was a connoisseur of wines and a gourmet. He loved to drive through town in a great coach with lackeys liveried in white and blue, flanked by outriders and attendant gentlemen on horseback. His crimson coats, gold braid, and sky-blue waistcoats of moiré silk were the oriflamme of elegance in Massachusetts, and his state of mind was congruous. In the autumn of 1789, during Washington's tour of New England, Governor Hancock precipitated a crisis in state-etiquette of the most painful sort. Instead of calling upon Washington he wrote inviting the President to stop at his house, and when the invitation was declined he sent a more breezy note asking the President to dine *en famille*. Again Washington frostily refused, and the whole town waited agog for the governor to call and pay his respects. At last several aides appeared from Hancock with excuses on the score of illness, but as Washington wrote in his diary, "I informed them in explicit terms that I should not see the Gov. unless it was at my own lodgings." Such an ultimatum having been given on Saturday evening with all the dignity of the Master of Mount Vernon, Governor Hancock turned up bright and early Sunday with his respects. Not since Gouverneur Morris had slapped him on the back at the Constitutional Convention in 1787 to win a dinner from Hamilton, had Washington's traditional majesty been so nearly imperiled.

Colonel Thomas Handasyd Perkins, typical of the Yankee trader who

---

[31]Cf. *Republican Court*, pp. 8 ff. Regarding Boston on the eve of the Revolution, Griswold gravely asserts: "In Boston there was undoubtedly more real respectability than in any other town of its population in the British empire." For more French impressions of Boston 1770–90 see Sherrill, *French Memories*, pp. 153–54, and Jones, *French Culture*, p. 250 and *passim*. Great naiveté regarding the French aristocracy existed outside towns like Boston and Newport: "the Comte de Moré, on his way to join Lafayette's army in 1777, stopped overnight at a New England house; his host said he would be very glad to have a Frenchman in the house, since now he would have somebody to shave him; and Moré says that a Frenchman having forgotten his boots, they were exhibited 'comme une merveille' in a museum in New York." H. M. Jones, *op. cit.*, p. 250, from Moré's *Mémoires*, Paris, 1898.

became a Boston magnifico and founded an important family, was born in 1764, son of a vintner and grandson of a hatter, from whom he gained his distinctive middle name. As a supercargo he went to China in 1789, and learned the tea and spice trade which accompanied the exchange of furs. On a visit to France he saw Robespierre beheaded, and at Mount Vernon spent several days with the aged Washington. Prospering greatly he became president of the United States Bank in Boston, was elected to the Massachusetts Senate, gave heavily to the Boston Athenaeum and the Massachusetts General Hospital, founded the Perkins Institute for the Blind, and was so open-handed with private charities that some accused him of being a poor judge of human nature. In Brookline he laid out a great estate where his fruits and flowers were tended by European gardeners to whom he paid $10,000 a year. Living upon a spacious scale, with the commerce of the seven seas borne by his sails—in a fashion that recalls the Venetian merchant-princes of the Renaissance—Colonel Perkins could be seen abroad any morning in the company of Harrison Gray Otis, Peter Chardon Brooks, and Israel Thorndike, as described by an eyewitness, "trudging homeward for their eight o'clock breakfast with their market baskets containing their one o'clock dinner." Such was the still provincial homeliness of Boston—as revelatory of its era as, in the 1850's, was the sudden dimming of gas of an evening in every parlor, which betokened that the big chandelier of the Boston Museum had been lighted, and that it was time to collect one's wraps for the theatre.

The most distinguished family in American history, though of minor social activity, is that of the Adamses of Massachusetts.[32] Most of them, as Henry Adams wrote of himself and his brother Brooks, have had "the passion for companionship and the antipathy to society." A certain cross-grained pride and cantankerousness has been their chief social characteristic. James Russell Lowell once wrote: "The Adamses have a genius for saying even a gracious thing in an ungracious way." Of sturdy Somersetshire yeoman stock, the Adamses did not begin to attract notice until the fifth generation, when they produced Sam, "the man of the Town Meeting," a great political agitator but so impecunious that his friends took up a collection to send him to the First Continental Congress via New York, where for the first time he and his cousin John met Livingstons,

[32]George III, receiving John Quincy Adams in 1795, asked Lord Grenville, "'All the Adamses belong to Massachusetts?' To which Lord Grenville answered, they did." J. Q. Adams's *Diary,* ed. Allan Nevins (New York, 1929), p. 12.

Planter, Puritan, and Patroon

Jays, Lows, Scotts, and Bayards, and the latter wrote home that "I have not seen one real gentleman, one well bred man, since I came to town." John Adams was even more famous—a man of sterling merit but increasingly tinctured with social vanity. In 1774 he wrote from Philadelphia concerning his native Massachusetts: "The morals of our people are much better; their manners are more polite and agreeable; they are purer English; our language is better, our taste is better, our persons are handsomer; our spirit is greater, our laws are wiser, our religion is superior, our education is better." As the first Vice-President, in the spring of 1789 waiting in New York for the arrival of Washington, he sat under his canopy of crimson velvet in the Senate chamber and grew giddy with his own magnificence. He invited the Senate to consider the problem whether he could open a letter incorrectly addressed to him as "His Excellency," and somewhat distressfully asked the Senate to weigh another punctilio: "When the President comes into the Senate, what shall I be? I cannot be President then. No, gentlemen, I cannot, I cannot. I wish gentlemen to think what I shall be." In private Ralph Izard of South Carolina dubbed him "His Rotundity," while John Randolph of Roanoke many years later did not forget that his brother had been "spurned by the coachman of the Vice-President for coming too near the arms emblazoned on the escutcheon of the carriage." It is worth speculating where John Adams found his coat of arms, for later Adamses have scrupulously denied owning one. Upon his election to the Presidency eight years later a jingle ran:

> See Johnny at the helm of State,
> Head itching for a crowny;
> He longs to be, like Georgy, great,
> And pull Tom Jeffer downy.

The same autocratic reputation pursued his son, John Quincy, in whose Presidency was circulated a *jeu d'esprit* called "The Adams Catechism, for the use of Noble Families and Good Society." Yet all this evidence may be a little misleading; the Adamses were perhaps a shade too self-conscious in their new dignity, but their worth was solid, their devotion to principle uncompromising. Wealth first came to the family in the seventh generation with Charles Francis Adams, who married the daughter of Boston's first millionaire, Peter Chardon Brooks, the merchant;

The Saga of American Society

he became Minister to the Court of St. James and probably saved England from intervention on the side of the Confederacy. Though possessed of the same stiff Puritan manner as his forbears, he had by marriage entered into Boston financial and social circles where earlier Adamses from Quincy had been anathema. His sons included Henry, noted historian and autobiographer, who with his wife Marion Hooper once collected a brilliant cènacle in Washington of diplomats, scholars, and litterateurs; Brooks, learned and eccentric, who married a sister of the late Mrs. Henry Cabot Lodge; and Charles Francis II, railroad president and stockyards promoter, who, after making a fortune, retired bitterly disillusioned with the successful American business man. The present head of the family is the third Charles Francis Adams, yachtsman, lawyer, former Secretary of the Navy, known to his friends as "the Deacon," and called in Boston clubs "the right one" to distinguish him from Charles Francis ("Pop") Adams, an improbably remote cousin who sponsors hockey and the Boston Braves. His daughter, Catherine, in 1923 married Henry Sturgis Morgan, younger son of J. P. Morgan. Other living Adamses are lawyers, college professors, authors, and men of business and civic affairs. This family, with two Presidents of the United States, two signers of the Declaration of Independence, three Ministers to England, and a galaxy of eminent private citizens, takes without question the primacy in America's intellectual artistocracy.[33]

The topic of genetics reminds one that the notorious family of prostitutes, paupers, epileptics, and criminals which sociologists have discreetly veiled under the name of "Jukes" is descended from early Dutch stock settled in New York State. It is perhaps a Lenten thought for Knickerbockers. The earliest white settlers of Manhattan—some thirty families of sturdy Walloons, chiefly artisans, who came over in 1623 in the *Nieu Nederlandt* under the governorship of Cornelis Jacobsen May—were in

---

[33]Among American strains which have lost their distinctive patronym, none delights the eugenist more than that of Richard Edwards, merchant of Hartford, and his handsome, brilliant, sensual wife Elizabeth Tuttle (whom he finally divorced for her immoralities). They were grandparents of the great Jonathan Edwards, and from him descended a multitude of presidents of Yale, Amherst, Union College, deans of law and medicine and divinity schools, authors, a chief justice of the Supreme Court, a signer of the Declaration of Independence (Robert Treat Paine), and two Presidents (Grant and Cleveland). The eugenist always points out that the descendants of Richard Edwards and his second wife, plebeian and commonplace Mary Talcott, were all mediocrities. Cf. Davenport, *Heredity in Relation to Eugenics*, pp. 226–28.

John Adams, in Court Dress

Minister plenipotentiary from the United States, as he called upon King George III
at St. James Palace in 1785

From a painting by Copley owned by Harvard University—photographed while at the
Copley Exhibition, Metropolitan Museum, N. Y.

After Gilbert Stuart

Mrs. William Bingham (Anne Willing)　　　　Mrs. James Beekman (Jane Ketaltas)

The two upper portraits are from "Republican Court."　D. Appleton & Co., 1859

Mrs. Roger Morris (Mary Philipse)　　　　Mrs. John Jay* (Sarah van Brugh Livingston)

From "Some Colonial Mansions."　Coates, Phila.　　　Copied by Daniel Huntington from a small medallion

*Mrs. Jay's portrait reproduced from "The History of the Centennial Celebration of the
Inauguration of George Washington."　D. Appleton-Century Co.

general vigorous pioneer stock. They are well described by Augustus Van Buren, who writes in the *Proceedings of the New York Historical Society,* vol. xi, p. 133: "Most of them could neither read nor write. They were a wild, uncouth, rough, and most of the time a drunken crowd. They lived in small log huts, thatched with straw. They wore rough clothes, and in the winter were dressed in skins. They subsisted on a little corn, game, and fish. They were afraid of neither man, God, nor the devil. They were laying deep the foundation of the Empire State."

Holland was just then in her renascence of commerce, learning, and political independence after the long tyranny of Spain, and there was little reason for anybody save those at the bottom of the ladder to leave. Hence the early Dutch settlers were of lowest social rank, unlike the middle and occasionally upper class colonists of Virginia, New England, New France, and New Spain.[34] Illiterate, quarrelsome, fond of cheating the Indians and each other, they were nevertheless tough and plucky, like most men with their backs to the wall. Their descendants are with us today; Walter P. Chrysler, automobile manufacturer, states in *Who's Who in America* that he is descended from the first male child born in New Amsterdam, Tuenis Van Dolsen.

Financial power in the planting of this colony came from the Dutch West India Company, composed of self-made Amsterdam merchants who—despised by the old aristocracy—longed to become founders of great estates and feudal barons, even by proxy in lands beyond the seas. One of them was Kiliaen Van Rensselaer, who had made a fortune trading in pearls and precious stones. In 1629 he and others persuaded the States General of Holland to encourage settlement by making any man "a patroon with all the rights of lordship" who within a space of six years should found a colony of fifty adults. The next year Van Rensselaer's agents bought from the Indians in exchange for "certain quantities of duffels, axes, knives, and wampum," a tract of some 700,000 acres along the west bank of the Hudson. The title was vested in him and his heirs for ever, and he was entitled to an oath of fealty from all tenants, a fortress with cannon and soldiery, and a flag which every passing vessel was required to salute. He himself never set foot in this great domain, but ruled through Van Curler, a deputy in New Amsterdam whose letters to his

[34]Cf. Herbert I. Priestley, *The Coming of the White Man* (New York, 1927), pp. 321 ff.

master began in this vein: "Laus Deo! At the Manhattans this 16th June, 1643. Most honorable, wise, powerful, and right discreet Lord, my Lord Patroon—" which must have applied flattering unction to the soul of this lapidary. Yet Van Rensselaer took a keen interest in the welfare of his tenants, sending them supplies which included "a wooden model of a small church" enclosed in a box, and also "one brandy-still weighing 115 pounds" with condensing coil. After his death in 1647 the patroonship passed to his son Johannes, then to Johannes's half-brother Jeremias who had married Maria Van Cortlandt. Thence to their son Kiliaen who in 1685, under the new English regime which supplanted patroonships with manors, became first Lord of the Manor of Rensselaerwyck. The Van Rensselaers, who had long ago left Holland to follow the rising star of their fortunes in the New World, intermarried with newly prosperous families like their lessees the Schuylers and the Livingstons, and firmly entrenched themselves in the destinies of the Hudson Valley.

The Dutch system was more autocratic in political than in social ways, largely because the colony was directed by bourgeois enterprise and because one's status as a "great" or a "small" burgher was quite frankly bought in cash.[35] Most high-handed of the governors was Peter Stuyvesant, whose blood still flows in the veins of New York lawyers, congressmen, and bankers. Suffering a sea-change from his mediocre status in Amsterdam, he arrived in New Netherland with a bearing described as that "of a peacock," kept the good burghers standing with uncovered head for more than an hour in his presence, and a little later dispersed a popular delegation which had come to offer suggestions about the defences of the colony with the words "We derive our authority from God and the Company, not from a few ignorant subjects, and we alone can call the inhabitants together." With the final overturn of Dutch power and the Treaty of Westminster in 1674 which gave the colony into English hands, the lineage of royal governors began. Sometimes they were cultivated and just like William Burnet, but often venal like the notorious

---

[35]In 1657 the two-fold burgher system in New Amsterdam was inaugurated with the words: "Whereas in all beginnings some thing or person must be the first so that afterward a distinction may take place, in like manner it must be in establishing the great and small citizenship." So many of the thrifty Dutch refused to buy the more expensive burgher right that in 1668 the distinction was abolished, and payment of fifty guilders was demanded for all burgher privileges, which were both political and social.

Planter, Puritan, and Patroon

Fletcher, or bankrupt rakes trying to recoup their fortune like Lord Cornbury. Though some of the Dutch families refused sullenly to admit it at first, the "governor's set" with its tone set from London society, assumed the social hierarchy and in time assimilated to itself the more prosperous and eligible Knickerbocker families—Beekmans, Schuylers, Cuylers, Van Rensselaers, Van Cortlandts, and a few others.

Although the attempt to create an aristocracy of patroons had failed—for indeed Rensselaerwyck was unique in its success—the impulse toward a landed gentry was still strong. And so, corresponding to the Spanish encomiendas, the French seigniories, and the Virginia plantations, arose the English manors of the Hudson Valley. Among the new creations was Livingston Manor, which went to Robert Livingston in 1686, Pelham Manor to Thomas Pell a year later, Philipsborough to Frederick Philipse in 1693, Morrisania to Lewis Morris and the Manor of Cortlandt to Stephen Van Cortlandt in 1697, and Scarsdale to Caleb Heathcote in 1701. Together with Rensselaerwyck, and early grants to John Archer and Thomas Chambers, this completes the tally of the nine actual manors—though for more than a century later heads of families up the river who owned large tracts, like the Schuylers around Albany, were popularly styled "patroons."

Most aggressive of the new barons was Robert Livingston, born in Scotland in 1654, son of a poor Presbyterian preacher who was driven into exile in Holland, where young Robert grew up with certain Dutch mannerisms. In 1674, out to seek his fortune, he turned up in Albany where he became town clerk and by shrewd trading and practice of law began to lay the timbers of his future wealth. According to an oft-repeated story, he was once called on board a yacht on the Hudson to draw up the will of a man who lay dying. When the stricken man's eyes fell upon young Livingston he groaned in a flash of second-sight, "I had rather it were any one but you, for you will marry my widow." Certainly in 1679 Livingston married the rich widow of Nicholas Van Rensselaer, Alida, sister of Peter Schuyler. He curried favor with governors, turned his coat with every administration, loaned money at 10 per cent, held a succession of political sinecures, was an army contractor addicted—as the current phrase ran—to "pinching the bellies of the soldiers," had a large share in that shady transaction of Captain Kidd's privateering which ended in piracy, exploited 3000 German refugees from war and famine whom he contracted to feed, built flour- and saw-mills and a bakery and brewery upon his manor. He steadily enhanced a reputation thus described by Governor Fletcher in 1696: "He has made a considerable fortune . . . never disbursing six pence but with the expectation of twelve pence, his beginning being a little Bookkeeper, he has screwed himself into one of the most considerable estates in the province . . . he had rather be called knave Livingston then [sic] poor Livingston." He had changed his coat of arms from that of the Scotch Livingstons—a cadet branch of the family which became Earls of Linlithgow—to a device of his own: a "ship in distress with the motto *Spero meliora";* somewhat later, with the apparent fulfilment of his hopes, the device was changed to a "ship in full sail." His death in 1728 left a vast estate to his less canny but more courtly son Philip, who had married Sarah Van Brugh; their son, Robert, third Lord of the Manor, lived till 1790, when under the new principles of democracy the entail to the estate was broken and the manor lands parceled out among his children. A certain lordly halo shone about the Livingstons: according to an old family tradition the hosts of black slaves who served them—and who now lie buried in a plot near "Clermont" above the Palisades—were all African kings or the offspring of headmen in exile. To be valeted by kings was a thought worthy of Tamerlane. From the days of Chancellor Robert R. Livingston, lawyer, diplomat, one of the committee of five who drafted the Declaration of Independence; of Chief Justice John Jay, whose wife was Sarah Van Brugh Livingston, daughter of the Governor of New Jersey; and of Edward Livingston, "Beau Ned," who left home under a cloud, prospered in New Orleans, married a Creole belle, and became United States senator and Secretary of State under Jackson, this confraternity set out to gain political and financial power by astute calculation. For several generations they had a representative, connected either by blood or marriage, on the Supreme bench, and one or more highly placed officials in the councils of both great political parties. This characteristic union of politics and financial power is best represented in our own day by Ogden Livingston Mills, former Secretary of the Treasury.

Another family which was rising more slowly abreast of the first Robert Livingston was the clan of Beekman, founded in the New World by Wilhelmus of that ilk, a German transplanted into Holland, who came over with his friend Stuyvesant in 1647, bought the unpromising land

Built by Richard Van Rensselaer in 1666 and conveyed to the Schuylers in 1672

Left: Caleb Heathcote, 1692–1721

From "Caleb Heathcote, Gentleman Colonist." Scribners

Right: Robert Livingston, First Town Clerk of Albany, N. Y.

The Van Rensselaer Mansion, Albany, N. Y.

This and the one at the top of the page reproduced from "Some Colonial Mansions," by Henry T. Coates & Co., Philadelphia, Pa.

Design by Major John
André on the Meschíanza
ticket

**The script appeared upon
reverse side of ticket**

Courtesy New York Public
Library

Major John André's
portrait of
Margaret. Shippen

Courtesy of the Historical
Society of Pennsylvania

The Chew House at Germantown, Pa.

From Godey's "Lady's Book," December, 1844

around Corlear's Hook which was then a salt meadow, and became a tanner. He rose to hold several important offices, and is thus jocularly described as lieutenant-governor by Irving in the *Knickerbocker History:*

This great dignitary was called Mynheer William Beekman, or rather *Beck*-man, who derived his surname, as did Ovidius Naso of yore, from the lordly dimensions of his nose, which projected from the centre of his countenance, like the beak of a parrot. He was the great progenitor of the tribe of the Beekmans, one of the most ancient and honorable families of the province; the members of which do gratefully commemorate the origin of their dignity; not as your noble families in England would do, by having a glowing proboscis emblazoned in their escutcheon; but by one and all wearing a right goodly nose, stuck in the very middle of their faces.[36]

Beekman's daughter married a son of Peter Stuyvesant, while among his male heirs was the well-known physician Doctor Gerard Beekman and Colonel Henry Beekman the affluent landowner, though the Beekmans have never been notably rich. Intermarried in colonial times with De Peysters and Livingstons, the Beekman family tree has had endless later ramifications, often with loss of identity to any save the genealogist, since daughters have rather remarkably outnumbered sons; of approximately fifty historical New York families, more than half possess Beekman blood. The stock within its own right has produced doctors, merchants, lawyers, jurists, clergymen, and philanthropists. Doctor Fenwick Beekman the surgeon is its most distinguished living member. It is perhaps worth comment that the president of the Social Register Association is Charles Keller Beekman, who for some years has also been secretary of the Union Club, ranking social club of America.

Doctor Cadwallader Colden, writing of New York during the mid-

[36]The *Knickerbocker History* glows with genial satire of Van Cortlandts, Suydams, Schermerhorns, Rutgers, Brinkerhoffs, and other "beavers of the Manhattoes," who he says are "after all, the only legitimate nobility and lords of the soil," even though the Sons of the Pilgrims "out-bargain them in the market, out-speculate them on the exchange, out-top them in fortune, and run up mushroom palaces so high, that the tallest Dutch family mansion has not wind enough left for its weathercock." Although one lady of Albany set out with a horsewhip in search of Irving, and a scion of the Dutch—with phlegmatic delay—denounced the author nine years after the book's appearance before the New York Historical Society, the satire was in general accepted with good grace—and Irving was a welcome guest at dinnertables of the Hoffmans, Schermerhorns, and Verplancks. See S. T. Williams, *Life of Irving* (New York, 1935), vol. II, pp. 92 and 275.

eighteenth century, observes: "Several of the principal families, I have been told, took their first rise from their commerce with the Pirates." This is true, regrettably enough, in respect to two prosperous Huguenot families which settled in New York around 1700, the De Lanceys and the Bayards, and to Frederick Philipse, a Dutch carpenter, who by the additional stratagem of marrying two heiresses in succession, rose to be lord of "Castle Philipse" near Sleepy Hollow. Ruling estates in West-chester, Dutchess, and Putnam counties, the Philipses were known among their tenantry as the *Junkers,* or gentlemen par excellence, from which the name of Yonkers is derived.[37] Great are the miracles of gold.

Another aristocratic commentator in the eighteenth century, Colonel Lewis Morris of Morrisania, wrote that "as New England excepting some Families was ye scum of ye old, so the greatest part of the English in the Province [New York] were ye scum of ye New." The Morrises had risen to such impeccable financial and social prestige by the middle of this cen-tury—as the only family of New York Society which was not engaged in "trade"—that such hauteur was almost inevitable. The founder was Richard Morris, a Welsh soldier who fought in Cromwell's army, then left Monmouthshire for Barbadoes, where he set up as a merchant and married an heiress, Sarah Pole. Migrating northward he bought a tract of 500 acres north of the Harlem River, but died in 1672 on the threshold of his life in New York, leaving a son one year old, named Lewis. Lewis Morris grew up to a sizable inheritance, increased in 1691 by lands bequeathed him from an uncle; in that same year he married Isabella Graham, daughter of the attorney-general of New York. With great good fortune in respect to what later economists would call the unearned increment, Morris saw his holdings in real estate appreciate rapidly. He became the first Lord of Morrisania, and set his heart upon being governor of New Jersey—an ambition which after many disappointments was finally achieved in 1738. He was a man of integrity, but excessively vain. His grandson Lewis, signer of the Declaration of Independence, was the last Lord of the Manor before its breaking-up by the laws against entail;

[37]For the subject of commerce with pirates see Dixon Ryan Fox, *Caleb Heath-cote: Gentleman Colonist* (New York, 1926), pp. 23-4 and 28. Huguenot families of perhaps more unimpeachable record settled in New York included De Forests, Gallandets, Freneaus, De Rhams, and Lispenards. In general they helped to raise the tone of Dutch and English Society; cf. Lucian J. Fosdick, *The French Blood in America* (New York, 1906), p. 235.

less aggressive than his forbears, he loved aristocratic leisure and feudal pomp, but added to the family fortune by marrying rich Mary Walton, daughter of Jacob and Maria (Beekman) Walton, in 1749. His half-brother was Gouverneur Morris, whose mother Sarah Gouverneur was a Huguenot. Gouverneur Morris feared the coming American Revolution as "the domination of a riotous mob," but took the American side when hostilities actually broke forth—though another brother, Staats Long Morris, became a major-general in the Tory army and eventually solaced his defeat by marrying the Duchess of Gordon. Gouverneur Morris's snobbish adulation of titles, his dandified air, and habit of carrying two French valets with him wherever he went to the astonishment of many a country innkeeper, led Hamilton to call him "an exotic." Appointed Minister to France in 1792, he witnessed a less savory revolution with boiling rage, and came home to air his cynical contempt for democracy in a way that antagonized many.[38] His marriage in 1809 in the Indian summer of his life to Anne Cary Randolph, who bore him a son, united perhaps the two most aristocratic clans of New York and Virginia.

But outside the pale of Morrisania, trade claimed all the prosperous families of eighteenth-century New York. The Bayards, Van Cortlandts, Roosevelts, Livingstons, Cuylers, and Rhinelanders were in the sugar-refining business. The Rhinelanders also imported crockery, while the Schuylers sold merchandise from Europe and India. Barclays, Rutgers, and Lispenards were brewers. General traders and shippers were Ver-plancks, Whites, Murrays, Baches, and Franklins, while Beekmans, Van Zandts, Clarksons, Setons and Buchanans were importers or dealers in dry-goods. The Goelets and the Brevoorts were ironmongers and the Schermerhorns were ship-chandlers. The Gouverneurs traded with the West Indies, and the Keteltas family operated warehouses. Gerard and Nicholas De Peyster were merchants. James Alexander, of the family of Lord Stirling, ancestor of the Duers, had a thrifty wife who eked out the income by running a small shop.[39] In the files of New York newspapers

---

[38]While a member of the Continental Congress, Gouverneur Morris suffered an accident which caused the loss of a leg, which was replaced by a stump. Years later, during the riots in Paris his carriage was attacked by the mob with cries of "Aristocrat!" Thrusting the stump out of the window Morris shouted: "An aristocrat! Yes—who lost his limb in the cause of American liberty." He was cheered to the echo, and drove off unmolested.

[39]Cf. *The Memorial History of New York*, 1893, vol. IV, pp. 524-25.

at the close of this and the beginning of the next century one finds humble advertisements bearing names long since divorced from the squalor of trade: Peter Goelet from his shop in Hanover Square offers the public saddles, hardware, pewter spoons, hair trunks, "and a consignment of playing cards"; Isaac Roosevelt advertises "loaf, lump, and strained sugar and sugar-house treacle"; plain Jacob Astor in Queen Street calls attention to guitars, fifes, and pianofortes; similar solicitations appear from Archibald Gracie, Abraham Brevoort, Leonard Kip, and others.

The social life of New York, like that of Boston, was still homely when the Tuckahoes of Virginia were laying down Madeira and building terrapin pounds and shooting-boxes. Knickerbockers sat and visited on benches beside the front door in good weather, skated in winter and held ice-carnivals. In early summer, as we are told quaintly in 1670, the Long Islanders "rushed violently into the fields" to gather ripe strawberries. The young people got up picnic and boating parties, and in some communities like Albany had organizations called "companies" which were rather exclusive cliques, made up of lads and maidens who took hunting and fishing excursions and traditionally found their life-mates. They were the provincial equivalent of the début, in the days when necessity of chaperones had not occurred to a guileless world. There was the Kissing Bridge over an inlet of the East River, with its perquisite of passage, and a famous tulip tree in Brooklyn near the ferry where many a jolly party was held. Callers were cordially pressed to "take a syllabub" before going home, a beverage of milk beaten to a froth with cider or wine. When due allowance for humor has been made, Washington Irving's description of tea-parties in high life is instructive:

These fashionable parties were generally confined to the higher classes, or noblesse, that is to say, such as kept their own cows, and drove their own wagons. The company commonly assembled at three o'clock, and went away about six, unless it was in winter time, when the fashionable hours were a little earlier, that the ladies might get home before dark. The tea-table was crowned with a huge earthen dish, well stored with slices of fat pork, fried brown, cut up into morsels, and swimming in gravy. The company being seated round the genial board, and each furnished with a fork, evinced their dexterity in launching at the fattest pieces in this mighty dish. . . . The tea was served out of a majestic delft tea-pot. . . . To sweeten the beverage, a lump of sugar was laid beside each cup—and the company alternately nibbled and sipped with great decorum.

Planter, Puritan, and Patroon

So late as 1838 James Silk Buckingham, visiting Stephen Van Rensselaer, "last of the Patroons," with an income "said to be a million dollars yearly," wrote of these old upstate families unchanged by the metropolitan ways of Manhattan:

These, in their number and ramifications, give a great gravity and decorum to the general tone of society here. There is less of show in houses, carriages, and horses; less of ceremony and etiquette in visiting; very early hours for meals: seven for breakfast, two for dinner, and six for tea; plainer and more simple fare at each than in the larger towns . . . every family here lives much within its income, and lays by accumulated means for the succeeding generation.[40]

In fact the simplicity of life in colonial New York made ostentation almost impossible, though keeping one's own carriage was the notable badge of social plutocracy. Maria De Peyster Spratt, whose husband was president of the Council, seems to have been the first woman to own her own coach and four; the Van Rensselaer patroons imported Dutch coaches in which they rumbled down to New York for the winter season; and Levinus Clarkson, a young blood of the 1760's, imported the first cabriolet from England and drove through town with a groom in green livery. The coach owned by Mrs. James Beekman in 1798 is now exhibited by the New York Historical Society.

But New York lost its social simplicity during the later eighteenth century with perhaps more celerity than Boston. Its brief regime as the national capital, and its enduring status as the national metropolis, attracted rich and sophisticated visitors from the South, England, and the Continent. Like all great commercial ports it was washed by the tides of world culture, and lacking the Puritan reënforcement soon succumbed to the Parisian elegance and frivolity brought home by Mrs. John Jay and her circle. In its brief heyday in 1789 as the capital city, the Boston *Gazette* rejoiced that "our beloved President stands unmoved in the vortex of folly and dissipation which New York presents." Among other

[40]*America: Historical, Statistic, and Descriptive* (New York, 1841), vol. II, p. 43. On the other hand Buckingham found that the "remote and real cause" of the Panic of 1837 was "the habit which all classes seem within the last few years to have contracted, of speculating beyond their means, of living beyond their income, of spending money before it was acquired, and of keeping up the appearance of men who had realized large fortunes while they were only in the act of accumulating them." (I, 52.) This was also the burthen of Miss Martineau's criticism in the same decade.

worldly influences should not be forgotten the presence of Brillat-Savarin, who spent the years 1793–96 in New York as an emigré from the horrors of Girondist cookery. He gave French lessons, played in theatre orchestras, and taught Julien in Boston to cook eggs with cheese. Though Fraunces Tavern was the favorite spot of George Washington, Brillat-Savarin preferred Little's Tavern, where the turtle soup was unexceptionable, and where he might regale his American friends with partridges *en papillote* and gray squirrels cooked in Madeira. Other exiles of more conventional rank added to the gaiety of Manhattan, and impoverished as they were, received eager welcome from Hamiltons, Morrises, Wolcotts and Livingstons—Louis Philippe and his two brothers, the Duc de Montpensier and the Comte de Beaujolais, who spent the winter of 1798–99 in New York in lodgings over a bakery, where the painter Copley attended a distinguished dinner given by Louis Philippe at which one half of the guests sat upon the side of the bed because there were no more chairs and indeed no room for them.

Louis Philippe while in Philadelphia—where he wore his rue with a difference, and lived over a barbershop—once proposed to a daughter of Senator William Bingham, but was refused by her father the financier patrician, who told the Duke: "Should you ever be restored to your hereditary position, you will be too great a match for her; if not, she is too great a match for you." That reply is redolent of the solid assurance which has always characterized Philadelphia Society. The founder of Pennsylvania, William Penn, was the son of a British admiral; while receiving an aristocratic education at Christ Church, Oxford, he began to attend Quaker meetings, renounced the scarlet coat for gray, and in 1681 received a charter to found a colony of Friends.[41] The Quaker movement was itself essentially democratic—the use of "thee" and "thou," for example, and the occasional startling habit of riding naked through the streets "shouting for King Jesus" being symbols of the attempt to strip away the trappings of rank. The colonists whom Penn brought over were, at their best, of the thrifty, prosperous middle class. These were the Logans, the Shippens, the Pembertons, the Norrises, the Lloyds, the

[41]Among the Penn papers in the Historical Society of Pennsylvania are some twenty preliminary drafts of a constitution which the governor drew up for his intended colony. The first provides for government by a landed aristocracy, while others become successively more liberal until the most democratic, which he adopted, is reached.

Wynnes, and the Peningtons. Up to the Revolution they were the leaders in finance, trade, and law-making in the Commonwealth, though in numbers they had soon been swamped by Germans and Scotch Irish. Often they built massive houses, comfortable but not showy—like Edward Shippen's on South Second Street, with its gardens, summer-house, and deer-park, or country places like Cliveden, Stenton, Belmont, and Landsdowne, seat of the Penns. Here they entertained simply but substantially, with dinner at the traditional hour of four which was maintained down to the Civil War. Most famous and socially minded were the Morrises, descended from Anthony Morris, convert to Quakerism who settled in Philadelphia in 1683 and made money in brewing. Among his descendants were Cadwalader and Anthony Morris, eighteenth-century merchants, and Caspar Morris, well-known physician of the next era. Present head of the family is the octogenarian Effingham B. Morris, president of the Girard Trust Company. This family is not to be confused with the Morrises of Morrisania or with Robert Morris of Liverpool and Philadelphia, financier of the Revolution, who later spent three years in jail for bankruptcy. Descendants of Anthony Morris have never been so indiscreet.

These Quakers, as a group, had little knowledge of or interest in Society, and in the course of the eighteenth century a strong social leadership was assumed by families of later settlers—merchants, lawyers, government officials—who were chiefly Church of England folk. These were Allens, Chews, Tilghmans, Plumsteds, Hamiltons, Lawrences, Hackleys, Inglises, Simses, Francises, Masters, Bonds, Peterses, Conynghams of Conyngham, Chancellors, Maddoxes and last but not conceivably least the Willings. Joseph Willing of Gloucestershire in the seventeenth century married Ava Lowre, an heiress whose coat of arms he took for his own. Their son Thomas married Anne Harrison, granddaughter of Major-General Harrison in Cromwell's army—the same General Harrison, by the way, whom Pepys watched with fascination as he was hanged, drawn, and quartered for treason, "he looking as cheerful as a man could do in that condition." In 1720 Thomas Willing visited America, and seeing the business opportunities brought over his son Charles in 1728, and set him up in commerce in Philadelphia before returning to England. Charles prospered, married a rich Quakeress of the Shippen family, and left a large fortune to his son Thomas, president of the first

Bank of the United States. Allied in late colonial times with Binghams of Philadelphia and Byrds of Virginia, the Willings early took the social leadership of Philadelphia which through succeeding generations they have shared with Cadwaladers, Wisters, Biddles and Yarnalls. With an assured footing in English Society that extends from Anne Willing Bingham, wit and beauty who was the toast of Georgian *ton,* to the present Lady Ribblesdale, born Ava Willing, this family was a precursor of "the international set."

The Cadwaladers and Biddles belong in origin to the same Colonial trading period. Though a Philadelphia saying runs that "when a Biddle gets drunk he thinks he's a Cadwalader," yet the Biddle family has enjoyed perhaps more national importance, thanks to a resourceful line of bankers and men of public affairs. The founder was William Biddle, a shoemaker who joined up with Cromwell's troops, became a Quaker, was imprisoned for Nonconformity at the same time as John Bunyan, and as a friend of Penn sought asylum in the New World in 1681. His descendants prospered in trade; one of them was Owen, patriot in the Revolution and watchmaker by profession: *The Pennsylvania Chronicle* for November 30, 1767, contains an advertisement in which he proffers the public "Mainsprings, Glasses, Verges, cantred Wheels and Pinions, Buttons, leaded and unleaded, Silver and Pinchbeck Bows," and offers to repair clocks "on the most reasonable Terms." A watch made by him is now in the possession of Mrs. Maurice Brix of Philadelphia. Other Biddles include his brother Clement, merchant and Revolutionary soldier; James, noted naval officer in the War of 1812; and Nicholas, president of the second Bank of the United States, "that hydra of corruption" which Andrew Jackson like a new St. George destroyed amid the plaudits of democracy. Thereafter Nicholas Biddle retired philosophically, settled at "Andalusia" on the banks of the Delaware, and became famous as a host to the social and intellectual lights of America and Europe. Notably intermarried with the descendants of Francis M. Drexel, an itinerant Tyrolese portrait-painter who in nineteenth-century Pennsylvania discovered an unsuspected flair for stocks and bonds, the Biddles would by now be regarded as a very old family in every American city except, perhaps, Philadelphia. Their tradition of public service, as well as their amiability in conferring this noble name upon gilded parvenus, is illustrated in the present generation by Anthony J. Drexel Biddle, Jr., United

Planter, Puritan, and Patroon

States Minister to Norway, who in 1915 married Mary Duke (tobacco, $50,000,000) and upon their divorce in 1931 married Margaret Thompson Schulze in London (mining, $85,000,000).

In Colonial Philadelphia as in New York a coach and four occupied the place of the steam yacht in modern Society. About the middle of the century Mrs. McIlvaine wrote with more pith than poetry—

> Judge Allen drove a coach and four
> Of handsome dappled grays,
> Shippens, Penns, Pembertons, and Morrises,
> Powels, Cadwaladers, and Norrises
> Drove only pairs of blacks and bays.

In 1772 Du Simitière reports that there are nearly a hundred carriages in Philadelphia, although Thomas Willing and William Peters claim the distinction of driving the only landaus in town. When the British occupied Philadelphia during the War, Sir William Howe commandeered the Cadwalader house for his headquarters, and for his transportation the smart coach and pair belonging to Mrs. Israel Pemberton. Having no choice, that imperious lady assented, but upon the condition that it be driven to her door first; hence, a full hour before it was ever placed at the disposal of General Howe, the glittering equipage stood before the house of Mrs. Pemberton.

Although we hear disparagements about Philadelphia ladies of quality from the Prince de Broglie down to James Silk Buckingham,[42] and although La Rochefoucauld assures us in 1797 that Society is indiscriminately mad after European visitors—philosophers, preachers, literary men, princes, dentists, wits, and idiots,[43] we cannot accept such crabbing

[42]The former wrote: "The ladies of Philadelphia, although magnificent enough in their costumes, generally do not wear them with much taste. . . . While they have good figures, they lack grace and make their curtsies badly." Cf. Sherrill, *Memories,* p. 61. Although Buckingham, a generation later, approved of Nicholas Biddle as "the most perfect specimen of an American gentleman that I have yet seen in the U. S.," yet he states that the ladies did not "appear to us so graceful and perfectly well-bred . . . we did not find in either sex that hearty frankness and cordial generosity which exist so generally at Baltimore." Buckingham came over, like so many of his compatriots, on a lecture tour, and one cannot help wondering whether, as he reports, the fact that in Baltimore his lectures were "extremely well attended" and "highly appreciated" while Philadelphians were colder, may have colored his opinion. Cf. his *America,* vol. I, 298 and 364.

[43]The *ipsissima verba* of La Rochefoucauld are worth preserving: "Voilà le véritable état de la société à Philadelphia: grands dîners, grands thés, pour les arrivons

too seriously. According to general opinion, Philadelphia at the close of the Revolution shared with Charleston the social palm among American cities—thanks in large measure to the effective leadership of Mrs. Bingham. Among the most celebrated parties of the century were the fête called the Meschianza, held during the War, and a little later the grand ball given by M. Luzerne, the French Minister, to celebrate the birth of the Dauphin. He erected a building just for the occasion, in the midst of a garden "with groves and fountains, spacious walks and numerous seats. . . . For ten days before the event nothing else was talked of in the city. The shops were filled with customers; hair-dressers were retained . . . and so great was the demand on their attention, that many ladies were obliged to have their heads dressed between four and six o'clock in the morning." There were cotillions, fireworks at nine, supper at twelve prepared by thirty cooks borrowed from the French army, and a merry good-night at three. Doctor Rush, among those present, writes of the 700 guests: "Here were ladies and gentlemen of the most ancient as well as of the most modern families." After all, the diplomatic set is usually compelled to be somewhat catholic in its invitations.

But nothing if not exclusive was the Philadelphia Assembly, first held in 1719 when Governor Hamilton led off with the mayor's wife, though not established as a fixture till 1748 by fifty-nine of the first families. The Master of Ceremonies—in the early days usually a distinguished army officer, like Colonel Mitchell—would give each dancer a folded ticket drawn by lot, with a number corresponding to that of one's accidental partner for the evening, "leaving nothing," says a. naïve chronicler, "to the success of forwardness or favoritism. Gentlemen always drank tea with their partners the day after the assembly,—a sure means of producing a more lasting acquaintance, if desirable." During the decade when Philadelphia was the nation's capital the Assemblies achieved their utmost éclat. They were held at O'Eller's, in a ballroom sixty feet square with a music-gallery at one end and the walls papered in French style. Their suppers were excellent, though the specialty of the house was iced punch

d'Europe, Anglais, Français, étrangers de tous pays, de toute classe, de tout caractère: philosophe, prêtre, homme de lettres, prince, arracheur de dents, homme d'esprit ou idiot." He adds, that after the first fine careless rapture the newcomer is often dropped, though if he be a prospective land-purchaser the festivities are prolonged. Again one wonders if Philadelphia had failed to make over the Duke all the ado he deserved in his own opinion.

with pineapple juice. Young ladies often brought along two pairs of slippers, in case they danced one pair out. The subscription lists of the Philadelphia Assembly have been guarded for almost two hundred years with unparalleled jealousy. Although in the United States women have been the chief social custodians, the practice of the Assembly in respect to admissions is European rather than American. The social rank of the man determines that of his wife. Thus a young woman who married a jeweler was instantly expelled from the list, but a gentleman who saw fit to wed his cook brought her into that august company. The apparently accidental admission of a barber in the late eighteenth century caused a furious controversy which raged in the columns of *The Pennsylvania Gazette*. Intensely conservative, the Assembly has stricken from its rolls the name of every person divorced and remarried; it is in this respect like the Court of St. James's. Bids to the receiving line are still trophies in Philadelphia Society, and both the matron who heads the line and the "bride of the year" who receives with her stand together upon a dizzy summit. Although there is some evidence that the Assembly is growing a little aware of business expediency—dating definitely from the admission some years ago of Mr. and Mrs. Edward T. Stotesbury, over the bleeding bodies of the Cadwaladers—it has still bravely refused any traffic with Wideners, Elkinses, Dorrances, and Atwater Kents in their own right.

Before closing the account of eighteenth-century aristocracy one cannot well overlook the part it played in the Revolution. The mainspring of rebellion came from the encroachment of a stupid Parliament upon the rights of trade. Organized by the prosperous merchant class with the help of lawyers—who were just gaining for their profession a certain amount of social recognition—the impulse to revolt spread among backwoodsmen, "buckskins," and farmers, who when victory was once gained suffered repudiation from the councils of the nation. After the unsuccessful attempt of Shays's Rebellion to make themselves heard, they lapsed into utter neglect under a "Republican Court" unbroken till the election of Andrew Jackson. The avalanche of Revolution had been started in Virginia, for example, by such patricians in the House of Burgesses as Peyton Randolph, Richard Bland, Robert Carter Nicholas, John Robinson, and George Wythe. They drew into the campaign a young backcountry lawyer, Patrick Henry, who stirred the simple folk and sounded the alarm more clearly than they—aware of their aristocratic bonds with Britain—had ever dared to do. The same collaboration between two classes, the humbler discovering that it was just as good as the British excisemen sent to tax it, and the prouder knowing its superiority, may be seen among the Signers of the Declaration and the Framers of the Constitution. On the one hand was the roster of blue blood and gold—Rufus King of Newburyport, Elbridge Gerry, an early captain of finance, Alexander Hamilton ("The People, your People, Sir, is a great Beast," as he observed later, in a dictum as famous and irritating to the populace as William Henry Vanderbilt's "The Public be damned"), Governor William Livingston, Gouverneur Morris, Robert Morris the banker, George Washington, James Madison, and two Pinckneys from South Carolina—and on the other Roger Sherman the shoemaker turned lawyer, John Langdon the farmer's son, and Benjamin Franklin whose ancestry of Northamptonshire blacksmiths may have shod the horses of the pink-coated Washington gentry. According to Balzac, Franklin was the man who invented the lightning-rod, the hoax, and the republic.

In all civil wars people of fortune and hereditary rank are apt to cling to the old order, and although the circumstances of the American Revolution created a multitude of exceptions, yet the Loyalist cause attracted many of the proud and rich—Fairfaxes, Galloways, Penns, Dulaneys, Philipses, Whites. The De Lancey family, for example, was split into two branches: one, intermarried with the Livingstons, remained anchored to these shores, while another because of its fidelity to the Crown removed to England, held important offices, and married into the noble houses of Southampton and Abingdon. Perhaps a little exaggerated is the pessimism of Mr. Porter Sargent, native Bostonian, in the preface to his annual *Private Schools: 1936:* "The aristocrats of Boston all left with Lord Howe. The old Boston families of today are for the most part derived from the rabble of smugglers and privateers-men who poured in as the Tories left with the British fleet."[44]

Some of the French allies, coming over to fight a war for oppressed classes, expected to find complete absence of social distinction. They were

[44]An anonymous play published in Boston in 1779, *The Motley Assembly,* ridicules the belief among certain circles of Boston Society that hearty support of the Revolution was incompatible with secure social standing. Among the Tories are Turncoat, one of the managers of the Assembly, Mrs. Flourish, Mrs. Taxall, and Mrs. Bubble, leaders of fashion.

mistaken. In Philadelphia Lambert Cadwalader had organized and out-
fitted a band of young blue-bloods to give their all for the self-evident
truth that men are created free and equal, called the Silk Stocking Com-

The Public Be ——!
Front page of *The Daily Graphic*, October 12, 1882
A Vanderbilt cartoon

pany. George Washington—who in 1777 had reminded Congress that it
would be necessary to receive the Marquis de Lafayette well because of
his high social standing—wrote to a friend about the choice of officers:
"Take none but gentlemen." In 1779 a captain in the American army
was tried by a brigade court-martial and dismissed from the service for
having persistently associated in a social way with the wagon-maker of

his brigade.[45] Lord Howe once went so far as to send the Commander-in-chief of the rebels a letter addressed "George Washington Esq. &c. &c.," and Washington agreed to see the officer who brought it. Dressed in full uniform and carrying a long sword in a scabbard of white polished leather, Washington in his stateliest manner listened to the awed envoy explain that "&c. &c." meant everything, including military titles. With an august smile the commander-in-chief replied that the symbols might include terms of insult too, and declined therefore to take the letter. Congress, to whom he referred the question, agreed that he could not open an envelope disrespectfully inscribed. The War went on.

George Washington—of whom a London newspaper during the War generously said, "There is not a king in Europe but would look like a *valet de chambre* by his side"—never forgot his Virginian pride. His very leadership of the cause was in fact a tribute to the aristocratic British tradition of public service, to which he was faithful in his fashion. Although he did not warm to the proposal of Colonel Lewis Nicola that he should become King George I of America,[46] probably looked with disapproval upon Gouverneur Morris's suggestion that members of the United States Senate be chosen for life, and despite inner sympathy passed over Hamilton's frank plea that "the rich and well-born" be given "a distinct, permanent share in the government," Washington was no democrat by heredity or taste.

In 1789 just before the opening of Congress in New York, a group of Philadelphians and Virginians—Chief Justice McKean, William Bingham, Madison, Page, and Richard Henry Lee—dined with Doctor Ship-

[45]Yet Dupetit-Thouars, a French visitor during the Revolution, was astonished to see a shoemaker who had become a colonel, and an apothecary a general. Cf. Sherrill, *French Memories,* pp. 46–7. Henry Knox of Boston rose from bookseller to General, and Secretary of War in Washington's Cabinet. Baron von Steuben, to the surprise of his American aides, sought to introduce greater democracy into the army by drilling with his men and making commissioned officers, as well as non-coms, directly responsible for the welfare of the men under them. In general however the practice of the United States Army, notably crystallized with the founding of West Point, has followed the British system by which "every officer is a gentleman" and a class apart from privates, rather than the modern French system which weakens this traditional barrier.

[46]Cf. L. B. Dunbar, *A Study of "Monarchical" Tendencies in the U. S. from 1776 to 1801* (Urbana, Illinois, 1922), who discusses also the proposal of the Comte de Broglie that an elective monarchy be set up, with a "Prince" as generalissimo of the American army. This was in 1776, and de Broglie obviously hoped the choice would fall upon him.

pen in Philadelphia, and over the port and walnuts gravely pondered the proper title for Washington as President of the United States. " 'Yes, sir,' replied McKean, 'he must have a title, and I have been examining the titles of the princes of Europe to discover one that has not been appropriated; "Most Serene Highness" is used, but Serene Highness, without the "Most," is not; and I think it proper that our Chief magistrate should be known as His Serene Highness the President of the United States.' "[47] General Peter Muhlenberg states that Washington himself wanted to be called "High Mightiness," a title used by the Stadtholder of Holland, but that while the question was being debated in Congress Muhlenberg dined with the President and by an unseemly jest ruined the possibilities of this title: "Among the guests was Mr. Wynkoop of Pennsylvania, who was noticeable for his large and commanding figure. The resolutions before the two houses being referred to, the President, in his usual dignified manner, said, 'Well, General Muhlenberg, what do you think of the title of High Mightiness?' Muhlenberg answered laughing, 'Why, General, if we were certain that the office would always be held by men as large as yourself or my friend Wynkoop, it would be appropriate enough, but if by chance a president as small as my opposite neighbor should be elected, it would become ridiculous.' "

General Armstrong of Rhinebeck—whose daughter, incidentally, married John Jacob Astor's son and brought that family into Society—reports that even honest Roger Sherman the shoemaker "had set his head at work to devise some style of address to the President more novel and dignified than 'Excellency.' " On April 23, 1789, committees had been appointed in both Houses to grapple with this problem; in the Senate, Izard suggested "Excellency" and Lee "Highness," while John Adams, who frowned upon "President" because there were "presidents of fire companies and cricket clubs," toyed with the lower ranks—proposing that the sergeant-at-arms be called "Usher of the Black Rod," and that Washington's cook be dubbed "Steward of the Household."[48] Finally the Senate committee

[47]Cf. Griswold, *Republican Court*, p. 153 for this and the quotation following.

[48]When Washington sent a questionnaire on presidential etiquette to Jay, Madison, Hamilton, and Adams, the last replied: "Chamberlains, aides-de-camp, secretaries, masters of ceremonies, etc., will become necessary. . . . Neither dignity nor authority can be supported in human minds, collected into nations or any great numbers, without a splendor and majesty in some degree proportioned to them." Hamilton, though characteristically deprecating "the notions of equality," counseled Washington to cultivate informality for the sake of tact and popular suffrage.

recommended "His Highness the President of the United States of America, and Protector of their Liberties," but finally by the more democratic House of Representatives this formula was pared down to "The President of the United States," so that in actual practice he was known simply as "Mr. President" or "The President"—a title so bare that on at least one occasion Washington was refused lodgings at a village inn upon the assumption that he was the President of Rhode Island College.[49] At the first session of Congress there was also talk of providing Washington with a throne, from which he might address the legislators, but the proposal came to naught and instead he used the Vice-President's chair for such purposes. Later, under the more democratic Jefferson, the President's messages were sent rather than delivered to Congress, to avoid the appearance of a "speech from the throne"—a precedent of long standing which has been broken in our own times by Woodrow Wilson and Franklin D. Roosevelt.

The most widely resented impulse toward aristocracy in which Washington had a hand was the establishment in 1783 of the Order of the Cincinnati, a society of American and foreign officers in the Continental Army, in which membership should be transmitted through the eldest male posterity, as a kind of patriotic perpetuation of '76. The Cincinnati were invested with elaborate insignia, rather like the Knights of the Garter. They chose as their Patron Louis XVI, who gave them his royal sanction at Versailles in December, 1783, and thus banded together the military aristocrats of Virginia and New England with Lafayette, Count de Grasse, Count Rochambeau, Viscount de Noailles, and a dozen more. Like most socially exclusive groups in a republic, the Order sought to justify itself by good works: "the principal end of the Society is to maintain their indigent officers and their widows, and to maintain and educate their indigent children," say the Rules and By-Laws. But a cry of outraged liberalism immediately went up from Sam and John Adams, Jefferson, and others; pamphlets were written to expose its sinister char-

---

[49]Cf. Griswold, pp. 185–86. Washington however disliked being announced brazenly by his title. According to Thomas Jefferson's *Anas,* at his first levee Washington entered the presence-room preceded by Humphreys, his majordomo, who called out "with a loud voice, 'The President of the United States!' The President was so much disconcerted by it that he did not recover in the whole time of the levee; and when the company was gone, he said to Humphreys, 'Well, you have taken me in once, but, by God, you shall never take me in a second time.'"

acter;[50] and though it continued for awhile under presidents like Washington, Hamilton, Charles Cotesworth Pinckney, Thomas Pinckney, Aaron Ogden, and Hamilton Fish, popular disapproval in New York created a rival organization founded on "pure democracy" called Tammany Hall. Under such pressure most of the state societies dwindled away during the early nineteenth century, though the national body managed to survive. From 1893 to 1902 the state chapters were revived and now meet annually in each of the thirteen states, with a present hereditary membership of about 980. Belonging to the Cincinnati is again a proud distinction, recorded by every Social Register in the country, and it has sometimes been provocative of a little vanity. Ward McAllister in his memoirs called *Society as I Have Found It* describes a ball given in Florence in 1856 by the Austrian minister, at which the host saw an American wearing a peculiar decoration, to which he called McAllister's notice: "We approached my countryman together, and, after a few words, the minister most courteously put the question to him. He drew himself up and said, 'Sir, my country is a Republic; if it had been a Monarchy, I would have been the Duke of Pennsylvania. The Order I wear is that of the Cincinnati.' The minister, deeply impressed, withdrew, and I intensely enjoyed the little scene."

The Revolution had an immense effect upon American Society. On the one hand the presence of French allies, officered by the cream of Gallic nobility, speeded the urge toward new worldliness and luxury—even though some French visitors professed themselves scandalized by the extravagance of American ladies of fashion.[51] So widespread was the blossoming of French taste and the corresponding *savoir faire* it implied, that —so Chateaubriand tells us at any rate—even the Iroquois tribe had their

[50]Notably by Aedanus Burke, an Irish judge on the Supreme Court of South Carolina, who published under the name of "Cassius" a widely read pamphlet, *Considerations on the Society or Order of Cincinnati . . . Proving that it creates a Race of Hereditary Patricians, or Nobility*, 1783.

[51]Brissot de Warville, dining at the house of President Cyrus Griffin of the Continental Congress (who, as he reports, had been called to his face "a tavern keeper" by the French Minister, the Marquis de Moustier), reports: "I saw at his house, at dinner, seven or eight women, all dressed in great hats, plumes, &c. It was with pain that I remarked much of pretension in some of these women; one acted the giddy, vivacious; another, the woman of sentiment. This last had many pruderies and grimaces. Two among them had their bosoms very naked. I was scandalized at this indecency among republicans." Q. in Griswold, *Republican Court*, p. 90: for charges of extravagance see Jones, *French Culture*, p. 249.

The Saga of American Society

French dancing-master, M. Violet. In the second place the Revolution, like all wars, pullulated with profiteers, while incomes based on permanent investments in mortgages and the like hit bottom. In the year peace was declared James Bowdoin wrote from Boston to ex-Governor Pownall: "When you come you will see scarcely other than new faces. The change which in that respect has happened within the few years since the revolution is as remarkable as the revolution itself." It was a story to be repeated in 1865 and 1918. Some of these parvenus at first were as uninstructed as that senator in the first Congress, of whom we read that having set up a coach he soon found the "inconveniency of being fashionable," because the irregular adjournments left him stranded for two or three hours in the Senate Chamber "in a state of ennui" waiting for his carriage to take him three or four hundred yards. Upon riches there was a sharply growing emphasis, which happens in every epoch of shattering and remoulding. Chastellux describes an assembly in Philadelphia at which, "on passing into the dining room, the Chevalier de Luzerne presented his hand to Mrs. [Robert] Morris, and gave her the precedence, an honor pretty generally bestowed on her, as she is the richest woman in the city, and all ranks here being equal, men follow their natural bent, by giving the preference to riches."[52] Talleyrand once

[52]Philip Mazzei, another visitor to America in 1785, quotes this passage from Chastellux and comments that precedence of wealth is accorded only in private parties, where no public officials and their wives are present: "An American in reading this account by the marquis would not be deceived; from the precedence yielded to Mrs. Morris he would understand that the wife of the President of Congress was not at the fête, nor yet the wife of the President of Pennsylvania, nor the wife of the Speaker of the General Assembly." But Ferdinand M. Bayard, *Voyage dans l'Intérieur des Etats-Unis,* Paris, 1797, trans. Sherrill, p. 47 says in detail: "The inhabitants of Philadelphia, like all the citizens of the United States, are classified by their fortunes. The first class is composed of carriage folk. Almost all these gentry, whatever their origin, have their coats of arms painted upon their carriage-doors. The son of a deported thief has liveried servants just like everybody else. Nobility having been abolished by the Constitution alone, it is not astonishing that so many individuals pretend to be descended from ancient English families. This fad becomes a sort of mania in mercantile cities. The second class is composed of merchants, lawyers, and business men without carriages, and doctors who pay their visits on foot. In a third class are found people who exercise the mechanical arts. Ladies who possess carriages never so far forget themselves as to receive in their homes those of the third class! . . . Business is mentioned with the same enthusiasm which the French employ to describe some generous action, or to give a panegyric." Bayard's view is extreme, but a residue of fact remains. It is unfortunate that the writing of books about America was for so long left to the foreign visitor, rather than the native son.

was talking to a man in Maine who had never visited Philadelphia, the capital. "When you go there you will be glad to see General Washington." "Yes," the man answered, and with his eyes sparkling added, "and I also want to see Bingham who they say is so rich!"

CHAPTER THREE

ARISTOCRACY IN RETREAT

L E ROI EST MORT; VIVE LE ROI!" might well be the rallying-cry of all
aristocrats. After one type of privilege is destroyed by the radicals,
democrats, and socialists of an era, another rises like the phoenix
from its ruins. Sometimes the radical himself becomes the new
king, and insensibly climbs up the chromatic scale from red to purple—
Cæsar, winning the *populares* by lavish public entertainment and agitating
for a more democratic judiciary, gains the honors of an emperor and even
a god, and the Socialist editor Benito Mussolini becomes Il Duce. Or else
the panoply of aristocracy is changed, so effectually at first that simple
souls are deceived—the frail beak-nosed noble, great-grandson of a strong-
thewed warrior or freebooter, reels to the guillotine amid the cheers of
the rabble, while a new strong man like Napoleon or Lenin prepares
another dynasty for his heirs or friends. In terms of less violent melodrama America during the early nineteenth century witnessed the liquida-
tion of one type of plutocrat and—while the plaudits of democracy rang
loud for three decades—the upsurge of another. To Thomas Jefferson
the dangerous aristocrat was the great landowner, devouring small farm
after farm, and passing on this vast feudality to his eldest son and so on
to the end of time, preventing "that equal distribution of property which
was the legitimate reward of industry"—and therefore to tear out "every
fibre of ancient or future aristocracy," as Jefferson wrote in his Autobiography, he took aim squarely against primogeniture and entail, against
Carrolls, Livingstons, Schuylers, and Van Rensselaers, and made it quite
certain that these at any rate would never be the great American fortunes.
Then he rested from his labors. And behold, on a new horizon another
plutocrat arose, the Federal banker—Nicholas Biddle in Philadelphia,
Robert Lenox in New York, Colonel Thomas H. Perkins in Boston—
and against this "hydra" of "moneyed capitalists" Andrew Jackson
charged as savagely as he had assaulted the British at New Orleans, and
with temporary success. But from the hydra other heads were to spring—

the international banker, the great real estate speculator, the Civil War profiteer, the railroad magnate and Wall Street operator, the manipulator of trusts in oil and steel—which became objects of passing democratic indignation, were attacked, and often died in the hope of a glorious resurrection.

These vicissitudes belong not only to the history of American economics but to Society as well—a connection which has existed to some extent everywhere, but which in the United States is peculiarly compelling because of that development in the national state of mind traced in the previous chapter. Yet the years from the death of planter and patroon to the final solidification of the city industrialist are years of rampant theoretical democracy, of renewed earnestness in attempting to achieve the ideal of the Declaration of Independence. As a result, social records during the first forty years of the nineteenth century are more barren and inglorious than in any other span of our national life. It was not by any means a period of proletarian rule in the Marxist sense, but one dominated by a rising bourgeoisie. Significantly Fredrika Bremer wrote in 1849 that "here, where almost every person works for his living, one cannot properly speak of a working class, but quite correctly of people of small means and somewhat limited environment and circumstances—*a class which has not yet worked itself up.*"

Every ambitious shopkeeper in shirt-sleeves regarded himself as a potential John Jacob Astor or Stephen Girard. In his Sunday clothes he even tried to look as though he had already arrived, thanks to the short-cut of a detachable collar or shirt with a "dicky," while his wife hung her gingham apron behind the pantry-door and appeared by his side in a dress copied by a third-rate mantua-maker from the *Petit Courier des Dames de Paris.*[1] Even in the last years of the eighteenth century La Rochefoucauld found that workingmen and their families ordered sedan-

[1]As early as Revolutionary times Chastellux observed: "So it is that the salary of a workingman must not only provide subsistence for his family, but also comfortable furniture for the home, tea and coffee for his wife, and a silk dress to put on every time she goes out." Bayard notes that "the wife of a laboring man wishes to vie with the merchant's wife, and she in turn will not yield to the richest woman in Europe." Later Beaujour writes: "Elsewhere luxury is only to be found in the upper ranks of society, but here it is everywhere, and it has even penetrated to the cottage of the workingman and the country laborer, so much so that in the United States there is no distinction in dress. The maid is dressed like the mistress, and the poorest workingman like the First Magistrate."

chairs on holidays and were conveyed to public-houses in the neighborhood, to take their gin-sling or threepennyworth of stout, while a generation later Tyrone Power in Mobile saw a merchant's lady, whose
French ball-dress cost $150, dancing in the same set with the modiste who
made it up. Lavish expenditure seems to have received popular approval
save when it came from those who could really afford it. Sir Charles
Lyell tells of an Alabama girl, daughter of a prosperous candidate for the
legislature, who after visiting Mobile returned home with a dress made
with Parisian flounces à la mode—wherefore her father lost the election.[2]
A wiser candidate for office in the same state, well able to afford a carriage,
chose instead to stump the rural districts on foot. In this era arose the
American paradox of the gentleman of classical education feigning illiteracy to get votes—like the Jim Fergusons and Alfalfa Bill Murrays of
a later day—and for the first time in our history the comedy of slang,
cracker-box philosophy, and smoke-house humor came to seem irresistibly
delightful, heralding the cult of Arkansas, Bill Nye, Hosea Biglow, and
Mark Twain. It was the discovery of a great common denominator, a
backhand blow at the precise and supercilious East. The grand manner
was on the wane everywhere, except perhaps in a few drawing-rooms in
Beacon Street or Washington Square and a score of stately houses in
Charleston and New Orleans.

The stronghold of political and social democracy was the frontier,
where, as it used to be said, "the rifle and the axe made all men equally
tall"—the original democratic thesis in America. Bacon's Rebellion,
Shays's Rebellion, the Whiskey Insurrection, and other protests against
the rich and powerful seemed to brew there, as storms in a cyclone belt,
and move eastward. What had been true of an earlier time grew even
more valid in the nineteenth century as the frontier grew longer and the
seaboard more entrenched in tradition. A gentleman of the British
Court, Charles Augustus Murray, in his book of travels published in 1839,
noted that while distinctions of fortune and family were sharply felt in
conservative circles of the East, in the West he saw the clerk of a steam-

[2]The new nationalism repudiated the spirit of Old World courtliness while frequently aping its trappings—often, it would appear, throwing away the grain to keep
the chaff. H. M. Jones in his study of *America and French Culture,* to which I
am indebted for various examples in this chapter, remarks, p. 266: "French manners become less and less important, French dresses become more and more conse-
quential."

boat and a grocer in a small Missouri River town sit down to grog and a game of cards with a Congressman and an army officer—all chatting, swearing, laughing, and calling each other by their first names.

The manner in which the spirit of frontier democracy asserted itself in national affairs, and to some extent deflected the course of American Society, might be sketched. First of all, the Revolution itself not only helped to set up new plutocrats, as has been noted, but also broke down much of the reverence that hedged the old. Major Anbury, a British officer held as prisoner of war in Virginia, remarked it keenly:

An instance of it I saw at Colonel Randolph's at Tuckahoe, where three country peasants, who came upon business, entered the room where the Colonel and his company were sitting, took themselves chairs, drew near the fire, began spitting, pulling off their country boots all over mud, and then opened their business, which was simply about some continental flour to be ground at the Colonel's mill. When they were gone, some one observed what great liberties they took; he replied it was unavoidable, the spirit of independence was converted into equality, and every one who bore arms esteemed himself upon a footing with his neighbor, and concluded by saying: "No doubt, each of these men conceives himself, in every respect, my equal."

Today, incidentally, the term "peasant" has almost died out of aristocratic usage in America—though at least one member of the Coolidge family, owning a distinguished connection with Harvard University, employs it privately. Early in the Revolution, on July 13, 1776, the radical *Pennsylvania Evening Post* called upon Americans to abandon all titles of Excellency and Honorable,[3] and a little later *The Boston Daily Advertiser* declared "Americans should have but one denomination—the People." The Constitution was careful to provide that the United States should grant no titles of nobility, and that no office-holder should without the consent of Congress accept any title, office, or present from a king or foreign power. Jefferson insisted, in the teeth of Federalist opposi-

---

[3]*The Evening Post* a few months earlier, April 27, 1776, got in a few licks at the aristocrat in politics, with his ingratiating methods of vote-getting: "A poor man has rarely the honor of speaking to a gentleman on any terms. How many poor men, common men and mechanics have been made happy within this fortnight by a shake of the hand, a pleasing smile and a little familiar chat with gentlemen who have not for these seven years past condescended to look at them. Blessed state which brings all so nearly on a level!" Cf. Gustavus Myers, *History of American Idealism* (New York, 1925), p. 54.

tion, that no titled foreigner could be admitted to U. S. citizenship until he had renounced his title. One of the noble emigrés who found refuge in Philadelphia, the Vicomte de Noailles, was much criticized in the public press because he insisted that a notary give him his full title and honors, including Chevalier de Saint-Louis and Knight of Malta. Less snobbish Frenchmen glowed at the new egalitarian spirit. Lafayette—whose democratic memory is still anathema in the Faubourg St. Germain—wrote to his young wife: "The richest and the poorest are on a level, and although there are immense fortunes in this country, I defy any one to find the slightest difference in the manners of one toward the other."[4] Other visitors like Brissot praised such a detail as the American stagecoach, in which everybody rode side by side and talked with the greatest ease, laborer with Congressman, mechanic with the son of Governor Livingston, the humbler trying "to rise to the level of the other." It is not without significance that Americans ever since have travelled—whether by river steamer, canal boat, railway train, streetcar, or bus—in a long narrow saloon, thrown together in close but casual association, without the invidious partitions and compartments known to other countries.[5]

During George Washington's Administration echoes of riot, borne from the far-away Tuileries and Bastille, stirred the more excitable democrats, and the arrival of Citizen Genet in 1793 well-nigh stampeded them. Even in sedate Charleston, when a statue of Lord Chatham which was being moved out of the way of traffic, fell and snapped off its head, the newspapers inanely rejoiced in the incident as ".ominous to the aristocrats." In Philadelphia it became the rage to call everybody "Citizen"

[4]Lafayette—who by the way later bore his share of suffering for the Crown—was a kindly idealist. Equally enthusiastic over the perfection of American democracy was William Cobbett, who lived here from 1817 to 1819 and wrote: "The American labourers, like the tavern-keepers, are never *servile*, but always *civil*. Neither *boobishness* nor *meanness* marks their character. They never creep and fawn, and are never *rude*. . . . Full pocket or empty pocket, these American labourers are always the *same men;* no saucy cunning in the one case, and no base crawling in the other. This, too, arises from the free institutions of government. A man has a voice *because he is a man,* and not because he is the *possessor of money."*

[5]For a very brief period the earliest American railroad coaches were on the style of later European cars, with compartments and exterior running-board, but the type was soon abandoned, and from 1840 till today there has been no essential change in our railway architecture. Cf. Fish, *Rise of the Common Man* (New York, 1927), pp. 82–83. The modern Pullman drawing-room and the even rarer private car are, of course, highly special exceptions which aristocracy has achieved.

and even in the press to announce marriages as partnerships formed between Citizen Jones and *Citess* Smith. Governor Mifflin was present at a dinner where a roast pig was served, labelled "Louis XVI," and after the head was severed from the body it was carried round to each guest, who, placing a liberty-cap upon his own brow, would cry out "Tyrant!" and with the knife from his plate mangle the hapless head. A tavern displayed as its sign a picture of the bloody torso of Marie Antoinette, to attract democratic trade. Politeness, we are told, "was looked upon as a sort of *lèse republicanisme*," while the word "aristocrat" became an epithet of vilest abuse. Citizen Genet himself, upon going to call at the President's house, saw in the vestibule a bust of the late King, and complained of it as "an insult to France." In the end, however, he heard news of the ill-success of his own faction in Paris, feared to go home, and somewhat ignobly ended his crusade for liberty, equality, and fraternity by marrying the homely but rich daughter of Governor Clinton and settling down as an amateur farmer and inventor of a balloon propelled by steam.

The great schism between the Jeffersonians and the Hamiltonians had distinctly social overtones—though by an unforgettable piece of irony the claims of blue blood and wealth found their champion in Alexander Hamilton, a West Indian of illegitimate birth who had started life with neither money nor prospects, "the bastard brat of a Scotch pedlar" as John Adams called him with more envy then scorn. Burning with insatiable ambitions, Hamilton as a boy had prayed for a war to break out so that he might rise upon the upheaval, and when it did come he took his chances magnificently, gained the friendship of Washington, Jay, and the Livingstons, received the Treasury portfolio, built up a brilliant law practice, married a Schuyler, and founded a family which has never lost the frank arrogance of its grandsire. Hamilton adored caste and riches, with an intensity perhaps unknown to those who inherit them. He will always stand as the apologist par excellence for the industrial rich, of whom he said: "Their vices are probably more favorable to the prosperity of the State than those of the indigent, and partake less of moral depravity." As Gouverneur Morris wrote after Hamilton fell by the pistol of Burr, he was "in principle opposed to republican and attached to monarchical government," and had espoused American Independence out of the shrewd instinct of an opportunist. Frequently he and his friends—like John Jay, who believed that "those who own the country ought to govern it"—coquetted with the idea of a crown and sceptre in America, but also knew how implausible a scheme it was.

With equal irony, his enemy Thomas Jefferson, whose eight-year Administration ushered in the Golden Age of democracy, was a scion of the Randolphs. Jefferson once said that they traced "their pedigree far back in England and Scotland, to which let every one ascribe the faith and merit he chooses." But from his father, of stout yeoman stock partly Welsh, as well as from his early schooling in Louisa County, a veritable hot-bed of frontier radicalism and Presbyterian dissent, Jefferson seems to have drawn the pungency of his political and social views, which comported so well with his red hair, angular frame, and preference for carpet-slippers to silver buckles—those notorious slippers in which he received foreign ambassadors as well as ladies of quality. Upon witnessing the French Revolution he told his friends "there is not a crowned head in Europe whose talents or merits would entitle him to be elected a vestry-man by the people of any parish in America," and also added some dark words about once in twenty years watering the tree of liberty with the blood of tyrants. Snubbed by Philadelphia Society in the 1790's for the radicalism of his opinions, Jefferson today would be considered hopelessly stuffy in those modernistic drawing-rooms of the amusingly radical rich, in Mayfair, on Park Avenue, and along the Main Line. For his was an agrarian doctrine, having no commerce with what he called "the *canaille*" of European cities, but grounded in the belief that farmers "are the true representatives of the great American interest, and are alone to be relied upon for expressing the proper American sentiments."

The fair distribution of land seemed to the gentleman farmer of Monticello to be the most vital safeguard of political and social equality, and therefore he set out to crush all vestiges of primogeniture and entail. Their destruction has had an almost incalculable effect upon American Society. It meant that the tap-root of the British gentry, the county families, would have no counterpart in modern America. Such growth as had already been made, in tidewater Virginia, Maryland, and the Hudson Valley, was weeded out within a generation. Also it meant, in collaboration with an industrialism which Jefferson did not foresee, the rise of an urban plutocracy, which for all its summer homes at Southampton, Easthampton, Lenox, Prides Crossing, Nahant, and Newport, was bound indissolubly with the cities from which its strength was drawn. In England a

George Washington

From a painting by Gilbert Stuart,
in the Metropolitan Museum of Art

Martha Washington

From a lithograph, probably after Gilbert Stuart's
unfinished painting

Lady Washington's Reception at the White House

After a painting by Daniel Huntington

Alexander Hamilton

From a painting by James Sharpless

Thomas Jefferson

From a painting by Gilbert Stuart

James Madison

From a portrait by Gilbert Stuart

James Monroe

From a painting by Gilbert Stuart

gentleman is traditionally Sir John Smith of Ashton Park, Staffordshire, no matter how imposing a house he may keep in the West End, whereas in the United States, to the disregard of his country villas for summer or winter residence, he is essentially Mr. John Smith of New York or Philadelphia. This usage is more than a convention; it is a symbol of the almost inescapable shackles of business. For the English week-end—that institutional convalescence upon which, it is said, the calm and assurance of British politics are based—we have sought, somewhat wistfully, to substitute the country-club, or the life of the commuter attempting daily to serve the God who made the country and Mammon who made the town. And finally, the breaking up of large landed estates in favor of younger children and potential spendthrifts has speeded the social turnover of America generation after generation. Despite efforts of the first Astor and the first Vanderbilt to concentrate their fortunes in the hands of the ablest son, both vast accumulations have now been scattered through a dozen families on both sides of the Atlantic, while Jay Gould's seventy-seven million have evaporated even faster. Although several states have left notable loopholes in the Rule against Perpetuities—such as "the Massachusetts spendthrift law" which since 1830 has enabled canny Bostonians to tie up family funds against creditors, business risks, and prodigality—the solidification of great fortunes *en bloc,* in land or in gold, has come to be frowned upon. The will of the first Marshall Field, with provisions for extending accumulations in trust until thirty-nine years after his death and denying his grandchildren possession until that date, was disclosed in 1906 and caused a storm of disapproval; the Illinois legislature responded by passing an act prohibiting such accumulations beyond the time when the heirs living at the testator's death shall come of age. As early as 1839 Francis J. Grund, an inquiring young German who made a special study of aristocracy in America,[6] predicted that no sort of permanent caste would ever be possible because "scarcely one fourth" of the then rich men had inherited their wealth and the traditions of wealth, while their heirs scattered it as quickly as it had been gathered. Unlike the *ancien régime* in Europe, the American plutocracy was not self-perpetuating. The present drift toward the confiscation of large fortunes through in-

[6]In 1837 he published in the United States and in England his book called *The Americans: in their Moral, Social, and Political Relations,* and two years later from a press in Stuttgart appeared *Die Aristokratie in Amerika aus dem Tagebuch eines deutschen Edelmanns.*

The Saga of American Society

heritance-taxes is but another and finally decisive step in the same direction. At first bound by a few strands of Lilliputian cord of which he was scarcely aware, the titan of wealth now finds himself so beset with legal hindrances against accumulations that he can no longer make the gesture of handing intact a princely fortune to his heirs.

Jefferson was the first who dared challenge the old hereditary principles of Europe. Primogeniture, long entrenched in English common law, was of very slow growth in America during the seventeenth century, partly because land was cheap and abundant, partly because there were so few means of livelihood other than farming for younger sons. But in the eighteenth century its practice was on the increase, especially among families of great pride, like the Byrds, Carrolls, Calverts, Livingstons, and Van Rensselaers, who wished to keep up their name in suitable style. Entail, which made properties inalienable, added security to pomp. In New England entail was not unknown, though in place of primogeniture the more democratic principle of the "gavelkind of Kent," with equal division among the sons, was followed. But in Virginia, the stronghold of both, Jefferson mobilized his energy and rhetoric for the attack, and in 1776 by a small majority the Legislature prohibited entail. Exultingly Jefferson said:

> To annul this privilege, and instead of an aristocracy of wealth, of more harm and danger than benefit to society, to make an opening for the aristocracy of virtue and talent, which nature has wisely provided for the direction of the interests of society, and scattered with an equal hand throughout all its conditions, was deemed essential to a well-ordered republic.[7]

To the scandal of his maternal relatives the Randolphs, Jefferson went on to assail primogeniture. When his friend Pendleton begged him to compromise on a law allowing the eldest son a double share of land, Jefferson retorted, "Yes, when he can eat twice the allowance of food and do double the allowance of work." In 1785 the Virginia Legislature

[7]In his *Memoirs* Jefferson wrote: "At the time of the first settlement of the English in Virginia, when land was had for little or nothing, some provident persons having obtained large grants of it, and being desirous of maintaining the splendor of their families, entailed their property on their descendants. The transmission of these estates from generation to generation, to men who bore the same name, had the effect of raising up a distinct class of families, who, possessing by law the privilege of perpetuating their wealth, formed by these means a sort of patrician order, distinguished by the grandeur and luxury of their establishments."

rewarded his efforts by making primogeniture illegal. In 1784 North
Carolina abolished both "principles of the European feudal system . . .
to raise the wealth and importance of particular families and individuals,
giving them unequal and undue influence." By 1787 the remaining states
had followed suit. The death of Charles Carroll of Carrollton in 1832
with the breaking up of his 80,000-acre estate in Maryland, Pennsylvania,
and New York, and the death in 1839 of Stephen Van Rensselaer, heir of
a grant which originally comprised 700,000 acres, now dispersed so effectually that within fifty years every acre had passed into the hands of
strangers[8]—these were the crashing of the last giant oaks. In South
Carolina no more great houses like Fairlawn or Newington were built,
and planters soon found that their inheritance was no longer ample
enough to send their sons to the English universities.[9] In 1835 Edward
S. Abdy asked a Virginian how long estates remained in the same family,
and was told: "The longest period may be three or four generations. I
do not think I could point out one in possession of an estate that belonged
to it at the Revolution. The poor and industrious soon succeed to the rich
and extravagant, and a perpetual change is going on between them."

Of course there were makeshifts left to the most stubborn clans—such
as marriage of cousins, or the convention of leaving the "home place"
to the eldest son while the rest of the property was parcelled out among
the others, or a scheme of piecemeal reversion which Miss Martineau discovered as an occasional ruse, but in general she records that by 1834–36
"the popular feeling is so strong against transmitting large estates, and
favouring one child, that nobody attempts to do it."[10] Another British

[8]William Stephen Van Rensselaer, for example, one of the few remaining
descendants to bear the family name, died in 1930 leaving an estate of $2500. Other
Van Rensselaers however have done better through marriage, because there are
few American names so attractive to arriving heiresses.

[9]To Banister, Jefferson wrote: "But why send an American youth to Europe for
education? . . . If he goes to Europe he learns drinking, horse-racing, and boxing.
These are the peculiarities of English education." And as typical of results from
all European education he named "contempt for the simplicity of his own country,"
fascination with aristocracy, and un-American dress, manners, and pronunciation.
Cf. S. E. Forman, *Life and Writings of Jefferson,* Indianapolis, 1900, pp. 196–7.

[10]Yet in New York State certain feudal rights were claimed on the old manors
up to 1846, when the new State Constitution abolished them—*e.g.,* some leases
obliged the tenant to get permission in writing before he could entertain a stranger
in his house for the day, and he was often compelled to buy all his commodities
at the manorial store and to grind his wheat at the proprietor's mill. The U. S.
Commission on Industrial Relations in 1916 pointed out later vestiges in America
of the hereditary principle "which has bulwarked the British aristocracy for centuries."

visitor, Captain Basil Hall in 1827–28, deplored the passing of primogeniture as tending infallibly to vulgarize American Society, and indeed some evidence seems to bear him out. In an access of democratic enthusiasm in Maryland which followed the uprooting of old estates, we read that coats of arms were destroyed and even erased from family silver, and all evidences of pride of lineage frowned down by American patriots and their descendants, so that not to know the maiden name of one's grandmother was common. Beverley Tucker apologized for putting on record a brief history of his family, remarking that "at this day it is deemed arrogant to remember one's ancestors. But the fashion may change." The father of President Tyler, we are told, "used to say that he cared naught for any other ancestor than Wat Tyler the blacksmith, who had asserted the rights of oppressed humanity, and that he would have no other device on his shield than a sledge hammer raised in the act of striking."[11] A South Carolinian of the new school was that individual whom Alexander Mackay met in 1846, who, though resplendent in a yellow waistcoat and a swallow-tail coat of indigo blue, replied to Mackay's questions about genealogy by saying: "We don't vally these things in this country. It's what's above ground, not what's under, that we think on."

Though Jefferson dealt the old aristocracy its deepest wound by his overthrow of hereditary principles, he commenced in later life to flaunt gayer social heresies. Before he succeeded Adams as President in 1801, and for some weeks after inauguration until the White House was finished, Jefferson lived at Conrad's boarding-house on Capitol Hill, and there as his friend Margaret Bayard Smith recalled, he "occupied during the whole winter the lowest and coldest seat at a long table at which a company of more than thirty sat down." In vain the proprietress of the boarding-house attempted to coax him to a higher seat at least among the Congressmen, but with his usual exquisite courtesy the President of the United States declined, and continued at the foot. When the White House at last was opened, and he began giving dinner parties himself, he always seated his guests at a circular table—on the principle of *inter pares* which seems to have been invented by King Arthur. Straightway

[11]Cf. *William and Mary College Quarterly,* vol. I, p. 53. The watchword of Wat Tyler's Rebellion was the famous couplet
"When Adam delved and Eve span,
Who was then the gentleman?"

he abolished the weekly levees in which Washingtons and Adamses had rejoiced, and when a group of indignant ladies appeared in their best party-dresses at the customary hour of the levee they found Jefferson out riding. They grimly resolved to wait, and have a Presidential levee willy-nilly. Soon the President appeared in boots and dusty clothes, gracious and suave as only a Randolph of Virginia who had lived long at the Court of Louis XVI knew how to be, and treated the call as a delightful surprise, with such adroitness that the ladies left charmed, bewildered, and routed. In view of his lavish hospitality—which called for the best Madeira and champagne at every dinner, and the ministrations of eleven servants including a French cook, a French steward, and an Irish coachman, for such was Jefferson's idea of republican simplicity— John Quincy Adams observed that Jefferson's "whole eight years was a levee." Unlike Washington he assumed no trappings of royal dignity, but even when receiving foreign ministers remained dressed in "a blue coat, a thick gray-colored hairy waistcoat, with a red underwaist lapped over it, green velveteen breeches with pearl buttons, yarn stockings, and slippers down at the heels," and as Senator Maclay describes him, generally sitting "in a lounging manner, on one hip commonly." One foreign ambassador, going in the morning to pay him a visit of ceremony, was deeply shocked to find him blacking his own shoes; Jefferson explained that he hated to cause his servants needless trouble. To another diplomat, from Denmark, who mildly rebuked him for appearing in shabby slippers, Jefferson good-humoredly told the story of King Ferdinand of Naples who complained to one of his ministers that ceremonies were such a bore, and asked if some couldn't be dispensed with—only to receive the reply: "Ah, your Majesty must remember that you, yourself, are but a ceremony."

But most heretical was his new rule of etiquette that "all persons when brought together in society are perfectly equal, whether foreign or domestic, titled or untitled, in or out of office." In place of the old gradations, therefore, he inaugurated what he was pleased to call "the rule of pell-mell," that is "of gentlemen in mass giving precedence to the ladies in mass, in passing from one apartment in which they are assembled into another." Mr. Merry, the British Minister freshly come from London, and not a little vexed already at having been jolted over frozen roads in the carriage he hired at Alexandria, and at the discovery that the city of Washington was so primeval that partridges could be shot from the doorway of his house on K Street, was invited to dinner at the White House. He had never heard of "pell-mell" save as a tract in London with a different spelling, and no more had his masterful wife whom Jefferson in private came to call "a virago." Other guests were the Spanish Minister, the lofty Marquis de Casa Yrujo, and his wife, born Sally McKean of Philadelphia, the French Minister Pichon and his wife, and James and Dolly Madison. When dinner was announced Jefferson took in Dolly—the hostess of his widowed Administration—and seated her on his right, leaving the rest to straggle in as they might. Furious, the Merrys left as soon as dinner was over. A few days later at a dinner-party at the Madisons' they received what they regarded as a further insult when Mrs. Merry, in the chaos of pell-mell, was left without a partner. Unappeased even when told about New World etiquette, the sulking Merrys refused to attend the President's New Year's Day reception, and, as the amused Pichon reported, "Washington Society is turned upside down." Making one overture of conciliation, Jefferson invited the unhappy pair to "take a friendly and familiar dinner" with him, but when Mrs. Merry answered with a long, punctilious letter inquiring whether they were being bidden in their "public" or "private" capacity, Jefferson instructed Madison to send his regrets concerning "the points of form which will deprive him of the pleasure of Mr. Merry's company at dinner on Monday next." Merry, who never again appeared socially at the White House, announced that he had written his Government for instructions—while Sally McKean Yrujo, who sided with the aggrieved Britons, rushed into a drawing-room crying, "Oh, this will mean war." Of course it meant no such thing, but it is more than possible that the hatred which Merrys and Yrujos came to feel against Jefferson and his pell-mell made them listen so sympathetically to Burr's schemes of treason shortly thereafter, and give him unwarranted hopes that England and Spain might help to spike the guns of this preposterous democrat.[12]

In the great shadow of Jefferson the sapling of democracy grew, pro-

[12]The Irish poet Tom Moore, a guest of the Merrys, piqued likewise when Jefferson failed to make much over him, wrote some insulting couplets about Washington, where expectant visitors come—
"Though nought but woods, and Jefferson they see,
Where streets should run, and sages ought to be."

tected from the withering scorn of Federalism—which, like the sun at noonday in Washington's and Hamilton's time, sank rapidly after their death until it set about 1815. Jefferson passed on his protectorship to Madison (1809–1817) and to Monroe (1817–1825), who although at heart less zealous democrats than their master, could not but regard the trust as binding. If Hamilton had succeeded to the Presidency instead of Jefferson, and if his life had been spared on the heights of Weehawken, quite probably the aristocracy of wealth and privilege—with all the social effulgence it radiated—would have dominated the American skies instead of being reduced to the little cloud of "perpetual vapour above Niagara" of which Harriet Martineau speaks. There is no gainsaying the fact that Jefferson, more than any other man in American history, curbed at the crucial time the power and glory to which the Society of a new republic aspired. He belongs in fact at the well-spring of a tradition which so far has received little notice from our social historians—that of the radical aristocrat in America, the man or woman whose blue blood or wealth, or both, have lent a keener appreciation of social justice, together with the resources for doing something about it.

In this tradition belongs Judith Cary Bell, who at the time of the Virginia Convention wrote to her brother Colonel Archibald Cary urging that he help abolish primogeniture and disestablish the Anglican Church; Charles Pinckney of South Carolina, who stood shoulder to shoulder with Jefferson; Edward Livingston, who—as Oliver Wolcott enviously wrote—lived "in the style of a nabob," yet espoused the cause of Jacksonian democracy with such ardor that the lowly rallied round, and carried him repeatedly to high office. There was Albert Gallatin, descended from the premier family of Switzerland, who became a passionate democrat; and a small company of high-born abolitionists on the eve of the Civil War, like Julia Ward Howe—whose daughter Maude Howe Elliott still remembers how at Papanti's Dancing School in Boston she was called "a nasty little abolitionist." Boston, in fact, most patrician of American cities, has been a seed-bed for this exotic paradox—of advanced and often radical ideas springing from inherited wealth and the most intense conservatism in daily life. This is perhaps part of its invincible Puritanism, of which an observer has lately remarked that its own heretics are its saints. The last generation remembers Josephine Shaw Lowell, who early in the 1880's founded the Charity Organization Society of New York, worked for civil service reform, college settlements, the labor movement, and prison reform,[13] and Charles Mills Cabot with his effective agitation to get better working conditions and shorter hours for employees of U. S. Steel and his fruitful investigation of workers' lives in the cotton mills of the South. This is the Boston which in our own times rioted for war when women and children went down on the *Lusitania,* and seethed with rage at the subjugation of Manchuria. Even Sacco and Vanzetti found a handful of defenders in the Somerset Club, while the late President Charles W. Eliot belonged, as his best friends knew, somewhere to the left of center. Among milder paradoxes should not be forgotten Woodrow Wilson, somewhat finicky Virginia patrician, making the world safe for democracy, and Gifford and Amos Pinchot in the hidebound industrial East. And to continue into the debatable arena of our own times, Philadelphia has its William C. Bullitt and Francis B. Biddle, Michigan its late James Couzens, New Mexico its late Bronson Cutting, New York City that infra-red, Corliss Lamont. The President of the United States has drawn many of his friends from the less extreme Left. Even the great dynasty of Wilmington has produced its radical, Evan du Pont, who bequeathed his entire fortune to the Communist Party, leaving his two daughters to be brought up by charitable relatives. The exquisite irony of fate has given to Senator Bingham, as well as to Stanley Baldwin overseas, the possession of a Socialist son.[14]

[13]A collection of the letters and papers of this interesting woman was edited in 1911 by William Rhinelander Stewart. Cynics may remark that the Bostonian often directs his crusades against other geographical regions, notably New York, the Middle West, and the South. Even Major Henry Lee Higginson, whom some may regard as a Tory of Tories, wrote from Burlington, Iowa in 1870, whither he had gone to investigate his railroad properties: "Money, money, success in material pursuits! It is injuring our generation, but perhaps the next may be the better for it, more good and educated men and women may strive for the welfare and civilization of America." Among the great industrialists of a generation ago who were considered rather radical should be mentioned John H. Patterson, owner of the National Cash Register Company of Dayton, Ohio, who made his life-hobby the building of club-rooms, kindergartens and high schools, lecture-halls, rest-rooms and cooking schools, and the enhancing of social intercourse among his employees —to the extent of giving them a great annual summer party at Far Hills with a concert, supper, and a cotillion "led by a prominent New Yorker." Of course such benevolent paternalism as his and Mr. Henry Ford's arouses more than suspicion in the breast of the Union Square radical.

[14]It is of interest to recall that *The New Republic,* current forum for liberals and intellectual pinks, was founded in 1914 under the endowment of Willard D. Straight, late banker, international railway magnate, diplomat, and Morgan associ-

Aristocracy in Retreat

No one in his senses would dare pick the sincere from the poseurs in this goodly company, or distinguish the Red badge of courage from the dash of pink which many well-dressed minds are wearing this season. They all, however, have some claim upon the heritage of Monticello.[15]

After an interlude of four years under cold, well-meaning, but unpopular John Quincy Adams, the democrats returned to power with the first plebeian President of the United States, Andrew Jackson. Here at last were the theories of Jefferson in a tenement of common clay. Of poor Scotch-Irish squatter stock, Old Hickory never learned to speak or write correctly, chewed tobacco incessantly, and shifted from riding-boots to stocking feet. With his stout, florid wife, "Aunt Rachel"—who was given lessons in table-manners by Mrs. Edward Livingston, after the Battle of New Orleans—Jackson responded to applause at the grand ball given him by the flower of Creole aristocracy, by showing the city folks what real dancing was, to the tune of *Possum up de Gum Tree*. Following Jackson's election to the Presidency in 1828, the death in Tennessee that winter of Aunt Rachel was learned by Washington society circles, as a contemporary tells us, with "a sense of relief."

The Inauguration of Jackson on March 4, 1829 marks, beyond much

ate, and his wife, born Dorothy Whitney, daughter of William C. Whitney. She is now best known for the progressive school she has sponsored in England, her present home.

[15]The rage for democracy in the first third of the nineteenth century was so potent as to get some of the most entrenched reactionaries into the habit of paying at least lip-service to it. Thus William Jay in New York wrote to Fenimore Cooper in Paris, January 5, 1827: "I was much amused with the lively picture you give me of french Society. It entirely agrees with the opinion I had previously formed of it. . . . Vice and luxury lead to universal selfishness, and selfishness, by sacrificing the interests and happiness of others to individual gratification, mars and interrupts the general welfare. . . . May our republican simplicity and religious habits never be exchanged for the magnificence, heartlessness and wretchedness of France." *Correspondence of Cooper* (New Haven, 1922), vol. I, pp. 112–13. In January, 1834, after attending a great ball at Robert Ray's new house in "Fitz-ray Place" on Ninth Avenue and a sumptuous dinner at Mr. Spofford's with wine at "eight or ten dollars a bottle," Philip Hone—stiffest of all new-made plutocrats and men about town—meditated in his Diary: "It may be painful to reflect how far the cost of a single bottle of Mr. Spofford's wine or one of Mr. Ray's *pâtés de foie gras* might contribute to alleviate the distress of those miserable objects who stretch out the attenuated arms of wasted poverty, or display the haggard countenance of infantile deprivation, or the tattered habiliments incapable of resisting the inclemency of the winter's cold." After the probable touch of dyspepsia—which seems to be reflected in such flatulent rhetoric—had passed, Hone was consoling himself with the thought that lavish entertaining "is all right enough" if one is solvent financially, and probably helps prosperity. *Diary*, ed. Nevins (New York, 1927), pp. 785–86.

doubt, the low water-mark of official Society in America. It was the People's saturnalia. After the Oath had been taken, thousands of people —buckskins, poor whites, cross-roads politicians, mulattoes and blacks, who had come to Washington to see the investiture of their idol—made a wild dash for the White House. When the doors were jammed the assault was carried to the windows. Waiters bearing trays of orange punch, saw the glasses snatched away before they were well into the room. Many were borne to the floor to scramble helplessly among rivulets of punch and shards of broken glass and china. Clamoring to be served, men in muddy boots stood upon damask-covered chairs, knocking mirrors and bric-a-brac from the walls with their gesticulations. One witness remarked: "It would have done Mr. Wilberforce's heart good to have seen a stout black wench eating in this free country a jelly with a gold spoon at the President's House." Somebody dragged a few tubs of punch out on the White House lawn, and about them eddied late-comers and those who had retreated with smarting noses from the main salon. It was feared at one point that the President himself would be suffocated by his devoted following; the smashing of a window afforded timely relief. Twenty thousand people, it was said, who had broken "cut glass and china to the amount of several thousand dollars . . . in the struggle to get the refreshments." "What a pity—what a pity!" wrote Margaret Bayard Smith to Mrs. Kirkpatrick. "Ladies fainted, men were seen with bloody noses and such a scene of confusion took place as is impossible to describe—those who got in could not get out by the door again, but had to scramble out of windows." Pell-mell indeed.

Good form was now in eclipse. Every guest at a White House dinner was provided with two forks, steel and silver, to take his choice; Jackson preferred steel. Friends dropped in before breakfast, or in the evening, as inclination prompted. At the later hour they were sure to find him in the White House living-room, smoking a reed pipe with a red clay bowl, with his niece Mrs. Donelson sewing, and half a dozen children playing on the floor. His critics, especially the feminine precursors of the later "cave-dwellers" of Washington, were uncommonly severe. When he gave large parties they complained of the presence of "Irish laborers . . . in their shirt sleeves," and when parties were small they sneered at "a little set of exclusives . . . under the immediate patronage of the President. . . . The scale established by the President is peculiarly arbitrary;

for instance, clerks with three thousand dollars salary are invited; those of two thousand are excluded." Any stranger with a scintilla of standing could, however, get an invitation to all the soirées by the simple expedient of leaving his card inscribed with his local address a few days beforehand. The Washington hotel-books were combed eagerly for distinguished foreign names before invitations were posted.[16] And Old Hickory did indeed have his pardonable vanities; for example an artist named Earl was hired to live at the White House during the eight years of his Administration, and do nothing but paint one picture after another of the President.

Jackson carried out two crusades against entrenched privilege. The first was his overturn of all office-holders who had imagined themselves inviolate from administration to administration, with the then novel cry "Turn the rascals out!" To insure political office from aristocratic tenure the spoils system was frankly begun, as party henchmen picked for blind loyalty rather than brains swarmed like rats to the corn-crib. Of course not all officials before Jackson's day had been gentlemen of uniform birth, breeding, and integrity—but now with security completely gone, and blue blood become the gravest of handicaps, the aristocrat said good-bye to public service and retired to his ivory towers on Commonwealth Avenue or Gramercy Park, from which ever since he has been loath to emerge. The few who stayed, like Francis Preston Blair, editor of the Administration paper *The Globe,* learned to sling the new political billingsgate while their patrician families blushed in silence.

The second was Jackson's destruction of the second Bank of the United States, chartered in 1816 for twenty years as the authorized financial agent of the Government, with a monopoly on the issue of all legal-tender money except that coined directly by Federal power. With a branch in

[16]George Bancroft, one of the social impeccables of Washington, with a sincere liking for Jackson's rugged honesty but a feeling of outrage at his levees, wrote in 1831: "The old man stood in the center of a little circle, about large enough for a cotillion, and shook hands with everybody that offered. The number of ladies who attended was small; nor were they brilliant. But to compensate for it there was a throng of apprentices, boys of all ages, men not civilized enough to walk about the room with their hats off; the vilest promiscuous medley that ever was congregated in a decent house; many of the lowest gathering round the doors, pouncing with avidity upon the wine and refreshments, tearing the cake with the ravenous keenness of intense hunger; starvelings, and fellows with dirty faces and dirty manners; all the refuse that Washington could turn forth from its workshops and stables."

every state, its headquarters were in Philadelphia, where its president since 1823, Nicholas Biddle, brooded over its heap of $35,000,000—the bad rich dragon of his day. Jackson, who in 1817 had refused to sign a petition "got up by the aristocracy of Nashville" for a branch in that city, promised the voters in 1828 and again in 1832 that he would never renew its lease. Amid cheers from the frontier and groans from the seaboard, this pledge was kept, and in 1836 the Bank of the United States expired— to reappear of course under a state charter as the Bank of the United States of Pennsylvania, and to pave the way for the dominion of Wall Street and those international financiers like George Peabody, Joshua Bates, Anthony J. Drexel, and the first J. P. Morgan. Fortunately for his peace of mind Jackson had no gifts of prophecy, and at the close of his Administration exulted in the stand he had taken against "the combined talents, wealth, and power of the whole aristocracy of the United States." Mr. Biddle—who according to William Cullen Bryant in the New York *Evening Post* should have passed his declining years "in the penitentiary" —withdrew quietly from public odium. In fact so completely had bygones become bygones in the Administration of Jackson's protégé Van Buren that the banker was received in Washington as an honored guest. However, the slings and arrows of outrageous fortune still pursued Mr. Biddle, inadvertently as it were, for concerning this occasion we read: "At supper he was seated next to a lady next the President, at the head of the center-table. At the close of the supper, a rush was made for the roses with which the chandeliers were ornamented. One hung over the head of the President, and so eager were those who contended for the spoils, that they broke the fastenings of the chandelier, and down it came on Mr. Van Buren's head, roses, grease, and all, causing him to retreat to his carriage with his whole outward man in disorder. Mr. Biddle and Mr. Clay saved themselves and the ladies under their charge." Again Mr. Biddle had escaped by the skin of his teeth, like a hero of melodrama.

There was no end in sight to the horrors of democracy—Philip Hone, who had worked himself up from the auction business to be a founder of the Union Club, a mayor of New York City, and father-in-law to a Schermerhorn, was kept awake the night after the Democratic landslide of November 5, 1834 "by the unmanly insults of the ruffian crew from Tammany Hall, who came over to my door every half hour and saluted me with groans and hisses." Yet political exuberance was not altogether on the side of Tammany, for when the Whigs won the next big municipal election the New York *Sun* for December 30, 1837 carried the following announcement:

THE BIGGEST FIRE YET

The Springfield (Illinois) *Journal* gives notice, that on the eighth day of January next—wind, weather, and snow permitting—the Grand Prairie will be set on fire, in commemoration of the great Whig victory in New-York. The prairie is about three hundred miles long, with an average breadth of from ten to twenty miles. The fires to be lighted at eight o'clock in the evening.

Indeed the newly re-formed conservative party, the Whigs, showed a quickness in learning tricks to stampede the electorate which would have done credit to the great Conservative Party in modern England, with its Zinoviev forgeries and protection of Ethiopia. Its first act, by a feat of almost accidental magic, was to stick the hated label of aristocracy on Jackson's smug little disciple in the White House, Martin Van Buren. Although Van Buren's levees seem to have been, heaven knows, democratic enough—for we hear from Miss Martineau of men in plaid cloaks and leather belts, and women in bonnets and shawls poking about the White House on reception days, and two country girls "being lifted up by their escorting gentlemen, and seated on the two ends of the mantelpiece, like lustres, where they could obtain a view of the company as they entered"—yet "Little Van" himself loved good food and a handsome plate off which to eat it, and that proved his downfall. He had also spent an appropriation of $60,000 in cleaning and redecorating the White House. On April 14, 1840, with election day a little over six months away, Congressman Ogle, a Whig from Pennsylvania, made his historic oration immediately published under the title, *Speech on the Regal Splendor of the President's palace.* Let observation with extensive view, said he, ". . . survey its spacious courts, its gorgeous banqueting halls, its sumptuous drawing-rooms, its glittering and dazzling salons, with all their magnificent and sumptuous array of gold and silver, crimson and orange, blue and violet, screens of Ionic columns, marble mantels." He lingered over the inventory of silver tureens and gold spoons, the Royal Wilton carpets, chairs at $600 the set, the Blue Elliptical Saloon, and the maroon coach with outriders. He exposed to a ribald world the secrets of Van Buren's dressing-table, which included such requisites as "Double Extract of Queen Victoria, Corinthian Oil of Cream, Concentrated Persian Essence and Extract of Eglantine." The response with which the public greeted his information astounded even Representative Ogle. The President of the United States had become overnight a laughing stock, an effeminate social swell. The blade of the political guillotine was whetted.

Quick to seize their chance, the Whigs in convention assembled passed up majestic old Daniel Webster—even though at Patchogue in 1840 he "offered to strike with his great fist any man who called him an aristocrat"—and came to rest upon that great Indian fighter, General William Henry Harrison, hero of Tippecanoe, then in his sixty-sixth year. Although he was descended from Pocahontas and John Rolfe, proudest of native genealogies, and lived in a fine mansion beside the Ohio River on an estate of 2000 acres and had been known to quote Latin tags, he could easily be built up into a candidate who was gratifyingly rough, and at least moderately ready. The old gentleman obligingly discarded the silk hat which he customarily wore, donned a soft broad-brimmed model, and awaited further instructions. They came—from the press of his opponents. The Baltimore *Republican,* in a moment of pitiful indiscretion, pointed out that poor old General Harrison might be content to sit at home in a log cabin drinking hard cider instead of sallying into national politics. The election was won. After that for many a generation nobody could jeer with impunity at a log cabin, from which the Voice of God might call a beloved president any time it pleased, as it demonstrated with Lincoln and Garfield. The Wall Street bankers like Hone and his friends saw to it that there were great parades, showing the barrel of cider, the cap of coonskin, and the cabin with latchstring hanging out to one and all, while in a carriage behind rode an effigy of Van Buren holding up the golden teaspoons he had bought for the White House service. Banners proclaimed that the Whigs would "teach the palace slaves to respect the log cabin," and by torchlight thousands marched and sang such pæans as:

> Old Tip he wears a home-spun coat,
> He has no ruffled shirt—wirt—wirt;
> But Mat he has the golden plate,
> And he's a little squirt—wirt—wirt.

Aristocracy in Retreat

With an increase of 800,000 votes over the previous presidential election, that of 1840 first brought out the full voting strength of a great people— with Van Buren and his golden spoons at the bottom of the heap. It had been a campaign in which tariff, monetary policy, slavery, and international affairs had played little or no part; to the voters at large the paramount issue had been social snobbery.[17]

In Washington, meanwhile, socially minded optimists predicted with every change in the White House that at last the golden age had come. We find a prophecy about aged General Harrison in 1840: "He will make these gorgeous halls reverberate with merry peals of laughter, refined repartee, excruciating anecdotes and sparkling bonmots"—but, without much chance to show of what social mettle he was made, old Tippe- canoe died just one month after his inauguration. Tyler, who succeeded him, turned out to be so excessively democratic that several ladies of *ton* in Washington boasted they had not set foot in the White House since General Harrison's death. One of these ladies, "the wife of a government printer," issued invitations to a supper party on the same evening the President held his first levee, "inviting those she regarded as belonging to the first set, and intimating that their non-attendance would be fol- lowed by expulsion from the coterie."[18] As a sample of the touch that

[17]The lithograph by Edward W. Clay, made in New York in 1844-45, called "A Riotous Election," shows an orator in overalls haranguing the mob: "Feller Citizens! down with the monied aristocracy." A motley rabble fights its way into a polling- place, plastered with broadsides in Gaelic and German, while an old-fashioned aristocrat standing aloof says to a friend: "My dear sir, I have been a voter in this ward thirty years, but since rowdyism rules the day, I cannot vote with safety to my person, and until we can have more efficient police I must relinquish my privilege of Citizenship."

Radical newspapers had had their share in stirring up class feeling; thus the New York *Evening Post,* under the leadership of Leggett and the Loco-Foco Party, the supposed people's faction before tables were turned in the Log Cabin Campaign, pictured the period as a running war between the masses and "silk-stocking, moroc- co-booted, high-living, white-gloved gentlemen, to be tracked only by the marks of their carriage wheels."

[18]Tyler's hostess was then his daughter-in-law, Mrs. Robert Tyler, daughter of an actor named Cooper. Her letters are full of ingenuous delight at her new eminence, her chagrin over fainting at a Cabinet dinner and being carried away in the arms of Daniel Webster, her exultation in new dresses, "one a pearl-colored silk that would set you crazy," and her perplexity over the punctilios of leaving cards. Cf. Ellet, *Court Circles of the Republic,* pp. 301 ff. A typical contretemps of the period is thus related by another Washington observer: "On the 8th of February [1844] Madame Pageot, the wife of the French minister, entertained her friends. Lemonade and sponge cake were handed about, but sparingly tasted; for whispers

makes the whole world kin, we read: "A story was told of the appearance of a new face at the President's table, whom Mr. Tyler asked to take wine with him, but who preferred brandy and water. The stranger was discovered to be a sturdy butcher from Wilmington, Delaware, who had presented a noble sirloin of beef, and the finest mutton in the world, to the Chief Magistrate, and had been honored with an invitation." Little wonder that during Tyler's Administration the new Washington Assemblies were formed by "a club of resident gentlemen, composed of the first class," to consolidate fashionable Society. Near the close of his term Tyler married young Julia Gardiner of Gardiner's Island, New York, and once more it was predicted: "Possessed of the highest order of beauty and intellect, with manners the most elegant and popular, she will draw about her a court circle rivalling that of Louis le Grand,"[19] As perhaps something of an anticlimax we read thereafter that she "threw open the executive mansion at stated periods. Other magnificent entertainments were in progress. John Quincy Adams delivered a lecture in one of the Baptist churches. Some concerts were given at the President's mansion."

The next Administration brought in James K. Polk, who was interested in Manifest Destiny but very little else, and his wife, whose "amiable and cheerful disposition won universal admiration." She was not however disposed to pander to cheerfulness in others, and being a staunch Presbyterian she forbade dancing and swept the card-tables out of the White House. Yet we begin to hope that the sovereign people are slowly learning, when we find Mrs. Maury, an Englishwoman who attended the New Year's Day reception at the White House in 1846, reporting: "The democracy behaved like a lady." But our hopes are soon dashed by this

of a 'Parisian supper,' 'pâtés périgord,' &c., were heard faintly; and the thermometer was below freezing point. About twelve, one of the elder ladies took the arm of the hostess, for the purpose of going to the dressing-room for a moment. It was understood that supper was ready; and two by two, with steady step, the company followed to the dressing-room. Supper there was none; and to return to the drawing-room would have been ungraceful; so everybody went home."

[19]Elegant manners, in individuals and at parties, are always commented upon, as if they were traits somehow unusual and wonderful. And occasionally the adjectives chosen are a little startling, as in this description of a fête given by the Russian Minister, M. de Bodisco, at the closing of Congress in March, 1839: "Among the ladies, Miss Adele Granger of Canandaigua was noticed particularly. Her naïve manners and original, discursive imagination marked the brilliancy of her intellect. This lady afterwards married Mr. Thayer, a gentleman of Boston, and is now the wife of Robert Winthrop." Ellet, *Court Circles*, p. 273.

contemporary account of General Zachary Taylor's Inaugural Ball in 1849: "Suddenly there was a crash. 'What's the matter?' Only the contact of a lady, whirled with all the enthusiasm which the merry waltz and Gung'l's music combined inspire, against an unfortunate wight in the way. 'Oh, my poor fan! It's smashed to pieces!' 'Dear me! there goes half my skirt!' 'Stop, sir! stop a moment! You're pulling that lady's head off!' 'Where's my bracelet?' 'There goes my bouquet!' etc. 'Ain't it delightful?' 'What, do you think it too crowded?' etc."

President Taylor was another superannuated soldier who pushed his spectacles on his forehead, seldom combed his hair, and sometimes appeared with a large pair of woolen socks drawn over his boots—married to an aging wife who refused to entertain but quietly smoked her corn-cob pipe in a back parlor. After a year President Taylor succumbed under the weight of these new dignities, leaving the White House to a kindly gentleman named Millard Fillmore. He was another exemplar of what Walt Whitman was to call the Divine Average; he was nothing if not popular, and, as was soon discovered, he was not popular.

The next election brought in Franklin Pierce, whose wife—daughter of President Appleton of Bowdoin College—was unlike many of her predecessors a perfect lady, shy, delicate, and sickly. Although she entertained much, and in better taste, the real leader of Society in the capital during this brief interval was Mrs. Aiken, wife of the Governor of South Carolina—thus described on the night of her farewell fête to Washington: "Mrs. Aiken, a graceful woman, with a form of perfect symmetry, draped in embroidered brocade which fell around it in heavy waves of silver, and splendid in diamonds, received the guests with her daughter, a young girl in white illusion with white lilies in her hair, with a quiet manner and air of gentleness." Another favored belle was Miss Woodbury, of New Hampshire and Newport, who in public sometimes appeared with as many as "six large bouquets which had been presented." In 1857 Buchanan's Administration got off to an almost aristocratic start by the apotheosis of Democracy at a gala inauguration. His carriage headed a procession that included a "Liberty car" with "the Goddess of Liberty, magnificently attired, supported by a liberty pole fifty feet high, and drawn by six horses"; fifteen thousand tickets were sold for the Ball. His hostess was his niece Miss Harriet Lane, who seems to have had a real social flair. It was she who on October 4, 1860, took the Prince of Wales away from a Presidential reception that bored him, and played ten-pins with him in the gymnasium of Mrs. Smith's Institute for Young Ladies. To her belongs the credit in Jefferson Davis's remark to Doctor Craven: "The White House under the administration of Buchanan approached more nearly to my idea of a Republican Court, than the President's house has ever done before since the days of Washington." To enhance the Court was a circle of brilliant Southern women including Mrs. Roger Pryor of Virginia, Mrs. Chestnut of South Carolina, and Mrs. Clay of Alabama.

In general it may be said that, despite tight little coteries in New York, Philadelphia, Boston, and Charleston, the keynote of social intercourse in *ante bellum* America—particularly as set by the nation's capital—was one of breezy camaraderie, founded at its best upon the theory that everybody could be a gentleman or a lady. At its worst it was characterized by Thoreau, the hermit of Walden Pond: "What men call social virtues, good fellowship, is commonly but the virtue of pigs in a litter, which lie close together to keep each other warm."[20]

Democracy had its moments of vainglory, as in Calvin Colton's boast in 1844: "This is a country of self-made men, than which nothing better could be said of any state of society." The same spirit filled the simple soul of Andrew Johnson, the Tennessee tailor who learned to read and write after he was grown, and by tragic accident became President, when he declared in 1865: "I believe man can be elevated; man can become more and more endowed with divinity; and as he does he becomes more God-like in his character and capable of governing himself. Let us go on elevating our people, perfecting our institutions, until democracy shall reach such a point of perfection that we can acclaim with truth that the voice of the people is the voice of God."

Upon the one hand this spirit engendered a new pride among the working classes. Servants refused to wear livery, that "badge of servitude,"[21] and Miss Martineau, visiting at the British embassy in 1835, re-

---

[20]Emerson, sometimes thought to be the apostle of rugged individualism, wrote in his Journal: "No man would consent to live in society if he was obliged to admit everybody to his house that chose to come."

[21]In Anna Cora Mowatt's popular play *Fashion* (1845) we find this colloquy between a social aspirant and the true homespun American hero:

Mrs. Tiffany. Let me tell you, sir, that liveries are all the fashion!

Trueman. The fashion, are they? To make men wear the *badge of servitude* in a free land—that's the fashion, is it? Hurrah for republican simplicity!

Aristocracy in Retreat

ports that the Ambassador "makes what compromises he can, allowing his people to appear without livery out-of-doors except on state occasions," and even then has to scour the town for newly arrived foreigners who have not yet become heavily tinctured with democracy. Mrs. Trollope discloses that in Cincinnati the servants—or the "help" as they prefer to be called—come to work in party dresses trimmed with roses, and often bridle at having to dine in the kitchen. She notes that laborers on the canal, draymen, and butchers' boys are referred to as "gentlemen," and that one mentions "the lady over the way who takes in washing," while Mrs. Trollope herself—an English gentlewoman who had ventured bravely to penetrate far into Ohio, to sell needles, thread, and cushions to the pioneers of the Western Reserve—is called "the old woman." And she adds that American democracy is "claimed in accents that breathe less of freedom than of onions and whiskey."[22] She was not the last Briton to carry back such tidings from the wilderness—many years later Philip Burne-Jones found the assumption of equality with himself by Boston cab-men "startling," while a more sympathetic critic, Doctor James F. Muirhead, who wrote Baedeker's Guide to America, recorded: "I have hailed with delight the democratic spirit displayed in the greeting of my friend and myself by the porter of a hotel as 'You fellows,' and then had the cup of pleasure dashed from my lips by being told by the same porter that 'the other *gentleman* would attend to my baggage'!"

Indeed the democratic theory was often accompanied by a vicious snobbery from below, on the assumption that (as Mr. Mencken has paraphrased it in his translation into the Vulgate of the Declaration of Independence) "you and me is as good as anybody else, and maybe a damn sight better." *The New York Review* for October 1838 observes: "How edifying to see the auctioneer asserting his superior gentility to the grocer, and the wife and daughters of the man who sells by the bale in Pearl-street refusing to associate with the wife and daughters of the man who sells by the yard in Broadway!" A man in Cincinnati enlightened Mrs. Trollope on the subject of an important social distinction which had

[22]Mrs. Trollope, a greatly prejudiced observer, found society to her taste in only a few cities, notably New York. She writes: "The small patrician band is a race apart; they live with each other, and for each other; mix wondrously little with the high matters of state, which they seem to leave rather supinely to their tailors and tinkers." *Domestic Manners of the Americans* (ed. Sadleir, New York, 1927), p. 358.

excluded the daughter of a mechanic from a ball on Washington's Birthday; a mechanic, he said, "assists in making the articles he sells; the others call themselves merchants." On the other hand in New Orleans Mrs. Trollope was surprised at "my being introduced in form to a milliner . . . in the very penetralia of her temple, standing behind her counter, giving laws to ribbon and to wire," and equally astonished when at Memphis she was seated at a boarding-house dinner opposite her own servant, William. It was, in fact, an era of social chaos, with almost everybody from below pushing, scrambling, and scratching to get ahead as they had done at the Inaugural party of Jackson.

Thus was the American Dream converted into a nightmare of fevered aspiration. Those who had tried to climb and received a kick in the face swelled the ranks of the disgruntled, defeated, and savagely impatient who made this an era unparalleled in American history for riots, street-fights, and incendiarism.[23] Those who met better luck and mounted steadily upward had only one gauge of measuring distance—the whispered commentary which Fredrika Bremer heard as she walked the streets of Boston in 1850: "He is worth so many dollars. . . ." Though she did hear of a small remote band, almost as mythical as the Lost Tribes, who were "above fashion"—probably because their money was made so long ago that the public had lost track of its exact amount. At large however that cult was evolving—less known to a frugal Colonial New England or a gay, spendthrift Virginia—which William James to-

[23]After the great New York fire of December 17, 1835 Philip Hone was "alarmed by some of the signs of the times which this calamity has brought forth: the miserable wretches who prowled about the ruins, and became beastly drunk on the champagne and other wines and liquors with which the streets and wharves were lined, seemed to exult in the misfortune, and such expressions were heard as 'Ah! they'll make no more five per cent dividends!' and 'This will make the aristocracy haul in their horns!'" De Tocqueville, Lyell, and others comment upon the widespread jealousy of the rich, which however turned to bitterness and hate only rarely and among desperate men. Not unrelated to Jacksonian democracy, inflammatory journalism, and the influx of restless immigrants, were such riots in New York as the Park Theatre riots in 1831 and 1836, the Irish-American election riots of 1834 and 1838, and the "stonecutters' riot" and the abolition riots of 1834; there were bread riots against the monopolists in 1837, anti-German demonstrations in 1840, and bloody fights in the same year among Irish laborers on the Croton aqueduct. The election of Robert H. Morris in 1842 caused a riot, and the following year a mob attacked the tracks and property of the Harlem Railroad; and perhaps most notorious of all was that frank demonstration of class hatred, the Astor Place Opera House riot of 1849. Philadelphia, Baltimore, and Boston witnessed riots against bankers and monopolists.

Mrs. Elbridge Gerry   Elbridge Gerry   Mrs. Charles Carroll (Harriet Chew)

The Gerry portraits are from the Harold Seton Collection. Mrs. Carroll's portrait is from "The History of the Centennial Celebration of the Inauguration of George Washington." D. Appleton-Century Co.

Richard H. Lee   Dolly Madison   Francis Lightfoot Lee

The Lee portrait is by C. W. Peale, 1791. Dolly Madison is from a miniature credited to one of the Peales. In the possession of Mrs. John Hill Morgan

Mrs. Richard Stockton   Mrs. John Quincy Adams   Mrs. Alexander Hamilton

From a portrait by Copley   From a miniature in the possession of   From a painting by Ralph Earle, 1787
                                 Mrs. Henry Parker Quincy

Jacob Ashdor, of Waldorf, Germany,
father of the first American Astor

Jacob Ashdor's second wife, stepmother
of the first John Jacob Astor

Here reproduced through the courtesy of The Harvard Graduate School of Business Administration
and the present owner, Miss Katherine L. Wilks, Cruickston Park, Galt, Ontario

John Jacob Astor

From a painting by E. D. Marchant, 1836

(See Chapter IV)

ward the end of its cycle called "the moral flabbiness born of the exclusive worship of the bitch-goddess success." It was inevitable that in a democracy which plumed itself on equal opportunities for all, the hero should be the man who had made the most of his golden chances. Moreover, already in the making was that peculiarly American psychology—symbolized in the great caravans moving westward—of keeping up with one's neighbors, of regarding solitude and independence as a little eccentric, if not dangerous. In business and mechanics the most daring of innovators, the American was already developing that social and personal timidity, that love of conformity, which is the hallmark of the parvenu. Only the born aristocrat takes for his motto that saying with which the grandest of Boston *grandes dames* used to explain herself, "C'est mon plaisir." Only the most honest plebeian makes the reply Abraham Lincoln did when a waiter at his first state-dinner inquired whether he would take white wine or red. "I don't know," said Lincoln simply. "Which would you?"

On the eve of the Civil War two kinds of aristocracy were struggling for mastery in America. In the North it was a plutocracy of bankers, mill owners, shipping magnates, and most notable of all, speculators in city real estate. The Astors, Goelets, Schermerhorns, and Rhinelanders in New York had had the good fortune in the early nineteenth century to hitch their family carriages to the rising star of Manhattan real estate, and already they were looking down their noses at such upstarts as A. T. Stewart, first great department-store owner, a sandy-haired commonplace Scotch-Irishman, who during the Civil War was making five million dollars a year, and to glut his appetite for grandeur built a two million-dollar marble palace on Fifth Avenue before which Mrs. Astor's carriage never blocked the way. Meanwhile Emerson, pale and ascetic in Concord, was committing to his Journal a fear lest the swiftly increasing power of great wealth "upset the balance of man, and establish a new, universal monarchy more tyrannical than Babylon or Rome."

Despite intersectional marriages—for Governor Wise of Virginia had married a Sergeant of Philadelphia, the Roosevelts of New York had mingled with the Barnwells of Charleston, Stephen A. Douglas had married a North Carolina heiress with a plantation in Mississippi and a hundred slaves, and Mrs. Jefferson Davis was the granddaughter of a governor of New Jersey—the North and the South had gone socially along divergent paths, the result largely of geography and economics. Thanks to the eloquence of orators like John Randolph of Roanoke, legal support like that of Chief Justice Marshall, and such brilliant scholarship as that of Thomas R. Dew, President of William and Mary College, who in German universities had been taught that inequality and social stratification were not only just but necessary—the South had come with increasing boldness to repudiate Jefferson. Setting out to justify slavery it ended by vindicating social gradations everywhere. Chancellor Harper of the Supreme Court of South Carolina declared that "through the evolution of men in society . . . each man or class of men comes to find the proper place and level, and society then crystallizes and legalizes the resulting differences."

At the top were the plantation aristocrats, comprising the approximately one thousand families who in 1850 received over $50,000,000 a year, while the remaining 666,000 families all together had an income of only $60,000,000. In the ranking class belonged some of the old eighteenth-century grandees—Lees, Bollings, Carters, Randolphs, and others—who had salvaged enough despite laws against entail to keep the family name in style,[24] and with them newer and even richer slave-owners and planters like the Hairstons with 1700 slaves and vast plantations in three states, Howell Cobb of Georgia with his thousand slaves, and millionaires like the Aikens of South Carolina and Joseph Davis (brother of Jefferson Davis) in Mississippi. As usual, rich parvenus had chosen brides from old families like the Rhetts and Pinckneys of Charleston. They blazoned old coats of arms on bright new carriages trimmed with brass and gold, in which they swayed proudly along the sandy roads driven by a black coachman in livery who was the king-pin among his fellow-slaves. The parvenu learned also to affect shabby or outmoded suits, since that was the current fashion among the Virginia gentry—who held that the secret of being well-dressed was to wear new clothes as if you despised them, and old clothes as if you were proud of them.

Below them was the numerous middle class: small slave-holding farmers, professional men, and prosperous tradesmen, and like the corresponding group in the North they looked emulously toward their betters. Hundley writes in 1860 in his *Social Relations in Our Southern States* that they "sometimes from sheer envy and jealousy entertain a most

[24]Nathaniel Heyward of Charleston, for example, upon his death in 1851, left fourteen rice plantations, 2087 slaves, and a total wealth of $2,000,000.

cordial hatred of those whose attainments and good breeding they despair of ever being able to emulate." Descending the ladder one came upon the petty farmer who did all his own work and lived on "hog and hominy," the "poor white," and finally the Negro, free or slave. Social lines in the South were everywhere sharply marked, because of a slavery which made the rich much prouder and the poor more scorned.

At first the Civil War, like other great conflicts, caused an acceleration of pulse, a gaiety, a hectic flush of prosperity even in the doomed South. Officially the premier hostess of the Confederacy, Mrs. Jefferson Davis— born Varina Howell, daughter of a Natchez merchant—launched in Richmond a furious round of sparkling dinner-parties with costly wines and food, resplendent with gold braid and scarlet-lined military cloaks, lovely with jewels and bare shoulders—the "giddy gaiety" of which the Richmond *Examiner* spoke in 1864, with the reproachful exclamation, "Five balls advertised, and flour 125 dollars per barrel!" Few outsiders knew that Mrs. Jefferson Davis was not only trying to keep up the morale of the officers in gray, but also waging her private battle against Carters, Byrds, and Lees who looked coldly upon her an an interloper. Even during the black winter of 1864-65 when the real aristocrats were giving "starvation parties"—cheerful foregatherings without food or drink—Mrs. Davis continued to startle Virginia with her midnight suppers and inexhaustible cellars of champagne. Seldom has display been more unfortunately timed; as the Richmond *Whig* noted shortly before the surrender at Appomattox: "While battle and famine encompass us on every hand . . . upper-ten-dum is as gay as though peace and plenty blessed the land."

At that, Mrs. Davis was not so abysmally impossible as her rival in the White House, stout, ill-dressed Mary Todd Lincoln, who appeared at her first levee in pink silk décolletage with a floral headdress "which ran down to her waist," and at a reception given to her husband in New York appeared carrying "a small ivory fan with which she occasionally fanned some of the gentlemen who paid their respects to her, playfully telling them 'not to get too warm in the cause.'" Her admirers in Springfield, who had given her as a farewell present "a splendidly ornamented sewing machine," had a sense of practical irony. The later career of Mrs. Lincoln grew darker even to insanity. She flew into a rage against Mrs. Ulysses Grant because on one occasion Mrs. Grant forgot herself and sat down unbidden in the Presence; after Lincoln's death his widow put up at auction on Broadway all the dresses she had worn in the White House. She was in some ways the heaviest cross borne by her patient and great-souled husband. An interlude of humility came to the White House with Andrew Johnson, inept though his Presidency was, for his daughter and hostess Mrs. Patterson silenced social criticism with the honest words: "We are a plain people from the mountains of East Tennessee . . . and we do not propose to put on airs." Her successor, Mrs. Grant, of lower middle-class origin, enjoyed too unctuously the spectacle of herself as First Lady, and so indoctrinated her family with a sense of their own importance that, when the Grants took the World Tour after retirement from the White House their young son Jesse in his 'teens stuck up manfully at Windsor for his right to join father and mother at Queen Victoria's table, and not eat his dinner with the mere gentlemen of the Royal Household.

Throughout the North, the Civil War ushered in an epoch of lavish money-making and spending, which, unlike the tarantella of Mrs. Davis, was more prolonged and secure.[25] Wives of war profiteers, called by Knickerbocker aristocrats "the Sybarites of 'shoddy,' " began to appear at Pike's Opera House and at Wallack's with more diamond stomachers and tiaras of emeralds than had ever been seen in public before. To show the wealth of their husbands, ladies took up the fashion of powdering their hair with gold and silver dust. Men, heralding the tastes of Jim Brady and H. A. W. Tabor, sported waistcoat buttons made from diamonds of the first water. In smart turn-outs they drove to Jerome Park and the races at a scintillating clip. New opera houses, theatres, luxury hotels, and a fresh crop of brownstone mansions along Fifth Avenue arose—for, as we are told by a sober historian, a hundred thousand New Yorkers were now making some pretense to "fashion." We read that during the season of 1865–66 six hundred balls, "more or less public," were given in New York City, with the cost to ball-goers estimated at seven million dollars, "the average cost of a suitable dress being a thousand dollars, without jewelry." Relieved from the scourge of bread-winning and penny-pinching, life came perhaps unduly to revolve about the luxuries—sport and

[25]The installation of stock tickers in 1867 marks a significant milestone in Wall Street finance; in the following year securities to the value of three billion dollars were being dealt with upon the exchange.

social concourse and the exploration of the senses. One hostess, we are told, "who is building a splendid house near Central Park, is said to get herself up with hasheesh for dissipation. Another, overturned in a pony drive, and almost swooning, faintly exclaimed, 'Take me to my children!' —'She'll have to be introduced to them,' observed a cynical bystander."

It was in fact the threshold of what Mark Twain christened "The Gilded Age," and which the late Vernon L. Parrington with even more felicity renamed "The Great Barbecue." There was much elbowing and jostling to seize the juiciest joints, though for a while it seemed as though there might be enough for everybody. At first occurred a brave barring of doors along Chestnut Street and in the genteel hush of Gramercy Park, but the parvenu was on the march like an army with banners. It is well, therefore, to pause and consider briefly the great fortunes of America, the writing of its Golden Legend. We do well to remember an English proverb of the seventeenth century, "Honour is but ancient riches."

CHAPTER FOUR

THE GOLDEN BOOK

THE new-rich man and his wife have been figures of fun ever since the days when Petronius wrote the *Satyricon* or Clement of Alexandria spoke of "riches wriggling in the grasp of inexperience." But the period required before crude ore is transformed into acceptable social grace has often grown shorter through the centuries. At an early date the Republic came to be known as "a democracy of opportunity which created an aristocracy of achievement." During the nineteenth century old New York Society took refuge in saying that "it takes three generations to make a gentleman," though liberals shortened it to two, and in our own time many have contended that one is enough. Ward McAllister, who posed in the popular eye as a snob of snobs, defined aristocracy in America as "the possession of hereditary wealth" but ignored his own definition in practice. The Right Honourable G. W. E. Russell, British social historian, wrote in 1901: "Probably in all ages of history men have liked money, but a hundred years ago they did not talk about it in society. . . . Birth, breeding, rank, accomplishments, eminence in literature, eminence in art, eminence in public service—all these things still count for something in society. But when combined they are only as the dust of the balance when weighed against the all-prevalent power of money. The worship of the Golden Calf is the characteristic cult of modern society."[1]

The assimilation of plutocracy to aristocracy has been the vital problem of Society in America since its beginnings, but particularly since the rise of great industrial fortunes. It has been imperative somehow to translate *richesse permet* into *noblesse oblige*. Behind endless manuals of etiquette and blue books of behavior, scrapbooks of culture and outlines of knowledge, and all the nostalgia for European titles as well as Old

[1]In America as early as 1808 John Adams defined the coming trend when he noted: "We have one material which actually constitutes an aristocracy that governs the nation. That material is wealth. Talents, birth, virtues, services, sacrifices, are of little consideration with us."

Masters, lies the aspiration of a rising middle class attempting to seize, even by casual symbols, upon some guiding wisdom, upon the art of being rich gracefully, which Americans are accused of lacking. "Who knows how to be rich in America?" demanded Godkin in *The Nation* in 1866. "Plenty of people know how to get money; but not very many know what best to do with it. To be rich properly is indeed a fine art. It requires culture, imagination, and character." And Henry Adams a little later spoke for the older aristocracy of cultivation when he observed that the lives of the very rich were "no more worth living than those of their cooks."

Of course to the mass of people, in the time of Jackson as well as in the time of McKinley, the individual of dazzling wealth was the happiest, most glamorous, and most enviable of men—just as he is today to the avid reader of Society Notes in the tabloid newspapers, going home on the six o'clock subway to his walk-up flat or hall bedroom. Admiration of the millionaire, which survives a thousand disillusionments and a dozen depressions with their cries against "hydras of corruption" and clamors to "soak the rich," always stirs a democracy where gold is the visible ensign of power. The hereditary aristocrat, to whom Marco Millions is an old story, is perhaps the only sort who comes close to freeing himself from this servility to mere wealth—even more than the professed Communist of water front and ghetto who has made a gospel of defeat. Theodore Roosevelt once wrote: "I am simply unable to make myself take the attitude of respect toward the very wealthy men which such an enormous multitude of people evidently really feel. I am delighted to show any courtesy to Pierpont Morgan or Andrew Carnegie or James J. Hill, but as for regarding any one of them as, for instance, I regard Professor Bury, or Peary, the Arctic explorer, or Rhodes, the historian—why, I could not force myself to do it even if I wanted to, which I don't." Yet it is probable that Theodore Roosevelt's ancestors, when they were founding their fortunes in sugar, trade, and real estate, looked with vast respect and emulation toward Kiliaen Van Rensselaer or Robert Livingston.

A review of the older commercial families may well begin with the Roosevelts, who trace their descent from one Klaes Martensen van Rosenvelt, who came to New Amsterdam about 1649 as a "settler," which as his descendant the twenty-sixth President of the United States remarked, was "the euphemistic name for an immigrant who came over in the steerage of a sailing ship of the seventeenth century." The progress of the Roosevelts from steerage to peerage was at first a slow and laborious climb. The immediate descendants of Klaes added to the family tree by marriage with the stock of a Puritan wheelwright and several strains of Scotch-Irish and Quaker origin. Not until the times of Johannes Roosevelt, forbear of Theodore, and his nephew Isaac, great-great-grandfather of Franklin Delano, in the eighteenth century did the family begin to acquire wealth and power. Isaac set up the first sugar-refinery in America, in Queen Street, New York, near the Walton house, and thanks to his increasing prestige became president of the Bank of New York—already the family was blending *dulce et decorum*. His son James bought and sold New York real estate,[2] and left a substantial fortune to his own heir Isaac, who practised medicine briefly but gave it up to live as a country squire at Mount Hope on the Hudson. Isaac's son James, born in 1828, father of the present President of the United States, increased his accumulation by a venture into railroads and settled at Hyde Park. He married first Rebecca Howland, and had a son James who married Helen Astor, aunt of Vincent Astor; the father married secondly Sara Delano, who still survives. Other Roosevelts, sprung from Johannes, showed a preference for Southern wives, usually of aristocratic blood and wealth, and entertained New York Society with conservative dignity in brownstone houses filled with black hair-cloth furniture, mahogany sideboards, and ornate gas chandeliers—belonging distinctly to the "nobs" rather than the "swells."

After the Roosevelts come the great fortunes in real estate which were amassed between the Revolutionary War and the heyday of the railroads. Up to about 1825 it was doubtful whether New York, Philadelphia, Boston, or Baltimore would yield the richest harvest to landlords, but the opening of the Erie Canal determined the future of New York. The Schermerhorns, represented by Peter the ship-chandler who after the

---

[2]Philip Hone's *Diary*, February 8, 1847, records: "Died yesterday, Mr. James Roosevelt, in the eighty-eighth year of his age; a highly respectable gentleman of the old school, son of Isaac Roosevelt, the first president of the first bank of New York, at a time when the president and directors of a bank were other sort of people from those of the present day. Proud and aristocratical, they were the only nobility we had (now we have none); powerful in the controlling influence they possessed over the commercial operations of the city, men could not stand straight in their presence; and woe to them who bowed not down to the representatives of a few bags of gold and silver, the potential dispensers of bank favors."

Revolution began buying Manhattan real estate with every penny he could scrape, and his shrewd son Peter "the Younger" who was a director of the Bank of New York from 1814 to his death in 1852, rose rapidly in importance, and through marriage to Hones, one-time auctioneers, and to Astors, carried even newer families along in their triumphant march. Francis B. Cutting and Robert Bayard were other speculators in early nineteenth-century real estate who enriched their intermingled families. William and Frederick Rhinelander, who kept a German bakery in William Street during the Revolution, thriftily expanded into the sugar industry, built ships, did a thriving commission business, and even more successfully bought land. Later generations reaped the benefit, purchased a castle on the Rhine near Oberwesel to justify their name, went much into New York Society, and became famous for their punch made by a secret family recipe. William Rhinelander, gathered to his fathers in the crypt of St. Mark's in 1907, left behind an estate of fifty million dollars and the Rhinelander Real Estate Company—which during the past generation was ably administered by William Rhinelander Stewart, lawyer and noted philanthropist, father-in-law to the Pretender to the Throne of Portugal, and Lispenard Stewart, his bachelor brother, aristocratic clubman of New York. Patriarch of the clan still surviving is T. J. Oakley Rhinelander, born 1853, who has long helped to conserve the real estate holdings of the family. Most social of the younger generation are Frederic W. Rhinelander and his wife, born Constance Satterlee, of Newport, current sponsors of the Buchman cult in American Society, while another living Rhinelander, Philip Mercer, is the former Episcopal Bishop of Pennsylvania.

Of even greater social luster are the Goelets, whose name is pronounced with no Gallic frills. They derive from Peter Goelet, ironmonger during and after the Revolution, who also had the good judgment to buy several acres on what were then the northern fringes of the young city. He had two sons, Peter and Robert, who alike married daughters of a rich Scotch merchant of New York and director of the United States Bank, Thomas Buchanan. These Goelets became a byword for parsimony, and transmitted their habits to the third generation—even though from 1850 to 1870 with the great migration uptown, their tract of land reaching from the present Union Square to 47th Street and Fifth Avenue advanced their fortune to well over a hundred million. This generation consisted of Peter, a bachelor who died in 1879 at the age of seventy-nine, who had mended his own clothes, saved the backs of envelopes for his stationery, kept a cow which he milked with his own hands, but allowed himself the sole extravagance of buying and breeding exotic birds, such as peacocks, pheasants, and storks; and his younger brother Robert, whose two sons Robert and Ogden, born in 1841 and 1846 respectively, received all the colossal inheritance. They at last welcomed the social tradition, ordered steam yachts, sent their sons to Harvard, and began to entertain at Newport. The two branches of the family are now represented by Robert Goelet, director of many corporations and cousin of younger Vanderbilts, Wilsons, and Herberts, and by Robert Walton Goelet, owner of railroads, hotels, and real estate, who in 1921 married Anne Marie Guestier, heiress of the famous wine-makers of France. The Dowager Duchess of Roxburghe, born May Goelet, the sister of Robert, latterly spends much of the year in New York and has inherited the first box in the Diamond Horseshoe of the Metropolitan Opera.

The Lenox and the Lispenard fortunes also came largely from the golden days of real estate. And there was the senior Henry Brevoort, who owned a tract stretching from 8th Street and Fourth Avenue to 13th Street and a line a little west of Sixth Avenue; its value soon raised him to the status of wealth, though he seems never to have been upset by that fact. He was very fond of pets, and enjoyed notoriety among the small boys of New York in the early nineteenth century because of the bear which he kept chained in his watermelon patch west of Broadway. He departed little from the way of his ancestors who had run a truck farm and dairy, and carried daily loads of vegetables, butter, and milk to market. His son Henry Jr. was in youth an employee of John Jacob Astor, and made long trips into the West collecting pelts; a man of some wit and cultivation, he became a boon companion of Washington Irving. He married a Charleston girl, Laura Carson, whose gifts for entertaining helped to raise the family to high social rank. The Brevoorts have not, however, been a prolific stock and have long been absent from public notice and the pages of *The Social Register*. The relatively modest scale of New York fortunes in the days of Henry Brevoort, Jr., is shown by the fact that his estate of $1,000,000 left at his death in 1848 was regarded with great admiration and comment; only five years before, upon the death of Pierre Lorillard, snuff- and cigar-maker, the newspapers coined the word *millionaire* to denote such affluence.[3]

But aside from the fortune of Stephen Girard of Philadelphia, left to found the Girard Institute and therefore of no concern to the annals of Society, the fabulous accumulation of the early nineteenth century was that of John Jacob Astor. According to a genealogical table published in *The Pall Mall Magazine* by his great-grandson, William Waldorf, who wrote romances of Renaissance Italy and had a Gothic imagination, the family derived from Jacques d'Astorga, a Spanish cavalier who came to France in 1085. Unfortunately this pedigree was investigated immediately by a professional genealogist, Lothrop Withington, who published his findings in the New York *Sun* for July 30, 1899, and called it pure fabrication. It may be stated however beyond cavil that the father of the first American Astor was Jacob Ashdor of Waldorf, Germany, whom Parton, earliest of reliable biographers, describes as "a jovial, good-for-nothing butcher . . . much more at home in the beer-house than at his own fireside." The Harvard Graduate School of Business Administration possesses a pair of authentic paintings showing Jacob with his basket of poultry and his second wife, stepmother of young John Jacob but ancestress of the Wendels of New York, holding up an egg from the nest. She was not always found in attitudes of such benevolence, and her frequent tantrums caused her stepson to run away to the neighbors, a ragged and often hungry little boy. Finally leaving home afoot with a few crowns from his father as his sole patrimony, John Jacob went to London where his elder brother George was a maker of musical instruments. But in November, 1783, with seven German flutes as his only stock in trade, the lad came by steerage to America, landing in Baltimore after a most tedious voyage prolonged by the break-up of the winter ice, in March, 1784.

He went to New York, where another brother Henry was a prosperous butcher. There the boy peddled cakes for a baker until he found employment in Robert Browne's fur store, beating furs to keep out moths.

[3]In his Diary for May 23, 1843, Philip Hone noted: "Died this morning at his seat in Westchester County, Mr. Peter Lorillard, in the eightieth year of his age. . . . He was a tobacconist, and his memory will be preserved in the annals of New York by the celebrity of 'Lorillards Snuff and Tobacco.' He led people by the nose for the best part of a century, and made his enormous fortune by giving them that to chew which they could not swallow."

The Saga of American Society

Having resolved from the start "to be honest, to be industrious, and not to gamble," he soon saved enough to begin to buy furs himself, and presently set up his own business. In 1785 or 1786 he married Sarah Todd, an impoverished distant relative of the Brevoorts, a strapping girl accustomed to the hardest kind of labor in her mother's boarding-house where the young couple first settled, in a spare room. As her dowry she brought him a few dollars in cash, and of much greater value, a hoard of practical sense and a knowledge of judging furs. The expansion of Astor's business, slow at first and then increasing prodigiously, is a legend as fabulous as the rise of London's Dick Whittington. Astor sent ships to Europe and to China, exchanging furs for musical instruments, silk, tea, and other commodities; soon he had set up the village of Astoria on the Columbia River as the trading-post of his American Fur Company. He bought New York real estate and heavily mortgaged farms in the environs. As he fondly remembered in old age, "the first hundred thousand were the hardest" and nobody suspected him of being so rich when he quietly reached his first million. The Panic of 1837 and the steep climb of land values in Manhattan increased that fortune many-fold, but he still remained the lower-class German immigrant, barely able to read and write enough for business purposes; Albert Gallatin, former Secretary of the Treasury, declined to manage his estates because "he dined here and ate his ice cream and peas with a knife." He liked beer, tobacco, and a game of draughts, but except for the fact that in autumnal days of wealth he was flattered to visit the courts of petty German princes along the Rhine, he neither had nor sought any notice by Society.

Living till his eighty-fifth year, Astor grew feeble in body though the ruling passion of gold was still strong upon him. Under the care of "his train-bearer and prime minister Mr. Coggeswell," Philip Hone saw him at dinner at Mr. Blatchford's house at Hell Gate in October, 1844: "His life has been spent in amassing money, and he loves it as much as ever. He sat at the dinner table with his head down upon his breast, saying very little, and in a voice almost unintelligible; the saliva dropping from his mouth, and a servant behind him to guide the victuals which he was eating, and to watch him as an infant is watched. His mind is good, his observation acute, and he seems to know everything that is going on. But the machinery is all broken up, and there are some people, no doubt, who think he has lived long enough." Near the end, which came in 1848, he suffered from stomach trouble, and by order of his doctor was tossed gently in a blanket as his only means of exercise; the only food he could take was milk from the breast of a wet-nurse. But even when the eternal shadows were drawing near, he was directing his son William in the foreclosure of mortgages. And although Bennett in his blatant *Herald,* calling him "a self-invented money-making machine," might propose that Astor's estate restore to the people of New York half the fortune he had squeezed from them, Astor had become a name that stirred the envy of millions, and as Hone notes in his Journal, the great funeral was conducted by "six Episcopal clergymen." His heir could have mustered as many bishops.

For the Astor fortune grew from twenty to fifty million under the care of William Backhouse Astor, whose elder brother John Jacob lived, a hopeless imbecile, for seventy-six years. William, born in 1792, had attended public schools till the age of sixteen, helping his father at the store after school hours; then he was sent to Germany for a university education. His marriage in 1818 to Margaret, daughter of General John Armstrong of Rhinebeck, New York, gave him a footing in Society. It was General Armstrong, by the way, who in his bachelor days just after the Revolution wrote to General Gates: "I am not yet married, nor likely to be so; the truth is, that I am too poor to marry a woman without some fortune, and too proud to marry any woman I know who possesses one." However, he soon swallowed his pride, married the noted heiress Alida Livingston, and became Minister to France. His daughter became the wife of "the landlord of New York," a hard worker who inherited not a little of the first Astor's penny-saving. His unsanitary tenements were the scandal of that day. A contemporary, Matthew Hale Smith, describes him as "a tall, heavy built man, with a decided German look, a countenance blank, eyes small and contracted, a look sluggish and unimpassioned, unimpressionable in his feelings, taciturn and unsocial. . . . He was somber and solitary, dwelt alone, mixed little with general society, and abhorred beggars." He left one-third of his fortune to his younger son William, husband of Caroline Schermerhorn, "the Mrs. Astor" of the Four Hundred, and two-thirds to his elder son John Jacob. The latter's marriage in 1846 to the daughter of Thomas L. Gibbes of the South Carolina gentry occasioned a grand reception—"the spacious mansion in Lafayette Place," writes Philip Hone, "was open from cellar to garret, blazing with a thousand lights." The Astors were becoming magnificent.

Although the grandson John Jacob in the midst of his tireless devotion to business would often take time to rewrite a telegram to save a single word, he did become something of a host and epicure. His son William Waldorf, named for the town of the ancestral butcher-shop which had received a legacy of $50,000 from the estate, inherited a hundred million dollars and developed delusions of grandeur. Defeated in New York State politics, he was appointed Minister to Italy by President Arthur, and spent the term of his ministry chiefly in writing *Valentino: an Historical Romance of the Sixteenth Century in Italy.* His wife, born Mary Dahlgren Paul of Philadelphia, tried unsuccessfully to wrest the social leadership of New York from his aunt, and this circumstance, combined with fears fomented by the press that kidnappers were after the Astors, caused him in September 1890 permanently to remove his family to England—leaving the site of his former town-house to the new Waldorf Hotel. He became a sharp critic of American life and customs during his flyer in British journalism. In July, 1892, hoping to find out what Americans thought of him, he had a false report of his death published in the United States, but the hoax was discovered before any obituary appeared. Perhaps it was just as well. In 1899 he became a British subject, and launched upon a series of vast expenditures in an effort to buy social recognition in England. At a cost of ten million dollars he restored the Anne Boleyn castle at Hever, Kent, and in the New Year Honors for 1916 had the satisfaction of appearing as Baron Astor of Hever; on June 3, 1917, he became Viscount Astor, amid jeers from a large section of the British press which accused him of buying the title outright. Vain and quarrelsome, "a strange, crotchety man," he provoked incessant squabbles. The affront which he offered to Admiral Sir Berkeley Milne gave him a bad odor in English Society, and after that he had the belated good sense to retire from social skirmishing. Upon his death in 1919 his son William Waldorf Astor became the second Viscount Astor. He has shown better taste than his father. In 1906 he married Nancy Langhorne of Virginia, whose first husband was the late Robert Gould Shaw.[4] Her travels with

[4] She is the daughter of the late Colonel Chiswell Dabney Langhorne, a civil engineer who made a comfortable fortune in railway construction, and kept open house with lavish hospitality at "Mirador," Greenwood, Virginia. After his daughter's brilliant marriage Colonel Langhorne used to startle London drawing-rooms by his bluff partiality for chewing-tobacco.

such intellectual friends as George Bernard Shaw and the Marquis of Lothian, her doughty preachment of Prohibition in England which is as readily forgiven as other eccentricities of this charming woman, and her speeches salty with the invective of platform politics, have made her, as all the world knows, the most picturesque of current Astor wives. When she arrived in the House of Commons in 1919 as M. P. from Plymouth, one reverend member bitterly remarked that his sensations upon her entry could only be compared to those of a gentleman in his bath who is invaded by a company of Cook's tourists. Yet with an armor which Horace would have described as *æs triplex,* Lady Astor has weathered all criticism and made many staunch friends. She is also London's most famous hostess from overseas, and has endeared herself to several generations of young Americans for the gay music and generous champagne of her parties for Rhodes Scholars in St. James's Square.

The Astor family is now represented in America in the male line solely by stock descended from William and Caroline Astor. Their son the fourth John Jacob, born in 1864, married Ava Willing of Philadelphia, built the Astoria section of the Waldorf Hotel in 1897, had a yacht the *Nourmahal* whose name has become an Astor tradition even as the *North Star* has been to Vanderbilts, was divorced from his first wife after she had borne him the present Vincent Astor, and in 1911 married Madeleine Talmage Force of Brooklyn. Returning from an extended honeymoon in April, 1912, on the *Titanic,* he saw his bride safely to the life-boat, and then tipping his hat he returned to finish his cigar with friends on the sinking deck while the band alternated "Alexander's Rag-time Band" with "Nearer My God to Thee." His wife bore him a post-humous child, the sixth John Jacob, and married William K. Dick in 1916, and Enzo Fiermonte, prizefighter, in 1933. Vincent Astor, present head of the family and childless, was a phlegmatic youth at St. George's School and Harvard, but has developed by slow and steady degrees, plus hard work and serious-mindedness, until he has become the most progressive of all the Astors—founding model farms and building model tenements for the poor, as well as running de luxe apartments and the St. Regis for the rich. His wife, Helen Dinsmore Huntington of a Hudson Valley family, has loyally shared these interests. With such hobbies as oceanography, practical science, and liberal journalism, and his preference for men of affairs over sacrosanct Society, has gone Mr. Astor's passionate

Americanism in speech, clothes, and habits which sets him sharply apart from his transatlantic cousins.

Among the great real estate fortunes outside the pale of New York should be mentioned that of the Longworths in Cincinnati, contemporary with the second generation of Astors. Nicholas Longworth, born in 1782 to a family of Dutch origin whose Tory sympathies during the Revolution caused all its property to be confiscated, had to begin from scratch. Clerking awhile in his brother's store in South Carolina, he moved to the frontier village of Cincinnati about 1803 and studied law. His first case, resulting in the acquittal of an alleged horse-thief, was paid by his client with two second-hand copper stills which young Longworth traded for thirty-three acres of land afterward valued at $2,000,000. He continued to buy and develop land around Cincinnati until by 1850 he paid, next to William B. Astor, the highest taxes on realty in the United States. Famous as an early cultivator of the Catawba grape he became known as "the Bacchus of the New World"—but not assuredly because there were vine-leaves in his hair or debauchery in his heart, for he was a stern Whig and Presbyterian. Although he lived in a "princely establishment, occupying a large square with fine gardens on the skirts of the town," where Hone called to see him in June 1847, Nicholas Longworth scoffed at stiff-bosomed Society and loved to deride the hypocrisies of a materialism he knew so well. He was much more generous to drunkards, prostitutes, down-and-outers, and ex-convicts than to his business rivals, or possibly to himself. On one occasion when a beggar came to his office and pointed to his gaping shoes, Longworth kicked off his own pair, gave them to the man, and sent his office-boy out to buy another for himself but under no circumstances to pay more than a dollar and a half. Naturally, as his great-granddaughter the Countess de Chambrun tells us, he preferred to be known as "Old Longworth" rather than "Old Nick." After his lifetime the great Longworth estate "Rookwood" was laid out, with its spacious gardens, groves, and baroque architecture—and there today lives the widow of his great-grandson, Nicholas Longworth, late Speaker of the House, who in 1906 married "Princess Alice" Roosevelt at the White House in the most brilliant wedding which the capital has ever seen. Though the memory of the Longworths is still powerful in Cincinnati, along with that of the more recent Tafts, they have been neither prolific nor too provident, and at present

The wedding of Alice Lee Roosevelt, daughter of President Theodore Roosevelt, to Nicholas
Longworth at the White House, Washington, D. C., February 17, 1906

The New York Central locomotive named *Commodore Vanderbilt*, with a portrait of the Commodore on the headlight. The name is painted in large letters on the tender

Reproduced by courtesy of the Publicity Bureau of the New York Central System

Cornelius (Commodore) Vanderbilt

the fortune is greatly shrunken; the young daughter Paulina is its heiress.

Among dynasties founded in early nineteenth-century America that of the Du Ponts of Wilmington should not be forgotten. The founder, Pierre Samuel du Pont, was a French watchmaker of bourgeois origin, whose keen intelligence and marriage to Nicole Louise Le Dée gave him an excellent start in life. He moved to Paris, became one of the "physiocrat" philosophers, and to identify himself geographically took the name "de Nemours"—which has never been used by his descendants except in the commercial title of the firm. Present Du Ponts find that upon their visits to France all hotel clerks and porters add "de Nemours" in addressing them, to their mild annoyance; they are, however, particular that the name Du Pont shall be accented upon the final syllable. Pierre's elder son, Victor, born in 1767, came to the United States in 1787 as attaché to the first French legation in this country. The younger son, Eleuthère Irénée, born in 1771, became a good friend of the great chemist Lavoisier, chief of the royal powder works, who gave him secret formulæ for making gunpowder. This Du Pont against the opposition of his family married a girl considerably beneath him in rank, after fighting two duels over her. When during the Revolution the publishing business of the Du Ponts was suppressed, the father and his son Irénée set out for America, encountering Victor at the port of embarkation and persuading him to return with them. Soon after his arrival in the United States Du Pont de Nemours, having gone hunting with friends, was struck with the poor quality of gunpowder obtainable, and decided to found a powder-mill near Wilmington, Delaware. Thomas Jefferson gave them government contracts, and the War of 1812 arrived to seal their new prosperity. Victor's son Henry (1812–1889) successfully continued the business, and his son Henry Algernon (1838–1926), United States Senator from Delaware and long-time patriarch of the family, forbade the marriage of cousins which for awhile threatened the Du Ponts with excessive inbreeding. Lately Du Pont heiresses have been encouraged to choose able but penniless young husbands—Copelands, Lairds, Carpenters, Sharps, Mays, Rusts, and Greenewalts—who have been admitted to this great industrial dynasty. Several members of the clan have shown a marked flair for military and naval careers. One of them was Admiral Samuel Francis du Pont, commander of the Union Fleet at the battle

The Saga of American Society

of Hampton Roads in 1861, for whom Du Pont Circle in Washington is named—though, to the chagrin of his family, his statue has now been removed in the interests of traffic. Present members include Pierre S. du Pont, head of the family, and famous for his annual garden parties at Longwood which have become a rite of the clan; Irénée, who is perhaps best described as the liaison officer between the family and the public; Lammot, serious, hard-working president of the Du Pont Company; Alfred Victor, able young architect; and Henry F. du Pont of Wilmington and Park Avenue, who with his wife, born Ruth Wales, is the most socially metropolitan of the family. The Du Ponts have traditionally preferred the simple yet baronial life of Wilmington—described by Henry S. Canby in his recent book of reminiscences called *The Age of Confidence*—to the social game of New York and London; the family's current choice of Fisher's Island instead of Bar Harbor or Southampton for the summer season is perhaps typical. The vast ramification of the Du Ponts through diverse marriages and prolific families is a new phase, hardly more than a generation old; it has gone hand in hand with that colossal expansion of their enterprise in new industrial fields, ranging from General Motors to cellophane, which has taken place since the Great War. Yet a surprising family solidarity is still maintained, despite a rift between young and old upon the wisdom of such stratagems as the Liberty League.

Certain American fortunes are linked with social names, while others are not—a difference doubtless explained by the time and circumstances of foundation, the personality and ambition of the founders. Thus the great wealth amassed in iron and steel by Andrew Carnegie, grandson of a Scotch shoemaker, has had very little impact upon American Society; though a portion of it is now pleasantly united to America's most intellectual ex-prizefighter, who speaks with a Harvard "a." On the other hand the older fortune made by another Scot, Henry Burden, who came to Troy, New York in the early nineteenth century and started the Burden Iron Company, belongs high upon fashion's roster, thanks to successive generations of James A. Burdens and I. Townsend Burdens with their heiress wives. In general however, wealth accumulated through banking and brokerage has been the sort most easily to escape the odium of manufacture or trade. Among the elder banking families still prominent in Society should be named the Iselins, of Swiss origin. One of their ancestors, Isaac Iselin (1728–1782), was a distinguished scholar, philosopher, and educator of Basle. The first great banker in the family was another Isaac, associated with the house of LeRoy, Bayard, and Company, who traded largely on the Paris Bourse; Hone records his death in the *Diary* for January 15, 1842, at Basle where he had long lived "in the dull, aristocratic style of the dullest and most aristocratic city in Europe." The founder of the American branch was the first Adrian Iselin, who married a wife of good Maryland Irish stock, Eleanora O'Donnell. Their son Adrian (1846–1935), who joined the banking house in 1868, yachtsman and zealous Catholic layman, and his sisters, Miss Georgine Iselin, a Papal countess, and Mrs. De Lancey Kane, were long familiar in New York Society. Young Swiss cousins, pink-cheeked and promising, have appeared from time to time to serve an apprenticeship in American brokerage, for their solidarity, like that of other international bankers, has been apparent. Iselins have intermarried notably with Jays, as illustrated in the present family by William Jay Iselin and by Mrs. Arthur Iselin, born Eleanor Jay.

The Drexels of Philadelphia and New York owe their fortune to Francis Martin Drexel, a portrait-painter from the Tyrol, who first came to Pennsylvania in 1817, worked at his art for ten years, and then wandered about South America and Mexico with his brushes and easel painting the *caballeros* of silver mines and ranches with their beautiful wives. Returning to the United States in 1831 he discovered in a burst of inspiration the profit to be made from buying and selling state bank notes, so-called "wildcat" currency. In 1838 he established himself in Philadelphia on a street significantly known as the "Coast of Algiers" where he promoted a great business in buying bank currency, financing corporations, and "shaving" commercial paper. His son, Anthony J. Drexel, whose slim, quiet, gentle and delicate appearance belied the keen financial brain and aggressiveness behind his actions, was one of the greatest bankers of the century—head of Drexel & Co. of Philadelphia, and senior partner of Drexel, Morgan & Co., of New York and of Drexel, Harjes & Co., of Paris. Intermarried with Biddles, Whartons, Van Rensselaers, Dahlgrens, and other social families, the Drexels reached their greatest prominence in the Gilded Age just before the War, thanks largely to Mrs. John Drexel and to Elizabeth Drexel Lehr, now Lady Decies, who has lately published a *chronique scandaleuse* of her times, in which malice and fantasy appear to struggle for mastery.

But greatest of American bankers were the Morgans. Although the late J. P. Morgan used to assert with the shadow of a smile that he was descended from Henry Morgan the pirate, the authentic family tree is not a gallows. The Morgans were a Welsh line of farmers and innkeepers, settled in America since one Miles Morgan emigrated to Springfield, Massachusetts in 1636. Great-grandfather of the present banker was Joseph Morgan, who did well in stage-coaches, a hotel in Hartford, Connecticut, and the Ætna Fire Insurance Company. His son, Junius Spencer Morgan, clerked in a Hartford dry-goods store, went to New York to learn something of finance as an employee of A. and M. Ketchum, brokers, and got together sufficient funds to buy an interest in the firm of J. M. Beebe in Boston. He proved so able that in 1854 the Anglo-American banker George Peabody invited him into partnership, and henceforth the Morgan fortune was assured. He married the daughter of the Reverend John Pierpont (1785–1866), poet, impecunious clergyman, and fiery reformer. Mr. Pierpont was the son of a clothier. After failing in the retail dry-goods business he had been ordained a Unitarian clergyman, and quickly took up spiritualism and the cause of temperance—much to the disapproval of his parishioners of the Hollis Street Church, Boston, who rented the church cellar to a rum merchant as a warehouse, thus cutting the ground from under his feet, as it were. After several fierce battles and an arraignment before a Unitarian church council on the charge of preaching on "exciting subjects," Mr. Pierpont resigned with honor, and at the time of his death at the age of eighty-one had been for some time a clerk in the Treasury Department at Washington.

From this discordant heredity the great John Pierpont Morgan was born in Hartford in 1837. Of frail health in boyhood, he was sent to the University of Göttingen where he took mud baths and showed a marked aptitude for mathematics. As his one act of romantic quixotry he married Amelia Sturges of New York as she was dying of consumption; despite his furious efforts to stave off the inevitable, death came three months after their wedding-day. Three years later, in 1865, he married Frances Louise Tracy, mother of the present John P. and Anne Morgan. Although he made several serious blunders in business, notably in management of the New York, New Haven, and Hartford Railroad, and was seldom so astute as Carnegie, Rockefeller, or Harriman, the first J. P.

The Golden Book

Morgan had tremendous vitality, ruthlessness to enemies but loyalty to friends, and a genius for magnificence—which led him on the one hand to organize U. S. Steel, the first billion dollar trust, on the threshold of the twentieth century, and on the other to exclaim impatiently on occasion to the trustees of Columbia, "Do something big!" One of his biographers, Atwood, says that the adjective "princely" was "applied to him more often perhaps than to any other American." Among his idiosyncrasies it is related that, whenever he found a personable young man to adopt as a protegé in the House of Morgan, he signalized the fact by sending the lucky youth a collie from his kennels; sometimes, as in the case of Robert Bacon, he picked his associates with surer knowledge of their social polish than of financial brains. Indeed the House of Morgan has never been built of timber unacceptable to the Social Register —unlike that, for example, of Kuhn, Loeb & Co. Morgan did nevertheless learn the trick of apportioning important work among his elder partners: Coster, who literally died in the Morgan harness, and after him Baer and Mellen, attended to the railroads, Griscom to steamships, Perkins to finance, and Morrow and Davison to the interrelation of departments. The great Morgan was equally the idol and bogey of public opinion. Just as the "trust-busting" era commenced under Theodore Roosevelt, a current musical hit on Broadway showed a glowing griddle in Hades tended by a chorus of demons who blew the flames with loving solicitude and chanted to all comers:

> This seat's reserved for Morgan,
> That great financial Gorgon.

Yet in the Panic of 1907 Wall Street turned piteously to him to avert disaster, including his enemies, "like atheists who do not parley with their principles but call for the sacrament at the last moment," as Max Lerner wrote some years ago. Some people saw a sinister import in the name of his famous yacht, the *Corsair,* without understanding that he was first and foremost a lover of Byron, whom he resembled in certain aspects of his private life. Although he hated photographers and despised public opinion—as one might do who counted among his familiars the King of England, dukes of the blood, the ·Archbishop of Canterbury, and the Episcopal hierarchy of America—he bitterly resented any remark, from whatever lowly wit or caricaturist, on his hideously inflamed nose. He never recovered from the phrase "a ruby-visaged magnate." Yet when Count Witte once ventured to suggest that German surgery might help him, Morgan replied: "Everybody knows my nose. It would be impossible for me to appear on the streets of New York without it." One biographer observes that Morgan felt his nose "was part of the American business structure." Gruff of speech, fond of ordering his car driven onto the curb in his impatience to avoid obstacles and get places, he was the last great imperialist of Wall Street. In his more genial moments he was a commodore of the New York Yacht Club, and a connoisseur of books, manuscripts, paintings, ivories, bronzes, wood-carvings, and tapestry. At his death in 1913 in Rome—preceded by the hiring of the specialist Bastianelli at a retaining fee of $100,000 and a dash from Egypt on the *Adriatic* at a cost of $25,000 for eight staterooms—Morgan was without doubt the dominant figure in world finance. "He was a great and good man," said Pope Pius X upon his passing, and perhaps he spoke with more authority than the librettists of Broadway.

For three generations the Morgans have been entitled, by reason of their great wealth and almost overpowering respectability, to as much social position in New York as they cared to claim. But neither Juliet Pierpont Morgan nor Frances Louise Tracy Morgan chose to assume the social leadership whose weight would have been to them—with their quiet, simple, reticent lives—more of a cross than a crown. And the same was true of the late Jane Grew Morgan, wife of the present J. P. Morgan and daughter of the solid Boston banking family which has also produced Joseph Clark Grew, Ambassador to Japan. Socially the most eminent of living Morgans are Mrs. Herbert Livingston Satterlee, born Louisa Pierpont Morgan, and her sister Miss Anne Morgan, noted social worker in war and peace, decorated with high honors by the French Government, and president of the American Woman's Association. Head of the family is John Pierpont Morgan, born in 1867, who continues his father's customs, such as the annual distribution at Christmas of six tons of China tea under mildly mysterious circumstances, and the wearing of a large bloodstone attached to a cable-like watch chain which cartoons in the *New Masses* never tire of picturing. He has also perpetuated the love of things English which has been a family trait since the days of Junius Spencer—the Church of England, represented at home by St. John's of Lattingtown Church in Locust Valley, and abroad by the current Archbishop of Canterbury, a welcome guest on the *Corsair;* London clubs and a house in the West End; the Morgan estate of Wall Hall in Hertford-shire, and the hunting lodge of Gannochy on the Scottish moors, where Mr. Morgan and the present King, when Duke of York, often shot grouse in August. Here his royal Scots retainers have invented a "Morgan tartan," to give authentic Caledonian flavor to the descendants of Welsh innkeep-ers. Within the past four years the Morgans have gained popularity before that great public which loves to be wooed, even in small particulars, by the lords of this earth. Miss Anne Morgan has endorsed Simmons Beds, and her brother has held a midget on his knee. The first of these wonders is susceptible of some explanation: Miss Morgan is keenly interested in a settlement house for New York working girls, and this project was given valuable publicity by the advertising agency employed by Simmons. The second, which apparently has so mitigated the shyness of Mr. Morgan that he recently announced, "I like newspaper men now," is probably more complex. What burst of sudden intuition caused Charles Leef, assistant press agent for Ringling Brothers Circus, to plant a female midget upon the lap of John Pierpont Morgan, while he awaited the Senate Banking and Currency Committee of Inquiry in 1933, will doubt-less never be known. It is as inscrutable as the inspiration which led Shakespeare to write *Hamlet.*

A family of less national fame, but well known in annals of the Gilded Age, is that of Oelrichs. Hermann Oelrichs, born in 1809 in Bremen, the son of a merchant, came to this country in the flood-tide of American shipping and found employment as a clerk in the office of H. H. Meier & Co., a New York mercantile firm with Bremen connections. In 1834 young Oelrichs was admitted to the firm, and proved so successful that within five years he was its dominant member. In 1844 his brother Edwin came over from Germany, and between them they gained entire posses-sion, under the title of Oelrichs & Co. Both brothers were at heart strongly sentimental Germans, and upon growing old returned to the Fatherland to die there. But their younger brother Henry was the parent of the American stock; he saw the firm, whose diverse interests spread from shipping Virginia tobacco to importing guano from the Chincha Islands, suddenly grow rich from the wool trade during the Civil War. The next greatest coup was the organization by Oelrichs & Co. of the North German Lloyd, which except for the interregnum of the Great

War has enjoyed steady prosperity. Henry's son the second Hermann, who began clerking in the firm in 1871 and was admitted to partnership after five years, became the rich, dapper sportsman and clubman of the Nineties. The Oelrichs family, though by no means belonging to the old patrician stratum, did by means of wealth, lavish entertaining, houses on Fifth Avenue and cottages in Newport, cut a broad swath in American Society during its most extravagant epoch.

A few families in the United States have long and excellent pedigrees, of which only a small segment is plated with gold. The enterprising grandson in a line of distinguished clergymen, educators, or men who have rendered notable public service, will suddenly have the chance and ambition to make or marry great wealth. This conversion has already been seen in the case of the Adamses, and it appears also in annals of the Whitneys. William Collins Whitney, with a heritage of intellectual New England ancestors, was born at Conway, Massachusetts in 1841. At Yale he had a brilliant career, splitting the honors with William Graham Sumner. Suave, handsome, persuasive, he went to New York and built up a notably successful law practice. In 1869 he married Flora Payne, sister of his college roommate Oliver, future treasurer of Standard Oil. He came to be known as the implacable foe of Tammany, and as an idealist in politics. He worked hard for the election of Grover Cleveland, became a close friend of that President, and was appointed Secretary of the Navy. He rendered valuable public service in advancing the Navy to new strength and efficiency. Then upon his return to private life, after he had passed his fiftieth year, Whitney's love of wealth and luxury got the better of him. As early as 1884 he had made a few overtures to Widener, and now he surrendered wholly to expediency, joined forces with Tammany, helped organize the great Metropolitan Street Railway Company of New York in 1893, and garnered vast wealth from this virtual monopoly of street cars. His closest associate now became Thomas Fortune Ryan, an Irish farmer's son from Virginia who was climbing financially and socially by leaps and bounds. With the aid also of Standard Oil in less than ten years Whitney amassed a fortune of $40,000,000. He built a palace on Fifth Avenue, and to furnish it brought art treasures from Europe, carvings, tapestries, and whole staircases and ceilings dismembered from mediæval castles. The Whitneys began to entertain with a splendor which left breathless even the spendthrift Four Hundred of

Ward McAllister's day. Their old Yankee pedigree was impeccable, and the marriage of the late Harry Payne Whitney to Gertrude Vanderbilt, daughter of the senior Cornelius Vanderbilts, in 1896, conferred marked prestige upon the latter aspiring family. The second son Payne married the daughter of John Hay. Of William C. Whitney, Henry Adams wrote that "after having gratified every ambition and swung the country almost at his will . . . [he] had thrown away the usual objects of political ambition like the ashes of smoked cigarettes; had turned to other amusements, satiated every taste, gorged every appetite, won every object that New York afforded, and not yet satisfied, had carried his field of activity abroad, until New York no longer knew what most to envy, his horses or his houses." Henry Adams always looked upon Whitney with wonder, because he was one of the very few men of real education, cultivation, and intellectual charm to achieve social success in his generation. It may be added that the sporting tradition, which led to the establishment of great stables and the crowning triumph of an English Derby winner, has been carried on by the Whitneys to the present day—when the family is represented by John Hay Whitney and Cornelius Vanderbilt Whitney.

Almost a hundred years ago Captain Marryat noted the sudden transformations and replacements wrought by American wealth: "The stream flows inland, and those who are here today are gone tomorrow, and their places in society filled by others who ten years back had no prospect of ever being admitted. All is transition, the waves following one another to the far west, the froth and scum boiling in advance." This was peculiarly true of the great fortunes founded during the gold rush and early railroading days of California, from 1849 to shortly after the Civil War. The social history of the California nabobs, mirrored in fiction by Mark Twain and Bret Harte, is in its sober truth a fantastic saga. The story is told of a newcomer on the streets of San Francisco in 1850 who offered a boy fifty cents to carry his valise, and got the reply: "Here's a dollar; carry it yourself." For a short time after the discovery of gold in Sutter's Mill there was complete social democracy, or perhaps one should say anarchy. Cooks and waiters mingled freely with lawyers and generals in the United States Army; some of the richest clung to their ragged overalls and denims, while others blossomed into dandies and sent their ruffled shirts and cambric handkerchiefs to be laundered in the Hawaiian Islands or China. At first it was a society without women, and one of the most injudicious consignments made by a Yankee firm in 1850 was a shipload of women's bonnets. In one camp at the Saturday night dances it was the invariable rule to regard as ladies those miners who had patches on the seats of their trousers. Yet women good and bad quickly flocked to California, and as early as the rise of the Vigilantes San Francisco was already sponsoring a magazine, patterned on *Godey's Lady's Book,* called *The Hesperian.* Soon balls of great magnificence were being given, while the playhouse and opera were in full swing, offering to the new rich the hastily constructed equivalent of a golden horseshoe with boxes draped in silk. Handsome carriages wormed painfully along the sandy, garbage-littered streets. The mud was so prodigious in the main streets of San Francisco that occasionally a horse or mule team with its load sank out of sight and was suffocated—until for paving, quantities of unwanted merchandise were used, bags of Chilean flour, tierces of tobacco, and across one thoroughfare a row of cook stoves was sunk in the mud to afford footing for pedestrians. The greatest luxury was found in gambling houses and their adjuncts the brothels, with tremendous plate-glass mirrors, oil paintings of epic size, and immense crystal chandeliers and girandoles.

In this milieu was founded the fortune of James Graham Fair, born in Ireland in 1831, who had picked up the rudiments of a business education in early Chicago. In California he pooled his energies and a few dollars with three other poor Irishmen, Mackay, Flood, and O'Brien, and reaped a golden harvest in the Comstock Lode exploited by their California & Consolidated Virginia Mining Company. Fair became a United States senator in 1881, startling Washington with his gaudy irregularities; while his two daughters "Tessie" and "Birdie" married Hermann Oelrichs and William K. Vanderbilt, and came to play a conspicuous rôle in the Gilded Age of Newport; both have lately died after worldly careers. Another partner, John W. Mackay, born in 1835 in Dublin, of the humblest origins, emigrated to the United States in his boyhood, worked in shipyards and saloons, and reached California in 1852 in time to keep a rendezvous with luck. He married the daughter of Daniel Hungerford, a Canadian barber; she had been stranded in Nevada by the death of a first husband, and when some miners taking up a collection to send her home approached Mackay, he interested himself in her plight, and shortly married her. Later she went to Paris and London and astounded the

Old World with the magnificence of her jewels and carriages; her daughter by her first marriage became the Italian Princess of Colonna. Mr. Mackay himself, like many other self-made Americans, shared little of this enthusiasm for Society, though his son the present Clarence Hungerford Mackay, who married Katherine Alexander Duer in 1898 and is now husband of Anne Case and father-in-law of Irving Berlin, has long enjoyed the pomps of New York and Long Island fashion. He has passed through many financial vicissitudes after investing his patrimony largely in cable and telegraph lines. The last two members of the quadrivirate of the Comstock Lode, O'Brien, who early dropped out, and James C. Flood, a poor gamin of the New York streets, who steppped from a "gin-mill" of San Francisco into the possession of several million, are of small interest to the annalist of Society.

Among the new California fortunes, that of the Crockers—founded by Charles Crocker, a blacksmith, who by means of success in trade rose on the stepping-stone of the Central Pacific Railroad to great wealth—struck deeper root in California than it ever obtained in New York, though some social advancements were made through marriages. Similarly Collis P. Huntington and Leland Stanford, also magnates of California railroads with humble origins, are of scant social importance though Huntington for several years before his death in 1900 stormed the citadels of New York. The Spreckelses, with a fortune from sugar, have stayed chiefly on the West Coast. But the one California nabob who hurdled all barriers was Darius Ogden Mills (1825-1910). The Millses were a North of England family who emigrated to America before the Revolution, and settled in a small community up the Hudson River. On account of poverty young Darius had to leave school and go to work. After a venture in running a hotel, he and his brother sailed to California with a cargo of merchandise in which they had invested their all. They set up a store in San Francisco, prospered in those piping times, and passed on to mining stock and banking. Darius Mills, then shaking all but the gold dust of California from himself, returned east and bought a great house opposite St. Patrick's Cathedral on Fifth Avenue. Giving a decorator *carte blanche* during a short absence from New York, Mills returned to find himself in possession of the most sumptuously appointed house in the city, together with a bill for $450,000; somewhat dashed, he attempted to bargain with his decorator but succeeded in getting "only a slight reduction."

The Saga of American Society

With an innate gift for the amenities of living, and an acute social consciousness, Mills travelled abroad, learned the nuances of English fashion, and was soon hobnobbing with nobility. His son Ogden in 1882 married Ruth Livingston, scion of one of the proudest New York families, and upon the marriage of his daughter to Whitelaw Reid, Mills bought the $400,000 Villard palace on Madison Avenue and bestowed it as a wedding present. Present Millses combine the affluence of Pacific gold with the hauteur of Atlantic blue blood which has come from the distaff side.

But the richest of social families in the United States remains to be described, the Vanderbilts. They however had no connections with the gold fortunes of the West, with the exception that Commodore Vanderbilt for a short time after 1849 ran a "transit" system across the swamps of Nicaragua to carry those prospectors seeking to avoid the covered wagons or the long voyage round the Horn, and that his second son and namesake Cornelius ran off to California at the age of eighteen but returned empty-handed, whereupon his father had him locked up in the Bloomingdale Insane Asylum. After his release the lad continued for years to sponge upon Horace Greeley, and borrowed as much as $50,000 from that editor —who apparently sympathized with any one who had taken his classic advice to young men. He, the younger Cornelius, an inveterate gambler and epileptic, who sometimes had seizures at the faro table, would recover consciousness, and go on playing with eternal bad luck, was one of the few unfortunates in a family whose history is the most brilliant of success stories.

The father, Cornelius Vanderbilt, was born in 1794 on Staten Island, the fourth of nine children of a Dutch farmer and ferryman who spelled his name Van Der Bilt, and his wife Phebe Hand, a New Jersey farmer's daughter. The Van Der Bilts were miserably poor squatters who had come over in the seventeenth century, to wrest a living through four generations from a stony and sandy soil. The mother, Phebe, was superior in brains and industry to her husband. She kept a dairy and garden, ran a little butter and egg business of her own, and kept her savings in an old clock. According to Margharita A. Hamm's *Famous Families of New York,* 1902, a collection of adulatory lives of the rich, old and new, "From her youth, tradition says, she was a leader of Staten Island Society. According to the records of the time, she attended all the weddings, christenings, funerals, and other functions." This assertion leads one to suspect that the state of Society upon Staten Island may have been comparable to that of the snakes in Ireland. Yet Phebe Van Der Bilt was a remarkable woman, who lived to a ripe old age in her little farmhouse and had the pleasure of being saluted with rockets and guns by her devoted son the Commodore as he passed the Island on his European cruise of the *North Star* in 1853. She alone could move his inflexible will, as she demonstrated by ordering him to release his wife Sophia from the Bloomingdale Asylum where he had committed her for nagging and lack of co-operation.

Hard-working and ambitious, Cornelius at the age of sixteen had his own boat, a periagua, for ferrying passengers and freight, and was soon saving a thousand dollars a year. During the War of 1812 he was given a small Army contract. In 1818, owner of several sailing boats, he sold them all and staked his future upon steam navigation; soon he was running a line of ships on the Hudson. In those early days of steam, ships raced for records against their competitors, often in the excitement of the race failing to pause at advertised stops; sometimes when the coal gave out the crew would burn bunks, furniture, and partitions before the course was finished, while one captain made no bones of keeping a rifle to shoot at overhauling rivals. Into this rough and tumble "Captain" Vanderbilt entered with zest: on shipboard he often took the wheel himself after laying steep bets on the outcome, while from his little business office he fought the Eastern shipping interests, the Fulton-Livingston group, and conquered—even as his grandchildren were to storm the Knickerbocker Society which that group represented. His two oft-repeated maxims were, "Never tell nobody what yer goin' to do, till you do it," and "Don't you never buy anything you don't want nor sell anything you hain't got." Secretive, aggressive, hot tempered and perhaps the greatest master of swearing in his generation,[4a] "Commodore" Vanderbilt—as he was soon acclaimed by popular promotion—was not too scrupulous in his business ethics, but yet remained staunchly loyal to those whom he liked, for, as a Wall Street broker said at the time of the Gold Conspiracy in 1869, "the

[4a]This fact, to which many contemporaries bear awestruck testimony, gained piquancy in 1882 after his death, when his son William Henry, vigorously denying to the newspapers that he had ever said "The Public be damned," added that it would have been an impossible utterance—since, like his father, he never sullied his lips with profanity. For a recent full account of this episode see Lloyd Lewis and H. J. Smith, *Oscar Wilde Discovers America*, New York, 1936.

old rat never forgets his friends." From Hudson River shipping he soon expanded into the North Atlantic and presently the Pacific, and made his first ten million.

And although he refused to replace the shabby carpets in his house at 1 Washington Place, whence he had moved his wife and twelve children from Staten Island, he did give his family a prodigious treat in 1853. He built the first yacht on which Vanderbilts had ever set foot, the *North Star*, 2000 tons, with a satinwood saloon furnished in rosewood upholstered with green plush, and a dining saloon decorated in polished ligneous marble panelled with Naples granite and adorned with medallions of Washington, Franklin, Webster, and Clay on the ceiling, framed in scroll work of purple, green, and gold. It cost $1500 a day to operate; the Commodore later boasted that the whole cruise came to nearly half a million. It was the one recklessness of a lifetime. He wanted to show Europe what grandeur a self-made American could achieve. He hired John Keefe, fashionable New York caterer, as steward, together with cooks and a doctor. As chaplain and historian of the voyage, he invited the Reverend J. O. Choules and his wife to come along, stipulating that there should be grace at every meal and evening prayers at nine o'clock. In London Doctor Choules, as he records in his promptly published *Cruise of the North Star,* herded the Vanderbilts from one Baptist chapel to another—while the Commodore, who was on his best behavior, benignly submitted. The Vanderbilts were not presented at Court, though thanks to Peabody the banker they occupied a box at Covent Garden and had a glimpse of Victoria and Albert, whose appearance, they decided, "was anything but aristocratic. . . . We searched scrutinizingly among the noble circles to discover something in form or feature marking the stamp of hereditary nobility; but in vain." Taking his cue from London Society, Mr. Ingersoll the American Minister was very cool toward the Vanderbilts—though the Lord Mayor did invite them to a soirée at the Mansion House, and the merchants of Southampton honored the Vanderbilts by an elaborate banquet, interspersed with hymns and glees, according to Doctor Choules, who prints all the notes of regret received from the American Minister, Mr. Peabody the broker, the Lord Mayor of London, and other acquaintances they had just made, but adds that the festivities were attended by many of "the leading tradesmen of the town and their ladies." The popular newspapers also made much ado over the

The Golden Book

Commodore, the London *Daily News* commenting in an editorial on June 4:

America . . . is the great arena in which the individual energies of man, uncramped by oppressive social institutions, or absurd social traditions, have full play, and arrive at gigantic development. . . . Those who ought to be the Vanderbilts of England would shrink from employing their wealth in the magnificent manner employed by their American friend. They would dread the effect of making any unusual display, which would surely subject them to the reproach of being millionaires and parvenus. Here is the great difference between the two countries. In England a man is too apt to be ashamed of having made his own fortune, unless he has done so in one of the few roads which the aristocracy consent to travel by—the bar, the church, or the army. . . . It is time that the *millionaire* should cease to be ashamed of having made his own fortune. It is time that *parvenu* should be looked on as a word of honor. It is time that the middle classes should take the place which is their own, in the world which they have made. The middle classes have made the modern world. The Montmorencis, the Howards, the Percys, made the past world,—and they had their reward. Let them give place to better men.

After a cruise to Russian, French, and Levantine ports the *North Star* turned homeward, and the great excursion was over. One relic of that event still survives, a wooden star with rays, salvaged from the old ship, which now hangs in the dining saloon of the *Winchester,* General Cornelius Vanderbilt's steam yacht.

After the death of his mother, and of his favorite son George in the Civil War, the Commodore began to frequent Mrs. Tufts, a spiritualist medium of Tompkinsville, Staten Island. He believed in "spells" and in homeopathic magic wrought with a lock of hair; on one occasion late in life he called up the ghost of Jim Fisk to advise him on a business deal. Yet with all these sallies into the invisible world, Vanderbilt never lost his mastery of reality, and it was now after the close of the Civil War that he astonishingly increased his wealth from ten to one hundred million dollars within twelve years through dazzling speculations in railroads. The New York Central became, and still remains, the backbone of the Vanderbilt fortune. Though the Commodore's tight-fisted control was broken after another generation, and the accumulation dissipated by extravagance and titled marriages, between 200,000 and 300,000 shares of stock still remain in the family.

The Saga of American Society

Vanderbilt's egotism was boundless. Over six feet tall, with a muscular physique built by his boyhood at the oars, fiery black eyes and red cheeks, a shock of white hair and flowing sideburns, he boasted to Ward McAllister that the sculptor Powers had said of his head, "It is a finer head than Webster's!" He printed his picture on all the Lake Shore bonds, gave a ship named the *Vanderbilt* to the Government during the Civil War, had a locomotive on the New York Central christened "Commodore Vanderbilt" with his portrait on each side of the headlight, put up a large statue of himself in his new Hudson River station in St. John's Park, and proposed to New York City the erection of "the tallest monument in America" which should be dedicated to the joint glory of George Washington and Cornelius Vanderbilt. He loved trotting horses, gambled all night at whist in Saratoga, read only newspapers, and professed to scorn the Society which—outside the Stock Exchange—would have no traffic with him because of his illiteracy and crudity. A few days before his death in 1877, when ulcers of the stomach and other ailments were pressing hard upon him, the physician recommended champagne. "Champagne!" groaned the Commodore. "I can't afford champagne. A bottle every morning! Oh, I guess sody water'll do." He died with a family group about his bed singing "Come, Ye Sinners, Poor and Needy."

His eldest son William Henry, apparently sluggish and unpromising, had finally won his father's admiration by living for years in a small two-story house with a lean-to for a kitchen, in the midst of a truck farm on Staten Island, and haggling with the old man over the price of manure from the horse-car stables of the Vanderbilts. He married Maria Louisa Kissam, daughter of a Brooklyn clergyman of an old and good family. Hard working and tenacious as grim death, he reaped the rewards of drudgery by inheriting almost all the estate of his father, who hoped thus to keep intact the makings of a dynasty. The son increased the fortune to two hundred million, but split it equally between his two sons Cornelius, who married Alice Gwynne of Cincinnati, and William Kissam, married first to Alva Smith of Mobile, later Mrs. O. H. P. Belmont, and later to Anne Harriman Sands Rutherfurd. Each successive generation marked a gain in social grace and the uncommercial interests. William Henry, who according to his early biographer Croffut, "liked pictures which told a story, with either strong or cheerful subjects," bought Meissoniers, Millets, and Rosa Bonheurs at the rate of some $1,500,000; he loved horses and owned the famous trotter "Maude S."; he moved Cleopatra's Needle from Egypt to Central Park at the cost of $100,000; and he built the great twin mansions on Fifth Avenue between 51st and 52nd Streets for himself and his daughters, employing 600 artisans for a year and a half. Of him Gladstone is said to have remarked to the Vanderbilt lawyer, Chauncey Depew: "The Government ought to seize his property and take it away from him, as it is too dangerous a power for any one man to have." Yet he lived with sobriety, and dying in 1885 was buried in the Vanderbilt mausoleum which he had built at New Dorp, Staten Island—whence the family came, and whither they all finally return. Designed by the fashionable architect Richard Hunt, it cost $300,000, and in those times was watched day and night by a guard who punched a clock every quarter-hour.

His grandsons included the late Alfred Gwynne, noted horseman, who married Margaret Emerson, heiress of Bromo-Seltzer, and met death on the *Lusitania;* the late Reginald, whose wife Gloria Morgan belongs to the "international set" and is much in the headlines because of her dashing beauty and her contest with Gertrude Vanderbilt Whitney over custody of her only child; the present General Cornelius, engineer and inventor of railway appliances, a kindly, shy, quiet gentleman of increasingly infirm health; the present William Kissam, yachtsman and industrious business man who dislikes the Newport crowd; and Harold Stirling, an even more noted sportsman and bridge expert. His granddaughters are Consuelo Balsan of France and Palm Beach, former Duchess of Marlborough, and her cousin Gladys, Countess Lâszló Széchényi, wife of a Hungarian diplomat, and hostess of Washington and Newport Society. In 1908 in his memoirs *Fifty Years in Wall Street* the broker Henry Clews noted that the young Vanderbilts exhibit "a high degree of refinement, showing how fast human evolution under favorable circumstances progresses in this country." The family passed through a phase of running after European titles and recognition which gave them a temporary though unfortunate notoriety; the youngest generation seems however to have grown blasé to such pomps and vanities. Its only liability is found in the person of Cornelius Vanderbilt, Jr., with his cheerfully irresponsible career of rash books and marriages; he nevertheless offered an *amende honorable* for a harsh saying attributed to his great-grandfather by starting a tabloid newspaper in Los Angeles in 1923 with the slogan "The Public Be Pleased." That revision is perhaps significant of the growing humility among American plutocrats, as well as of the fact that sixty years after the great Commodore the Vanderbilt family has rapidly completed the typical cycle into the sere and yellow leaf of wealth, vigor, and enterprise.

The next greatest fortune reaped from American railroads was probably that of Edward H. Harriman. His cousins the Oliver Harrimans and their immediate connections long looked upon him as their unfashionable kin, since they themselves had won recognition among Hudson River families a generation before. The late Elliott Roosevelt was briefly engaged to Anne Harriman, daughter of Oliver, and future wife of William K. Vanderbilt, to the surprise of his conservative Roosevelt relatives who even then regarded him as something of a pioneer. Edward H. Harriman was born in 1848, the son of a poor Episcopal clergyman of sound but modest ancestry who spent the latter days of his life as bookkeeper in the old New York Bank of Commerce. At the age of fourteen young Harriman got a job as office-boy with DeWitt C. Hays, a Wall Street broker. Widening his acquaintance rapidly, he became intimate with Lewis Livingston and his son James, of the Knickerbocker aristocracy. As soon as Harriman had worked himself up to bookkeeper of the Hays firm, he persuaded James Livingston to go into stock brokerage with him, the Livingstons supplying the capital. The firm attained rapid success, and soon Harriman dissolved the partnership to strike out alone. Cultivating people with means and social standing, he came to number among his clients and business associates Astors, Goelets, Cuttings, and Fishes, whose pet investment was the Illinois Central Railroad. Furthermore, his marriage in 1879 to Mary Averell, daughter of a small railroad owner in Ogdensburg, New York, helped draw his interests toward that field where keen business audacity and skill found full play. A small, nervous, restless, and taciturn man, Harriman became first the ally and then—according to tradition, goaded by his wife's social pique— the bitter enemy of Stuyvesant Fish, the big, forthright patrician president of Illinois Central, known in Wall Street on account of his blondness, ineptitude, and physique as "the White Elephant." Eventually the mouse sent him crashing to defeat in 1907. Equally relentless was Harriman's feud with James J. Hill of St. Paul, the builder of another colossal fortune in railroads, who however never crossed the social threshold. A familiar story tells that after coming out from the ether of an appendectomy Harriman immediately asked for a telephone and announced to Hill: "This is Harriman. I wanted to tell you the operation's over and I'm all right." Dying in 1909 Harriman left $100,000,000 and his vast responsibilities in the remarkably able hands of his wife, who lived to her eighty-first year in 1932. Their children include W. Averell Harriman, industrialist and polo-player, E. Roland Harriman, another well-known sportsman of today, and the late Mary Harriman Rumsey, founder of the Junior League.

While some of the old families, like the dull but canny De Peysters, the proud and retiring Livingstons, the colorful Van Cortlandts, the practical and unimaginative Schuylers, and the proverbially parsimonious Winthrops, were clipping coupons, living upon a fraction of their income, and snubbing the new millionaires of shipping and railroads, other ancient families were slipping slowly but perceptibly, like the kind and friendly Beekmans and the charming but indolent Van Rensselaers, who since the first patroons have never gained any money except by marriage. But all of the old fortunes were being dwarfed, in fact and in publicity, by the new riches which accrued between the Civil War and the Great War—the longest crescendo in the history of American wealth. The rise of dynasties like the Vanderbilts, Fields, Rockefellers, and McCormicks and the fabulous legends with which the press invested them bore a close relation to the great labor unrest of 1886, which witnessed a noteworthy labor campaign in New York politics and the bloody Haymarket Riot in Chicago. The era of muck-raking journalism, of Ida M. Tarbell and Lincoln Steffens, as well as of trust-smashing from the White House, was not far away. Alternating were the typically American spasms of great accumulation and moral indignation.

Nobody was more bitterly cursed as a predatory plutocrat than a shy, sallow, frail little man with the face of a disappointed poet, who spent twenty years dying of consumption, and often—wracked with chest-pains, bleeding from the lungs, and unable to still in sleep the spinning gyroscope of his brilliant mind—would pace the sidewalk before his Fifth Avenue house, under the eye of a night-watchman. Jay Gould had been born in 1836, son of a dairyman of Roxbury, New York. Henry Adams was to call him "the complex Jew," and most of his associates in Wall Street regarded him as a Shylock in habits and probably heredity.

The Saga of American Society

Certain it was that he descended from one Major Nathan Gold, who settled in Fairfield, Connecticut in 1646, and that the spelling of the family name was first changed to the less suspicious form in 1806. But the elaborate and in some respects eminent pedigree of the Goulds of Fairfield gives no unequivocal answer, and it is quite possible that Israel has been blamed unfairly for this broker who came to call himself, with weary candor, "the most hated man in America." Jay Gould received a scant education at Beechwood Seminary, where on April 9, 1850, he wrote a theme which is still preserved on "Honesty is the Best Policy." Many years later before a Senate investigating committee he recalled with pathos how, as a poor farm boy, he drove the cows to pasture and stung his bare feet on the thistles. After a short season as surveyor and manager of a tannery, Jay Gould came to New York City at the age of seventeen hoping to sell a mouse-trap he had invented. Later he related: "It was in a pretty mahogany case which I carried under my arm. I went into a Sixth Avenue car, I think, and every now and then I ran out on the rear platform to see the buildings, leaving the case containing the mouse-trap on the seat." He came back to find it gone, and upon a hint from the conductor ran after and collared the thief, who turned out to be a notorious criminal; the incident got half a column in the New York *Herald*. Though the world showed no inclination to beat a track to the inventor's door, it was soon learning to respect this daring young man who floated bond issues with the greatest of ease—who with slender capital had risen so quickly in a brokerage house, and begun to launch into railroad speculation. He found a partner in the ex-patent medicine showman and barker Jim Fisk, jovial, florid, beplastered with "kiss-curls," who took over Pike's Opera House for their offices, and dressed up in admiral's uniform to see passengers off on their Fall River steamboat line. Such exploits as the Erie Railroad scandal of 1868 and the "gold conspiracy" of 1869, when Gould double-crossed Fisk and barely escaped lynching at the hands of a mob, belong to the chronicles of finance rather than Society. He and his wife, born Helen Miller, were cuttingly ignored by Mrs. Astor and the so-called Four Hundred; after being blackballed overwhelmingly by the yacht clubs, Gould soon gave up whatever social hopes he may have had. Dying in 1892, he left more than $77,000,000 to his four sons and two daughters, with no such concentration in the hands of a favorite heir as early Astors and Vanderbilts had provided.

Viscount William Waldorf Astor

Berry Wall

C. Oliver Iselin

J. P. Morgan

Wm. C. Whitney

Andrew Carnegie

August Belmont

James Gordon Bennett

E. H. Harriman

Mr. E. T. Stotesbury and daughter John D. Rockefeller, Sr., and son

Both photographs by Brown Bros.

Mrs. Harry Payne Whitney (Gertrude Vanderbilt), 1909

From the Harold Seton Collection

The Golden Book

His children had to battle every inch of the way against their father's unsavory name. The eldest son, George Jay, though no paragon, was admitted to the New York Yacht Club, even as the junior James Gordon Bennett was taken in after the repute of his father had been a trifle obscured by time. George Gould built an imposing house named "Georgian Court" at Lakewood, N. J., with a great elliptical staircase of marble and bronze, a bedstead worth $25,000, Italian sunken gardens, and a palaestra costing $250,000 with a great tanbark hippodrome, shooting gallery, and Turkish and Russian baths. Other children of Jay Gould are Helen, Mrs. Finley J. Shepard, known for the charities of a simple, kindly heart; Edwin, former chairman of the board of the St. Louis and Southwestern Railway; Howard, an expatriate in England; Frank Jay, the croupier de luxe of the Riviera; and Anna, who married first the elegant poseur Boni de Castellane, and secondly the Duc de Talleyrand-Périgord. George Gould, who reputedly broke his sister Anna's attachment to the actor Frank Woodruff, chose his own wife, Edith Kingdon, from Augustin Daly's noted troupe, and begot eight children, including Vivien, first wife of Lord Decies. In his will George Gould acknowledged three natural children by a less successful actress, Guinevere Jeanne Sinclair, whom he married just after his wife's death and a year before his own. This was the era when many plutocrats waited with orchids at stage-doors— though, unlike Gould, they often married the homely daughters of their business partners. Although newspaper columnists and their readers have long genuflected at the name of Gould, that family has never been admitted into conservative Society in America. The Goulds have been made, in fact, the scapegoats among parvenus. In conclusion it might be mentioned that one of the more innocent stories circulated about them was that they had solid gold faucets in their bathrooms, a report which has also been made concerning the William Fahnestocks at Newport and the Hugh Dillmans at Palm Beach; it would appear to be the classic legend of ostentatious wealth in America, the land which above all others has promoted the amenities of lavatory and latrine.

Among newer Philadelphia fortunes the names of Widener and Elkins loom large. Peter A. B. Widener, born in 1834, began his career as butcher's boy in the shop of his elder brother, but soon worked up to the ownership of his own meat market. In post-Civil War days the meat markets in some American cities vied with saloons and billiard parlors as loafing places for ward politicians, who often would foregather in a back room for beer and dominoes—especially if the proprietor were as jovial as Peter Widener, member of "The All-Night Poker Players." Widener himself soon took a hand in municipal affairs, and observing their obvious connections with the franchises of street-railways, he set out successfully to become city treasurer of Philadelphia in 1873. Meanwhile he found his ideal partner in shrewd, enterprising William L. Elkins, who had worked up from clerk in a grocery store, through his own fruit and vegetable business, to investments in the young oil and natural gas fields of Pennsylvania. Elkins and Widener soon controlled the street-car system of Philadelphia, and then joining forces with Ryan, Whitney, and Brady, extended their empire to New York, and made vast accumulations of wealth. Widener's son George married Elkins's daughter Eleanor; their son Harry Elkins Widener and his father were lost with the *Titanic*. Saved by one of the life-boats, Eleanor Elkins Widener gave to Harvard its Memorial Library in memory of her son, who had been a lavish bibliophile. Three years later she married Doctor Alexander Hamilton Rice, rich geographer and explorer of South America. At "Miramar," most elaborate of all Newport estates, the Rices live in the grand style, and their annual ball during Tennis Week is the high watermark of the season; they also maintain establishments in New York, Palm Beach, and Paris. Mrs. Rice, nearing seventy, is impressively the grande dame against every social horizon save that of her native Philadelphia, while her husband belongs to the Mayflower Descendants, the Society of Descendants of Knights of the Most Noble Order of the Garter, and six other genealogical societies. *Honi soit qui mal y pense.*

Another Pennsylvania fortune which long figured in Newport Society was that of the late Edward J. Berwind, son of a German immigrant who found employment as a cabinet-maker in the Meyers Piano Factory in Philadelphia. The son secured an appointment to Annapolis, but left the Navy to enter the coal business. Dour, tenacious, close-mouthed, and illiberal with employees, he gained great wealth. At "The Elms" in Newport and on Fifth Avenue he and his wife entertained with heavy magnificence, and were much better known to gilded Society than to the popular press. Equally shy of publicity in earlier days, though less smartly social, was Andrew Mellon, whose immigrant grandfather from Ireland had settled on Turtle Creek near Pittsburgh, and whose father was a jurist with a flair for money-lending and saving. So quietly did he make his immense fortune in coke, steel, aluminum, and oil, that his name had never been printed in the New York *Times* up to 1921, and Harding had never heard of Mellon until he was ordered to make him Secretary of the Treasury. However, his children, Paul Mellon and Mrs. David K. E. Bruce, daughter-in-law of former Senator William Cabell Bruce of Maryland, received much publicity during their father's belated fame.

No phase of American industry has yielded a more spectacular harvest of fortunes than Standard Oil. Yet aside from some of the older hoards which were further enriched by investment here, the billions derived from Standard Oil have not mixed notably in Society. The lion's share fell of course to the Rockefellers, who unlike Vanderbilts and Astors have had little to do with foreign titles, Newport, and lavish pageantry, but have stuck loyally by their business origins and made a career of hard work, simple living, and planned philanthropy. According to a family anecdote, the young sons of John D. Rockefeller, Jr., Winthrop and David, were ragged by a playmate for tinkering with a dilapidated row-boat, for, he suggested, they might at least ask their father for an outboard motor; they are said to have replied indignantly, "Who do you think we are, Vanderbilts?" The Rockefellers are of rather obscure German origin, Johann Peter Rockefeller and his son Peter coming from Sagendorf about 1722 and settling in New Jersey. The father of the present John D. Rockefeller, Sr. and of the late William was an itinerant peddler of patent medicines, who moved his impecunious family about in New Jersey, New York, and Ohio, finally anchoring in Cleveland. As a boy John D. clerked in a forwarding and commission house, while William was hired as bookkeeper by a small Cleveland miller; eventually the brothers joined forces in the produce business, and then hearing reports of the Pennsylvania oil fields made the choice which shaped their destiny. In 1867 the firm of Rockefeller, Andrews & Flagler was incorporated, and altered three years later to the original Standard Oil Co. William, who died in 1922, was a genial and companionable man, something of a *bon viveur,* who liked a box at the opera and was not averse to a little innocent social climbing; he was lacking in both the pieties and charities of his more famous brother. John D. has been always a simple, frugal, God-fearing Baptist, with no change except that years have altered the keen preoccupations of business into those of a valetudinarian. His son and namesake, now the arbiter of the family, has felt little attraction to the social game; no doubt the kindly, charitable, intelligent, but unfashionable wives whom they married—the father the late Laura Spelman, the son Abby Greene Aldrich, daughter of the self-made and distinguished Senator Nelson W. Aldrich—have fully acquiesced in their tastes. Among the first Rockefeller's associates Henry Flagler, son of a poor Presbyterian dominie, came to dine at the tables of social New York, blazed the trail to Palm Beach which Society was shortly to follow, and after divorcing his insane wife married Mary Lily Kenan of an excellent North Carolina family.[5] Yet the Flaglers were far from being social leaders, and the same attitude is found in another great Standard Oil family, the Harknesses, of respectable Scotch origin, who have taken no conspicuous rôle either in their native Ohio or in New York. Emulating the Rockefellers, Edward S. Harkness, son of the founder, has given immense sums to medicine and education.

The fortunes drawn from United States Steel have gone either to enhance older coffers, as in the case of the Morgans, or else have played a distinctly minor part in social history. The Fricks, the Garys, and the Phippses have had interests of their own—sport, Palm Beach estates, art, philanthropy—but whether from choice of compulsion have never gone far in formal Society. Other Pennsylvania fortunes have flashed briefly like meteors upon the social horizon, like that of the Wanamakers derived from department stores; and that of the Edward T. Stotesburys from stock brokerage, which, thanks to the ageing Mrs. Stotesbury, long ruled with imperial power over Palm Beach and Bar Harbor, was unknown in Newport, and was looked at a trifle askance in Philadelphia.

[5] In *'King' Lehr and the Gilded Age* the present Lady Decies tells a romantic and wistful story—that Mary Lily Kenan, a poor relation of the Pembroke Joneses, was brought by them to Newport to do the family sewing, and that she sat with needle and thread "somewhere at the top of that enormous house, in a tiny room among the servants," dreaming of a Prince Charming who should appear one day—until Henry Flagler saw her, asked that she sew a button on his coat, proposed, and married her. For the sake of truth it should be recorded that the Pembroke Joneses, rich arrivists from North Carolina, were extremely proud of their gently born but less prosperous relative and had induced her to live with them in Newport as the visible sign of their pedigree. Well provided for after the death of Henry Flagler in 1913, she married, in 1916, Robert W. Bingham of Louisville, present Ambassador to the Court of St. James's. Upon her death in 1917 she left him $5,000,000 out of her total fortune of $70,000,000.

Philadelphia Society has probably the longest record of snobbish exclusiveness in America; more compact and effectively implemented than New York, it is more lavish and overtly more materialistic than Boston. It has offered therefore a cruel sun in which sapless gentility may wilt, and a stony soil where the parvenu seldom strikes successful root.

On the other hand the paradise of parvenus is Chicago. In this midwest metropolis one's social passport is given a more perfunctory glance, particularly if it bears the visa of wealth. The name of its long-fashionable district, the Gold Coast, is significant. A very old family are the Potter Palmers; the founder came to Chicago in 1852, the year of the first railroad connection, and opened a dry-goods store in Lake Street. Successful, he retired temporarily from business after fifteen years, leaving his firm in the hands of Marshall Field and Levi Leiter; he travelled abroad in leisurely style, and returned to Chicago to speculate in real estate along the Lake Shore Drive, and built shops and hotels, dying a multimillionaire in 1902. His wife, most famous hostess of the Midwest in the 1890's, was the daughter of H. H. Honoré, a Kentuckian of French patronymic who had come to Chicago and done well in real estate. For her Potter Palmer built in 1885 a huge turreted castle of limestone, which, in tribute to her remote Gallic origins, had a Louis Quatorze salon and a gallery of French paintings; it also contained a Japanese room and a music-room in Moorish style. Iowa housewives read with astonishment in Mr. Medill's *Tribune* that Mrs. Palmer was waited on hand and foot by six servants, an eminence shared by no other Chicagoan. Called by her social friends "the Queen," Mrs. Potter Palmer was called by destiny to be president of the Board of Lady Managers of the Chicago World's Fair in 1893. With éclat she drove a nail of precious metals into the Women's Building, and at the opening of the Fair on May first she rode in the procession of twenty-three carriages, right behind President Cleveland and at her side the Duke and Duchess of Veragua. Not all the flower of Spain behaved cordially to Mrs. Palmer—for the Infanta Eulalie, wearing a spun-glass dress of 2,500,000 threads that weighed less than a pound, snubbed Mrs. Palmer on her own dais. Even her fellow-members on the Women's Board threatened recalcitrance some weeks later; there was a tense scene, a public quarrel from causes almost unknown in the midsummer hysteria, while Mrs. Palmer rose and referred darkly to "certain ladies who mortify me." Some one cried out, "You, our queen—," and for no clear reason everybody began to cry, and the tempest blew over.

Mrs. Palmer's castle remained Chicago's social capital up to her death in 1917. For awhile the mansion stood empty, until her son Potter bought the interest of his brother Honoré and reopened it in time for the début of his lovely but shy daughter, Pauline. Later it was sold to Vincent Bendix, inventor, sportsman, and symbol of the new riches of the motor age. The second landmark of the family was the old Palmer House, built in 1871 and rebuilt after the Fire in French style, containing a famous barber-shop whose floor was inlaid with silver dollars. Rudyard Kipling wrote in *From Sea to Sea:* "They told me to go to the Palmer House, which is a gilded and mirrored rabbit-warren, and there I found a huge hall of tessellated marble, crammed with people talking about money and spitting everywhere. A man who had drunk quite as much as was good for him told me that this was 'the finest hotel in the finest city on God Almighty's earth.'" Today chronic illness and increasing reticence have kept the Palmers from their old social domination of Chicago.

Palmer's partner and successor Marshall Field was born in 1834, of plain New England stock which had come over in the early Puritan migration. Young Field clerked in a dry-goods store in Pittsfield, Mass., until in 1856 he joined the westward trek and got a similar job in the Chicago shop of John V. Farwell. He slept on a pallet in the store to save lodgings, and lived on half of his $400 a year salary. By 1861 he had worked up to the post of general manager, was admitted as partner, then with Levi Leiter joined Potter Palmer and ultimately came to dominate the firm. Of Field one of his partners said, "His business was his passion," and from the world of commerce were drawn his closest friends—notably P. D. Armour, George M. Pullman, and N. K. Fairbank, with whom he lunched daily at the old Chicago Club. His death in January, 1906, following shortly after the mysterious death of his son and heir, left an estate of $120,000,000 in trust for his two grandsons, of whom only Marshall Field III now survives. His contacts have been largely with New York and Long Island, where he prefers to live, and with England, where at Eton and Cambridge he received his education.

The third partner, Levi Ziegler Leiter, was born in 1834, and as a boy clerked in the village store at Leitersburg, Md. He arrived in Chicago in 1855, and by hard work and astuteness rapidly rose in trade. In 1866 he married Mary Theresa Carver of Chicago, and had by her four children, including Mary, whose charm and grace won social admittance for the Leiters even among the rocky battlements of Newport, and gained for herself a brilliant marriage to the proud, autocratic Lord Curzon of Kedleston. Her only brother was Joseph, who tried disastrously in his fledgling days to corner wheat in the winter of 1897-8, but failed sensationally with a loss of nearly $10,000,000. After that the Leiters withdrew from speculation and moved to Washington, along with newspaper-owning McLeans, gold-mining Walshes, and other new families attracted by its more accessible and necessarily shifting Society. Levi Leiter, who devoted his old age to the collection of Americana, always recalled with amusement and wonder the long road he had travelled. The daughter of a late President of the United States remembers his turning to her at a magnificent dinner-party of American and European notables and saying with a wry smile, "I suppose you wonder, as I do, at seeing a gnarled little Jewish peddler being host to a table like this." Mrs. Levi Leiter, although she was a woman of some education, had a most unfortunate predilection toward gaucheries and slips of the tongue which the wits of Washington Society repeated with glee and probable embellishment—how her husband attended a fancy dress ball "in the garbage of a monk," how the Leiter house contained "a spinal staircase" and "sexual book-cases," how she pressed President Theodore Roosevelt to take another helping at dinner saying "You'd better have some more —you don't get anything at home like this." To a friend in reduced circumstances she complained about the rats which were infesting her house, adding, "And my dear, I suppose even you are troubled by mice in *your* little house." It appears that every American city whose Society is relatively new, small, and compact sports its legend of a malaprop, whose daily doings and sayings are followed by sardonic humorists like seagulls in the wake of a ship. For example in the Western city where the author lived for some years, a worthy lady delights her contemporaries by reporting how she has spent the day "in running pro and con" or remarks of her wistfully facetious husband, "You know, everything Horace says has to be taken with a dose of salts." Her type is a definite symbol in the social comedy of the United States; what would the English-speaking world have done had not Richard Brinsley Sheridan given her a local habitation and a name?

Probably the greatest of Chicago fortunes is that of the McCormicks. Thomas McCormick came from Ulster to settle in Pennsylvania in 1734; he was a weaver and soldier in the Indian wars. His grandson Robert (1780–1846) was the first inventor of the family, though never a very successful one; but it was his son, Cyrus Hall McCormick, who in 1834 patented the first practicable reaper and in 1847 wisely chose Chicago as the site of his future great factory. These McCormicks were a practical-minded family, with marked gifts for industrial organization, and a deep strain of Presbyterian piety. The affairs of the International Harvester Company have been well managed by the second Cyrus, who died in 1936, and his younger brother Harold Fowler McCormick, now chairman of the board, sponsor of grand opera in Chicago, husband of the late Edith Rockefeller and secondly of Ganna Walska. The Virginia branch produced a distinguished diplomat, Robert Sanderson McCormick (1849–1919), Ambassador to Austria, Russia, and France, who married the daughter of the Chicago publisher Joseph Medill; they had two sons, the late Senator Medill McCormick, whose widow Ruth Hanna is now Mrs. Albert G. Simms, eminent in the politico-social set of Washington, and Colonel Robert Rutherford McCormick, staunch Republican and somewhat dictatorial owner of the Chicago *Tribune*. His cousin Joseph Medill Patterson, who wrote *Confessions of a Drone* to reproach his own life among the gilded youth, helped organize a Municipal Ownership League, and in 1909 ran for office on the Socialist ticket, now owns the New York *News* and belongs in the camp of the mildly radical rich discussed in a previous chapter. Though the family has not been without gestures of grandeur—as when, some years ago, the wife of Cyrus McCormick III chartered a special train to carry her at top speed from New York to Chicago to attend a meeting of Christian Scientists, or on the other hand the publicized glamor attendant upon Eleanor or "Cissy" Patterson of the Washington *Herald*—the McCormick-Medill-Patterson clan has a solid rather than a purely social reputation, founded upon public service and rather simple, conservative living.

The late Mrs. Rockefeller McCormick, who after her divorce studied with Carl Jung, psychoanalyzed all her friends, and gave her worldly affairs into the hands of a psychic Swiss who remained her steward and *cicisbeo,* started a cultist fad in Chicago Society. Christian Science, Buchmanism, Theosophy, Rosicrucianism, New Thought, "metaphysics," and *yogi* flourished fashionably in her wake, in a manner known only to one other American city, Los Angeles. After her death the ranking grande dame in Society, in a less spectacular tradition, became Mrs. Martin Ryerson.

The great meat-packer who founded the Swift fortune compelled his wife and sons to take turns at keeping books, as a measure of economy and discipline. Thrifty, sluggish, bourgeois, with a gloomy vein of Teutonic pessimism, the Swifts have added little to the social gaiety of Chicago —though an element of fashionable Bohemia entered their doors with the marriage of Charles Swift to the noted German *lieder*-singer Claire Dux. Armours and Cudahys have produced both hard-working business men and sporting sons, but no preëminent leaders of Society. Indeed the meat-packing families of the Middle West have suffered unduly from that mysterious malady which stamps a family with an indelible trademark, like one of their own admirable hams. Just as Society finds it difficult to dissociate Dorrances from Campbell's Soup, Manvilles from asbestos and tar, Brokaws from ready-made clothes, Hartfords from the A. & P., and Mr. Frazier Jelke from butterine. Perhaps the wisest course has been followed by Mr. and Mrs. Robert Woods Bliss of Washington, who, it is reported, at one time ordered the advertising of Castoria to cease in the District of Columbia under the theory—as their less fortunate social rivals phrased it —that ignorance is bliss. It may be solace for these families to reflect that grandfathers of those who profess to sneer at trade-names were in their good time ironmongers, watchmakers, and chandlers. In America, as has been shown, almost all the great fortunes sprang from trade, and living them down has been a matter of two or, at the most, three generations.

In Detroit the so-called old fortunes of Newberrys, Algers, Trowbridges, and Russells derive chiefly from lumber and real estate. The new ones are naturally those from the motor-car industry, which now invade Grosse Pointe, the Detroit Country Club, the Yondotega Club for gentlemen, and the Colony Club for women. A recent family with cultivation and a record of public service, like the Chapins, is accepted readily, while polo and steeplechasing have furnished entry to Briggses and Fishers. Families like the Knudsens which do not fall into the social patterns approved by Society are still outlanders. Henry Ford has never attempted to scale the summits, in accord with the oldest of pre-War jokes about the Model T, that "the Ford can go everywhere except in Society." His son Edsel is much more aware of Society because of an ambitious wife, born Eleanor Clay, niece of a department-store founder of the nineties. Most fantastic of Detroit millionaires are the Dodges, whose wealth was amassed by two brothers, Horace and John, after beginning as struggling mechanics in 1900; during the last decade their business was sold for $146,000,000. The widow of the latter, Matilda Rausch Dodge Wilson, is a keen business woman and philanthropist who has no social interests and is not found in *The Social Register*. But the relict of the former, now Mrs. Hugh Dillman of Detroit and Palm Beach, has devoted herself to the game with intense absorption. Her only daughter, Delphine Dodge Cromwell Baker Godde, was one of the most sensational post-War débutantes in America; she married in succession the present husband of Doris Duke, then the late Raymond T. Baker, and most recently a French-born husband. The daughter of John Dodge by his first wife is Isabel Dodge Sloane, who out of all the Dodge women achieved the status of *The Social Register,* by marriage to George Sloane, since divorced. Though she does not ride and is extremely frightened of horses, she maintains a magnificent stable and seeks to rival Mrs. Payne Whitney as first lady of the turf in America. According to the social column she is a sportswoman, and according to the sports writers a "socialite." The current heiress of the Dodge family is Frances, who achieved much celebrity by wearing a black orchid at her début. Botanists confessed themselves somewhat nonplussed until it was revealed that the hue had been achieved by the painter's art.

Two distinct social layers in St. Louis have been merging for the past generation—one with grandfathers and no dollars and the other with dollars and no grandfathers. The former are the French Creoles who came in soon after 1760 when the Marquis Pierre de Laclede-Liguest and his young stepson Auguste Chouteau founded the city. The Marquis and his friends came at length to be fascinated by the democratic philosophy of Rousseau, destroyed family documents, and erased coats of arms. Like many other New World radicals they sired Tory grandchildren. Later Chouteaux went into the fur trade with John Jacob Astor, while others— with names like Cabanné, Berthold, de Balivière, de Mun, Sarpy—with the expansion of the town reaped comfortable fortunes from large real estate holdings. In the Indian summer of French St. Louis after the Civil War these families created aristocratic cliques—such as the "Home Circle" dancing group and a little later the "Imperial," which gave great balls two or three times a year. In 1878 the St. Louis Club for men was founded, with a membership of 500, and in the same year the Veiled Prophet's Ball began. The Prophet's identity was always kept darkly secret, but his Queen was invariably a débutante from the old families— though the most conservative ones forbade their daughters to pay too much notice to so public an occasion. Mrs. Gerald Mark Borden, now of New York, born Lucille Papin, was compelled in the summer of 1892 by her mother to decline the Queenship and its gift of a diamond tiara—though to avoid offence and to make valid her excuse the family had the annoyance of remaining in Canada until late autumn when the ball was over. A generation ago among the social leaders of St. Louis were two sisters of the Sarpy family who had been presented at the court of Napoleon III: Madame Armand Peugnet, cold, patrician and aloof, and Mrs. James Lowry Donaldson Morrison, gay and fond of large, jovial parties. Mrs. William Maffitt, great-granddaughter of the Marquis, and her daughter, Mrs. Edward Walsh, as well as Mrs. James Scanlan and Mrs. George Castleman, were other aristocrats of a vanished day. The newer stratum in St. Louis dates from German waves of immigration, the first after 1848 and the second in the seventies. They lived on the South side, brewed beer, milled flour, manufactured shoes, had their Turnverein and Sänger-bund, ate marzipan and regarded a *kaffeeklatsch* as the acme of social frivolity. Creole children were sometimes driven in the family carriage, with the coachman to answer their curious questions, through streets where Anheusers, Busches, Fausts, and Lemps lived. Prosperity slowly but surely achieved intermarriages. Blackballed by the St. Louis Country Club, dating from 1892, the Busches founded the Bridlespur of their own and by lining the treasury of the ball committee with a sum said to be $50,000 had a Busch débutante crowned Queen—even though at the moment of coronation Creole women turned their backs. When the first member of that family was admitted to the Junior League, Mrs. Morrison drew the shutters of her drawing-room, and from that time on seemed cheerfully resigned to her end.

In Denver the largest fortunes today, contrary to vague impressions in the East, are seldom survivals from the gold and silver rushes of 1859–70.

The Saga of American Society

Though mining has enriched through the years many old conservative families, the most blatantly rich discoverers of bonanzas usually left the West to attempt assault upon New York, Newport, or Paris, and ended their careers in social disaster or alcoholic extravaganza. They rose in tornadoes and sank like sandstorms. Cooks in mining camps, bartenders, clerks in drugstores, and prospectors with donkey and pick amassed wealth which seemed more fabulous at the time than it really was, and they spent with prodigality. Gene Fowler has lately retold the story of J. J. Brown, who cached $300,000, from the sale of a mine, in an unused stove during the late summer, awoke to find that his wife unwittingly had burned the banknotes, but cheerfully bestirred himself to stake out an even more dazzling claim, and gave her a life income upon which to be snubbed at Newport. It was a time of social anarchy. George Tillinghast Clark, a descendant of Governor Stephen Hopkins of Rhode Island, came to Colorado in 1860 in a buckboard to try his luck. He married an aristocratic young lady from New York, and to do their cooking and washing hired an Irish girl named Katie. The maid, innocently proud of her mistress' fine lace petticoats from Stewart's in New York City, used to hang them to dry on the highest hilltop of the mining camp. Later she became the wife of an Irish flour-miller who made millions, and upon being introduced to her former mistress by the proprietor of the department store of Daniels & Fisher, cut her dead with a swish of her own lace petticoats. Today her daughters live in magnificent houses. The most distinguished record of civic service in Denver belongs to the descendants of a physician, John Evans, who founded Evanston, Illinois, and was appointed by President Lincoln to this new territorial governorship. Cautious, conservative, dignified, enriched by railroads, proud of their Methodist loyalties, the Evanses share honors as Denver's traditionally premier family with the Kountzes, bankers descended from the same German stock known in New York and the Middle West. The Hills with their fortune in mining, the Morrises related to the Hudson Valley clan with money from Western railroads, the Reeds from Colorado Springs with wealth from oil and an exemplary sense of philanthropy, the Chappells and Cranmers who employ a patrimony from public utilities freely in the sponsorship of music and drama, and a dozen other families have played their part in the social life of the West. Denver also boasts its Italian prince and a French noble who has renounced his title; both have taken Denver brides, and devote themselves to a variety of pursuits from investments to raising turkeys for the market.

At present the newest fortunes which Society is finding most difficult to assimilate are those from the movies of Hollywood. Several of the most personable and amusing cinema stars and the people who write for them, both American and English—like Mary Pickford, Charlie Chaplin, Cole Porter, Noel Coward—have been adopted eagerly by the most blasé group in world Society, the "international set," under the sponsorship of such globe commuters as Mrs. Reginald Vanderbilt and her sister Lady Furness, Lady Louis Mountbatten, the Duff Coopers, and Lord and Lady Milford Haven; this group also enjoys the royal patronage of the Duke of Windsor, who was inducted into it upon his visit to Long Island in 1924 when the Jazz Age was in its most seductive phase. Its effect upon his hitherto sheltered life, and upon the politics of an empire, has lately been demonstrated.

Conservative American Society has other criteria besides sheer wealth, and to neglect this fact would be a grave injustice. Among the new families who have obtained a measure of social notice, one can trace year by year an upward or downward curve, usually conditional upon the behavior of their members. It is perhaps discouraging to add that, aside from judicious entertaining of the right people, the art of quietude is the recipe for success. An aspirant makes the lower rungs of the social ladder by getting his name in the newspapers, but achieves the higher levels by keeping it out of them. The Woolworth heirs, for example, have suffered during the past three years by the floodlights focused upon Countess Barbara von Haugwitz-Reventlow, though after her less flashy second marriage and increasing domesticity, her standing is now convalescent; the rather obvious social ambitions of her good-humored, rowdy kin the Donahues have been even more maladroit, while their discreet relatives the McCanns have been in *The Social Register* since 1928. On the other hand the Dukes are rising steadily; though publicity has not spared the heirs of such an immense fortune, it has been of the better sort. They are descendants of a Scotch-Welsh couple, Taylor and Dicie (Jones) Duke, who had settled in the tobacco country of North Carolina in the early nineteenth century. Their son Washington was an unprosperous farmer who fought in the Confederate Army, and returned home with a single half-dollar and two blind mules. He and his two boys "Ben" and "Buck" pounded out leaf tobacco with hickory sticks in a small log barn, and packed it in small cartons labelled "Pro Bono Publico"; drawn by the blind mules they sold it from farmhouse to village through southern North Carolina. They began to supply stores in their native and then in adjoining states, pioneered by installing cigarette machines, and by 1889 were producing half of the cigarettes smoked in the United States. Benjamin Duke branched out into hydro-electric power, and did valuable service in promoting the rehabilitation of the South; upon his death in 1929 he left an estate of sixty million dollars. His brother James Buchanan, who had died four years before, joined him in giving heavily to Trinity College, now Duke University. Buchanan Duke's widow, born Nanaline Holt of Atlanta, has been favorably received at Newport. That Society has always had something of a predilection for Southerners, who are adopted quickly—as were the rice-milling Pembroke Joneses of North Carolina a generation ago. Mrs. Duke's daughter Doris is now the wife of James H. R. Cromwell, son of Mrs. E. T. Stotesbury.

Before closing a brief and necessarily selective account of the great fortunes in American Society it is necessary to add a few words about the history of Jewish wealth. The present anti-Semitism of Society—as expressed in visiting lists, club memberships, and personal attitudes—is markedly keener in the United States than in England or France, where Rothschilds for example seem to find virtually no doors barred against them. It is probably an aspect of that insecurity, that timidity and conventionalism, which looms so large in our social picture. But much of it unquestionably arises from waves of successively poorer and less desirable Jewish migration, chiefly from Poland and Russia, which have had a most damaging effect upon the social standing of the Jew in America. Today the anti-Semitism of Society is invariably prefaced by the apology, "Why, some of my best friends are Jews, but—." It is unfortunately true that bumptious Jews in business—hated by the Sephardic aristocracy with trancendent hatred, such as even Hitler has scarce achieved—standing shoulder to shoulder with such diverse cousins as the grandiose movie magnate in his orchild vest, and the intellectual Marxist with his sallow face and unkempt hair, have conspired to give Society its prejudices. A few masochistic Brahmins have even toyed with the idea that they themselves might be long lost tribesmen—like James Russell Lowell who had an *idée fixe* that the name Russell had sprung from a clan of red-haired Israelites, while all people who bore the names of countries and towns or somewhat fantastic compound names were originally Jewish. With half-serious and half-whimsical ingenuity he pursued the thesis, especially during his ambassadorship in England, and conjured up Jews everywhere by a kind of multiple image of Disraeli—even as some naïve persons enjoy life by seeing a conspirator in every Catholic, a Negro in every brunette with curly hair, or a homosexual in every youth who carries his handkerchief up his sleeve.

In the eighteenth century, when the only Jews known to American society were Spanish and Portuguese, with a light sprinkling of Dutch and German, anti-Semitism was practically unknown. Thus Rebecca Franks, daughter of a rich Philadelphia merchant, was one of the most popular belles of the Revolution; General Lee called her "a lady who has had every human and divine advantage." She was one of the princesses of the great Tory fête the Meschianza, visited and corresponded charmingly with Chews, Allens, and Penns, married Lieutenant-General Sir Henry Johnston, and finished her days as the grande dame of Bath, most aristocratic of English watering places. Her two sisters married Oliver De Lancey and Andrew Hamilton of "Woodlands." Throughout the nineteenth century Hebrews of pure Sephardic stock, like the Lazarus family, occupied a quiet but distinguished position in New York Society; even the doors of the Union Club admitted them, as they did an occasional Jewish visitor from the Southern gentry like Judah P. Benjamin, whom the Union Club refused to expel with his fellow-Confederates at the time of the Civil War and thus drove the more rabid patriots into founding the Union League Club.

The last Jew to enter the arcana of smart New York Society before the bars went up was August Belmont, born in 1816 in Germany to Simon and Frederika (Elsaas) Belmont—a name more familiar in Frankfort in its German equivalent, Schoenberg. According to a hoary legend which may as well be discounted, August was an illegitimate scion of the House of Rothschild; but at any rate, at the age of fourteen he entered the employment of those bankers at Frankfort. His first duties consisted of sweeping out the offices, but soon he rose to a position of trust, moved on terms of social familiarity with his employers, and in their household learned the arts of epicure and sportsman which he later taught New York and Newport. The Rothschilds sent him to the United States as their agent, and again he discharged his task so successfully that after the panic of 1837—still with the approval of the greatest banking house in the world—he set up his own firm of August Belmont & Co. The duel as an early technique of social climbing, of establishing one's status as a gentleman, has already been mentioned, and it was by this route that Belmont first attracted widespread comment. On August 26, 1841, after a quarrel which occurred at Niblo's over a subject too trite to be mentioned, Belmont fought a duel with Edward Heyward of South Carolina.[6] Belmont was shot in the thigh, declared that his honor was satisfied, and walked with a patrician limp for the rest of his life. He became a United States citizen, was appointed consul-general to Austria and served from 1844 to 1850, and with steadily rising wealth and prestige married in the interval Caroline Slidell Perry, from the family of naval heroes. From 1853 to 1857 he was Minister to the Netherlands, and returned to render valuable financial service to the Union during the Civil War. He was a collector of paintings, porcelains, and objects of art, a somewhat rakish man-about-town, and a noted connoisseur of horse flesh. One of the founders of Jerome Park, he was for many years president of the American Jockey Club. He died in 1890, but his eldest son Perry, born in 1851 —aristocratic diplomat and sportsman—still survives. The second August Belmont married the celebrated actress Eleanor Robson, with the benediction of *The Social Register;* the third married Elizabeth L. Saltonstall.

Since the first August Belmont set foot in America, no member of that family has ever married a Jewess, but invariably a Gentile of social standing. In this way, plus an exchange of the synagogue for Episcopal communion, a constant association with non-Jews, and the adaptability of Nature which has given Belmonts scarcely any Semitic cast of feature except in their patriarchal age, a complete break with their Old World background has been successfully effected. In social acceptance no later Jewish family can compare with them, though marriage with an eligible Gentile is still the most potent entrée—as illustrated by the case of James

[6]The usually trustworthy *Dictionary of American Biography* states that the duel was fought at Elkton, Indiana, with William Hayward [*sic*]. But compare Hone's *Diary* for Friday, September 3, 1841: "A duel was fought on Thursday of last week at Elkton in Maryland between two well-known New Yorkers, Mr. August Belmont, an agent of the Rothschilds, and Mr. Edward Heyward, one of the exquisite sons of Mr. Wm. Heyward of this city." He proceeds to give further circumstantial details. This was the well-known Heyward family from Charleston, whose most famous living member is DuBose Heyward, novelist and playwright.

The Golden Book

Speyer, German Jewish banker who made a fortune in the pre-War generation. He married the late Ellin Prince Lowery, daughter of John Dyneley Prince and niece of the noted lawyer and wit William R. Travers. Her background, enhanced by great charm and popularity, caused the Speyers to be much sought after by social New York. Mr. Speyer, who belongs to one smart club, the Racquet, has often voiced his disapproval of those clubs and private schools which make racial discriminations. The late Otto H. Kahn, sometimes facetiously called "the flyleaf between the Old and the New Testament," was a German who came in 1893 to the United States as an employee of Speyer & Co.; three years later he became a partner of Kuhn, Loeb & Co., and through the years grew to be a multimillionaire. Sponsorship of the Metropolitan Opera did more to advance his social standing than the ostentatious Norman castle he built at Woodbury on Long Island, on a hill which took landscape gardeners and workmen two years to build, with a staff that once comprised 125 servants, with a Georgian dining-room that seated 200, and so many guest rooms with sunken baths that before each door was a silver rack for the guest to fill with his card so that he might be identified in the multitude. Such magnificence was on a parity with that of Randolph Guggenheim, who while president of the Municipal Council of New York, in February, 1899, gave at the Waldorf what the *Herald* called "New York's most costly dinner" at $250 a plate, with nightingales singing in a grove of transplanted rose trees, arbors hung with hothouse grapes, liqueurs bottled before the French Revolution, and richly jewelled matchboxes and vinaigrettes as favors. A few gestures like these, outstripping the pomp of even the Gilded Age, have unfairly given conservative Society in New York the impression that Jewish life is one of barbaric splendor. As a matter of fact, Jewish families of caste have their own criteria of admission to small clubs and country clubs that are every whit as exclusive as those of best Society among the Gentiles. A few old Sephardic families like the Cardozos are the inner circle, surrounded by German Jews of chiefly banking antecedents like Warburgs, Schiffs, and Strauses; on the outside and barred from any possible social standing, whatever their new wealth, are Russian Jews. Certain Jewish families, like those of some Gentiles, have degenerated under excessive prosperity and actually lost rank—such as the Fleischmanns of Cincinnati, of Viennese rabbinical stock with rather aristocratic traditions, who after a gen-

155

eration of prosperity in distilling and yeast-making joined the great commercial classes of remote social suburbs, though the late Julius was a lifelong friend of Nicholas Longworth. Mixed marriages are still favored by socially-minded Jews—thus John M. Schiff is married to Edith B. Baker and Gerald F. Warburg to Natica Nast while the daughters of Otto Kahn became Mrs. John C. O. Marriott and Mrs. John Barry Ryan, Jr. On the higher levels, at least, and in metropolitan surroundings there is an absorption between the races unknown to more insular and provincial communities. The Ullmans in Baltimore and several well-bred Jewish families of Minneapolis move freely in best Gentile Society; unlike most American cities, these communities tend to pass upon Jews simply as human beings, and either accept or reject them outright.

CHAPTER FIVE

THE BOOK OF ETIQUETTE

SUCCESSIVE invasions of new wealth have long made adult instruction in "good form" a necessity in America. A Victorian manual calls etiquette "the barrier which society draws around itself, a shield against the intrusion of the impertinent, the improper, and the vulgar." Its deepest *raison d'être* is of course consideration for the feelings and safety of others. Because mediæval houses were built with overhanging stories from which slops were thrown into the street, and mud was splashed from passing carriages, etiquette decreed that a gentleman give a lady the wall. The conservatism of etiquette has always demanded, upon the same principle, that a gentleman walking with two ladies must never sandwich himself between them—though this rule, especially among the young and informal, is often ignored today, in illustration of the fact that when tradition clashes with convenience it may be tacitly waived.

Throughout the ages etiquette is forced into continual compromise with common-sense, expediency, and changes in the physical environment of life. A simple example is the use of tobacco, which for more than two centuries after King James's *Counterblaste to Tobacco* was regarded in many circles as a loathsome indulgence of the male, barely within the pale of tolerance. Cecil B. Hartley, in *The Gentleman's Book of Etiquette* (1860), says: "One must never smoke, without consent, in the presence of a clergyman, and one must never offer a cigar to any ecclesiastic"; after smoking, a gentleman should change his clothes, rinse his mouth, and brush his teeth before joining the ladies. Of course Mr. Hartley's severity was extreme; smoking was not unknown at a much earlier day among strong-minded ladies of the highest quality, like the Revolutionary belle, Lady Kitty Duer, daughter of Lord Stirling, who smoked a clay pipe in her own house. But Victorianism came to outlaw such habits as unspeakably improper among the gentry, whatever the backwoodsman's wife might continue to do with her shag tobacco and Duffy's snuff. Not indeed till the waning of the Gilded Age did the American society woman begin to follow her pioneering cousins in Mayfair, and take cigarettes at the dinner table, the races, or on the country club veranda with complete assurance.[1] Promoted by advertisers in tactful stages—which first showed a wistful girl inviting her fiancé to "blow some my way," then ventured a manicured hand holding a lighted cigarette, and finally caught a sophisticate brazenly in the act of smoking—society women dared to smoke in public, sorority houses at the more advanced colleges opened smoking, rooms, and in their wake the shopgirl and stenographer eagerly followed. Today any mentor of etiquette who attempted to reassert the old conventions would be howled down.

Though it is safe to say that among decent people a man will always offer protection to women and children, and spare the feelings of the unfortunate and deformed, some of the less cardinal conventions—like taking soup from the antipodes of the plate, sitting in one's proper corner on the back seat of a motor car, or sending cards *pour prendre congé*—are pleasant amenities which to many minds are invested with a little snobbery. Society, like freemasonry or any other cult of exclusion, has its own marks of identification, passwords and phrases, inflections and gestures, likes and dislikes. Its taboos are even more vital than its sanctions. A center light in the drawing-room, a rocking-chair, a butler who takes a card in his fingers or a maid who removes more than one plate at a time, the high hand-shake, "made up" dress-ties and the word "tux," or such locutions as "Meet Mrs. Blank" and "Pardon my glove"—these things are sufficient to cause a *frisson* along the spine. Yet one may say "Oh, my God," or "damn" or "hell"—except perhaps as Mr. Hartley would caution, to an ecclesiastic—and indulge a few approved gangster-isms, especially if piquant and not too threadbare, as well as an occasional remark savoring of the acceptable kind of physical frankness. In fact to

---

[1] In Edith Wharton's *House of Mirth* (1905) part of the comedy turns upon the desperate efforts of Lily Bart, a young lady of ambition in the top flights of sophistication, to conceal her vicious habit of smoking from rich, conventional Percy Gryce who gives a "startled glance" at the mere mention by a woman of the word tobacco.

Women began to smoke in public in the first decade of the twentieth century. The pioneer seems to have been Mrs. Frederick Lewisohn, who was asked to throw away her cigarette at Sherry's—a social crisis which Caroline Harding reported dramatically for the New York *Herald*. In conservative Charleston even in the 1920's some gentlewomen who smoked ordered their cigarettes from tobacconists in other cities, to save the shame and revelation of local patronage.

be a shade audacious in word and deed shows that one is neither a hopeless stay-at-home nor a timid parvenu. Only the self-consciously genteel live in "residences," sign their letters "Cordially yours," and fear to "go to bed" or to put their elbows on the table when they feel inclined. Simplicity is always the best taste, with the ease and absence of affectation which it implies. It has become during the past generation a gratifying symbol of our break with the Gilded Age, or with the Victorians—who had their own symbols too which now seem to us less worthy, like the corset which signified unbending rectitude, the huge crinoline hoop-skirt which occupied social space, and the trailing garments too impractical for walking which implied a carriage at the door. Today we have only the mandarin's fingernail which avows unfamiliarity with dishpan and keyboard.

The history of American folkways cannot be treated within a narrow compass, but a review at least is possible of some manuals written to help the aspirant along the road to Best Society. Such books are found in almost every modern language, but nowhere have they been published so copiously and absorbed so eagerly as in these United States during the past century. Tart criticisms of our social behavior by visitors like Mrs. Trollope, Captain Basil Hall, James Silk Buckingham, Charles Dickens, Oscar Wilde, Bernard Shaw, Paul Bourget, Rudyard Kipling, G. Lowes Dickinson, and others, have played no small part in creating the demand. Upon their visits to the United States—that "nation of nobodies," as Sir Philip Gibbs calls us—English lecturers in particular have given America a better example of good manners in the breach than in the observance. Being very conservative, they have continued to regard America in the same light as did exploring Britons three hundred years ago—as a wilderness which, though filled with material riches, is inhabited by a race of quaint but friendly savages with whom one may profitably parley, and whose customs may be examined as one would study life among Maori headhunters or the platter-lipped natives of the Congo Basin. Many of these flippancies have been inspired less by ill-nature than a desire to utter bright and pungent remarks, and write books which will circulate in the vortex of controversy. Yet such generalizations, rank and over-stated as they generally are, have had some good results among the upper strata, always hypersensitive to English opinion. As a casual instance, the New York *Evening Post* reported at a performance by Fanny Kemble in September, 1832, shortly after the publication of Mrs. Trollope's scathing

The Saga of American Society

Domestic Manners of the Americans, that between acts an individual in the audience assumed a sprawling posture upon a box railing:

> Hissings arose, and then bleatings, and then imitations of the lowing of cattle: still the unconscious disturber pursued his chat—still the offending fragment of his coat-tail hung over the side. At last there was a laugh, and cries of "Trollope! Trollope! Trollope!" with roars of laughter, still more loud and general.

The immense effect of English surveillance upon the speech, clothes, dining, sport, and religion of American Society will appear later. But in regard to manners, the prevailingly British rather than Gallic inheritance of our Society is a fact of utmost importance. One of our kindest critics, Lord Bryce, wrote in 1888: "The manners of the 'best people' are exactly those of England, with a thought more of consideration towards inferiors and of frankness towards equals." In the same decade, with somewhat more harshness, Matthew Arnold compared English and American manners, complaining in the latter "the absence of the discipline of respect" as well as "a false smartness," though he approved the democratic spirit which had erased the invidious social distinctions between "Mr." and "Esquire."[2] A dozen years later Doctor James F. Muirhead observed: "It seems to me that I have met in America the nearest approaches to my ideals of a Bayard *sans peur et sans reproche;* and it is in this same America that I have met flagrant examples of the being wittily described as *sans père et sans proche*—utterly without the responsibility of background and entirely unacquainted with the obligations of noblesse." A statement like this is probably the fairest appraisal which has come from overseas of that huge paradox, the social behavior of Americans.

The chronicle of *politesse* in theory—as reflected in the book of etiquette —is of course not the exact history of its practice. The great impact upon manners of business, with its haste, informality, and camaraderie mingled with a flair for "contacts," is one aspect of American life which etiquette manuals do not mirror. Certainly Emily Post is not likely to join Professor Thomas Nixon Carver of Harvard in remarking that "we may take a certain genuine satisfaction in the fact that we have no leisure class

---

[2]Arnold's grievance about "the absence of the discipline of respect" is probably not unconnected with his shock upon seeing his arrival in Chicago announced by the *Tribune* under the caption "MATTHEW HAS WHISKERS."

and are never likely to have one . . . and must therefore content ourselves with such arts and graces as can be cultivated by busy people." Professor Carver's attitude, so alien to the concepts of any aristocracy, is undoubtedly shared by millions of Americans recruited not only from department stores, quick-lunch counters, and real estate firms, but also from the higher financial levels which are always impinging upon Society. Replenished constantly from those successful in trade—the jovial, the crude, and the aggressive—Society in America has tried heroically to digest its bumper meal, with such help as may be afforded by the enzymes of etiquette.

Practically all books on manners published in America during Colonial times were reprints from England and France. The first seems without doubt to have been Richard Lyngard's *Letter of Advice to a Young Gentleman leaving the University concerning his behaviour and conversation in the World,* New York, 1696.[3] In 1715 at New London a manual was published called *The School of good manners,* and the following year in Boston a work with the more godly title of *A Sermon for the reformation of manners,* by Benjamin Colman. Benjamin Franklin, most enterprising of Colonial publishers, brought out in Philadelphia in 1745 a work which ran into at least six editions within five years, with reprints in New York and Boston; it was also of London origin and bore the title *The Friendly Instructor: or, a companion for young ladies and young gentlemen.* Young George Washington at the age of fifteen copied out in a manuscript, which still survives, the *Rules of Civility and Decent Behaviour* written by French Jesuits and first published about 1595, Englished by Francis Hawkins around 1640, and widely popular among the British gentry. These rules are mostly sensible, matter-of-fact, and timeless, though some reflect the crudity of the times, such as—

Spit not in the Fire, nor Stoop low before it neither Put your Hands into the Flames to warm them, nor Set your Feet upon the Fire especially if there be meat before it . . . bedew no mans face with your Spittle, by approaching too near him when you Speak.

Kill no Vermin as Fleas, lice ticks &c in the Sight of Others, if you See any filth or thick Spittle put your foot Dexteriously upon it if it be upon the Cloths of your Companions, Put it off privately, and if it be upon your own Cloths return Thanks to him who puts it off.

[3]This *Letter,* addressed to Lord Lanesborough, was first published in London in 1670. Cf. C. Evans, *American Bibliography* (Chicago, 1903), vol. I, p. 117.

The Saga of American Society

Being Set at meat Scratch not neither Spit Cough or blow your Nose except there's a Necessity for it.

Cleanse not your teeth with the Table Cloth Napkin Fork or Knife but if Others do it let it be done w^t. a Pick Tooth.

Among the rules touching upon social discrimination:

In Pulling off your Hat to Persons of Distinction, as Noblemen, Justices, Churchmen &c make a Reverence, bowing more or less according to the Custom of the Better Bred, and Quality of the Person.

When one is out walking in company with another,

if he be a Man of Great Quality, walk not with him Cheek by Joul but Somewhat behind him; but yet in Such a Manner that he may easily Speak to you.

Such were the precepts given young Washington, probably typical of the most polished society on Southern plantations. One of the most popular manuals of etiquette for eighteenth-century children, patterned upon the mediæval *Babees' Booke,* was called *A Pretty Little Pocket Book.* Some prescriptions in Colonial handbooks of behavior suggest a finesse unknown to modern days:

How all must regret to hear some Persons, even of quality say, 'pray cut up that Chicken or Hen,' or 'Halve that Plover'; not considering how indiscreetly they talk, when the proper Terms are, 'break that Goose,' 'thrust that Chicken,' 'spoil that Hen,' 'pierce that Plover.' If they are so much out in common Things, how much more would they be with Herons, Cranes, and Peacocks.

Yet actual manners left much to be desired by the critical. Mrs. John Adams wrote from august Philadelphia when it was the nation's capital that in regard to etiquette "it was not to be found," while Brissot de Warville noted of Virginia planters "that they do not understand the use of napkins, that they wear silk scarves, and that instead of using handkerchiefs they blow their noses with their fingers, or with a silk handkerchief which serves as cravat, napkin, etc." At the fashionable resort of Bath in Virginia, Bayard observed at a five-o'clock tea-party "an elderly American, to whom this new style of serving tea was inconvenient, who after having taken a cup in one hand and tartlets in the other, opened his mouth and told the servant to fill it for him with smoked venison!" Many French visitors failed to understand one of the nuances of American etiquette, the so-called "tea-signal," by which the hostess continued to refill the tea-cup until it was turned upside down in the saucer and the spoon placed on top. Bayard reports that "a Frenchman who spoke no English, and knew nothing of this sign language, was distressed to see the sixth cup arriving for him, so he decided after emptying it to put it into his pocket until the replenishments had been concluded," while Chastellux, whose cubic dimensions seem to have been greater, writes:

Monsieur de la Luzerne took me to drink tea at Mrs. Morris', wife of the Treasurer of the United States. . . . I drank some excellent tea and would have taken more, I think, if the Ambassador had not charitably warned me at the twelfth cup that I must put my spoon across my cup, whereupon this sort of hot water torture was ended. 'It is almost rude,' said he, 'to refuse a cup of tea when it is offered, but it would be indiscreet for the host to offer you more when the ceremony of the teaspoon shows what your intentions are upon this point.'

Society in the young Republic took its punctilios very seriously, as is illustrated by the furore over Jefferson's "pell-mell," and by such an episode in non-official circles as the dinner given for Joseph Bonaparte by Madame Stephen Jumel, whose gay entertainments in the old Jumel mansion on a high bank of the Harlem River were the apogee of "fast" Society in the early nineteenth century. She refused to enter her own dining-room ahead of a prince, and he declined to precede a lady, while the guests stood by keenly interested in the *impasse*. The actual decision is unknown, but it is significant that soon afterwards Madame Jumel had wider doors cut in her house. During this first quarter-century fashionable districts, with their own codes and conventions, were becoming more clearly delimited in all the Eastern cities. Philadelphia was typical, where, as Harriet Martineau discovered in 1834, the Chestnut Street ladies would have nothing to do with the Arch Street ladies, "the fathers of the Arch Street ladies having made their fortunes, while the Chestnut Street ladies owed theirs to their grandfathers"—a superiority which found expression in the etiquette of the curtsey, "the Arch Street ladies rising twice on their toes before curtseying, while the Chestnut Street ladies rose thrice."

As one travelled westward however he felt a perceptible thawing of decorum, until along the frontier the absolute melting-point was reached. Mrs. Trollope noted with horror that Kentucky colonels picked their teeth with pocketknives, while in Cincinnati—where "the custom of making interminable calls had its origin"—at evening parties "the gentlemen spit, talk of elections and the price of produce, and spit again." It must be remembered that Mrs. Trollope was prejudiced at all times, with a dreadful gift for seeing the seamy side—even in Washington on the evening she went to the theatre "one man in the pit was seized with a violent fit of vomiting, which appeared not in the least to annoy or surprise his neighbors." But still along the Mississippi, which she found malarial to the body and abysmal to social intercourse, Americans were trying to learn etiquette as soon as they achieved a small margin of time after exterminating redskins, clearing stumps, and reaping their first crops. Works like *The Young Man's Own Book* (1832), *A Manual of Politeness for Both Sexes* (1837), *The Laws of Etiquette* (1839), *A Manual of Good Manners* (1844), Maberley's *Art of Conversation* (1844), and Docine's *Manners Maketh Man* (1852), streamed from the presses of Boston and Philadelphia, the capitals of etiquette publishing, to the outposts of the West. In old attics they may still be found alongside *The Last Days of Pompeii* and the Wesley hymnals.

Yet despite Elias Howe's widely popular *Ball-Room Hand Book,* which gave minute instructions on asking a lady to dance and prescribed all grace requisite to "the poetry of motion," we have Augustus Baldwin Longstreet's report in *Georgia Scenes* (1840), of an assembly among the new-rich of Georgia, where the ladies' dancing resolved itself "into the three motions of a turkey-cock strutting, a sparrow-hawk lighting, and a duck walking," while that of the gentlemen "resembled the action of cleaning mud off one's shoes on a door-mat." Similarly Baldwin's *Flush Times,* describing social life in the South just prior to the panic of 1837, tells the story of a traveller named Beechim from Tennessee who "had a great penchant for fashionable life, and fashionable life was the life of the coteries, the upper-tens of Knoxville." Going to New Orleans he fell in with a cosmopolitan wag named Cousins. After putting up at the St. Charles Hotel, both went downstairs to dinner, and

got along pretty well until just as B. had taken a piece of pine-apple on his plate, the waiter came along and put a green-colored bowl before every guest's plate with water and a small slice of lemon in it. Beechim asked Cousins what *that* was. C. replied, 'Sop for the pine-apple.' B. said he thought so. 'That's the way it used to be served up at "The Traveller's Rest" in Knoxville.' Beechim took the bowl and put it in his plate, and then put the pine-apple in the bowl, and commenced cutting up the apple, stirred it around in the fluid with his fork, and ate it, piece after piece. B. kept his eyes on the bowl—did not observe what was passing about him. Many persons at table—five hundred at least—ladies, dandies, foreigners, moustached fellows; began to be an uproar on the other side of the table; everybody got to looking down at Beechim—eye-glasses put up. . . . B. got through with the pine-apple. Cousins had been laughing with the rest—composed himself now, and asked B. 'how he liked the pine-apple?' B. answered in these words: 'I think the pine-apple very good, but don't you think the sauce is rather insipid?' . . .

[When an old Englishman told B. he had been eating out of the finger-bowl] Beechim got out—forgot where his hat was—ran bare-headed to the bar—called for his bill—never got his clothes—ran to the steamboat—shut himself up in the state room for two days;—thing out in the *Picayune* next morning—no names given. B. came home—saw Cousins when *he* came up—licked him within an inch of his life with a hickory stick.

There seems to have been keen national sensitiveness upon this subject, for of all the indiscreet comments Fanny Kemble made upon her return to England, the one which rankled deepest among fashionables who had entertained her was her remark that upon no New York dinner-table had she seen a finger-bowl. In all probability she was forgetful, since finger-bowls seem to have been common enough even when their function was abused. T. C. Grattan, British consul in Boston from 1839–46, gently reproves the universal custom of "splashing in the 'finger-glasses,'" while contemporary etiquette books often caution their readers against "rinsing and gargling from finger-bowls." One victim of tall tales about American manners in the 1840's was the celebrated dancer Fanny Elssler, who at the suggestion of friends in Europe brought a supply of her own napkins to carry to American dinner-parties.

One of the most widely circulated books, so typical of this period, was Mrs. John Farrar's *The Young Lady's Friend,* Boston, 1838. Most carefully does she fortify the neophyte for that ordeal called "a ceremonious dinner." "With erect carriage and firm step, enter the drawing-room" and allow yourself to be distracted by nobody till you have curtsied to your hostess. "A child, a picture, an animal, a worked ottoman, a bunch of flowers, may furnish topics for conversation, till dinner is announced.

Observe next, whether a blessing is to be asked, that you may not sit down before the rest and have to rise again." Directions follow:

When fairly seated in the right place, spread your napkin in your lap, to protect your dress from accident; take off your gloves and put them in your lap, under the napkin. . . .

If you should happen to meet with an accident at table, endeavour to preserve your composure, and do not add to the discomfort you have created, by making an unnecessary fuss about it. The easier such things are passed over, the better. I remember hearing it told of a very accomplished gentleman, that when carving a tough goose, he had the misfortune to send it entirely out of the dish, and into the lap of the lady next to him; on which he very coolly looked her full in the face, and, with admirable gravity and calmness, said, 'Ma'am, I will thank you for that goose.'

Such presence of mind as this, we do not expect from very young persons; but even they may refrain from all exclamations, when anything is spilt on their clothes.

Mrs. Farrar surprises us by endorsing as an American prerogative a habit upon which Best Society has frowned for some time, namely using the knife to carry food to the mouth:

When you send your plate for anything, whether by the hand of a servant, or friend, take off the knife and fork, and lay them down on the cloth, supporting the ends on your bread, or else hold them in your hand, in a horizontal position. If you wish to imitate the French or English, you will put every mouthful into your mouth with your fork; but if you think, as I do, that Americans have as good a right to their own fashions as the inhabitants of any other countries, you may choose the convenience of feeding yourself with your right hand, armed with a steel blade; and provided you do it neatly, and do not put in large mouthfuls, or close your lips tightly over the blade, you ought not to be considered as eating ungenteelly.

We are warned particularly against the mischievous interludes of a dinner, when eating is temporarily impossible:

When not engaged in eating, do not let your fingers find employment in playing with any of the table furniture, or in making pellets of bread. If you would be very refined, you must avoid blowing your nose at table, or touching your hair, or adjusting a comb; those are, in some persons' eyes, great offences. I once heard a gentleman describe a young lady as having every virtue and every charm that could be desired, and then he added with a sigh, 'She would be perfect were it not for one thing.' I eagerly asked what that was; and he replied, 'She blows her nose at dinner-time.'

Mrs. Farrar tells her young charges what to do when dinner is over:

Be sure to get through with your dessert, and have your gloves on, all ready to move, by the time the lady of the house gives the signal. . . . A dinner, well performed by all the actors in it, is very fatiguing, and, as it generally occupies three hours or more, most persons are glad to go away when it is fairly done. After dinner, you are expected to take leave more generally and sociably, than after any other kind of party, except it be a small supper party.

She goes on to reprimand certain affectations of current Society:

Some girls have a trick of *jiggling* their bodies (I am obliged to coin a word to describe it); they shake all over, as if they were hung on spiral wires, like the geese in a Dutch toy; than which, nothing can be more ungraceful, or unmeaning. It robs a lady of all dignity, and makes her appear trifling and insignificant. Some do it only on entering a room, others do it every time they are introduced to anybody, and whenever they begin to talk to any one. It must have originated in embarrassment, and a desire to do something, without knowing exactly what; and being adopted by some popular belle, it became, at one time, a fashion in New York, and spread thence to other cities.

One wonders if this peculiar affectation of Society had any relation to that decorous see-saw for ladies, called "a joggle-board," which Philip Hone saw under the apple trees on Ochre Point, Newport, during this same period; it offered perhaps a moral equivalent for jiggling. Mrs. Farrar also cautions young ladies against undue eagerness to reach the supper-table at late and sophisticated parties:

Gentlemen often feel their pride engaged in doing their utmost to provide well for the ladies on their arms, and so press on too violently; it is, therefore, incumbent upon a lady to repress the earnestness of her cavalier, to say she is in no haste, she will go presently, when there is more room.

After a week-end, the perfect guest will send the hostess "some little offering of gratitude," for, "though it be only a pincushion or a guard chain, of your own making, it will have a certain value as the expression of the gratitude which it becomes you to feel." Mrs. Farrar provides for most of life's contingencies, including the proper behavior "in a carriage, when the horses run away with it." To scream and jump up and down is both dangerous and unladylike; from experience she counsels relaxation —"I have been overturned so often, that I know exactly how to fall; and when I feel the carriage tipping over, I draw myself all up together and make myself as much like a bag of wool as possible." Surely the solicitude of a mentor could go no farther.[4]

The unacknowledged levy which almost every book of etiquette makes upon earlier manuals can be appreciated by the chronological reader alone. Thirteen years after Mrs. Farrar, Mrs. L. G. Abell in *Woman in her Various Relations: containing Practical Rules for American Females,* New York, 1851—a book whose directions run the gamut from housekeeping hints to methods for rescuing a child that has fallen into a well—echoes *verbatim* the rule about prompt departures: "A dinner well performed occupies two or three hours, and if you are not warned to expect an evening party added to it, the sooner you depart the better, when all is ended." Mrs. Trollope's barb about "interminable calls" had apparently struck home. But in the midst of Mrs. Abell's strictures on "rocking eagerly" we still find cautions against "affected 'jiggling' of the body," especially at "evening parties." It is a little discouraging to think that, on the eve of the Civil War, females were jiggling yet.

A patent example of lending is found in *How to Behave: a pocket manual of Republican Etiquette,* 1850: "If a lady chooses to seat herself upon the ground, you are not at liberty to follow her example unless she invites you to be seated. She must not have occasion to think of the possibility of any impropriety on your part." Such advice, savoring of a curiously prudish sex-consciousness, is reiterated almost word for word with added emphasis in *The Bazar Book of Decorum,* by Robert Tomes,

---

[4]Mrs. Farrar directs some of her most vigorous rebukes toward steamboat manners: "One of the worst features in steam-boat travelling is the struggle for the best places at meals, and the rude elbowing and pushing of those who call themself ladies." Mrs. Trollope's experiences in this regard were harrowing, while even the kindly Miss Martineau wrote: "I never saw any manner so repulsive as that of many American ladies on board steam-boats. They look as if they supposed you mean to injure them, till you show the contrary . . . the bristling self-defence the moment you come near; the cool pushing to get the best places."

M.D., in 1870. In fact the tone of American books on etiquette during
this period is still dictated from London, and across their pages falls the
prim gray shadow of Queen Victoria. These American guides merely
amplify the succinct phrase of a popular Victorian manual which warns
that young ladies should not "come into a room like a whirlwind." This
was the era in Britain when ladies never attended the Derby, nobody
of standing was ever seen on the street with a parcel, no one in Society
ever travelled anything but first-class, and after August 1 if for any reason
people were obliged to be in London they concealed themselves in the
back of the house.

In America the slowly increasing pomp of formal Society, winning
its way over Jacksonian democracy, may be seen not only in books of
etiquette but also diaries, letters, and newspapers from the 1820's to the
post-Civil War era. On February 17, 1829, for example, Philip Hone
records the death of Simon, "the celebrated cook":

He was a respectable colored man, who has for many years been the
fashionable cook in New York, and his loss will be felt on all occasions of
large dinner and evening parties, unless it should be found that some
suitable shoulders should be ready to receive the mantle of this celebrated
cuisinière.

Such was the simplicity of catering in an era where evening parties lasted
from seven to ten, with a cotillion or two, music on the piano-forte, and
singing—ending with a supper of shredded ham and grated cheese, jellies,
oranges, nuts, coffee, and sometimes as a special treat an oyster stew.
Upon the side-board were good Madeira, port, and sherry; champagne
was extremely rare, even at weddings. During the 1830's beaux and belles
strolled to Contoit's Ice-Cream Garden on Broadway between Leonard
and Franklin Streets. Very few of the old and established families had
liveried coachmen for ordinary occasions; a buggy and pair often sufficed.
A box at the Italian Opera House, opened in 1833, and a pew in Grace
Church gratified a solid sense of property.

But soon there were signs of change. Buckingham, attending a New
York soirée in 1837, noted the "affectation of indifference, which is considered to be more genteel than vulgar vivacity—a weakness, no doubt,
copied from the English," and observed that "the most fashionable persons, though invited for eight, rarely come till ten or eleven," so that

some parties are prolonged till two o'clock. In January, 1838, Philip Hone went to his first dinner *à la française,* at Mr. and Mrs. Olmstead's, where one's plate arrived empty, rather than served to order from the array on the table—a novelty which he found disagreeable.

The dishes were all handed round; in my opinion a most unsatisfactory mode of proceeding in relation to this important part of the business of a man's life. One does not know how to choose, because you are ignorant of what is coming next, or whether anything more is coming. Your conversation is interrupted every minute by greasy dishes thrust between your head and that of your next neighbor, and it is more expensive than the old mode of shewing a handsome dinner to your guests and leaving them free to choose. It will not do. This French influence must be resisted.

Two years later, however, Hone had grown so blasé over European innovations that he welcomed the new custom, begun by Mr. Douglass, of giving one o'clock breakfasts, as "the last imitation of European refinement." The actual consumption of "coffee and chocolate, light dishes of meat, ice cream and confectionery, with lemonade and French and German wines," did not begin till two; while breakfast was in progress, "an aviary of singing birds" was heard from the conservatory, while at the head of the stairs a band played, to which the young people danced cotillions and waltzes before leaving at four o'clock. "In taste, elegance, and good management," adds the aristocrat of this divertisement, "it goes beyond most things of the kind in Europe, and seems to be placed as a bright object in the overwhelming flood of vulgarity which is sweeping over our land." Perhaps it was significant of change that the newest book of etiquette just then appearing in the book-shops of London, republished in America in 1843, was the famous *Etiquette: or, A guide to the usages of Society . . . By Count Alfred D'Orsay.* Falsely ascribed to that exquisite, it was actually written by one Charles William Day. A smattering of Gallic manners and phrases grew very popular among those out to make an impression in Society. In Mrs. Mowatt's play *Fashion* (1845) the central character is an ex-milliner, Mrs. Tiffany, whose husband has struck it rich. Saying of her station in life, "Forget what we *have* been, it is enough to remember that we *are* of the *upper ten thousand,*" she dresses in exaggerated Parisian fashions, mispronounces French after a week's perusal of *French Without a Master,* and hails the new "at home" custom: "This mode of receiving visitors only upon one specified day of the week is a most convenient custom! It saves the trouble of keeping the house continually in order and of being always dressed. I flatter myself that I was the first to introduce it amongst the New York *ee-light.*"

Mrs. Tiffany's real existence is proved by newspapers and etiquette-books of the time. The New York *Herald* for example in 1848 remarked that vulgarity was the chief trait of "fast" Society in America—"loud talking at table, impertinent staring at strangers, brusqueness of manners among the ladies, laughable attempts at courtly ease and self-possession among the men—the secret of all this vulgarity in Society is that wealth, or the reputation of wealth, constitutes the open sesame to its delectable precincts." Among miscellaneous manuals published in this decade we find young ladies rebuked for the common habit of "audibly sipping up" the liquor of stewed oysters, while "We have seen a young gentleman lift his plate of soup in both hands, hold it to his mouth and drink, or rather lap it up. This was at no less a place than Niagara." We read that "the rising generation of elegants in America are particularly requested to observe that, in polished society, it is not quite *comme il faut* for gentlemen to blow their noses with their fingers, especially when in the street—a practice infinitely more common than refined." The reader is warned against "taking a person by the buttons or collar; whirling a chair around on one leg; and shaking with your feet the chair of a neighbor," and one learns that "ladies should never dine with their gloves on unless their hands are not fit to be seen." If at dinner a lady "should raise an unmanageable portion to her mouth you should cease all conversation with her and look steadfastly into the opposite part of the room." When a bachelor married it was understood that all former acquaintanceship ceased, "unless he intimate a desire to renew it by sending you his own and his wife's card."

But the topic invariably discussed and reprehended is the habit of chewing tobacco and spitting. "What an article is a spittoon as an appendage to a handsomely furnished drawing room!" exclaims one writer on etiquette. The British journalist Alexander Mackay, here during 1846–7, and full of praise for most American customs, detested the universal tobacco-chewing of men, and reported that he had once seen an individual take the quid from his mouth and with it draw ornamental figures

The Saga of American Society

on the window-pane. British visitors two generations later were to express as great surprise though less revulsion over its successor, chewing-gum. Perhaps, as some have suggested, chewing tobacco and gum, gulping food, and bolting from the table were symptomatic of the new nervous tempo of American life and business. Our business civilization was already on the march; and its material accomplishments were so evident that even the patrician Hone, rejoicing that after the Mexican War Americans are being spoken of more respectfully abroad, adds complacently: "The Yankees may be ignorant of the most approved method of using the knife and fork; but it cannot be denied that they are competent to make a good use of the sword and musket. They eat fast, but they go ahead wonderfully; they use some queer expressions, but in defense of their rights are apt to talk much to the purpose." Such was the imperialist apology for bad manners.

Yet it is only fair to cite tributes in this era to the innate chivalry of Americans, which existed apart from the nuances of etiquette. Harriet Martineau in 1835 declared that "the manners of Americans (in America) are the best I ever saw," while Charles Dickens in 1842, for all his grumbling, recalled that never once did he see a woman "exposed to the slightest act of rudeness, incivility, or even inattention." And Fredrika Bremer in 1850 had nothing but praise for the generosity and hospitality of American life, complaining merely that the "incessant bustle of serving" and habit of urging a guest to take more and more food marred the suavity of dining. Miss Bremer's constant battle to maintain her gastric equilibrium reminds us of this rule in Miss Leslie's *Behavior Book* (1853):

> While at table, all allusions to dyspepsia, indigestion, or any other disorders of the stomach, are vulgar and disgusting. The word "stomach" should never be uttered at any table, or indeed anywhere else, except to your physician, or in a private conversation with a female friend interested in your health.

Miss Leslie, it might be added, informs us that "the fashion of wearing black silk mittens at breakfast is now obsolete," cautions the female reader to "avoid saying anything to women in showy attire, with painted faces, and white kid gloves" when travelling alone, admonishes that "you will derive no pleasure or advantage from making acquaintance with females who are evidently coarse and vulgar, even if you know that they are rich," and advises constant vigilance against the promiscuous spitter:

A lady on the second seat of a box at the Chestnut-Street theatre found, when she went home, the back of her pelisse entirely spoilt, by some man behind not having succeeded in trying to spit past her.

Such is the jumbled story of good and bad manners in mid-nineteenth-century America.[5]

Although the most widely read etiquette book of that era, which reached its twentieth edition after the Civil War, was *Sensible Etiquette of the Best Society,* written under the pseudonym of Mrs. H. O. Ward by Mrs. Clara Sophia (Jessup) Bloomfield-Moore, the greatest single influence on the side of social grace and sophistication was not a manual but a magazine, *Godey's Lady's Book.* Louis Godey, a self-educated New Yorker, founded it in July, 1830, but its real success came under the editorship of Sarah Josepha Hale beginning in 1837. Mrs. Hale, tolerant of a superficial crudity which she preferred to the old Puritan strait jacket, wrote several handbooks of etiquette, notably *Manners, or Happy Homes and Good Society All the Year Round* (Boston, 1868). Other books had addressed themselves to such problems as whether a "genteel female" should insist upon a gentleman's wholly "restraining himself in demonstrations of affection," but Mrs. Hale got down to essentials with her insistence that "a certain formality of manner, or etiquette as it is usually called, is both a mark of respect for others and of one's own self-respect," and her remark that "the first indispensable requisite of good society is education."[6] In the pages of *Godey's,* Mrs. Hale waged a campaign for sensible manners freed from pedantry and affectation. Her

[5]One of the most curious reports which several European visitors took home was regarding etiquette on Fifth Avenue omnibuses. The Scot, William Chambers, in *Things as They Are in America* (1853) says that when these vehicles become crowded "the gentlemen either stand, or take the ladies on their knee." According to Constance Cary Harrison, *Recollections Grave and Gay,* in the 1870's M. Simonet recorded in the *Revue des Deux Mondes* that he was "told in New York" that it was customary for ladies upon getting into a full omnibus on Fifth Avenue to sit upon the knees of gentlemen already in the possession of seats.

[6]Similarly the anonymous *Manual of Politeness for Both Sexes* had taken pains to acquit politeness from the charge of being merely an aristocratic whim; rather, it declared, good manners were "one of the most essential elements of a placid and happy life."

encouragement of satire against false gentility produced the "Aunt Magwire" stories of Frances M. Whitcher which appeared in *Godey's* during the late '40's and early '50's. As a sample, "Aunt Magwire's Visit to Slabtown," in December, 1849, described a small town where everybody "had got their ideas raised a good deal, and had some wonderful curus notions about ginteelity"—which they went to work to achieve with the earnestness of pioneers. The crooking of the little finger while taking tea, for example, was an exertion which made one so self-conscious that he was sure not to forget himself and drink like a pig.

Social customs among conservative families of Boston, New York, and Philadelphia changed grudgingly during the era of post-Civil War prosperity, even as they had done during the real-estate boom of the late 1830's and '40's. The late Mrs. John King Van Rensselaer remembered New York in her girlhood during the Civil War, "a serene, simple, self-satisfied circle." In her own family, the Kings, Saturday evenings were "at home," with salad and punch, candy and cake, served by the hostess herself, for "with Sunday so near at hand, it was unthinkable that the servants should be asked to share the burden of entertainment." Indoors were games and dancing, while in summer one went boating or driving and in winter organized skating or sleighing parties. In the 1860's, when bridle paths were laid down in Central Park, riding was at last sanctioned for women; though Miss King, driving a smart pony phaeton on Fifth Avenue, was glared at disapprovingly through the plate-glass windows of the Union Club. Soon Colonel William Jay, DeLancey Kane, Roosevelt Roosevelt, and Frederick Bronson startled the quiet streets with their dashing four-in-hand coaches. No girl thought of going farther downtown than Canal Street if she were unescorted. Everybody dressed for dinner *en famille,* and the clan assembled gravely in the drawing-room to await the head of the family, like troops for review. The table was completely covered by a white cloth and adorned with heavy silver clustered about an epergne. Grace was asked before the supremely solid meal. Afterwards the young played, sang, and coquetted in the parlor, while their elders sat down to whist. If a ball were in view, the women retired at nine o'clock to dress. Everybody who mattered read books from the Society Library, and occupied subscription seats at Wallack's Theatre and for opera a box at the Academy of Music. It had long been *de rigueur* to sit in a box at the opera, but bad form to take a box for the play.

Divorce, whatever the provocation, meant social exclusion. Drinking, upon occasions like weddings, anniversaries, and New Year's, with great punch-bowls of March & Benson or Constitution Madeira and a growing vogue for champagne, was quite *au fait,* with a man's capacity assumed to be unlimited and a woman's reckoned at two glasses. Upon days not in the rubric women were supposed to have no alcoholic appetites; though for men in some households there was a genial custom called "taking the oath," which signified that a decanter of bourbon and a pitcher of ice-water might be found behind a statuette of the "Greek Slave" or a Rogers group in the library.

Fashionable women strove for the posture called the Grecian bend, though assuredly the Hellenes never had a word for it. In hairdressing the chignon and waterfall were cultivated. Men revelled in beards, and during this era arose the saying that "kissing a man without a moustache was like eating an egg without salt." Trouser creases were bad form, because they implied that clothes were store-bought. It was the day of the Turkish Cozy Corner and the pyramidal whatnot, of the portière, the lambrequin, the antimacassar, and Berlin wool work. The rubber plant enjoyed favor, piano legs were adorned with baby-blue sashes, coal scuttles as well as china were painted with floral designs by young ladies with time on their hands, and in affluent suburbs iron statuary on the lawn was the acme of taste. Decorative catholicity included the gilded rolling-pin, which, as Mr. Henry Collins Brown has pleasantly observed, showed "that the family no longer made its own bread, but was financially able to endure the strain of purchasing ready-made loaves at the grocer's." Final triumphs of sophistication comprised peek-a-boo waists and the novelty of toilet-paper. In the late 1870's fashionable Eastlake furniture, with its incised gilt designs, was supplanted by the "æsthetic taste"—wafted from England where the arts and crafts of William Morris, the Venetian Gothic of John Ruskin, and the refined languors of the Pre-Raphaelites were regnant. The new style glorified vases filled with cat-tails, gilded chair legs, lilies of the valley, Japanese fans, and embroidered "throws," with medieval armor just around the corner.

The history of fashion—which Oscar Wilde defined as "a form of ugliness so intolerable that it has to be changed every six months," and which a less flippant critic, Doctor C. W. Cunnington, calls "a taste shared by a large number of people for a short space of time"—is indispensable to the records of Society. Worth, Lelong, Schiaparelli, Poiret, Chanel, Hattie Carnegie, and a few other names are as potent in the annals of American Society as an incantation. In the longer view, milestones may be traced by the feathered coiffure of the Revolution (which with its inflammability by candle-light afforded a pleasing hazard to social intercourse), the "polka fashions" of the 1840's, the audacious bloomer mode introduced in 1851 by the journalist Amelia Bloomer and the social light Elizabeth Cady Stanton (whose young son addressed a stern letter from boarding-school to his mother, requesting her not to visit him "in a short dress"), the introduction of hoop-skirts in 1853 with the august patronage of the Empress Eugénie, the innovation of mascara in 1865 at Newport and Saratoga ("the Sodom and Gomorrah of our Union" as *Godey's* called them), and a dozen later fashions. To illustrate the potency of vogue, it might be added that the rise of the hobble-skirt, just before the Great War, caused the invention of a new type of streetcar, the so-called "hobble-skirt car," in which the floor sloped to a low entrance. There were however very few of them built, because the rage was transitory. After it had passed from ladies of quality down to those who ride in street-cars—a remarkably quick percolation in America— the style was already declassé, the War was on, and the angular outlines of the mannish girl could soon be glimpsed through the clouds of battle.

But indisputably the 1870's had their "culture"—which was then a term of the highest fashionable praise, as *ton* had been to the eighteenth century, or "elegance" to the early nineteenth. Nowadays "culture" is a ghost of utmost derision, having long been supplanted by its twin-heirs "cultivation" and "sophistication." Godkin of *The Nation* aptly called the Seventies a "chromo civilization," filled with more social garishness and bad taste than any other decade in American history. He put his finger upon an example—"the action of the Plymouth Church in Brooklyn, on the day Henry Ward Beecher came to trial for his alleged intimacy with Mrs. Tilton, in sending flowers to decorate the courtroom; like placing wreaths about the open manhole of a sewer."[7] One fancies that it breathes through etiquette books of the time, like this rule in Doctor Robert Tomes's *Bazar Book of Decorum* (1870): "When you salute a lady or a gentleman to whom you wish to show particular respect, in the

[7] Cf. *The Nation*, February 4, 1875; cited by Nevins, *The Emergence of Modern America*, pp. 226-7.

The Polka Fashions, Godey's "Lady's Book," November, 1845

Editor's Note: "The subscribers of the 'Lady's Book' will be enabled to accomplish with ease and grace this exquisite dance without the aid of a master," which was followed by a description of the step

Saratoga Springs, 1851

From a lithograph by Wm. Endicott & Co., on the cover of sheet music entitled "Saratoga Schottisch"

Both are from the New York Public Library

Grand Ball given by the citizens of New York to the Prince of Wales,
at the Academy of Music, October 12, 1860

From *Harper's Weekly,* New York Public Library

The Prince of Wales with cane and high hat

Group of leading citizens at the Academy of Music with the Prince

From a photograph supplied by Brown Brothers

(*See page 209*)

street, you should take your hat entirely off and cause it to describe a circle of at least ninety degrees from its original resting place." It was only a short step to one of the most curious patents taken out at the U. S. Patent Office during this era. This was an automatic hat-tipping device, by which an ingenious spring inside a bowler hat responded to slight inclination of the wearer's head and raised the hat impressively without the assistance of his hand. Equally redolent of the age is this admonition from the *Bazar Book of Decorum:*

The nose should never be fondled before company, or, in fact, touched at any time, unless absolutely necessary. The nose, like other organs, augments in size by handling, so we recommend every person to keep his own fingers, as well as those of his friends or enemies, away from it.

Yet in such an epoch social conventions had worked out an elaborate system of dog-earing calling cards, an Anglo-Saxon code which rivals the language of the flowers among Latins. As Mark Twain and Charles Dudley Warner recorded in *The Gilded Age* (1874), the turning up of the lower right-hand corner meant "called in person," while the upper left-hand conveyed "congratulations" and the upper right "condolence."

Dick's *Society Letter-Writer for Ladies . . . on All Subjects and Occasions Incident to Life in Good Society* (1884) provides for such exigencies as "Letter Refusing a Donation to an Old Ladies' Home" ("I am compelled to contribute only to such objects as have my warmest sympathy"), "Letter Congratulating a Friend upon Finding a Lost Child" ("God bless Essie!"), and "Answer to a Letter of Condolence on the Loss of a Limb" ("Hoping to see you soon, maimed as I am"). Hill's *Manual of Social and Business Forms* (1887) offers extremely practical suggestions upon what the age regarded as the most difficult of all situations, that of proposing to a young lady:

He may write to the lady, making her an offer, and request her to reply. He may, if he dare not trust to words, even in her presence write the question on a slip of paper, and request her laughingly to give a plain 'no' or 'yes.' He may ask her if in case a gentleman very much like himself was to make a proposal of marriage to her, what she would say. She will probably laughingly reply that it will be time enough to tell what she would say when the proposal is made. And so the ice would be broken.

The same *Manual* cautions that "visits should not be over two hours in length. The custom of remaining until a late hour has passed away in genteel society." It adds a word of extreme circumspection: "Do not, if a lady, call upon a gentleman . . . unless he may be a confirmed invalid."

FIG. 11. BAD MANNERS AT THE TABLE.

No. 1. Tips back his chair.
" 2. Eats with his mouth too full.
" 3. Feeds a dog at the table.
" 4. Holds his knife improperly.
" 5. Engages in violent argument at the meal-time.
" 6. Lounges upon the table.
" 7. Brings a cross child to the table.

No. 8. Drinks from the saucer, and laps with his tongue the last drop from the plate.
" 9. Comes to the table in his shirt-sleeves, and puts his feet beside his chair.
" 10. Picks his teeth with his fingers.
" 11. Scratches her head and is frequently unnecessarily getting up from the table.

From Hill's *Manual of Social and Business Forms, 1887*

The same book prescribes an elaborate code of etiquette between husband and wife, including these rules:

Never should both be angry at the same time.
Let the angry word be answered only with a kiss.
Always leave home with a tender good-bye and loving words. They may be the last.

The 1880's added appreciably to the growing mountain of behavior books. At the threshold of the decade came anonymously *The Social Etiquette of New York,* and in 1884 Mrs. John Sherwood's *Manners and*

Social Usages, revised in 1887, again in 1897 (in which edition we learn that "gentlemen now wear pearl-colored gloves embroidered in black to dinner, and do not remove them until they sit down to table"), and given

FIG. 12. GENTILITY IN THE DINING-ROOM.

The evidences of good breeding with a party of ladies and gentlemen seated about a table, who are accustomed to the usages of polite society, are many. Among these will be the fact that the table is very beautifully and artistically spread. This need not require much wealth, but good taste is necessary to set it handsomely.

Again, the company evince gentility by each assuming a genteel position while eating. It is not necessary that an elaborate toilet be worn at the table, but careful attention should always be given to neatness of personal appearance, however plain may be the dress which is worn.

Another evidence of good manners is the self-possession with which the company deport themselves throughout the meal.

From Hill's *Manual of Social and Business Forms, 1887*

final form in 1900. Mrs. Sherwood frankly announced in her preface that the book's intention was to help the ambitious parvenu. In 1880 appeared *Manners that Win,* in 1887 *The P. G., or, Perfect Gentleman,* and in 1888 *Success in Society.* In Howells' novel *The Rise of Silas Lapham* the wife and daughters of this successful paint manufacturer, invited to dine with the Corys on the water side of Beacon Street, consult not merely one but several etiquette books to fortify themselves. Incidentally, among other memorable vistas of the age which this book reveals, there is a scene in which Silas Lapham, accompanied by his family, is showing a young man through the expensive house he is building, and points out one scaffolded room as his daughters' bedroom. The novelist adds: "It seemed terribly intimate. Irene blushed deeply and turned her head away." This was the era which has been termed that of the Plush Age Man, in which manners and morals were similarly upholstered.

The sumptuary curve of Society meanwhile was going up and up. In New York and Newport, Ward McAllister bumbled about like a slightly adipose Petronius Arbiter revelling in the new elegance. "Success in entertaining," he wrote, "is the ladder to social success." With pride instead of regret he recalled: "I myself once lost a charming friend by giving a better soup than he did. His wife rushed home from my house, and in despair, throwing up her hands to her husband, exclaimed, 'Oh, what a soup!'" By way of counsel to beginners he warns that "in planning a dinner the question is not to whom you owe dinners, but who is most desirable," and also says with solemnity: "A dinner invitation, once accepted, is a sacred obligation. If you die before the dinner takes place, your executor must attend the dinner." Lovingly he debates the merits of soups, *tortue claire* being finally elected; discusses the shortcomings of salmon, and listens to the controversy between the terrapin recipes of Baltimore and Philadelphia; considers the *pièce de resistance,* which must be a *filet de bœuf,* a turkey, or a saddle of Southdown mutton; judiciously meditates upon salads and the proper sequence of sauces; and arrives at the sweet, preferably a *pouding Nesselrode,* and cheese. The subject of wines merits of course the devotion of a lifetime. Of a very well-known literary woman of New York McAllister once scathingly exclaimed to Mrs. Burton Harrison: "*She* write stories of New York Society! Why, I have seen her, myself, buying her Madeira at Park & Tilford's in a demijohn!" One of the most unforgettable episodes in McAllister's life was a dinner he attended at Delmonico's on February 17, 1873, given by Henry Lukemeyer, a rich German who had arrived in New York to start a bank and resolved to begin with proof of his solvency. Upon this dinner for seventy-two guests he had spent $10,000—for in addition to an incredible menu and priceless wines, the table had been transformed into billows of blossom by violets and "bolder sorts," says McAllister, and in the center an oval pond thirty feet long with "four superb swans brought from Prospect Park." Although the swans had been drugged by veterinary art, in the hope of rendering them more tractable with no loss of majesty, as the dinner wore on it was enlivened "at one time by a fierce combat between these stately, graceful, gliding white creatures." McAllister was in ecstasies; he felt like the monarch in *Alexander's Feast*. A little later, he remembered, it was his privilege at Newport to assist at a fête where the ballroom had been transformed into a vast grotto of ice in huge

© *Life Publishing Co.*

A Senseless After-Dinner Custom
So thinks the young man who must listen to her father's friends during the next hour
C. D. Gibson in *Life* in 1899

blocks, rendered iridescent under electric lights: "Then as the blocks of ice would melt, they would tumble over each other in charming glacier-like confusion, giving you winter in the lap of summer; for every species of plant stood around this immense floor."

Such were the blandishments which the Gilded Age carried to perfection. At one party we are told that orchids, "being the most costly of flowers, were introduced in profusion." Frederick Townsend Martin recalled a New York dinner-party at which "each cigarette was rolled, not in white paper, but in a one hundred dollar bill, the initials of the host were engraved in gold letters," while at another "each guest discovered in one of his oysters a magnificent black pearl." Poultney Bigelow in his *Seventy Summers* evokes an era when flunkeys in knee-breeches and powdered wigs passed around jewelled cotillion favors from Tiffany's "as though they had been bon-bons or glasses of lemonade." He once attended what he calls "the social eruption" of a certain family after "picking up from the top of my father's wastepaper basket a beautifully engraved invitation to a reception at their palace just completed. I said nothing, but went from curiosity, nor was I disappointed. Everybody there seemed surprised at seeing everybody else there, and the usual greeting was 'Hello, what brings you here?' It was a man-only reception . . . a quasi *ballon d'essai*. . . . Even the bathroom was referred to as having the walls daringly decorated; nude nymphs, after the engaging manner of Boucher or Fragonard. I did not see these, for the bathroom was always packed; and if there was one part of the palace even more dense it was near the tables, where champagne flowed freely. . . . . There was a host—so I learned afterwards—but I did not see him at any time." A fashionable boredom, assigned to that contagious malady of Paris and London called the *mal du siècle,* is mentioned in literature of the period; to overcome it gayer and more costly entertainments were prescribed.

Whereas to the present day there is little dining in public by Society in conservative Boston, threadbare Charleston, and a few other cities, the rage for restaurants captured Manhattan at an early date. In Philip Hone's time Niblo's restaurant, in the midst of its exotic garden, was the great setting for dinners to celebrities like Webster and Jackson; its "vaudevilles" were precursors of floor-shows in the night-club era. Destroyed by fire in 1846, Niblo's had a pompous but not socially exclusive tradition. The latter sort was attained by the dining-rooms of John Delmonico in William Street soon after foundation in 1829. After his death in November, 1842, from heart failure while on a deer hunt, Delmonico's widow, brother, and nephew issued a black-bordered card of thanks for tender expressions of sympathy, adding "the establishment will be reopened today under the same firm of Delmonico Brothers, and no pains of the bereft will be spared to give general satisfaction. Restaurant, bar-room, and private dinners No. 2 South William Street; furnished rooms No. 76 Broad Street, as usual." Though gentlemen had long given stag dinners at Del's when they wanted the best of French cuisine and wines, it was not until 1870 that the first balls for "the coming out" of young ladies were given there, under the pioneering of Archibald Gracie King.

Soon Delmonico's, at Fourteenth Street and Fifth Avenue, was launching all the ranking débutantes in its great mirror-lined hall. Lorenzo Delmonico, enterprising nephew of the Swiss founder, was quick to enhance its reputation for exclusiveness. He refused to allow any guest in the restaurant whose social standing was not, at least, fair; parvenus were almost as anxious to conciliate him as if he were Ward McAllister. In this plastic age, New York Society was frantically eager to adopt any earmarks of social distinction, as well as any arbiters of the "ins" and the "outs" without inquiring too deeply into their qualifications; the two men who profited most, therefore, happened to be a vulgar snob and a restaurateur. Following the march of fashion Del's moved first up to 26th Street, and then in 1899 as far as 44th—keeping, up to the Great War, its high favor among Society which distrusted flashy places like Rector's and Martin's. The début in public rooms preceded public dining however by about thirty years; a few irreproachable friends from the smart set might gather for lunch at Sherry's—a newer establishment which became Delmonico's only serious rival—but the first dinner-party there, given by Mrs. Ogden Mills at the turn of the century, was looked upon as delightfully audacious. To stage formal entertainments under a public roof was quite different from the gathering of small, casual groups, and at first Mrs. William Astor was dubious. But very soon the vogue caught on, and Sunday suppers at Sherry's became the special favorite of the Gilded Age—with Mrs. Fish, Harry Lehr, Mrs. Mills, Stanford White, and their friends dining under the awe-struck gaze of social climbers who were lucky to get tables at all.

Entertaining in public restaurants or dancing in their "private rooms" was not a mere whim, but a serious early symptom of the restlessness, disintegration, and informality of present Society. The minute planning and elaborate domestic machinery required to achieve a great dinner-party or ball at home was a delight to Mrs. Astor, but her daughter-in-law found it irksome. Society had tired of its own game. If caterers, decorators, stewards, headwaiters, and *sommeliers* were glad to shoulder the whole responsibility, and one were spared the ordeal of living intimately with the party before and after it was given—then surely this was the New Freedom idealists were always talking about. Long ago, of course, in the era of the Civil War the fashionable wedding had moved from the home of the bride's parents into church, less perhaps from a sacramental impulse than a feeling that pews, stained glass, high altar, and the pipe organ were a better show than one could produce *chez soi,* and that the rector in his way was a specialist too, like Lorenzo Delmonico and Louis Sherry. "House weddings" came to be regarded as the shabby expedients of Baptists and Methodists, who had neither altar nor liturgy.

Julia Ward Howe in her lecture "Is Polite Society Polite?" published in 1895 after being read before the New England Women's Club in Boston, answered her question by saying: "I do not think that the manners of so-called polite society today are quite so polite as they were in my youth. . . . On the other hand, outside this charmed circle of fashion, I find the tone of taste and culture much higher than I remember it to have been in my youth. . . . So the community gains, although one class loses,—and that, remember, the class which assumes to give to the rest a standard of taste." Certainly since Mrs. Howe's day Society has grown less courtly, less starched and florid; one can only hope that the true spirit of manners has not been sacrificed. Plainly there has been a gain in lightness and pace. Begun by the so-called Four Hundred, who were growing jaded in their brownstone or French châteaux and craved a freer, jollier comradeship with brighter lights, and were not averse to exploring the fringes of that *vie Bohème* which Murger and Puccini had rendered so attractive, the same compulsion appeared in different guises in inland cities and humbler societies. On the one hand, as Schlesinger writes, "Nothing was more revolutionary, perhaps, than the wide-spread abolition of the parlor, a ceremonial room which, darkened with drawn shades and closed doors, had hitherto served as a sort of mortuary chapel for the reception of guests." Gloomy wallpaper, furniture of mahogany and black walnut, upholstery of glossy black horsehair, were suddenly discovered to be hideous. Rugs supplanted carpets, sunshine and a little taste were admitted—and lo, the parlor had become a drawing-room. A corresponding change in manners occurred more slowly. But indubitably the decline of the parlor knelled also the death of the chaperon, the vestal virgin of its social hearth.

Chaperonage—a traditional Continental device not merely for safe-guarding a young girl against the wiles of a male world assumed to be uniformly wicked, but for enhancing her value in the eyes of Society—

arose in smart circles at a much earlier time than is often supposed. We read in Nathaniel P. Willis's *The Rag-Bag* (1855): "Of late, for instance, it is not considered *Fifth-Avenue-able* for an unmarried young lady to ride unattended in an omnibus—nor to be seen in Broadway without a carriage or servant—nor to go unchaperoned to the play with a young gentleman—all of which newly forbidden things, and others of the same

© *Life Publishing Co.*

AUNT JANE (from the country): If you children want to go anywhere evenings while I'm here, don't hesitate about asking me to chaperon you

C. D. Gibson in *Life* in 1925

kind, were considerable and innocent privileges of the restrained sex." And Willis rightly attributes the new mode to aping of European customs. In smaller cities, especially in the Mid-West, and almost everywhere in the country, chaperonage was scarcely known—and even through late Victorian times buggy-rides alone in the moonlight were sanctioned occasions, where many an honorable proposal was made presaging domestic bliss and ten children. But in New York, Boston, and Philadelphia mores were very different. To describe the chaperonage of a party, the term "to matronize" was coined. In an album which the author has been privileged to see, of invitations, calling cards, autographed dinner-menus and the like kept by Miss Dora Thayer, a belle of New York in the '70's, one finds a note from Peter Marié, most famous of the old-time beaux, requesting the pleasure of her company at dinner on 27 January, 1875, and adding that "Mrs. Brockholst Cutting will kindly matronize the party." Another gentleman asks on February 1, 1878, "Will you do me the honour to dine, in a small and frugal and strictly proper way with me, under the kind supervision of Mr. and Mrs. Phipps on Monday evening next at seven to say farewell to the Earl of Dufferin on his way back to the frozen North?" Of course dining alone with a man in his rooms would have been compromising in any era of Society, but such phrasing as the above was characteristic of the new Continental mode brought home by cosmopolites. Mrs. John Sherwood writes in 1884 of the chaperon:

She must accompany her young lady everywhere; she must sit in the parlor when she receives gentlemen; she must go with her to the skating rink, the ball, the party, the races, the dinners, and especially to theatre parties; she must preside at the table, and act the part of a mother, so far as she can; she must watch the characters of the men who approach her charge, and endeavor to save the inexperienced girl from the dangers of a bad marriage, if possible.

These last words are eloquent of the whole philosophy of chaperonage. In her revised edition of 1900 Mrs. Sherwood adds that, although in some circles an unmarried woman of increasing years is thought to be exempt from vigilance, yet an "elderly girl" of thirty-five is very unwise to visit an artist's studio alone, even though "there is in art an ennobling and purifying influence which should be a protection." Betrothal meant not relaxation but tightening of chaperonage:

A chaperon is indispensable to an engaged girl. . . . Nothing is more vulgar in the eyes of our modern society than for an engaged couple to travel together or to go to the theatre unaccompanied, as was the primitive custom. . . . Society allows an engaged girl to drive with her fiancé in an open carriage, but it does not approve of his taking her in a close carriage to an evening party.

Once the wedding invitations are issued, says Mrs. Sherwood, the bride-to-be must withdraw from public gaze, allow herself only an occasional quiet walk during daylight hours with her fiancé, and behave with extreme prudence. Florence G. Hall in *Social Customs,* Boston, 1887, relates: "A young lady at the seashore greatly shocked public opinion by going down to the surf beach and bathing on the morning of her wedding day."

In Philadelphia James G. Huneker in the 1880's found that for a girl to go alone with her suitor to a ball or the theatre would have damaged her name beyond redemption; whereas in Baltimore she might attend the theatre alone with a man, and always expected him to see her home after a ball. A Boston girl going to evening parties might dispense with the chaperonage of a maid if she took one of Kenny & Clark's hacks, whose coachmen in dark green coats with silver buttons bearing a stag's head were regarded as stable as the foundations of Beacon Street. Of course no old-fashioned girl owned a latchkey, and upon her return a servant opened the door and parents waited to greet her before the fireplace. Perhaps the most extreme example of Victorian mores is reflected in Henry James's story "A London Life" in which a young woman desperately expects a man, who does not love her, to marry her and save her reputation, because the two have been left alone in a box at the opera.

Naturally some girls rebelled at this convention, while their beaux secretly grumbled at having to pay for dinner or tickets for a third person. A few voiced their grievance by calling it un-American. *The Designer Magazine* in 1902 rejoined:

There are many, of course, who resent the innovation, as savoring too much of the duenna system of Europe; yet, taking into consideration the changed social conditions which now environ us, it seems but right that we should surround our American young womanhood with the all-enveloping protection that all young womanhood needs.[8]

Even Mrs. Burton Harrison in *The Well-Bred Girl in Society* (New York, 1904)—a wise and kindly book on social attitudes, rather than knife-and-fork manners—expresses the consensus of the East in saying of chaperonage that "a girl of the present generation would not venture to combat it without the risk of sharp criticism from alien tongues."

But the growing informality of society, accentuated by the freedom of

[8]This same arbiter remarks, with delightful supererogation, about the etiquette of broken engagements: "Presents that have been received during an engagement must be returned without delay if the engagement be broken, a similar plan being followed in regard to such correspondence as has been preserved. This rule cannot be applied to gifts such as flowers."

The Saga of American Society

War years and the jazz decade, gave the *coup de grâce* to chaperonage in the old rigid sense. The Victorian cult of "keeping up appearances" came to seem a shade hypocritical, or else insultingly sceptical of the decent impulses of young men and women. Sages added that if a girl is determined to have her pre-nuptial fling, no elderly kinswoman or maid in mufti is likely to stop her. Since 1922 when Emily Price Post first published *Etiquette: the Blue Book of Social Usage* there has been such an additional relaxation of chaperonage even in smart metropolitan custom that she has had to record successive changes, a little reluctantly, in an appendix.[9] At present the chaperon is extinct in the society of most inland cities; in New York, débutantes and their friends usually arrive at parties in a group, and hence avoid much of the old-time need for supervision by elders. A few from the most conservative families—patrons for example of the Metropolitan Dancing Class—still have their chaperons, maids or professionals hired from an agency like Miss Dignum's at $4 an evening, who read in the lobby or dressing-rooms of the Pierre or Waldorf until the stars pale and "Home, Sweet Home" brings their unexacting vigil to a close.

A christening, wedding, or funeral may happen to anybody, but the modern début is a rite belonging to Society alone, or at least to those who covet its prizes. Serving notice upon the social world that a daughter has become nubile, the début has immemorial roots which may be traced to coming of age in Samoa and Polynesia. In eighteenth-century America, Southern belles came out at an appreciably earlier stage of life than their Northern cousins—like Margaret Herbert of Alexandria, Virginia, granddaughter of the Carys, who was presented to Society at fourteen. Débuts at fifteen or sixteen were common, with marriage following as soon as an eligible suitor presented himself. The traditional purpose of the début is to introduce a girl to Society of all ages, especially the friends of her family—whom, as cynics remark, she knows already and probably never wants to see again. In the mid and later nineteenth century the medium might

---

[9]The original title of this the most famous contemporary work on manners was *Etiquette in Society, in Business, in Politics, and at Home.* Written with marked charm, common-sense, and readability, and enhanced with little fables about the Bobo Gildings and the Smartlingtons, *Etiquette* was followed in 1928 by the same author's half-serious parody, *How to Behave—Though a Débutante,* reflecting the franker manners of the youngest generation and fittingly illustrated by John Held, Jr. The only serious rival to Mrs. Post's manual is *Vogue's Book of Etiquette,* first published in 1929.

be an elaborate dance, but more typical was the afternoon reception, at which the débutante received with her mother and father and a few of her best girl friends, greeting not only young men but a liberal assortment of dowagers and old gentlemen. After the crowd had gone, an informal dinner followed, and lastly a dancing or theatre party for her intimates. The conventional age then, as now, was eighteen. In New York a girl might make her bow at any time during the season, which began in mid-November with the Horse Show—a curiously analogous occasion—and closed at Lent. Today the really smart season is shorter, for although it begins officially with the Tuxedo Autumn Ball, Society prefers to display its leisure by waiting till after the opening night of the Metropolitan Opera; soon after New Year's Day the bloom has already faded. This abbreviation means of course a great congestion of parties around Thanksgiving, Christmas, and January first, multiplied by the influx from private school and college. Occasional débuts take place after Easter and as late, or as early, as June. In New York the Ritz-Carlton has kept ever since the War its pre-eminence among débutantes, while in Philadelphia the Bellevue-Stratford enjoys high favor. The management of other hotels angle for trade with complimentary "débutante luncheons," but results sometimes disappoint their hopes. Today the début is much more the exclusive property of the young, with a plethora of dancing men and champagne. Like other entertainments of Society under a public roof it is generally entrusted into the hands of a specialist, the professional social secretary, like the nationally known Miss Juliana Cutting. So-called "Society publicity organizations," with their dossiers and morgues compiled from newspapers, seek to share the profits also, but have little save phantom services to offer the gullible client.

In New York Society alone there are approximately 250 débutantes each year, with a seasonal budget estimated at three to five million dollars. The average cost for hotel rental, food and drink, service, music, and flowers runs at present from $5000 to $10,000. Excessive spending, which transformed ballrooms into Southern gardens and tropical jungles in December, with tons of gardenias, orchids, monkeys, and parrots, with bills for $75,000 to $100,000, reached its crest in the season of 1928–29. A début reported to have cost the maximum figure was that of Miss Helen Lee Eames Doherty, step-daughter of Henry L. Doherty, oil millionaire, at the Mayflower Hotel, Washington, on December 26, 1930. As

The Saga of American Society

an added touch Miss Doherty on the eve of the début gave a dozen Ford cabriolets—whose sides she had painted with hunting scenes—to her intimates at dinner and to one absent acquaintance, the King of Spain. Senator George W. Norris, viewing the breadline in the same block as the Mayflower Hotel, told the press, "I can't help thinking that this is exactly the same situation as existed prior to the French Revolution." Subsequent events however were much kinder to Miss Doherty than to her friend the King of Spain. Tribal pomp of this kind—associated with the introduction to Society of such young ladies as Charlotte Dorrance, Eleanor Post Close, Gloria Gould, Barbara Hutton—has now ceased to be good form, if in fact it ever was. Stories are told however of anxious fathers and mothers who have taken the début with almost pathetic seriousness since the Depression; well known is the case of a father who borrowed $10,000 on his $50,000 life insurance policy to launch his daughter fittingly in the depths of financial winter, though today he is clerking in Wall Street while she, unmarried, earns her own living. With the increasing financial wariness of these times it is perhaps not surprising to learn from a recent tally made in New York City that only some 30 per cent of a season's débutantes now marry within the year, and about 20 per cent the following year.

With such discouraging returns from their investment, many parents at present prefer one of several cheaper alternatives: an afternoon tea with dancing, which is still quite smart; a dinner-dance for 150 or 200 of the younger set at the Ritz or Pierre's, in place of the old guest-lists of 1200, which in these days serves very well; a small tea without music, which mother's friends declare to be "very sweet"; or finally the mere sending out of cards bearing the daughter's name engraved below that of her mother's, known simply as "slipping out." With cruel irony, the girl who most needs the fanfare of début often can afford it least, while the worldling who is already well known—from school at Foxcroft, Miss Chapin's, or Brearley, and summers at Newport, Bar Harbor, or Southampton—will be invited to the best parties and treated as a débutante though her family make few overtures or none.

The old *Town Topics* of horrid memory loved to grade débutantes like certified milk, into categories which are still current among the ruthless. Grade A was the girl who had three generations of family, with money and personal charm. Grade B was a mixed lot into which were swept girls with background but scant attractiveness, reckless girls with money and position, and nice girls whose antecedents were a little tarnished by the wrong kind of divorces and financial scandals; it was in fact a class demoted largely on the score of behavior, either one's own or one's parents'. Stamped with Grade C were children of the new-rich, still odorous of oil, paint and varnish, or the stockyards; theirs was a frankly hopeful campaign for a step on the escalator. Eligible young men often liked them better than the products of Class B, because their candor was disarming, their sense of fun less stereotyped, their 'scutcheon bare but clean, and their father's wealth generous and consoling. The début, as achieved in the larger American cities with clannish and competitive social groups, has long been a school for hopes and tears, exultation and bitter disappointment—and inevitably, since its *mise en scène* is that time of life when heartbreak is so poignant, victory so sweet, popularity so vital, and even the best of children are so sadistic.

Indeed without some mention of the dictatorship of the young, any chapter on American manners would be incomplete. No other country in the world has made so much of its children, or given them so free a hand in shaping its customs and lending their exuberant naïveté to its social scene. As early as Revolutionary times, French visitors in the more aristocratic households, like the Schuylers', for example, reported that children were "spoiled" and "self-willed." Yet social precocity was one evident result of the attention paid them; Bayard describes the master of a country house near Winchester, Virginia, where, "dinner hour having sounded, we sat down at a round table, his daughter, nine years old, doing the honors very gracefully in the absence of her mother." Beaujour poetically says that the children "sparkle in the streets of American towns like field flowers in the springtime," and nobody denied the fact that children of the rising classes often had greater charm and *savoir faire* than their self-made parents. This situation is partly responsible for the reign of youth in America, for, possessing superior opportunities, it has often set up its own authority in social matters. Frequently, as we are told in the early nineteenth century, the mother, bowed by household cares and eclipsed by her daughters, failed to appear at parties given in her house—leaving the honors to be done by "pert young misses of sixteen." Emerson quoted a man who said it was a misfortune to have been born in an age when children were nothing and to spend maturity in an age when children were everything.

Buckingham in 1837 says that "the old seem either to be left on the shelf altogether, or only brought upon the stage to look on, bestow their approbation, and pay the expense." At Saratoga, he reports, "young children of six and seven years of age are here seen at concerts, balls, and 'hops' at hours when they should be in bed; and passing the day in the most frivolous amusements, playing at checkers or backgammon, coquetting and flirting in the gardens, eating and drinking of everything at table." The spectacle of flirtations in the garden at the age of six is one over which we may be a trifle incredulous, despite Doctor Freud and the Bertrand Russells. Other visitors, like Mary G. L. Duncan in 1852, were impressed with the straightforward manners of American children: "They come, not with a 'make your bow,' or 'curtsey to the lady'—that is not republican fashion; but with a becoming courage, looking straight into your eyes, and extending the right hand for a cordial handshake." Among the rich, however, French governesses have for generations helped to teach young girls something of Continental grace, while the dancing-master of Society—like the celebrated Papanti in Boston—served the same end for both boys and girls. Today, the curtsey, the bow from the waist, and the almost audible click of heels are seldom found in America save among children of a few old cultivated families. They are marks of caste, like a college boy's use of "Sir" in addressing tutors, which shows that he has attended Groton or St. Paul's—or else is adroitly imitative.

The surprise of visitors from abroad over the autocracy of our youth has never ceased. At the turn of the century Doctor James F. Muirhead, compiler of the American Baedeker, was immensely struck; he tells of a little girl, aged five, who appeared alone in a hotel dining-room, ordered an indigestible breakfast, and told the doubtful waiter, "I guess I pay my way." He noted particularly the tyranny of the American débutante, who coolly assumed the center of every stage, accepted homage as her undoubted right, allowed her young admirers to spend far too much upon her, and moved a little too insolently against a background of orchids and American Beauty roses. Henry James, revisiting these shores in 1906 after many years of absence, saw American Society as

The Book of Etiquette

"a great circle of brilliant and dowered débutantes and impatient youths, expert in the cotillion, waiting together for the first bars of some wonderful imminent dance music." The eagerness yet unsureness, the lack of discipline and restraint, the wandering attention and quick boredom, the susceptibility to suggestion and whim—all these things impressed him as characteristic of Society in the United States, with "the sawdust of its ripped-up dolls" still in its hair. "The immensity of the native accommodation, socially speaking, for the childish life, is not that exactly the key to much of the spectacle?"

Few things are so revealing of this state of mind as the popularity of the word "sophistication." As a term of praise it is unknown in other languages and even in England, except in certain circles which have consciously borrowed from us. The great Oxford Dictionary defines it in no sense but a vicious one, meaning adulteration, impurity, specious value, or an affectation of wisdom. Yet in America—where sophistication may mean anything from painted toe-nails to intellectual urbanity—it was for some years the rallying-cry of tailors and dressmakers, the appeal of advertising in those magazines which address the gentry of sport and fashion, and the envy of college sophomores and parvenus from the middle class. Its rise as an epithet of praise dates from the post-War years, particularly after Gertrude Atherton's *Black Oxen* in 1923, though ground had been prepared for it by the Yellow Nineties. For in that era wicked Oscar Wilde was defining a gentleman as "one who never inflicts pain unintentionally,"[10] and Huysmans was writing *A rebours* with its decadent hero who expresses his utter disenchantment by playing symphonies upon his palate with a pipe-organ of liqueurs, encrusting the shell of a pet turtle with jewels, growing tropical flowers into revolting and obscene shapes, and cultivating a taste for street-gamins. Such people now seem in the light of psychopathology to be morbid examples of arrested adolescence. The worship of diabolism has never amounted to much in America—though, as the Black Mass of "fast" Society, it has sometimes unduly alarmed the serious-minded. But the fevered quest for experience which it represented once found congenial company in fashionable Bohemia and among the internationals of Mayfair and Long Island. Just after the War the bright young people of America, in

[10]An irreverent amendment to Cardinal Newman: "It is almost a definition of a gentleman to say that he is one who never inflicts pain."

their myopic search for wisdom, seized upon sophistication instead. One of the minor poets, Mark Turbyfill, wrote a "Prayer for Sophistication":

> Close all open things, O God!
> Close the rose,
> The throats of flutes and birds.
> Close all eyes
> To tears not yet fallen.
> Close my heart.
> Close all open things, O God!

Miss Frances Newman, a provincial spinster who wrote a novel called *The Hard-Boiled Virgin* to shock the elders of Atlanta, was engaged at the time of her death in 1928 in compiling—out of materials which one can only conjecture—a *History of Sophistication*.

It flourished naturally in little coteries of its own, because nobody can be sophisticated all by himself, for example a man climbing into an unshared bed—after, of course, his valet has left him. This generation blissfully believed that it had invented sophistication, without realizing that the most blasé societies of history—the Age of Pericles, the times of Confucius, and the reign of the Roi Soleil—had not talked about it because they took it completely for granted. The fledgling preens its feathers most frequently. Chief among social traits was its cynicism about morals. Even in the Gilded Age, when a hapless young millionaire had sought advice from Joseph Choate concerning a married woman who was chasing him around Newport, "Tell her," counselled the witty lawyer, " 'Madam, I have no time for a liaison, but I am willing to oblige you, if you promise that our adultery is not to be of a serious nature.' " The tastes of "advanced" Society in the post-War years, as reflected in the drama, the novel, and the quality magazine, ran to sexual comedy— the peccadilloes of husbands and wives, the finesse of seduction, the humors of divorce, the innuendoes of perversion. Situations which once would have called for the problem play or reform novel became fit topics for jest in the dialogue of Noel Coward and Philip Barry, or the caricatures of Peter Arno. The disillusionment of returned editors of *The Stars and Stripes* and the keen satire of young Jews founded *The New Yorker;* its wit—best described as the uprush of the under-dog—has given a strange nervous enjoyment to the upper classes. The advent of the talkies in the closing years of this decade introduced the great inland public to a dash of the irony, the *double entendre,* and gay flippancy of the Broadway theatre. For the first time, perhaps, the citizen of Middletown or the sophomore of Siwash College could observe through the none too accurate lens of Hollywood how the smart set talks and behaves. The effect upon the population at large was not so great as one might have supposed, partly because the double meanings went unperceived by the majority, including the censors; partly because the plain man continued to find more thrill in the ocular simplicities of musical comedy; and finally because the onset of the lean years had a far more powerful effect in bringing to a close the excesses of that era. Now, with the waning of great fortunes and the vast uncertainty of our economic and social future, "sophistication," with its thin veneer of Byronism, has already passed its peak. In fact, the paradox is dawning upon a rather serious younger generation that sophistication may also be enlisted upon the side of virtue, as it appears in that wittily urbane letter which Madame de Sévigné wrote to her cousin Bussy, when he urged that she revenge herself upon an unfaithful husband by embarking upon an affair with him.

At any rate, despite its early kinship with pose and cheap cynicism, the word has fought hard for an honorable place—evidently because a need is felt in America to express some undefined aspect of the art of living. Mere etiquette is not enough; there must be charm, suavity, and distinction besides. In this sense sophistication is one of those additional bulwarks which minorities continue jealously to build in the midst of a democracy.

CHAPTER SIX

THE BLUE BOOK

THE formation of cliques happens inevitably in human relations. It has been remarked that if three men were shipwrecked on a desert island, two presently would be found foregathering under the best banana tree and looking askance at the third. Butlers in Newport recognize the social primacy of Mrs. Henry White's Stryde, while in New York and London they have their annual Butlers' Ball under the patronage of masters and mistresses, and in the approved plutocratic way set aside the profits for charity. A hostess in Washington recently hired a colored girl as second cook, though warned by her prospective employee, "I'll have to ask you for lots of my evenin's off, Ma'am—you see I'se a débutante this year." Within their clan charwomen recognize superiors and inferiors, while the inmates of brothels among themselves are notoriously snobbish. It need cause no surprise then or remonstrance that in Society efforts are continually made to limit the quota of immigration by those who have not only arrived but have disembarked.

Social distinction often appears in unexpected guises. Take the circulating library, which seems in itself a guileless instrument of pastime and knowledge. In the eighteenth century such lending collections were set up in the larger towns by printers, stationers, and enterprising individuals. The present Library Company of Philadelphia goes back to 1731 and Benjamin Franklin's little group called the Junto, which from a band of intelligent 'prentices, mechanics, and clerks, progressed until "reading became fashionable," as Franklin remarked, and assumed a restrictive character. Its shares have long been hereditary, and though today its reading-room is almost bare of patrons and its character moribund, the Library Company is rich in funds and social tradition. In 1748 seventeen young gentlemen of Charleston pooled their resources to send £10 to a London bookseller for pamphlets and magazines. Chartered in 1755 after stubborn opposition from the Royal Governor, the

Charleston Library Society elected the Governor to its presidency and became a social club of most exclusive aspect. Impoverished by the Confederate War—as that event is always called in Charleston—the Library Society still carries on bravely, recruiting its spinster librarian and her assistant from the roll of the St. Cecilia. Financial succor came in 1900 when Major Theodore G. Barker, president of the South Carolina Jockey Club, proposed, since the great days of racing were over, that this equally aristocratic organization dissolve and bequeath all its property to the Library—assuring it an income of some $2000 annually. More prosperous New England peers include the Providence Athenæum, the Redwood Library of Newport, and richest of all the Boston Athenæum founded by William Smith Shaw in 1807—within whose cloistered walls the late Gamaliel Bradford wished whimsically to be buried, as the Yankee equivalent of the Ivory Tower. In accord with the formula *otium cum dignitate* the Athenæum rules that "No person shall put his feet upon a table or window seat." It is also probably the only reading club in America to have an authentic ghost, that of the Reverend Thaddeus Mason Harris, seen by none less than Hawthorne, "reading the newspaper as was his wont."

In 1754 a circulating library was incorporated in New York, under the sponsorship of Alexanders, Livingstons, and De Lanceys; eighteen years later under royal charter it became "The New-York Society Library." From its inception it was cradled in exclusiveness. The *Mercury* for May 12, 1755, reported: "No sooner were the Subscriptions compleat, and a Day appointed for the Election of Trustees, than a dirty Scheme was concerted, for excluding as many English Presbyterians as possible, from the Trusteeship; concerted, not by Trinity Church in this City, but by some of her unworthy Members."[1] Episcopalians were already in the social saddle. The original shareholders—Beekmans, Crugers, Keteltases, De Peysters, Ludlows, Stuyvesants, and a few others—were joined in 1790–96 by such new subscribers as Jay, Astor, Lenox, LeRoy, Roosevelt, Schieffelin, and Schermerhorn. Descendants of these shareholders, who today number approximately 800, know no prouder privilege than hereditary membership in the Society Library, now housed upstairs in pleasantly gloomy quarters in University Place, little more than a stone's

---

[1] The writer of this indignant Calvinist remonstrance was probably the Rev. Aaron Burr, president of the College at Princeton.

throw from the turbulent proletarianism of Union Square. Though its rules are ostensibly uniform, shareholders are said to enjoy virtually unlimited privileges unknown to mere subscribers; any one with a Knickerbocker pedigree can with impunity keep a book out at least a year. For the last forty-two years its librarian has been Mr. Frank B. Bigelow; his assistant for more than thirty years and present active librarian, Marion D. Morrison, married one of the Society Library's most faithful patrons, Mr. Frederick Gore King (Harvard '75)—who, after long solitude as a bachelor, used to be seen with mild surprise by his Iselin relatives pushing a perambulator in Central Park while his wife presided over the august shelves of the Society Library.

Another organization whose name is covered with a fine old Dutch patina is the New-York Historical Society. The hyphen is as sacred as the tombstones in Trinity Churchyard. Yet it was organized as late as 1804, by DeWitt Clinton, Anthony Bleecker, Samuel Bayard, Peter G. Stuyvesant, and seven others, to preserve historical records and maps, letters, newspapers, books on genealogy and history. It has been greatly enriched by the Gates, Stirling, Duer, Lamb, and Steuben manuscripts on the Revolution, and by the Gallatin papers for the succeeding period. For generations the New-York Historical Society has arranged series of evening lectures, at which the members doze gently after the lights are turned low, wake up at cessation of the hypnotic voice, and go downstairs where they drink cocoa among the mummified bulls and sacred cats in the Abbott collection of Egyptology, which the Society bought in 1859 for no very clear reason after James Lenox had presented some Nineveh sculptures in 1857. Shortly after the Civil War, when plans were on foot to organize the Metropolitan Museum, the New-York Historical Society declined a suggested merger because, as Mr. Nicholas Fish effectively pointed out, some of the sponsors of the Metropolitan Museum were not gentlemen. Today the president is John Abeel Weekes, and the officers include R. Horace Gallatin, Lucius Wilmerding, Doctor Fenwick Beekman, and Stephen H. P. Pell. Although the destinies of the Society have always been controlled by De Peysters, Stuyvesants, Schieffelins, Kips, Satterlees, Kings, Hoffmans, and their friends—who in recent years gravitate also to the Lords of the Manor Society, under the sponsorship of Kiliaen Van Rensselaer—its bars are not so high as to have shut out the late Collis P. Huntington, George Fisher Baker, and a few other captains of industry upon whose pedigrees expensive genealogists had labored and not in vain. Excessively rich, the New-York Historical Society is safely beyond the need of sustenance through dues—charging only a nominal $20 initiation fee and an annual assessment of $10.

Lacking the compasses of an hereditary peerage and gentry, which mark so sharply the bounds of Burke, Debrett, and the *Almanach de Gotha,* social groups in America have drawn their magic circles in a variety of ways. To review them all is impossible. One may select however the history of social New York, as offering probably the richest assortment of those methods—through visiting-lists, directories of wealth and fashion, blue books, dancing groups, personalities or arbiters of Society, and professional social secretaries—by which the sheep have been sorted out and earmarked. From time to time of course one may glance into neighboring folds, where the flocks of other cities have been impounded.

The first representative visiting-list which survives was that kept by Mrs. John Jay—the proud and brilliantly social wife of the Secretary for Foreign Affairs when New York was the capital, during the season 1787–88. It is therefore her "official" list, including not only her own Livingston relatives and intimate friends, but also ranking members of Congress and foreign diplomats. Called "Dinner and Supper List for 1787 and 1788" it reads as follows, with the occupation of each gentleman so far as can be ascertained supplied in parentheses:

Mr. John Alsop (merchant)
Mr. and Mrs. Allen (perhaps from the mercantile family of Philadephia)
General John Armstrong (soldier, future Minister to France)
Mr. and Mrs. Van Berckel (Dutch Minister to U. S.)
Mrs. Bruce
Mr. Barclay (James, merchant)
Miss Browne
Mr. Egbert Benson (lawyer, Attorney-General of New York State)
Mr. William Bingham (banker, Senator from Pennsylvania)
Major Beckwith (aide-de-camp of British staff)
Mr. Pierce Butler (South Carolina planter, Senator)
Mrs. and the Misses Butler
Major Butler
Colonel Aaron Burr (lawyer)

Mr. Bronson (probably Isaac, banker)

Miss Bayard

Mr. Blount (probably William, son of wealthy North Carolinian, delegate to Constitutional Convention of 1787)

Mr. Constable (merchant)

Dr. and Mrs. John Charlton (physician)

Mr. and Mrs. Augustus Van Cortlandt (inherited income)

Miss Van Cortlandt

Mr. Van Cortlandt (probably Pierre, Lieutenant-Governor of New York)

Mr. and Mrs. Colden (probably David, well-known scholar, son of Dr. Cadwallader Colden)

Miss Cuyler

Governor George Clinton (soldier, politician, speculator)

General James Clinton (brother of George, professional soldier)

Mr. Freeman Clarkson ⎤
Mr. Stratfield Clarkson ⎬ (members of well-known New York family
Mr. Levinus Clarkson ⎦ in importing and dry-goods business)

Mr. Henry Cruger (merchant)

Mr. Lambert Cadwalader (merchant, soldier, statesman)

General Clarkson (Matthew, soldier, politician, philanthropist)

Mr. Corbit (probably of family descended from Abraham Corbit, N. Y. Alderman in 1686)

Colonel Carrington (Edward, Congressman from Virginia)

M. Chaumont (French diplomatic service)

Colonel William Duer (merchant)

Lady Kitty Duer (wife of the above, and daughter of the self-styled Earl of Stirling, whose title the House of Lords rejected in 1762)

Mr. and Mrs. James Duane (lawyer, Mayor of New York)

Miss Duane

Mr. Dowse

Mr. Nathan Dane (Massachusetts Congressman)

Mr. Frederic De Peyster (inherited income, married Mary Justina Watts)

Miss De Peyster

M. de la Forest (French consul in New York)

Colonel William Few (Georgia Congressman)

Mr. Franklin (Samuel, director of Bank of New York)

Don Diego Gardoqui (Spanish Minister)

Mr. and Mrs. William Grayson (Senator from Virginia)

Mr. Gouverneur (Isaac, merchant)

Mr. and Miss Gorham (Stephen, Claims-Commissioner for New Hampshire)

Mr. Elbridge Gerry (Massachusetts Congressman)

Mr. Gansevoort (probably Peter, on roll of Cincinnati Society of New York)

Mr. Nicholas Gilman (New Hampshire Congressman)

Mr. Richard Harrison (lawyer)

Mr. Hindman (William, Maryland planter, lawyer, politician)

Colonel and Mrs. Alexander Hamilton (lawyer, Secretary of the Treasury)

Mr. Haring (John, Congressman from New York)

Mr. Daniel Huger (South Carolina Congressman)

Mr. Hawkins (Benjamin, North Carolina Senator, son of a wealthy planter)

Mr. and Mrs. Houston (perhaps John Houstoun, lawyer, former Governor of Georgia)

Mr. Hobart (John Sloss, Justice of New York Supreme Court)

Mr. Ralph Izard (Senator from South Carolina)

General Irwin (probably the New York merchant)

Dr. William Samuel Johnson (lawyer, son of first president of King's College, later Columbia)

Mr. and Mrs. Frederick Jay (auctioneer)

Mrs. James

Mr. S. Jones (real-estate lawyer)

Chevalier Paul Jones (the great naval hero, son of a Scotch gardener)

Mr. Kemble (probably Peter, merchant)

General and Mrs. Henry Knox (bookseller, soldier, Secretary of War)

Mr. and Mrs. Rufus King (lawyer, statesman)

Mr. Kean

Dr. and Mrs. Benjamin Kissam (physician)

Mr. and Mrs. Daniel Ludlow (merchant, later president of the Manhattan Bank)

Mr. and Mrs. Morgan Lewis (lawyer, later Governor of New York)

Mrs. Judge Livingston (wife of Brockholst Livingston, lawyer)

Mr. and Mrs. William Livingston (Governor of New Jersey; these Livingstons were the parents of Mrs. Jay)

Miss S. Livingston

Miss Maria Livingston

Miss Eliza Livingston

Mr. Philip Livingston (probably son of Philip, merchant and Signer of Declaration of Independence)

Chancellor Robert R. Livingston (lawyer, distinguished jurist)

Mr. John Lawrence (lawyer)

Mr. and Mrs. Richard Henry Lee (Senator from Virginia)

Mr. and Mrs. John Langdon (merchant and Senator from New Hampshire)

Mr. C. Ludlow (probably Charles, broker)

Mrs. Ludlow

Major John Rowland Livingston (State Assemblyman from Albany)

M. Lattinière (probably French diplomatic service)

Mr. and Mrs. Arthur Lee (Commissioner of the Treasury)

Miss Marshall

Mr. Meredith (Philip, banker, first U. S. Treasurer)

Marquis de Moustier (French Minister to U. S.) and Madame de Brehan (his sister)

Mrs. Montgomery (widow of General Richard Montgomery)

Mr. Mitchell (probably Samuel Latham Mitchell, "a buckish young oracle, half dandy and half philosopher," a dilettante in medicine)

Mr. and Mrs. Mason and Mr. Mason, Jr. (the senior is probably the Rev. John Mason, Presbyterian clergyman; his son John M. Mason, recently graduated from Columbia, became one of the most fashionable pulpit orators of the next generation)

Mr. and Mrs. Moore (probably the Rev. Benjamin Moore, Episcopal clergyman)

Mr. J. Marston (Tory merchant)

Mr. Matthews (probably George Matthews, Georgia Congressman)

General Morris (Lewis, third lord of Morrisania, given rank of brigadier-general in 1776)

Mr. Gouverneur Morris (diplomat)

Mr. James Madison (lawyer, Virginia Congressman, future President)

Major William North (merchant and soldier, married daughter of Mayor James Duane)

Mr. Samuel Osgood (Postmaster-General)

M. and Mme. Otto (Louis Guillaume Otto, French *chargé d'affaires*)

Mr. and Mrs. Pintard (Major in the Westchester Light Horse)

Miss Pintard

Mr. and Mrs. Pierce (John, Paymaster General)

The President of Congress (Cyrus Griffin of Virginia, married to a Scotswoman of noble birth and styled Lady Griffin)

Colonel Parker (probably Daniel, auctioneer)

Mr. Parker (probably Josiah Parker, Virginia Congressman)

Mr. Pinckney (both Charles and Charles Cotesworth Pinckney, South Carolina planters of legal training, were eminent in public life after their delegacy to the Constitutional Convention)

Bishop and Mrs. Samuel Provoost (first Episcopal bishop of New York)

Mr. and Miss Pratt (probably Matthew Pratt, fashionable portrait-

painter, who moved much in Society; see Dunlap, *Arts of Design*
1918 ed., vol. I, p. 114)

Mr. John Rutherfurd (lawyer)

Mrs. Rutherfurd

Mr. Rodgers (probably Dr. John Rodgers, Presbyterian clergyman)

Mr. Read (probably Senator George Read of Delaware)

Miss Van Rensselaer

Mr. Rickets

Colonel Ross (perhaps James Ross of Pittsburgh, afterwards Senator;
business agent of George Washington in Pennsylvania)

Governor John Rutledge (famous South Carolina jurist)

Mr. Henry Remsen (secretary to John Jay)

Mr. Sears and family (Isaac, merchant and Revolutionary leader)

Mr. and Mrs. Melancthon Smith (merchant, lawyer, member of Continental Congress)

M. de Saint Glain (probably French attaché)

Mr. Philip Schuyler (son of General Philip John Schuyler, *infra*)

Baron Steuben (famous German officer)

Mrs. Swan

General Schuyler (patroon, soldier; father of Mrs. Alexander Hamilton, Mrs. Van Rensselaer, and Mrs. Church)

Mrs. Symmes (sister of Mrs. Jay, and wife of John Cleve Symmes, New
Jersey Congressman)

Sir John and Lady Temple (British Consul General)

Mr. Charles Thompson (Secretary to Congress)

Mr. and Mrs. Turnbull (Mrs. Turnbull, née Susan Van Horne, was
a noted New York heiress and belle)

Mr. and Mrs. Van Horne (probably Abraham, New York Assemblyman)

Mr. C. Van Horne

Miss Betsey A. Van Horne

Miss Cornelia Van Horne

Colonel and Mrs. Richard Varick (lawyer)

Mr. Cornelius Verplanck (banking)

Mr. and Lady Mary Watts (the son-in-law of Lord Stirling, thus
amusingly relegated to the minor rôle, was Robert Watts)

Mr. John Watts (lawyer, Recorder of New York)

Mr. and Misses White (probably the rich Loyalist family of Henry
White, whose daughters were famous belles of New York during
this era; one of them lived to a great age as the dowager Lady
Hayes)

Dr. Williamson (Hugh Williamson, Presbyterian clergyman, professor
of mathematics in the University of Pennsylvania, scientist, physi-

cian, North Carolina delegate to the Constitutional Convention;
during this season he married an heiress, Miss Apthorp)
Dr. Witherspoon (president of Nassau Hall, New Jersey)
Colonel Jeremiah Wadsworth (banker, wool-manufacturer, Congress-
man from Connecticut)
Mr. Paine Wingate (Congregational clergyman and Senator from New
Hampshire)
Judge Yates (Robert, Justice of New York Supreme Court)[2]

This list, in which men of affairs predominate, shows in comparison
with the century-later roll of Ward McAllister's "Four Hundred" several striking changes. The removal of the national capital from New
York in the following year decreed that its future Society, unlike that of
London, Paris, Rome, Berlin, Vienna, and other great cities, should be
divorced from statesmanship. Political careers henceforth would not
parallel social ones in the metropolitan pattern, which was to become
increasingly gilt-edged, and perhaps more clannish, frivolous and indolent
than a Society interwoven with public service. In McAllister's list it will
be seen that lawyers have held their own, bankers have multiplied, phy-
sicians have dwindled to a single representative, and clergymen have
dropped out altogether from the Smart Set. Ward McAllister's is of
course the most publicized, rather than the most judicious, of lists; still
when set beside Mrs. Jay's it is significant of a rather profound shift
in the occupations of Society—which from 1790 to 1890 in New York
had taken on the character of a leisure group with certain meretricious
aspects, a class made up of coupon-clippers, sportsmen living off their
fathers' accumulation, and a stratum like the Astors and Vanderbilts
trying to renounce their commercial origins as quickly as possible.

Midway between these dates arose the first "millionaires," reflected
in the pioneer guide-book to credit and marriage, published by Moses
Yale Beach, proprietor of the New York *Sun,* in 1844. *The Wealth and
Biography of the Wealthy Citizens of the City of New York* passed

---

[2]With minor corrections this follows the transcript as given in Griswold's *Republi-
can Court,* pp. 98–99 n. In an incomplete list from Mrs. Jay's papers given in *The
Memorial History of New York,* vol. III, pp. 87 ff. additional names include Robert
Troup, John Lansing, Josiah Ogden Hoffman, and James Kent, lawyers; Doctors John
Henry Livingston and William Linn, Reformed Dutch clergymen; Robert Morris,
Philadelphia banker; Charles Carroll, Maryland planter; and statesmen, largely self-
made and sprung from farmer and merchant stock, like Roger Sherman, Benjamin
Huntington, and Elias Boudinot.

through ten editions in two years, and was revised twice during the next decade. It lists some 850 names, of citizens with fortunes of $100,000 up—lawyers, merchants, auctioneers, newspaper publishers, tailors, patent medicine manufacturers—with the computed wealth of each, and a brief biography. Beach is not the most flattering of compilers. He reminds old John Jacob Astor that he used to beat moths out of furs in his shirt-sleeves, brands the Kernochans as shanty Irish who started as colliers and teamsters but worked up in the iron business, recalls to James Gore King the fact that in spite of his aristocratic airs his grandparents were of the humblest sort, notes that the Posts spring from butchers and mechanics and that the Schieffelins descend from a Hessian mercenary who after the Revolution had the good luck to capture an heiress, calls Thomas Suffern "a respectable Irish gent" who has done well in the tobacco trade, and points out that the Wilmerdings run an auction business formerly Haggerty & Wilmerding.[3] Overshadowed by the Astor millions the Goelets are listed at $2,000,000; A. T. Stewart, department-store owner, $2,000,000; Cornelius Vanderbilt, $1,500,000; Peter Cooper, Moses Taylor, ancestor of the Pynes, and the Lorillards, one million each. These are the millionaires of 1844, and in comparison with the Gilded Age their fortunes seem paltry. On the other hand, in Mrs. Jay's time there was not a single New Yorker worth a million dollars—such a prodigy being reserved for Maryland with its Charles Carroll, and Philadelphia with its William Bingham. Beach's guide also gives us transparent glimpses of the conversion of plutocrat into aristocrat. For example we read concerning John W. Moffat: "The founder of the celebrated 'Life Pills and Phœnix Bitters,' by the manufacture and sale of which he has amassed his present fortune. He has now retired from active business and is succeeded by his son William B. Moffat." And of the latter, who with a

[3]He also reproaches Henry Brevoort, Jr., for scorning the "basse classe," "profanum vulgus," and "sans culottes" who were "the boon companions of his venerable mother ... whose weather-beaten features bore the brunt and pitiless peltings of many a piercing wintry northeaster of sleet and rain, as she sat vending her vegetables, and carrots, and York salad and olycakes, under the unsheltered eaves of the market-house in the Bowery." Concerning Doctor David Hosack who married the widow of Henry Coster, but died of apoplexy brought on by the shock of seeing some of his new property burn up, Beach solemnly concludes: "But for David's marriage with a widow of extreme wealth, he would have been now and for years hence at the head of his profession, and of eminent usefulness—all of which and his life were suddenly arrested by the potent influence of gold."

magnificent house on Broadway and a profit of $60,000 annually, was making quite a dash in New York circles: "An only son and the successor in business of his father as stated above. Possessed of that greatest mine of wealth—a thorough and complete education—his recent travels in Europe have so polished the jewel that its owner must shine in future years as a distinguished man."[4]

In New York, flood-gate of world commerce and industry, the social evolution occurred more rapidly than in Philadelphia, Charleston, and Boston. Yet even in Boston the lifetime of Henry Cabot Lodge spanned the transition. In *Early Memories* he recalled that in his boyhood a hundred thousand dollars was considered a very comfortable property, while a little earlier, in 1830, the richest citizen was taxed on possessions worth only $350,000, with the rest far below: "Society, as I first remember it, was based on the old families; Doctor Holmes defines them in the 'Autocrat' as the families which had held high position in the colony, the province, and during the Revolution and the early decades of the United States. They represented several generations of education and standing in the community. . . . They had ancestors who had filled the pulpits, sat upon the bench, and taken part in the government under the crown; who had fought in the Revolution, helped to make the State and National constitutions and served in the army or navy; who had been members of the House or Senate in the early days of the Republic, and who had won success as merchants, manufacturers, lawyers, or men of letters. In many places people of this sort have been pushed out of sight, if not actually driven against the conventional wall. Unless they were able to hold on to a certain amount of money or to add to their inherited fortune, they have been swept away." This class is the backbone of Mrs. Jay's "Dinner and Supper List," while that of McAllister's Four Hun-

---

[4]It might be noted, as a symptom of the same condition, that the *Wealth and Biography of the Wealthy Citizens of Philadelphia, by a Member of the Philadelphia Bar,* appeared in 1845. The new criteria of society were thus bluntly stated twenty-five years later by George Makepeace Towle, an American consul, in his two-volume *American Society,* London, 1870, vol. I, p. 292: "You may easily procure an entrance to its most gorgeous saloons—only you must be rich enough to keep pace with their frequenters. You are not asked who your ancestors were; it is hardly a recommendation that you are university-bred; but the more a man or woman of the world you are, the more *recherché* your manners, the more chatty and piquant your conversation, the purer the breed of horses you drive in Central Park, the more faultless your toilette, the more fashionable your taste and criticism of pictures and operas, the more familiar you are with the social events and gossip of the hour, the more you will be welcome."

dred is of persons able and willing to play what came to be known as "the social game."

Long before the emergence of Ward McAllister, Society in America had been searching for a Beau Nash—an arbiter of elegance and exclusion like that celebrated Master of Ceremonies in the pump-room at Bath. Thus in staid Charleston in 1794 there was so much bickering over socially desirable boxes in the theatre, aggravated by a fashion of wearing obstructive feathers in one's coiffure which Mrs. Izard had brought home from Paris, that *The City Gazette* for October 18 suggested that the municipality "appoint a Master of Ceremonies, as they have done in Boston, to settle all kinds of social disputes, especially over the possession of stage boxes, for one unfortunate misunderstanding has resulted in a duel." A fashionable resort of the earlier nineteenth century, the White Sulphur Springs, did have its arbiter, called "the Metternich of the Mountains," in the person of Mr. Caldwell, an old gentleman with white hair and small cue carefully tied with a black ribbon. Although he owned the one hotel and all available cabins, which held a total of 700 guests, Mr. Caldwell "was never intended for an innkeeper" as James L. Pettigru wrote to Susan King, and any guest was flattered to be asked to take wine in his rooms. Captain Marryat found him "as despotic as all the lady patronesses of Almacks rolled into one. . . . Spa, in its palmiest days when princes had to sleep in their carriages at the doors of the hotels, was not more in vogue than are these White Sulphur Springs with the élite of the United States. And it is here, and here only in the States, that you do meet what may be fairly considered as select society." People adored the discipline which admitted only those families who travelled in their private carriages, yet charged them only eight dollars a head per week for board and lodgings. Also unless guests were known in person or descent to Mr. Caldwell, they generally were sent away discomfited to join the *canaille* at the Blue Springs. In his benevolent smile Mrs. Caton took the cure, and queened it over the season—for was she not the daughter of Charles Carroll of Carrollton, and mother-in-law of three British peers?

The closest approach to Beau Nash which New York then could boast was Dominick Lynch, "the greatest swell and beau that New York had ever known," as Ward McAllister called him many years later in ascribing his own ambitions to the anecdotes of Lynch which McAllister's father used to tell. Celebrated as "the only Irishman who brought money to America," Lynch set up a wine-importing firm in New York during post-Revolutionary times. In 1793 he bought a large estate in Westchester County, at Clason Point, and built an imposing mansion with a Carrara marble fireplace; for many years his townhouse stood at No. 1 Greenwich Street. He was a devout Roman Catholic, with a Continental grace of manner and a passionate devotion to music. He was often asked to sing at dinner-parties, such as the Hones's party on September 15, 1832 in honor of Fanny Kemble; in her book she wrote contemptuously of her hosts and their question "whether I had heard of his singing, or their musical soirées, and seeming all but surprised that I had no revelation of either across the Atlantic." He had gone over to London several years before and collected the first real grand opera troupe which New York had ever had, accompanied their voyage over on the packet-ship *New York,* and helped coach them for the "Barber of Seville" at the Park Theatre on November 29, 1825. Epicures were grateful to Dominick Lynch for having also introduced Château Margaux to American palates. Hone lamented his death from dropsy in Paris in 1837, and wrote of him as the most sought-after and brilliant diner-out of his generation, while the noted physician Doctor John Wakefield Francis eulogized Lynch before the New-York Historical Society as "the acknowledged head of the fashionable and festive board, a gentleman of the *ton.*" In the small, compact New York coterie of that day, Dominick Lynch probably never though of himself—in McAllister's self-conscious way—as the Good Shepherd of Society, but his charm, cultivation, and European knowledge of the arts apparently made him the center of that group, the Celtic leaven in the Knickerbocker lump.

The typical "clubman" of that day—as described in the jargon of modern tabloids—was Philip Hone himself. The son of a carpenter or joiner, Hone embarked with his brother on a lucrative auctioneer's traffic, and after twenty years of faithful money-making retired in 1821 to learn how to be a gentleman. He travelled abroad, witnessed the coronation of George IV, taught himself art, history, and literature, and later lamented that "I would give half I possess in the world to enjoy the advantages of a classical education." He rode in a barouche drawn by two horses, entertained visiting peers, helped build the Italian Opera House and founded the Union Club, was a governor of the New York Hospital, trustee of

Columbia and of the Bloomingale Insane Asylum, and saw his children marry into the Dutch aristocracy. Adoring everything traditional, he loved above all other sights "the Stuyvesant pear-tree" on Third Avenue at 13th Street, and was in ecstasies in June, 1838, when after he had dined at Mr. Fish's house with Stuyvesants and Winthrops, "they very politely had some of the blossoms gathered and sent to me, which I intend to preserve as a specimen of long-lived vegetation, and a floral reminiscence of the Stuyvesant dynasty." Embalmed for all time in his *Diary* Philip Hone is symbolic of the older parvenu, eager to adopt the ways of a social Tory, a hater of newspapers and reporters, politicians and mobs, and a votary of rich men's tables, fashionable weddings and funerals, sedentary clubs, and the Episcopal Church. The modern arrivist often relishes publicity, prefers night clubs to the Union or Knickerbocker, and thinks it hardly worthwhile to dance attendance upon, and risk rebuff by, the cave-dwellers.

Still another type in the social pageantry of old New York was represented by Isaac Brown, sexton of Grace Church, "the most fashionable and exclusive of our metropolitan Courts of Heaven," as N. P. Willis wrote in the 1850's in describing him. For two generations New York Society came to depend upon his faultless memory for names, pedigrees, and gossip. Hostesses about to issue invitations would summon honest Isaac Brown to tell who was in mourning, who had gone bankrupt, who had friends visiting them, who were the new arrivals in town and in Society. Generally he could foretell with exactitude just what acceptances and refusals one might expect, and as Willis adds, "suggest the possible and advisable enlargements of acquaintances." He was then charged with the leaving of cards upon distinguished strangers, as well as the bearing of invitations to all elected guests. He was often asked to inspect the premises before a party, to check the accommodations and refreshments, and upon high occasions was present in the rôle of steward—such as at the ball for the Prince of Wales at the Academy of Music, October 12, 1860, where the floor started to collapse just before the entry of His Royal Highness, and workmen under the masterful direction of Isaac Brown got it repaired in the nick of time. At other parties he presided at the doorstep under the canvas awning, gruffly calling and despatching carriages; some one called him "the connecting link between Society and the curbstone." In view of the then fashionable district he told one host-

The Saga of American Society

ess that he really couldn't undertake "to run Society" beyond 50th Street. He grew quite arbitrary in later years, sometimes accepting employment at the door of a *nouveau riche* but advising any of his old patrons who turned up to go elsewhere, adding, "This is mixed, very!" Wits of the time claimed that he possessed a list of "dancing young men" for the benefit of newly arrived party-givers, and the eligibles of New York were styled "Brown's Brigade." McAllister had great respect for Isaac Brown, but upon his passing had a Cerberus of his own in training—known always under the simple name "Johnson"—who stepped into the breach, and became the watchdog of Patriarch Balls. Occasionally there were mix-ups in invitation cards, and as McAllister told a reporter from the *Tribune* on March 25, 1888: "An error of this kind caused some annoyance to Miss Elsie de Wolfe last winter, the ticket being irregular, and she was stopped by Johnson, until the matter was satisfactorily explained."

But all these attempts at social discipline from various levels pale before the name of Ward McAllister himself, "The Autocrat of Drawing-Rooms" as he rejoiced to be known, though "ringmaster" might have been more accurate. He claimed descent from the French family of Corday, which gave Charlotte to the annals of history; her distant cousin proved to be equally ruthless, but preferred to stab in the ballroom rather than the bath. He was born in Savannah, Georgia in 1827, the son of a lawyer famous for hospitality but none too prosperous.[5] After a sketchy education, young Ward went to New York to visit a relative, a rich old spinster. Basking in great expectations, he began early to court Society, and upon receiving a thousand dollar legacy paid by the New York Life Insurance Company, spent it all on a costume for his first fancy-dress ball, given by Mrs. John C. Stevens—born Maria Livingston, and wife of the first commodore of the New York Yacht Club. The youth was at this time drudging at the desk of a bookkeeper, but his soul rebelled. A further indignity came when his relative died and left all her fortune to charity. He went home to Savannah, read law in his father's office, and as

[5]This lawyer and planter, Matthew H. McAllister, was defeated when he ran for Governor of Georgia in 1845. In the course of the campaign he was described as belonging to "that class in Savannah known as the 'Swelled Heads' who think the up-country people no better than brutes." His wife, Louisa Charlotte Cutler of New York, Ward McAllister's mother, was related to General Francis Marion and was the aunt of Julia Ward Howe and the epicurean lobbyist "Uncle Sam" Ward who married Emily Astor. F. Marion Crawford was another scion of this rather distinguished family.

he characteristically relates in his autobiography, spent his leisure "breathing soft words to lovely Southern maidens, in the piney groves that surround that charming city."

In 1850 father and son followed the gold rush and opened law offices in San Francisco. Always an exquisite, McAllister recalls amid the hurly-burly of the Barbary Coast that "my bed-quilt cost me $250; it was a lovely Chinese floss silk shawl." Under his father's tutelage and favorite maxim, "Be sure, my boy, that you always invite nice people," the young man learned to give sumptuous turkey dinners—with turkeys at $16 apiece—to European clients of the firm. By 1852, having made a small fortune in flush times, McAllister turned eastward, paused in Washington long enough to give a few dinners and serve on the committee for the Inaugural Ball of Pierce in 1853, married a self-effacing heiress named Sarah T. Gibbons, and sailed for Europe on a tour which was less honeymoon than social apprenticeship. He visited Windsor Castle, "dining at the village inn with Her Majesty's *chef*," off partridges which he hoped had been shot by Prince Albert, and was given a peek at the dining-table actually laid out for Queen Victoria, though his mystic communion was cut short by the flurry presaging her imminent arrival. In Paris he saw the baptism of the Prince Imperial in 1856, and in Florence hired an English doctor at $2 a day to supervise his health and get him into Italian Society. He was scandalized by an American girl, who while dancing with him punched the King of Bavaria in the ribs with her elbow, just for the deviltry of it; McAllister, regarding the act as *lèse majesté*, never asked her to dance again. At Baden-Baden "we dined daily within a table or two of the then Prince of Prussia, afterwards the Emperor William, whom [*sic*] I soon discovered was no judge of wine, as I drank the best and he was evidently indifferent to it." Returning to America in 1858 flushed with connoisseurship, he set about transforming the sleepy summer resort of Newport, where he had spent childhood summers, into a kaleidoscope of fashion. He began to give champagne picnics at his newly bought "Bayside Farm," and to simulate rusticity would hire a flock of Southdown sheep and several cows "for half a day, to give the place an animated look," when he was expecting guests from New York. His fishing parties and clambakes, which always ended miraculously around a band and an elevated platform for dancing, were—as he curiously calls all successful *fêtes champêtres*—"English life to perfection." Occasionally he had the luck to snare a strayed British lord, and the cordiality shown him by the Prince of Wales in 1860 helped to consolidate his position.

In New York McAllister saw that Society was divided into the "nobs," old crustacean families who had position without fashion, and the "swells," who had to entertain and be smart in order to win their way. By a skilful mixture of both, he decided, Society might be given that

© Life Publishing Co.

The Social Ladder

C. D. Gibson in *Life* in 1902

solidity needed to resist invasion of the flashiest profiteers. As a matter of fact, McAllister was the only man of his time willing to give his days and nights to the study of heraldry, books of court etiquette, genealogy, and cookery, to getting up balls and banquets, to the making of guest-lists and the interviewing of ambitious mothers with débutante daughters. These things he came to love as a miser his gold. It did not occur to him until near his death in 1895, when Society had dropped him after the publication of his fatuous book, that perhaps he had really been the glorified butler of the Four Hundred rather than its master. But meanwhile—set off against the coruscations of Mrs. Astor's jewels, and the pedigrees of his friends the Riveses, Kanes, and Livingstons—McAllister cut a very imperial figure, and his fame was borne so far by newspapers that, upon his rare travels through the hinterland, yokels would walk miles to catch a glimpse of "the world's greatest dude." In sober truth he was not an imposing sight, with his paunch, a weedy little Van Dyke, rapidly thinning hair, and expensive clothes which he wore so badly that they looked as if they had been thrust upon him. The secret of his success was the immense seriousness with which he took himself and his part as Grand Patriarch. "Fashion," he wrote, "selects its own votaries. You will see certain members of a family born to it, as it were, others of the same family with none of its attributes. You can give no explanation of this; 'One is taken, the other left.' Such and such a man or woman is cited as having been always fashionable. The talent of and for Society develops itself as does the talent for art." With his Huguenot blood, it came to seem to McAllister much like the dogma of predestination.

The means for organizing Society, he saw, lay in a revival of the old assemblies. The New York Dancing Assembly, coeval with the Philadelphia Assembly, had flourished in the eighteenth century; John Jay was one of its ablest managers. In the early nineteenth century the Bachelor Balls had overshadowed all else. When they too declined, a great City Ball, so called from being given at the City Hotel, was organized by subscription among 150 young bloods for the night of January 24, 1841 to revive the "old *noblesse*" of the assemblies. It had been one of the memorable fêtes in the history of New York, with 2000 candles illuminating the ballroom, and 800 guests. The newspapers in their discreet way give us a glimpse of the beautiful Miss H., "one of the fair daughters of a widow lady up town," and the ravishing daughters of Mr. W., the Wall Street financier, who "adorned the room by their presence, hanging carelessly on their father's arm." But after several years, assemblies with new names and brave notions of exclusiveness would begin to languish; a series was held at Delmonico's, and according to tradition disbanded after "a Wall Street banker, not even a native American," crashed their party by threats only to find himself left in solitary grandeur.[6] Others, with more modest subscription price and supper, called themselves the

---

[6]Mrs. Van Rensselaer relates that he told the invitation committee: "I have been investigating the accounts of you gentlemen on the Street. I can assure you that either I get an invitation to the Assembly this year, or else the day after the Assembly each of you will be a ruined man." Curiously enough, the unsavory financial implications of this story escape Mrs. Van Rensselaer. The legend itself is one of the canards of New York social history; in Mrs. Van Rensselaer's account the villain is pretty obviously August Belmont, while according to the version current in the Morris and Coster families, the interloper was a Vanderbilt.

Cheap and Hungries, and to avoid coercion operated through a secret invitation committee.

In 1866–7, shortly before Archibald Gracie King brought the début to Delmonico's, Ward McAllister got up a series of cotillion suppers there— where he sat among *grandes dames* at the head of the table and whispered confidential forecasts about the social fate of newcomers. Encouraged by these successes, and mindful of the great London tradition of Almack's, McAllister in the winter of 1872–73 organized the Patriarchs, a committee of twenty-five men "who had the right to create and lead Society" by inviting to each ball four ladies and five gentlemen on their individual responsibility, which McAllister stressed as a sacred trust. These were the original Patriarchs in the order given by the vizier himself:

John Jacob Astor	Edwin A. Post
William Astor	A. Gracie King
DeLancey Kane	Lewis M. Rutherfurd
Ward McAllister	Robert G. Remsen
George Henry Warren	William C. Schermerhorn
Eugene A. Livingston	Francis R. Rives
William Butler Duncan	Maturin Livingston
E. Templeton Snelling	Alexander Van Rensselaer
Lewis Colford Jones	Walter Langdon
John W. Hamersley	F. G. D'Hauteville
Benjamin S. Welles	C. G. Goodhue
Frederick Sheldon	William R. Travers
Royal Phelps	

For the benefit of juniors—he himself had a very homely daughter—McAllister formed The Family Circle Dancing Class, held in private houses during the first season, and later at Dodworth's and Delmonico's. In accepting or rejecting applicants McAllister had recourse to two touchstones—first and foremost, the pleasure of Mrs. William Astor, special adviser to the Patriarchs, and secondly his own investigations into the candidate's pedigree on the principle that "in my opinion, four generations of gentlemen make as good and true a gentleman as forty." Happily it did not occur to him to examine the pedigree, for example, of William Astor in any such light. It sufficed that Mrs. Astor, who wore a distinguished black wig to dinners and Patriarch balls, was "the Mystic Rose." The Patriarchs continued until 1897, and then finding, with so many

Mrs. Stuyvesant Fish

From a photograph by Brown Brothers

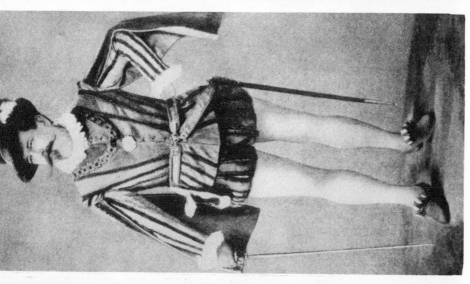

Ward McAllister

In costume at the W. K. Vanderbilt Ball, March 26, 1883

Harold Seton Collection

Mrs. William Astor

From the painting by Carlos Duran

Photographed by Brown Brothers

Guests at Fancy Dress Ball given by James Hazen Hyde at Sherry's

Left to right: Mrs. James Henry Smith, Francis L. V. Hoppin (seated), J. Francis A. Clark, Mrs. James A. Burden, Stanford White, James Henry Smith, Norman Whitehouse, Mrs. Stuyvesant Fish

A Fancy Dress Ball at Delmonico's, 1875

Left to right: Fredericka Belmont, William A. Duer, Lulu Rutherford, Edith Fish
Seated: John Balfour, Isaac Bell

Both photographs from the Harold Seton Collection

other exclusive groups, that outside pressure was forcing them to enlarge, they chose to disband and thus commit honorable *hara-kiri*.

McAllister's flowering time was in the 1880's at the threshold of a new social extravagance, when because of national economics gold replaced silver plate, the orchid dwarfed the rose, music was played between the courses of private dinners, butlers' wages rose from $40 a month to $75, and canvasbacks formerly $2.50 a pair went up to $8 within a decade. McAllister's own vulgar materialism and snobbery—"the mean admiration of mean things," as Thackeray defined it—blended with real knowledge of wines and cooking, and interlarded with anecdotes about the Grand Duke of Tuscany's receptions, suited to perfection the taste of this era. Also, in common with his age, he prided himself upon belonging to the smallest possible groups but giving the largest possible parties: the climax of his book is the New Year's Ball of 1890, given at the Metropolitan Opera House for 1200, which he staged with the assistance of 300 servants in livery. He also encouraged a passing whim in New York—"to build an addition to one's house, to be used but for one night, and to be made large enough to comfortably hold, with the house, one thousand or twelve hundred people."

Yet to the newspapers his greatest fame lay in frequent statements like this to a reporter from the *Tribune* on March 25, 1888: "Why, there are only about 400 people in fashionable New York Society. If you go outside that number you strike people who are either not at ease in a ballroom or else make other people not at ease. See the point? . . . When we give a large ball like the last New Year's ball for 800 guests, we go outside of the exclusive fashionable set, and invite professional men, doctors, lawyers, editors, artists and the like." The Four Hundred caught the fancy of the time. There were endless speculations about its membership, reports that it had been whittled to 150, and the contrary announcement of *Life* in 1890 that it had risen to 1500 because Wall Street had got control and watered the stock. The same magazine proposed to run Ward McAllister and Albert Wettin of Wales on a Society ticket for President and Vice-President, and published a Gibson drawing whose caption divided New York into "the Bohemian set, all brains and no style, Society proper with a fair amount of each, and the Four Hundred, all style and no brains." Gibson caricatured McAllister as a goose-girl rounding up the flock, and as a marshal on a hobby-horse leading the parade of 400 marchers bearing 'scutcheons blazoned with "fur," "lumber," "groceries," and the like.[7] When McAllister's memoirs, *Society as I Have Found it,* appeared, *Life* showed a patrolman who had just collared two drunks in white ties:

> *Captain.* What's that you've got, O'Hara?
> *Roundsman O'Hara.* Society as Oi have found it, sorr.

After tantalizing the public for years McAllister finally gave the official list of his Four Hundred to the New York *Times* on the occasion of Mrs. Astor's great ball, February 1, 1892—for, according to popular report, the dimensions of her ballroom coincided exactly with the limitations of gilt-edged Society. His list, it will be seen, comprises just over 300 names; perhaps, as has been suggested, the rest were abroad, had retired from social activity on account of age or mourning, or else belonged to the unstable fringe which fluctuated from season to season. As a matter of fact, his commitment to "Four Hundred" was probably the whim of a moment, under that genial intoxication which a press-reporter always evoked in McAllister; the list he had in mind was simply the roll-call of Patriarch Balls with its 250 requisite names, and a sprinkling of eligible visitors from other cities and abroad.[8] Again, with corrections made in spelling, and, for comparison with Mrs. Jay's list, the ascertainable occupations of the gentlemen—a sordid detail which McAllister would never have supplied—the authentic Four Hundred were as follows:

Fred H. Allen (lawyer)
Mr. and Mrs. F. R. Appleton (watch manufacturer)
Mr. and Mrs. John Jacob Astor (real estate, railroads)
Mr. and Mrs. William Astor (New York real estate and later Florida
    development; at this time retired capitalist)
Miss Baldwin

[7]Perhaps it was fortunate McAllister could not foresee that Miss Irene Langhorne of Virginia, whom he selected to lead the grand march with him at the Patriarch Ball of 1893, was the future wife of the satirist Charles Dana Gibson.

[8]McAllister somewhat vaguely said of his own computation to the interviewer: "Let me explain, don't you know. There are three dinner dances, don't you know, during the season, and the invitations, don't you see, are issued to different ladies and gentlemen each time, do you understand? So at each dinner dance, you know, are only 150 people of the highest set, don't you know. So, during the season, you see, 400 different invitations are issued."

© *Life Publishing Co.*

For the Centennial Parade

Since the unfortunate Mr. Ward McAllister has nothing else to do, why not allow him to embellish the procession?

C. D. Gibson in *Life* in 1889

C. C. Baldwin (banker)
C. C. Baldwin, Jr. (sportsman)
Miss Louise Baldwin
Mrs. Barbey
Miss Barbey
Mr. and Mrs. James L. Barclay (trustee; fortune largely mercantile)
Mr. and Mrs. Edmund L. Baylies (lawyer)
Miss Amy Bend
Miss Beatrice Bend
Mrs. Cavendish Bentinck
Miss Berryman
Miss Bishop
Heber Bishop (banker; of him McAllister told the *Times* reporter: "You ask me how it is, catch the point, that Heber Bishop is in the inner circle list, although he comes from California and is not of our old New York families. There are two answers to that: his millions and the fact that he is Ogden Mills' in-law. Then, Heber Bishop works for it, dontcherknow. He's an old man, but he will work away dancing all night")
Mr. George S. Bowdoin (banker)
Mr. Temple Bowdoin (banker)
Mr. and Mrs. Frederic Bronson (lawyer)
Harold Brown ⎫
William Harold Brown ⎬ (visitors from Baltimore)
Mr. and Mrs. Lloyd Bryce (editor)
Edward Bulkeley (retired broker)
Miss Burden
Mr. and Mrs. I. Townsend Burden (iron manufacturer)
General and Mrs. Henry L. Burnett (lawyer; U. S. District Attorney)
The Misses Cameron
Duncan Cameron (merchant)
Sir Roderick Cameron (merchant; British consul)
Mr. and Mrs. Harry Cannon (president, Chase National Bank)
Mr. and Mrs. Charles Carroll (income from family trusts)
Mr. and Mrs. Clarence Cary (lawyer)
Mr. and Mrs. Winthrop Chanler (great-grandson of William B. Astor, no occupation)[9]
The Misses Chanler
Mr. and Mrs. Edward Cooper (iron and glue manufacturer)
Mr. Harry Coster (fortune from brokerage)

[9]The Winthrop Chanlers lived in New York during 1891–92 for the purpose of launching three Chanler sisters in Society; see Mrs. Chanler's *Roman Spring*, pp. 232–4, for her comments on the Four Hundred that season.

The Blue Book

William B. Coster (Morgan partner)
Rawlins Cottenet (brokerage)
Miss Crosby
Col. J. Schuyler Crosby (U. S. A.)
Mr. and Mrs. James Cross (English merchant)
Mr. and Mrs. S. Van Rensselaer Cruger (real estate)
Miss Edith Cushing
Mr. Thomas F. Cushing (lawyer)
Mrs. Brockholst Cutting
Mr. F. Bayard Cutting (income from real estate investments)
F. Brockholst Cutting (the same; these Cuttings belonged to a group
    of eight sporting and affluent young bachelors called "the Dudes")
Mr. and Mrs. W. Bayard Cutting (lawyer)
Robert L. Cutting, Jr. (broker)
William Cutting, Jr. (income from real estate)
Mr. and Mrs. Paul Dana (editor, New York *Sun*)
Mr. and Mrs. George B. De Forest (retired merchant)
Miss Delafield
Dr. and Mrs. Francis Delafield (professor of medicine, Columbia)
Mr. and Mrs. Chauncey M. Depew (law, railroads, politics)
Mr. and Mrs. Frederic J. De Peyster (lawyer)
Mr. and Mrs. Elisha Dyer, Jr. (brokerage)
Mr. and Mrs. Duncan Elliott (real estate)
Mr. and Mrs. Hamilton Fish, Jr. (lawyer)
Mr. and Mrs. Stuyvesant Fish (railroads)
H. De Courcey Forbes ("clubman" and sportsman)
Mr. and Mrs. C. G. Francklyn (brokerage)
Theodore Frelinghuysen (treasurer Coats Thread Co.)
J. C. Furman (broker)
Mr. and Mrs. Ogden Goelet (real estate)
Mr. and Mrs. Robert Goelet (law and real estate)
Miss Grant
Miss Greene
Alister Greene (lawyer)
Frank Gray Griswold (Long Island gentleman farmer; horseman;
    formerly in shipping and Lorillard Tobacco Co.)
Augustus C. Gurnee (brokerage)
Alexander M. Hadden (social work, philanthropy; married to a proba-
    tion officer)
John A. Hadden, Jr. (inherited income)
Miss Hall
Mr. and Mrs. Valentine G. Hall (real estate)
Mr. and Mrs. Charles F. Havemeyer (sugar and banking)

The Saga of American Society

Robert F. Hawkes (no business; died young)

Mr. and Mrs. Peter Cooper Hewitt (iron manufacturer)

Miss Hoffman

Mrs. Charles P. Hoffman

Robert Hone, Jr. (securities)

Meredith Howland (inherited fortune made in shipping by Gardiner G. Howland)

Mr. and Mrs. Thomas Howard ("clubman," cotillion leader)

Mr. and Mrs. Richard Irvin (merchant)

Langdon Irving (known as "Sunbeam"; reformer, who courageously incurred much banter by accompanying Dr. Parkhurst on his investigations of red-light districts)

Mr. and Mrs. Columbus Iselin (banker)

Isaac Iselin (broker)

Miss Jaffray

Mrs. William Jaffray

Col. and Mrs. William Jay (lawyer, sportsman)

Miss Beatrix Jones (future landscape architect, now Mrs. Max Farrand)

Mr. and Mrs. F. Rhinelander Jones (real estate investments)

Shipley Jones (broker)

Mr. and Mrs. De Lancey Kane (sportsman)

S. Nicholson Kane ⎫
Woodbury Kane ⎬ (inherited income; sportsmen and "dudes")
           ⎭

Elizabeth Kean

Julian Kean (lawyer)

Mr. and Mrs. Frederick Kernochan (lawyer)

Mr. and Mrs. J. P. Kernochan (merchant)

Col. and Mrs. Lawrence Kip (Civil War service; retired capitalist)

Miss Kip

Miss Knowlton

Mr. and Mrs. Luther Kountze (banker)

Mr. and Mrs. James Lanier (banker)

Arthur Leary (merchant)

Miss Leiter

Miss Clarissa Livingston

Edward Livingston (banker)

Edward De Peyster Livingston (lawyer)

Mr. and Mrs. Henry B. Livingston (broker)

Mrs. Maturin Livingston

Miss Lusk

Clement March (real estate)

Peter Marié (broker)

Mr. and Mrs. Charles H. Marshall (merchant)

The Blue Book

Mr. and Mrs. Bradley Martin (retired capitalist)
F. T. Martin (brother of above, investments, "clubman," amateur author)
Miss McAllister
Ward McAllister (retired lawyer)
Mr. and Mrs. H. W. McVickar (real estate; amateur caricaturist)
Mr. and Mrs. Ogden Mills (mining stock and other investment)
Mr. and Mrs. Clement C. Moore (cotton broker, grandson of the theologian who wrote "'Twas the Night Before Christmas")
Miss Anne Morgan
Mr. and Mrs. A. Newbold Morris (income from real estate and family trusts)
Miss Eva C. Morris
Mr. and Mrs. R. Mortimer (real estate)
Charles Munn (editor of Munn & Co., publishers of *Scientific American,* and patent agents)
Mrs. Frederick Nelson
Mr. and Mrs. Thomas Newbold (retired capitalist)
Mr. and Mrs. Charles M. Oelrichs (banker)
Stephen H. Olin (lawyer)
Miss Otis
James Otis (broker)
James V. Parker
Mr. and Mrs. Francis Key Pendleton (lawyer)
Miss Perry
Mrs. William A. Perry
Richard Peters ("clubman" and cotillion leader)
Miss Pierson
General and Mrs. J. Fred Pierson (iron manufacturer)
Mr. and Mrs. Benjamin C. Porter (artist)
Mr. and Mrs. Charles A. Post (lawyer)
Edward C. Post (inherited income)
Mr. and Mrs. George B. Post (architect)
Clarkson Potter (lawyer; U. S. Congressman)
Mr. and Mrs. H. N. Potter (architect)
Julian Potter (broker)
Miss Cora Randolph
Goold H. Redmond (sportsman)
T. J. Oakley Rhinelander (lawyer, real estate administrator)
Robert Kerr Richards (broker)
Mr. and Mrs. S. D. Ripley (broker)
James W. Ritchie (inherited income)
Mr. and Mrs. George L. Rives (lawyer)

The Saga of American Society

Mr. and Mrs. Christopher Robert (importer, son of merchant philanthropist who founded Robert College, Constantinople)

Mr. and Mrs. H. Robins (*sic,* probably Henry P. Robbins, lawyer)

D. T. L. Robinson (broker)

Mr. and Mrs. Douglas Robinson, Jr. (real estate)

Randolph Robinson (lawyer)

Mrs. Burke Roche

Miss Rogers

Mrs. Rogers

Mr. and Mrs. James Roosevelt Roosevelt (sportsman, retired capitalist)

Mr. and Mrs. Lewis Rutherfurd (astronomer, with inherited income)

Miss Sands

Mr. and Mrs. Philip Schuyler (lawyer)

Miss Shepard

Mr. and Mrs. Edward Shepard (lawyer)

Mr. and Mrs. William Watts Sherman (banker)

Miss Adele Sloan

Mr. and Mrs. William D. Sloane (carpets, interior decorating)

J. Clinch Smith (lawyer)

Mr. and Mrs. Byam K. Stevens (broker)

Miss Elizabeth Stevens

Lispenard Stewart (lawyer, "clubman")

Mr. and Mrs. William Rhinelander Stewart (lawyer; trustee of real estate)

Miss Stokes

Mr. and Mrs. Anson Phelps Stokes (real estate investment; copper)

Mr. and Mrs. F. K. Sturgis (banker)

Mr. and Mrs. Walter Lispenard Suydam (broker)

Miss Tailer

E. N. Tailer (real estate)

Marquise de Talleyrand

Belmont Tiffany (investments, sportsman)

Miss Tooker

G. Mead Tooker (lawyer)

Mr. and Mrs. Hamilton McKown Twombly (manufacturer of lighters)

Mr. and Mrs. Cornelius Vanderbilt (railroads)

George W. Vanderbilt (gentleman farmer of "Biltmore," North Carolina)

Mrs. A. Van Rensselaer

Miss Alice Van Rensselaer

Miss Mabel Van Rensselaer

James Varnum (lawyer)

Mr. and Mrs. James M. Waterbury (manufacturer of cordage)

The Blue Book

Alexander S. Webb (broker)
General and Mrs. Alexander S. Webb (president C. C. N. Y.)
Miss Carrie Webb
Mr. and Mrs. W. Seward Webb (railroads)
Mr. and Mrs. Benjamin Welles (inherited wealth; parents of present
    Sumner Welles, State Department, Washington)
Mr. and Mrs. W. Storrs Wells (manufacturer of scales)
Miss Wetmore
Governor and Mrs. Wetmore (banker in house of George Peabody,
    later Senator from Rhode Island)
Mr. Worthington Whitehouse (real estate)
Mr. and Mrs. William C. Whitney (lawyer, organizer of street rail-
    ways, president Manufacturing Investment Co.)
Mrs. C. A. Whittier
Matthew Astor Wilks (inherited real estate)
Miss Willing
Barton Willing (from Philadelphia; inherited income)
Miss Georgiana L. Wilmerding
Miss Grace Wilson
Mr. and Mrs. Orme Wilson (banker)
Richard T. Wilson, Jr. (cotton broker)
Miss Winthrop
Mr. and Mrs. Buchanan Winthrop (lawyer)
Egerton Winthrop (banker)
F. B. Winthrop (lawyer)
Mr. and Mrs. J. J. Wysong (trustee)

When he divulged this list McAllister was already waning in authority.
He himself had written, in urging "clever men and politicians" to play
the game of Society as they do in Europe, that "there is no power like
the social power; it makes and unmakes." Soon he began to feel the
edge of his own remark, when after the ridicule heaped upon his book
by the press, Society began to laugh at his pompous ways and continued
pronunciamentos—such as his advice to the Faithful in 1893 that they
might go and see the World's Fair without much social hazard if they
associated only with moneyed Chicagoans.[10] His fall, like that of

[10]McAllister's position was on the wane even before the publication of his book. He
had grandiose schemes for the Centennial Ball of 1889 in New York, but the committee made up of Hamilton Fish, Elbridge T. Gerry, Colonel William Jay, and their
friends relegated him to the discard. "McAllister is a discharged servant. That is all,"
Stuyvesant Fish curtly told the press. Piqued, McAllister went down to Washington

The Saga of American Society

Humpty Dumpty, was irrevocable—and after forty years the mention of his name to the children of his Patriarchs, who today are the Old Guard of Newport and Fifth Avenue, awakes a patronizing smile. Who could ever have taken him seriously?[11]

McAllister was by no means the sole dictator of taste and fashion in his own day. In clothes there was E. Berry Wall, known for a generation as the best-dressed man in New York; while August Belmont the epicurean banker, William K. Vanderbilt the yachtsman, and Pierre Loril-

and sulked until the ball was over. Then he returned to deride it: "A young lieutenant, mind you, dancing with Mrs. Astor! I don't wonder the country laughs! And young Harry Cannon, forsooth! And, mind you, young Creighton Webb! Why, as a dance of dignity the thing was a farce! I am glad that I had nothing to do with such a Fishball." For the nonce he succeeded in convincing the newspapers that the Centennial Ball without him had been ludicrous indeed, and the next season he was allowed to manage the great New Year's Ball to his heart's content. But the boredom of his own Four Hundred was increasing, and after the publication of his silly memoir McAllister found himself definitely cashiered.

[11]Yet one who did was that strange individual, the Rev. Charles Wilbur de Lyon Nichols, or Nicholls as he spelled his name in later life. An Episcopal clergyman of New York City, he was intensely proud that a newspaper once called him "Ward McAllister's first Apostle on the Philosophy of Society," and attempted to capture the mantle by publishing in 1904 *The Ultra-Fashionable Peerage of America, with a few appended Essays on Ultra-Smartness*. In this volume he selects 150 as "the ultra-smart," with Mrs. Astor still queen and flanked by the "viceregal leaders" Mrs. Ogden Mills, the younger Mrs. Cornelius Vanderbilt (the Grace Wilson of McAllister's day), Mrs. John Jacob Astor, and Mrs. Ogden Goelet. The next of his concentric circles embraces the 400, with a few fashionables from "the provincial towns" like Philadelphia, Chicago, San Francisco; the final group, the 600, includes "the outer fringe" and some Knickerbocker families with their "coarse Holland Dutch market gardening blood," together with "society in the crude." The test of belonging to the 400 is an invitation to Mrs. Astor's ball; of being in the sacred ranks of 150, a dinner invitation from Mrs. Astor. "Not to have dined at Mrs. Astor's virtually debars one from eminent leadership in that surpassing coterie known as national and international American society." He cautions his readers that the inner circle never speak of themselves as "the 150" or "the 400," but merely know that there is where they belong. In this quaint book the Rev. Mr. Nichols mingles genealogies with fashion notes—*e.g.,* he condones Mr. T. Suffern Tailer's devotion to green suits because "when one has the blood of both a Suffern and a Tailer coursing through his veins, he can do a variety of things with impunity."

Among more recent attempts to divide American Society (that is, the Society of New York and Newport) into restrictive pens, should be mentioned that probable transcript of his mother's visiting lists which Cornelius Vanderbilt, Jr., gives in *Farewell to Fifth Avenue,* pp. 102 ff. He presents 75 names as comprising "The Backbone of American Society"—Vanderbilts, Astors, Whitneys, Millses, Iselins, Schermerhorns, Morgans—and about 150 more comprehending "The Outer Fringe"—Mackays, Rockefellers, Van Rensselaers, Condé Nast, Mr. and Mrs. Harrison Williams, Frank Crowninshield, and others—who are recognized because of wealth, traditional prestige, or journalistic power. It is a curiously naïve document.

The Social Push—Almost In

C. D. Gibson in *Life* in 1902

lard of Tuxedo Park, a septuagenarian of today who has always been a master of arts and graces, represented other facets of Society. The Pepys of the age was E. N. Tailer, keeper of a voluminous diary of social events, and its wit was William R. Travers—*bon vivant,* judge of wines, patron of horse-racing, member of twenty-seven clubs, and host over five luxurious establishments. Samples of his wit which convulsed Society in the decade before his death in 1887 now seem a little tarnished—like his explanation for stuttering worse in New York than in his native Baltimore, "this is a d-d-damned sight b-b-bigger city," or his blank question addressed to the Siamese twins after he had wonderingly examined the ligature between them, "B-b-brothers, I presume?" Though Travers's ability in law and business was unimpeachable, his fame in repartee rested too exclusively upon the affinity between stammering and drollery which Charles Lamb and Lewis Carroll had built up as a great English-speaking tradition. The most celebrated diner-out during this era of New York was Peter Marié, descendant of French West Indian stock and heir to a comfortable fortune. A perennial bachelor, with the tastes of an exquisite, he collected fans, snuff-boxes, card cases, and other *bijouterie;* he was an amateur poet and loved to give such parties as the one described in his invitation for February 14, 1870, as "an Intellectual Tea, on St. Valentine's Day, after the manner of the Hotel Rambouillet, and no guest can hope for Tea, until he has undergone the reading of one of Mr. Peter Marié's Poems." He was a popular house-guest at Southampton, Bar Harbor, and Lenox—where he always offered prizes in contests ranging from foot-races to essay-writing on the subject "What is Charm?" Best-known was his platonic seraglio of 300 miniatures painted at his command by the best artists of the time, to illustrate every type of feminine beauty. The belles of two generations in New York, Philadelphia, Boston, Baltimore, and New Orleans were flattered to be asked to sit to a miniaturist commissioned by Mr. Marié. Rather characteristically he changed his intention of bequeathing his collection to the Metropolitan Museum and instead gave it to the New-York Historical Society, doubtless feeling that his toasts of yesteryear would never be ogled disrespectfully. Though Marié would have been horrified to receive any of the publicity which attended Ward McAllister, he also had his share in the moulding of New York Society—as contemporary letters and memoirs testify—with his fastidious entertaining and gallantly archaic eighteenth-century grace. American Society has had its few dandies in the sense known to Savile Row and the boulevards of Paris —the faint aura of cologne upon cambric, the *boutonnière* ordered daily from the florist, "the nice conduct of a clouded cane" or more accurately the malacca stick. Richard S. Fay in Boston of the 1850's and 1860's was such, with his fine dancing and horsemanship, his taste for water-colors, and his distinguished manner; today the type lingers there with Mr. Hooper Hooper and a few members of the Tavern Club. Philadelphia has produced no exotic beaux; Williams Carter, handsome, charming man-about-town, was typical of its ideal a generation ago. One of the greatest of bachelor dandies was the late Walter De Courcey Poulteney of Baltimore, invariably called by his full name; his audacities included stiff Alice-blue dress shirts with pink ties. For his fine collection of early American glass Henry Ford recently paid $175,000. Dropped in 1885 for obscure reasons from the dinner-list of Mrs. David L. Bartlett—noted *grande dame* who had risen from the ranks—Walter De Courcey Poulteney was finally re-invited in 1929, and just before the guests sat down at table, while the hostess' attention was briefly diverted, he turned over a plate and inspected it with the characteristic and audible comment, "Ha, the same old china." Among New Yorkers of the *ancien régime* who still remain, Mr. Creighton Webb is most noteworthy, since the greatest exquisite of the Gilded Age, James Hazen Hyde—heir of the Equitable Life Assurance fortune built by his father, and a noted whip, book-collector, gourmet, patron of opera and the theatre, with a French and Harvard education—has spent the last thirty years in Paris, after newspaper disapproval of his $200,000 *bal masqué* at Sherry's threatened to wreck public confidence in the Equitable.

Another major-domo of Society, who took his leadership rather in the spirit of Puck than a Patriarch, was Harry Lehr. Born in Baltimore in 1869, the son of a tobacco and snuff importer, he was left almost penniless in his 'teens. During this phase of his life he came to hate the drabness and poverty of boarding-houses, and grew into a youthful opportunist resolved to live by his wits. He got his social start by female impersonations at the Paint and Powder Club in Baltimore, and then was invited to Newport by Mrs. Townsend Burden and Mrs. Elisha Dyer. He set out to amuse rather than dictate to Society, and made rapid progress among the bored and idle. Ward McAllister he professed to regard, with attenuated blasphemy, as "the voice crying in the wilderness who prepared the way for me." He sent a bruised flower to a hospital by special ambulance, and by a score of increasingly outrageous pranks made excellent copy for the press. Liking his wit and impudence, Society undertook to support him by drinking the champagne he sold on commission, and lending him such *réclame* that tailors, jewellers, and restaurateurs gladly supplied his wants, until his marriage to Elizabeth Drexel Dahlgren secured him a permanent income. Harry Lehr's forte was mimicry, usually with a dash of bitters: thus when a rumor was circulating about the Indian blood of Adèle Stevens he turned up as the dinner-partner of that lady dressed in feathers and war-paint. His frequent impersonation of women and the wardrobe of dresses and wigs upon which he drew for such occasions, his shrill high-pitched voice and fluttering mannerisms, led to conjectures about his private life which his widow recently pointed up in her book based supposedly upon the "locked diary" which he kept. But among the dozen living New Yorkers who knew him well and observed the actions of a frivolous but patently transparent existence, such rumors are persistently denied; they report Harry Lehr as apparently sexless, an ephemera who adored scintillating and witty women—their perfumes, silks, and snobberies—even as Alexander Pope, whom he resembled in malice though not in genius.

During the dozen golden years before the Great War the dominant type of "society" man was the cotillion leader—Elisha Dyer, Worthington Whitehouse, Thomas Howard, Richard Peters, Craig Wadsworth, Alexander Hadden, Phœnix Ingraham. The usual divertissement of Society consisted of an elaborate dinner, followed by a dance usually with a cotillion, giving way to a champagne supper and more dancing, with a breakfast-party at sunrise. Hostesses vied with one another in the costliness of cotillion favors; each man was given a favor to present to the girl of his choice, and each lady received a corresponding favor for a man. At the cotillion given in 1910 by Mrs. George Gould to announce the engagement of her daughter Marjorie to Anthony J. Drexel, Jr., the souvenirs of gold and precious stones—jewelled pins, charms, and rings for the women, and jewelled scarf-pins for the men—were the sensation of the town; the leader of the most intricate figure in this cotillion was the late Justice Phœnix Ingraham. Other hostesses supplied gold cigarette-cases for the men and millinery boxes containing smart Paris hats for the ladies; often the total cost of cotillion favors for a single party ran as high as $10,000. Cotillions generally began with a Grand Right and Left to exchange greetings all around, and then followed with a basket figure; great ingenuity in costumes, lighting, and pantomime appeared in these later figures—such for instance as the batting of iridescent tennis balls by the dancers, across a net shot through with multicolored spangles. This was the epoch in American Society which might be called the Field of the Cloth of Gold, and such dancing-groups as the old Assemblies which continued at the Waldorf up to 1903, and the Bachelors which inherited the tradition of the Patriarchs, took on new vivacity and luster.

Since the Great War and successive waves of jazz, tango, and swing time, the dancing of Society has changed as sharply as its frocks, but certain groups remain in serene possession of the old social traditions. Of these the New York Junior Assembly, heir of the one-time Junior Cotillions, is chief, recruited from débutantes bearing the names of old New York families—who are allowed to remain in the coterie for its two dances on first Fridays between December and February at the Ritz, and then after a season must give place to new débutantes. Its executive committee is invariably made up of Morgans, Satterlees, Osborns, and Kings, and to the social mongrel its fences appear formidable indeed. Yet even more exclusive is the Metropolitan Dancing Class, the "Met," whose graduates are always welcomed into the Junior Assembly as its inmost ring. So called from a brief season at the Metropolitan Club, the Metropolitan Dancing Class selects sixteen girls annually out of some 400 candidates; they are between sixteen and eighteen years of age, and only one child can be taken from each impeccably pedigreed family. Six letters are written in behalf of each applicant, and receive the most careful scrutiny from Mrs. Herbert L. Satterlee and Mrs. James Gore King. The "Mets" are not exciting, and indeed are not meant to be; but they successfully induct the sub-débutante into the adagio paces of Old Society. Dancing begins at nine-thirty, and closes at one. Girls appear in long white gloves, and dance sedately with blue-blooded lads also in white gloves. Alcohol and cheek-to-cheek dancing are strictly forbidden, and any girl on the "Met" list who is reported seen in night clubs or other queer places is immediately dropped. Parvenus seldom attempt this ultimate arcana of New York Society for a variety of reasons, among others being the fact that they have never heard of it. It remains therefore in undisputed possession of De Peysters, Livingstons, Van Rensselaers, Morgans, and Jays like a somewhat juvenile ark of the covenant. In preparation for entering it and several other less impregnable coteries the fashionable dancing classes of New York flourish, teaching youth to make its bow, waltz, and enter a room gracefully. Of these the most eligible are run by Miss Edith M. Benjamin, lately retired from active teaching, and by Miss Adeline King Robinson.

The Philadelphia Assembly is richly traditional, the Creole balls of New Orleans long kept their historic place, and the Boston Assemblies, held first at Copley Hall and later at the Somerset Club, inherit luster. Fairly exclusive is the Richmond German, founded in 1870 at the house of the late John H. Montagne. In Baltimore the Bachelors' Cotillion, started soon after the War of 1812 in the heyday of Pattersons, Olivers, Carrolls, Catons, and Browns, is still the incontrovertible test of Society. Its managers, who are either bachelors or else benedicts who have married after the age of fifty, dictate its admissions; wealth and poverty cause no tremor of the scales, and on occasion the managers have presented party-dresses with their compliments to impoverished young ladies who otherwise could not attend. In Baltimore too, it may be added, running a boarding-house "for gentlemen" does not disqualify socially, as the Warfields have fully demonstrated. Reporters from New York find this attitude difficult to digest. Baltimore Society—now under the control of aging Mrs. Henry Barton Jacobs, wife of the great tuberculosis specialist, and her junior affiliates, ex-Ambassador and Mrs. John W. Garrett—is as conservative as any in America. It is there, after a quarter-century, that a light still burns day and night and a butler stands in readiness to welcome the long-lost prodigal son of a social family. And there too intermarriages and identical names have so entangled old clans that a custom, much like that found in Mexico City and Spanish aristocracy, has arisen—of forming a legal signature by adding one's mother's maiden initial to the full name, e.g., "John Eager Howard of J.," or Edgar Allan Poe of M.," to distinguish an individual from his flock of cousins. There also a late famous hostess ate her dinner upon a sort of planchette, set upon the dining-table before her, to assert her eminence over her guests; among malicious people it was reported that she had been originally her millionaire husband's laundress, while the more charitable maintained she was once his housekeeper. In Baltimore too lingers the custom known among the Dutch families of New York, of New Year's Day visiting by gentlemen in cutaway and silk hat, while their ladies remain at home to receive callers and dispense egg-nog, apple toddy which was laid down the previous year, and black fruitcake. In Baltimore, Society encourages such locutions as "he don't" and "acrost the street"; furthermore, any one who pronounces the "ti" in "Baltimore" is either an outsider or an insufferable æsthete. It may be noted that in common with New Orleans and St. Louis, Baltimore Society is warmly sympathetic toward Catholics. That is, Catholics who meet its traditional standards; for the Raskobs, with the catapult of their General Motors millions, have found it as unassailable as the Capitoline Hill.

The most celebrated annual balls in America are still the St. Cecilias of Charleston. The St. Cecilia Society began in 1737 as an amateur musical club which gave a concert each year on St. Cecilia's Day. Not until 1762 was it formally organized; in the later eighteenth century Charles Cotesworth Pinckney and Ralph Izard played in its orchestra. For generations the Society met invariably on Thursdays at nine P.M., with the sole exception of a grand concert and ball given on a Saturday in 1819 in honor of President Monroe. Gradually the concert became less important, and the dancing more so, until after 1821 the ball reigned alone. For many years the first St. Cecilia was held in January, with two more following in February before Lent; since the Depression only one St. Cecilia is given. In its heydey prior to the Civil War the Society held its festivals in St. Andrew's Hall, where it kept a private cellar of Madeira and champagne, as well as plate, damask, glass, and china. To serve its suppers every butler and footman among the slave population who could obtain a swallow-tailed coat was mobilized; upon coming to his own "fambly" he always grinned proudly. Although cynics today speak of the St. Cecilia as a carefully fostered device for advertising picturesque old Charleston, and tell stories of occasional Yankees who have bought their way by threatening to fire their aristocratic clerks, it is a fine fragrant tradition and virtually impervious to commerce. It is not impossible for the outsider to be invited—and indeed its members are expected to bring their house-guests, up to the grand total of fifty non-subscribers, unless they happen to be Jews, actors, or divorcés. If he becomes a resident of Charleston the newcomer may find himself elected to membership, but it will be because Hugers, Rhetts, Rutledges, Pinckneys, and Manigaults approve of him as a human being rather than as a financial factor. Charleston has a gay, quixotic contempt for great riches, and proffers in its St. Cecilias the social equivalent of the needle's eye to the Biblical camel. Sons and grandsons of members are elected without challenge unless they are sheep of notorious blackness. Once a man is approved, the names of ladies in his household are put on "the list," and only death or permanent removal from the city erases them. Apparently nobody has ever been dropped from the St. Cecilia, though the possibility remains awesome. This is practically the only assembly outside Philadelphia and Baltimore in which women have no voice or share— its managers, elected for life, are remarkably deaf to feminine persuasion and intrigue. The president chooses for his supper-partner the latest bride, to share with him the honors of that brave and stately occasion. Early in the 1920's, the St. Cecilias threatened to yield before the first great Yankee invasion since Sherman; but with a gallantry worthy of Fort Sumter the defences were tightened, and today the "débutantes" (as old families speak of the newcomers) are somewhat more scarce.

Other means of social differentiation exist besides dictators and dancing assemblies in the United States. Perhaps most important of these is *The Social Register.* Its precursors were such publications in New York City as Maurice M. Minton's expansion of the visiting-list of his mother, Mrs. Charles A. Minton, which he called *The List: a Visiting and Shopping Directory.* Containing over 3000 names in 1880 and thereafter, Minton's *List* provided a dilatory domicile section ("Not located" and "Not permanently settled for the winter"), and admitted advertising. A similar publication called *Society* was merged with it in 1884 under the title *Society-List and Club Register;* more ambitious, it added club addresses and "the maiden names of married ladies." Other social guides followed, including Miss E. D. Bininger's *Manhattan Visiting List,* begun in 1899, which arranged the inhabitants of fashionable New York by their street-numbers for the convenience of callers and footmen, in that age of furious card-leaving; more lasting popularity has attended the series of Dau's *Blue Books,* offering a list of "permanent residents arranged alphabetically and by streets and much other valuable social information."

But the most signal success came to an enterprise begun in 1887 by Louis Keller, the son of a patent lawyer of French origin, Charles M.

Keller, who had left him a small life-income and a sound though inconspicuous social standing. Louis Keller, then thirty years old, dined regularly at the Calumet Club and spent most of his time in scheming gentlemanly ways of enhancing his livelihood. He was a gunsmith, a farmer and proprietor of the Wat Nong Dairy, and an innovator of golf at Baltusrol, N. J., where he owned a modest acreage and ran a one-locomotive railway between Summit, Baltusrol, and Newark, nicknamed by his friends "Keller's Baltusrol & Pacific." Seeing the rapid expansion of New York Society among the rich, the curiosity awakened in the populace by Ward McAllister's teasing allusions to the *crème de la crème,* and the possibility of supplying advertisers with what a less kind age would dub a "sucker list," Keller launched into journalism. On the one hand he sired a gossip sheet which turned into a prodigal, *The American Queen and Town Topics,* and on the other a list of the Best People from which advertising was wisely excluded but which merchants might buy, *The Social Register.* The latter gratifyingly became a white hope. It has been suggested that the rise of the telephone directory, so useful yet democratic and unwieldy, helped Keller's *Social Register,* as did the hearty support of his friends among New York clubs like the Calumet and the Union. Here at last, unencumbered with advertisements of dressmakers and wine-merchants, enhanced by large clear type and a pleasant binding of orange and black—which, if anything, suggested the colors of America's most elegant university—was a convenient list of one's friends and potential friends. It gave names, addresses, telephone numbers, maiden names and wives' names by previous marriages —a boon in the dawning day of divorce—as well as clubs, colleges, summer residences, and yachts. It was an immediate triumph.

Keller copyrighted the name and appearance of his volume, and in 1910 entrusted a Boston edition into the trustworthy hands of Mrs. John J. Attridge, sometime clerk in the vital statistics office of the State of Massachusetts and secretary to the Society editor of the Boston *Herald.* Other expansions took over Philadelphia, Washington, Baltimore, and Chicago. In 1922 Louis Keller died of cancer; it was fitting that among the mourners at his funeral reporters noticed the daughter of Ward McAllister, Mrs. Albert Nelson Lewis. But *The Social Register* went on and on, claiming a maximum of twenty-one cities at its peak in 1925; though nine of these were dropped later, "for lack of interest." Keller's heir, his nephew Charles Keller Beekman, has managed *The Register* with superior business ability, though as is well known he would be glad to sell it for $600,000 to responsible persons and relieve a busy lawyer from carrying the keys of a social St. Peter. Still, the routine of reading application forms which all candidates are required to file, the appraisal of endorsements from friends already listed, and the actual acceptance or rejection of an estimated 75 per cent of all aspirants, fall to Keller's trusted secretary, Miss Bertha M. Eastmond. She lives quietly at Summit, N. J., near the Baltusrol Golf Club and visits about once a month the offices of the Social Register Association at 381 Fourth Avenue. She has never inserted her own name in *The Social Register,* and is believed by most metropolitan society editors—who long to penetrate the mystery so essential to her success—to be the daughter of a railway conductor. But this, perhaps, is because of her business association with that incubus "Keller's Baltusrol and Pacific," otherwise the Rahway Valley Railroad, so long entangled with the destinies of *The Social Register.*

An efficient impersonality, detachment, and air of secret inquisition surround *The Social Register.* A certain anonymity is essential to its continued success and prestige. Yet it has been reliably reported that its decisions are made by Mr. Keller's former stenographer, with occasional help from Mr. Beekman and his law partner Morton Bogue and a third lawyer, Ralph Wolcott, attorney for the Keller estate; and that its correspondents in cities outside New York are chiefly decayed gentlewomen or ex-society reporters, who for a salary averaging $25 a month are willing to check the credentials of local applicants, keep track of births, marriages, divorces, scandals, and deaths, and read proofs of their respective editions. Among Society's more naïve members, various superstitions exist about *The Social Register.* Its august tribunal is thought to meet and examine testimony gained from a terrifyingly unknown espionage, whereas its chief source of information is the newspapers. It is safe to say that any one who keeps out of their columns—whatever his private life may be, or clandestine rumors may report—will not fall foul of *The Social Register.* Another pious error believed by many is that a copy of *The Social Register* may be owned only by those persons whose names occur therein, although in truth its publishers rejoice to sell a New York *Register* in exchange for $7, and for $50 to supply the entire repertory—Washington, Philadelphia, Chicago,

The Blue Book

Boston, St. Louis, Pittsburgh, Cleveland, Cincinnati and Dayton, San Francisco, Baltimore, and Buffalo. Newspapers, magazines, shops, hotels, steamship lines, and dude ranches find *The Social Register* well worth the money. About 10 per cent of its total 33,000 copies for all cities go to commercial firms. At present it lists some 90,000 names and addresses in its November issue. The annual profit to the Association is estimated at $50,-000; other rewards, such as the quiet sense of power, and of an apparently needful work well done, are intangible.

According to *The Social Register,* in New York approximately 27,000 out of more than 6,500,000 people are in Society, or four in every thousand. Washington, where the President and Vice-President, the Supreme Court and Cabinet, the diplomatic corps, and all United States senators are listed automatically, runs to the highest percentage of distinction, 14 per thousand. In a former preface *The Social Register* described its eligibles as "those families who by descent or by social standing or from other qualifications are naturally included in the best society of any particular city or cities." This statement is both vague and elastic, as policy demands. If it is hard to codify the principles of admission, it is even more difficult to dogmatize about expulsions—which the penny press regards somewhat luridly as the equivalent of social ostracism or the pillory. Unfavorable publicity seems as near as one can come to the reason for banishment, but this again is applied with more intuition than logic. More than a decade ago James A. Stillman and his wife, later Mrs. McCormick, were dropped because of their quarrel over the paternity of young Guy Stillman; yet Mrs. Reginald Vanderbilt has never imperiled her status by disputes with Mrs. Harry Payne Whitney over the custody of Gloria Vanderbilt, nor by the scandalous allegations involving European nobility. *The Social Register* remained loyal to Samuel Insull and to the principals in the Massie case, yet dropped Cornelius Vanderbilt, Jr., after the publication of *Farewell to Fifth Avenue. Mésalliances* are almost always grounds for exclusion, but just what constitutes a socially impossible marriage is debatable. Although the stage is customarily regarded as beyond the pale, distinguished actresses like Eleanor Robson, now Mrs. August Belmont, and even an occasional musical comedy girl like Mae Daw upon her marriage to a son of Louis G. Kaufman, have found themselves in *The Social Register;* while Miss Jane Wyatt of the Van Rensselaer clan, on the Broadway stage and in Hollywood, is gladly retained. Mrs. Post, author of

The Saga of American Society

Etiquette, wrote to the Social Register Association in 1925 at the time it recorded the marriage of Leonard Kip Rhinelander to the Negress Alice Jones, preparatory to dropping Mr. Rhinelander forever from its pages: "I happen to know that you announce all the *mésalliances* of those on your list; that ends them, and unsuitable behavior ostracizes—a stand which I greatly admire, and one which in certain prominent cases has shown no little courage of principle on your part." *The Social Register* not infrequently forgives its misbehaving children when they divorce ineligible mates and remarry into the fold—as happened to Katharine Harris, expelled for marrying John Barrymore in 1910, but reinstated after her divorce and retained as Mrs. Alexander Dallas Bache Pratt, and to Blanche Oelrichs, who married John Barrymore in 1920, but is now Mrs. Harrison Tweed; later wives of Mr. Barrymore have offered no problem to *The Social Register*. Within the past season it has patiently borne the levity of Mrs. George L. K. Morris (Estelle C. Frelinghuysen), who included the name of her four-year old Pekingese, Rose, in the *Summer Register* for 1936. Insult was added to injury because Rose was unpedigreed.

Doctor Harvey W. Zorbaugh, sociologist who made a careful study of *The Gold Coast and the Slum* eight years ago for the University of Chicago, reported concerning the metropolis of the Mid-West: "One of the amazing things about *The Social Register* is the utterly unquestioning acceptance which Society accords to its verdicts. While talking with several of the acknowledged leaders of Chicago society one afternoon the writer asked what was the criterion of social position. It was agreed that acceptance by *The Social Register* was perhaps the safest criterion. Yet no one had the faintest idea who selected the names for *The Social Register,* or upon what basis they were included." Even those cities which are too small or apathetic to support a *Social Register* have customarily a private enterprise which issues a "Social Record," "Social Blue Book," or some other imitative volume of less dignity, sustained—unlike the authentic *Registers*—by advertising and levies upon the gullible.[12] The newest

[12]The customary procedure is to telephone a non-subscriber, leave the impression that his or her name is under consideration, and suggest the payment of perhaps $5 to ensure its inclusion and prompt delivery of the forthcoming volume. The true *Social Register* operates in no such shady fashion. Everybody whose name is printed, with a few *ex officio* exceptions like the President of the United States, must make application himself and submit credentials. In regard to distribution, the Association sends a copy of the *Register* each year to all families whose names appear in it, together with return postage for use "if not interested." It employs no solicitors.

venture to be launched in 1937 is *The Social Register of Virginia,* sponsored entirely by Mrs. Clifford Randolph Caperson of Richmond, cousin of Mrs. Warfield Simpson. Mrs. Caperson is also a Colonial Dame, and a founder member of the Descendants of Knights of the Garter. According to its prospectus, "invitations are to be extended only to those men and women who are, by virtue of their position in the state and in their respective communities, entitled to be classed among the best people of Virginia." The greater or less authority which these books possess, with their characteristically American compromise between Bradstreet and Debrett, is convincing proof of our quest for social assurance in black and white.

The most important personality in the crystallization of metropolitan Society today is Miss Juliana Cutting of New York. Miss Cutting herself says modestly that she is attempting to fill the place created some forty years ago by the first professional social secretary, Maria de Barril. The daughter of John Joseph de Barril, rich Latin-American settled in New York City, and niece of Frederic Barreda, Peruvian Minister to the United States, who owned the Newport villa "Beaulieu" which passed to the Astors and is now the home of General and Mrs. Vanderbilt, Miss Maria de Barril was born into the ranking aristocracy of New York *emigrés.* When in 1893 disaster overtook her family's fortune, she acted upon the suggestion of a friend and became the pioneer social secretary to New York and Newport—preparing invitation lists, ordering flowers, attending to the music and catering. Still a patrician to her fingertips, she insisted that clients come to her for consultation in her rooms at the Hotel Stratford, and bent many a self-important parvenu to her yoke. Her fine Spencerian backhand upon envelopes and invitations became the superscription of quality; with expanding business she taught a secretary to imitate it exactly, and that secretary, whose penmanship still brings nostalgia to the sentimental, is now a valued employee of Miss Juliana Cutting. The death of Miss Maria de Barril in 1919, leaving a modest fortune to Catholic charities, caused a perceptible lack in New York affairs which Miss Cutting began to fill three years later.

Miss Cutting is the granddaughter of Robert Livingston Cutting. He had inherited wealth from two great real estate families, including that amassed by William Cutting after far-sighted purchase in 1803 for $25,-000 of the present Manhattan theatre district, in partnership with John

Jacob Astor. Miss Cutting's mother was a Pomeroy. Her heritage of position was such that upon her début in the nineties the New York *Herald* remarked, with even greater clairvoyance than it suspected: "Her education has been completed abroad and her family connections alone, without her rare personal charm, would insure her a complete and triumphant career in Society." After passing years had brought gray hair and an almost matchless knowledge of social ramifications, Miss Cutting in November, 1922 entered into partnership with Mrs. Thomas Blackford, but in 1924 went into business for herself, announcing that she would "supervise the preparation and sending out of invitations to social entertainments of all kinds." She has, however, sedulously avoided advertising. Her first assignment in 1924 was the wedding of Miss Eleanor Margaret Green to the Danish Prince Viggo, and a little later she was sending out invitations to meet the Prince of Wales under the roof of Burdens, Mackays, and other Long Islanders. Soon Miss Cutting was in demand for great parties evoked by the full tide of post-War royalty—Swedish, Spanish, and Roumanian—until Queen Marie provided a somewhat Barnumesque finale. Meanwhile Miss Cutting had become an institution.

In 1884 George du Maurier under the caption of "Alarming Scarcity" had drawn three top-hatted bucks lounging before the fire of a club smoking-room:

First Young Swell. Aw!—going anywhere?
Second Ditto. No!—asked to ten 'Hops' tonight! The Idea has completely floored me!"
Third Ditto. By Jove! I've been thinking of letting myself out at Ten Pounds a Night. A Fellow might recoup himself for a bad Book on the Derby.

The day had not yet come of the "professional escort" as supplied by certain London agencies and in New York by the ingenious Mr. Lucius Beebe, but already the dearth of dancing men was being felt. The tired young business man was beginning to find difficulty in keeping pace with the giddy débutante.[13] The disparity between eligible boys and girls,

[13]In 1904 in *The Well-Bred Girl in Society* Mrs. Burton Harrison complained at the notable "lack of dancing men" which caused many girls, left without cotillion partners, to retire crestfallen to the dressing-room until their carriages came. She ascribes it largely to the early hours which young men in Wall Street have to keep. The social apathy of the American male, discussed elsewhere, should also be blamed.

Drawn by George DuMaurier for "Punch," 1874

Alarming Scarcity—Scene—Club Smoking Room

FIRST YOUNG SWELL: "Aw!—Going anywhere?"
SECOND YOUNG SWELL: "No!—Asked to ten 'Hops' tonight! The idea has completely floored me!"
THIRD YOUNG SWELL: "By Jove! I've been thinking of letting myself out at ten pounds a night. A fellow might recoup himself for a bad book on the Derby."

upon which Miss Cutting has risen to fame and fortune, is even more pronounced on Park Avenue than in Mayfair, being greatly accentuated by the modern custom of "cutting in."[14] That practice arose during the War years when soldiers bound overseas found at the big farewell parties that there were too few girls to go around. After the War, when Prohibition lent the stag line its solace of a pocketflask, "cutting in" and the gay irresponsibility it implied eluded all challenge. Continuing its appeal to the new informality of society, "cutting in" is now firmly entrenched; a moralist might call it the ballroom equivalent of divorce. To rescue the desperate hostess Miss Cutting attempted to build up a list of about 2000 personable young men, in and about New York, to cope with its 200 annual débutantes. In practice she estimates that for a dinner-dance there should be a boy and a half to each girl, and two boys to a girl for supper-dances; to ensure success, however, she recommends a ratio of three to one.

In September most eligible young men in the metropolitan area receive a printed notice, which reads in part:

MISS CUTTING

would like to have your full name, also nickname, if any, and the address to which you wish invitations sent for the coming season, in order that you may receive any invitations sent you by her office.

She makes no charge to place a name upon her list, contrary to the belief of many outsiders, but is quick to drop one if her request is ignored or rudely answered, or if a hostess complains about the conduct of any young man who was invited through her office. She asks for nicknames in case a girl wishes to ask to parties some "Bud" or "Sandy" whose Christian name she cannot recall. Miss Cutting keeps on file several thousand names and family records, and has her private system of grading—according to tradition into the A, B, and C categories which correspond to the three orders of débutantes. Her office is also a clearing-house for future dates, with a calendar on which débuts have been slated two or three years in advance. Services include the social counselling of a début, the use of dancing lists,

---

[14]In her article "From Cotillion to Jazz," *Saturday Evening Post*, April 1, 1933, pp. 10 ff., Miss Cutting expressed her private disapproval of "cutting in." However, as Emily Post observes in the latest edition of *Etiquette*, it is "the only behavior known in smartest New York society."

the writing and sending of invitations, and the assurance that a débutante will be invited to her quota of those charity balls which are so important to *jeunes filles en fleur*. Her charges for launching a débutante with lists and good advice are reported to run up to $1500, while for arranging a party with the hotel, decorators, florist, musicians, and liquor dealers, her commission is reckoned as high as 20 per cent of the total cost. Miss Cutting's social power is undeniable, and within the region of New York comes as near to benevolent dictatorship as one can discover in this rebellious and chaotic age.[15]

To enumerate all social criteria known in the United States would be well-nigh impossible. There are fashionable tailors, automobiles, perfumes, furs, magazines, cocktails, styles of letter paper. And of course conventions. Did any one in society ever dot an "i" with a circle? Except perhaps during her first year at Foxcroft, Farmington, Westover, Miss Chapin's or Miss Walker's,—for these are the topmost girls' schools. Chaperonage is rigidly maintained, the simplicity of sleeping bags and bare tables is often cultivated, and an ice-cream soda is a monthly or semiannual orgy. With their quaint mixture of riding to hounds and revelling in lacy-valentine crushes, they are the complement of those boys' schools, said to be sentimental and barbarous, Episcopal in the chapel service and bawdy in barrack-room ballads. At any rate, Groton, St. Paul's, St. Mark's, and Choate are patterned somewhat artificially upon Eton, Harrow, and Winchester, even to the introduction of "fives" at Groton and a modified fag system at St. Mark's, are richly significant of social Anglophilia. Within the past few years several American critics have pointed out with dismay that our prep school tradition has neglected to borrow the British concept of public service or social obligation in the larger sense. For Groton has given to America, in spite of itself, President Franklin D. Roosevelt.[16]

[15]Many women of wealth have their private social secretaries, whose duties are a custom-built version, so to speak, of Miss Cutting's. Often employed jointly by three or four hostesses, the private social secretary will keep the engagement book, record invitations sent and received, write impersonal notes for her employer, take longer letters in shorthand, telephone informal invitations and other messages, audit bills and draw cheques which are brought to her employer for signature, and file receipted bills. Upon a smaller scale, she may make her own lists of dancing men; check addresses, marriages, and deaths; and even devise entertainments after a large dinnerparty or supervise the decoration and catering. And finally—as upon the recent death of Mrs. William Goadby Loew—the secretary may take charge of arrangements for her mistress' funeral. Her rôle is another evidence of the vast complexity of society today.

[16]The concept of social service in the education of the rich has taken an important

The Saga of American Society

Symbols of fashion have grown more important during the past generation than at any other time in American history. This is partly because the break-up of old-time solidarity has destroyed so many other marks of identification, and partly because of the usefulness of such signals in "the social game." The new blue book of society, beginning in the Gilded Age, has been compiled more and more frequently from the names of those who play it. Except in such back-waters as old Baltimore, Charleston, and Virginia, where no one is dropped from society on the score of poverty, the social game is a vital means to success, and to keep at it the only security against being forgotten. Boston and Philadelphia may look somewhat dubiously upon new money; yet they give short shrift to the old patrician who has gone bankrupt. In ruthless metropolitan centers like New York and Chicago, where money is so abundant that it is casually assumed as a *sine qua non,* nobody would be so foolish as to glance toward society unless he could pay the piper, and that handsomely. It is increasingly true that one is no longer born to social position, but achieves it by waging the social battle. Ours is the age of specialization, and an ironic corollary is the fact that society—among those who care about it—is less an enjoyment or recreation than a profession. With its town and country houses, yachts, private planes, imported motor-cars, boxes at the opera, and world travel, it is the most expensive hobby in the world. And with the accumulation of taxes and the world drift toward socialism—whether we like it or not—it appears that the next generation may find this sport as obsolete as the mediæval tourney. Meanwhile, in the shadow of the *Götterdämmerung,* its costs are still formidable. In New York, for example, at the present time a conservative estimate made to the author by Mr. Frank Crowninshield sets the minimum for playing

though rather belated hold in America. Thus the Headmaster of Middlesex, Mr. Winsor, makes a hobby of stressing community obligations to his charges, and for a time ruled that they should make each other's beds, wait on tables, and the like, but abandoned the scheme after finding what inroads it made upon study-hours. At Kent, one of the less fashionable schools, Father Sill has consistently maintained the idea of self- and communal help. Among girls' schools Westover has emphasized the responsibilities of wealth and position, and sponsors a program of relief work among the neighboring poor of Middlebury. At Miss Walker's there is a social-service committee in charge of eleven needy families, while at Foxcroft under the direction of a professional social worker a girl helps look after poor children, black and white. She sews for them, gives Christmas presents, and earns $5 for them during the school's Lenten period, by running errands, selling candy, and doing other chores.

the game at $60,000 annually; to prosecute it on the international scale requires at least $100,000.

What does it mean to play the social game? Briefly, to entertain frequently and well the other best people who can return the favor; and to be seen on every fashionable occasion.[17] To dress in smart clothes, a little ahead of the popular style, and to be gay and amusing are very important.

© *Life Publishing Co.*

Mrs. Steele Pool's Housewarming

C. D. Gibson in *Life* in 1901

A young Chicago couple who devote themselves systematically to its pursuit are typical. Born of good families and educated at fashionable schools, they are not too rich and therefore have to plan their disbursements with care. They live in a suite in the city's most eligible hotel, and entertain at carefully thought-out intervals and in novel ways. Their lists of guests are painstakingly made, involving no social risks, but mixing just the right celebrity of literature, art, or drama, with the fashionable set. The wife specializes in services to friends, from helping select the

[17]Mrs. John Drexel, notable in the Gilded Age of New York and Newport, later a fashionable expatriate in Paris, is quoted as saying, somewhat incoherently to be sure: "This having to keep *en evidence* the year round, we society women simply drop down in harness." Nichols, *The Ultra-Fashionable Peerage*, p. 32.

latest ball gown to arranging flowers at a funeral; in social life she plays her charming and highly keyed part as skilfully as a comedienne, and after a dinner or dance at which she has been the life of the party is as drained and dispirited as though she had borne the ordeal by footlights. The husband, who, unlike many American men, keenly relishes society, is tall, handsome, graceful, and an excellent dancer and bridge player. "I always drink one good glass of champagne before this sort of thing, and stay in bed the next day," he says, admitting that late hours and nervous effort "take it out of me," and adding that if his business life were less flexible he would find the training for society almost an impossibility.[18]

It is a game which implies also the art of social climbing. Rare indeed is the type of hostess who once remarked to the author: "If I ever do any social climbing I shall have to start by climbing down." If one belongs merely to the industrial rich, whose social consciousness is just being stirred out of the lethargic commerce of chain stores and soothing-syrup, one begins to aspire toward that group which has been called "exclusive bar society"—the unattached socially who eddy about El Morocco and Bradley's Casino. Next one may pass to the Palm Beach and racing set, with a dash of smart Bohemia and the reward of a nod from Beatrice Lillie. If one gambles sportingly, dances well, and uses horses up the hill of social difficulty, he may graduate into the international set. By this time he will bestow a patronizing smile as he passes the locked portal of the old guard, for ahead of him stretches presentation at Court and hob-nobbing with Mountbattens or Athlones. The royal family of Great Britain is the *ne plus ultra* of American Society—for after that, one has only death to apprehend, and the ultimate presentation.

The grossest technique in social climbing is known as gate crashing. Apparently it was sponsored first by Socrates, who persuaded Aristo-demus to assist at Agathon's party by suggesting that "to the feasts of the good, the good unbidden go." Its great modern vogue seems however to date from the Great War and the attendant social disintegration. When

---

[18]Concerning the let-down and disillusion which follow departure, Logan Pearsall Smith in his *Trivia* has this delightful note called "Social Success":

"The servant gave me my coat and hat, and in a glow of self-satisfaction I walked out into the night. 'A delightful evening,' I reflected, 'the nicest kind of people. What I said about finance and French philosophy impressed them; and how they laughed when I imitated a pig squealing.'

"But soon after, 'God, it's awful,' I muttered, 'I wish I were dead.'"

society was a small, compact group of those who knew each other well and entertained sedately, gate crashing was seldom inspired by either opportunity or desire. An unknown man or woman in the ballroom of Mrs. Astor would have been as uneasy as a sinner upon the griddle of hell. But the War brought in large parties of casual, even indiscriminate guests, and the private dances of the 1920's for a thousand or more people —approximating the numbers hitherto known only at subscription fêtes— relieved the interloper, who had come to see the sights, hear the music, and drink the champagne, of any discomfiture.[19] Sometimes a hostess had only the vaguest ideas about the people to whom she sent hundreds of her invitations. The story is told of a Harvard undergraduate who replied in writing to a hostess of whom he had never heard, "I should be pleased to accept your invitation, but I think I ought to tell you that I am a Negro." Early clients of Miss Cutting in 1924 complained that at 2 or 3 A.M. "it would be discovered that a raffish swarm of men and women in evening clothes had infiltrated the gathering of young dancers." Crashers of the better sort were uninvited friends of legitimate guests, but many others were curiosity seekers from Broadway night clubs or even professional gamblers and underworldlings. Sometimes they gave false names at the checking list, purloined return checks, went in back entrances, or posed as members of the orchestra. Ambitious young men, upon reading about a forthcoming party in the newspapers, would promptly send their acceptance to an unwary hostess. This flood of anarchy was stemmed by the vigilance of Miss Cutting and other social secretaries through rigid examination of lists, scrupulous identification at the door, the stoppage of "leaks," and merciless expulsion of the unwanted. Today the problem of gate crashing is much less acute than a decade ago, for the fashion during the depression of entertaining smaller groups in private houses rather than in hotels and casinos aided its solution.

There are wiser methods of social climbing. Ward McAllister gave a few hints in his day:

[19]During wartime young soldiers and sailors, about to die for their country, felt an unusual sense of social privilege. For example, at a dance given at "Wakehurst" by Mrs. James Laurens Van Alen in August, 1918, a wholesale invasion of ensigns in uniform from the Newport Naval Base was routed with great difficulty by the hostess, her butler, and footmen. "Think of my feelings," exclaimed one youth. "Think of mine," replied Mrs. Van Alen.

The Saga of American Society

If you want to be fashionable, be always in the company of fashionable people. . . . If you see a fossil of a man, shabbily dressed, relying solely upon his pedigree dating back to time immemorial, who has the aspirations of a duke and the fortunes of a footman, do not cut him; it is better to cross the street and avoid meeting him.

It is well to be in with the nobs who are born to their position, but the support of the swells is more advantageous, for society is sustained and carried on by the swells.

A gentleman can always walk, but he cannot afford to have a shabby equipage.

When you entertain, do it in an easy, natural way, as if it was an everyday occurrence, not the event of your life.

Yet with unconscious irony McAllister closes his chapter called "Entering Society" with the summation: "I think the great secret of life is to be contented with the position to which it has pleased God to call you." Even Emily Post offers a few demure suggestions to the "outsider": "The better, and the only way if she has not the key of birth, is through study to make herself eligible. Meanwhile, charitable or civic work will give her interest and occupation as well as throw her with ladies of good breeding, by association with whom she cannot fail to acquire some of those qualities before which the gates of society always open." The patronage of charity, church settlement work (Episcopalian), the financial support of hospitals, clinics, and opera are probably the safest route which the newcomer can travel. After she has given her cheque for a substantial sum and shown her eagerness to work for the cause, she will be asked to become a sustaining member and sit on the board with women she has wanted to know. Probably they will begin to ask her to tea, then to large parties and luncheons, and finally to dinner. If fortune has blessed her with a small daughter, let her be sent to a fashionable day school, where she will have classmates to be invited to a birthday party, and given expensive souvenirs; in this way a little child may lead them. No climber should overlook the broadening influences of travel; in crossing the Atlantic, cruising the Mediterranean, or circumnavigating the globe, one may get a good table by generous tipping and promptness, and then maneuver eligible acquaintances and celebrities into sitting there. Deck stewards also can do much for one, since during the course of a long voyage propinquity is almost irresistible.

The Blue Book

Some have obtained help from patronizing a fashionable doctor; others have been rewarded by negotiating for a yacht from the right people, or having their houses redecorated by society women. It is only fair warning, that a few businessmen and women with social rank are wary of being impresarios: one of the leading landscape architects of America, who lives at the Colony Club, has developed a tactful routine of refusal to clients from the Middle West who add, as an afterthought to ordering a formal garden, what a great convenience membership in the Colony Club must be to an out-of-town visitor. Better results are usually obtained with musical celebrities, whose Bohemianism makes their social consciences more supple; they may be hired to sing or play for private musicales, to which many snobs will come as martyrs to art if the artists are only great enough. These stars will usually help patrons to meet other celebrities and social lights. A professional entertainer who knows all the smart people and makes a specialty of breaking the ice, like Elsa Maxwell, is a godsend to parvenus. But let nothing in jest or in art suggest inadvertently the past which you have buried; at the début five years ago of a very rich young lady whose grandfather had founded a great mercantile chain the orchestra was bound by solemn instruction to avoid a current favorite called "I Found a Million Dollar Baby in a Five and Ten Cent Store."

Older stratagems included the cultivation with kindness and champagne of society reporters, who sometimes inserted in party lists the names of their well-wishers whom hostesses had overlooked; the hiring of a press agent to chronicle the opening of one's Long Island house, or one's departure and return from abroad, another somewhat outmoded practice; the summer custom of living upon a yacht if one felt insecure, so that one carried along a picturesque background for parties, yet if snubbed in Newport could sail on to Bar Harbor; the play for visiting noblemen; and *par excellence* the advantageous marriage. One ambitious mother moved her household of marriageable daughters into a country house to be near an aristocratic young convalescent; after the most attractive girl had captured him upon his emergence from a plaster cast, her sisters found fresh possibilities for themselves. Once it becomes fashionable to marry, for example, a Wilson from Georgia, or a Mdivani from another Georgia, society quickly rallies round. Most questionable of all perhaps was the method of a pretty young wife who gained position for herself and her willing husband by becoming the mistress of a rich and distinguished New York bachelor.

The social sponsor is often highly effective. As early as 1870–80 a handful of well-connected young men in New York made a good living from advising the newly rich about their problems, and paving the way into the best drawing-rooms and clubs. They were nicknamed by Mrs. Van Rensselaer Cruger "the little brothers of the rich." Late Victorian society in London offered sympathetic mentors in Lady Cork, Mrs. Cavendish Bentinck, and the Duchess of Manchester. When Mrs. John W. Mackay found her advancement in social New York stalemated by malicious rumors of wash-tubs, she wisely moved to Paris and placed herself in the capable hands of Mrs. Robert Hooper, wife of a diplomat of small means, and then transferring her campaign to London rented a great house facing Buckingham Palace, called in the Duchess of Manchester, and within the season was entertaining the Prince of Wales. A similar course was followed by Mrs. John J. ("Leadville Johnny") Brown of Colorado, who, scorned as illiterate Irish by the Sacred Thirty-Six of Denver, left a glittering wake in Paris and London, did credit to her social tutors by learning to speak French and charming the decadents of Europe with her salty speech and exhibitions of pistol shooting, and by her resourcefulness in the *Titanic* disaster gained immortal fame as "the Unsinkable Mrs. Brown." In New York a generation ago Miss d'Angelo Bergh ran a kind of social coaching school, not only providing contacts with "the smart musical set" but also training the ambitious to speak with what was called "the society intonation," to enter and leave a drawing-room gracefully, to entertain, and to employ "the latest society badinage." The cultivation of physical grace was rightly regarded as important, and among others Mrs. Burke Roche carefully studied Delsarte to achieve graceful entrances and exits. There have also been sponsors of social aspiration who responded out of kindness and sympathy rather than an eye to gain. Among these was Mrs. Oliver Harriman, a dashing Louisville belle and beauty of the 1900's, who once defended her tolerance by asking, "Why should we ridicule a person who wants to improve himself through contact with another sphere?" And indeed, among those of certain temperament and interests, social ambition is as honest, simple, and natural as the heliotropism of a sunflower. Its ugly side appears only in that type of climber whom Thackeray described as "licking the boots of those above him and kicking the faces of those below him on the social ladder."

A chapter on social discriminations would be incomplete without some reference to the relation between master and servant. It need hardly be said that on account of the milieu in which they live, servants of the rich are as keenly sensitive to social gradations as their betters. The personal maid of a British millionaire's wife gave notice after several years of apparently contented service, explaining: "Well, it's like this, Madame; we constantly stay at the country houses of the nobility where most of the guests have titles. You are an excellent mistress and I have been very happy with you for four years, but I am quite tired of going in to dinner last." Furthermore, the best English servants of Fifth Avenue and Newport have an expert knowledge of social amenities, an excessive conservatism and cautiousness, a hatred of idlers and reporters, and a very real distinction of manner. Karl Marx and *The Daily Worker* are not their saviors; when naturalized they generally vote the straight Republican ticket. Although an estimated 95 per cent of American families have not a single servant—with a proletarian preference for spending money on cars, radios, and silk dresses rather than in buying an increased margin of leisure—the rich have come to value a good servant above all other luxuries, for this is essentially the aristocratic as it is the European viewpoint. To many a parvenu, a well-trained servant is priceless not only on the score of efficiency but because to have him in the house is a liberal education. In Chicago during the first great emergence of the meat packers there was a frantic demand for butlers—those princes of their guild— who had been formerly employed in ducal families.[20] American society has also adopted the English attitude toward its servants, a formal and impersonal one, in preference to the chatty comradeship found in Continental and particularly Latin countries.

The quest for the good servant in America is a very old one, as well as an inexhaustible topic of conversation among employers—for without small talk centering about their servants the lives of the rich would be vastly more barren. It is a subject which comes midway between the objectivity of the weather and the intimacy of disclosing one's digestive

[20]A roster of famous butlers in American society, who almost invariably are British, would include J. P. Morgan's Physick and Biles, Marshall Field's Hider, Herbert L. Satterlee's Beany, Mrs. Henry White's Stryde, Newbold Morris's Slattery, and Wildgoose in the household of the late E. J. Berwind.

problems. The best servants have always come from Europe, ever since those unhappy days when the well-to-do on Massachusetts Bay attempted vainly to train the Indians—and, as James Russell Lowell wrote, "your cook might give warning by taking your scalp or chignon, as the case might be, and making off with it into the woods." The stigma of servitude has always rankled with native-born Americans, except of course among Negroes in the South. The controversy over livery, knee-breeches, and powdered wigs in the first age of political democracy has already been noticed; in new guise it cropped up again in 1896 when George C. Boldt, manager of the Waldorf, decreed that all waiters and other hotel employees, as well as the cabmen who attended patrons at the 33rd Street curb, should be clean-shaven. Up to that time many American servants had bedecked themselves with beards and sideburns, and a furious controversy ensued. Appealed to for his opinion, Governor Flower of New York replied: "It was not so many years ago that I was a servant myself, and I used to wear my beard as I pleased and my hair as long as I pleased. Had any man dictated to me that I should put a French twist to my beard or a Spanish curl to my hair I would have taken it as an insult. I will veto any bill regulating men's beards." Nevertheless customs were changing; in more fastidious private houses only the clean-shaven servant was coming to be employed, and within a few years hotel after hotel followed the precedent set by the Waldorf. The coeval disappearance of beards and side-whiskers among their masters probably helped to reconcile the disaffected. Today a servant with beard or moustache would be a solecism unspeakable.

The present retinue of a wealthy household in America follows the British mode. Its head is the butler, who under no circumstances wears livery, but striped trousers and swallow-tail coat at lunch and the door, and at six o'clock changes into a dress suit almost indistinguishable from a gentleman's except for the absence of braid on trousers and the presence of black waistcoat with a white tie. Under orders from him are the house footmen, who wait on table, clean the dining-room and pantry, polish silver and set the table, move furniture, carry wood, and often valet junior members of the family and house guests. They wear livery in the colors of the house, and for high feasts may don knee-breeches—much less frequent than in the Gilded Age, though sometimes they are still seen at formal dinners and balls in New York, but rarely elsewhere. The pow-

dered wig for footmen, favored in grandiose society of the 1890's, is quite
déclassé. Other indispensable servants include the cook, often assisted by
a second cook who prepares food for the domestics, and one or more
kitchenmaids, sometimes known as "sculleries"; a parlormaid, whose
province is the drawing-room and library, with occasional service to the
front door and telephone; a housemaid, who attends to bedrooms, dress-
ing-tables, and bathrooms; and a lady's maid, whose duties include hairdressing, packing, mending and keeping her mistress' clothes in order.
Similar functions belong to the valet, who is often the butler in a more
humble rôle. With vigilance he watches over his master's wardrobe, puts
studs in shirts and lays out clothes for the next change, runs the bath, and
may shave his master and help him dress. Most intimate member of the
family's domestic staff is the nurse, who as companion of the children
shares some privileges of equality, especially if she is a veteran in the
house. One must add also the chauffeur, who may drive with an outside
footman to open doors and hold umbrellas. The staff of a country place
is naturally much larger, and comprises grooms, gardeners and assistant
gardeners, nurseryman, head farmer, poultry and kennelsman, night
watchman, carpenters, and laborers. The world of domestic service has
of course its own rigid conventions and exactitudes: a "useful man" never
waits upon table, and a woman servant never announces guests or opens
the doors of automobiles. Its way of life is perhaps the most stereotyped
and carefully ordered of any stratum in American life, and probably the
least typically American. It is in fact the expensive and smooth-running
imported mechanism without which the social race could not be run.

CHAPTER SEVEN

THE GENTLEMAN AND HIS CLUB

ROM the eighteenth century when the Duc de la Rochefoucauld observed "with melancholy" that American men were too busy "for the enticements of polished society," to the twentieth when Charles Eliot Norton startled a class of Harvard undergraduates by the opening remark "I suppose that none of you young men has ever seen a gentleman," a good deal of material has been accumulating to show that the gentleman in the more courtly sense is almost as rare in North America as the heath-hen drumming in solitude upon the dunes of Martha's Vineyard—another victim of our national ruthlessness. Though Aristotle sketched the lineaments of the gentleman, with his twelve public and twelve private virtues in the Nicomachean Ethics, he was really the creation and darling of feudalism. He was a soldier or shield bearer, as the word *esquire* still faintly commemorates. He was also a horseman and sportsman, a *caballero* or *chevalier,* and the smell of saddle leather still clings about him. Steering a middle course between fop and sloven, scholar and boor, he lived by the classic maxim of "nothing in excess." He found courage, patriotism, loyalty, and generosity more attractive than the churchly and commercial preachments like sobriety, prudence, thrift, and chastity.[1] Not always consistent, he enshrined women of his own social class in idealism and exquisite homage, but was not above seducing a few peasant girls on his way home from the Crusades. But committing even his peccadilloes with liberality and

[1]The old-style gentleman is always adored by servants, who love his charm and the easy, imperious ways which set him at the antipodes to the middle classes. They are his born retainers and, like hunting-dogs upon the sound of a gun, at his voice they feel the age-old stirrings of blood. Lord Randolph Churchill in an extremely indiscreet speech at Paddington once said: "The best class and the lowest class in England come together naturally; they like and esteem each other; they are not greasy hypocrites talking of morality and frequenting the Sunday School while sanding the sugar. They are united in England in the bonds of a frank immorality." It is no secret that the late King George, with all the middle class virtues, roused less vital enthusiasm among Welsh miners and Manchester mill-hands than his father Edward VII or his son the abdicated Edward VIII.

The Gentleman and His Club

rakish grace, he relied both here and hereafter upon the plenary grace of a hearty life. A French lady of the old régime once said: "Depend upon it—God Amighty thinks twice before he condemns persons of quality!" While none less than Shakespeare assures us that "The Prince of Darkness is a gentleman." What, between the blunted horns of such a dilemma, has one to fear?

The cult of materialism in America and the furore of competition during its building era conspired against the gentlemanly character, for, as William Butler Yeats has lately said, "A gentleman is a man whose principal ideas are not connected with his personal needs and his personal success." Yet at the heart of American conduct there is surely as much essential kindness, generosity, and desire to do the right thing as was found when knighthood was in flower. Often it appears quite independently of grammar, occupation, and affluence. It has been justly remarked that the filling-station attendant has done more to raise the standard of courtesy *en masse* in the United States than all the manuals of etiquette. The wife of a master at Groton, spending a winter's holiday in South Carolina, was startled when—upon the stalling of her automobile near a remote country crossroads—the engineer of a "mixed" train stopped his locomotive, repaired her motor, and tipped his greasy cap as he climbed back into the cab. Not all of those who have salvaged bits of the gentlemanly character from the wrack of industrialism are behind plate glass on Commonwealth Avenue.[2]

Yet the social club in America has done a great deal to keep alive the gentleman in the courtly sense. Here is his peculiar asylum from the pandemonium of commerce, the bumptiousness of democracy, and the feminism of his own household. Here he is technically invisible from the critical female eye—a state of bliss reflected in the convention that a gentleman never bows to a lady from a club window, nor according to the best form discusses ladies there. The club is his Great Good Place, with its comfortable and slightly shabby leather chairs, the pleasantly malt-like effluvium of its bar, the newspaper room with a club servant to

[2]Lord Bryce in *The American Commonwealth,* Part VI, chap. cxiii, wrote: "The nature of a man's occupation, his education, his manners and breeding, his income, his connections, all come into view in determining whether he is in this narrow sense of the word 'a gentleman,' almost as they would in England, though in most parts of the United States personal qualities count for rather more than in England, and occupation for hardly anything."

repair quickly the symptoms of disarray, the catholicity of magazines from highbrows to *La Vie Parisienne* which in less stately company would seem a trifle sophomoric, the abundant notepaper, the good cigars and hearty carnivorous menus, and the waiters who are not to be tipped from New Year to Christmas. And perhaps most important of all, the friends with whom one sits down to a rubber of bridge after five o'clock, on the way home. They are the men with whom one grew up, saw through prep school and college, attended at their weddings—and whom the survivors will accompany decently in gloves to their long home in Mount Auburn or Sleepy Hollow. They are the good fellows in whose essential infallibility one is bound to believe. Here we have no poor losers, bounders, muckers, or cads—and if one should take a cocktail too many and speak with loosened tongue, nobody outside is the wiser. And if by inconceivable chance one finds himself unable immediately to go home, there is always a pleasant bed upstairs in a room of bachelor's asceticism still redolent of pipe tobacco and toilet water.

One is likely to meet doctors here and almost certainly surgeons, but never a dentist. There will be many lawyers—barristers, as they style them in Pall Mall, but not solicitors. Bankers and brokers, of course, who come from the best Nordic families, and wholesale merchants rather than retail. Retired military officers, with their excellent horsemanship, their erect carriage, white hair, and fine apoplectic flush, are also in the best Piccadilly tradition. Two or three Episcopal clergymen, preferably deans, lie lightly upon the consciences and the budget of the club. Artists, musicians, and authors are regarded with suspicion unless their family names and background are quite trustworthy, and set them clear of raffish bohemia. The Union, the Knickerbocker, the Racquet, and the Metropolitan condescend to the Century, where achievement outweighs blood and wealth.[3] A stage player is very seldom seen, though the fashionable architect—as the tradition of Richard Hunt and Stanford White, or even Addison Mizner in Palm Beach, demonstrates—may be quite a swell and an amusing fellow. With what Henry James called "a certain light of the fine old gentlemanly prejudice to guide it," the preëminently social club welcomes the serious frivolity of horses, hounds, foxes, and

[3]Mr. W. C. Brownell, who spent most of his leisure at the Century Association, but actually slept at the Athletic Club for change of air, once overheard one member there say to another, "Did you know there was a club down on Forty-third Street that chose its members for intellectual eminence? Isn't that a hell of a way to run a club?"

The Gentleman and His Club

boats, but not the effeminate frivolity of æstheticism. Pedantry is also frowned upon; except for the *Social Register, The World Almanac,* and Lloyd's *Register of American Yachts* not a volume in the club library has been taken down since the cross-word puzzle craze. It is comforting to think that one's sons and grandsons will sit in these same chairs, and firelight will flicker on the same steel engravings and oil portraits of past presidents—and though the stars may wheel in their courses and crowned heads totter to the guillotine, this little world will remain, so long as first mortgages and Government bonds endure. One of the youngest of the really top-flight clubs has taken for its motto the sentiment of its elders—the Brook, which boasts, with the help of Tennyson, that

> Men may come, and men may go—
> But I go on for ever.

The earliest clubs in Colonial America seem to have been small groups united by racial or professional bonds and a community of taste which met in private houses or taverns for dinner and an evening of talk. Such organizations as the Irish Club and the French Club in New York, which John Fontaine visited in 1710, the French Club founded in Charleston in 1737, the St. Andrew's Society in Philadelphia which published its Rule Book in 1751, and the German Society of Pennsylvania which was founded in 1764, were not strictly social groups; most of them mixed conviviality of no very exclusive kind with the purposes of a fraternal and charitable order. Doctor Alexander Hamilton on his journey north in 1744 chronicles his adventures with a "drunken club" at a tavern in Maryland, the "Governor's Club" in Philadelphia, the "club at Withered's" in Boston, and the Philosophical Club at Newport where the worthy doctor "was surprised to find that no matters of philosophy were brought upon the carpet," but that punch and tobacco were staples together with much talk about shipbuilding and privateers. During this decade, with growing leisure at home and news of coffee-house wits and beefsteak clubs in London, dozens of imitations sprang up throughout the Colonies. *The Maryland Gazette* for March 24, 1747 prints a wistful letter from a gentleman on the East Shore who finds himself involved in a new club with no very clear idea of its nature, except that its purpose is to avoid "an Omnium Gatherum who are neither capable of improving or being improved"; he would be grateful for a copy of the rules of some

255

good club elsewhere. He hears there are scores of them in western Maryland.

The oldest group for the sport and association of gentlemen which survives is the Fishing Company of the State in Schuylkill, best known wherever punch is brewed as the Fish House Club. It was founded in 1732 on the estate of a Quaker, William Warner, where opportunities were offered not only to the angler but also the hunter of rabbits, partridges, and pheasants. Under its first governor, Thomas Stretch, it was organized like a miniature commonwealth—"the State in Schuylkill"—with executive, legislative, and judicial branches represented among its thirty members, who were called "citizens." There was an assembly of five, a secretary-treasurer, a sheriff, and a coroner. Elections were held annually, and after settling affairs of state the electors dined royally rather than democratically on barbecued pig, rounds of beef, and steak, suffused with punch and Madeira. The invention of planked shad should also be mentioned among the *gestes* of the Fish House Club. Membership is still limited to thirty, with the addition of a few honorary members of which the last, elected in 1920, was General John J. Pershing. A prospective joiner must wait until resignation or death thins the ranks. The castle where the club meets for its epicurean meals on alternate summer Wednesdays is no longer upon the Schuylkill, but near Torresdale upon the Delaware. Formerly the special straw hat of the club was *de rigueur* for fishing, and the straw worn by Lafayette is a venerable relic. Apprentices, as newly elected members are called, wear· a cook's apron and are taught the mysteries of club recipes; from dishwashing they graduate to the spit and the oven. Mr. John White Geary, banker, is its head, and for generations Cadwaladers, Chews, Biddles, Wrights, and Welshes have been happy to serve in its kitchens.

The most noteworthy band of epicureans in early New York was called the Social Club. For some years prior to its dispersal in 1775 its twenty-seven members met every Saturday evening in winter at the famous tavern in Broad Street kept by "Black Sam" Fraunces, who later became steward to President Washington. Fraunces was the best cook of his day, and according to advertisements sold "portable soup [*i.e.,* solid broth made from beef, veal, or chicken, often taken on sea voyages], catchup, bottled gooseberries, pickled walnuts, pickled or fryed oysters fit to go to the West Indies, pickled mushrooms, currant jelly, marmalade." John Jay,

The Gentleman and His Club

Gouverneur Morris, Robert R. Livingston, Morgan Lewis, Gulian Verplanck, Stephen De Lancey, James Duane, and Leonard and Anthony Lispenard were among the connoisseurs of this fare; those who had been bred to the bar belonged also to the Moot Club, which flourished simultaneously. Most members of the Social Club were passing rich, and for their pleasure in summer could afford to build "a neat large room for a club house" at Kip's Bay. Post-Revolutionary dining clubs on the same pattern included the celebrated Barbecue Club of Richmond in which Chief Justice Marshall was the ruling spirit, and the Cossack Club of Charleston centering about General Charles Cotesworth Pinckney. The annalist of the Cossacks, Charles Fraser, calls them "the remnant of a peculiar race of people," aristocrats by birth and Englishmen by education, but staunch patriots of the Republic: "Such men were, in their proper element, at the head of society—it was theirs to maintain and transmit the ancient character of Charleston for intelligence, refinement, and hospitality."

The gentleman's clubhouse, an anchorage distinct from mere fraternal groups or periodic dinners, evolved from the London coffee house of late Stuart and Georgian times. In fact the properties of coffee—discovered, according to tradition, by an oriental shepherd who watched his goats grow frisky beneath a coffee-bush—made that drink best among mild solvents of Anglo-Saxon phlegm. Favorite coffee-houses of Tory or Whig gentlemen, like White's opened in 1698 and Brooks's in 1764, or of fox-hunters who began to frequent Boodle's in 1762, began as the property of a publican—but soon those guests who wanted exclusive privileges paid him a fixed sum to close his doors to all others. The first coffee-house in New York was opened about 1700, and quickly became a rendezvous of the *ton*. Though few if any American taverns were converted into clubhouses in the manner of Brooks's, they did bring to focus the social life of Colonial gentlemen, and built barriers of price and custom which effectually excluded the riff-raff. The Green Dragon and the Bunch of Grapes in Boston, Little's Tavern in New York, and the French establishment called "Lebanon" in the suburbs of Philadelphia for "orderly, genteel and reputable people," were all locally famous.[4]

[4]Of course coteries of gentlemen continued to meet in private houses, and these were long more select than most tavern groups, like the celebrated "Wistar parties" in Philadelphia, or that club of sixteen Bostonians described by both Chastellux and Brissot in

The Saga of American Society

The oldest gentlemen's club in the United States which has lasted without a break is the Philadelphia Club. As early as 1830 a few gentlemen met at Mrs. Rubicam's Coffee-House at Fifth and Minor Streets to play cards. Joined by friends they organized the Adelphia Club in 1834; it soon came to be called the Philadelphia Club. Henry Bohlen, George Cadwalader, James Markoe, and Henry Pratt McKean were among its guiding lights. In 1835 the club rented the old house where Joseph Bonaparte, King of Naples, had lived in exile, and became officially the Philadelphia Club. For the past eighty-six years it has occupied its present stately brick dwelling at Thirteenth and Walnut, built originally as a residence for Thomas, only son of aristocratic Major Pierce Butler of South Carolina. Ladies have been admitted only three times in the club's history, for balls in 1851 and 1869, and a centenary tea in 1934—at which Mrs. John Markoe, last belle of the ball of 1869, poured tea for the distinguished veterans. Most members of the Fish House Club belong also to the Philadelphia Club, and its link with the old Assembly is very strong since members traditionally come here for their nightcap after the ball is over. Bounded by these three sides of a triangle lies probably the most compact and inviolable little group of aristocrats in America. Its most dangerous schism broke with the Civil War, when a Unionist entered the club remarking that "this place reeks of Copperheads." A fellow-member promptly knocked him down, was expelled, reinstated by court order, again expelled and again reinstated by Federal command; he then entered the club, ordered a drink, and handed in his resignation for ever. One of its most picturesque habitués was Chief Justice Gibson, whose habit was to sit till all hours with good whiskey and better company, and then needing to get up early to render decisions would order the boy who waked him to bring "Coffee, hot as hell and strong as the wrath of God."

The Philadelphia Club has had its crusty characters so typical of club life. There was the member who used to sleep in the library every afternoon, and left instructions to be called for dinner. A waiter once came for this purpose, but found that the mere human voice—raised to the

the late eighteenth century. Meetings were held in members' houses by rotation, with the privilege of bringing one guest each; election required a unanimous vote. "They assemble after tea-time, play, converse, read the public papers, and sit down to table between nine and ten," says Chastellux. A few bottles of Madeira and a round of songs were the lyric passages in these meetings.

maximum loudness thinkable in the Philadelphia Club—was unavailing. Of course he could not touch the reverend member with his hand, but being a waiter of resource, just then he spied the Club's cat strolling in. Picking up the cat he deftly placed it in the sleeper's lap, hid behind the door, and returned a few seconds later with his respectful announcement. And there was the late William Read Fisher, who stoutly opposed a plan for converting the former coat-room into a tea-room about 1900; his protests were out-voted and the alteration took place, but until the day of his death in 1913 Mr. Fisher upon entering the Club would walk straight up the marble steps and—before going in to lunch or bridge— deposit his hat and coat aggressively on a chair in the new tea-room. Such intransigence calls to mind the Oxford legend of the ghost in Pembroke College, of a seventeenth-century don who is always seen walking apparently on his knees in the neighborhood of his old rooms. Such peculiar behavior was explained when the present bursar, digging among old records, discovered that the floors in that wing had been raised eighteen inches in early Victorian times; the ghost, being a conservative, was simply haunting the old level.

And the Philadelphia Club, like others of its kind, has had its celebrated wagers. John T. Montgomery, a wag who died forty years ago, once casually remarked over the card-table that he had a brother thirteen feet high. Bets were immediately placed by sceptical friends. "I suppose it is generally admitted that two halves make a whole?" ventured Mr. Montgomery mildly. When everybody had assented to this axiom he concluded, "Well, I have two half-brothers, each six-foot-six-and-a-half." After ocular proof of this fact he collected his winnings. Another sort of ruse was once practised in the Union Club of New York, before removal from Fifth Avenue to its present quarters at Park Avenue and 69th Street had invalidated its old custom of reviewing the town from behind its plate-glass windows. A favored sport was to bet upon the number of Negroes who would pass the Club windows during a specified time. A member who lost a good many dollars by this pastime once had the good luck to meet a parade of colored delegates starting far up Fifth Avenue. Hastily calling a taxi he arrived at the Union Club, and with great success bet with all comers on the apparently insane proposal that 500 Negroes would pass within the next half hour.

The Union Club ranks in antiquity a close second to the Philadelphia

The Saga of American Society

Club. Francis Gerry Fairfield in his book *The Clubs of New York* (1871) recalls the year 1836 as an *annus mirabilis*: "Tradition preserves the record of the season under the designation of the cold summer. Weird

The Lotus Club Arrives

Aristocratic clubs greet the advent of the new Lotus Club with lofty sneers, and are righteously rebuked by the proletarian press:

Mr. Jeunesse Doré of the Union Club, loquitur: "See heah! What—ah—means this procession? 'Lotus'—'Lotus'—yaas—I comprehend. These awtists—these fellahs that wite and dwaw and puffawm at shows—puhsons on salaries! Good gwacious! Awthuth ah vulgah! Cahn't keep dawgs. B'long to no high familith. Wuk for living! I think it 'orrid of them to come up wound heah."
Daily Graphic, New York, April 19, 1870

auroras did not forbear to lift themselves in mountains of fire along the north, even in July; and more than once the canopy-aurora hung like a mock sun in the very center of the heavens. People predicted strange things." Rather as an anticlimax we learn that the only prodigy brought forth was the Union Club. More and more New Yorkers, travelling abroad, were observing the social clubs of the West End in London, and of these the Union was an express imitation. "If this club can be gotten up like the English clubs it may succeed; little short of that will meet the views of the members," Philip Hone writes in his diary on December 7, 1836, after dining with the governing committee at Windust's.[5] In earlier times New York citizens had lived and entertained for the most part at home, and in post-Revolutionary days had looked upon the St. James's Square type of club with actual disfavor. But now with increasing congestion in the city, further distances from home to business, and the rise of a class of worldly bachelors and men-about-town whom Hone mentions as the chief beneficiaries of the new Club, attitudes were changing.

The entrance fee was set at $100, and annual dues $20. In midsummer, 1836, a committee made up of Hone, Thomas J. Oakley, Ogden Hoffman, J. De Peyster Ogden, and a few others had sent out invitations to membership. One of them was received by an up-and-coming Scotchman who had just started a newspaper, and whose blatancy had not yet been fully revealed; five years later he could not have bought his way into the Union Club at any price. James Gordon Bennett early adopted the habit of inviting the readers of his *Herald* to share his personal problems and affairs: in 1840 he was to announce his forthcoming marriage under the headline "Declaration of Love—Caught at Last—Going to be Married—New Movement in Civilization." Now, with the engraved invitation from the Union Club upon his desk Bennett could not resist the

---

[5]Hone's earliest entry regarding the Club is under June 17, 1836: "A new club is about being established, at the head of which are a number of our most distinguished citizens, to consist of four hundred members, and to be similar in its plan and regulations to the great clubs of London, which give a tone and character to the society of the London metropolis." At the December meeting he was offered the chairmanship of the committee but declined. Hone was a perennial joiner, a "clubable man" in Doctor Johnson's famous phrase; he belonged to the Reading Club with Duers, Hoffmans, Kings, and Washington Irving, and was a frequent guest of the Kent Club of noted lawyers, "with oceans of champagne." Although his own antecedents were humble French-German ones, he was asked to join in 1835 a Knickerbocker Society which in 1875 was re-christened as the St. Nicholas Society to consolidate the Dutch aristocracy of Stuyvesants, Rapeljes, Fishes, Costers, and Schermerhorns. And his friends paid him the rare tribute of forming a Hone Society in 1838, of twelve gentlemen who met at each other's houses: "A sumptuary law was enacted confining the dinner to soup, fish, oysters, four dishes of meat, with a dessert of fruit, ice-cream, and jelly." Religion, party politics, and gossip were interdicted topics, but Daniel Webster was a revered guest since he stood for "government founded on cautious legislation and conservative policy." Upon Hone's death in 1851 it disbanded.

possibilities of "copy"; on August 17, 1836, in an editorial he pondered:

"Shall I, or shall I not, accept the invitation?

"What is the use of any social system in which women do not participate? In which their petticoat is not seen—where glossy ringlets cannot enter and make it Paradise? . . .

"The Union Club, now proposed, is the first attempt of this kind in this country. Can it succeed? Will it promote principle, taste, philosophy, talent and genius? It may aid eating, cooking, and conversational powers, but one hour of solitary bliss of true genius is worth an eternity of meretricious social happiness . . .

"Still I shall take the matter, as requested, into consideration, and reply to the secretary in a few days."

At this time Bennett was eager to increase circulation, and seized at every straw to ingratiate himself with the 300,000 New Yorkers who were not being invited to join the Union Club. In November he criticized the Union Club sharply and ended with the flourish, "Down with all Clubs say we." For months afterwards he fired desultory salvos at the extravagance, over-charging, and likely degeneration of the Union Club into a "mere gambling association," until some of the more faint-hearted subscribers actually dropped away.

Early in 1837 the Club hired M. Julien, a chef from Paris, who gave satisfaction in every respect except turtle-soup and terrapin—later to become a *spécialité de la maison,* along with clams southside and French pancackes. A cellar of excellent wines was laid down, and gourmets began to flock to the Union. Its first president was Samuel Jones, Chief Justice of the Superior Court of New York City; he was succeeded by John C. Stevens, noted pioneer of yachting, and in turn by Governor John Alsop King, son of Rufus King. In 1842 the Club moved to William B. Astor's former house on Broadway, which, says Philip Hone, is "an excellent lounging place for young and old beaux, each of whom would fain be thought what the other is; where horse racing and politics are discussed by those who know little about either of those abstruse sciences; where the 'young idea' is taught to shoot billiard balls and study the mysteries of whist; and where I frequent, notwithstanding the satirical tone of the present remarks."

The roll of early members shows a predominance of merchants, with lawyers a close second; today brokers lead the field. In 1855 the in-

The Gentleman and His Club

vincible Bennett referred to the Union as "an eating and drinking establishment of merchants, old fogy speculators, stock jobbers, Wall Street bulls and bears, lame ducks, and kite-flyers . . . this nursery for old bachelors." Aside from female servants few women have ever set foot within the Union Club; even its historic mascot was a tom-cat, Kibosh. The wife or widow of an ex-president is allowed to see her husband's portrait when it is hung, and on one memorable occasion the wife of an inveterate whist-player knocked aside the doorman and forced her way into the card-room. The historian of the Club relates that the luckless husband "retained his presence of mind. Gravely he introduced his wife to his fellow members at his table. Then he turned to her, and courteously and politely asked her to be seated until the rubber was ended. When this had been accomplished he offered his arm to his wife, bowed gravely to the other members and left the Club—never to set foot inside the clubhouse again."

Although Goelets, Pynes, Schermerhorns, Iselins, and Wilmerdings do not make history if they can help it, the Union Club has not been wholly barren of dramatic episodes. Refusal of the demand in 1861 to expel Judah P. Benjamin—not that he was a Jew but because he had become the financial brains of the Confederacy—led to the secession of hotheaded patriots to form in 1863 the Union League Club, composed, as a Democratic paper sneered at the time, "of able-bodied gentlemen, whose purpose is to induce other able-bodied men to enlist." Its politics have always been more outstanding than its pedigrees. And the expulsion from the Union of Count Joseph Loubat in 1882 became a *cause celèbre*. In 1891 another rift occurred in its ranks when the late J. P. Morgan, piqued by the blackballing of a business associate, inspired a few friends to join him in founding the Metropolitan Club. Popularly known as the "Millionaires' Club," the Metropolitan is made up on the one hand of a stratum acceptable to the Union Club and on the other of gentlemen whose wealth is a little too cumbersome to pass through the mid-Victorian doorway of the Union and the Knickerbocker. As a matter of history it may be recorded that even its founder came in later years to make amends to the Union Club, when the partner he had championed turned out to be hardly worth the trouble. But the red-letter day in the life of the Union Club occurred in the autumn of 1920, when the Cork Men's Benevolent and Protective Association, issuing from St.

Patrick's where they had been attending Mass for the repose of the soul of the martyred Terence Macswiney, saw the Union Jack flying from the mast over the door of the Union Club in commemoration of the 300th anniversary of the *Mayflower*. Storming the Club with sticks and stones, they broke plate-glass windows and exchanged bloody noses with Club members who bravely stood their ground and refused to lower the ensign. Police finally routed these Irish patriots with gentle firmness, while over the fortress still waved the symbol of St. George and St. Andrew. Mr. Telfair Minton, the Union Club member who sustained greatest mayhem in the shape of two black eyes, was consoled by a cablegram from a friend in London, "O say, can you see?"

The various dining clubs within the Union which have sprung up, flourished and died during the last century illustrate the cellular division so frequently seen in club life. A *petit comité* will form inside even the most exacting group, commandeer a room for itself, and begin to build an enclave of tradition. Usually taking the guise of an informal dining club, it specializes in appeal to gourmets who are also good fellows—like the Decanter and the Pee Wee Clubs within the Philadelphia, the Kitten and the late Zodiac Clubs of the Union, and the Beacon Society within the Algonquin Club of Boston. Three members are probably the minimum which can still remain "clubable"—exampled by the late but famous little group of Harry Payne Whitney, Francis P. Garvan, and Finley Peter Dunne in New York, called "The Meeting-House."

The Union is proud to call itself "the mother of clubs." The most aristocratic of its children is the Knickerbocker, organized in 1871 by a company of young men who were either members of the Union Club or securely upon its waiting-list—Alexander Hamilton, who was the first president from 1871 to 1890, John J. Astor, William Cutting, Robert S. Hone, Philip Schuyler, and a few others. According to the version told at the Union, several of those young bloods grew impatient with the ten years' waiting-list at the elder club; today, with less arrogance, the Union acts upon candidacies with reasonable promptness. According to the story of the Knickerbocker Club, these young men felt that the Union was getting too mixed, democratic, and resolved to found an association whose name should stress the requisite of family. Its membership is limited to 750, and for a time its critical demands were ex-

The Gentleman and His Club

ceedingly high. Like so many other symbols of solidarity the Knickerbocker has relaxed its standards, decorously and almost imperceptibly
over a span of the last twenty years. Today, since the opening in 1933
of the Georgian club-house of the Union with fine athletic facilities, the
Knickerbocker appears to be waning in favor. With its sedate quarters

The Knickerbocker Club House on Fifth Avenue at Thirty-second Street
in the eighteen-nineties

on upper Fifth Avenue it seems just now to be a relic of those sedentary
times when, as Holmes declared in Boston, "Society would drop a man
who should run round the Common in five minutes."

Another club legend of New York records that the Brook was started
by two youngish gentlemen expelled from the Union for the unappreci-
ated prank of putting a poached egg upon the head of its most revered
patriarch. Founded in 1903, it has chosen to remain a small but very
smart club with a sporting and cavalierish bonhomie among its members. Its guiding spirit and current president is Mr. Percy Rivington
Pyne. A much larger club with even greater stress upon the sporting
tradition is the Racquet and Tennis Club, founded in 1890 by Isaac
Townsend, R. J. Cross, H. De Coppet, H. S. Hoyt, Edward La Montagne, and Rutherfurd Stuyvesant, and merged with the earlier Racquet

Court Club founded in 1875 under the inspiration of William R. Travers. Among young men of New York, especially those who must concentrate upon membership in a single important club, the Racquet is today

The Manhattan Club at Madison Avenue and Twenty-sixth Street. At the time this drawing was made by Otto H. Bacher in 1890 it was the home of The University Club

the most attractive socially, though tales of its exclusiveness are somewhat exaggerated when ascribed to a club which numbers 2100 members.

Every American city with a vestige of tradition has one eminently respectable men's club, housed behind brownstone or substantial brick, heavy but impressive in architecture, food, and membership. The Chicago Club, the Pacific Union Club in San Francisco, the Denver Club, the Boston Club in New Orleans, the Metropolitan in Washington, and the Maryland Club in Baltimore are all impeccable. Young men often profess scorn of their stodgy ways, but are immensely flattered when an old fogy offers to nominate them. Local conditions played of course an important part in the time and circumstances of their origin.[6] Thus the Pacific in San Francisco began at the surprisingly early date of 1852, a year after the Somerset of Boston and five years before the Maryland Club, because of socially minded Peytons, Wards, Colemans, and McAllisters who had arrived in the wake of the Forty-Niners. Because the club idea is Anglo-Saxon rather than French, New Orleans was tardy in adopting it; and because it is urban rather than rural, Virginia social life, even in its capital Richmond, was long oblivious. Even today in a small and clearly delimited aristocracy like that of Charleston, clubs on the London pattern have never struck root.

In addition to the social club *par excellence,* most larger cities have at least one intellectual and celebrity-garnering club which usually meets around a long table for lunch, and once or twice a year—preferably midsummer or the Christmas holidays—stages a play, or carnival, or gala party. The most picturesque of these is the Bohemian Club of San Francisco, founded in 1872, and worthy disciples are the Cactus Club of Denver, the Tavern Club of Chicago, and the Cosmos in Washington. Eastern clubs of this type often assume most functions of the staid social club as well; of these the pioneer is the Century Association of New

[6]The great multiplication of clubs occurred at the close of the nineteenth and beginning of the twentieth century. Thus in New York alone, as we learn from Rossiter's *Club Men of New York*—an annual of club membership begun in 1893—during the eight years of its publication up to 1901, clubs had increased in number from 119 with 24,000 members (excluding some 32,000 repetitions) to 157, with 38,000 names. The editor ascribes this growth chiefly to "prosperous conditions," and points out the significant fact that the majority of club members belong to more than one organization —foreshadowing the "clubman" of the tabloids. Rossiter's is an extremely catholic list because of his inclusion of athletic clubs and fraternal groups.

Somewhere between the palmary social club in every community, and the plebeian athletic club in whose lounge dominoes and pinochle tend to supplant bridge, lie various strata of relative social exclusiveness. Most cities have for example a University Club, which requires a college background and modest social standing; of this order the best and most critical is the University Club of New York. Several of the larger cities have also their Harvard, Yale, Princeton, and other college clubs, whose rank is generally secondary.

The Saga of American Society

York, founded in 1847, and without doubt the most aristocratic is the Tavern Club of Boston, begun in 1884. Excessively reactionary in the matter of electric lights and pedigrees, the Tavern has for its core a group even more socially fastidious than the proverbial Somerset—a noble Boston tradition which began in 1851 under the presidency of Francis B. Crowninshield, with a membership of 600 whose names— Amory, Appleton, Codman, Coolidge, Cushing, Dexter, Endicott, Gardner, Hooper, Minot, Perkins, Sears, Thayer—are still the incantation of its sesame. Probably the Somerset is the only club in America whose members do not trouble to sign checks.

Shortly after the foundation of the Tavern Club, Doctor Tilden canvassed for funds to buy a bear-cub to which he had taken a great fancy in a dime musem of freaks, kept by a giant who was proprietor as well as one of the curiosities. But a cool-headed Executive Committee vetoed the scheme out of hand, and diverted the fund to purchase a massive punch-bowl which became one of the prized possessions of the Club. Yet the "jolly brown bear" lingered in song and story, and remains the Club symbol today. One of several rousing Tavern Club bacchanals has as its burthen

> Vive la bear, vive la bear!
> Vive la, vive la, vive la bear!
> Joy we share; down with care!
> Vive la compagnie!

For the Tavern is nothing if not lyrical, with such past and present littérateurs as M. A. De Wolfe Howe, Arlo Bates, Bliss Perry, George Pierce Baker, Owen Wister, Arthur Stanwood Pier, and Charles Eliot Norton. William Dean Howells was one of its founders, aided by less literary and more traditionally Brahmin souls like Colonel Henry Lee, Major Henry Lee Higginson, and Cameron Forbes. Its present most actively venerable member is President Emeritus Abbott Lawrence Lowell, "Cousin Larry" to Beacon Street, and among its non-resident members is Mr. J. P. Morgan, exceedingly *persona grata* in Boston and at his alma mater Harvard. The Tavern Club has a long record of theatricals capably done —chiefly Elizabethan plays, and Beaumont and Fletcher in particular— and is so securely Bostonian that in 1905 it could well give a dinner in honor of Booker T. Washington with a panegyric in verse by Le Baron

The Gentleman and His Club

Russell Briggs. Some years ago Winthrop Ames celebrated the Tavern in pleasantly invidious lines:

> Every worthy club in Boston
>   Has its proper point of pride:
> At the Botolph Sunday Concerts,
>   At the Somerset 'tis "side";
> And the graveyard gives the Union
>   Its distinctive clammy calm,
> But the Dry Martini Cocktail
>   Is the Tavern's special charm!

The St. Botolph is a more democratic version of the Tavern; the Union is the bankers' and lawyers' lunch club. The Tennis and Racquet is favored by sporting youth, while for costly epicurism nothing can compare with the annual dinner of the Massachusetts Humane Society, founded in 1780 to furnish life-boats and preservers, and to award medals for acts of heroism. Extremely rich and patrician, it now devotes its surplus income to hospitals. With it should be compared the Philadelphia Skating Club and Humane Society, organized in 1849 to skate on the Schuylkill; its members always carried rope to save people who had fallen through the ice. Though owning a less ambitious program of service to humanity, it still flourishes and now does its skating indoors.

Of the resort clubs, halfway between the urban and the country club, those of Newport are examples of exclusiveness. There is the Reading Room, chartered in 1854 by William S. Wetmore, William B. Lawrence, and Edward King when Newport was a quiet summer home for a few Northern and many Southern families of quality who lived chiefly in boarding-houses. In that day Bailey's Beach was regarded as very "fast" because it licensed mixed bathing—"I confess I thought this," wrote Alexander Mackay in 1846, "more in accordance with the social habits of Paris and of Vienna than those of the United States." Women in ankle-length pantalettes and red frocks with long sleeves, and men in knee-length suits, disported themselves in the foam—the gentlemen, as Charles Augustus Murray observed in 1839, "handing about their pretty partners as if they were dancing water quadrilles." Only the walrus and the carpenter were missing, for a later generation saw the Clambake Club appear in 1897 under the sponsorship of Henry F. Eldridge, James

The Saga of American Society

Otis, Center Hitchcock, Prescott Lawrence, Frederick Paine, and others. Its shield displayed a clam above a lobster rampant, and the waggish device *Ex litore clamavi*. The Gooseberry Island Club, devoted to fishing, drinking, bathing in the nude, and dressing in time to welcome the ladies to lunch, is Newport's most *recherché*. Its dozen members today include Ogden Mills, Doctor Alexander Hamilton Rice, Doctor Henry Barton Jacobs, and others of the utmost social gravity. These are also among the present Governors of the Spouting Rock Beach Association, otherwise Bailey's Beach, which manages adroitly to be exclusive in repute and democratic in practice. For it was here that Evelyn Walsh McLean hired two private detectives to patrol the plage while she bathed, explaining, "Good Lord! I've got to be watched!" But the Governors disapproved, and Mrs. McLean abandoned her Newport campaign forever, leaving its dowagers in possession of their citadels and its tradesmen in a quandary. An earlier explorer of Newport who left a cairn to mark the spot was James Gordon Bennett, Jr., who for a time courted society as sedulously as his father had insulted it. A British army officer, Bennett's guest, on a dare rode his polo pony up the steps and into the hall of the Newport Reading Room. Indignant old members of the Reading Room, sensing the presence of a horse in their midst as the beginning of social disintegration, revoked the officer's guest-card. In reprisal Bennett resigned and built a club of his own, the Casino, on Bellevue Avenue opposite his own house. Tennis is its chief interest, an annual invitation tournament marking the height of the Newport season. On Tuesday nights in its ballroom Broadway plays are presented by the original cast, for the pleasure of an intimate group.

The country club, though few of its patrons realize it, is a peculiarly American concept. Some years ago it spread to Canada and Mexico City, and at present—viewed with conservative disapproval—is gaining a foothold in the suburbs of London, at Richmond and elsewhere. Its infection of England is somewhat ironic, because the country club is essentially the communal, telescoped American equivalent for the British week-end. A gentleman must dig his toes into the turf with fair regularity, and his children must romp in sun and wind if they are to be future empire-builders. Hence before Long Island was rediscovered with such acclaim, the country club began. Today its chief support comes from those vice-presidents of small banks, moderately successful lawyers,

The Gentleman and His Club

and busy doctors who cannot well maintain a great rural estate. Henry James, revisiting the Hudson Valley after long absence in 1906, seized upon the country club as a deeply significant American symbol—the only known organization which accepted the Family in "its extension, its *whole* extension, through social space"—father, mother, offspring of collegiate or tenderest years, with relatives and guests, and no discriminations of age or sex. To the family, in all its majestic eld or jam-smeared adolescence, it offered "new forms of felicity," as James observed with European wonder. Here he saw on golf links and tennis courts, in swimming pools and gymnasia, in restaurants and ballrooms and piazzas, "the sovereign People, as a pervasive and penetrative mass, 'doing' themselves on unprecedented lines." Of course, as he added in afterthought, there are a few people who cannot belong to country clubs, because "even the most inclusive social scheme must in a large community always stop somewhere." Happily for his own peace of mind James had not the prescience to analyze the night-club era.

The history of the country club is bound by several links with the popularity of golf. Said to be derived from the Dutch *kolf,* club or stick, this game was first imported from Holland, and played in New Netherlands with such zeal that the authorities forbade it within thickly settled areas. Dying out in its more ferocious form, the game was later revived upon the Scotch model. Charleston in 1795 had the first recorded golf club and clubhouse, on Harleston's Green; Savannah and Augusta both had golf clubs at the beginning of the nineteenth century. The Savannah Golf Club had a house on East Common where it gave banquets and balls— one of its invitations, dated December 20, 1811, for a New Year's Eve dance, hangs on the walls of the Denver Country Club. After 1818 it apparently dissolved. Such groups in general were made up of loyal Scots, who putted on a stretch of turf, drank whiskey under the apple trees, reminisced fondly about the Old Country, and entertained at rare intervals their Caledonian friends. None of these organizations lasted long. Not until the idea of the country club had already germinated near New York and Boston, with hunting, riding, and shooting as its staple sports, did golf return to America and powerfully re-enforce the need for acreage. The first golf club in the modern sense was the St. Andrews Club of Yonkers in 1888; soon thereafter its members built a suitable clubhouse. In the same year the Meadowbrook Hunt Club, organized in

1881, declined to sponsor golf, but in 1890 two young swells who had picked up the game at Biarritz, Duncan Cryder and Edward S. Mead, introduced it to Southampton and the following year founded the Shinnecock Hills Golf Club—the oldest club in America which has used continuously the same terrain. These were the "dude years" in the development of golf, which saw expensive courses laid out at Brookline as the property of "The Country Club"—only one of its kind which has never assumed a name, under the proud impression that it is *sui generis,* like the roc's egg—and at the Newport Country Club under the sponsorship of Whitney Warren, and at Westchester, whose pioneering Country Club had been founded by James M. Waterbury, sporting son of a rich New York merchant, in 1884. Not until the early twentieth century did golf reach the upper middle class, and create demands for country clubs from Detroit to Houston, Atlantic City to Los Angeles—"turning cowpastures into rich tourney fields," as Sinclair Lewis has recorded. Golf therefore was not the initial provocation for the country club, but the most potent agent in its spread.

Tuxedo, though not as sometimes stated the first country club in the United States, soon followed Westchester, and ever since its foundation in the winter of 1885–86 has remained the prince of its type. The first Peter or Pierre Lorillard in 1814 foreclosed a mortgage upon part of its territory, then a wilderness of thickets and boulders beside the lake which Indians had named Ptuck-sepo or Tuxedo. The Lorillards, successful manufacturers of cigars and snuff, continued to buy land until Pierre Lorillard III came into possession of 600,000 acres by inheritance, purchase, and winning at poker from his relatives. After consultation with his friend the architect Bruce Price, he decided in 1885 to convert this rugged but picturesque site, then reached by railway from New York, into a resort of individual cottages where the Best People who were growing tired of resort-hotels at Saratoga and Richfield Springs might come to hunt, fish, and skate. He built roads, a water and sewage system, a Park gatehouse or keeper's lodge "like a frontispiece to an English novel," twenty-two cottages, stables, swimming tank, and the clubhouse itself—a huge gray wooden structure with wide porches surrounding a ballroom where on Saturday evenings Lander's band was hired to play. A contemporary description reads: "There is a brown plush divan around the room between the windows, and a row of camp chairs where a few chaperons sit while slim girls in gauzy skirts and long corset-like silk bodices circle about in the arms of men whom an all-afternoon tramp in the stubble after birds has not fatigued." Its gala opening on May 30, 1886, drew 700 guests from New York, who were impressed to find a staff of game-keepers in green and yellow with Tyrolese hats who started self-consciously from the underwood as the liveried coachman drove past in his smart yellow buckboard. William Waldorf Astor, Grenville Kane, Peter Cooper Hewitt, and Sir Roderick Cameron, merchant and British consul in New York, were among the first cottagers. In the best English tradition Sir Roderick maintained a shooting-box there; for native partridge and woodcock were abundant, though the imported pheasants and turkeys failed to stay within the pale of the Park and were given up in despair. Mr. Lorillard spent the balance of $2,000,-000 in laying out in 1889 a golf course whose location has been changed several times, in building a race track whose grandstand is now used solely for horse and dog shows and Fourth of July sports, in constructing an electrically lit toboggan slide nearly a mile long, and in introducing court tennis in 1899 under the sponsorship of T. Suffern Tailer. The Kanes promoted fox hunting, and Mrs. James Brown Potter—then known as a relative by marriage of the saintly Bishop Potter rather than the sensational actress she later became—helped with amateur theatricals and breathed her first demoralizing whiff of grease-paint.

The first of a famous series of autumn balls, which came to mark the beginning of New York's social season, was held in October, 1886. A society reporter wrote: "Young Griswold Lorillard appeared in a tailless dress coat and waistcoat of scarlet satin, looking for all the world like a royal footman. There were several others of the abbreviated coats worn, which suggested to the onlookers that the boys ought to have been put in strait-jackets long ago." Tradition asserts that the tailless dress coat originated at a small dance given by one of the egregious Chowder and Marching Clubs in the Bowery, at which certain leaders of Irish fashion decided that swallow-tails impeded the vigor with which real dancing ought to be done, and that young Lorillard and his friends adopted the style. It is more probable however that the inspiration for the "Tuxedo"—as it was first called in society and still remains to the uninitiate—was the new English dinner-coat which the Prince of Wales and his cronies had recently adopted. Even as the distinguished black garb affected by the hero of Bulwer-Lytton's popular novel *Pelham* in 1828 had forever shamed out of favor the claret, purple, crimson, and indigo dinner-clothes of the Regency, so the semi-clerical coat affected by a most unclerical heir to the Crown and his imitators at Tuxedo changed permanently the style for informal dining and country-house parties.

Today Tuxedo has 246 members and a new clubhouse designed by John Russell Pope which was opened in 1928, built in the style of an English country place, with open terraces instead of porches. Its old architecture survives, however, in scores of provincial country clubs which had accepted it as their cynosure. Its honorary president is the present Pierre Lorillard. Other conspicuously fashionable country clubs are the Piping Rock at Locust Valley, Long Island, the Saddle and Cycle in Chicago, and the Burlingame in San Francisco. One of the most critical is the Myopia Hunt Club, founded by a near-sighted group of Bostonians in 1892 for golf, hunting, and polo. In the tradition of high living and hard riding the premier American country club is the Meadow Brook in Nassau County, Long Island, with a hunting area of some twelve by twenty miles along the Jericho Turnpike. Fox hunting was inaugurated in 1890 during the Mastership of Thomas Hitchcock, Sr.; its present president is an almost equally famous sportsman, Mr. Devereaux Milburn. Its 200 members have their distinctive evening dress, a scarlet coat with robin's egg blue facings and hunt buttons, worn with white waistcoat. Upon its field the International Polo Matches have been held since the beginning of the present century. Even more narrowly sporting is the Turf and Field Club at Belmont Park, incorporated in 1895. The Creek Club, founded later upon Long Island by Vincent Astor, Marshall Field, Clarence H. Mackay, and the late Harry Payne Whitney, is both costly and aloof. These clubs have evolved in such specialized fashion and are so heavily buttressed with wealth that they have little in common with the average pedestrian country club in America.

In the clubs heretofore mentioned, the most acute of all discriminations between the "ins" and "outs," namely secrecy, has played no part. But somewhere in the broad domain of human action it is bound to appear. To the young it gives a sense of personal power, and to the elder it satisfies the mingled hunger for fancied superiority and the pomp of ritual. Secret societies in the United States—so far removed

The Myopia Hunt Club, Hamilton, Mass.

Drawn by F. S. Coburn in 1895

from the subterranean religious and political melodrama of Latin countries—usually attract either the young or the socially underprivileged adult, who finds in the password, the grip, the cabala, a sense of exclusiveness denied him by humdrum reality. In former times and circumstances, a few secret societies enjoyed considerable social favor. The first reference to Free Masons in America occurs apparently in 1715 in a letter from the collector of the port of Philadelphia mentioning "a few evenings in festivity" with his Masonic brethren. In the days of George Washington many a Virginia planter and New England merchant was a Mason, and so much democratic distrust was long brewing against the Order that in 1826 the mysterious disappearance of an apostate Mason named William Morgan enabled Thurlow Weed to exploit the furore and form the Anti-Masonic Party in politics. During the nineteenth century, particularly in the smaller cities and towns, all prominent business men of Protestant faith regarded membership in Masonic lodges as extremely important. Today Masonry is ignored by many young men of worldly, sophisticated background, and its social standing appears to be steadily waning. Odd Fellows and Maccabees represent successive steps downward in the social scale, whatever their useful charities may be. The craving for honors and distinctions among masses of commonplace Americans was reflected in the amazing proliferation of secret societies at the close of the last century. Schlesinger computes that at least 124 new secret orders were formed between 1880 and 1890, 136 within the next five years, and 230 more by 1901. Knights of Pythias and Elks arose during the decade of the Civil War, and a little later—with a characteristic wedding of regal splendor and camaraderie in title —the Knights and Ladies of the Golden Rule, the Sons of Malta, the Royal Society of Good Fellows, the Prudent Patricians of Pompeii, and the Concatenated Order of Hoo-Hoo. Negro societies were even more magniloquent.

But the social standing of the best college societies is quite a different story. Most of them have been tinctured with secrecy and conspiratorial airs at some time in their history, and the majority—whether national fraternities or local clubs—still guard an arcana of ritual, though hardly with the grimness of half a century ago. The premier college club is without much doubt the Porcellian at Harvard. No other group which its members may ever join—and Porcellians always belong to the

The Gentleman and His Club

best clubs in every city—will claim their affection half so much. No matter how insouciant and disillusioned about life in general they may become, the most urbane feel a lump in their throat and a catch at the heart upon thoughts of the Porcellian—even as the masses are said to respond to the evocation of Home and Mother. A well-known novelist of the Philadelphia aristocracy, who was elected to the Porcellian Club fifty-seven years ago, patiently tried to describe to a questioner the nature of this feeling. "Nothing has ever meant quite so much to me. It is a bond," he added after a long minute of hesitation, "which can be felt but not analyzed." Others reply to inquiry with language faintly suggestive of mysticism, as St. Francis might speak of stigmata or Dante of Beatrice. Not only is the Porcellian a sacred subject, but belonging is a career in itself, a cultus. In the houses of members on Commonwealth Avenue, Long Island, or the Main Line, one finds that they prize and frame photographs of Club groups, while across the glass suspended from a green and white ribbon hangs a silver medal in the shape of a star with eight points, bearing crossed swords, the two dates 1791 and 1831, and the motto *Dum vivimus vivamus*. A Porcellian who lives in Greenwich has filled his handsome house from mud-scraper to rear garden with suckling pigs, hogs, and wild boars in iron, clay, china, papier-mâché, and chromium. And between the fledgling of twenty and the veteran of seventy exists an extraordinary rapport. This is of course the ideal of scores of similar clubs, but few outside Porcellian at Cambridge and Skull and Bones and Scroll and Key at New Haven seem really to achieve it.

The Porcellian is not the oldest of Harvard clubs, being outdated by the Institute of 1770, which is also patrician at an earlier stage of college life. In 1791 a few intimate friends, Harvard juniors and seniors —Joseph McKean, Charles Cutler, Henderson Inches, Robert Treat Paine, John Curtis Chamberlain, Francis Gardner, Francis C. Lowell, William Jones, and Charles Jackson—fell into the habit of meeting in each other's rooms on alternate Friday nights for talk and supper, and first called themselves the Argonauts. But one evening a member of the company invited them in to discuss the merits of a roast pig, with such jollity and success that the band came to be known briefly as The Pig Club. With a consciousness of their eminent social position they also dallied with the name of Gentlemen's Club, but soon with a happy compromise between dignity and delicatessen hit upon the name Porcellian. Charles Cutler was the first Grand Marshal and the second Joseph McKean. In 1831 a similar order of equal impeccability, the Knights of the Square Table, founded in 1809, was merged with the Porcellian by mutual desire. In those early days a strong South Carolina strain in the Porcellian mingled names like Pinckney, Huger, Rutledge, and Alston with the rock-ribbed patronymics of Saltonstall, Sedgwick, Winthrop, Codman, Perkins, Sturgis, Brimmer, Hunnewell, and Crowninshield. When the Southern tradition of Harvard waned and was finally broken forever by the Civil War, Knickerbocker and Philadelphia scions supplanted the flower of Dixie's chivalry. Famous sons of the Porcellian include Wendell Phillips, Channing, Story, Everett, Prescott, Charles Sumner, Doctor Oliver Wendell Holmes, James Russell Lowell, John Lothrop Motley, Justice Holmes, Theodore Roosevelt, and Owen Wister. Some eight to ten members are chosen from each Harvard class, generally in their sophomore year though in recent years increasingly from the upper-class brackets.[7]

Another distinguished club at Harvard is the A. D., established in 1836 as an honorary chapter of the national fraternity Alpha Delta Phi, founded at Hamilton College four years previously. In 1846 it became a regular chapter and so remained until 1859 when a great hue and cry against fraternities so assailed it that, with characteristic Harvard anti-nomianism, it defiantly became secret, highly desirable, and quite illegal —known among its members as the "Haidee," after the name of a college boat and, incidentally, Don Juan's mistress. In 1865 the chapter handed in its national charter and became the A. D. Club of Harvard alone; a later attempt to revive Alpha Delta Phi from 1879 to 1907 failed but left as its progeny the Fly Club. In view of the failure of national fraternities to strike root in Cambridge one recalls the boast of William James that "our irreconcilables are our proudest product," or

[7]That ominous gaps may sometimes occur in such solid ranks is at least suggested by early Catalogues of the Porcellian Club, which for many years give a notable dash beside the name of the Librarian for 1836. Beginning with the Catalogue of 1887, after this fifty years' mysterious silence, the names of Christopher Columbus Holmes and John Francis Tuckerman are supplied.

Another socially acceptable organization is the Hasty Pudding Club founded in 1795 "to cherish the feelings of friendship and patriotism." It is best known for its theatricals of the lighter sort, and with its miscellaneous functions includes many members of the Porcellian, Fly, and A. D.

The Gentleman and His Club

the half-serious attempt which one critic made to explain the difference between Harvard and Yale by pointing to William Graham Sumner as the timeless model of all good Yale men, with his preoccupation with

The Hasty Pudding Club, Harvard
From a drawing by Otto H. Bacher in 1897

folkways and mores, the gospel of social conformity—and over against him William James, Harvard man *in excelsis,* experimentalist and rebel living by the lights of individual judgment.

Undergraduate life at Cambridge has not lacked for bitter passages, which compel notice from any anatomist of society. On the one hand there has long been a snobbery moulded of New England pride and juvenile cruelty which is probably more savage than any known to Fifth Avenue and Newport. Its favorite illustration is the time-worn tale of the lonely lad who to feign that he had *one* friend used to go out as dusk fell over the Yard and call beneath his own windows, "Oh, Reinhardt!"[8] And on the other it has had moments of mad, terrible loyalty —exampled by the episode which is still recalled, awesomely without names, over the coffee and liqueurs when Harvard men meet in Beacon Street or the South Seas. It is the true story of a Harvard senior at a party in Brookline, who suddenly enraged by a jocular remark made concerning the girl whom he later married, publicly slapped the face of his best friend—and then in an access of remorse walked to an open fire and held his offending hand in the flame until it shrivelled away to the wrist. *Réclame* is added because the self-martyr, who spent agonizing days in the hospital, was related to the proudest of Hudson Valley families and became a noted essayist and critic, and because the young jester bore Boston's premier social and intellectual name, and achieved future high honors in science.

Of the senior societies at Yale only two matter socially, the Russell Trust Association, known as Skull and Bones, founded in 1832, and the Kingsley Trust or Scroll and Key, begun in 1842. In May members of each junior class lounge about the Memorial Quadrangle, trying to look as nonchalant as possible under the eyes of several hundred spectators, and furtively watching seniors dressed completely in black save for a gold insignia at the throat—who, after glaring about with zest, suddenly catch sight of a favorite and with a solemn blow on the shoulder, which is never a slap, bestow the highest of all possible accolades. The lucky fellow grins nervously, flushes to the ears, and runs to his room, followed by the Hound of the undergraduates' Heaven, who there gives him private instructions. Such is Tap Day, currently known as "desire under the elms." Some twelve to fifteen are chosen by each society, "the

[8]The implications of this story were not lost during its greatest currency fifteen years ago when Harvard College, panicky over the magnetism of the School of Business Administration, was attempting with supposed subtlety to limit the quota of Jews. On the authority of a late registrar of Yale, the Harvard Admissions Board at that time was examining one day the candidacy of a young man whose aspect was suspiciously Semitic. Among other arch questions he was asked, "And what language do you speak at home?" "Oh," said the candidate simply, "we always speak English, but I think I can soon pick up enough Yiddish to get around in the Harvard Yard."

The Gentleman and His Club

best men of the year" in social background, wealth, good fellowship, athletic or literary prowess—preferably a combination of two or more qualities. Skull and Bones is a national byword, but young gentlemen of great social fastidiousness have been known to prefer Scroll and Key. The latter pre-eminently represents caste and "seasoned wealth," while the former specializes in achievement—editors of *The Daily News* and *The Lit.*, football captains, and brilliant young scholars who at times have to be coerced into wearing neckties, cleaning finger nails, and brushing hair; it also taps Heinzes and Manvilles of less seasoned wealth. Skull and Bones has even been known to smile upon graduates of high schools; to Scroll and Key this anarchy would be unthinkable.

Members traditionally avoid all reference to their own or rival societies in the presence of outsiders. On their way to Saturday night dinners in the "tombs"—massive windowless façades encased in ivy and Virginia creeper, with iron doors secured by padlocks—they bid good-bye to whatever friends may be with them, and with a sharp turn march the last few steps alone and in reverent silence. Never do they allude to anything which happens within those Lethean portals, and according to a standing joke even the black servants and the grocer's boys who penetrate those tombs through the postern gate are inviolable Bones or Keys men. Years ago Skull and Bones built a great fortress of brown sandstone with a terraced playground behind its tomb, intending to afford members a place of permanent domicile so that during their senior year in Yale College they need never set foot on unhallowed ground save to attend lectures. Opposition from Faculty and Corporation was so strong, however, that the scheme was abandoned, and today that grimly feudal structure houses the Yale School of Architecture. Both societies are immensely rich through gifts, and their old members so potent in American finance that it is said no neophyte has cause ever to worry about a future job. Both have weathered many storms of democratic opposition and mockery. Bottles of ink used to be smashed against their doors and the chains torn from their staples. A bogus society called Bowl and Stones used to divert itself by comic songs, posting derisive hand-bills, stealing ice-cream prepared for inaugural banquets, tapping simple-minded classmates and instructing them to knock on the door at given times, and travestying the supposed ritual in the manner of the Black Mass. Not more than six years ago the editor of a sheet called *The Harkness Hoot* virulently attacked senior societies in general and Scroll and Key in particular, with the stock democratic

Scroll and Key Club House at Yale
Drawn by Orson Lowell in 1896

arguments. Quietly Scroll and Key claimed him on Tap Day, secured his prompt acceptance, and left him to abysmal obloquy. Cynics whispered that his elder brother had gained admittance five years before to a senior society by similar tactics. Such victories are Pyrrhic.

Under President McCosh Greek letter fraternities had been extirpated from Princeton. But in the fall of 1877 sixteen sophomores, disgusted with the food at the one village restaurant, and having just been expelled from Commons for rough-housing, bought a stove, hired a cook, and in Ivy Hall set up the first eating club. David M. Massie, a future judge, Blair Lee, later U. S. Senator, and Henry W. Frost, destined to

Skull and Bones Club House, Yale
Drawn by Orson Lowell in 1896

become a Doctor of Divinity, were its first officers. The Ivy Club began to invite likable fellows to join them and share expenses as old members dropped out, and soon was self-perpetuating. Within five years, largely through the efforts of Pliny Fiske, Arthur H. Scribner, and

Charles A. Munn, it was installed in its own clubhouse. During the next decade it gained further power from the presence on its Board of Governors of Junius Spencer Morgan, C. Ledyard Blair, and Horatio Turnbull. The devotion which Ivy could inspire is best illustrated by George Kerr Edwards, a graduate of '89, who years later stricken with an incurable disease returned to Princeton and the Ivy Club to die, bequeathed it his worldly goods, attended his last Annual Dinner and passed away during Commencement Week. Among his last acts was the writing of a letter to the Board of Governors praising "this one devoted spot, this dear old Ivy Club of ours. Thus in this clumsy fashion may I be allowed to set forth my feelings in regard to Princeton as a whole and our dear old Club as an integral part of that glorious whole. Let me be so bold as to urge upon each Ivy man, past, present, and those to come, to earnestly and continually strive to push onward and expand our present prestige by word and deed, so that amongst Princeton men, to say 'I am an Ivy man' shall correspond to the proud declaration of the ancient Roman, 'I am a Roman citizen.'"

Endowed also by Cuylers, Van Rensselaers, Osborns, McCormicks, Winants, and Brokaws, and numbering among its literary and scholastic lights Henry and Paul van Dyke, Booth Tarkington, and James Boyd, Ivy continued to flourish—and inspired later clubs like Cap and Gown, the Colonial, and Tiger Inn, along Prospect Avenue. A new President of Princeton, Woodrow Wilson, grew alarmed at their power. In his report to the Trustees in December, 1906, he wrote: "It would be difficult to exaggerate the importance in the life of the undergraduate of the question whether at the end of his Sophomore year he is going to be taken in to one of the upper-class clubs. His thought is constantly fixed upon that object throughout the first two years of his university course with a great intensity and uneasiness whenever he thinks either of his social standing, his comradeship, or his general social considerations among his fellows. The clubs do not take in all the members of the Junior and Senior classes. About one-third are left out in the elections; and their lot is little less than deplorable. . . . It often happens that men who fail of election into one of the clubs at the end of the Sophomore year leave the University and go to some other college or abandon altogether the idea of completing their university course." Believing that "the side-shows" were swallowing up the circus, and that "any organi-

The Gentleman and His Club

zation which introduces elements of social exclusiveness constitutes the worst possible soil for serious intellectual endeavor," the great idealist undertook to make Princeton safe for democracy. For three turbulent years, ending only in 1910 with his resignation to run for Governor of New Jersey, Wilson fought to abolish "bicker week," to supplant eating-clubs with quadrangles where rich and poor, senior and freshman, high and lowly, might live and dine together. Mingled also in his epic war was a crusade against an isolated graduate school, and the dominion of wealth represented by a conditional gift of $500,000 from a wealthy soap manufacturer, William C. Procter. Social and financial power was represented in the heart of Princeton by Moses Taylor Pyne, who from the "Momo" of Wilson's affectionate letters became his suave but inflexible enemy. A trustee of different mettle was David B. Jones, a Welshman who had risen to business success in Chicago; ever loyal to Wilson and the democratic idea he wrote in November, 1907: "If Mr. Pyne thinks it best to withdraw his support, I shall be very sorry, but I shall be infinitely more sorry to see the University dominated by the club men of New York, Philadelphia and Pittsburgh." Wealth and aristocracy fought back: Mr. Procter withdrew his offer, Wilson was excoriated in the New York press, even Mrs. Wilson as the President's wife was not invited to a place in the receiving line at a notable reception at the 1910 Commencement. Only Wilson's translation to public spheres brought the struggle to a close—leaving the Ivy Club unliquidated and at peace, with Dean West to select appropriate Latin mottoes to inscribe over its two great fire-places. But it had been the fiercest of all struggles between aristos and demos in the American college. Today Wilson's "Quad System," called the House Plan at Harvard and the College Plan at Yale, financed by Edward S. Harkness, is more subtly undermining the old undergraduate gods. That new ones will arise in their place no realist can doubt.

Snobbery is inseparable from the college campus. Forty years ago before the decline of Greek and Latin the majority were called by the anointed *hoi polloi;* twenty years ago they were "the Great Unwashed," and during the Jazz Age "wet smacks." Today they are known as "black men," "drips," and "meat-balls." Always to fraternity men they have been "barbarians" or "barbs"—as the Hellenes of old regarded the Persians, so termed in mockery of their outlandish gibberish. College fraternities in America have initiated well over 800,000 members, of whom half a million are still living. They embrace approximately 200 societies, with a total of 4500 chapters located at 660 colleges; of these about 1000 are honorary or semi-honorary, and therefore chiefly intellectual rather than social. Some $30,000,000 are invested in fraternity and sorority houses and furnishings. The first Greek letter society was Phi Beta Kappa, founded at William and Mary in 1776 by a young classical scholar dissatisfied with the local Society "F. H. C.," possibly because it overlooked him. Adopting the motto, long treasured as a precious secret, of φιλοσοφία βίου κυβερνήτης, "philosophy the guide of life," he took its initial letters Phi Beta Kappa as the name of a society with ritual, grip, oath of fidelity, and badge. Ambitions of expansion were soon achieved at Yale and Harvard. In 1831 after the great agitation of the Anti-Masonic Party, John Quincy Adams and Judge Story gravely debated and finally decided that Phi Beta Kappa should abandon any pretense to secrecy. This was done first at Harvard and later at Yale, completely transforming the character of the society, which soon became the organization of high scholastic honor which it has since remained.

The real pattern for the American fraternity system was set at Union College in 1825 by John Hunter and his friends, who established Kappa Alpha; stimulated by democratic and faculty opposition it prospered, and in imitation Sigma Phi and Delta Phi arose two years later. In 1832 at Hamilton College was founded Alpha Delta Phi, whose reputation particularly in the East has been rather fashionable and literary, though the withering of its hopes at Harvard and later at Yale has been a heavy blow. Psi Upsilon was started at Union College in 1833 and has long enjoyed a prosperous history, though it likewise has witnessed the withdrawal of its eminently rich and social Yale chapter from national affiliation to become "The Fence"—even as Delta Kappa Epsilon ("Deke"), begun at New Haven in 1844, and associated with the hearty life, has shown no great enthusiasm of paternity for its provincial offspring, while the Harvard chapter has become "The Dickey." Fraternity men in the older and more snobbish colleges are often a little proud of not knowing the grip of their order, incline to laugh at its naïve initiations with red devils and phosphorescent skeletons, and pointedly snub the eager, puppy-like advances of their brethren from Maine and Iowa. Fraternities which had the misfortune to originate in the Mid-West, such as Beta Theta Pi at Miami University in Ohio, are still regarded as socially second-rate in the complacent East. Chi Psi, begotten at Union in 1841, ranks high in the West but elsewhere has rarely risen to a parity with the earlier Union College foundations. Socially damned in most universities are fraternities like Alpha Chi Rho and Alpha Sigma Phi; their members, unable discreetly to boast that they turned down all the bids of Rush Week, are hopelessly confirmed in mediocrity. The first sorority was the I. C. Sorosis at Monmouth College, Illinois, in 1867, which soon took the name Pi Beta Phi; three years later Kappa Kappa Gamma began upon the same campus. The same year saw the foundation of Kappa Alpha Theta at a college which is now De Pauw University, with Delta Gamma following at Oxford, Mississippi, in 1872. Collegiate fraternalism has its banalities—not the least of these being the dull and occasionally smutty songs of males, the thinly saccharine lyrics of females, piously sung between courses at dinner—and its occasional abuses in the matter of hazing and even more smarting social brutality. Formerly in some Southern and Western colleges the haste to secure desirable members was so keen that "preps" were pledged and even initiated before entering the university, and pledge-pins were even handed out to boys in grammar-grades; today such behavior is outlawed. Yet one who has lived much in a college town cannot but feel kindly toward fraternities: on the whole they are a civilizing influence and a discipline, and their idealism though ingenuous is not without excellence.[9]

Of the making of clubs there is no end. The curious American blend of business and social intercourse, of comradeship with an eye to "contacts," appears most clearly in those boosters' luncheon clubs formally begun by the Rotarians in Chicago in 1905. They attempted to select one representative of each business, profession, and institution in the city. For some years the movement languished, gained momentum with the foundation of Kiwanis in 1915 and of the Lions in 1917, and reached its zenith with the post-War prosperity. The hornets of satire were not far behind, and stung with such pungence that for several years Elks and

[9]An attempt to found a kind of social register of fraternity men was begun but abandoned by one Will J. Maxwell from 1898 to 1903. He compiled and published a series called *Fraternity Men* or *Greek Letter Men* of the following cities and regions: Albany, Baltimore, Boston, Chicago, Minnesota, New York, St. Louis, Syracuse, Washington, Rocky Mountain States, Pacific Coast. The standard reference work for American college fraternities is Baird's *Manual,* begun in 1879, now in its 13th edition. *Banta's Greek Exchange* (1913–   ) is the chief periodical now serving the pan-Hellenic group.

The Saga of American Society

Rotarians came to be the most enthusiastic followers of *The American Mercury*. Today Mr. Sinclair Lewis turns his gaze upon shapes of things to come more alarming than Babbitt's waistline, while Mr. Henry L. Mencken appears to have been stranded, like the Ark upon Ararat, by the receding tide of the Zeitgeist. Yet the bourgeois business man we have always with us, even as he seems to have existed in 1781 at Salem, Mass., where the Marquis de Chastellux noted: "Stopped at Good-hue's inn. There was held in this inn a sort of merchants' club. Two or three of its members came to see me." Obviously they were greeters. Only last year the proprietor of an enterprising hotel in the West, an incarnate Rotarian, informed the writer that he personally attended to the welcoming of every guest in its 1000 rooms, adding "And, by God, when *I* greet them they *stay* greeted!"

It is in fact no far cry to the club-like aspect of the American luxury hotel. As early as 1846 Sir Charles Lyell observed their "tacit recognition of an aristocracy" in the head-waiter's reservation of certain tables or rooms for the *ton*. Under no circumstances could the ordinary commercial traveller tip his way into the Ladies' Ordinary. In Boston there was the old Tremont House, later the Revere House, upon which the Prince of Wales set his approval, and still later the Parker House. New Orleans had its Saint Charles, St. Louis its Planters Hotel, Denver the Brown Palace Hotel, and Chicago its Palmer House. All in their day bore the social cachet. In New York the Astor House in the 1840's was termed by a journalist "that simple and chaste, though massive establishment which for centuries to come will serve as a monument to the wealth of its proprietor." Little did he dream of that later and greater hotel built upon land owned by the same resplendent family, demolished at length only to rise elsewhere in superior glory, the Waldorf-Astoria— which, as the late Oliver Herford blandly observed, finally "brought exclusiveness to the masses."

CHAPTER EIGHT

WOMEN IN AMERICAN SOCIETY

IN every age where women have been given relief from labor and an honorable place, society has bloomed; as soon as they have been ordered to shut their mouths and sent back to the kitchen, it has waned. The reasons are not far to seek. Society is feminine in that it ranks strategy above directness, and grace above strength; moreover woman—custodian of the cultural as well as the physical germ-plasm—has an instinctive appreciation of the codes, barriers, patterns, and traditions which the formation of social classes creates. In fact the ultimate aims glimpsed through the mechanisms of society—the achievement of leisure without boredom, the sheltering of a fastidious minority behind walls of economic and social security, and the preservation of caste through marriage—usually appeal more strongly to woman the great conservative than to her husband.

Byron, approving the old Greek idea of women as drudges and brood-mares, noted: "They ought to mind home—and be well fed and clothed —but not mixed in society." As might be expected, social life among the freemen of Athens and Sparta was simple, democratic, disorganized, highly individualistic, while woman's place was in the home, or, even more specifically, in the bed. Not till the days of Imperial Rome, when the newly rich Cæsars began to feel that an idle wife was the conspicuous measure of a man's extravagance, did the Society Woman first arise —bringing in her wake the nuances of snobbery and intrigue, the elegances of bath and boudoir, the art of dining, and the private collection of jewels, pictures, and statuary. Even the society page seems to have begun with the Acta Diurna, over which the lady of quality whiled away the forenoon, while the rise of the clubwoman or bluestocking is shadowed in Juvenal's weary protest: "Let a husband be allowed to make a solecism in peace." Later, Christianity confirmed the higher place of woman, and the Middle Ages enshrined the lady of noble birth in its cult of chivalry. With the rise of the *salon* she became a patroness of the arts and graces as well as the mistress of repartee, which became to her what the duello was to the gentleman. The eighteenth-century woman of breeding came to express herself in terms of a new confidence that made her ancestresses seem like a lineage of milksops. Abigail Adams, queen of America's premier intellectual family—who incidentally used to call the people of this country "the mobility"—wrote in 1776 with grave playfulness to her husband, who was in Philadelphia helping draft the Declaration of Independence: "If particular care and attention are not paid to the ladies, we are determined to foment a rebellion, and will not hold ourselves bound by any laws in which we have no voice or representation." Shortly the Industrial Revolution endowed the lady of leisure with undreamt-of luxuries, changed her life slowly from that of a country chatelaine to a metropolitan hostess, and released a great host of parvenus to batter the gates of a small, serene, largely hereditary citadel. And finally the so-called political and economic "emancipation" of women in the next century gave to the arbitress of fashion a larger background of assurance; significantly, one of the *grandes dames* of American society, who by marriage increased the fame of both Vanderbilts and Belmonts, was among the first sensationally to break precedents by demanding her rights to divorce and the ballot.

With mingled admiration and amusement, the fashionable European visitor for the past century and a half has been calling the American woman a new type, a spoiled child, a benevolent but costly tyrant, a paragon of charm, a beauty "nonchalante et froide." Even more valid are the opinions of occasional American men like N. P. Willis and Henry James, whose fastidious, slightly epicene temperament made them sensitive to changes in the social climate. The former wrote in 1855:

The present is the first century, and this is the first country, of the world, in which *the female sex* is (collectively, and all qualities taken into account) *superior to the male*. . . . It is the women who regulate the style of living, dispense hospitalities, exclusively manage society, control clergymen and churches, regulate the schemes of benevolence, patronize and influence the Arts, and pronounce upon Operas and foreign novelties; and it is the women . . . who exercise the ultimate control over the Press.

Half a century later Henry James, repressing a shudder at the typical American plutocrat, thus paid his respects to the wife:

Women in American Society

Nothing, meanwhile, is more concomitantly striking than the fact that the women, over the land—allowing for every element of exception—appear to be of a markedly finer texture than the men, and that one of the liveliest signs of this difference is precisely in their less narrowly specialized, their less commercialized, distinctly more generalized, physiognomic character. . . . It is at all events no exaggeration to say that the imagination at once embraces it as *the* feature of the social scene.

Every generation complains anew that the American business man is too deeply absorbed in making money to take part in social leadership. As early as 1824 Betsy Patterson Bonaparte, a Baltimore merchant's daughter, whose marriage in 1803 to Jerome the brother of Napoleon founded a family which has been fitfully prominent in American society, wrote from her native city after a long sojourn abroad that "the men are all merchants; and commerce, although it may fill the purse, clogs the brain. Beyond their counting-houses they possess not a single idea; they never visit except when they wish to marry."[1] Typical of a later day is the "French criticism" of an American girl quoted in *Gems of Deportment* (1882). We learn that she must resign herself to hearing "at night nothing except discussions about patent machinery, unexplosive petroleum, chemical manures" from her male relatives, however eager she may be for gaiety and flirtation. Indeed the clumsiness and social torpor of the successful business man have been the butt of satirists for well over a hundred years. Sometimes the men themselves have endorsed the

[1] Betsy Patterson, who according to gossip recorded in J. Q. Adams's Diary had "seduced" the nineteen-year-old Jerome into marriage, to the boundless rage of Napoleon, was during the period of her first return to America (1805-1815) the sensation of society. Mrs. William Seaton, friend of Dolly Madison, writes: "Madame Bonaparte is a model of fashion, and many of our belles strive to imitate her"—though her perfect back and shoulders were conceded to be inimitable. The Yankee Puritan Simeon Baldwin wrote to his wife from Washington, January 12, 1805: "Her dress at a Ball which she attended has been a general topic of conversation in all circles. Having married a Parissian [*sic*] she assumed the mode of dress in which it is said the Ladies of Paris are clothed—if that may be called clothing which leaves half of the body naked & the rest perfectly visible— Several of the Gent^n who saw her say they could put all the cloaths she had on in their vest pockett. . . . Tho' her taste & appearance was condemned by those who saw her, yet such fashions are astonishingly bewitching & will gradually progress, & we may well reflect on what we shall be when fashion shall remove all barriers from the chastity of women." Divorced by orders from Napoleon, she had another social whirl abroad, but finally returned to Baltimore to spend her last eighteen years in a cheap boarding-house and bequeath a fortune of $1,500,000 to her only son Jerome Napoleon Bonaparte.

charge, as in the famous outburst of Charles Francis Adams II, sometime President of the Union Pacific and of the Kansas City Stockyards, against his fellow-directors: "Not one that I have ever known would I care to meet again either in this world or the next: nor is one of them associated in my mind with the idea of humor, thought, or refinement." The dreariness surrounding the old self-made millionaire echoes in the wistful confession of the great banker James Stillman at the close of his career—words which Sinclair Lewis consciously or unconsciously put into the mouth of Babbitt—"I have never in all my life done anything I wanted."

Yet the grubbing which kills social grace as well as the soul is not unrelated to the demand for diamonds and sables. The business man himself has found sympathy since the days when Harriet Martineau noted in New York that merchants rose early, gulped a cup of coffee, and toiled in the dust and heat of Pearl Street all day in order that their wives might wear bonnets costing $100 apiece. James Silk Buckingham in 1837 observed the "morning promenade" of "beautiful and gaily-dressed ladies" down Broadway unaccompanied by any such gentlemen of fashion as one would find in Regent Street; he found their fathers and husbands instead drudging behind desks or on the stock-exchange with pallid, anxious faces. In *Fashion* (1845) Mrs. Mowatt has the French maid comment to the footman: "Monsieur is man of business, —Madame is lady of fashion. Monsieur make the money,—Madame spend it. Monsieur nobody at all,—Madame, everybody altogether." Fifty years later Paul Bourget found that in America the business man had undergone an almost complete social self-effacement: he felt most at home not in his glittering château built by Richard Hunt on Fifth Avenue, but in his office or club or at the bar of some downtown hotel— while for his smartly groomed wife and daughters he felt more pride than affection. They ranked with his yacht and stables as the visible badge of good fortune, of what Thorstein Veblen was to call "the ability to withstand pecuniary damage." By this time the "hostess" had completely eclipsed the "host" in the columns of society news, and the presence of "extra men" at dinner and dancing parties was coming to be regarded as a triumph. Of course with the faster tempo of business competition during the same era, the millionaire sometimes worked himself literally to death, especially if he attempted to play the social game until

Women in American Society

the stars paled. In contrast with such ripe octogenarians as the first John Jacob Astor and the first Cornelius Vanderbilt, and the present nonagenarian Rockefeller, with their simple, even homely ways of life, one recalls the scores of notably rich Americans who have sunk at middle age under the accumulated burden of business worries, late hours, strong cocktails and rich food, leaving a surplus of bridge-playing dowagers who are perhaps the most striking feature of our social landscape.

Man has usually submitted without challenge to the woman's rule of American society. In the first place he has never really abandoned the attitude, old as pioneer days, that hard daily toil is man's unremitting portion, even when there is no longer the spur of need—like the rich young heir of the 1830's who, we read, "wearied out with his solitary leisure . . . could find no other relief than to open a fancy-goods shop." The first fabulous merchant-banker, Stephen Girard, once confessed that "my love of work is the only pleasure I have on this globe" and held piously that "every man should labor to the last hour of his ability." The American kings of industry, usually married to the queens of society, have seldom made a fine art of leisure, self-cultivation, and social amenity, in the tradition which practically disappeared from the New World with the Virginia and Carolina planter—a tradition in which the second William Byrd stood shoulder to shoulder with Lord Chesterfield, and in which John Randolph of Roanoke wrote: "The muck-worm whose mind knows no other work than money-keeping or money-getting is an object of pity or contempt." A little near-sighted socially, the typical American plutocrat has seldom been able to tell a gentleman of leisure from a trifler. In consequence the *arbiter elegantiarum* of real taste and manliness, like Dominick Lynch in post-Revolutionary New York, was supplanted by a mannered snob on the pattern of Ward McAllister or an effeminate dandy like Harry Lehr. Moreover, the very qualities which made a man successful in the hurly-burly of the Gilded Age—ambition, boldness, and an eye to the main chance—were not necessarily those which fitted him for either the cultivated life or graceful frivolity. Hence the boisterous attempts at geniality, the dearth of small-talk, and the ill-suppressed yawns after dinner which our foreign critics maliciously set down in their notebooks. In fact, building a great material empire seems to have drained the elder American of that color, imagination, charm, and sense of play as necessary to the creation of an attractive social

personality as to the creation of art. He exhausted his fantasy by expressing it in steel and stone.

There is perhaps still another cause for the insignificance of man in
American society, as compared with his traditional rôle at the Court of
St. James's and in the coteries of the Faubourg St. Germain. The total
destruction of primogeniture and entail just after the Revolution robbed

© Life Publishing Co.

Mr. Meeker doesn't object so much to his wife's entertainments as he does to the way
she uses his room for the gentlemen's things

C. D. Gibson in *Life* in 1902

man of the hereditary importance he had possessed under the European
system with the founding of a great house, the accumulation of broad
acres, and the transmission of his name attached to that estate forever.
In Old World aristocracies the male was the vessel in which social values
were conserved. Although wife and daughters might add to the wit and
beauty of drawing-rooms, man was the mainstay of the peerage and wore
the larger strawberry leaves in his coronet and the superior ermine on
his cloak. In marriage he endowed the woman with his social rank, like
King Cophetua and the beggar-maid, or, as in the modern parable, the peer
and the parvenue. Furthermore, today, any Englishwoman who acquires

a "dignity" by marriage loses it legally upon remarriage to a commoner. Quite different has been the trend of American society, by which rich Astors, Vanderbilts, and Belmonts have risen from social nobodies to nobility by marriage with patrician women from the Livingston, Armstrong, Schermerhorn, Kissam, and Perry families. American millionaires who have chosen generations of worthy but not socially dazzling

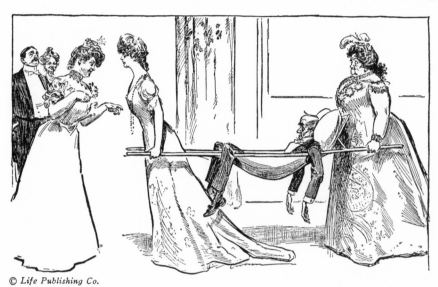

© *Life Publishing Co.*

Pillsbury does not care for Society, but his wife will not go without him

C. D. Gibson in *Life* in 1902

or ambitious wives, like the majority of Rockefellers and Du Ponts, have never moved in the top flight of fashion—while new merchant princes, beer barons, and pork packers, bursting upon the scene with dowdy wives, have seldom got within hailing distance of the Smart Set. The first Mrs. John Jacob Astor, who swept her mother's boarding-house and helped her young husband in the curing and appraisal of furs, and the first wife of Commodore Vanderbilt, who ran a little water-front hotel called Bellona Hall, patiently bore her husband twelve children, but complained when he moved her from Staten Island to the bright lights of Manhattan, illustrate the *raison d'être* of the proverb that in America it takes two generations to make a gentleman. The first generation seldom arrives married to a lady. Also there is the potent American tradition that, while a self-made man who slaps friends on the back, scatters cigar ashes and mistakes in grammar, and chews with mouth ajar may be indulgently excused or even praised as a diamond in the rough, yet his wife, who says no more than "pleased to meet you," is damned as the flashiest kind of rhinestone, usually by her own sex. If on the other hand the man is single there is always a chance, at least, that he will marry a social mentor.

The attempt to make America safe from democracy has been very largely a feminine enterprise. Of course there are rare exceptions, like Sarah Franklin Bache, only daughter of Benjamin Franklin, who took a rather important part in late eighteenth-century society, but inherited enough of her father's homespun doctrine to rebuke a schoolmaster who had treated her children obsequiously because they were "young ladies of rank," whereupon Franklin's daughter tartly observed, "There is no rank in this country but rank mutton." Later Baches have foresworn such radical notions of equality. The difference between the prevailing social attitude of man and woman in America has been frequently noticed. Mackay, a shrewd Briton of the mid-nineteenth century, commented: "The professional man may be on the very best of terms with the blacksmith, but ten chances to one if the daughters of the professional man know the blacksmith's daughters, or if they would acknowledge it if they did." Mrs. Woolson in 1873 believed that "If our government were delivered wholly into the hands of women of fashion and society, we should have a monarchy and an hereditary order of nobility established within a twelvemonth." In 1912, a writer in the Paris *Gaulois* remarked that American society was divided sharply in two—on one side the men, "eager democrats, genial merchants, who spend their time in making money," and on the other the women, "petted children of aristocracy, who amuse themselves in spending the fortunes of the men." Certainly a whole crop of native novels from *The Rise of Silas Lapham* to *Dodsworth* supports this point of view.

Surrendering the social dictatorship to wives and daughters with a distinct feeling of relief, men have seldom tried to enforce their more democratic bias in the drawing-room. To be sure there have been isolated cases—such as President Andrew Jackson's long campaign to get recognition among the ladies of Washington for "Peg" (or, as the newspapers called her, "Bellona") Eaton, an innkeeper's gay daughter who had married one of his Cabinet officers. Jackson easily enlisted bachelors and widowers, but found inflexible opposition from all the women, including the hostess of the White House, his favorite niece Mrs. Donelson, whom he sent packing to the hills of Tennessee for her refusal to call on Mrs. Eaton. What the press described as "keeping Bellona afloat socially" became a major problem of Old Hickory's administration, and finally split the Cabinet asunder. Ironically enough, Mrs. Eaton went to Spain with her husband as Minister, grew to be a favorite of the Queen, and married off one daughter to a Randolph of Virginia and another to the French Duc de Sampayo; a granddaughter became the Baroness de Rothschild of Austria. And of course there have been random gestures of defiance against the feminine idea of polite society—like that of the late B. P. Hutchinson ("Old Hutch"), gaunt sardonic meat packer and banker of Chicago, who once invited a horde of workingmen to dine at his house on the evening his wife had arranged a large dinner-party for society: with the result that the men in shirtsleeves ate and drank noisily in one part of the mansion "while the people in evening clothes dined, rather uneasily, in another." But woman's social power has in general been uncontested. Furthermore, in accord with their social rôle, women have been the chief genealogists of America—as guiding spirits of the Mayflower Society, Colonial Dames, Daughters of the American Revolution, and the Order of the Crown of America bear witness—and in recent years they have built a structure of clubs, leagues, societies, and sororities which is unparalleled throughout the world. Realists suggest that any woman who is blackballed by a club retaliates by starting one of her own. Certainly the American woman's sense of social place is often extraordinarily acute: the author recalls the remark of a dowager in Denver that her family plot in Fairmount Cemetery was "right there among the Kountzes and the Evanses and the other best people, with whom we have always associated."

A chronicle of notable women in American society is rather meager in respect to Colonial New England. Wives of the Puritan theocracy worked hard, minded their tongues, feared God, and frequently died in childbed. The women of spirit and social antecedents about whom we hear— Anne Bradstreet the poetess, or Lady Deborah Moody who came to the New World because she took her theology earnestly, but quarrelled with Boston on the subject of infant baptism, and finally settled on Long Island among the more congenial Stuyvesants, or Lady Arbella Johnson, who, according to Cotton Mather, "left an earthly *paradise* in the family of an Earldom, to encounter the sorrows of a *wilderness,* for the entertainments of a *pure worship* in the house of God; and then immediately left that *wilderness* for the Heavenly paradise"—these are hardly the stuff from which a smart set is made. Yet we have the record of at least one unnamed social aspirant from John Dunton, the English bookseller who visited Boston in 1685; he tells of a dame who "takes as much state upon her, as wou'd have serv'd six of Queen Elizabeth's Countesses; and yet she's no Lady neither."

Despite the patrician claims of their descendants, the Dutch women of Colonial New York were less distinguished for social charm and grace than for thrift, initiative, and commercial shrewdness. Judith Bayard, wife of Peter Stuyvesant, spoke several languages and served as interpreter for the citizens of New Amsterdam; Margaret Philipse owned and operated a fleet of transatlantic merchantmen; Anne Van Cortlandt laid down one of the first cobbled streets in the metropolis to protect her house from the dust of brewery wagons; Maria Provoost Alexander, ancestress of the Duers, drove a sharp bargain for £30 a few hours after giving birth to a child, and eventually achieved a fine house on Broad Street with a blue and gold leather room, a green and gold leather room, and a large staff of servants. Maria de Peyster, famed in nursery rhyme as Mrs. Jack Spratt, kept the only coach and four with the exception of the Governor's, and was the cynosure of the social plutocracy. According to tradition these women had their literary club, "The Rose," at which they read original verses and essays, while most of the men smoked and drank beer in another room; they share with a little group of goodwives who met at Anne Hutchinson's house in Boston to discuss theology and current events the place of pioneers in the women's club movement. The terror of New York Society in the early eighteenth century was Lady Cornbury, wife of the governor, who (we are told) "had fallen in love with her ear, which was very beautiful." Marriage brought disillusion, and even her ear ceased to please him; in fact he treated her so shabbily that she was forced to gratify her taste for luxuries by calling in state upon wealthy burghers, admiring clothes and bric-a-brac which she asked to "borrow"—with the knowledge that no one could refuse her, and the equal certainty that she would never return them. Hence the rumbling of her Ladyship's coach through the streets came to be the signal for hiding all movable treasure. Lady Cornbury would also flatter young ladies of quality by inviting them to spend a few days at the governor's mansion, and end by inveigling them into mending and housecleaning. Probably few women have ever exploited their social status more shamelessly. It might be added that her husband was even more extraordinary: having been told that he was being sent to New York to represent his cousin Queen Anne, he fancied that he must do so literally, often dressed himself in skirts and high-heeled shoes, and in the cool of the evening loved to pirouette upon the ramparts, fan in hand.

Society in Colonial Virginia can claim the first personal maid to set foot upon this Continent—one Anne Burras, who arrived in the service of Mistress Forrest, wife of Thomas Forrest, Gent., in 1609 in the second Virginia Supply. It can also claim the first presentation at the British Court, that of Pocahontas in 1616 under the social sponsorship of Lady De La Warr—first of a long line of American princesses who have been received there with polite astonishment. With the burgeoning of society in tidewater Virginia the hostess flourished. Noteworthy was Mrs. Alexander Spotswood, wife of the Governor of Virginia in the first quarter of the eighteenth century, who ruled a great feudal estate on the banks of the Rapidan, "an enchanted Castle" Colonel Byrd called it, where she dispensed royal hospitality, and "to cheer her Solitude" had a brace of tame deer running about the house which occasionally broke a pier glass or upset the tea-table "with a terrible Fracas among the China," which, adds Colonel Byrd, the hostess bore with "moderation and good humour." Boundless *savoir faire* and resourcefulness were expected of the Colonial lady in the South, and often she rose magnificently to the occasion. In South Carolina Eliza Lucas as a girl of sixteen managed three plantations during her father's absence, besides devoting herself to music and gardening; to her South Carolina owes the introduction of one important crop, indigo. Meanwhile she was the belle at gay parties at Drayton Hall and in Charleston, where she fell in love with and married Chief Justice Pinckney, over whose household she presided for many a year with fine social grace. Upon her death at a venerable age George Washington requested the honor of being a pallbearer. The wives of Southern planters and of patroons along the Hudson, in their dual rôle of manager and hostess, seem to have led lives of a spacious, aristocratic style which has been equalled nowhere else in America. Not perhaps the most brilliant social life—since, according to the code of that time, gaiety belonged to the brief day of the débutante alone—but one of simple dignity and charm. Its classic picture is found in Mrs. Grant's *Memoirs of an American Lady* (1808), describing the widowhood of Mrs. Philip Schuyler in the later years of the past century—dwelling on her large old manor near Albany, entertaining with old-fashioned largesse, ruling the affairs of her tenants with a blend of the matriarch and Lady Bountiful, "not having the smallest solicitude about what people thought of her," reading her Milton and knitting placidly under the oaks near the grave of her late lord.

American women were coming to regard the social arts and graces with more seriousness. The Marquis de Chastellux, present in 1781 at the already exclusive Philadelphia Assembly, tells of the Master of Ceremonies shouting to a damsel who had allowed a bit of gossip to interfere with her turn in a contra-dance, "Come, miss, have a care what you are doing! Do you think you are here for your own pleasure?"[2] Two years later we find Thomas Jefferson writing to his daughter Martha, aged eleven, who was at boarding-school in Philadelphia:

With respect to the distribution of your time, the following is what I should approve: From 8 to 10, practise music. From 10 to 1, dance one day and draw another. From 1 to 2, draw on the day you dance and write a letter next day. From 3 to 4, read French. From 4 to 5, exercise yourself in music. From 5 till bed-time read English, write, &c. . . . Inform me what books you read, what tunes you learn, and inclose me your best copy of every lesson in drawing. . . . Take care that you never spell a word wrong. . . . It produces great praise to a lady to spell well.

Yet this severe regimen in the case of Martha Jefferson produced a paragon of grace and charm; she married Thomas Mann Randolph of Tuckahoe, and from her have sprung several distinguished families, including Randolphs of the Old Dominion and Jefferson Coolidges of Boston, who also have inherited the blue blood without the egalitarian heresies of their grandsire. One significant index is the greater attention paid to dancing,

[2]Baron Closen, aide-de-camp to Rochambeau, notes in his manuscript journal now in the Library of Congress, that unlike the generality of American women those of Philadelphia are a little too serious-minded, caused, he thinks, "by the presence of Congress in that city."

the art of those balls and assemblies which were the apogee of life in
society, as distinguished from the utilitarian amusements—husking bees,
quilting parties, house-raisings, church bazaars, and infares—of provincials. Thus Fithian in 1773 describes a class held by one Mr. Christian at
Nomini Hall, seat of the Carters, at which the dancing of "young misses"
and "young fellows" under a sternly critical eye occupied the day from
breakfast till two o'clock; dinner came at half-past three, and "soon after
dinner we repaired to the dancing-room again."[3] Even staid Boston,
which in 1686 had expelled a dancing-teacher named Stepney, welcomed
Charles Pelham in 1754 and flocked to learn the minuet, as well as jigs,
reels, marches, and hornpipes, on three afternoons a week.[4] Perhaps
dancing and the parties it evoked were more highly prized as the competition for husbands became keener. Unattached women in American
society were already beginning to outnumber men to a surprising extent
—whether as evidence one takes the gross census figures that in Boston
in 1750 there were 1200 widows out of 18,000 inhabitants, or the statement in 1785 of Hannah Thomson, wife of the Secretary of Congress, that
in New York City the ladies of fashion outnumbered the gentlemen "ten
to one." This was probably one important reason for the rising sumptuary
standard among fashionable women during the late Colonial and Revolutionary period—a standard which, for example, enabled mantua-makers
in New York, Philadelphia, and Boston to charge five shillings a look at
dolls from London or Paris "drest after the Newest Fashion of Mantues
and Night Gowns & everything belonging to a dress," caused a French
hairdresser in Annapolis to earn as much as a thousand crowns a year, or
boomed the trade in cosmetics even though a Massachusetts clergyman
might assure his flock that "at the resurrection of the Just there will no
such sight be met as the Angels carrying Painted Ladies in their arms."[5]

[3]During the same period, with that emulation after fashion so characteristic of the
American middle class, the daughters of an innkeeper at a ferry on the Shenandoah
"went regularly three times a week, seven miles, to attend the lessons of one De Grace,
a French dancing master," as we learn from George Grieve.
[4]The traditional notion that the Puritans were inflexibly opposed to dancing on
principle has lately been corrected by Percy A. Scholes, *The Puritans and Music in
England and New England,* London, 1934, Chapter IV.
[5]In respect to hairdressing it may be noted that during the 1790's fashionable
American ladies discovered a passion for wigs, of which the costliest models are advertised as made of human hair imported from France, *i.e.,* from the foot of the
guillotine. An ironist might reflect on the thought that the crowning glory of an old
regime was thus literally descending to the parvenue.

The Saga of American Society

Before the Revolution the queens of society had been *ex officio* the wives of Royal Governors, and most of them, while not quite so unpopular as Lady Cornbury, seem to have looked down their noses upon the court of their provincial exile. But with the Revolution a throng of notable women, chiefly wives of generals and statesmen, suddenly supplanted the Governor's lady. Most celebrated in history, though not the most scintillating socially, was Martha Dandridge Custis, the dignified, kindly, phlegmatic widow of wealth and rural gentility whom George Washington had married in 1759. She once described herself as "an old-fashioned Virginia housekeeper, steady as a clock, busy as a bee, and cheerful as a cricket," and in the midst of her career as First Lady commented rather wistfully "that I, who had much rather be at home, should occupy a place with which many younger and gayer women would be extremely pleased." Amidst her family she was a person of extreme simplicity; we catch a glimpse of her at breakfast in the summer of 1794, through the eyes of Henry Wansey, the English manufacturer:

Mrs. Washington herself made tea and coffee for us. On the table were two small plates of sliced tongue, and dry toast, bread, and butter. . . . There were but slight indications of form, one servant only attending, who had no livery; and a silver urn for hot water was the only expensive article on the table. Mrs. Washington . . . was short in stature, rather robust, extremely simple in her dress, and wore a very plain cap, with her gray hair turned up under it.

Yet Martha Washington at heart was a country aristocrat, and in the public view assumed those privileges which befitted her birth and the eminence of her majestic husband. During the War she had followed him from camp to camp "in a plain chariot, with postillions in white and scarlet liveries," which after his elevation to the Presidency was exchanged for a cream-colored state coach in "the shape of a hemisphere . . . ornamented with cupids, supporting festoons, and with borderings of flowers around the panels," drawn by four horses for ordinary occasions and six on formal ones. Generally addressed as "Lady Washington" in the President's household, this imperious lady once came upon her granddaughter Nelly Custis—who should have been practising at the harpsichord—entertaining instead a young suitor who fled at the approaching footfall, but left behind a blemish on the freshly painted wall above the

Women in American Society

settee. "Ah, it was no federalist!" exclaimed Lady Washington. "None but a filthy democrat would mark a place with his good-for-nothing head in that manner!"[6] Although she did not reach New York in time for the first ball of the Administration—given May 7, 1789, in the Assembly Rooms on Broadway near Wall Street—the First Lady did arrive in state three weeks later, in a barge hung with red curtains and manned by thirteen pilots dressed in white with blue ribbons. Two days later she held the first of her levées which Colonel Stone describes as "numerously attended by all that was fashionable, elegant, and refined in society; but there were no places for the intrusion of the rabble in crowds, or for the mere coarse and boisterous partisan—the vulgar electioneer—or the impudent place-hunter—with boots, and frock-coats, or round abouts, or with patched knees, and holes at both elbows." To instance her social punctilio, we learn that she always returned visits on the third day, preceded by a footman who knocked and heralded her approach. The present rule of etiquette, that the President's wife is exempt from the duty of paying calls, was then unknown, thanks chiefly to the smallness of the Republican Court.[7] Moving from very plain quarters in Cherry Street to a more sumptuous house near fashionable Bowling Green at the then outrageous rental of $2500 per annum, and then to the even grander mansion of Robert Morris in Philadelphia, Lady Washington gracefully adjusted her life to a rising scale of luxury, and ordered the family plate from Mount Vernon to be melted down and recast into "more elegant and harmonious forms" bearing the Washington arms. Perhaps it was little wonder that democrats sourly objected to her drawing-rooms "as tending

[6] Her successor, Abigail Adams, shared the same feeling. During that Administration Albert Gallatin—himself a democrat, though he sprang from one of the most distinguished Swiss families—wrote to his wife: "I dine next Tuesday at Court. Courtland dining there the other day heard Her Majesty, as she was asking the names of different members of Congress of Hindman, being told of some of the aristocratic party, say, 'Ah, that is one of OUR people.' So that she is Mrs. President, not of the United States, but of a faction."

[7] However, the President himself claimed such exemption from the start. The title "Republican Court" dates from the early years of Washington's administration; its most elaborate description is found in Rufus W. Griswold's *The Republican Court: or American Society in the Days of Washington,* New York and London, 1856. Daniel Huntington, early nineteenth-century portraitist and president of the National Academy of Design, painted 80 square feet of canvas called "The Republican Court," portraying a levée of Mrs. Washington, with likenesses of sixty eminent guests.

to give her a super-eminency, and an introductory to the paraphernalia of courts."[8]

The case of Mrs. Knox, who assiduously cultivated the friendship of Lady Washington, proves that social climbers were on the march. Sprung from a commonplace family named Fluckner, she had married an ambitious Boston bookseller, Henry Knox, who upon the outbreak of hostilities organized a regiment, finally attained the rank of general, and became Secretary of War in Washington's Cabinet. Hitherto a slattern in appearances, Mrs. Knox suddenly developed social yearnings, grew neat as a pin, and came to be known as a formidable whist-player—though at the same time she had the misfortune to become so enormously fat that Abigail Adams Smith confessed in 1788 that "I am frightened when I look at her." Described as

a lively and meddlesome but amiable leader of society, without whose co-operation it was believed, by many besides herself, that nothing could be properly done, in the drawing-room or ball-room, or any place indeed where fashionable men and women sought enjoyment,

Mrs. Henry Knox is the subject of a malicious story thus told by Thomas Jefferson:

At the first public ball which took place after the President's arrival there [at New York], Col. Humphreys, Col. William S. Smith, and Mrs. Knox were to arrange the ceremonials. These arrangements were as follows: a sofa at the head of the room, raised on several steps, whereon the President and Mrs. Washington were to be seated; the gentlemen were to dance with swords; each one, when going to dance, was to lead his partner to the foot of the sofa, make a low obeisance to the President and his lady, then go and dance. . . . Mrs. Knox contrived to come with the President, and to follow him and Mrs. Washington to their destination, and she had the design of forcing from the President an invitation to a seat on the sofa. She mounted up the steps after them, unbidden, but unfortunately the wicked sofa was so short, that, when the President and Mrs. Washington were seated, there was not room for a third person, and she was

[8]Few American hostesses were ever scrutinized so naïvely as Mrs. Washington. Maclay of Pennsylvania, who kept a Journal during the years 1789–1791, records that at the close of one state dinner a trifle was served which, as everybody soon discovered, had been made with rancid cream. All the ladies immediately began to watch Mrs. Washington to see what she would do—and, as was related all over town the next day, she was seen to taste and swallow her portion in self-martyrdom. *Noblesse oblige.*

obliged, therefore to descend in the face of the company, and to sit where she could.

Evidently Jefferson mistook the date at which this episode occurred, since, as has been remarked, Mrs. Washington was not present at the first public ball after the Inauguration; but there is no reason to doubt that it happened at some later reception and is reported with substantial accuracy. In Jefferson's *Anas* it stands as a solemn social warning to the *embonpoint*.

The leader of smart society in New York during this period was Mrs. John Jay. Born Sarah Van Brugh Livingston, daughter of Governor William Livingston of New Jersey, she married John Jay in 1774 and accompanied him on important diplomatic missions to Madrid and Paris. Among the French aristocracy her innate social gifts made her an immediate favorite, and in Madame de Lafayette she found a lifelong friend. With good looks, modish clothes and jewels, and a regal bearing, she was once mistaken for Marie Antoinette by the audience in a Paris theatre. Upon returning to New York John Jay was appointed Secretary for Foreign Affairs, and his wife with equal ease became the reigning queen of the capital. Linked by birth with the old Knickerbocker families, and enhanced by her acclaim abroad, Mrs. Jay had a glitter denied to Martha Washington. As her inner circle she gathered about her those ladies who still clung to their British titles, dubious though some of those titles were—Lady Stirling, Lady Mary Watts, Lady Kitty Duer, Lady Temple, and Lady Christiana Griffin.

Yet with all her gifts Mrs. Jay was soon eclipsed by a hostess of the second capital of the United States, Philadelphia. During the decade of 1790 Mrs. William Bingham achieved a leadership of society which for wit, taste, and brilliant worldliness has never been surpassed in America. Anne Willing was the daughter of a rich Philadelphia banker who was the partner of Robert Morris. Her grandfather, Charles Willing, was a prosperous Gloucestershire merchant who had settled in America in 1728, married Anne Shippen, and became mayor of Philadelphia. The Willings also had allied themselves with the premier family of Virginia, Anne's aunt having married the third Colonel William Byrd of Westover—who on January 1, 1777, committed suicide rather than take further orders, it is said, from his mother-in-law. In 1780 at the age of sixteen Anne Willing married William Bingham, who "possessed larger estates than any other person in the Colony" and later became United States senator from Pennsylvania. In 1784 he took his young wife abroad. With the face of a Fragonard beauty, the chic of a Pompadour, and the social ambition of a Willing, she was destined to go far. Presented at the Court of Louis XVI, she became the toast of Versailles—where young Abigail Adams, with her simple New England background, thought her "possessed of greater ease and politeness in her behavior than any person I have met." She conquered other hearts at the Hague and at the Court of George III in 1785, where Abigail's brother John Quincy, future President of the United States, called her "the finest woman I ever saw," of superior beauty to the celebrated Georgiana Duchess of Devonshire—though as a Puritan afterthought he laments that she has "a passion and thirst after all the luxuries of Europe." After five giddy years abroad she returned to Philadelphia, and built, at Third Street above Spruce, the Mansion House, a replica "somewhat enlarged" of the town house of the Duke of Manchester. Its grounds covered three acres, with parterres, walks, and statuary in a garden of lemon and orange trees shut off by oaks and Lombardy poplars from the common gaze. Her house contained the first "self-supporting broad stairway of fine white marble" in America, French wallpaper, carpets from Moore's in London, pictures from Italy, and chairs from Seddon of the newest taste, the back in the form of a lyre, with festoons of yellow and crimson silk. Here and at Lansdowne—the country seat of the Penns on the Schuylkill, which they had abandoned upon the fall of the Crown—Mrs. Bingham entertained Chews, Allens, Shippens, and Cadwaladers upon a scale of luxury hitherto unknown to Philadelphia. The Cabinet was at her social beck and call, and as for Washington himself it was she who persuaded him to sit to Gilbert Stuart.[9] "Unquestionably at the head of American society," as Griswold wrote half a century later in *The Republican Court,* Mrs. Bingham often startled the town with her French innovations. Her chef evoked soups and sauces novel to Republican palates, though few guests were so churlish as Judge Samuel Chase who at a formal dinner in the season of 1795–

---

[9]But when Washington sat to Stuart in 1796 he took with him not Mrs. Bingham but Harriet Chew, daughter of a noted Philadelphia family and bride of the junior Charles Carroll of Carrollton, "whose conversation he said should give his face its most agreeable expression." Cf. *Republican Court,* p. 355.

6 told his hostess that he couldn't eat such folderol—whereupon Mrs. Bingham suavely ordered the footman to bring a haunch of roast beef and a couple of bottles of brown stout, which the judge downed with surly satisfaction. She also introduced to America the custom of having a lackey announce arriving guests, to the discomfiture, among others, of James Monroe.

"Senator Monroe," proclaimed a flunky near the door.

"Coming," said the senator.

"Senator Monroe," cried another flunky down the spacious hall.

"Coming as soon as I can get my greatcoat off," patiently replied the Senator.

With rare social tact, Mrs. Bingham seems to have been all things to all friends. Jefferson admired her intellect and common sense, and from Paris wrote her a letter contrasting her own domestic cares that "fill every moment with a healthy and useful activity," with the frivolity of a Parisian belle. On the other hand we get a somewhat different picture of her at dinner with Otis, the Clymers, and the Willings, an intimate little circle which had no objection to a lady's swearing, and loved the naughty *double-entendre*. Some one mentioned the Duke of York, a gentleman so embarrassingly rotund that he "was compelled to cut a semi-circle out of his table to give access to his plate," whereupon Mrs. Bingham demurely solicited the company's sympathy for the plight of his new bride, the Duchess of Württemburg. Equally adroit in grave company and in gay, Mrs. Bingham seems impartially to have enchanted everybody; as Griswold remarks, "really exclusive in her associates, she gave to none the slightest offence; with great social ambition at the basis of her character, no aspirant for the eminence of fashion felt that she was thwarting her aims." And with her relish for the sophisticated innuendo —a taste which has amused society in both the eighteenth and the twentieth centuries—she herself was never touched by the breath of scandal throughout a sparkling career which closed in 1801 when she was carried on a stretcher aboard ship for Bermuda, there to die of tuberculosis at the age of thirty-seven.

Yet such a course was not wholly free from social disappointments. There were trivial ones, such as the sharp refusal of Wignell, manager of the new theatre opened in Philadelphia in 1794, to sell her a box "to which nobody would be admitted save with her consent." Her aspirations after a Diamond Horseshoe met with a stern democratic veto, against "a prestige impossible and unfit to be asserted or allowed for an aristocracy here"—and Mrs. Bingham took the only revenge possible to a great lady, viz., she never set foot in Wignell's playhouse. After all, we remember, this was the decade of the French Revolution, and even in Philadelphia the rabble in theatre galleries would often demand that some luckless "aristocrat," chosen at random in the pit below, doff his hat to them; upon being ignored they would shower him with apples, sticks, and the lees of beer-bottles. Hence Wignell's refusal of Mrs. Bingham may be not unrelated to the immediate popular success of his theatre. A more serious blow to her pride was the runaway match of her fifteen-year-old daughter Marie with an aging, down-at-heels roué, Count de Tilly, who was found in bed with the girl at a French milliner's, after the Binghams' frantic midnight search. Although the marriage was annulled after a substantial cash settlement on the Count, Mrs. Bingham was cut to the quick at the shame and publicity, and never quite recaptured her old-time assurance and vivacity.

If, as unprejudiced travellers tell us, Philadelphia at this time was the social capital of the North, Charleston undoubtedly was that of the South. It boasted at least two women of remarkable social qualities and leadership. The first was Mrs. Ralph Izard, *née* Alice De Lancey of New York, daughter of a well-known Huguenot family, who in 1767 had married a rich young Carolina planter lately returned from schooling in England.[10] Like most of the *ton* in eighteenth-century America, Mrs. Izard had spent a prolonged interval abroad with her husband, where she was received freely in the Court circles of London and Paris, though her husband refused to be presented at Court because, said he, he would never "bow the knee . . . to mortal man." Witty and handsome, painted by Gainsborough and Copley, Mrs. Izard returned to "the Elms" in Charleston in 1780 after an absence of nine years to assume the social primacy of that debonair, half-Continental city. During the Revolution she is said to have outwitted a band of British marauders in search of her husband, who contented themselves with plundering the Izard wardrobe of its silk and satin court regalia. Like other aristocratic patriots, the Izards es-

[10]Ralph Izard (pronounced Rāfe Ízard) was descended from the original bearer of that name who had emigrated from London in 1682. The Izard male line will be extinct in America after the passing of the present Ralph Izard of Richmond, born in 1860.

poused the Revolution less from conviction that all men were created free and equal, than from the belief that they themselves were superior to Tory bureaucrats.[11] After Ralph Izard was chosen one of the two original senators from South Carolina, his wife accompanied him to New York and joined the inner coterie of Mrs. John Jay.

The second and younger hostess of Charleston was also by origin a New Yorker, the beautiful Theodosia Burr, heroine of romantic legends. Her father Aaron Burr, who adored her from her earliest years, had her instructed not only in conventional subjects like French, music, and dancing, but also in Greek, Latin, and mathematics. He wrote on one occasion to his wife: "If I could foresee that Theo would become a mere fashionable woman, with all the attendant frivolity and vacuity of mind, adorned with whatever grace and allurement, I would earnestly pray God to take her forthwith hence." Yet he carefully educated her in the arts of pleasing people and taught her a precocious *savoir faire,* so that at the age of fourteen she became his hostess at Richmond Hill, and at sixteen was a belle of New York society. A year later, in 1800, she married Joseph Alston, a Charleston cavalier of birth and wealth, and somewhat to her father's vexation shortly became the young queen of fashion in South Carolina. But in the dark days of Burr's disgrace and exile she turned away from the gaieties of St. Cecilias in a gallant attempt to effect her father's recall, using all her charm, intelligence, and social strategy upon Dolly Madison and others in power. Successful at last, she embarked in December, 1812, to meet her returning father in New York, but the ship—the prey of pirates or storms—never reached port.

Dolly Madison herself was a notable figure in society for one of the longest reigns on record—beginning with her marriage to James Madison in 1794, and, except for interludes of retirement, extending to her death in 1849 at the age of eighty, as the grand old lady of Washington, "the queen of this new world" as Philip Hone called her. As a Quaker in Virginia, little Dolly Payne had been nurtured in elegances unknown to

---

[11]Parson Ellington of Goose Creek Parish, where the Izards worshipped, was a valiant Tory during those stormy days. According to Mrs. St. Julien Ravenel's *Charleston: the Place and the People,* 1906, p. 299, one Sunday Mr. Ellington with great unction uttered the petition, "That it may please Thee to bless and preserve our Sovereign Lord King George," and waited for the response, "We beseech Thee to hear us." After an ominous silence a voice from the depths of the Izard pew answered sonorously, "Good Lord, deliver us!"

the more austere households of Friends—with a white linen mask to shield her cheeks from the wind, a sunbonnet sewed on her head by her mother every morning before she set off to school, and long gloves covering hands and arms. As the wife and shortly the widow of a sober Philadelphia lawyer, she led a simple, retired life, and not until her marriage with the "great little Madison" (as she called him) did she discover those abundant social gifts which flowered in his term as Secretary of State and as President.

Neither a wit nor a snob, but a pleasant, easy-going, gracious, simple, somewhat superficial woman, she had the rare knack of attracting people of all sorts and political creeds. She was not herself the shaft of brilliant sunlight, but rather the lens which drew other beams into social focus. With increasing worldliness she became an Episcopalian, but never learned to dance—even at her own Inaugural Ball, where she "looked a queen" in pale buff-colored velvet with a long train, and a turban with two bird-of-paradise feathers. On all dress occasions for the next forty years Dolly Madison is always described wearing a turban, long after it had ceased to be fashionable; perhaps to her it was the mundane equivalent of the Quaker cap. At this the first Inaugural Ball of any Republican Court, James Madison—whom Irving later called "a withered little apple-John"—cut beside his superb wife a pretty sorry figure, with a face that Margaret Bayard Smith described as "most woe-begone" and the whispered confession that "I would much rather be in bed." According to general knowledge, he owed his second term in the White House to Dolly's vast popularity.

Her appearance in the visitors' gallery of the Supreme Court always caused a ripple even in that august chamber; we are told that "one day Mr. Pinckney had finished his argument and was just about seating himself, when Mrs. Madison and a train of ladies entered—he recommenced, went over the same ground, using fewer arguments, but scattering more flowers . . . the women here are taking a station in society which is not known elsewhere." Though the envious wife of the British Minister thought Mrs. Madison's generous meals resembled dinner-parties less than harvest-home suppers, most people adored her entertainments, more jolly and informal than Lady Washington's. At dinner she always took the head of the table, with Madison halfway down, and one of his secretaries at the foot. Her warm-hearted tact was proverbial; at one of her receptions a backwoods youth was standing about acutely ill at ease, fiddling nervously with his coffee cup:

Mrs. Madison's keen eye had noticed his embarrassment, and she wished to relieve it. She walked up and addressed him. The poor youth, astounded, dropped the saucer on the floor, and unconsciously thrust the cup into his breeches pocket. 'The crowd is so great'—remarked the gentle lady—'that no one can avoid being jostled. The servants will bring you another cup of coffee. Pray, how did you leave your excellent mother? I had once the honor of knowing her, but I have not seen her for some years.' Thus she continued, till the poor youth felt as if he were in the company of an old acquaintance. He took care, secretly and soon, to dislodge the protuberance in his pocket.

After some years of absence she returned to Washington as a widow, and in her old-fashioned gowns with leg-of-mutton sleeves and her Roman shawls, entered once more into the social round which she had grown to love with an almost child-like simplicity. As a septuagenarian oracle, she was consulted by such an inexperienced hostess of the White House as young Mrs. John Tyler, on the propriety of "visiting in person or sending cards; Mrs. Madison says, 'Return all my visits by all means.'" At the age when most women take to their knitting by a sunny window, Queen Dolly was once again the toast of Washington society; but as for being its dictator, she had never possessed enough ruthlessness to qualify.

Under the rough-and-tumble materialism whch filled the second quarter of this century, women of fashion seem to have lost much of the dash, verve, and smartness of the previous era. Of course there were a few shining exceptions, like Mrs. Harrison Gray Otis I, *née* Sally Foster, daughter of a Boston merchant and wife of the distinguished orator, who in the midst of bearing eleven children found time to carry on the courtly traditions of an earlier day, in Boston and Washington, up to her death in 1836.[12] And there was the fair Octavia Walton of Georgia, whom Irving called "such a woman as occurs but once in the course of an empire," who married rich Doctor Le Vert of Mobile, entertained the Duke

[12]The Otis family, long prominent in New England society and national affairs, descended from one John Otis, of whom nothing is known save that he emigrated from Somersetshire about 1630; his son John in 1675 was fined forty shillings for selling cider. Samuel Otis in 1764 married the only daughter of Harrison Gray; her grandfather, a ropemaker, had settled in Boston in 1686.

of Rutland's daughter on her Alabama plantation, visited the noblest families in England in 1853, and was apparently the only American woman whom Queen Victoria ever invited to a state ball without a previous presentation. And there was Cornelia Van Ness, a favorite of the Queen of Spain and of Parisian fashionables, whom the great La-fayette gave away in marriage to James J. Roosevelt, and who led a clique of aristocrats in New York City prior to the Civil War. But women of this stamp appear to have been rarer than in the days of Mrs. Bingham and Mrs. Jay; the upsurge of demos, and the growing provincialism of insular America in spite of its new canals and railroads and steamboats, weakened the free intercourse which earlier New World aristocrats had enjoyed with Versailles and St. James.

Away from the Atlantic seaboard at any rate, women and society were in a state of eclipse together. Mrs. Trollope tells us for example that in Cincinnati in 1829 she went to an elaborate ball on Washington's Birth-day, where the gentlemen supped at a splendid table, while in another room the ladies received plates and were served standing up their "sad and sulky repast." At dinner-parties she saw the gentlemen all seated along one end of the table, and the ladies at the other, though as a rule men dined, played cards, and enjoyed music-parties and suppers without any feminine intrusion. "In Baltimore, Philadelphia, and New York, I met with some exceptions to this," she writes, "but speaking of the coun-try generally, it is unquestionably true," and she goes on to deplore "the lamentable insignificance of the American woman." Neglect seems to have gone hand in hand with forgotten niceties of the toilette, if we can believe her statement that, thanks to laziness and a dearth of personal maids, ladies were addicted to wearing masses of false hair and powder-ing themselves "immoderately, face, neck, and arms, with pulverized starch—the effect is indescribably disagreeable by daylight, and not very favourable at any time."[13] The Duke of Saxe-Weimar, touring the United States in the same decade, found society "uncommonly fine and lively, especially when ladies are not present." We can well believe it, when we read after a contemporary account of a notable party given by Mrs.

[13]Fifty years before, the Abbé Robin had a different complaint to make respecting the cosmetics of American women: "Instead of using powder they wash themselves with soap, which does not always suit them. . . . The most fastidious are learning, however, to adopt European fashions."

Women in American Society

Macomb, wife of the major-general of the armies of the United States, in Washington in the season of 1836–37:

> Mrs. Macomb is a leader in fashionable society, but attends church regularly. She is the daughter of a clergyman who formerly lectured to a congregation in Georgetown. Under the droppings of his sanctuary she grew up, and retains her early impressions. She gives splendid parties with a military air about them, and goes to soirées, but not to balls, having some religious scruples on that head.

And from our foreign visitors we hear more and more remarks on the cold, spiritless character of Americans. It begins certainly by the close of the eighteenth century when St. Méry, in America from 1793 to 1798, expresses surprise at the lack of chaperonage: "Young people sit up spooning after their elders go to bed, and sometimes a late returning servant will find them both asleep and the candle burned out—so cold is love in that country." James Silk Buckingham, visiting Saratoga, that center of worldly sophistication, in 1838, writes that

> although probably the American women make the most faithful wives and most correct members of society that any nation or community can furnish, I do not think they love with the same intensity as the women of Europe, or would be ready to make such sacrifices of personal consideration, in rank, fortune, or conveniences of life, for the sake of obtaining the object of their affections, as women readily and perpetually do with us.[14]

The charge is echoed frequently, up certainly to the present generation when Mr. G. Lowes Dickinson writes:

> The Americans are the only great nation that has not produced a single lyric of love worth recording. Physically, as well as spiritually, they are a people of cold temperament. Their women, so much and, I do not doubt, so legitimately admired, are as hard as they are brilliant; their glitter is the glitter of ice. Thus happily constituted, Americans are able to avoid the immense waste of time and energy involved in the formation

[14]Yet in the same era Alexis de Tocqueville, *Democracy in America,* concluded that thanks to democracy marriage was possible between almost any man and woman in America, to the lessening of those clandestine relationships which sprang up in the Old World when passion drew together those whose socially recognized union would have been impossible.

and maintenance of subtle personal relations. They marry, of course, they produce children, they propagate the race; but, I would venture to say, they do not love, as Europeans have loved.

It would perhaps be too impertinent to inquire in what way our critical visitors acquired their evidence. Some of it is the easy generalization in which writers of travel books indulge, but its increasing emphasis during the last century offers at least a straw in the wind. The Victorian concept of the "lady" had struck socially aspirant America with terrific impact. Love without passion, sentimentalism without humor, and the holy fear of vulgarity—these had become the watchwords of the genteel female. Mrs. L. S. Bodichon wrote in 1859: "In America, in that noble, free, new country, it is grievous to see the old false snobbish idea of 'respectability' eating at the heart of society." In both England and the United States the rise of a commercial and industrial middle class, timorous about the proprieties of taste and behavior, and tinctured with the ethics of Calvinism, developed the cult of the lady under the benign patronage of the good Queen herself. As Harold Nicolson has pointed out in regard to Tennyson, the keynote of the age was fear—fear of sex, fear of economic insecurity, fear of death, fear of God. Naturally the qualities of originality, piquancy, and individual brilliance were discouraged in favor of conformity. To be respectable was everything. "Be good, sweet maid, and let who will be clever," is not the hallmark of a socially dazzling epoch; Mrs. Bingham's set would have greeted such advice with polite derision. Yet the effect which this woman-sponsored conformity has had upon America—traditionally the land of dissenter, rebel, pioneer, and rugged individualist—is perhaps incalculable. Here is the social counterpart of our impulse toward standardization in industry, with its slogan that uniformity is the label of merit. The influence of socially ambitious classes, and especially of the women who direct them, has been deeply felt for the last century in regard to conformity in speech, etiquette, folkways, and dress. One recalls the confession of a society woman that "the consciousness of being well dressed (*i.e.,* dressed like 'the best people'), imparts a peace of mind greater than is obtained from any religion." A critic is tempted to go farther afield and track that same spirit in the feminine patronage of art, music, and literature which is so largely responsible for what James Truslow Adams calls our "anæmic, uncreative cultural atmosphere."

The Ladies' window at the New York Post Office

From the American Sketches series drawn by the English artist, Arthur Lumley. Engraved by Henry Linton for *Harper's Weekly*

The Saga of American Society

The incessant stress upon the word "lady" is an index to these new standards of respectability. Harriet Martineau, visiting the United States from 1834 to 1836, quotes the rhetorical question of a preacher: "Who were last at the Cross? Ladies. Who were first at the Sepulchre? Ladies." When she asked the warden of the Nashville prison whether she might visit the women's cells he replied: "We have no ladies here at present, madam. We have never had but two ladies, who were convicted for stealing a steak; but, as it appeared that they were deserted by their husbands, and in want, they were pardoned." By 1845 New York boasted a Ladies' Oyster Shop, a Ladies' Reading Room, and a Ladies' Bowling Alley elegantly equipped with carpets and ottomans and girls to set up the pins. Banks and post-offices afforded a ladies' window where the fair sex would be untouched by greasy elbows and tobacco-laden breath. Mrs. A. J. Graves in her book *Woman in America* (New York, 1855) reports that our cities are crowded with "females in their ambition to be considered 'ladies'" who employ their lily hands only "in playing with their ringlets, or touching the piano or guitar." We are told that a poor Irish prospector, John H. Gregory, who struck the fabulous lode of gold near Central City, Colorado, on May 19, 1859, flung down his pick and exclaimed with instant fervor: "Thank God, *now* my wife can be a lady!"

The word "woman" had become of course a term of depreciation if not downright abuse; it was however sufficient for that foundation in Philadelphia named "The Lying-In Charity for Attending Indigent Women in their Homes," and in such a euphemism as the phrase "fallen women." "Female" was at least noncommittal as to the financial, social, and moral standing of the person designated; this nice distinction appears in the title of a charity organization started in 1833 in the frontier town of Jacksonville, Illinois, "The Ladies' Association for Educating Females." Yet for the lady *in excelsis* a term of even higher praise was reserved. Of Mrs. Paulding, wife of Van Buren's Secretary of the Navy, we read in Mrs. Ellet's *Court Circles of the Republic,* 1869: "The word 'lady' hardly defined her; she was a perfect gentlewoman."

Who then was the lady? In the first place she was a woman excused from toil, economic worry, and competition; while against poverty, impurity, and crudity in any form she was carefully shielded. Secure in that station in life to which it had pleased God and the *Zeitgeist* to call her, she ruled her little sphere with serene assurance, patronizing those below her and moving at ease among her peers. Unlike the fashionable woman of other times and places, the *salonière,* or the bluestocking, she was not expected to radiate sophistication, wit, or wisdom. In fact these qualities had all come to seem a trifle unladylike. Her insulation from the world and the purity of her sex were the keys to her social place. That such purity was founded upon pervasive sex-consciousness seems not to have disturbed these Victorians, who in their worldly mood invented the Eleventh Commandment, "Thou shalt not be found out," and in their more naïve moments left behind such conventions as one finds in Lady Gough's *Etiquette* (1863):

The perfect hostess will see to it that the works of male and female authors be properly separated on her bookshelves. Their proximity unless they happen to be married should not be tolerated.[15]

Delicacy became the lady's prime requisite. Literature during this era is filled with heroines owning "that peculiar charm which no healthful comeliness can ever confer," and in a popular story of the 1850's called "Angelina's Fainted" we read that in the common opinion "to faint was feminine. Eve . . . was made for *sal-volatile!*" To achieve the desired pallor young girls were advised to drink strong vinegar and eat quantities of chalk—though in separate doses lest the joint effect be explosive. Virgins sometimes dined right well on roast beef and turnips in the privacy

[15]In America, Hiram Powers' nude statue "The Greek Slave," modelled in 1843, thrilled yet shocked the gentlefolk of the period. In Augusta, Georgia, and elsewhere, she was exhibited first to the public and then at a soirée "for ladies only," but in Cincinnati, before exhibition was allowed, she was dressed in calico blouse and flannel drawers reaching to the ankles, by thoughtful ladies of the city. At a fancy-dress ball at Delmonico's, December 26, 1874, Miss Beckwith, later Lady Leigh, daringly impersonated "The Greek Slave"—fully clothed. A painting of Adam and Eve, naked, was permitted only because it was a "sacred subject," just as the crucifix pendant from the Greek Slave's chain had indisputably raised her above the status of a bar-room hussy; but an exhibition of corsets in the show-windows of A. T. Stewart in New York brought a flood of letters denouncing him for "immorality." Among the more sophisticated, however, the prudery of the times was a standing jest, not always recognized as such by credulous European visitors. Thus the old chestnut about clothing the legs of the piano in pantalettes seems to have been invented by John Van Buren, son of the President and a noted wit about New York City in the 1830's and 1840's; slyly he repeated it to Captain Marryat, who recorded it as a fact in his *Diary in America* (1839), whence it has descended to posterity.

of their boudoir so that they might affect languor and indifference at table.[16]

All this fragility seems to have been acquiesced in readily enough by doting fathers and husbands, who admitted with complacence that they themselves were coarser clay, morally as well as physically. Yet their wives termed them "the lords of creation," obeyed meekly in all temporal matters, and long after marriage continued to address them as "Mr." This was at least the middle-class ideal. Amid the pearls of political wisdom which Charles Ingersoll gathered from the lips of the great Calhoun we find this memorandum: "Mr. Calhoun thought ladies should always be dressed in white, and wear a girdle." It was the age of the clinging vine, when a preference for the rambler would have been thought unspeakable—the age of *Godey's Lady's Book,* of bathing-machines, and of the "lady's pompadour *porte-jupe* or dress-elevator" which by means of a cord around the waist could raise the bottom of a skirt to avoid mud or display a pretty ankle. The bustle, soon to follow, proved more intractable, since, as we read, it "has the drawback of being liable to slip out of place, being situated in a region on which the fair wearer is unable to keep an observant eye."[17]

[16]That an eighteenth-century miss affected no such modesty in pecking at her fare is suggested by this extract from the *Journal of a Young Lady of Virginia: 1782* (Lucinda Lee), ed. Emily V. Mason, Baltimore, 1871, pp. 41–43: "I must tell you of our frolic after we went to our room. We took it into our heads to want to eat; well, we had a large dish of bacon and beef; after that, a bowl of Sago cream; and after that, an apple pye. While we were eating the apple pye in bed—God bless you! making a great noise—in came Mr. Washington, dressed in Hannah's short gown and peticoat, and seazed me and kissed me twenty times, in spite of all the resistance I could make; and then Cousin Molly. Hannah soon follow'd, dress'd in his Coat. They joined us in eating the apple pye, and then went out. After this we took it into our heads to want to eat oysters. We got up, put on our rappers, and went down in the Seller to get them: do you think Mr. Washington did not follow us and scear us just to death. We went up tho, and eat our oysters. We slept in the old Lady's room too, and she sat laughing fit to kill herself at us." Perhaps one should add that the Mr. Washington here mentioned is not the Father of His Country, but Corbin Washington, whose grandson was the last master of Mount Vernon.

[17]The rôle of the lady led woman to stress her differentiation from man, and also her doll-like helplessness, by padding hips and breast in a manner which the generation of single-standard women, suffragettes, and bachelor girls was quick to repudiate. Concerning the later Victorian era Charles Macomb Flandrau in *Loquacities,* 1931, has written: "The bustle and the 'form improver' moulded not only anatomies, but entire lives; they determined female fates—changed destinies. In my hearing at an early age a young man passionately declared that he had decided never to propose to a certain girl because, as he delicately expressed it, 'I think, by God, that there's deception in that bust.' "

Women in American Society

The pastimes of a lady included oil-painting and painting on china, charcoal sketching, designing on burnt leather, knitting all manner of useful articles including "netted covers for horses' ears," and perhaps even a flirtation with conchology, which, as we read in a Victorian magazine, "is a study peculiarly suited to ladies; there is no cruelty in the pursuit, the subjects are so brightly clean, so ornamental to a boudoir." And of course among social delights there was the art of the amateur musician; in Hill's *Manual of Social and Business Forms* we are told:

Amateur performers upon the piano should thoroughly commit to memory a few pieces to play independently of notes, as to take sheet-music to a party is a hint that they expect to be invited to play. If possible, have the voice in good condition also, so as not to be obliged to complain of a cold. To eat a small amount of horse-radish just previous to reading, singing or speaking, will quite effectually remove hoarseness.

But such arts and graces were still not enough for the genteel female, and it is during this period that we find beginning the modern woman's club—that organization, in Edith Wharton's words, of "ladies who pursue Culture in bands, as though it were dangerous to meet alone." It is the peculiarly American version of the French salon. The coteries of Madame du Deffand, Mademoiselle de Lespinasse, and the Maréchale de Luxembourg had been of immense social importance—under them, as Emily James Putnam has written, "the theory and practice of good society were brought to perfection, under the formative influence of the lady." However erudite a woman like Madame du Deffand might be, she wisely learned the art, in Tennyson's phrase, of

> wearing all that weight
> Of learning lightly like a flower.

She imitated Rousseau's heroine Sophie, who had *du goût sans étude, des talents sans art, du jugement sans connaissance.*[18] Beneath the petticoats of frivolity she concealed the blueness of her stockings, unlike Mrs. Montagu and Hannah More, who followed her in England with pedantic imitation, or those literary ladies of Connecticut about whom Samuel

[18]D'Alembert wrote to Mlle. de Lespinasse, in words which seem to describe the ultimate secret of social success: "What distinguishes you above all in society is the art of saying to each one that which suits him; and this art, though little common, is very simple in you; it consists of never speaking of yourself to others, but much of them."

Peters remarks in 1781 that they know naught of plays, operas, whist, or quadrilles, "but will talk freely upon the subjects of history, geography and the mathematics."

Every ambitious hostess has yearned perhaps at some time or other to found a salon—a fountain of wit and wisdom, a meeting-place for celebrities in the fine arts and sciences. Although American society has never given so hearty a welcome to the artist as the more socially secure groups of the Old World, it has always shared to a small degree the Continental tradition that a salon is, after all, the brightest jewel in any hostess's diadem. Philadelphia was the cradle of the salon in America. There in the late eighteenth century one found *conversazioni,* blending the intellectual and the social, at Mrs. Robert Morris's, Mrs. Samuel Meredith's, the Shippens', and Mrs. Samuel Powell's. Mrs. George Logan, wife of a rich Quaker, and thus disposed toward converse rather than dancing and cards, collected at her country-place "Stenton" a notable company of brains and fashion, including the lion of that day, Doctor Caspar Wistar.[19] And Miss Elizabeth Graeme, daughter of the town's leading physician, returned from a whirl in London society to open a salon at her house in Chestnut Street above Sixth, which attracted scientists and writers as well as members of the Dancing Assembly; after her unhappy marriage to Hugh Ferguson it continued to be the ruling passion of her life. A generation later the social palm was captured by the "Saturday mornings at eleven" of Mrs. James Rush, born Phoebe Ann Ridgway in 1799, daughter-in-law of Doctor Benjamin Rush, signer of the Declaration of Independence. With a Continental education in music, art, and literature, Mrs. Rush brought also to American society the custom, common in Europe, of an "at home"—first decried as decadent and unpatriotic, but finally accepted by fashion, partly because Mrs. Rush had a way of her own. Known as "a second Semiramis" who ruled Chestnut Street with an iron hand, she fostered her legend with eccentricities:—she loved to eat oysters at outdoor booths, wore green velvet mantillas and florid dresses at home, but dressed in nothing but black bombazine during her annual appearance at Saratoga and immediately gave away her trunkful

[19]The well-known anatomist and amateur botanist, for whom the wistaria was named. In his honor a masculine type of salon sprang up, the celebrated "Wistar parties" which continue in Philadelphia to the present day, with 24 members recruited from the American Philosophical Society, meeting for monthly suppers on Saturday nights during the winter.

of funereal garments upon returning to Philadelphia. She snubbed presumptuous women with chilling hauteur, but toward all men was much more clement. A bowl of her calling cards is still preserved, and shows that among her visitors were Joseph Bonaparte, Moncure Robinson, Bancroft, Channing, Van Buren, Dickens, Harriet Martineau, and Longfellow, besides of course the elect of Philadelphia. Parvenus schemed in vain to get invitations to her celebrated Saturday mornings—gate crashing being then unimagined—but Mrs. Rush took great pains to keep them as exclusive as the Assembly. Of these salons a contemporary writes: "Sometimes it would be a fashionable tenor; sometimes children who recited verses; and on one occasion the Aztecs were shown, before they became common in public exhibitions." Always to Mrs. Rush belonged the *récherché*.

Boston, future cradle of women's clubs and Browning Societies, nurtured several nineteenth-century salons—the most eminent socially being that of the junior Mrs. Harrison Gray Otis. Born Eliza Boardman, daughter of an East India merchant, and married in 1817 to the son of Boston's post-Revolutionary social queen, she was left a widow while still young. Styled "the dashing Mrs. Otis," she became an aggressive figure in Washington, Saratoga, and Boston—where her Saturday morning receptions and her midnight suppers, which popularized cake and non-alcoholic punch, were famed. Samuel Breck writes disapprovingly of her in April, 1832:

This lady, a widow and mother of five children and already of a certain age, has been displaying and flirting during the winter in Philadelphia and Washington, giving the tone and assuming the lead. . . . This lady-traveller inherited about one hundred and fifty thousand dollars from her father, and is, for the rest, a light-hearted woman, not destitute of wit and smartness, and has been much attended to by the fashionable circles of our city.

He reports that in Boston she frequently goes visiting on foot in the evening, accompanied by a sturdy Irish servant; at her order he once knocked down a certain courtly beau who had challenged the right to squire her home. Noteworthy were her Thursday soirées, with tea and cakes and the invariable ingredient of celebrities: at one triumphant party, we are told, she had "President Fillmore, Lord Elgin, and an Indian chief." The Civil War put a term to her gaieties—busy distributing Bibles to soldiers, she did not buy nor have made over a single dress during those four gruelling years. She loved to tell the story of the soldier lad who stilled the ribald mirth of comrades over a Bible they had discovered in his possession, with the simple words, "Mrs. Otis gave it to me." She contributed $50,000 to the Sanitary Commission, and raised additional war funds by selling kisses at $5 apiece. Her Otis relations looked upon her somewhat aghast; in fact, up to the days of Mrs. Jack Gardner Boston had seen nothing like her.[20] Of course there were more conservative hostesses, too, like Mrs. James T. Fields, whose biography M. A. De Wolfe Howe has charmingly written; she presided in the *post bellum* period over a fastidious salon, more literary than social, at her house in Charles Street which Henry James called "the little ark of the modern deluge."

Little would it profit the annals of either society or belles lettres to name all the ambitious ladies of this era who poured libations of China tea and Roman punch to the manes of Madame du Deffand. Most found themselves, alas, in the position of that hostess described by Oscar Wilde, who "tried to found a salon, but only succeeded in opening a restaurant." Typical of the literary patroness with scant social pretensions was Mrs. Anne Charlotte Lynch Botta (1815–1891), daughter of an Irish dry-goods merchant, who taught in the Brooklyn Academy for Women, and by her rather pallid bookish charm drew to her modest parlor at 25 West 37th Street in New York, Bryant, Greeley, Willis, Bayard Taylor, and Margaret Fuller; Emerson called it "the house of the expanding doors." Equally bare of material pomp, but socially more sparkling, seem to have been the little salons in Charleston in the 1850's of Mrs. Holland, an attractive widow related to the Turnbull clan, with an exotic beauty ascribed to a dash of Greek blood. Dressed always in Hellenic robes with her hair bound by a fillet, she was a favorite of South Carolina society. Though poor in purse Mrs. Holland held in her bedroom a little court of devoted gentlemen and ladies, who met to share conversation and songs accompanied on the guitar, and to drink lemonade or claret-sanger with sweet wafers. Once a gentleman inadvertently opened a closet door and precipitated a heap of clothes into the room in the midst of a song, but with a smiling apology for "the intrusion of my garments" Mrs.

---

[20]The Healy portrait of Mrs. Otis (*see facing page* 49) shows her dressed in the gown of old lace and purple velvet which she had ordered for the Boston Theatre Ball given in 1860 for the Prince of Wales.

Holland shut the door and resumed her guitar. Lacking enough chairs, her guests often sat on soap boxes—and loved it. Despite the airs of an Aspasia which she rather theatrically assumed, Mrs. Holland apparently came nearer than most of her rivals to the real spirit of the Hôtel Rambouillet. And the Middle West was not innocent of such aspirations: about the time of the Civil War, Mrs. Caroline M. Severance, champion of women's rights and patroness of the fine arts, had in Cleveland the beginnings of a salon, which evaporated after her removal to Boston. Chicago in the 1880's witnessed various inept attempts in the same direction, such as that of Mrs. H. O. Stone, daughter of a boarding-house keeper and relict of a beef-baron, who buttressed by her friends Mrs. Marshall Field, Mrs. Wirt Dexter, and Mrs. George M. Pullman, tried to collect a cénacle, to the ribald mirth of *Town Topics*.

The feminine pursuit of "culture" as a fashionable hobby sprang from an impulse akin to that which had produced the salon. If one were unable to blaze in the bright center of the drawing-room, at least one could glow in the penumbra of the lecture-hall. An observer in late eighteenth-century New York notes that "it has become the fashion to attend lectures on moral philosophy, chemistry, mineralogy, botany, mechanics, etc., and the ladies in particular have made considerable progress in these studies." This great thirst for information, especially among women who were just attaining a margin of leisure, was largely responsible for the spate of new magazines and newspapers which broke upon the Colonies shortly before the Revolution.[21] Later, about 1825, the lyceum appeared in Boston and New York, gaining rapid favor among people of *ton;* Philip Hone, referring to the lyceum courses at Clinton Hall, the Tabernacle, and the New-York Historical Society, remarks in 1841 that "lectures are all the vogue, and the theatres are flat on their backs." In 1844

[21]The *précieuses ridicules* among "middle-aged ladies" of America did not escape Harriet Martineau's keen observation. She writes: "A literary and very meritorious village mantua-maker declared that it was very hard if her gowns did not fit the ladies of the neighborhood. She had got the exact proportions of the Venus de Medici to make them by; and what more could she do? Again. A sempstress was anxious that her employer should request me to write something about Mount Auburn: (the beautiful cemetery near Boston). Upon her being questioned as to what kind of composition she had in her fancy, she said she would have Mount Auburn considered under three points of view: as it was on the day of creation, as it is now, as it will be on the day of resurrection. I liked the idea so well that I got her to write it for me, instead of my doing it for her." (*Society in America,* London, 1837, vol. III, p. 82.)

The Saga of American Society

John Robert Godley in *Letters from America* speaks of the Boston Lyceum as "most fashionable," and as offering "a little pleasing excitement of partly intellectual and partly sensual [*sic*] kind." Becoming in time outmoded, the lyceum was then discovered enthusiastically by the provincial middle class.[22]

The same cycle was followed half a century later by the women's clubs —that national passion so puzzling to Continentals like Thérèse Blanc, who observed that "the absence of men would make French women feel . . . as if they were eating bread without butter." Aside from a few Colonial precursors already noted, the women's club is forecast as early as 1818 in a group organized in Boston called "The Gleaners," composed of unmarried women who met "to discuss questions of the proper attitude to be maintained toward gentlemen." Short-lived, it ceased upon the marriage of the last of its members, who, we gather, had solved the problem of the proper attitude. Around the middle of the century the Ladies' Library Society of Kalamazoo, Michigan, the Minerva Club of New Harmony, Indiana, and the Friends in Council of Quincy, Ill., met to discuss worthwhile books and current events. But not until 1868 did the women's club movement get under way, in a national sense and with a certain social momentum, upon the organization of the New England Woman's Club and the New York Sorosis. The former was founded in Boston by Caroline M. Severance, the bluestocking from Cleveland; upon her removal to California, the presidency for the next forty years fell to that *grande dame* of Boston and Newport, Julia Ward Howe. Under her regime it maintained behind all the literary, artistic, and philanthropic schemes evolved in its Park Street clubrooms an air which was more socially exclusive than that of its compeer, the New York Sorosis, started by Jane Cunningham Croly in a fit of indignation when she was barred by reason of her sex from the banquet tendered Charles Dickens in 1868 by the New York Press Club. These two clubs are the prototypes of uncounted hundreds of women's organi-

[22]Mrs. John Farrar in *The Young Lady's Friend* (Boston, 1838) discusses in Chapter XIV the question of etiquette at the Lyceum. She cautions "the daughters of a rich man" that "you have, therefore, no claim to certain seats because you have before occupied them. . . . When anything is handed round at a lecture to be looked at, remember that your eyes are not at your fingers' ends, and be satisfied without touching the article. . . . A gentlewoman should never forget herself, should never do anything that is ungentle, should never run, jump, scream, scramble, and push, in order to get a good seat anywhere."

Headquarters of the Women's Centennial Executive Committee, 903 Walnut Street, Philadelphia

Mrs. E. D. Gillespie receiving reports from sub-committees

From Frank Leslie's Historical Register of the U. S. Centennial Exposition, published 1877

zations for study, discussion, creative writing, social work and philanthropy, which have since sprouted throughout the United States in all classes of society. For the past fifty years they have been most characteristic of American life. They have evoked innumerable luncheons of creamed chicken and banana salad, an infinity of papers on Duncan Phyfe furniture and the song-birds of New Jersey; and to minister to their pleasure they have created the male lecturer—a type *sui generis,* of which the pioneer was Hamilton Wright Mabie, who, according to Frank Moore Colby's obituary, "conducted young ladies into the suburbs of culture—and left them there."[23]

The Reverend Doctor Nichols wrote pontifically in *The Ultra-Fashionable Peerage of America* (1904): "A woman of fashion and a clubwoman are two mutually excluding entities—two totally distinct creations of Almighty God, although the latter often tries to palm herself off as the former." Indeed within a short time after its birth the woman's club movement was seized upon by social climbers, housewives, and vaguely unhappy widows from every quarter; its vast expansion during the twentieth century has been made possible by such triumphs of science as the vacuum cleaner and the electric washing-machine. Yet in most cities small socially select groups have arisen which bear kinship to either the salon or the club, sometimes both. In New York, for example, "Les Causeries du Lundi" was founded in the early 1880's upon the supposed pattern of the old Knickerbocker gatherings, by Mrs. Hamilton Fish, Mrs. John Jacob Astor, Mrs. William Griffin, Mrs. John Sutherland, and a few others; each member was expected at intervals to read an original composition; curiously enough, no Roman Catholic was ever admitted to membership. The Thursday Evening Club, though not an

[23]Professor William Orton, an urbane Briton on the faculty of Smith College, well observes in his study *America in Search of Culture:* "Most lecturers to American women's clubs have at times, I am sure, felt as if they were a species of eunuch admitted to circles where no normal male, whatever his motives, would dream of intruding." To illustrate the vicissitudes of this vocation the present author recalls a book-review of Werfel's *The Forty Days of Musa Dagh* which he gave laboriously for an hour's session to the Junior League of a Western city in December, 1934. At its close the president introduced him to several members of the audience—including the wife of a prominent young doctor, who remarked to make conversation that she had just returned from New York. The author asked what plays she had seen, and she named several; and among other trivia added, "Oh yes, and I browsed around the big bookshops on Fifth Avenue. Everywhere I went I kept seeing windows full of a new book called *The Forty Days of* Something-or-Other—have you read it?"

exclusively feminine enterprise, has still an honored place in the annals of New York society; in its heyday each hostess arranged a program of costly entertainment, such as readings by Coquelin or music by Paderewski, followed by an hour of talk or varied by occasional papers on travel, science, or civic topics, and ended by supper with champagne. During the 1900's the Entertainment Club met at the old Waldorf to study current events, and enjoyed a dignified and unruffled history save for the publicized excitement caused in March, 1906, by the resignation of Mrs. Rhinelander Waldo, "because she resented the suggestions made by members that her dress was not suitable for a lecture on Alaska." Elsewhere lectures and discussion-groups were sponsored by such socially limited organizations as the Chilton Club in Boston, where the late Amy Lowell often read poetry, the Fortnightly Club and the Friday Club in Chicago, Le Petit Salon in New Orleans, and the Fortnightly Club in Denver. Among national clubs devoted to special interests, the Garden Club of America has long maintained an air of exclusiveness.

But the most important offshoot of the women's club movement is the Junior League, started in 1901 by the late Mrs. Charles Cary Rumsey, then Miss Mary Harriman, daughter of the railroad-builder Edward H. Harriman who had arrived in the faubourgs of New York society in the post-Civil War era. First proposing that débutantes of her year donate their flowers to the city hospitals, after serious studies at Barnard College Miss Harriman worked out a program of welfare service and organized some eighty girls into a group which staged *tableaux vivants* for charity. Called the Junior League of the New York College Settlement, it was soon copied by similar organizations in Boston, Portland (Oregon), Baltimore, Chicago, and Philadelphia, until by 1921 there were thirty Leagues scattered throughout the United States with no formal connection. In that year in the club-rooms of the New York League the present Association of Junior Leagues of America was incorporated. With no coercive power over the member Leagues, its authority comes solely in admitting or rejecting groups from towns and cities where no Junior League already exists. In such a place, young women may band themselves together, study the technique of social service, map out a local program, and then submit their candidacy to the national Association. The quality of their work, and also the question whether they represent Best Society in their community, will be carefully scrutinized by the

Association. Chary of bestowing its honors, the Junior League Association has accepted only 32 out of 201 applications in the past seven years; hence its reputation for both exclusiveness and serious work is guarded. At present there are 135 Leagues in the United States, six in Canada, and one in Mexico City, with a total of 28,581 members. No Leagues are found in the following states: Vermont, New Hampshire, Mississippi, North and South Dakota, Montana, Wyoming, New Mexico, and Nevada.

The New York League with 2000 members, the highest annual dues ($120, in comparision with a national average of $13), and a handsome clubhouse on East 71st Street, is easily the largest and most pretentious; other Leagues have rooms in office-buildings, hotels, and apartment houses. The New York League is the only one which does not require its members to perform some type of community service. The New York social welfare program—including an expert housekeeper service for homes of the poor, a system for collecting and distributing clothing in large quantities, and a collaboration with the Children's Aid Society— is markedly efficient, though its equally pronounced trend toward worldly luxuries drew down its founder's disapproval a few months before her death from injuries suffered at the Middleburg Hunt. With New York patently in mind Mrs. Rumsey observed in February, 1934: "The Junior Leagues in the big cities are building these big clubhouses where the girls just go and swim and manicure their nails and the cost is too great." Yet, paradoxically, in the life of a metropolis the New York League is of scant social significance; its members—though unfailingly pleasant, popular, well-dressed young women—form by no means the exclusive roster of birth and fashion. But in the smaller inland cities, especially those where social lines have never before been clearly marked, and where the male relatives of Junior Leaguers dominate wealth and business—like Indianapolis, Kansas City, Dallas, Peoria, Omaha, Milwaukee, Oakland, and scores of others—membership in the Junior League is vitally important, especially to the daughters of the self-made. In certain towns, as we are told by a current reporter, "A girl who doesn't get elected might as well live across the tracks."

A girl whose background, personal qualities, and social "set" have met the approval of the local membership committee becomes a provisional member until she has attended a course of lectures given by social workers

Women in American Society

and has passed a not too difficult examination on the course, sometimes including questions like, "What would you do if your unmarried maid suddenly told you she was pregnant?" The age limits are eighteen and forty; at forty a Leaguer undergoes virtual retirement into the status of a sustaining member. The Charter of the League reads as follows: "The purpose of this League shall be to foster interest among its members in the social, economic, educational, cultural, and civic conditions of their community, and to make efficient their volunteer service." The Junior League in America satisfies a vague and hitherto unorganized impulse, in linking social eligibility with the theory of civic service, of reviving the old feudal dogma of *richesse oblige*. At its best the Junior League has done a limited but efficient stint of philanthropy, and even more important, has given many rich girls a chaperoned glimpse of how the other half lives. Even at its most snobbish, the Junior League has made society women eager to wait on tables, sell all manner of articles over the counters of bazaars, assist doctors in the clinics of slums, and perform other drudgeries because they are "exclusive"—a voluntary and aristocratic debasement like that of medieval kings who washed the feet of the poor on Maundy Thursday.

In the older cities, where social lines have been drawn and erased generation after generation, there are clubs for women whose exclusiveness makes the Junior League seem a trifle higgledy-piggledy—like the Vincent Club in Boston, the Acorn Club in Philadelphia, and the Colony Club in New York. The Vincent Club was in fact a pioneer of the social service theory, founded in March, 1892, and named after Mrs. Vincent, a leading actress of the Boston Museum Stock Company; upon her death a memorial fund was collected to build the Vincent Memorial Hospital for wage-earning women and girls. After the hospital was erected in 1891 and the fund was seen to be insufficient for its upkeep, the Vincent Club was organized to raise money from theatricals staged by Boston débutantes. Its shows were patterned on the musical comedies of the Hasty Pudding, and up until the time of the World War no men were ever admitted—with the exception of firemen, whose presence was required by law, but who wore masks so that members would never be embarrassed by recognizing their faces elsewhere. A few members of the Vincent Club, notably the Braggiotti sisters in 1922, have gone from amateur to professional stage with success.

The Saga of American Society

On the other hand, there is the exclusive women's club which has no program of social service or money-raising, but is modelled upon the gentlemen's club of Pall Mall and Fifth Avenue.[24] Of this the best example is the Colony Club of New York, the smartest of such clubs in the world. Started in December, 1903 by a little group of friends which included Anne Morgan, Elisabeth Marbury, Elsie de Wolfe (now Lady Mendl), and Mrs. William K. Vanderbilt (Anne Harriman), and housed in fitting quarters on Madison Avenue designed by Stanford White, the Colony has remained steadily at the social apex. Its resident membership is limited to 1350. Candidates are introduced by their proposers to the governors, who announce that they will be in the visitors' rooms of the Club for that purpose on several afternoons prior to elections. In common with most representative clubs throughout the world—as distinguished from the clubs of mere millionaires—the dues of the Colony Club are quite moderate. The entrance fee is $250, and annual dues for resident members $125.

In a private dining-room of the Colony Club meets the Sabbatical Club, composed of seven women who entertain seven men not their husbands

[24]Earliest English forerunner of this type—and almost the only kind of club known to the Victorian lady—was the Alexandria, founded in London in 1883, in which no man, not even the future King Edward VII when accompanied by the Princess of Wales, was allowed to set foot. Of course there had been "the female Almacks" of Horace Walpole's day, but the Alexandria was the first chartered women's social club. Imitators sprang up, like the Pioneer, the Victoria, the New Century, but none enjoyed palmary importance.

The Woman's Club of Wisconsin, founded some sixty years ago in Milwaukee, is said to be the first woman's club in the United States to own or build its own clubhouse; somewhat cautious in the beginning, it has grown steadily more free and easy. The first purely social club for women which has consistently maintained its rank seems to be the Acorn Club of Philadelphia, founded in 1889 by Miss Katherine Shippen, Miss Emily Williams Biddle, Miss Florence Sibley, and a few others. Parents and guardians compelled the resignation of some of the younger members because the first clubhouse was on Walnut Street where "the men walked past coming from their offices," and it was assumed that débutantes would ogle them from behind the window-boxes. Its present quarters—with dining and card rooms, reading-room and bedrooms—are on Locust Street. Present membership is 1156, and ordinarily it takes from five to seven years to become a member. Annual dues are $80 for residents.

One should also mention the more recent social clubs for both men and women, which followed logically from the country club. A good example is the River Club in New York, begun in 1930 by Kermit Roosevelt, Mollie M. Davis (Mrs. Joseph Edward Davis), Robert Sturgis Potter, Robert E. Strawbridge, Jr., and James W. Barney. At its clubhouse on East 52nd Street it offers such sports as tennis, squash, badminton, as well as the conventional restaurant, bar, and library.

Women in American Society

at dinner seven times a year. At eleven o'clock, looking somewhat sheep-
ish, husbands are allowed to call for their wives. Mrs. August Belmont,
Mrs. Archibald Roosevelt, Mrs. Wolcott, and Ethel Barrymore were
among its founders; Katherine Cornell is a lately added celebrity.

The women's club movement—though one of the most striking devel-
opments in social life since the Civil War—should not becloud a review
of those personalities who from time to time have left a striking impress
upon society. The Brown Decades, as Mr. Lewis Mumford has called that
era which opened in the 1860's—an age of brownstone fronts in architecture and of a correspondingly serious-minded and sedentary social pomp
—brought forth an array of leaders the like of which had not been seen
since the Republican Court of the Jays and Binghams. But, as happens
often in the American pageant, the surnames were mostly new. There
was the first Mrs. August Belmont, born Caroline Slidell Perry, daughter of Commodore Matthew C. Perry and niece of Oliver Hazard Perry,
hero of Lake Erie. A woman of singular sweetness, beauty, and social
grace, she was married in 1849 to August Belmont, the flashy Jewish
financier and *bon vivant* whose knowledge of cooking, wines, horses, and
dogs—learned in the household of his employers the Rothschilds—lent a
new dimension to the society of a rather provincial New York. Belmont's
fast-growing wealth and his worldliness, plus his wife's breeding and
charm, proved irresistible; and for two generations thereafter the name
of Belmont was a synonym for sport and sophisticated entertaining in
Continental style.

In the hierarchy of post-Civil War times was Mrs. Hamilton Fish,
whose husband became Secretary of State in Grant's Cabinet; she belonged to what was called "the Faubourg St. Germain set" of New
York—families entrenched since Colonial days in wealth and civic eminence, who could afford to live in tarnished magnificence on outmoded
Second Avenue, while the "swells" eddied like moths toward the luster
of Fifth Avenue. Equally assured was the position of Mrs. Theodore
Roosevelt, mother of the future President, born Martha Bulloch, of
Georgia. A famous beauty, Mrs. Roosevelt held court first in a modest
brownstone house in a street between Broadway and Fourth Avenue,
where, as Mrs. Burton Harrison remembered many years later, "her
afternoons at home seemed to convey a waft of violets." Afterwards the
Roosevelts moved to a large new mansion in West 57th Street, where

331

they gave a great ball for the coming out of their eldest daughter—issuing the then fabulous number of 1100 invitations. Another peeress was Mrs. Lewis Morris Rutherfurd, wife of the rich astronomer descended from Lewis Morris of Morrisania; she was born Margaret Stuyvesant Chanler, and eventually transmitted the Stuyvesant fortune to her son, who then reversed his name and became Rutherfurd Stuyvesant. According to the recollections of Mrs. Harrison, she "had the prettiest way in the world of putting people in their appropriate place"—a gift also hereditary with the Stuyvesants.

Mrs. Paran Stevens, *née* Reed, a tall dark handsome woman with marked social ambitions, was a conspicuous figure in New York and Newport for more than a quarter century before her death in 1895. She was famed for her thrifty musicales, at which the éclat was invariably superior to the music. William R. Travers, whose reputation for wit lent him a certain immunity in speech, once told her: "My dear lady, it is impossible for me to resist the magnetism of your charming society, although I know it only draws me back to cold tea, hot Apollinaris, and bad music." One of the typical crises of her career occurred on the night of October 22, 1883, when the new Metropolitan Opera House opened under sponsorship of the newly arrived Vanderbilts, in competition with the old Academy of Music long patronized by Cuttings, Beekmans, and Livingstons. Unable to decide where the greater glory lay, Mrs. Stevens divided her evening between the boxes of both houses.

But the primacy of leadership during this period lay between the two Mrs. Astors. Charlotte Augusta Gibbes, of a proud but rather threadbare South Carolina family, in 1846 had married the third John Jacob Astor —grandson of the doughty old fur-trader who had founded the fortune, but, in respect to the social pantheon of New York, found himself in the position of St. Paul's Ephesians who had not so much as heard if there be any Holy Ghost. Social standing had nevertheless been gained with the marriage in 1818 of his son and heir William Backhouse Astor to the daughter of General John Armstrong of Rhinebeck, N. Y., and his wife, born Alida Livingston. Their elder son, John Jacob III,[25] a genial, democratic gentleman who inherited two-thirds of the vast estate, was—under

[25]*The New York Times,* April 27, 1892, states that in addition to John Jacob III and William, there was a third brother, "but on account of a marriage of which the family did not approve, he has not been recognized for many years, and the public generally does not know of his existence."

the tutelage of his Southern wife—the first of the Astors to practise the art of living graciously. He became a popular host, a connoisseur of wine, and a collector of paintings, books, and old furniture. His wife, cordial and simple, "full of gracious sweetness and wide humanity," as she is described by Mrs. Harrison, occupied an important place in New York society up to her death in 1887.

Her nature was by no means so dominating as that of her rival, Mrs. William Astor—who became eventually the social leader of greatest fame and most undisputed authority in the history of the United States. Born Caroline Webster Schermerhorn, she was a descendant of Peter Schermerhorn the ship-chandler. In 1853 she married the second son of William Backhouse Astor, who had dropped the unhappy middle name of his sire, but succeeded to only a third of the Astor fortune. He and his wife were keenly aware of the secondary position which they occupied: Mr. and Mrs. John Jacob Astor were constantly played up by the press as head of the family, and in New York and Newport always received social precedence. In consequence William Astor, proud arrogant roué with a distaste for business and a weakness for horses, ships, and women, spent much of his time cruising in foreign waters on his yacht *Nourmahal,* leaving his wife to nurse a feeling of inferiority which at length was triumphantly sublimated. With unexampled determination she set out to rule New York society from her mansion at Fifth Avenue and 65th Street—with its picture gallery in cream and gold, its baronial dining hall panelled in old oak and hung with French tapestries while overhead in painted flowers and clusters of fruit blazed the Astor monogram in gold, and its even more celebrated ball-room which according to legend held "comfortably" only 400 people. She found her court chamberlain in Ward McAllister, whose lobbyist cousin Sam Ward—brother of Julia Ward Howe—had married the sister of William Astor. Eager to bask in the light of his distant kin, and, as a connoisseur of snobbery, relishing the ruthlessness of Mrs. Astor, McAllister dedicated all his talents in social strategy, the forming of cliques, and the planning of menus to the glory of his queen. He saw that she was the only woman in New York and Newport who had all the will, wealth, and ambition which social dictatorship demanded—the kind of dictatorship needed to complement his own rôle in the public eye. McAllister was then at the height of his powers, with much publicity at his command, and after he had assiduously paid her the royal honors at Patriarch Balls, grand dinner-parties, and *fêtes champêtres* at Newport, the habit caught on.

Meanwhile Mrs. William Astor herself, soon crowned by the journalists as "Queen of the Four Hundred," played up to the part so skilfully that by the early 1880's she had eclipsed all rivals. Upon the death of Mrs. John Jacob Astor she was quick to claim the title of "the Mrs. Astor," though Mrs. William Waldorf Astor, daughter-in-law of the deceased, did not relinquish it without a struggle. For a time the postmaster at Newport was in a most awkward plight, since both women insisted upon receiving all letters addressed "Mrs. Astor, Newport," and instructed their partisans so to write to them. Eventually the young Mrs. Astor covered her defeat by flight and permanent expatriation in England, while the elder continued on her majestic way with calling cards—that bestowed the final accolade upon whatever lucky salver she left them—engraved simply "Mrs. Astor." At the great Centennial Ball on April 29, 1889, in the presence of President and Mrs. Benjamin Harrison and all the Cabinet, she led the contra-dance, as a kind of national recognition.[26] Spectators often stood beside the *porte-cochère* on 39th Street of the Metropolitan Opera House, hoping to catch a glimpse beneath the ermine of her celebrated diamond stomacher, or to see the tiara on her brow—for, as *The New York Times* gravely observed, she always wore diamonds "with the most effective prodigality." Her skill in winning the press was shown in 1891 when her son John Jacob Astor IV, known in his Harvard days as "Jackastor," father of the present Vincent Astor, married Ava Willing of Philadelphia. Before the wedding Philadelphia journalists had begun to exploit the match as the union of Colonial blue blood with the not too impeccable lineage of a Waldorf butcher; but after Mrs. Astor gave a champagne and terrapin party at the Bellevue for reporters and cajoled them into believing it was the wedding-breakfast, Astors swept Willings from the headlines. Not too intimate with any one, Mrs. Astor built a tradition of social authority which no other hostess in America has ever quite achieved. Against such rank newcomers as the

---

[26]One of the largest semi-public entertainments ever attempted in this country, the Centennial Ball to commemorate the Inauguration of George Washington was not one of the most urbane. When the supper-rooms were opened, we read, "the food was scattered everywhere indiscriminately—on the ladies' costumes and on the walls. Men pushed through the crowd with bottles of champagne in their hands, providing wine for their chance acquaintances" (*N. Y. Times,* 30 April, 1889).

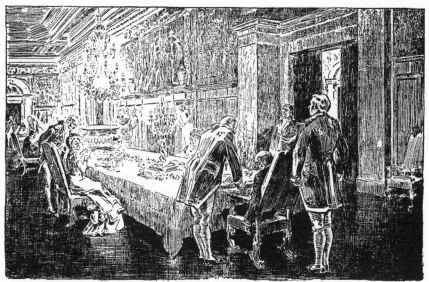

The Troubles of the Rich

At the last moment, several who were invited send their regrets

C. D. Gibson in *Life* in 1902

Castles in the Air

C. D. Gibson in *Life* in 1905

Goulds, for example, she set her veto so firmly that they have never overridden it. In her drawing-room Mrs. Astor habitually stood in front of a life-size portrait of herself by Carolus Duran when receiving formally —and there in the befogged sunset of her old age she often planted herself, greeting imaginary guests long dead, exchanging pleasantries with ghosts of the utmost social distinction.

The waning star of Mrs. Astor, finally quenched by death in 1908, left behind a small galaxy of lesser lights in New York and Newport. Her daughter-in-law Ava Willing Astor appeared briefly to be her successor, but in general preferred Bohemian friends and European ties to the pomp of the so-called Four Hundred; eventually her divorce in 1909 and her marriage ten years later to Lord Ribblesdale ended her life in America. Mrs. Ogden Mills, the former Ruth Livingston, with a full measure of the hauteur of that distinguished family, was the daughter-in-law of Darius O. Mills, the self-made California gold miner. Mrs. Mills longed for the coronet of the great Mrs. Astor, but with a cold sardonic nature and her reduction of the Four Hundred to "only twenty families," she was soon defeated as a representative social leader by her own exclusiveness. She never learned that the wise arbiter of society does not set impossible standards in America; after all, if one speaks only to God the opportunities for polite converse are somewhat limited. Mrs. Ogden Goelet, born Mary Reta Wilson, was the possessor of Box No. 1 in the Diamond Horseshoe of the Metropolitan after its reconstruction in 1893, and one of the smart hostesses of her generation.

But beyond cavil the outstanding personality of this era—though never the unchallenged sovereign of a *petit comité* as Mrs. Astor finally became—was the late Mrs. Oliver Hazard Perry Belmont, indefatigable duchess of the Gilded Age. To paraphrase the achievement of the Emperor Augustus, it might be said that she found the material structure of American society brick, and left it marble. Born in Mobile, Ala., in 1853, she was the daughter of Murray Forbes Smith, a cotton planter, and his wife Phœbe Ann, daughter of General Robert Desha of Tennessee. A more remote genealogical bond connected her with that Revolutionary hero, William Alexander, who without permission of Parliament styled himself Lord Stirling, and for whom her son, Harold Stirling Vanderbilt, yachtsman and bridge expert, is named. The Smiths were not too impoverished by the Civil War to send their daughter Alva to boarding-

Women in American Society

school in France. In Manhattan at the age of twenty-one she married William Kissam Vanderbilt, grandson of the old Commodore—who was still alive, and had himself at the age of seventy-three recently married a Mobile belle, the young Frances Crawford. The first two generations of rich Vanderbilts neither sought nor obtained much recognition; in fact, as Alva Smith was later to remark, "I was the first girl of my set to marry a Vanderbilt." She was always experimental. Her young husband, with a dawning appreciation of horse-racing, entertaining, and the glamor of European titles, was more than ready to underwrite the ambitions of his plump, energetic Southern bride, and together they set out to conquer the fortress of New York society.

The first move was to widen social acquaintance by several years of quiet but well-planned entertaining, though Mrs. William Astor might continue oblivious. The second step was to commission a house from Richard M. Hunt, who in the 1880's was wiping out the brownstone age with the French château style of the fifteenth and sixteenth centuries, and embellishing upper Fifth Avenue with the splendors of Chambéry and Chenonceaux, which he recalled had delighted the parvenu bankers and merchant-princes of the Renaissance. At the corner of 52nd Street he built for the Vanderbilts a $3,000,000 town house adapted from the Château de Blois, which they somewhat oppressively filled with medieval and Renaissance furniture, tapestries, and armor. As a house-warming Mrs. W. K. Vanderbilt planned the most sumptuous fancy-dress ball that had ever been given in America, for the night of March 26, 1883. Miss Caroline Astor, daughter of the Queen, the future Mrs. Orme Wilson, assuming that she would be invited, began to organize the "Star Quadrille" in which she and her friends planned to appear as pairs of stars, yellow, blue, mauve, and white. It was a charming idea. Hearing of Miss Astor's plans, Mrs. Vanderbilt intimated to common friends that, alas, it would be quite impossible for her to invite that young lady, since the Astors had never paid her a call. Mrs. Astor, admitting for once that her hand had been forced, summoned her carriage, left her card at the shining new portal, and thus made the Vanderbilts forever free of Best Society. The last of the 1200 invitations was dispatched immediately.

It was truly a victory ball. The hostess, dressed as a Venetian princess of the Renaissance, was photographed with white doves—perhaps symbolic of peace—fluttering about her.[27] She and Lady Mandeville, who as her social mentor had originally suggested the ball, received standing side by side. Her brother-in-law Cornelius appeared as Louis XVI, and his wife as "The Electric Light."[28] There was a plethora of Mary Stuarts, Marie Antoinettes, Black Princes and cavaliers, and one French nobleman in flesh and blood, the Duc de Morny, as well as an authentic ex-President, General Ulysses S. Grant. As often happened on such invidious occasions, Jay Gould and his family were out of the city on a Florida cruise. The halls and drawing-rooms were lined with roses, while upstairs the gymnasium where supper was to be served had been transformed into a tropical garden, with orchids swaying from palm fronds and bougainvillea encircling the dome. Dancing was in the Louis XV salon, with its Gobelin tapestries and wainscoting ripped from an old French château on the Loire, and also in the great dining-room adjoining. It was magnificent, marred only by a little grumbling from ladies in elaborate toilette, who found that their personal maids were not allowed to leave the carriages in which they had come. The ball opened with a *tour de force* called "The Hobby-Horse Quadrille," led by Mrs. S. S. Howland, in which the dancers, dressed in riding-habit, appeared to be mounted on hobby-horses; it had taken two months to get these costumes ready, for the horses were "of life-sizes, covered with genuine hides;

[27]To explain the photograph here reproduced, as well as to indicate the intricate costumes of the Fancy Dress Era, one might append this description published the following day: "Mrs. Vanderbilt's irreproachable taste was seen to perfection in her costume as a Venetian princess taken from a picture by Cabanel. The underskirt was of white and yellow brocade, shading from the deepest orange to the lightest canary, only the high lights being white. The figures of flowers and leaves were outlined in gold and lined with Roman red. Almost the entire length of the train was caught up at one side forming a large puff. The waist was of blue satin covered with gold embroidery; the dress was cut square in the neck, and the flowing sleeves were of transparent gold tissue. She wore a Venetian cap, covered with magnificent jewels, the most noticeable of these being a superb peacock in many colored gems." (*N. Y. Times,* March 27, 1883.)

[28]Illuminated costumes were one of the amusements of that ingenious age. Just before the close of the Civil War, for example, Mrs. Pierre Lorillard Ronalds gave a great costume ball at which she appeared as "Music," in her hair a harp made in Paris which was illuminated by tiny gas jets, "and she only removed the meter when dancing began." Many years later, in the age of Edison, she appeared at a costume ball given by the late Duchess of Devonshire in London, again as "Music," but this time wearing a harp lighted by "a convenient little battery which did not interfere with dancing in the least." *Cf.* Frederick Townsend Martin, *Things I Remember,* New York, 1913, p. 78.

Mrs. Bradley Martin (Cornelia Sherman)

Mrs. W. K. Vanderbilt: Hostess
(later Mrs. Oliver H. P. Belmont)

All three costumed for the W. K. Vanderbilt Ball, March 26, 1883

From the Harold Seton Collection

Mrs. James Brown Potter (Cora Urquhart)

Mr. and Mrs. August Belmont in Fancy Dress. Mrs. Belmont was Caroline Perry

The photographs are from the Harold Seton Collection

James Hazen Hyde and the Countess de Rougemont

had large, bright eyes, and flowing manes and tails, but were light enough to be easily and comfortably attached to the waists of the wearers, whose feet were concealed by richly embroidered hangings. False legs were represented on the outside of the blankets, so the deception was quite perfect." Then came the Mother Goose Quadrille, led by Mrs. Laurence Perkins and Mr. Oliver H. Northcote; the Opera Bouffe, organized by Mrs. Fernando Yznaga, sister of the hostess; then the Star Quadrille, Miss Carrie's indiscretion; and finally the Dresden Quadrille, in old German Court dress, arranged by Mrs. James Strong. All in all, it was the most ornate party in American social history, up at least to the Bradley Martin Ball of 1897, and every New York paper gave it precedence over other news. Henry Clews, the genial broker of Wall Street, in his memoirs admits that perhaps entertainments of Alexander the Great, Cleopatra, and Louis XIV may have been more magnificent—"but when viewed from every essential standpoint, and taking into account our advanced civilization, I have no hesitation in saying that the Vanderbilt ball was superior to any of those grand historic displays of festivity and amusement referred to, and more especially as the pleasure was not cloyed with any excesses like those prevalent with the ancient nobility of the old world." In short, it was an American triumph; Alexander had most certainly had his orgies, and, with equal certainty, had never achieved any such thing as "The Hobby-Horse Quadrille."

But Mrs. Vanderbilt, also unlike Alexander, had other worlds to conquer, and soon turned her magnificent energies toward Newport and a European title. In 1892 Marble House, greatest of Newport villas, was built as a birthday gift from her husband, at a cost of $2,000,000, with $7,000,000 more spent on furnishings and decoration. Designed also by Hunt, in white Italian marble, with pilasters and Corinthian capitals as large as those of the Temple of the Sun at Baalbek, with a marble driveway and surrounded by high marble walls, it was guarded day and night by detectives during its construction, so that neither the curious nor the felonious might enter. Through all the vicissitudes of her divorce, and the displeasure which her second husband took to her entertaining there, she clung to Marble House—though after 1914 it was boarded up like a cenotaph of departed glories, and finally, in August, 1932, a few months before her death, sold for $100,000 to Frederick H. Prince, Boston banker and yachtsman. The opening and the close of Marble House marked the limits of the most gorgeous social extravaganza America has ever known—with gold plate, banks of orchids, footmen in knee-breeches, and enough champagne, it seemed, to fill the harbor where the white sails of a hundred yachts ticketed the sky—Newport of the pre-War decades.

In 1895 she divorced William K. Vanderbilt, and the year following married O. H. P. Belmont. In those days such an act still savored of audacity, and its consequences still pursued her as late as 1926, when Bishop Manning demanded her resignation from the board of an Episcopal charity which she had founded, and precipitated an epic quarrel in the course of which she pointed out her sponsorship in baptism of the ducal heir of Blenheim and the high favor which she enjoyed with His Grace the Archbishop of Canterbury. Meanwhile Mrs. Belmont had traced a career of increasing social assurance. Sometimes she tested her powers by launching complete parvenus to whom she had taken a fancy, such as William B. Leeds, "the Tin-Plate King," and his fair young wife —who, it may be noted, was launched so effectively that after the death of her husband she moved to Mayfair, hobnobbed with nobility, and married Prince Christopher of Greece. Mrs. Belmont, piqued by the remarriage of William K. Vanderbilt in 1903 to the daughter of Oliver Harriman, embarked upon an implacable feud with her successor, refusing to receive at Marble House any one who had entertained Mrs. Vanderbilt, and seeking to outstrip her in good works—soup kitchens, clinics for the poor, model houses, campaigns against the drug traffic, and birth-control agitation. The rivalry became almost an international episode after the second Mrs. Vanderbilt retired to Paris and Deauville, where she became the premier American hostess in France, and during the War, working beside such friends as Miss Anne Morgan and Miss Elisabeth Marbury, won new laurels by establishing her great hospital at Neuilly where she slaved twelve hours a day.

Mrs. Belmont, after the death of her husband in 1908, devoted herself increasingly to causes, the most outstanding being the suffragette movement, which appealed to the deep Amazonian strain in her nature. Doubtless apocryphal is the story that she comforted a sobbing agitator— facing a jail sentence for smashing plate glass and pouring carbolic acid in letter boxes—with the words: "Brace up, my dear. Just pray to God— *She* will help you." But she did go to England to confer with Christabel Pankhurst, wrote a propagandist operetta produced at the Waldorf in

1916 with the late Marie Dressler in the cast, gave $100,000 to house the headquarters in Washington of the National Woman's Party, and led a great Women's Vote Parade which marched from 59th Street to Washington Square. In her later phase Mrs. Belmont belongs not unworthily to the company of Margaret Fuller Ossoli, Lucretia Mott, Elizabeth Cady Stanton, and Fanny Wright—those pioneers who voiced with conviction and courage the new self-sufficience of their sex. Always keenly interested in the arts of building, and the only woman ever to become a member of the American Institute of Architecture, Mrs. Belmont devoted her last years to the restoration of a great Renaissance château near Augerville which she had bought in 1926. She died in Paris in 1933 at the age of eighty.

Schopenhauer once remarked that a certain type of woman reminded him of "the holy apes of Benares, who, in the consciousness of their sanctity and inviolable position, think they can do exactly as they please." Such was the mettle of Mrs. Stuyvesant Fish. Born in 1853, daughter of William Henry Anthon, a prosperous New York lawyer, Marion Graves was married in 1876 to Stuyvesant Fish, scion of the Knickerbocker gentry and long-time president of Illinois Central—known as "the society railroad" of New York capitalists. For some thirty years before her death in 1915 Mrs. Fish was the delight of a small circle of intimates, and the *enfante terrible* of metropolitan society at large. With a malicious wit making up for whatever had been denied her in beauty, and a vividness of personality that startled the sedate Nineties like the flash of a scarlet tanager, Mrs. Fish helped greatly to revolutionize the art of fashionable entertaining in America. With a smart, efficiently served fifty-minute dinner she superseded the eight-course banquet with its fish, flesh, and fowl, baroque confections, and half-a-dozen wines which was deemed necessary in the Brownstone Era—"the sort of dinner," in Doctor Samuel Johnson's phrase, "you would ask a man to." Naturally the age of such dining had been coeval with the heyday of Saratoga, the White Sulphur Springs, Baden Baden, and Pau. Mrs. Fish was apparently the first hostess of the upper reaches who sprinkled her invitation list freely with the names of amusing, attractive, and talented people who had no social or financial claims—Mrs. Astor openly regarded her as a disintegrating force. Mrs. Fish offered her guests private theatricals with stars hired from Broadway, and in place of the old formal orchestra she introduced lighter, brighter music by a small band. She was in fact the harbinger of the Jazz Age. Deciding that life's major problem is the circumvention of bores and boredom, she saw no reason for enduring those tedious social farces which every one pretended to enjoy. Once, sated with one of her own parties, she stopped it at an early hour by ordering the orchestra to begin "Home, Sweet Home" and keep it up till all the guests got under way—and the musicians, still playing, followed on the heels of the last reveller downstairs to the door.

In accord with new informality, everybody was called by his first name at Mamie Fish's parties, and frequently there were name-callings of another sort—for the hostess's quick temper seemed intuitively communicated to her guests, and starting a row at the dinner-table was regarded as the best way of showing you felt entirely at home. Sarcasm was her forte, and she took no pains to conceal her dislikes. According to a well-known story, Mrs. Belmont confronted her one day in the Newport Casino, and in a great rage cried: "I have just heard what you said about me at Tessie Oelrich's last night. You can't deny it because she told me herself. You told everybody that I look like a frog!" "A toad, my dear; a *toad*," was the unruffled reply. Simpler souls even took pride in having served as the butt of Mrs. Fish's ridicule. Frederick Townsend Martin, brother of Bradley Martin, relates with relish in his pompously fatuous memoirs *Things I Remember* how at dinner he once told Mrs. Fish and company that he had spent the afternoon bringing cheer to the inmates of a blind asylum, and at the close of an hour's inspirational address had propounded the question whether they would prefer blindness or deafness. "And," he added, "they were unanimous in deciding in favor of being blind." "What!" retorted Mrs. Fish, "after hearing you talk for an hour?"

Just as the grandiose Mrs. Astor found her social majordomo in Ward McAllister, so did Mrs. Fish discover her affinity in the hysterical Harry Lehr—whose spite, mimicry, and elaborate practical jokes fitted perfectly into the pattern. The pair usually contrived to invest any occasion with a faint aura of delirium. Dressing up to caricature one's enemies, talking baby talk to a doll which one carried about, hiring horse-cars for a day's junket, giving a dinner-party for dogs, and wading in public fountains were for a while regarded as screamingly funny. Their most-talked-of exploit was the Monkey Dinner, at which a small pet monkey belonging

Women in American Society

to Joseph Leiter was introduced as a Corsican prince and seated at the table; the penny press seized upon the incident with outcries of glee and held it up to their readers as a sample of behavior in best society. Yet when one has discounted the distortion given this and similar episodes by the newspapers, the fact remains that Mrs. Fish cracked the impeccable dignity which the so-called Four Hundred had hitherto maintained in the public eye, and prepared the way for its dissolution into small groups each pursuing its own interests and amusements.

The more immediate effect was a vogue for sophisticated silliness, especially fun with fauna. Mrs. John King Van Rensselaer tells of seeing one ambitious Newport dowager driving down Bellevue Avenue in her victoria with a monkey on each shoulder and a well-washed pig staring from the seat beside her; in Boston Mrs. Jack Gardner terrified crowds in the main hall of the Boston Zoo by romping with a young lion named Rex, and sometimes appeared in the evening with two large diamonds called "The Rajah" and "The Light of India" mounted on waving antennæ in her hair; Mr. and Mrs. W. E. D. Stokes gave a dinner at which the gentlemen received as favors bullfrogs in grass baskets, which, escaping, hopped into plates and wine glasses; Mr. Paul Rainey from Indiana carried a jazz band with him wherever he went; and, on authority no less than that of Miss Juliana Cutting, a convivial guest once made his entry into a ballroom riding in a small cart drawn by a trained seal. F. T. Martin tells of a stag dinner served on horseback "on the upper floor of a fashionable New York resort," the guests dressed in riding clothes and the horses shod with rubber while they "pranced and clattered about the magnificent dining-room, each bearing, besides its rider, a miniature table."[29] After a brief flare-up in the early 1920's—which, like every period of post-war gaiety, distilled the champagne of its hilarity from the grapes of wrath—the Silly Season seems to have lost its former charm, except perhaps for youth home from Groton or Foxcroft for the holidays. Certainly one of the most painful social failures on record was

[29]This and a score of similar incidents are related in the opening pages of his book, *The Passing of the Idle Rich,* London, 1911. Incidentally, Mr. Matthew Josephson in his recent account of *The Robber Barons,* p. 338, draws numerous examples of scandalous waste from Martin, including this particular party which he startlingly transforms into "a ball on horseback." The mental image of a Quadrille of the Centaurs, as an improvement upon Hobby-Horses, would certainly have enchanted the Gilded Age—if they had only thought of it. This dinner on horseback, as a matter of record, was given by C. K. G. Billings at Sherry's in 1900.

a dinner given a few years ago in London by the then Ambassador, Charles G. Dawes, at which the comedian Leon Errol was hired to appear dressed as a waiter, to give advice on table manners, spill water on décolleté shoulders, and search with a flashlight for dropped forks under the table; a final explanation of the joke was not greeted with gales of laughter. That segment of present society which demands picturesque amusement has decided apparently that the whole thing had better be entrusted to a professional like Elsa Maxwell.

In summary it may be said that the quarter century before 1914 was the great age of the social leader in America, of the dominant personality who—by a mixture of wealth, family, aggressiveness, social skill, originality, and a measure of publicity—was able to shape into a more or less compact group the casual, scattered materials cast up by successive tides of new riches and luxurious living. The cycle of New York and Newport was repeated on a lesser scale elsewhere—Chicago in the regime of Mrs. Potter Palmer, Detroit under the Algers and the Newberrys of Grosse Pointe, St. Louis in the sway of Mrs. Morrison and Creole dowagers, Denver with Mrs. Crawford Hill and the "sacred thirty-six," San Francisco directed by a few hostesses of Burlingame, Palm Beach at the feet of a Mrs. Stotesbury unable to make headway with the more solidified society of Philadelphia, and Boston amused but scarcely dominated by Mrs. Gardner.

But the Great War, like every major upheaval, reshuffled social values. More decayed gentlemen sold their family plate, and Knickerbockers took suburban cottages; while along newly discovered Park Avenue flowered a crop of profiteers, oil promoters, motor-car magnates, tobacco princes, and chain-store millionaires. Fortunes in railroads, gold mining, shipping, and telegraph lines which seemed parvenu to the 1880's now inherited the immemorial dignity of the real estate and China trade of the 1830's, so swift was the pace of industrial expansion. Furthermore, city life had grown highly complex, and in accord with the transient spirit of the times the fashionable apartment had usurped the Fifth Avenue mansion with its enormous staff of servants, and all the sense of place and heredity it implied. The few owners of large houses lived and entertained in them but briefly: with a new volatility they flitted to Santa Barbara, the South Seas, or the Côte d'Azur, taking a cocktail shaker with them. Old lines had dimmed, and youth in its friendships and marriages often

Mrs. Burton Harrison (Constance Cary), a descendant
of the Virginia Fairfaxes

Mrs. Ogden Goelet (Mary Wilson)

Mrs. Ogden Mills and her twin sister, Mrs.
W. George Cavendish-Bentinck (Ruth and
Elizabeth Livingston)

Both photographs from the Harold Seton Collection

Mr. and Mrs. Charles Crocker of San Francisco

Mrs. Henry O. Havemeyer
(Louisine W. Elder)

Mrs. John Innes Kane
(Annie Schermerhorn)

All the portraits are from the Harold Seton Collection

Women in American Society

showed impatience with the castes, taboos, and social punctilios revered by an older society.

Under such circumstances the doom of the social arbitress had come. Here and there, to be sure, relics of the type remained—such as the late Alice Gwynne Vanderbilt, widow of the Commodore's grandson, known simply as "the Mrs. Vanderbilt," and sometimes called the loneliest figure in American society, who held court for a few aging friends at "The Breakers" at Newport; but her social power was negligible. Following her death in 1934 at the age of eighty-nine her place as dowager queen of the old regime has been taken by Mrs. Hamilton McK. Twombly, vastly rich, proud, frosty granddaughter of the Commodore. Since the War the old tradition of entertaining in the grand, spacious style has been carried on in America almost solely by Mrs. Cornelius Vanderbilt, Sr. Her father was Richard T. Wilson, a Georgian who, unlike most of his compatriots, became wealthy during the Civil War by selling cotton blankets and other supplies to the Confederate Army; later he moved to New York, where, although at first he was snubbed as a war-profiteer by the most idealistic, his son married Caroline Astor and his daughters wedded Ogden Goelet, Sir Michael Henry Herbert, and Cornelius Vanderbilt. Incurring the displeasure of his stern father by marrying the beautiful Grace Wilson in 1896, young Cornelius Vanderbilt was cut off with only a million dollars—though his brother Alfred, the future victim of the *Lusitania,* made it up to him after their father's death. A favorite of the late King Edward VII and subsequently *persona grata* with the House of Windsor, a fact of which she is justifiably proud, Mrs. Cornelius Vanderbilt, Sr., has always taken the social game very seriously, and with her gifts of strategy, charm, and ambition, has played it surpassingly well. For more than a generation she has occupied the place of America's first hostess, and has done much to keep together such fragments as still exist of smart society from the pre-War period. If the ghosts of Mrs. Bingham and Mrs. Astor revisit these glimpses of the moon, surely it is upon Mrs. Cornelius Vanderbilt out of all contemporary hostesses that their approval falls.

About the new society woman it is almost impossible to generalize, since she has ceased to represent any standard type. On the one hand there are women of inherited position and great wealth who are much more interested in projects of their own than in the mechanisms of society. An example is Mrs. Harry Payne Whitney, the former Gertrude Vanderbilt, a hard-working, highly gifted artist and patron of art, who has modelled such notable sculptures as the Titanic Memorial and the Aztec Fountain in Washington, a statue of the American doughboy at St. Nazaire, an equestrian statue to Buffalo Bill in the West, and the El Dorado Fountain in San Francisco. Representing another range of interests is Mrs. Vincent Astor, born Helen Dinsmore Huntington, who— often helped by her serious-minded and industrious husband—has ably carried out a dozen social service projects, such as a home at Rhinebeck for convalescent children, and is a keen sponsor of music.

On the other hand there is the new "socialite" of the rotogravure, the metropolitan Society Page, and the gossip syndicates throughout the land; it is she who now supplies the press with the best copy, and frequently with her guest lists as well. The most conspicuous name of this kind today is that of Mrs. Harrison Williams. Mona Strader, born about 1898 in Kentucky, is the daughter of a horse trainer in the blue-grass region. Upon the separation of her parents, she went to Lexington and for a short time attended Sayre Institute. Remembered even as a girl in pigtails for her marked personality and vivacity, she early developed an enterprise of her own which neither she nor her best friends have ever sought to deny. Her father was employed in the stables of Henry J. Schlesinger, a kindly German of Milwaukee who had grown rich in the iron-ore business, and whom she married in 1917. Plump, pretty, and a shade naïve during her Teutonic phase, she emerged in 1920 with a divorce. The following year she married James Irving Bush, Manhattan broker, and embarked upon a social career which has grown more dashing and masterful with the passing years. In 1925 she again sued for divorce, and in the next year married Harrison Williams, of humble Ohio origins, but grown extremely wealthy in public utilities and owner of the most beautiful estate in Palm Beach. There, on Long Island, and in her Manhattan apartment Mrs. Williams now entertains smartly and lavishly, with a flair for fun, excellent cocktails, and copious champagne; usually she is surrounded by a bevy of amusing young people who regard her as too divine. With innate taste for mannered décor, and possessed of beautiful clothes, jewels, and distinguished gray hair, Mrs. Williams has been twice crowned by Parisian dressmakers, although, as she tells the press, she spends but $20,000 a year on her wardrobe. Mrs. Williams, having a notable love of white houses and furnishings, is the foremost exponent of that cult of black-and-white which many modernists have discovered to be most effective in creating the grand manner. She can also claim the distinction of having appeared in full-length portraiture as the heroine of a modern novel, Ruby Wintringham in Louis Bromfield's *Twenty-Four Hours*. Helen of Troy had her *Iliad*, Beatrice her *Paradiso*, Mrs. Hargreaves her *Alice in Wonderland*, and Mrs. Harrison Williams need not complain. With her love of fashion, parties, publicity, and a tincture of snobbery, she does not—for a variety of reasons—take seriously the old social game as it is still played among the dowagers of Newport. They of course reciprocate. In many respects Mrs. Harrison Williams is typical of the lacquered new sophisticate found today in every cosmopolitan society from Honolulu to Half-Moon Street.

CHAPTER NINE

THE SOCIETY PAGE

IT IS seldom realized how greatly the Society Page has helped create social consciousness in the United States. In the first place, newspapers accentuate groups among readers merely by sorting out news according to politics, sport, finance, fashion, art, cinema, religion. Secondly, only the propagandist in wartime or the public relations expert in business can appraise fully the power of newsprint in awakening prejudices good or evil. The Society Page, which has flowered with peculiar luxuriance in American journalism, has often been sufficient to confer leadership on individuals or groups simply by printing their names day in and day out, or ascribing to them a dictatorship which is accepted first by the gum-chewing typist and finally by the enthroned dowager. In Denver for example the leading newspaper, from the days of the old *Republican* to the present *Post,* has always been owned outright by or else affiliated with the estate of Senator Nathaniel P. Hill, a professor of geology at Brown University who moved west in post-Civil War days and by science and good luck amassed a fortune in gold mining. The newspaper which he bought came quite naturally to hail his wife in preference to her rival Mrs. Anthony Sweeney as the uncrowned queen of Denver, and to print her guest-lists even for "a pink afternoon, or heliotrope tea, served by pink candlelight." Her ukases on fashion were also promulgated through *The Denver Republican,* as in this item of April 1, 1888: "There should be a rule established ostracizing dark felt and straw hats from the Opera House, particularly on such an occasion as the coming one. No woman thus hideously attired should be permitted to enter the portal." After her death it seemed fitting to the press that the purple mantle should fall upon her daughter-in-law, Mrs. Crawford Hill, born Louise Sneed of Tennessee. Hearing that her calling-list comprised only thirty-six names, *The Post*—which, among other services, prepared a daily digest of its news solely for Mrs. Hill's dinner conversation—was quick to build a cult of the Sacred Thirty-Six, with Mrs. Hill as

The Society Page

tutelary goddess. Like every other group in America during the era 1900–1914 it was called the Smart Set—which afforded the remark by a gentleman of sly wit, though he was a cousin of Ward McAllister and belonged to the inmost Denver circle, that it was so named upon the principle which had caused a tract in northwestern Colorado to be labelled the Rain Belt, because it held the state's drought record. Through the years *The Denver Post* has remained staunchly loyal to Mrs. Hill, though its less flourishing rival *The Rocky Mountain News* has long boomed the counter-claim of Mrs. Claude Boettcher, wife of a newer sugar and cement millionaire, lately presented at Court. So consistently has *The Post* dedicated itself to praising the septuagenarian beauty of Mrs. Crawford Hill, the Romanoff emeralds which she wears in a tiara suggesting the charioteer in *Ben Hur,* the exquisite taste of her house "the social capitol of Denver" done all in white and filled with the lilies which long ago became symbols of the Sacred Thirty-Six, and welcomed her home after visits to her sons in the East who are married respectively to the heiress of Campbell's Soup and to a granddaughter of the late George Fisher Baker—that Mrs. Hill is still the uncrowned queen of Denver. One recalls the similar rôle of a good press in building up Mrs. Astor, Mrs. Potter Palmer, and Mrs. Jack Gardner—of whom a Florida newspaper observed in 1901, "The Boston woman who is getting columns upon columns of free advertising out of her love of privacy is a genius in her way."

"Only the rich man is interesting," a noted journalist once told a class of college students. Certainly the glamour of the Society Page in a metropolitan daily is news about the dazzlingly remote, accompanied by the echo of sonorous names, and the innocent envy of a ragamuffin pressing his nose against the plate-glass window of a bakery. At the Marlborough-Vanderbilt marriage of 1895 *The New York Times* reported that "women and children almost threw themselves under the feet of the horses in their desire to get a look at the occupants of vehicles." Such is the compelling fascination of the social juggernaut, as editors know so well. Kindly souls from Flatbush to St. Petersburg, Florida, love the evanescent familiarity of "Gloria," "Consuelo," "Barbara," and "Wallis" dished up by the tabloid reporter. With no remote hope of crossing the threshold of Mrs. Cornelius Vanderbilt, they adore to read of the magic phantoms who do. That the magic phantoms themselves steal occasional glances at the *Herald Tribune* and the *Times* goes without saying. Thus the Society Page cuts with a double axe.

While the metropolitan press is highly selective, and gains its particular charm for the average reader by drawing the remote near, the provincial newspaper works upon the opposite principle, making itself as inclusive as possible to flatter the maximum number of subscribers, clothing the trivial and homely in the dignity of type. The obverse of the Society Page is the Personal Column, as found in country weeklies which report that "Ed Tibbetts is helping out at the A. and P. this week," or announce "Jim Bailey painted his barn last week. Good for you, Jim!" This last is an equally sound principle of business success, as the racket of "biographical encyclopedias" which blossomed thirty years ago in New York State and the Middle West richly testified. To see oneself in print is to the parvenu as enticing as was the ministry of portrait painter and daguerreotypist a century ago.[1]

But the society editor rejoices in barriers, cliques, snobberies, and invidious implications, knowing that these things make news and give the humble reader a sense of being "in the know" even though he may never dream of impinging upon that holy sphere. Long ago advertising

[1]New York, Cleveland, and Chicago were the centers of the biographical cyclopedia business in the 1900's. It has not wholly died out, but affluent customers have grown wary. Its method was simple. A plausible salesman who claimed to have been sent by common friends would call upon the widow of a rich citizen, or a citizen himself with known vanities, and represent the necessity for preparing a biographical sketch, a catalogue of achievements, and a photograph of this townsman for a cyclopedia of representative Americans soon to be published. To cover the cost and to supply the gilt-edged volume itself, a subscription ranging from $25 to $100 was mentioned casually. To avoid Federal prosecution, the book was generally printed, distributed to the several hundred subscribers, admired extravagantly in spite of its cheap paper and disintegrant binding, and added to the family library between grandfather's Bible and the poems of Ella Wheeler Wilcox.

As a sample of these cyclopedias one may take any of the dozens of volumes issued county by county, together with the ubiquitous and unchanging "Biographies and Portraits of all the Presidents of the United States," by the Chapman Publishing Company of New York and Chicago. Picking up the *Portrait and Biographical Record of Suffolk County, Long Island* one turns at random to the biography of William P. Howland: "In speaking of the different occupations in which the people of Suffolk County are engaged, we desire particularly to call attention to the industry in which Mr. Howland is engaged, that of duck-raising in Eastport. . . . On attaining his majority, he supported the candidates of the Republican Party, but in 1884 he found he had reason to change his views, and since that time has affiliated with the Prohibitionists, and is looking anxiously forward to the time when rum will be voted out of existence."

managers of newspapers learned that a little judicious buttering of Mrs. A, B, or C in their social column created much good will for themselves and their advertisers, from the ladies mentioned and also from husbands. Conversely a new respect for society editors has stirred within the bosoms of most hostesses since the twentieth century began. They have learned that the power of burlesque is a terrible revenge, while to be ignored is, if anything, even worse. A hostess who refused haughtily to give her guest-list to a society editor in the West some twenty years ago was repaid when that young woman made a survey of the automobiles parked on the night of the reception for several blocks away, checked the license numbers, and printed a roll of names which did include a majority of *bona fide* guests but also some piquant additions from apartment houses around the corner. This same reporter, meeting the curt denial of another lady, retaliated by describing her year after year, at luncheons, teas, the opera, and races, as wearing the same lavender dress and picture hat she had worn at the time of the fatal interview. Mary Margaret McBride, a journalist and radio commentator known under the pseudonym of "Martha Deane," practised a kinder stratagem during earlier days as social reporter for a newspaper in the college town of Columbia, Missouri; she called up local dairymen and confectioners to discover who had ordered extra ice cream, and then accused secretive hostesses of planning a party. Frequently reporters have faked news-stories beforehand, with hints of costumes to be worn and a liberal ingredient of conjecture—though seldom with such embarrassing results as the famous description in the past tense of the Coronation of King Edward VII reported in a London weekly six weeks before it occurred; no one could have foreseen His Majesty's sudden illness which postponed the event.

Miss Ishbel Ross in her recent book *Ladies of the Press* tells of a clash between an Amazon of the old *New York World* and her prey. Thirty-five years ago Nixola Greeley-Smith, granddaughter of the great Horace Greeley, achieved much success with a series of interviews with the hitherto sacrosanct leaders of society. Mrs. Stuyvesant Fish allowed herself to be cross-questioned, and with Harry Lehr she conversed by telepathy through a medium. Bearing a letter of introduction from Chauncey M. Depew, Miss Greeley-Smith gained access to the presence of Mrs. Astor, and with little difficulty persuaded her that she was to America what Victoria meant to England and Eugènie to France. Touched by the thought that perhaps she owed her admiring multitudes a proclamation, Mrs. Astor uttered several rather remarkable statements. After preparing her article for *The Sunday World* Miss Greeley-Smith, a novice, began to have qualms that she should obtain express permission for its publication, and under the derision of the city editor retraced her steps to Mrs. Astor's door. She was refused another appointment, but by the maid Mrs. Astor sent down a $2 bill with the message that "you work for a living and you've been put to some trouble in coming here." With hauteur the granddaughter of Horace Greeley replied: "Tell Mrs. Astor that she not only forgets who I am, but she forgets who she is. Give her back the $2 with my compliments and tell her that when John Jacob Astor was skinning rabbits, my grandfather was getting out *The Tribune* and was one of the foremost citizens of New York." After this pronouncement, more pungent than chronologically accurate, Miss Greeley-Smith put the finishing touches to the interview and had the satisfaction of seeing advance notices of her *coup* broadcast throughout New York. The dowager's son, the late John Jacob Astor, threatened suit against the proprietors of *The World* if the story were run. It appeared blithely as announced, and neither earthquake nor blue ruin followed. Emboldened, *The World* opened in its magazine section a new series which began with the time-worn query, "Is Fashionable Society Corrupt and Wicked?" Having marked social ambitions of his own, Joseph Pulitzer answered in the negative.

The genesis of the Society Page is remote and devious. In relatively modern times among its precursors were the *nouvellistes* or professional newsmongers who at the court of Louis XIV made it their business to gather and spread news, satire, and scandal about fashionable folk. They produced handwritten news-letters which were sometimes posted but often circulated surreptitiously. At this early date society reporting was already tinged with blackmail and innuendo, so readily invited by the private lives of public characters. In England the coffee house was not only the cradle for the gentleman's club, as has been remarked, but also for social gossip and the newspaper. Though bulletins at sporadic intervals and weekly gazettes were known early in seventeenth-century London, the first daily newspaper was *The Daily Courant* begun in 1702. *The Post Boy* followed hard upon its heels, and also Defoe's *Review of the Affairs of France* which featured an imaginary "Scandal Club." In

The Next Morning

C. D. Gibson in *Life* in 1902

Mrs. Innittor Dedd's Maid Reads: "Among those present was Mrs. Innittor Dedd, whose lovely face and splendid figure were enhanced by a tiara of diamonds and three ropes of pearls. She wore her famous rubies and was even more regal than at the Bullyons' Ball the night before," etc. etc.

the newspapers of Queen Anne's day, intermingled with essays on the unities in drama, intelligence from the Low Countries, advertisements of nostrums, and accounts of calves born with two heads, one finds intimations of the Society Page in the shape of decorous doings of the Royal Family, and hints of scandalous carryings-on in which the principals' names are veiled in initial letters, dashes, and asterisks. The highly proper Joseph Addison, "a parson in a tye-wig," was shocked at the liberties taken by his rival *The Examiner* under the editorship of Mrs. Manley: "No sanctity of character or privilege of sex exempted persons from this barbarous usage. Several of our prelates were the standing marks of public raillery, and many ladies of the first quality branded by name for matters of fact, which, as they were false, were not heeded, and if they had been true, were innocent." A generation later Horace Walpole complained to Mann, September 17, 1778, that newspapers have become "vehicles of lies, blunders, and scandals." In the limbo of unborn time *Town Topics* stirred.

Reports of fashionable life which newspapers featured almost from the beginning received both praise and rebuke. *The Weekly Journal* saw in this mirror held up to public gaze a satisfaction for the craving after pageantry, glory, comedy, and tragedy.[2] Even in those times the Society Page was the glass in which a humdrum spinster of Shalott might see the plumes of a gay Sir Launcelot, one hopes with no tragic consequences. On the other hand Henry Fielding in the *True Patriot* for November 5, 1745 remarks on the distortion, flattery, and exaggeration of social reporters: "the arrival of my Lord —— 'with a great equipage'; the marriage of Miss ——, 'of great beauty and merit'; and the death of Mr. ——, who was never heard of in his life." In the world of journalism every bride had already become ravishingly fair, and every clubman immaculately groomed.

The London Times from its first appearance on New Year's Day 1788 to its present ripe age under the ownership of Major John Jacob Astor,

[2]On 24 June, 1721, the *Journal* inquired: "Were it not for the Newspapers what would become of Herds of fine People, whose Transition from Amusement is constantly to Vice? . . . By their Assistance we are preserv'd from degenerating into Brutality, we are soften'd, civiliz'd, nay, humaniz'd. If a Lady or Gentleman lose their dear Spouses, the whole Nation is taught to grieve in Concert with them. . . . Fires, Executions, Casualties, Deaths, Promotions, etc. are constantly soliciting our Affections of Pity and Joy." All news has then its function of *catharsis* in the Aristotelian sense.

The Society Page

brother of the Viscount, has set the world a pretty consistent example in one type of social reporting. One may call it the court calendar style, of dignified items about the coming and going of important people beginning with the blood royal. These items are treated in a solemn, matter-of-fact way, far removed from the piquant sauce, the lurid garniture, and the impertinent curiosity of the ranker journalism. One finds *The Times* confirmed in discretion from its tenderest years: under the caption "London" the first issue records sedately the doings of royalty, and then follows with this item: "The great heiress, Miss Pulteney, the daughter of William Pulteney, Esq., came of age last Thursday.—The entertainments on the occasion were very splendid, and the celebration kept at Shrewsbury." No mention of the bonfires lighted by a loyal tenantry, the approximate number of bottles consumed, dressmakers' chit-chat, attentions paid by ambitious youths, and other details which an eighteenth-century Cholly Kickerbocker would have found irresistible. Turning to a slightly later issue, October 12, 1789, one finds that "the town of Poole is going to build a new very elegant Assembly Room." But after all, the eighteenth century was the eighteenth century, and even in this issue one comes upon a startling social detail, recalled by an obituary: "While Charlotte Spencer was *en famille* with the Duke of Devonshire, she produced his Grace a daughter:—The young Lady has ever resided under the Duke's roof, and ever experienced the most generous protection from the Duchess." Even Walter Winchell would have thought twice before recording so bluntly an event unblessed by clergy.[3]

With the Boston *News Letter* in 1704 the first American newspaper of any real hardiness was established. Colonial papers in the beginning showed little initiative; in respect to society they offered little more than clippings from London sheets of tittle-tattle about peers and the rich gentry. Soon weddings and funerals of quality folk were described in stock phrases of flattery. *The Charleston Gazette* before the Revolution is filled with marriage announcements such as: "Febr. 15. On Thursday last Mr. John Garret, an eminent Merchant of this Town was married to Mrs. Elizabeth Hill, a young, beautiful and genteel lady, with a con-

[3]In those days the social status of a journalist was undefined, but seems appreciably to have sunk since the coffee-house essayists. In 1808 the benchers of Lincoln's Inn adopted a by-law excluding all persons who had written for hire in the daily papers from being called to the bar. It was later rescinded.

siderable fortune," or the union of Lord William Campbell, younger son of the Duke of Argyll, to "Miss Sarah Izard, daughter of Walter Izard, Esqr., an amiable and accomplished young lady, esteemed one of the greatest fortunes of this province." Often the bride's specific price mark was affixed, "a most amiable young lady with ten thousand pounds to her fortune." During the late eighteenth century the New York *Weekly Museum,* aspiring to be a sort of society journal, specialized in personal notes and often got into hot water over its marriage announcements, for it appears that the editor was victimized by practical jokers, and once barely escaped the duelling field for his gullibility in printing errors. Typical of his more reliable reports was this: "On Monday the 31st of July, 1786, in Washington County, Maryland, Major General Horatio Gates to Miss Mary Vallance, a lady distinguished most deservedly for her good sense, liberal education, and amiable disposition, with a handsome fortune." When the bride lacked *dot* and social background, the newspapers made no bones about it; Rufus Griswold cites this notation of marriage in October, 1790: "At Philadelphia, Hugh H. Breckenridge, Esquire, a celebrated counsellor at law, to Miss Sabina Wolfe, a young girl of obscure German parents."

In reporting arrivals and departures American newspapers early adopted phrases which they deemed suitable to the pomp and circumstance of the person. In Boston in 1776 we find a zealous journalist writing, "arrived in Boston from Philadelphia, that most worthy and patriotic gentleman, the Hon. Samuel Adams, Esqu., a member of that august and united body, the right honorable the Continental Congress." Such was the unction of American Independence. With the onset of Jeffersonian democracy and the age of Jackson, baroque titles and phrases in the press appear to have suffered a decline, and with them waned reports of affairs in high life. James Boardman in *America and the Americans,* London, 1833, observes: "European news is copiously reported, and is as eagerly read; but no namby-pamby trash of fashionable movements, routs, and dinners finds its way into the columns of American papers, such absurdities being held up to ridicule." Soon the age of American Victorianism began, when, as Grattan remarked in *Civilized America,* London, 1859, "The newspapers . . . abstain, on a point of delicacy, from ever announcing the birth of a child, while marriages and deaths occupy their columns without reserve." Upon turning to the files of contem-

The Society Page

porary newspapers, even the most blatant of them all, Bennett's *Herald,* one finds this is true. Meredith's cynic pointed out that "birth and death are natural accidents—marriage at least we can avoid"; but the journalist in mid-nineteenth-century America chose to juggle with the epigram.

Impudence arrived with the elder James Gordon Bennett, a Scotchman who knew little about his ancestors except that "I have had bishops, priests, robbers and all sorts of people in my family; and, what is more, we were bright in ideas and saucy enough in all conscience." After several years of hand-to-mouth hack writing he began *The New York Herald* in May, 1835. At that time only one newspaper was read and approved by New York society, *The Courier and Enquirer,* edited by Colonel James Watson Webb, later a charter member of the Union Club.[4] Just a year after *The Herald's* foundation Webb and Bennett fought each other with fists in the middle of Wall Street, and a furious rivalry was on. Bennett early saw his chance to publicize and mock society; probably with tongue in cheek he announced on March 17, 1837: "No one ever attempted till now to bring out the graces, the polish, the elegancies, the bright and airy attributes of social life. . . . Our purpose has been, and is, to give to the highest society of New York a life, a variety, a piquancy, a brilliancy, an originality that will entirely outstrip the worn out races of Europe." In the same year the British temperance lecturer Buckingham, who had a personal grievance against *The Herald,* wrote: "Private dinner-parties, balls, and social meetings are pretended to be reported in its pages, some of them having no existence, and others wholly misrepresented; and the only way of securing exemption from the attacks of his slanderous pen is to advertise largely in the paper, at most extravagant prices, or to send the editor presents in money or other direct bribes." From Saratoga as well as New York Bennett picked up servants' tattle which vastly irked Hones, Aspinwalls, Cuttings, Schermerhorns and their set, until such ire was stirred that even after the Civil War Bennett was refused lodgings at

[4]Charles King, editor of the somewhat less impeccable *New York American,* was also favored by the Union Club. In general however the members of that club grew notoriously gun-shy of journalists, and in 1867 blackballed Manton Marble, editor of *The World,* merely because of his profession. A friend of Marble in indignation swore to blackball every proposed candidate until justice was done him, and, under this threat, Marble was finally admitted. James Gordon Bennett, Jr., was taken in after demonstrating his deference to social decorum, and became a most redoubtable patron of the Union, often ordering barrels of the club's oysters for long cruises on his yacht.

The Saga of American Society

Saratoga after guests at the hotel told the landlord that he must choose between the editor's patronage and their own.

On February 27, 1840, Bennett smuggled the first society reporter in America across the threshold of a fashionable party, with the reluctant connivance of its host. The occasion was a famous fancy-dress ball given by the Henry Brevoorts in their house at 9th Street and Fifth Avenue, to which Jones Schermerhorn went as Gessler, Eliza Russell as Lalla Rookh, Philip Hone's daughters Mary and Catherine as Day and Night, and Hone himself "as Cardinal Wolseley [*sic*], in a grand robe of new scarlet merino, with an exceedingly well-contrived cap of the same material, a cape of real ermine which I borrowed from Mrs. Thomas W. Ludlow, gold chains and cross, scarlet stockings." Arrayed in such splendor it was little wonder that Hone—whose earlier Diary is sprinkled with aspersions on "an ill-looking, squinting man called Bennett," and his penny paper "hawked about the streets by a gang of troublesome, ragged boys"—should express surprise at seeing at the ball "a man in the habit of a knight in armor," one William H. Attree, former sports writer for *The Herald*. Mr. Attree's costume was probably chosen with an eye to self-defence. Hone learned that Brevoort had agreed to the fellow's presence in order to avoid scurrilous abuse in *The Herald,* and his disapproval increased when "Mr. Charles A. Davis and other gentlemen made this Mr. Attree 'hail fellow well met.'" Hone regarded Bennett's attitude as subversive of all decency and order, since it obviously set out to ridicule wealth and fashion, and release that pent-up social revolution which Hone feared was simmering under the kettle's lid. He was right in predicting that journalism would help break down the old exclusiveness of a clique which once regarded its balls and dinners as no more the public's business than its bankruptcies and adulteries. But he did not foresee that society would pass from anger to tolerance and thence to secret pleasure in seeing itself written up. Within a short time even Bennett began to meet society halfway, subordinating mockery to descriptions of pomp and grandeur.

The simultaneous arrival in 1841 of Viscount Morpeth and the Prince de Joinville, third son of Louis Philippe, was a journalists' saturnalia. We read of Mrs. Mott's soirée for the Prince, at which she wore a diamond tiara and ruby-colored robe of Damascus satin, and queened it over her house in Bleecker Street, "filled with many evidences of the most refined

From a painting by Madrazo

Mrs. Cornelius Vanderbilt (Grace Wilson)   Miss Anne Morgan

Mrs. George J. Gould (Edith Kingdon) and her daughters, Mrs. Anthony J. Drexel, Jr. (Marjorie, eldest), Lady Decies (Vivien, 2nd), Lady Hector Macneal (Edith, 3rd), Mrs. Walter M. Barker (Gloria, youngest)

All three photographs from the Harold Seton Collection

Mrs. Medill McCormick   Lady Ribblesdale (Ava Willing)*

*The above photograph was made when the wife of Col. John Jacob Astor, with her daughter, Alice M. Astor, who later became Princess Serge Obolensky; still later Mrs. Raimund von Hufmannsthal

From a photograph in the Harold Seton Collection

Mrs. Joseph E. Widener and son

The Society Page

taste in the costly furniture and *bijouterie* scattered around," and of the following evening's entertainment which was even grander. It was a farewell dinner given the Prince by the Corporation of New York City, with the ballroom of the Astor House transformed by red, white, and blue draperies and golden pillars. The dinner was graced by endless toasts, of which this—to his frigate *La Belle Poule,* translated for the benefit of monolingual readers "beautiful chicken"—is a sample: "We give her a hearty Godspeed; may she always be successful whenever her cause is just, but otherwise unsuccessful, but if ever she is opposed to an American ship may she be unsuccessful right or wrong. And I give you the United States; may she be always right, but always successful, right or wrong."

Bennett set the custom of recording arrivals at the Astor House, since obviously anybody able to pay $2 a day for a room must be a person of consequence; he also chronicled a list of "Passengers Arrived" by first-class on boats from Europe and the South. He loved also to regale his readers with fables of high life. For instance on September 3, 1836 we find on the front page "A Tale for the Ladies" warning them against masked balls by the reputedly true story of a jealous husband who tracked his frail wife and her domino to "a fashionable assignation house" and there crashed in the door. The wife swooned across the bed which was to have witnessed her shame, but her spouse "had her placed in the carriage and drove home—a physician was sent for, but in vain—she was a *confirmed lunatic.*" After his reporters began to get entry into society, one finds no more stories of this kind.

Bennett's most ambitious news-story of society seems to have been "the Grand Fancy Dress Ball at Newport" on August 31, 1849, which, except for a fraction of a column on European politics, took up the entire front page of *The Herald* three days later. After thrilling accounts of preparations for the ball, of the three "Persian columns" labelled BEAUTY —LOVE—PLEASURE, and of the grand promenade itself, descriptions followed of some three hundred costumes. These from the front page are typical:

Miss Wright of Newark whose elegant manners and fine deportment were the topic of conversation at Newport, wore a *robe de bal* of pink satin of the *mielleur* [*sic*] *goût.*

The Saga of American Society

Miss A. Wilkins of Boston, a tall person with an intelligent look, was dressed as Fanny Elssler in the 'Cracovienne.'

Mrs. Currie Duncan, of Louisiana, wore a rich dress, and her amiability attracted around her many friends.

Already the society reporter had bought a copy of *French Phrases at a Glance*—even as today society editors on village newspapers, of which the Huntsville, Texas, *Item* is an example best known to the author, intersperse accounts of church sociables, strawberry festivals, and box-suppers with allusions to *savoir faire,* and to the *décor comme il faut,* with every one attired in a manner quite *soignée.*

After Bennett had broken the barriers of reticence, other New York papers like *The Tribune, The Times,* and *The Evening Post* after the régime of William Cullen Bryant, began to dish up social soufflé to their public. Yet Bennett himself never won the acceptance of society, while his wife—an Irish girl named Henrietta Agnes Crean who had emigrated with her family in 1838—was snubbed by New York so severely that she came to live almost wholly abroad, and in a sophisticated, indulgent French atmosphere brought up their son and heir James Gordon Bennett, Jr. Shortly after the Civil War he began to make himself felt in councils of *The Herald,* and upon his father's death in 1872 reigned supreme. A dandy in dress, a gourmet of brandy and plovers' eggs, member of the Jockey Club and future commodore of the New York Yacht Club, the second Bennett was quickly accepted by the sporting set in town—Heckschers, Howlands, Osgoods, Lorillards, and Oelrichs. He carried an Alderney cow with an electric milker, in a padded stall cooled by electric fans, on the grandest of a long line of Bennett yachts, the *Lysistrata,* named after "a Greek lady reputed to be very beautiful and very fast." But his favorite beverage, perhaps unfortunately, was not milk, for while in his cups he performed madcap pranks which were the talk of New York and Paris—kidnapping a theatrical company from Amsterdam and making them perform upon his yacht during a voyage of several days, driving a coach furiously through midnight streets while he sat stark naked upon the box, and pulling cloths off restaurant tables as he walked past but settling handsomely for broken crockery. On January 1, 1877, following the old Knickerbocker custom which had been praised

The Society Page

by none less than George Washington,[5] Bennett set out to make a round of calls and punch-bowls, but by the time he reached the door of Miss Caroline May, daughter of a distinguished and rather military family from Baltimore, he was flown with insolence and wine. His behavior was so profoundly shocking that two days later Miss Caroline's brother Frederick horsewhipped young Bennett in front of the Union Club. Bennett challenged May to a duel with pistols, which was fought in Delaware on January 7. May fired into the air, while Bennett, too nervous to take aim, declared himself satisfied. Amid the derision which the whole episode provoked, Bennett sailed for Paris, never returned except for flying business trips, and wore a coat of mail beneath his clothes whenever the Paris edition of *The Herald* reported that the Mays were visiting *la ville lumière*.

But alike before and after his disgrace, nobody took New York society more gravely than Bennett. Nicholas Biddle became social adviser extraordinary to *The Herald,* while the late William C. Reick, long its managing editor and weary of innumerable sacred cows, plaintively asked Don C. Seitz of *The World,* "How in hell can I be expected to carry the names of all the members of the Union Club in my mind?" In charge of *The Herald's* Society Page during the seventies and eighties was the adroit and socially erudite William B. Bininger, sprung from a German family which had risen to some wealth in New York through the grocery business. Under his vigilance no contretemps ever occurred such as happened after his retirement, when the make-up man mixed Mrs. Stuyvesant Fish's guest-list for a reception with the list of ringside seat-holders at a simultaneous prize fight. Mrs. Fish's caustic tongue lashed the managing editor most effectually and he decided to drop all future allusions to her from *The Herald,* but this oblivion so maddened her that she appealed to Bennett in person and was reinstated. Such an incident is eloquent of the fact that society had become reconciled to its Page. After journalism called a truce to mockery, society found little hardship in enduring the

---

[5]On January 1, 1790, when New York was briefly the nation's capital, Washington delighted to follow this tradition, observing: "The highly favored situation of New York will, in the process of years, attract numerous emigrants, who will gradually change its ancient customs and manners; but, whatever changes take place, never forget the cordial and cheerful observance of New Year's Day." Edith Wharton's novelette *New Year's Day,* New York, 1924, depends for its setting and initial action upon this custom as preserved in the later nineteenth century.

The Saga of American Society

increasingly personal tone—even though Walt Whitman in *The Brooklyn Eagle* as early as February 26, 1847 had rebuked the type of newspaper which informs its readers "whether A eats roast beef or Graham bread."[6]

From about 1860 to the close of the century England had witnessed a spate of society journals which flourished independently of staid newspapers like *The Times* and *Morning Post*. There was Thomas Gibson Bowles, a hustling journalist who without visible cachet founded *Vanity Fair* and promised to impart to his readers what were mysteriously called "the pass-words of Society." Enough people yearned to know these pass-words to make *Vanity Fair* an immense success. Edmund Yates, trained in the offices of *The New York Herald,* then started *The World,* often called "the pioneer of modern society journalism." He himself boasted and not without reason that "For the first time ladies—who, in publications which claimed to consult feminine idiosyncrasies exclusively, were hitherto obliged to be content with recipes for cookery, hints for illness, precepts for the nurture and training of infants, patterns for needlework, and mild facetiae culled from the records of district visitors—now found a journal which, proclaiming that it would not ignore them, interpreted their real wants, and supplied them too." Quite shamelessly he decided to make his journal amusing, "a quality which, to the majority of newspaper proprietors and editors of those days, was stamped with the mark of the Beast." He also invited contributions from the Court and the aristocracy, promising that "the spelling and grammar of nobility will be corrected, and manuscripts when done with, will be discreetly buried at midnight during a thunderstorm, in order that the capital sin of possessing intellect may never be brought home to anybody." Its features included a popular series called "Celebrities at Home," of interviews with the Prince of Wales, the Dukes of Cambridge and Edinburgh, Continental royalty, poets, famous jockeys and trainers. More sensational was the gallery of "West End Usurers," of notoriously rich and socially

[6]Herbert Spencer, interviewed by Professor Youmans upon his visit to the United States in 1882, remarked that Americans "do not sufficiently respect the individualities of others. . . . It is shown by the disrespectful manner in which individuals are dealt with in your journals—the placarding of men in sensational headings, the dragging of private people and their affairs into print. There seems to be a notion that the public have a right to intrude on private life as far as they like; and this I take to be a kind of moral trespassing." Professor Edward A. Freeman, the distinguished historian, visiting the United States in 1881–82, recorded the same impression.

vulgar individuals. Another sally into society journalism made by Yates, which began to encroach upon the domain of libel by the use of so-called "snaky" paragraphs, was *The Cuckoo;* ultimately it failed, in accord with the timeworn superstition of journalists that no newspaper named after a bird will ever fly far. Henry Labouchère's *Truth* had a mildly crusading purpose in ridding society of parasites; H. W. Lucy attempted a journal called *Mayfair;* and William Alison, a blade of the Junior Carlton Club, began the *St. Stephen's Review* and developed the brilliant caricaturist Phil May. The piquant brand of humor and satire, the light crisp fiction, the drawings, and the sophisticated interviews or profiles of the great, all had marked effect upon the quality journalism of the United States—from Charles Dana Gibson to Peter Arno, from the earliest American *Vanity Fair* to the present Condé Nast publications.[7]

Yates was right in analyzing the appeal of society journalism as essentially feminine, and in America it came to be recognized about fifty years ago that women by and large made the best editors of social pages. Tireless memory for names and family histories, ability to describe the intricacies of fashion, a sense of style and good taste, even the invocation of chivalry as a shield against rude refusal—these things showed woman as the divinely appointed steward. Even the dean of old-school society editors, the late Frank Leslie Baker of *The New York Times,* came at length to depend greatly upon feminine assistants—one of whom, Bessie I. Phillips, has now inherited his place. Among pioneer women were Sally Joy who in post-Civil War times wrote under the name of "Penelope Penfeather" for Bennett's *Herald* and had a boy from the staff detailed as her "escort" to all parties after 7 P.M., and Emily Edson Briggs or "Olivia" who worked for several Manhattan papers and undertook one of the first syndications. "Olivia" gallantly defended Kate Chase Sprague, who had always been most sympathetic to the press in Washington, when the hounds of scandal were snuffing out her friendship for Roscoe Conkling. Today the premier woman in society journalism is probably Ruth E. Jones, or "Jean Eliot," of *The Washington Herald,* owned by Hearst

[7]In 1925 the struggling *New Yorker,* for example, discovered its potential appeal to Park Avenue by happening to publish "Why We Go to Cabarets: A Post-Débutante Explains," by Miss Ellin Mackay, the year before her marriage to Irving Berlin. The significance of its notable success was not lost upon Harold Ross and his Fleischmann sponsors.

and edited by the vivacious Eleanor Medill Patterson. Miss Jones, daughter of a well-known Washington lawyer, attended fashionable schools in her girlhood and has always enjoyed the confidence of the cave-dwellers. After ripe apprenticeship to *The Washington Times* and *The Post,* she is now an authority on the shifting social pageant of the capital, with a keen news-sense but aversion to scandal. Mrs. Sallie Pickett of *The Star,* now in emeritus rank, and Evelyn Peyton Gordon of *The Post,* have also carried on the conservative tradition of the society page in Washington.

The tone of any society page depends vitally upon the interests of owner and editor-in-chief. It is inevitable that Mrs. Patterson—who once married a Polish noble, Count Gizycka, and today entertains lavishly on Du Pont Circle and at Dower House in Maryland—should have probably the best society editor in America, and sponsor other columns called "Peter Carter Says" and "These Charming People," and reproduce expensive photographs of débutantes, brides, and civic leaders. It is equally certain that *The New York Times,* carried on by Arthur Hays Sulzberger from the tradition of Adolph Ochs in the heart of German-Jewish aristocracy, will continue to treat society with grave respect, even though Frank Leslie Baker died in January, 1936. Mr. Baker was born in Lowell, Massachusetts, the son of a petty naval officer. As a schoolboy he carried a paper-route, and then after a brief and unhappy interregnum of rural school-teaching, entered journalism on Dana's *Sun,* went in 1889 to *The Tribune* under Whitelaw Reid, thence to Bennett's *Herald* for his longest term of service, and after further shifts to *The Times* in 1924. He worshipped the Four Hundred, attended opera in silk hat and white gloves, faithfully trailed dowagers with his camera-man at Newport and Southampton, and occasionally achieved a notable "scoop," as by his exclusive account of the Lăszlo Szĕchényi-Vanderbilt wedding in 1908. He bore no malice toward the mighty and arrogant who often wiped their feet upon him, and only his assistants had a glimmering notion of the stories he might have told had he been that kind of man and *The Times* that kind of paper.

The old *World* under Joseph Pulitzer and the present *St. Louis Post-Dispatch* under his sons belong also in the conservative wing, because the Pulitzers have always genuflected before society. In Josephine Robb, later Mrs. Frank S. Ober, the first Pulitzer found his ideal social editor.

The Society Page

Colonel Mann dearly loved to poke fun at "old Joey" under his gilded dome, crying repeatedly upon his staff to "redooze selleries," but learned a new respect after young Ralph married Fredericka Vanderbilt Webb in 1905. Today the only Pulitzer society page in America is edited in traditionally respectful fashion by Margaret Ruhl of *The Post-Dispatch*. *The Herald Tribune* is another newspaper which will never desert the court gazette for vulgar flippancies. Its column called "Personal Intelligence" and its longer news stories edited by Howard White speak not of storks or unhappy couples who have decided to "sleparate." Mr. Ogden Reid inherits the dignity of his father, the late Whitelaw Reid, Ambassador to the Court of St. James; his wife, a Wisconsin girl who made a brilliant record at Barnard and found employment as secretary to her future mother-in-law, has more intellectual audacity but holds firmly to the essentials of decorum.

Equally conservative is Olga E. Gellhaus of Philadelphia, who began her career as usher in Oscar Hammerstein's opera house. Reporters asked her to identify box-holders and collect costume-notes; soon, with the help of Alexander Van Rensselaer and other helpful patrons, she was reporting for *The Press,* and later for *The Evening Bulletin.* Her page is dignified, though of course it can never rival the stateliness of the late-defunct *Ledger* in the days of G. W. Childs Drexel's editorship, or the society notes of "Peggy Shippen" (Mrs. Cornelius Stevenson). If one is searching today for a society editor with the powers of a dictator he must go to *The Cincinnati Enquirer* and ask for Marian Devereaux, whose post was inherited from her mother and whose celebrity in Cincinnati is matched only by that of Mrs. Longworth. In Cincinnati it is believed that Miss Devereaux furnished Sinclair Lewis his model in *Babbitt* for Miss Elnora Pearl Bates of *The Advocate-Times* who rises "to her highest lark-note" on the visit of a real baronet to Zenith. Anne Bolton Ellis's thirty-five years of service upon the staff of *The New Orleans Times-Picayune* have lent her also an apostolic eminence. In Boston *The Evening Transcript*—whose readers, as T. S. Eliot so memorably wrote, "sway in the wind like a field of ripe corn"—has the reputation of investigating the social status and club membership of every prospective reporter. There is a familiar story of the butler who announced to his master, "Two reporters from the newspapers, sir, and a gentleman from *The Transcript.*" Yet Boston's best-known society editor was the late Caroline Hall Washburne of *The Herald,* who stemmed from an old family and dressed impressively in Paris fashions of the year before last. The San Francisco vicar of *The Social Register,* Mrs. Jacques Henrici, born Wanda Brastow, was formerly society editor of *The Examiner* in that city, but ceased after her indiscreet remarks at a cocktail party disclosed the approaching divorce of George Hearst. Once held by Kathleen Norris, who resigned after being refused a salary of $50 a week, the society editorship of *The Examiner* is now filled by Ethel Whitmire, a relative of the Hearst family. A generation ago Mrs. Austin Walton, now Mrs. Marshall Darrach, created the rôle of "Lady Teazle" on *The San Francisco Chronicle,* and amusingly recorded the Indian summer of the bonanza kings on Nob Hill. During the same decade, in 1909, Caroline Kirkland began the popular column of "Madame X" on *The Chicago Tribune;* today June Provines on that paper is read by every Chicago housewife, for she caters to a sympathetic curiosity about the rich which sets Chicago apart from the hard glitter of New York. Among recent *noms de plume* that of "Madame Flutterbye," Molly Thayer of *The New York Journal,* is best known.

The pseudonym of Cholly Knickerbocker was invented by a Hearst reporter soon after William Randolph Hearst entered New York journalism in 1895 with *The Journal,* and decreed that his staff should break the old formalities by calling Mrs. Fish "Mamie" and Mrs. Oelrichs "Tessie." Such Pacific breeziness was at first hotly resented, but the dignity of society—like that of its new collapsible opera-hat—proved surprisingly adaptable. Ivy Ross and her successor Isabel Fraser first made the name of Cholly Knickerbocker a byword. It is now continued in *The New York American* and in a syndicated column by Maury Paul, polished, capable, master of discreet innuendo and unresented impudence, but something of an outsider to the Knickerbocker society whose label he professes. Among the tabloids are "Barclay Beekman" or Howard Shelley of *The New York Daily Mirror,* and "Nancy Randolph" of *The Daily News,* in reality Mrs. J. Addison Robb, who comes from an Idaho ranch and fears no lorgnette—as she has demonstrated by outfacing Mrs. Joseph E. Davies and other imperious hostesses of Manhattan, Washington, and Palm Beach who have "forbidden" her to mention their names in her column. Valiant for the little stenographer, because she herself buys her hats in economy basements and gaily avows it, Nancy Randolph usually tells all. Among capable women in New York journalism should be mentioned Helen Worden of *The World-Telegram* and Scripps-Howard syndications, who is also from the West, but reports the geography, humors, and society of New York with relish and charm. She was among the first to treat society from a broad and generic viewpoint, as a succession of good news stories rather than a catalogue of resounding names.[8]

A study of the society page would afford rich materials to the social historian. There was a day, for example, when the phrase "poured without hats" was thought to convey the essence of *chic* at a tea-party; in the provinces social editors still use the term "seated tea" to describe a smartly sedate gathering at which one does not nibble and run. The society page of forty years ago embalms much information about those Sewing Circles which from Boston to St. Louis used to foregather twice a month amid extreme social exclusiveness to sew for the poor. The sewing was none too utilitarian. One dowager who grew up in that era lately remarked to the author that it was like the notions of charity possessed by young Lewis Carroll, for his sister relates that the boy used to spend hours peeling rushes with the idea that the pith would afterwards "be given to the poor," though to what possible use they could put it he never attempted to explain. Up till after the Great War sewing circles lingered on in Boston, though in time they came to do their sewing vicariously, by hiring professional sempstresses; finally the Junior League claimed them all. In glancing through the social files one sees also that locutions like "Mrs. Doctor A" and "Mrs. Ex-Senator B" were formerly common. And in many communities there was an era when every hostess stressed her garden, and in the midst built a pergola as the American equivalent of the Petit Trianon. The pergola was always mentioned whenever she poured tea outdoors, entertained the vicar and her fellow-parishioners, or welcomed Garden Clubs with their papers on Sicilian, Spanish, or Moroccan gardens which inevitably began with the line from T. E. Browne,

"A garden is a lovesome thing, God wot."

Mr. Canby has lately recalled in *The Age of Confidence,* from memories of Wilmington in the nineties, that the editor of personal notes always

[8]Parallel to the "radical aristocrat" noted in an earlier chapter should be set the even rarer type of Marxist society editor, represented by Julia Blanshard, one-time

placed a bar ———.——— "after the last item that belonged to Us, before the doings of the 'plain people' began to be set down." It was an eloquent, insuperable barrier.

Commenting upon the childish character of American life and society in the Age of Innocence, Henry James added, "the newspapers alone, for instance, doing so much to feed it, from day to day, as with their huge playfully brandished wooden spoon." This quality appears unmistakably in respect to the greatest society news-story in American history, the Bradley Martin Ball of February 10, 1897. It was an expensive and uncommonly vulgar display of wealth, but there was no very cogent reason for its becoming the wonder of the English-speaking world from Seattle to London. That was the caprice of the newspapers, languishing in doldrums between the Vanderbilt-Marlborough wedding and the Spanish-American War. It happened also to fall in the era of journalistic minutiæ, when every loop in a festoon, every bit of passementerie, and every restored feather on a pheasant served à la mode, was tallied in loving inventory.

The Bradley Martins came from Troy, New York, but seldom mentioned it. Mr. Martin—or Mr. Bradley Martin, as he became after the slow growth of an imaginary hyphen—was the son of a self-made lawyer who had invested his earnings with luck and skill. Mrs. Bradley Martin was born Cornelia Sherman, and like other members of her family believed in Society. Favored by Ward McAllister and Mrs. Paran Stevens's set, the couple flourished in Newport and New York. They learned to play the social game abroad, bought a town house in London and an estate in the grouse country near Inverness, and in 1893 had the satisfaction of seeing their daughter Cornelia, aged sixteen, become the bride of Lord Craven. One morning at breakfast during the winter of 1896-7 Mrs. Bradley Martin, reading of depressed conditions and the sufferings of the poor, suddenly decided to have a ball "to give an impetus to trade." As she pursued this ideal it grew grander and grander, until she ended by stimulating trade to the extent of $369,200. Couturiers in New York and even in far-off Paris set to work designing Renaissance, Elizabethan, Van Dyck, Pompadour, and Marie Antoinette costumes, with seed-pearls,

staff member of *The Rochester Democrat*. While writing of the *ton,* she lived among garment workers and mill-hands of that city, paraded with and agitated for them. Later she made several trips to Russia and became a warm advocate of the Internationale. She died in 1934.

cloth-of-gold tissue, and Mechlin lace. Mrs. Bradley Martin, who had appeared at the Vanderbilt Ball of 1883 as Mary Queen of Scots in a white bodice and head-dress of ruby-colored velvet, decided to surpass even herself, and again appeared as Mary Queen of Scots, in a bodice of black velvet lined with cerise satin, an overdress opened over a white satin petticoat, a richly jewelled stomacher, and a pointed cap of silver, together with a massive ruby necklace worn by Marie Antoinette and a cluster of diamond grapes which had belonged to Louis XIV. Her husband decided to go as Louis XV, perhaps unaware that Mr. Belmont was preparing to be the observed of all observers in a full suit of steel armor inlaid with gold which cost him $10,000. ("Were all the costumes ticketed with the price?" innocently asked *The London Chronicle*.) Miss Anne Morgan, a graceful débutante, appeared as Pocahontas in a beaded dress "made by Indians," though aboriginal honors really belonged to Mr. R. W. G. Welling personating an Indian chief, "whose costume was made under the eye of Prof. Putnam of Harvard." For fully two weeks before the Ball neither those invited nor the newspapers could talk of anything else. Hairdressers charged $15 an hour. Family jewels were borrowed from decayed aristocrats in the South: the Oglethorpe gems arrived from Georgia, and the Fairfax diamonds from Virginia. On the morning of the great day readers of *The Times* were told about carloads of orchids, roses, galax leaves, "and an almost incredible amount of asparagus vine," which arrived to transform the ballroom of the Waldorf into what was fondly supposed to be "a replica of a hall in Versailles." The presence of Pinkerton detectives somewhat marred the illusion, for it was rumored that anarchists had been caught planting bombs under the Bradley Martin mansion at 20th Street, and that others planned to throw infernal machines through the windows of the Waldorf. At any rate these windows were boarded up, ostensibly to foil spectators. Other horrid rumors were afloat, disclosed *The Times*. "A most alarming story was printed yesterday morning concerning the disastrous use of Lima oil by the Waldorf servants in polishing up the furniture . . . a very crude and cheap petroleum." Happily this was false, too.

Town Topics urged prospective guests to polish up on their historical characters, and avoid solecisms in conversation. Editors of London and Paris papers ordered thousands of words to be sent by cable. Hearst's *New York Journal* prepared to devote most of its first five pages to descriptions of the Ball, pen sketches of costumes, and still other illustrations captioned "Some of the Four Thousand Who Were Not in the Cotillion." Under the scare-headline "James Van Alen Cannot Go" *The Times* related how that gentleman had decided after some debate that the death of a relative would prevent his dancing in the *quadrille d'honneur* which had been rehearsing for days at Mrs. Astor's under the scrutiny of Professor Karl Marwig; his place was taken by Fernando Yznaga. In this quadrille were Mrs. Bradley Martin, Mrs. Stuyvesant Fish, Mrs. Orme Wilson, Mrs. Whitney Warren, Miss Madeline Cutting, Miss Angelica Gerry, and Mrs. T. Suffern Tailer, along with Messrs. John Jacob Astor, Robert Van Cortlandt, Lispenard Stewart, Craig Wadsworth, Harry Lehr, Center Hitchcock, and F. Townsend Martin, brother of the host, who in his memoirs *Things I Remember* recorded his impressions of the Ball for posterity: "The power of wealth with its refinement and vulgarity was everywhere." After the quadrille came a cotillion in which "for the first time since Colonial days the gentlemen danced with swords at their sides, feeling that the swords were a part of the costume," but paid the price of archaism by tripping frequently, "to the delight of the spectators."

The Herald and *The Times* gave over their front pages to such a prodigy, which seemed exactly like "a stately court function in one of the capitals of Europe," even to the liveried lackey who stood at the foot of Mrs. Bradley Martin's dais and announced every guest by name, character represented, and historical period, "in a loud tone." Newspapers also culled human interest stories like this: "A little man with a gray beard stood for a moment beside the awning watching the passage of the guests. He was told to move on. 'Bradley Martin and I were schoolboys together,' said he, but was again ordered to move on." Allowing for the difference in transatlantic time *The London Daily Mail* for February 11 informed its readers at breakfast: "Mrs. Bradley Martin, we have every reason to believe, is dressed at this very moment in a train of black velvet lined with cerise satin, and a petticoat, if it is not indiscreet to say so, of white satin, embroidered with flowers and arabesques of silver." Its contemporary *The London Chronicle* wrote: "We congratulate New York Society on its triumph. It has cut out Belshazzar's feast and Wardour Street and Mme. Tussaud's and the Bank of England. There is no doubt about that." Oscar Hammerstein produced a burlesque called "The Bradley-Radley Ball" at the Olympia, but others took criticism more seriously. Newspaper editors, clergymen, and college debating societies discussed the heartless extravagance of wealth, and even more effectively the New York authorities more than doubled the city tax assessments of the Bradley Martins. Under a storm of notoriety the Bradley Martins removed permanently to England, pausing long enough to give a farewell dinner for eighty-six persons costing $116.28 a plate—while *The New York World,* surveying the guest-list, computed that a dozen men were present at that dinner worth upwards of ten million, twice as many with five million, and among the grand total of forty men a bare half-dozen who were not at least millionaires, while among their consorts "there were enough diamond crowns to fit out all the crowned heads of Europe and have some over for Asia and Africa." Thenceforth American newspapers practised what they had learned from the Bradley Martins—that nothing so agitates mass circulation as stories of prodigality in high life. James Hazen Hyde's $200,-000 ball at Sherry's in 1905, which likewise drove its host into exile, and Harry Lehr's "dog dinner" at which his friends' dogs were invited reputedly to eat pâté and chicken, afforded magnificent copy to accompany the exposure of American finance beneath the muck-rake of Lincoln Steffens, Ida M. Tarbell, Ray Stannard Baker, and Samuel Hopkins Adams.

The era of exposure brought also the shearing of the black sheep in the fold of society journalism, *Town Topics,* and the downfall of its patriarchal shepherd of the flowing white moustaches, red bow-tie, and clerical frock-coat—a benevolent old gentleman who always carried lump-sugar in his pockets for truck horses, and adored cats. William D'Alton Mann was born in Sandusky, Ohio, in 1839. During the Civil War he organized the Seventh Michigan Cavalry, and gained the rank of Colonel to which he was predestined by nature. After the War he went to Mobile, erected a mill and refinery for cotton-seed oil, took a flyer in journalism, and to be sure that no one would confuse him with the generality of carpet-baggers joined the Ku Klux Klan. In 1872 he invented the Mann Boudoir Car, though a decade later his rights were bought up by George M. Pullman. Mann's only glory had been to build a sleeping-car for Leopold II of Belgium, a feat for which he vainly solicited a decoration for many years, from His Majesty by letter and from the Belgian Minister in Washington. He also invented a cannon, wrote a military treatise, and did a number of other interesting things which brought him indifferent returns. Then in 1891 the Colonel took over from his brother E. D. Mann a self-styled society journal named *Town Topics*. His brother had been convicted in 1887 of sending obscene matter through the mails, and was growing a little weary.

Begun in 1879 as Andrews' *American Queen, a magazine of art, music,*

The Dual Life

From *The New York Evening Journal*, January 23, 1906
Republished in "Collier's Weekly," February 10, 1906

literature, and society, this weekly aspired to be a pleasant dilettante; Louis Keller, future founder of the *Social Register,* James B. Townsend, and T. J. Oakley Rhinelander were among its exceedingly respectable early sponsors. Its first editor, Andrews, mysteriously decamped and left affairs in bad shape; reorganized in 1882 with Keller in control it lasted to 1885 simply as *The American Queen.* In that year it was bought by E. D. Mann, rechristened *Town Topics,* and launched on its career of metropolitan scandal-mongering. It hinted forthcoming divorce suits, broke news of bankruptcies in Wall Street, gossiped about dowries, advised certain débutantes to use less mascara, and printed bulletins from Chicago under the label of "Skunkville." Under January 13, 1887, we read that "Nobody in the Union Club was astonished to learn that Bob Townsend had married his cook. Unless he has reformed of late years, it is generally held among those honored with his acquaintanceship, that the sympathy of the public belongs to the cook." More risky gossip is couched in allusion, such as the story of "a Philadelphia clubman" married to a wife whose "social freedom with certain society youths in and about the Bryn Mawr Hotel a couple of summers ago would lead to the belief that her husband is mistaken when he says she is as cold as she is fair." But all this was merely the prelude to Colonel Mann's regime. Not that he printed items more offensive or daring than his brother had done; his forte was not libel but blackmail. The hidden threat, the card

Colonel Mann
From *The New York Press,* December 29, 1905
Republished in "Collier's Weekly," January 13, 1906

Knowledge is power. The more you know about people that are worth knowing about, the more you'll know that's worth knowing. Some people are worth knowing all about, and all people are worth knowing something about. A word to the wise is worth two in the bush

up the sleeve, the notorious locked safe in which he boasted that he kept the reputations of the Four Hundred, but when opened at last was found to contain several bottles of brandy—these were the tools of his trade.

Colonel Mann's Newport correspondent entered the homes of the rich as a musician, and he had another employee whose duty was to mingle with the butlers and chambermaids of Fifth Avenue. Harry Lehr, an inveterate gossip with mischievous inclinations, afforded occasional tips. But in general Mann found that the best spies were the hangers-on, who never quite entered the magic circle, and cherished a hundred petty grievances against those who had snubbed them. A small part of the information he gained appeared in *Town Topics;* he avoided libel laws by the simple ruse of printing an unpleasant paragraph about the doings of anonymous gentlemen and ladies, and then following it with a harmless "key" paragraph in which the missing names occurred. But to publish such items always grieved him; he much preferred to have the cash for their suppression. Nor was his motive purely selfish, for everybody in the office got his share of the blackmail, as Mann's assistant Ahle explained to Mr. Edwin Main Post—husband of the future authority on etiquette, who was "touched" for $500 but had an officer from the district attorney's office concealed during the interview. To his busy workers Colonel Mann would despatch billets like the following:

Dear Wooster:
  I believe you can get J. Edward Addicks if you go right after him. Did you try Arbuckle, the sugar man? You must go over and pin Governor Murphy. If you were to go over to the West End, Long Branch, and stop there a day or two so as to have time and catch John A. McCall, you can interest him, as his vanity will lead him to have that half-a-million dollar house handed down to posterity, and he would certainly go into the book when he finds that such men as Woodward, Whitney, Morton, Astor, Vanderbilt, Aldrich, Dryden, &c. appear.

The subscriptions here suggested were to the famous volume *Fads and Fancies of Representative Americans;* in view of its extreme costliness its solicitors boasted that it "required an entire hide for the binding of each volume." For several years Mann collected subscriptions whose cost was set at $1500 per copy, but frequently ran to a larger figure. The timorous paid to avoid exposure, and the vain paid to secure a flattering biography. From Justice Joseph M. Deuel of the Court of Special Sessions of New York City, shareholder in *Town Topics* and its legal adviser, went a demure reminder to Wooster: "You are seeding the garden, and I trust, with gentle cultivation, of which you are capable, we will yet fill our basket quite full of either flowers or fruit." After this letter was made public *The New York Evening Telegram* commented: "Sounds better than proposing to go out and violently shake a plum tree."
  Town Topics played up its favorites. There was James Hazen Hyde, whose Equitable Life Assurance Society had made a loan of $165,000 on the real estate owned by Mann and the Ess Ess Publishing Company (the initials stood for "smart set"). And there was Perry Belmont from whom Mann had "borrowed" $4000 on one occasion—behavior which appeared even more magnanimous because his brother O. H. P. Belmont had re-

fused to give a paltry $2000. On June 30, 1905 Mann wrote to his editor in charge:

Dear Wayne:—Use enclosed notes. I have especial reason to be nice to McCormick and Mrs. McC., and I also wish to show that Perry and Mrs. Belmont go to the best affairs here. All well. Kindest regards. W. D. M.

Was there ever a more thoughtful old gentleman? A few weeks before he had pencilled a memorandum which read, with lofty clemency, "Let up on Henry T. Sloane. W. D. M." He also admonished: "*T. T.* will be careful of anything said about Mrs. Inman of Atlanta. Nothing unpleasant." Thus considerately did he pave the social path for the future mother of Doris Duke Cromwell. Charles S. Wayne, the managing editor to whom these notes were addressed, testified that the following names were immune, and the Colonel once suggested posting the list on the office wall so that none should be "roasted" inadvertently: General Russell A. Alger, James Hazen Hyde, Perry Belmont, James R. Keene, W. K. Vanderbilt, George J. Gould, J. Pierpont Morgan, A. J. Cassatt, Melville E. Stone, August Belmont, Senator W. A. Clark, George H. Daniels, Stuyvesant Fish, Henry M. Flagler, Abraham H. Hummel, E. Clarence Jones, Harry Lehr, John E. Madden, Creighton Webb, Charles T. Yerkes, Thomas W. Lawson, Reginald Ward. Lawson for example was a parvenu from Boston who advertised heavily in the columns of *Town Topics* in order to obtain a good press, while Reginald Ward, about whom Mann had received disclosures from his Boston correspondent, paid 5000 shares of Rico Syndicate to have some pleasant paragraphs about him published in 1904.[9] Occasionally a name would be taken off the sacred list, and then restored when an "understanding" was reached. Robert A. Irving, who canvassed for the Colonel, was asked on the witness stand what had been his method of approach. He answered: "Well, I told them that Colonel Mann was a great fellow to get in with distinguished people." Nor could any one complain of less than value received,

[9]The almost tremulous thankfulness with which one hailed deliverance from the scourge of *Town Topics* is mirrored in Ward's letter:

"My dear Mr. Wooster—Thanks for your of the 5th inst., the contents of which I have carefully noted, and am looking forward with much interest to the paragraphs to which you refer. I wish you would please put my name down on the regular list of *Town Topics,* so that I will get it regularly, if not too much trouble.

REGINALD WARD."

The Saga of American Society

for sure enough in 1905 every one of the eight-six subscribers to *Fads and Fancies,* in addition to President Theodore Roosevelt, the Library of Congress, the New York Public Library, and the British Museum, received a handsome volume in red and gold with gilt edges, an "Introductory" by the patrician Mrs. Burton Harrison, and a series of adulatory biographies, handsome marginal pictures of the subjects, their houses, horses, dogs, and yachts—and from cover to cover not an unkind word. By far the longest biography is the eight-page account of Collis P. Huntington and his locomotives, plus a full-page portrait; although he had died in 1900, his widow subscribed $10,000 because she believed that her husband as the builder of the Golden West was entitled to more space than any one else. Few of its purchasers seem to have cherished their highly bought copies of *Fads and Fancies,* and today it is one of the rarest items in American bibliography.[10]

But the showing-up of Colonel Mann was soon to come. His references to P. F. Collier as a Bible peddler who had ridden into society behind a

[10]Its rarity may excuse an enumeration of its biographical subjects in order: Colonel John Jacob Astor; Peter Marié; Clement A. Griscom, shipping magnate; Daniel O'Day, Standard Oil; S. Osgood Pell, real estate; Washington E. Connor, broker; James M. Waterbury, sportsman and manufacturer; Charles T. Yerkes, financier; Howard Willets, country gentleman and sportsman; Harrison I. Drummond, tobacco; Clarence A. Postley, U. S. A., retired; Robert A. C. Smith, shipping, engineering; William K. Vanderbilt; Stanford White, architect; Henry M. Flagler, Standard Oil; Dean E. A. Hoffman, Episcopal clergy, to add a touch of consecrated wealth; James Henry ("Silent") Smith, inherited millions in coal, iron, railroads, and enjoyed a heyday as New York's most eligible bachelor; Perry Belmont the diplomat; Henry B. Plant, Florida development; Senator John F. Dryden, insurance; Charles M. Schwab, U. S. Steel; Chauncey M. Depew, legal counsel to the Vanderbilts, statesman; Collis P. Huntington; James T. Woodward, banker; Edward H. R. Green, son and heir of Hetty Green; Henry Siegel, department store owner (in place of giving the usual memberships in Union, Knickerbocker, Racquet, etc., the editor remarks: "The love of home is strong in Henry Siegel and he cares little for club life"); T. L. Woodruff, typewriters; Pembroke Jones, rice; Thomas Shaw Safe, English explorer, who penetrated Newport, R. I.; William Astor Chanler, amateur politician of Tammany Hall; Henry E. Huntington, nephew of late Collis P., railroads and street-cars, also completely self-made, future founder of the great Library at San Marino, California; James J. Hill, "colossus of railroads," who rose from the desk of a shipping-clerk to become a connoisseur of painting with "a particular affection for the Barbizon school," says *Fad and Fancies;* Lewis Nixon, shipbuilder; Oliver Gould Jennings, oil and sporting life; F. le Baron Robbins, coal; David R. Francis, banker and organizer of St. Louis World's Fair; Levi P. Morton, drygoods merchant, statesman; Julius Fleischmann, president of Fleischmann Co., Cincinnati; Grant B. Schley, broker; Daniel G. Reid, railroads, tin plate; A. D. Juilliard, self-made magnate of

pack of hounds had done little to gain the good will of the son Robert Collier, *bon vivant,* and owner of *Collier's Weekly.* Several members of his staff were interested in the social game, including his business manager, Condé Nast; and the editor-in-chief was a crusading young man named Norman Hapgood with wild hair and eyes. Bored by "a publishing business which should resemble the manufacture of corsets," as he now recalls, Mr. Hapgood's chivalry leaped up when Mr. Collier pointed to a pert paragraph in *Town Topics* in the summer of 1905. It mentioned Miss Alice Roosevelt's visit to New York as a guest of Mrs. Ogden Mills and the probable conformity of Princess Alice to the heavy drinking habits of that family. The first Young Lady of the Land had been insulted, and with gratuitous bad taste. In his issue for August 5th Mr. Hapgood penned a stinging rebuke to Judge Deuel: "He is part owner and one of the editors of a paper of which the occupation is printing scandal about people who are not cowardly enough to pay for silence." At such insults couched in Harvard English the plug-uglies of *Town Topics* gasped. Justice Deuel brought suit against *Collier's* for libel, and on Jan-

textiles and imports, future patron of music; George S. Scott, expatriate in Paris; Morton F. Plant, railroads and shipping; Harry S. Black, construction company; William C. Whitney; Anthony N. Brady, utilities, street-cars; Grover Cleveland; Theodore Roosevelt; Samuel Newhouse, mining engineering; John A. Drake, lawyer; Oliver Harriman, Jr., banker, inherited wealth from his father, a drygoods commission merchant; Thomas F. Walsh, Irish miner who "struck it rich" in Colorado; E. J. Berwind, coal; Alfred Gwynne Vanderbilt; Stephen B. Elkins, West Virginia coal, law, politics; John H. Patterson, Dayton cash registers; Levi Z. Leiter; Isaac F. Emerson, Bromo-Seltzer, which he invented when a drugstore clerk, to allay patrons' hang-overs, though the editor omits this detail; James A. Burden, iron; Benjamin N. Duke, tobacco; James Hobart Moore, corporation lawyer; Reginald C. Vanderbilt, great-grandson of the old Commodore, who "radiated pure sunshine in his life and character," as the editor remarks: Nelson W. Aldrich of Rhode Island, railroads and political service; Ohio C. Barber, match manufacturer; William Cornell Greene, ranching, Mexican copper; Charles W. Morse, ice, shipping; J. Pierpont Morgan; William B. Leeds, tin plate; Thomas Fortune Ryan, broker; Edward R. Bacon, lawyer; Alfred C. Harrison, Philadelphia sugar refiner; Paul G. Thebaud, president commercial house of that name; Charles H. Cramp, shipbuilding; Thomas W. Lawson, copper, banking; Clarence H. Mackay, cable and telegraph; Peter Lorillard, tobacco; F. T. F. Lovejoy, steel; A. L. Barber, asphalt, real estate investments; Alexander Van Rensselaer, sport and philanthropy; James R. Keene, broker and speculator; his son Foxhall Keene, sportsman; Bishop Henry C. Potter, spiritual pastor of the Four Hundred, who married more American heiresses to noblemen than any other cleric of his time; Henry C. Pierce, oil; Patrick Calhoun, law, railroads; José F. N. de Viaña, Spanish magnate in New York shipping and cement; Henry B. Hyde, life insurance.

uary 16, 1906, the case opened. *Collier's* hired away several employees from *Town Topics,* gave them jobs, and thus obtained matchless evidence, including many memoranda from Judge Deuel suggesting that his colleagues "bag" certain well-known persons, and "try to run down Marshall Field." To his agent in Florida His Honor wrote comparing their prospective customers to "Davy Crockett's coon—all you need to do is to point your gun and every high-tone, desirable citizen of Palm Beach may tumble in your basket." At first with reluctance, and finally with a touch of pride, the Colonel on the witness stand admitted that he had "borrowed" a total of $184,500 distributed as follows:

James R. Keene, $90,000
William K. Vanderbilt, $25,000
John W. Gates, $20,000
Doctor W. Seward Webb, $14,000
William C. Whitney, $10,000
Thomas F. Ryan (through Morton Trust Co.), $10,000
Collis P. Huntington, $5000
Roswell P. Flower, $3000
J. Pierpont Morgan, $2500
Howard Gould, $2500
Grant B. Schley, $1500
George S. Scott, $1000

James A. Burden, Jr., recently accosted for blackmail, gave convincing testimony, as did Edwin M. Post, Oliver Belmont, and Harry Lehr. With secret relief District Attorney William Travers Jerome saw the libel case against *Collier's* turn into a searing indictment of *Town Topics.* The jury returned a prompt acquittal. At an earlier stage of the game Amos Pinchot had proposed to several friends that the most effective treatment of the Colonel would consist in shaving off half his epic moustache and parading him down Fifth Avenue in an open carriage; on account of the Colonel's bad heart, and habit of carrying a pistol, the scheme was abandoned. Now it was proved unnecessary; he was discredited forever. Advertisers shrank away, many a distinguished New Yorker began to wonder why nobody had called the old rascal's bluff years ago, and even before the verdict *The New York Mail* gaily parodied a popular song:

> Everybody works but the Colonel,
>   He sits around all day,
> Reading spicy gossip
>   And *vers de societé.*
> Daniels and Justice Deuel
>   Get the best they can.
> Everybody works the public
>   But Colonel Mann.

In vain did the Colonel seek to rouse his spirits by pointing out that the name "Norman" had never occurred in the Hapgood family before, but that a great friend of the mother of *Collier's* editor was so named. In vain did he try to retaliate on Roosevelt for denying that the President had authorized his biography in *Fads and Fancies,* by criticizing "the absurd card" of invitation sent out for the wedding of Miss Alice Roosevelt to Mr. Longworth.[11] Colonel Mann knew that his day was over, but till his death in 1920 tramped the streets of New York in increasingly shabby frock-coats—a bogey-man which mothers sometimes used to frighten their self-willed débutante daughters. From Lucifer he had fallen to Mrs. Grundy. For awhile *Town Topics* was edited by his daughter, Mrs. E. Mann-Vynne, but expired beneath the depression in 1931. To old New Yorkers it may come as a surprise to learn that *Town Topics,* with its mid-Victorian mast-head in the hearts and flowers style, with the same old format, and a vague yearning after indiscretion, was revived in 1936 by one J. C. Schemm who had experimented with a tattle sheet in Washington called *The Mirror.* During the past Presidential campaign its strictures against the New Deal crowded out habitual coy allusions to "pre-nuptial romances" or to the graying hair and varicose veins of cer-

---

[11]It read "The President and Mrs. Roosevelt request," etc., whereas *Town Topics* maintained, with metaphysic wit, that "the President, unlike the Emperor or the King, is a temporary title, and, being incorporeal, can have no children." Hence the invitation should have read "Mr. and Mrs. Theodore Roosevelt request," etc. Yet in June 1910, Colonel Mann showed great eagerness to attend the marriage of Theodore Roosevelt, Jr., to Eleanor Butler Alexander. He wrote to the bride's mother, Mrs. Charles B. Alexander—by repute the most formidable and aloof of hostesses—requesting an invitation, and even more surprisingly she complied at once. Perhaps a certain sunset aureole still lingered about his hoary head.

tain dowagers on the sands of Palm Beach. It is safe to predict for the new *Town Topics* a quiet and innocuous future. Thanks to the syndication of columnists and the new floodlights of publicity in this modern age, society no longer begins to shiver upon over-exposure.

The best proof of this changing attitude is the flood of signed endorsements of cosmetics, cigarettes, pianos, whiskey, and other commodities which would have been unthinkable to an earlier generation. The nearest possible approach to that sort of thing a century ago is this advertisement of Indian Vegetable Elixir in Bennett's *Herald,* November 30, 1842:

☞   MYSTERIOUS.—A gentleman belonging to one of the most ancient and wealthy families of this city, who must be well known to numerous friends, having since the year 1818 been bent nearly double, and for several years confined to his bed, has been restored to good health. . . . We will give inquirers his address, and doubt not his humane feelings will excuse this liberty.

Occasionally, as time went on, the vendors of other nostrums ventured to claim a somewhat dubious social leadership for their users—such as an advertisement of Lydia E. Pinkham which appeared in 1902, captioned: "Miss Mary Lenghan, a Young Society Lady who lives in Brooklyn, N. Y., tells how Young Women May Escape those Terrible Monthly Pains . . . ($5000 Forfeit if the above Letter is not Genuine)." But why should Miss Lenghan, whoever she was, have hesitated to follow the steps of Henry Ward Beecher, Henry M. Stanley, and several ex-Presidents of the United States who had endorsed patent medicines? In the nineties Ivory Soap had rounded up more than half the members of the United States Senate into a single magnificent testimonial, while Sarah Bernhardt apparently never demurred to lend the stamp of her divinity to any trade-name. In fact it was as a potential actress that the first society woman sold her approval of a cosmetic for cash. This was Mrs. James Brown Potter, born Cora Urquhart of New Orleans, who married the nephew of Bishop Henry Codman Potter, and learned to recite at private parties such favorites as "Curfew Shall Not Ring Tonight," "The Charge of the Light Brigade," and "Paul Revere's Ride." Hell bent for elocution she added to her repertory a sentimental poem called "Ostler Joe" in which there was an allusion to an unmarried mother; its recital in Washington at a party given by a cabinet member's wife deeply shocked the

Whither?

A Well Wisher: "Excuse me, Madam, but your 'social influence' is taking you in a wrong direction"

C. D. Gibson in *Life* in the "Eighties"

maiden sister of President Cleveland. From amateur theatricals at Tuxedo, Mrs. Potter went on the professional stage. Oliver Herford commented that "actresses will happen in the best-regulated families," and Charles Dana Gibson drew her travelling down a steep path from the Temple of Fame, carrying an actress' wardrobe, amid the applause of a flock of geese dressed in white ties—with the comment of a well-wisher: "Excuse me, Madam, but your 'social influence' is taking you in the wrong direction." Amid this storm of notoriety she signed her name to an endorsement of Harriet Hubbard Ayer's cold cream written on the stationery of Tuxedo Park, left her husband, and went on the London stage. Her little daughter without a mother's care grew up to be the Fifi Stillman of the tabloids.

For more than a generation Mrs. Potter remained a scarlet example of the social leader who had sold her name to commerce. But always in the background remained that immemorial British precedent of "purveyors by Appointment to His Majesty the King," with the blazon of lion and unicorn. As early as 1840 "The Association of Her Majesty's Tradesmen" was formed, and met annually on Queen Victoria's birthday. It has now become "The Royal Warrant Holders Association." Members guard jealously the privilege—lawfully obtained after two years of supplying Buckingham Palace, Windsor, St. James's Palace, Sandringham, or similar households—of displaying the royal arms on their products. From 1900 to 1920, for example, some 4096 illegal users were summarily dealt with. Contrary to widespread supposition among American advertising men, no payment is made to the Crown. But in becoming gratitude for this privilege tradesmen have often subscribed en masse to royal memorial funds and charities, and on the occasion of the late Jubilee they presented George V with a £50,000 model house in Surrey, now occupied after Royal invitation by Admiral Tupper. To give American readers some idea of the multiplicity of trades and products which bear the royal arms of Britain, one might name among the oldest or most famous listed in the Blue Book: Bass's Beer; Brock & Co., fireworks; Bryant & May, matches; Cadbury's chocolate; Thomas Crapper & Co., sanitary specialists; Fortnum & Mason, grocers; Gosling & Co., poultry; Guy, Court haircutter; Doctor Jaeger's sanitary woollens; Runting, chiropodist; Sandow, physical training; John Ward, perambulators.

But not until the year 1923 did the advertisement based purely upon social eligiblity begin to take shape in the United States. In that year two leading New York advertising agents, J. Walter Thompson Company and William Esty, came to suspect that certain social leaders might not be unwilling to appear in advertisements.

William Esty first put his theory to the test in respect to pianos, instruments which the generality of buyers regard as "prestige furniture." He found that a number of women in society, beginning with Mrs. Oliver Harriman of New York and the Duchesse de Richelieu from Baltimore were glad to exchange old Steinways for new Hardman pianos. Photographs of these instruments in their drawing-rooms, preferably with the owner standing by, were used discreetly in advertisements. Two months later J. Walter Thompson—soon to become the sponsor *par excellence* of society appeal—inaugurated a new day for Pond's cold cream and lotions. Hitherto regarded as a poor relation of Elizabeth Arden, Pond's gained immeasurably in standing among the masses by a roster of users which was led by Mrs. Oliver Harriman, Mrs. Nicholas Longworth, and the senior Mrs. August Belmont. It was soon discovered that Goulds and lesser Vanderbilts entered sympathetically into the scheme, though Astors were wary. The Simmons metal bed, found heretofore in servants' quarters, began in 1927 to appear in milady's bedroom—for contrary to the assumption of sceptics, endorsers in general faithfully do use the products they recommend. Upon this point reputable advertising agencies insist, both for the sake of legality and for the probability of a check-up by competitors. In fact, most users in society discover a sincere though perhaps passing enthusiasm for the commodity they sponsor.[12] Perhaps the most

[12]Outside the pale of Society and especially in the early days of purchasing names, such scrupulousness was sometimes violated. The late Tex Rickard, who, as his associates knew, never smoked a cigarette in his life, endorsed a well-known brand, not Camels. An All-American fullback at a Texas college well known to the author signed a testimonial for the same brand of cigarettes in exchange for $500 shortly before his graduation, when his amateur standing was no longer important. Hearing of this fact, the president of the college called the youth into his office and with stern Puritanism observed, "You should be ashamed of yourself, my boy. You would have been a *better* athlete for dear old Siwash if you had never tasted nicotine." "But I don't, sir," replied the hapless athlete, "I just needed the money." "Even worse," snapped the president, "a piece of deliberate dishonesty." Vastly disturbed, the young man sought out the advertising agent who had ensnared him and told his tale of woe. "Oh, keep your money, son," he was comforted, "we'll fix that okay." Soon thereafter the billboards of the Southwest bloomed with posters showing a dauntless fullback breaking through the line, and beneath him the legend: "J— H—, All-American athlete, says: 'I do not smoke, but if I *did* TOASTIES would be my choice.'"

elaborate series, the Almanach de Gotha of American advertising, was that undertaken by Esty for the manufacturers of Camels. A partial list of endorsers follows: Mrs. John Gardner Coolidge II, Mrs. Hamilton Fish, Jr., Mrs. James Russell Lowell, Mrs. Adrian Iselin II, Mrs. Powell M. Cabot, Mrs. Potter d'Orsay Palmer, Mrs. Thomas M. Carnegie, Jr., Miss Anne Douglass Gould, Miss Mary Byrd. The geographical spread of these famous names is of course well planned. Other familiar endorsers include Miss Mary Taylor, daughter of Bertrand Taylor and niece of the Countess di Frasso, who has endorsed both cigarettes and cosmetics and has modelled clothes and also acted in the movies, Mrs. Anthony Drexel Biddle, Mrs. J. Borden Harriman, Mrs. T. Markoe Robertson, Mrs. Langdon Post, Mrs. William Wetmore, and Mrs. Rodman Wanamaker.

Why do women in society sign testimonials? The usual and in many cases truthful explanation is that their earnings are given to pet charities. From the top price of $10,000 with which the greater names were first lured, or the current maximum wage of $1000, down to $500 or even $250, many donations to milk funds, free clinics, hotels for working girls, homes for the blind, and other projects have been made, as well as to purely personal endeavors such as sending a worthy art student abroad. However, it is not too cynical to add that a good deal of this charity begins and ends at home. Some endorsers are the poor relations of great families in finance and society; Keokuk and El Paso cannot be expected to know the difference, and furthermore it is the headlined surname rather than the seal of aristocracy which interests the advertiser and his public. Others are juniors who desire to supplement their pin-money. Moreover, in the eyes of the most affluent, money earned bulks much larger than the monthly and semi-annual dividends which are accepted as inevitably as day and night. In 1892 Mrs. Jack Gardner earned ten shillings from *The London Times* by telegraphing an account of the première of the opera *Atenaïde* to its Rome correspondent; she had her gold half-sovereign made into a breloque and always cherished it as "the only money she ever earned." The æsthetic satisfaction of making money is therefore important. Furthermore, the agent's solicitation is often done through some impecunious friend, who receives a commission known or unknown to the endorser; the impulse to oblige may thus enter into one's motives. Finally, most of the endorsers really enjoy the publicity, which is a kind that appeals more strongly to women than to men. It is a

The Society Page

method of broadcasting one's social eminence, of being hailed as "a leader of smart society" or "distinguished sportswoman and hostess," and among married women of comparatively humble origin the proclamation of one's ability to bask in the shade of a great tree. The innate reticence of men has prevented their widespread success at this sport. But among ambitious women the endorsement of cigarettes and cold cream has come to be so attractive—in a world where conspicuousness passes for distinction—that some who have never been approached are known to complain among friends of the endless annoyance to which they are put by solicitors. It is well to remember that virtually every photograph and endorsement which an advertiser uses has been paid for; the ones which he might have *gratis,* though numerous, are worth little or nothing to him commercially. Probably mythical is the case of a certain "Mrs. Torchell" described by Arthur Train in his novel of social ambition called *Jacob's Ladder.* Sensing that she was slipping from the topmost rungs, and in need of the reassurance of being proclaimed in four colors as America's regnant queen of New York and Newport, she offered to pay for the privilege of endorsing something. "Mrs. Torchell" is a creature of fiction, but the wise will draw their own analogies.

CHAPTER TEN

IN QUEST OF CORONETS

SOME forty years ago the great steel magnate Henry Phipps, the son of a shoemaker, was one out of many American plutocrats who under the persuasion of their families lived largely abroad. Mr. Phipps in fact became a symbol, through the creation of Charles Dana Gibson's "Mr. Pip," a kindly, harassed, diminutive soul haled about Europe by his socially ambitious women. After exhausting the feudal possibilities of Knebworth the Phippses rented the Scottish estate of the Master of Lovat, descended from that famous Simon Fraser, Lord Lovat, who in 1745 was beheaded on Tower Hill for his loyalty to the Stuarts. Not only did the Phippses retain the piper to pipe them up for breakfast, but also kept on as their honored guest the master himself, to shoot his own deer and kill his own salmon at their expense. One day with a party of their house guests they were surveying the picture gallery of the Lovats and paused in front of a dark old portrait which through all its grime showed the Stuart face with its stamp of insolent grace. A New Englander there present, who has kindly informed the author of this circumstance, remarked in all innocence, "Why, there's the Old Pretender." A young lady who hitherto had remained silent glanced at him with a haughty flutter of the eyelid. "Here in the Highlands," she said with a gravity which would have done credit to Flora Macdonald, "we *never* speak of the Pretender. You mean, of course, the Chevalier de St. George." Quietly he took his reproof, but later inquired of a fellow guest who the fierce Jacobite might be. "Oh," he answered, "she is the daughter of William R. Grace, the Irish mayor of New York."

A certain tender devotion to the Stuarts—the last romantic swagger kings before Britain fell into the hands of Hanoverians and Wettins—was once popular in select social circles of America and England. Beatrice, sister of the Right Hon. Sir Austen Chamberlain and daughter of the celebrated statesman whose marriage into the American Endicotts was long regarded by that family as a shocking intrusion, has left on record a curious fact. It is that Queen Victoria never countenanced finger bowls on the royal table because she had heard of the old Jacobite custom of passing one's wine-glass over a dish of water before drinking to reigning Majesty—which meant a toast to "the King over the water," *i.e.*, the Pretender in exile. The Order of the White Rose, revived in England in 1886 to honor the Stuarts, spread shortly to the United States.[1] Every thirtieth of January, on the anniversary of the execution of Charles I, his statue in Charing Cross used mysteriously to blossom with a huge wreath of white roses bearing the legend "America Mourns Her Martyred King." In Boston the rector of the Church of the Advent—whose steps had been scrubbed in Lent by Mrs. Jack Gardner, who being a Stewart fancied herself as a Pretender too—used to send out black-bordered invitations to Holy Communion on that day. Although Philadelphia had a portrait of the Royal Martyr which had been dedicated by the Episcopal Bishop of Iowa, and New York boasted a coterie which drank a toast, standing, at midnight, to restoration of the Stuarts, Boston was the center of the White Rose. Its Prior was Ralph Adams Cram.

Perhaps a gentler Nemesis, which laid the witch-burning judges upon Hawthorne's conscience, sprinkled the blood of Charles I upon the restless heads of the Regicides' great-grandchildren. This was also the Boston of James Russell Lowell's grandmother, who upon every Fourth of July "would dress in deep black, fast all day and loudly lament our late unhappy difference with His Most Gracious Majesty." And the Boston of Henry Adams, who shrank from the Erie Scandal, the Gold Conspiracy, and the democratic ballot back to the court of Saint Louis the King.[2] In many ways the most British of Colonial cities, Boston suffered a temporary eclipse in 1776 and 1812, and again during the Civil War when England was expected to join the Confederacy, but always it has returned to its deep-rooted Anglophilia, which today is its great bulwark against Irish, German, and Jewish invasion. As Van Wyck Brooks has lately written: "The more the center of gravity of the nation

[1]Upon outbreak of the Great War, loyalty to the English-speaking tradition in preference to the current "Pretender," Prince Rupprecht of Bavaria, caused a virtual abandonment of the Jacobite cause. Even before that time it had begun to base itself upon the spiritual principles of noblesse rather than overthrow of the House of Windsor, but the *frisson* of treason had certainly been its initial charm. Today "the King over the water" is a better Edwardian than a Jacobite toast.

[2]"The true Bostonian," Adams wrote, "always knelt in self-abasement before the majesty of English standards."

shifted towards the West, the more the Boston mind, thrown back upon itself, resumed its old colonial allegiance." It kept the broad *a* in pronunciation, and the superfluous *u* in spelling, wrote its street addresses with a comma after the numeral, loved to trace its family trees to armigerous English stock, and felt that the world could not go wholly to the dogs so long as Anglo-Saxon gentlemen stuck together. Of course it had its provincialisms too; Mr. T. S. Eliot has described the society of Boston as "quite uncivilized—but refined beyond the point of civilization," and the wit Tom Appleton once retorted to a fellow-Bostonian who was wishing vapidly that he were a subject of the British Crown, "Why do you want to be a subject when you are already such an object?"[3] And there have been a few outright dissenters, like the great lady who refused to give a party for visiting Royalty on Thursday because Thursday was the cook's day out, or the Minister to England Charles Francis Adams, whose son Henry has recorded: "He was one of the exceedingly small number of Americans to whom an English Duke or Duchess seemed to be indifferent, and Royalty itself nothing more than a slightly inconvenient person."

Outside of colonies, no country in the world has depended so greatly upon another for its social customs as America upon England. It was a vital bond which continued to hold the upper classes of the two nations long after the umbilical cord of politics had been cut. In old Virginia everything salable in the shops was labelled of English manufacture, insomuch, adds Conway, "that fanciers used to sell the songsters unknown to England, if they sang particularly well, as *English mockingbirds.*" In 1798 John Bernard found remote planters "perfectly *au fait* as to the literary, dramatic, and personal gossip of London and Paris." Books, newspapers, and letters kept green the associations and friendships of Americans educated abroad. John Randolph of Roanoke, who as a boy had thrilled at the sight of ships from England entering the James River, and as a man kept an English coach, rode in an English saddle, wore English clothes, read English books, and dined off English plate, wept for pure joy upon his belated first glimpse of the white cliffs of Albion. A century before him, William Byrd of Westover had felt the

[3] As Professor S. Foster Damon has recently pointed out in his biography of Amy Lowell, it was Appleton who invented the most famous saying ever coined about expatriation, that "good Americans when they die go to Paris." Both Oliver Wendell Holmes and Oscar Wilde purloined the remark from him.

same way, while a hundred years later Walter Hines Page was to raise a diplomatic tempest by saying in 1913 in dedicating a monument to the Pilgrims at Southampton that the United States was "English led and English ruled." The timeworn saying, "Let me make a nation's songs, and I care not who makes its laws," lends significance to the fact—as everybody knows—that *America* is sung to the tune of *God Save the King,* that the *Star-Spangled Banner* bears the melody of an old English drinking song, and that *Home, Sweet Home,* the nostalgia of a wanderer through pleasures and palaces, is an old Sicilian air which Payne picked up in Italy. The very sentiments of our patriotism are set to European rhythms.

In Colonial times the American in England seems to have had much the same social status as the present Australian possesses—for he is vaguely classified with the kangaroo, the duck-billed platypus, and the wombat as another extraordinary manifestation of that Continent. Yet in the case of all Colonials there is enough resemblance to make the situation a trifling embarrassing, like the visit of a country cousin. From even the most favored provinces in the South families like Manigault, Izard, and Elliott removed to Europe for apparently indefinite expatriation; some like the Izards enjoyed at least a modest whirl, but travelled about rather restlessly and at length returned to bask in the light of real social primacy, while the family of Barnard Elliott—as shown by unpublished letters in the possession of Mrs. Drayton Grimke of Charleston—looked down their noses at their own lower middle-class relatives in England, and were in turn snubbed by the aristocracy they sought. The tradition of "the beautiful and lively American" in London society, with her extravagance, childishness, and eccentricity, was already well established when Fanny Burney committed to her Diary the antics of Mrs. John Paradise from Virginia. Among the small minority of Americans who received high social acclaim in the eighteenth century one may distinguish two marked types. The first was the rare cosmopolitan whose looks, dress, wealth, wit, and manners afforded ready entry to courts and salons; of these Mrs. William Bingham was the leader. And the second was the picturesque, homely, democratic American, of which Benjamin Franklin was the pure example and Jefferson the somewhat sophisticated product. The latter type got along much better in France, where equalitarian theories and the spirit of scientific inquiry were stronger than in England.

The Saga of American Society

Early in the next century the true cosmopolitan became almost extinct. New visitors to Europe were either gaping provincials with tin trunks and maps, or else servile imitators whom their models despised. "I am an American" had become either a chip on the shoulder or else a rueful apology.[4] As late as 1840 only 50 per cent of all books published in America were by native authors, and a great many of those were routine schoolbooks. The art movement was well under way which has filled our land with Palladian courthouses, copies of pupils of the Old Masters, and volumes of poetry which celebrated the nightingale and the faun. It was also the great heyday of French toilette waters—esprit de cédrat, sirop de Boubie, citromane, Micheaux's freckle wash—and the era when, as *The Ladies' Repository* for August, 1843, assures us, it was "a mark of the greatest vulgarity for a *lady* to wear anything but a Parisian slipper." In the 1860's after the memorable visit of the Prince of Wales, and the increasing fussiness of French fashions under the Second Empire, men turned to the patrician simplicity of English style and made Savile Row their arbiter. A generation later the introduction of trouser-cuffs evoked the popular taunt, "It must be raining in London!" High tea became a fashionable rite, pink coats came into favor among huntsmen, and many individuals experimented with saying "bēēn," "jolly well," "dontcherknow," "right you are," and "frightfully." A comic song of the late eighties carried the refrain

> O, the things that we say and the queer things we do
> Are "English, you know! Quite English, you know!"

and a few noted Anglophiles like Ward McAllister and James Van Alen sought to achieve that British public-school pronunciation which, as Stephen Leacock has described it, "sounds as if a whole flock of sheep had broken loose in your vocabulary."

Perhaps most significant of all was the widespread revival of interest in genealogies and coats of arms, the rediscovery of European roots. Few parvenus have had the courage of the late F. E. Smith, Lord Chancellor of England, who upon becoming Earl of Birkenhead took as his heraldic

---

[4]De Tocqueville in 1835 observed: "An American leaves his country with a heart swollen with pride; on arriving in Europe he at once finds that we are not so engrossed by the United States and the great people which inhabits them as he had supposed, and this begins to annoy him."

motto *Faber meae fortunæ,* "I am the smith of my own fortune."[4a] And even fewer have commented with the forthrightness of Julia Newberry from Chicago, a precocious child of fifteen, who upon being taken to New York in December, 1869, inscribed in her Diary: "Thursday evening last I went to my first dinner-party, & never in my life was I so bored. I had the illustrious Mr. Stuyvesant Fish who in spite of his having a Grand-Father is little less than an idiot." A good many people who pride themselves upon belonging to old families seem to lose sight of the fact that all families are equally old, and that the difference arises simply because some know or think they know the names of their ancestors at a particular time. It is of course natural that one should take pride in the heroism, the public services, and the intellectual attainments of his forbears—the extension of his personality through a fourth dimension—but the cult of ancestor-worship in the West has its obvious follies. One takes refuge up his family tree because he is incapable of standing upon his own feet in the throng; others may find inordinate satisfaction in ancestors who have little else to commend them than their predatory habits, like the first Astors and Vanderbilts, who merely carried into trade the imperialism of Kipling—

> Revere this simple maxim:
> That he who will not fight
> Gets smacked by the other fellow,
> And serves him damn well right.

The coat of arms, first adopted for identification in the days of armor, usually by the man himself in the way that a tradesman might invent a trademark, has been subject to much abuse. Old writers on heraldry gave blazons to the angelic host before the Creation, while the French family of Croy showed a picture of Noah about to enter the Ark, calling to a servant, "Sauvez les papiers de la maison de Croy." The Duc de Levis hung in his gallery a painting of the Blessed Virgin saying to his ancestor who bowed hat in hand, "Couvrez-vous, mon cousin," while the

---

[4a]In this connection the jest of Sydney Smith will be recalled: "The Smiths have never had any arms, and have invariably sealed their letters with their thumbs." On the subject of genealogical ignorance a memorable exchange of cross-fire occurred after the visit to the United States in 1893 of Paul Bourget, author of *Outre-Mer*. M. Bourget announced to the world that some Americans did not even know who their grandfathers were. Whereupon Mark Twain replied that the average Frenchman never knew who his father was. At the time it was considered a brilliant retort.

Colonna family had painted a Last Judgment with Colonnas rising from their tombs with the assistance of angels and claiming the exclusive attention of God the Father and His Son. Thoreau discovered a rare book called *The Blazon of Gentry* which reported: "Christ was a gentleman, as to the flesh, by the part of his mother . . . and might have borne coat-armor. The apostles also were gentlemen of blood, and many of them descended from that worthy conqueror Judas Machabeus; but, through the tract of time, and persecution of wars, poverty oppressed the kindred and they were constrayned to servile workes."

Coats of arms were known in America from the coming of the white man. As Brannon and other archæologists who have dug in South Carolina and Alabama report, the first traders gave medals, gorgets and arm bands in silver and bronze, bearing royal arms, "only to headmen"; plain ones could be bought by anybody. After one has sifted out the shamelessly inaccurate records of the Gore Roll in New England, Bolton's *American Armory*, Matthews's *American Armoury and Blue Book,* the *Magazine of American Genealogy,* and the books of William Armstrong Crozier, a visiting British genealogist who was much sought after by the fashionables of 1905, one still finds that at least a score of Virginia families and a dozen New England ones brought by the mid-seventeenth century authentic coats of arms registered with the College of Heralds, the patent-office for such trademarks. The custom of massing one's wealth into the relatively liquid form of silver plate—properly ornamented by such devices alone—caused many new families to adopt coats of arms already held by others. The Pages in Virginia took the arms of the Paget family, and in Massachusetts the Lowells eventually evolved a blazon by an effort of pure reason; the Adamses, being cross-grained dissenters, were proud not to do so. In the eighteenth century, painters like Jeremiah Theus in Charleston, George Searle in Newburyport, John Coles in Boston, and Thomas Pryse in Annapolis did a profitable business in adorning coaches with coats of arms; in the decade of 1790 Freneau's *National Gazette,* ridiculing the aristocratic airs of the Federalists, declared

> On coaches now, gay coats of arms are borne
> By some who hardly had a cent before.

Guillim's book on heraldry was the chief storehouse of plunder. In 1815

at Miss Pierce's School for Young Ladies at Litchfield, Conn., we find
that schoolgirls were picking out heraldic designs from Edmondson's
Complete Body of Heraldry, embroidering them on their dresses, handkerchiefs, and petticoats, and proclaiming them their own. In 1855 Robert Everest reported finding an "Office of Heraldry" flourishing in New
York, under the special patronage of new-rich traders, land speculators,

From Harry Whitney McVickers' *The Greatest Show on Earth: Society,* by permission
of Harper and Brothers

and railroad kings from the West. Not until a generation later did Tiffany establish its department of "Blazoning, marshalling, and designing
of arms complete." Mrs. Sherwood in her handbook of etiquette published in 1897 says: "The modern married belle at a dinner is apt to be
dressed in white, with much crystal trimming, with feathers in her hair,
and with diamonds on her neck and arms, and a coronet on her head,
which is not republican." At the Bradley Martin Ball—where the hostess
was called Queen and her partner the King[5]—and at lesser parties, cotillion

[5]"An ancient authority upon dancing points out that when no royalties are at
hand, the most prominent lady and gentleman present may take upon themselves

The Saga of American Society

favors were bejewelled with coats of arms or crests of miscellaneous selection.[6] Even though in the nineties it used to be said that Philadelphia asked the question, "Who was your grandfather?" while New York merely demanded "How much are you worth?" and Boston inquired "How much do you know?" the pride of ancestry was rapidly growing in New England. Mrs. Mary Baker Eddy, though in tune with the Infinite, still thought it worthwhile to parade a temporal coat of arms until her right to it was protested by the representatives of the family in Scotland. Another American arrivist, slightly changing the spelling of his name, claimed relation with an old English family, and in their parish church in England put up what was described as "a brazen tablet" to a mythical emigrant ancestor; the tablet was carefully tarnished and affixed secretly in the wall. It was discovered however by the local gentry, and much derision caused when beneath the edge was found the signature, "John Jones fecit 1879." Still another American family in the late nineteenth century claimed an extinct ducal title, and was mercilessly exposed by British genealogists and the College of Heralds.[7]

Noble and royal descent—computed through younger brothers, the female line, the bar sinister, and hypothetical gaps—has always charmed socially ambitious Americans as well as threadbare gentlefolk. Most impressively the Reverend Doctor Nichols wrote in 1904: "Mr. J. Pierpont Morgan, Mr. E. D. Morgan, and Mrs. Herbert Livingston Satterlee are scions of a dynasty of Welsh kings, the founder of which was Gynned Cymric, king of all Wales, 605 A.D. Mr. Morgan can by right use eighteen quarterings on his shield, but by choice shows only twelve." After this testament of exquisite humility, Doctor Nichols continues: "Mrs. John Jacob Astor, one of the most far-descended as well as beautiful leaders of the ultra-smart set in the United States, derives her patrician cast of family type. Ogden Mills, Mrs. Vanderbilt, Mrs. Oscar Living-

the royal character. Mrs. Bradley Martin, the hostess, properly received homage as Queen, John J. Astor, her partner, received it as King." *New York Times,* Feb. 11, 1897.

[6] In 1904 the Rev. Dr. Nichols, *The Ultra-Fashionable Peerage,* was shocked because so many parvenus "cannot distinguish between a coat-of-arms and a crest," and commit dreadful solecisms in ignorance of the fact that a coat of arms "should not be blazoned on any smaller vehicle than a big landau or the largest size of brougham."

[7] During this same period it may be noted that a British tax on armorial bearings reduced their number from 252,000 in 1880 to 39,315 by 1923.

ston, Mrs. James Francis Sullivan of Philadelphia, Mrs. Frank S. Wither-
bee, Lispenard Stewart, James Laurens Van Alen, Mrs. Royal Phelps
Carroll and Mrs. Vanderbilt descend gracefully from kings." Not pausing to notice that Mrs. Vanderbilt has descended twice from kings in
the same sentence, he concludes more wistfully: "In more than eight out
of a dozen instances a chasm yawns between the family in the mother
country and the first settler in this, which hundreds and sometimes thousands of dollars expended in genealogical research will not bridge over."[8]
Many American genealogists would not be deterred by the yawning of
any such chasm, but gladly would throw themselves like Curtius into the
breach; the United States has never known that old English law which
condemned the manufacturer of pedigrees to be docked of an ear. One
interested in this subject should consult such works as Charles H. Browning, *Americans of Royal Descent,* third edition, Philadelphia, 1894, a
voluminous work of 736 pages and thousands of names; or *The Royal
Lineage of the Hamlins arranged by Hon. H. F. Andrews, Exira, Iowa,
Author of the Hamlin Family and other works,* The Exira Printing Company, 1909; or *Of Sceptered Race,* Memphis, 1910, by Annah Robinson
Watson, author of *Some Notable Families of America, A Royal Lineage,*
and *Passion Flowers.* For those who take comfort in such things there
are books of more scientific pretension such as *Your Family Tree,* 1929,
by the late David Starr Jordan and Miss Sarah Louise Kimball, proving
that Calvin Coolidge was descended from Charlemagne, along with
Shakespeare; Grover Cleveland, Abraham Lincoln, and John D. Rockefeller from King Henry I of France; Ulysses S. Grant from William the
Conqueror; and William Howard Taft, David Starr Jordan, Ray Lyman
Wilbur, and J. P. Morgan from King David of Scotland. The average
reader may be a little baffled thus to discover that Mr. Morgan derives
from both Scottish and Welsh kings, by two entirely separate genealogies,
and astonished to learn that of the men on the *Mayflower,* thirteen "are
known to have been entitled to coat armor." These are indeed strange
words from a distinguished ichthyologist and pacifist. The ultimate solace
however may be afforded by the statement of Doctor E. M. Best of Mc-

[8]Yet he is very kind to *nouveaux riches* from the Pacific Coast, finding that Miss
May Fargo of San Francisco comes "in a direct line from both King William of
Orange and a long dynasty of Saxon kings," and that Darius O. Mills's lineage
runs "straight back to King Bruce."

The Saga of American Society

Gill University: "Every one of us is descended from William the Conqueror, and Anglo-Saxons are, all of us, at least thirtieth cousins to each other."

In 1890 Charles H. Browning, who, as we have seen, had written a book on this subject, founded the Colonial Order of the Crown, for such men as could trace their descent from Charlemagne; Miss Henrietta Lynde Farnsworth began a similar one, largely feminine, called the Order of the Crown of America, accepting the descendants of any blood royal. Today both sexes are admitted into the Colonial Order of the Crown, whose headquarters are at Wyncote, Pennsylvania. Its entrance fee is $65, which covers the cost of a parchment certificate and a Royal Crown Insignia suspended from a purple and gold ribbon. More catholic was an even earlier organization started by the same Charles H. Browning in 1867, the year in which he began compiling his *Americans of Royal Descent,* to admit "men and women whose lineages are traced to the legitimate issue of kings." Known as the Society of Americans of Royal Descent, it likewise was cradled in Pennsylvania, charges an admission fee of $100, and offers a ribbon of red, white, and blue, "suggestive alike of patriotism and royal achievement." Its president is Mrs. George H. Houston, born Mary Stuart Hoge, and its officers include Colonel Charles Wickliffe Throckmorton, John S. Wurts, George Steptoe Washington, and other genealogically minded people who are officers of most of these societies.

The pleasant lines from *Iolanthe*—

> Scorn not the nobly born
> With love affected,
> Nor treat with virtuous scorn
> The well connected.
> High rank involves no shame,
> We boast an equal claim
> With him of humble name
> To be respected,

might also apply to groups a little less encompassed by the divinity that doth hedge a king. There is the Society of Magna Charta Dames, founded in 1909 in Washington, but with present headquarters in Philadelphia. Its little brochure *A Priceless Heritage: A Sacred Trust* begins in arresting fashion. "KNOW YE THAT: Seven hundred and eighteen years ago your ancestor, a gallant knight, came with a group of other knights as gallant as he to challenge King John and to wrest from him the crushed liberties of his Anglo-Saxon subjects. In the meadow of Runnymede they assembled, dauntless and determined." Its best-known regents are Mrs. Finley J. Shepard, Jay Gould's daughter, Mrs. Theodore J. Hoover of California, Mrs. Alexis F. du Pont, and the Princess Pierre Troubetzkoy, born Amelie Rives, of Virginia. The Society of Descendants of Knights of the Most Noble Order of the Garter was organized by Mr. John S. Wurts in 1929; its presidents are the Duke of Sutherland (honorary) and Doctor Josiah H. Penniman of Philadelphia. As stated by its descriptive pamphlet, this society has taken as its chief task the preservation of St. George's Chapel at Windsor Castle, badly in need of repairs several years ago: "The fabric was so much decayed that, as the Dean of Windsor once remarked, 'We could find no scientific reason, when the work was started nine years ago, why parts of the roof should have stayed up so long.' The reason, probably, is tradition." Mr. Wurts fills the office of "Portcullis" in another order, the Plantagenet Society, incorporated in 1930, with Admiral Byrd as its honorary president; lineal descendants of Geoffrey Plantagenet are eligible. These groups hold receptions and teas from time to time, in Philadelphia, New York, Boston, Chicago, San Francisco, and elsewhere. On September 8, 1936 for example the Society of Descendants of Knights of the Garter, the Colonial Order of the Crown, the Plantagenet Society, and the Society of Americans of Royal Descent met for a "Pilgrim Supper at the Polly Darling Tea Room, Plymouth, Mass."

Societies which enshrine early American history rather than Old World glamour are the Colonial Dames and Colonial Sons and Daughters, Colonial Daughters of the XVII Century, the Ladies' Association of Mount Vernon,[9] Colonial Order of the Acorn, Daughters of the American Colo-

---

[9]The Mount Vernon Ladies' Association, founded by Miss Ann Pamela Cunningham in 1853, is perhaps the pioneer in women's groups which combined historical restoration with a certain social cachet. The founder herself stressed that each Vice-Regent, appointed in every State, "should be of a family whose social position would command the confidence of the State." "It would be safer and better for my country to add no more Vice-Regents to our number than to make unfortunate selections—an irremediable evil," she wrote on another occasion. Mrs. Justine Van Rensselaer Townsend of New York, Mrs. Phoebe A. Hearst of California, Mrs. Mary T. Leiter of Illinois, and Mrs. Rebecca M. Flandrau of Minnesota were among its most active Vice-Regents a generation ago.

nists, Descendants of the Signers of the Declaration of Independence, Society of Descendants of the Continental Congress, Huguenot Society of America, Holland Society of New York, Order of Colonial Lords of Manors in America, Order of the Founders and Patriots of America ("descendants of both founders and patriots in the same line"), the Society of Mayflower Descendants, the Society of Colonial Wars, Sons of the American Revolution, United Daughters of the Confederacy, and the New England Historic Genealogical Society which lately has become virtually the American College of Heralds with its benign survey of coats of arms. Of local groups the St. Nicholas Society of New York, founded in 1835, is most famous and bears the bell of social distinction; its members are descendants of New York inhabitants before 1785, "and qualified in other respects to join a society composed of gentlemen." Of national groups the most celebrated are the Daughters of the American Revolution, organized in 1890 to protect historical spots, erect monuments, encourage research in history, and celebrate patriotic anniversaries; its members are women descended from any man or woman loyal to American Independence "provided the applicant is personally acceptable to the society." A junior group called Children of the American Revolution was formed for the benefit of youths under eighteen. Members of the D. A. R. in recent years have been most notable for their advocacy of teachers' oath laws, more stringent investigation and deportation of radicals, and the banning of Marxist literature. They are in fact the vestals of our patriotic fires. Sometimes even Colonial history proves unpalatable; the late Secretary of the Virginia Historical Society was long harassed by a Richmond candidate for the D. A. R. who wished elaborate investigation of the ancestor upon whom she based her eligibility—in desperation he was compelled finally to inform her that the ancestor in question was a cobbler in Washington's army, but the shoes he made were so poor that he was finally told to go home. Several years ago before a D. A. R. meeting Mr. Archibald Rutledge of South Carolina read a letter from George Washington to his ancestor John Rutledge, dispatched by rider from Charleston, forty-two miles away, ending with the postscript: "For God's sake give my rider some grog." After the meeting was over Mr. Rutledge was privately requested to keep secret what was termed "Washington's weakness."

Ancestors may cause a great deal of hard feeling. Some ten years ago in St. Louis an exhibition of family portraits was held by the old French aristocracy; unhappily a great deal of bickering broke out over the illegitimacy of certain patriarchs there represented, and the exhibition ended in a bitter feud which has not yet been forgotten. In New Orleans the publication of George W. Cable's study of Creole origins awoke keen indignation; in a defensive speech in 1885 Charles Gayarré admitted that 160 immoral women were sent over from France in the early days as wives for colonists, and "although he did not explain this at the time, for fear of shocking the ladies in his audience, he was often heard to say privately that the lives these women had led made it impossible for them to procreate; that only one among them had had a child, and it died young; so that no Creole could be descended from any but virtuous women."[10] The recent publication of Herbert Asbury's *The French Quarter* has rekindled this old controversy.

The cult of noble titles in the United States had had some rather astonishing social results. Probably the only self-created nobleman which America can boast was Lord Timothy Dexter of Newburyport (1747-1806). A tanner who gained a small fortune by following the advice of wags—shipping coals to Newcastle and having them arrive in the midst of a miner's strike, sending mittens and warming-pans to the West Indies where the former were disposed of to Baltic traders and the latter eagerly bought as skillets for cooking—Timothy Dexter was urged by his fellow citizens to take out patents of American nobility and did so. "Ime the first Lord in the younted States of Americay, Now of Newburyport," he wrote in *A Pickle for the Knowing Ones* (1802). "It is the voice of the peopel and I cant help it and soe let it goe. Now as I must be Lord, there will foler many Lords pretty soune, for it dont hurt a Cat nor the Mouse." Getting rid of his foolish wife by the simple device of regarding her henceforth as a ghost, "Mrs. Dexter that was," "the ghost that was my wife," Lord Timothy Dexter passed to grander things. Hearing that every nobleman kept a poet, he made Jonathan Plummer his laureate and dressed him in a suit sprinkled with silver stars. He moved into the best house in Newburyport, named it "the Palace," bought a counterpane that once belonged to Marie Antoinette, searched a book of heraldry for several quarterings that henceforth adorned his coach—in

[10]Edward L. Tinker, "Cable and the Creoles," *American Literature*, V, 4 (January, 1934).

which, on one memorable occasion, he was driven in state to jail. Having built himself a fine tomb, and provided for "fier workes in the toume, pipes & tobaker & a speaking trumpet, and a bibel to read and sum good songs," he staged a mock funeral, and following the suggestion of some friend who proposed Lord North as one of the pall-bearers, he added gratuitously Lords East, West, and South. On pillars round the house he erected statues of Adam and Eve and Noah, Venus, Washington, Adams, Jefferson, John Jay, Rufus King, "the great Indian Chief Cornplanter," George III, Louis XVI, Bonaparte, Charles IV, Alexander I of Russia, the King of Denmark, Governor Gilman of New Hampshire, two greyhounds, four lions and a lamb to lie down with one of them, and a representation of Motherly Love. Although most relics of his glory have long since mouldered into dust, America may still be proud of her one autochthonous nobleman. Beside him pale examples of borrowed European pomp like Benjamin Thompson, of "Rumford," Concord, N. H., who for service to the Elector of Bavaria received the title of Count of the Holy Roman Empire, and whose daughter styled herself the Countess Rumford up to her death in 1852; or the gentleman in the oil business in Pittsburgh who in 1936 became the Earl of Thomond.

The search for feudal splendor has taken many shapes. The dazzling Meschianza held in Revolutionary Philadelphia, of which Major André left pen-and-ink sketches, was a recreation of chivalric pomp. The first fancy-dress ball recorded in New York society was given by Madame Brugière in her house on Bowling Green in 1829; the Schermerhorn Ball of 1854, the Vanderbilt fête of 1883, and the Bradley Martin Ball of 1897 followed in a crescendo of magnificence. The Veiled Prophet Ball in St. Louis and the Mardi Gras in New Orleans are survivals of the old Latin spirit of carnival, now grossly commercialized, and mingled also with the American quest for fantasy, for courtly mummeries of the Sun King, Elizabeth, or the Doges of Venice. It is a curious and ironic phase of the American Dream, in which every man is king. Even Arkansas Baptists sing "Will there be any Stars in my Crown?" In South Carolina and Georgia tourneys have long been held by youths who like Miniver Cheevy "missed the medieval grace of iron clothing." A typical antebellum tournament was held in April, 1851, at Pineville, S. C., with thirty knights "in complete steel" bearing such titles as the Knight of Ophir, the Hibernian Knight, and the Knight of South Carolina, with a King-at-arms on a charger "splendidly caparisoned in an azure horse cloth." Their negro servants were called Moors. The knights rode at the ring, and the victor then crowned a Queen of Love and Beauty; a banquet and a ball followed. With much less panoply than picnic, tournaments of riding at the ring are still occasional amusements of the Southern gentry. A miscellaneous catalogue of American nostalgia would include the complete works of Henry James, James Branch Cabell and the chronicles of Poictesme, the longer poems of Edwin Arlington Robinson that Maine Yankee at King Arthur's court, and many other imaginative symptoms—for the grandson of the Colonists, possessing intelligence without ripeness and poetry with little faith, has long cast wistful eyes upon the wake of the returning Mayflower. It would also comprehend the antique furniture market, the famous dinner set of Sèvres china painted by Dessard for the old Waldorf bearing the heads of all the rulers in Europe, and a great part of the history of design in America. Fortunately obscure is that American architect, drunk with eclecticism, who once proposed a building exhibiting a different historical style on every story.

It might also relate the history of those great feudal domains which a few Americans have built to satisfy their baronial appetite—James Gore King's "Highwood" at Weehawken in the 1840's, Jay Cooke's "Ogontz" which was erected after the Civil War at a cost of $2,000,000 and later converted into a girls' school, and George Vanderbilt's "Biltmore" in North Carolina which cost $6,000,000. George Vanderbilt, a fastidious and somewhat petulant romantic like William Waldorf Astor, was the biological sport of his family. He is said to have employed 300 stone-masons the better part of three years upon this project; and on one occasion he ordered uprooted an entire apple orchard in bloom "because he wished to see only forest trees from the windows of his house." The only tangible result of these labors was that many pedigreed hogs were raised here, and that here Paul Leicester Ford wrote *The Honorable Peter Stirling*. The greatest attempt ever made to achieve lordly splendor in America is William Randolph Hearst's 240,000 acre estate at San Simeon, Calif., with its estimated cost of $15,000,000 for furnishings and antiques alone. Its great dining-hall hung with Sienese banners and a magnificent Gothic chimneypiece from the Château du Jour, its sixteenth-century refectory tables, Flemish tapestries, seventeenth-century Spanish candlesticks and old English silver, six Gobelin tapestries costing $575,000, a notable collection of armor, and Cardinal Richelieu's own bed are witnesses to the spoliation of Europe. Mr. Hearst once bought a castle in Spain, and had it transported from Andalusia to New York in packing-cases. Many of his crated treasures remain for years unopened. To gratify his taste for antiquity *in situ* he purchased St. Donat's Castle in Wales. At San Simeon it has sometimes cost him thirty or forty thousand dollars to have a full-grown tree moved thirty feet. There is a private railway of three cars and a diner to convey the fifty or sixty guests who are generally in residence, and pending good behavior are never asked to leave though they stay for months. The paradox of dining off gold plate with a paper napkin in one's lap, and of mingling the *Risorgimento* with Hollywood movies, is peculiarly Californian. Poe might best have described this domain of Arnheim, where the Master has decreed that death shall never be mentioned in his presence.

The zenith of European influence upon American society came from about 1895 up to the Great War. This was the period when so many historic estates in England and Scotland were being bought by American capitalists in emulation of the squirearchy, that *Life* showed a view of the Thames bank with a well-known structure in the foreground: "The residence of Mr. John B. Grabb, of Chicago. This building is historically interesting as having been formerly the seat of the British Parliament." This era also saw the great invasion of titled bankrupts in search of American heiresses, than which nothing more sweeping had been known since the rape of the Sabine women. British peers have always met with flattering respect in the United States, where to the generality they seem as enchantingly fabulous as the griffins and unicorns displayed on coat armor. At home they are accepted as a matter of course. There it is known that, through the vicissitudes of time and circumstance, the present Duke of Northumberland, with a title redolent of the glory of the Percys, is really descended from Hugh Smithson, a London apothecary of the eighteenth century; that the Earldom of Essex was founded by a draper, and Craven by a tailor; and that the handsome Earl of Warwick, now in Hollywood and about to enter the movies under his family name of Brooke, has only a nominal bond with the Kingmaker Richard Neville, but is descended directly from William Greville, a worthy woolstapler.

In Quest of Coronets

American society has always greeted the visiting peer with a great out-cry, exceeded only by its trepidation at meeting royalty. Lord Adam Gordon's tour of the Colonies in 1764–65 caused prolonged excitement.[11] Sir William Draper, Knight of the Bath, was greeted by a whirl of par-ties in 1770, and ended by capturing the heiress Susanna De Lancey of New York. The Comte de Mosloy, who came as attaché to the French Minister in 1779, went much into society and married a very rich Liv-ingston in 1782, while the Marquis de Marbois, a great favorite in post-Revolutionary Philadelphia, took his bride from the well-to-do Moore family. A little later Frances Cadwalader of the same city mar-ried the future Lord Erskine, secretary to the British Legation, and in Boston the British Consul General, Sir John Temple, Bart., espoused Governor Bowdoin's daughter. The titled marriages of Binghams and Carrolls are well known, and also the match which made Sally McKean the Marchioness d'Yrujo and mother of the Duke of Sotomayor, Prime Minister of Spain. Even at the high tide of political democracy in 1837 the *Knickerbocker Magazine* noted the "abject reverence for foreign titles prevalent in our fashionable society." Sidons, Sealsfield, and the Comte de Saint Victor report the same thing; Auguste Carlier in his *Marriage in the United States* adds of the American girl: "Place before her two men, one of whom has but his noble title; and the other a man distinguished in science, in letters, or in business—there will be no doubt of the young American's choice." The marriage of Betsy Patterson to Jerome Bonaparte awoke great admiration, even though the Bonapartes had risen from sea-level in Corsica. His brother Joseph was long the lion of Eastern society, for his titles as King of Naples and King of Spain were dazzling, and few saw the exile with the eyes of the Briton Thomas Hamilton, who observed at Bordentown that "the ex-king took out his pocket handkerchief and deliberately mopped his bald

[11]The only dissenter on record was Mrs. Burgwin of Wilmington who wrote to her sister: "In my last I was going to tell you about the great people we had in town, really a collection of as ugly ungenteal men as I've seen, four in number. Lord Adam is tall, slender, of the specter kind intirely; Capt. McDonnel is a high-lander very sprightly; the other two are Americans just come from England where they have been educated, both very rich, which will no doubt make amends for every defect in Mr. Izard and Wormly." Of Lord Gosford's arrival in 1837 Mrs. Ellet, *Court Circles of the Republic*, p. 257, comments: "He created quite a stir. Though an Irishman, he was a lord; and invitations to dinner and supper awaited him on every side."

discrowned head with a hand that belonged rather to a spit than a sceptre."
The typical American naïveté is well expressed in a letter of Mrs. Robert Tyler, daughter-in-law of President Tyler and hostess of the White House, January 28, 1842: "I am afraid you poor Alabamian plebeians will expire with envy when I tell you that a real live English Lord was among the guests at the President's house last week; Lord Morpeth now, Earl of Carlyle that is to be, with the blood of all the Howards coursing through his noble veins!"

The visit of the Prince of Wales as Baron Renfrew in 1860—which required two "burthen cars" to carry his souvenirs by rail, and at the Academy of Music elicited such ten-minute bulletins from Bennett's *Herald* as "10.10 the Prince is Approaching," "10.20 He arrives," "10.30 He is now dancing"—was more pompous but not more exhilarating socially than the visit of his grandson under the same incognito in 1924.[12] Prince Napoleon, the Grand Duke Alexis of Russia, Dom Pedro, Emperor of Brazil, the Duc d'Orleans, Prince Henry of Prussia—who in 1902 had strong curiosities of his own and wanted to meet Morgan, Vanderbilt, and Marshall Field—Prince Louis of Battenberg, King Albert of Belgium, and a score of others have received notable ovations. Within the past ten years the social seasons at Palm Beach have been built around visiting nobility—it was there that the impending arrival of the Earl and Countess of Athlone caused the winter colony to consult its oracle, Mrs. Edward T. Stotesbury, on the question of curtseying to a brother of Queen Mary.

Richard Vaux, attaché of the American Legation in London, danced with Queen Victoria at the Coronation Ball, June 28, 1838; when the news was carried to his Quaker mother in Philadelphia she was silent for a moment, and then said, "I hope my son Richard will not marry out of meeting." Such demure snobbery has unfortunately been rarer than the other kind in America. Though, as has been seen, the pursuit of

[12]A few links between visits were diplomatically forged. One, generally unknown, is here told on the authority of the British Embassy in Washington. In 1860 H. R. H. had dined and danced with a belle of the capital, Miss Alice Riggs, and had recorded the fact in his private address-book. Upon the first hurried visit of his grandson just after the War, in 1919, the present Duke of Windsor called upon Miss Riggs, then an octogenarian, only to be turned away by an old colored butler who spent his spare time reading Thackeray in the pantry and never deigned to admit any one whose face he did not recognize. Not until long afterwards did Miss Riggs learn of her caller.

In Quest of Coronets

heiresses was not unknown to Colonial times, comparatively few rich families gave great dowries to their daughters, as Chastellux, Mazzei, Bayard, and others testify. During the early nineteenth century the marriage of convenience was looked upon with general disfavor by that romantic, democratic age. Not until the second quarter of the century do we find it stated that the credo of a young lady begins: "I believe in elder sons, a house in town and a house in the country, I believe in a coach and six, diamonds, a box at the opera, *point de Bruxelles* lace, and crinoline . . . " The increasing worldliness of marriage in society with a capital $, and the blandishment of the nuptial vow, "With all my worldly goods I thee endow," served greatly to deflect the course of romance. For two generations the decay of European nobility through economic causes was arrested to a marked extent by infusions of American money. Though even an approximate guess is necessarily wild, Myers in his *History of the Great American Fortunes* cited a computation in 1909 that "more than 500 American women have married titled foreigners. The sum of about $220,000,000, it is estimated, has followed them to Europe." A distinguished professor of English history who for years has made a canvass of England county by county, in connection with his researches, tells the author he has visited scarcely a village or small community in which the vicar or the landlord has not remarked to him, "There's a countrywoman of yours living hereabouts, the American wife of Sir —— who years ago brought him the money to mend his house." And if it is the landlord speaking, he often adds in a burst of confidence, "And they do say, sir, that she's had a bit of a hard life of it, too." Not only peers and knights but also many county families have been buttressed in this way. French, German, Hungarian, Greek, Russian, Georgian, Italian, and Papal titles have attracted a multitude of heiresses; that many of them are invalidated by republics, others not hereditary, and still others highly dubious seems to have mattered little.[13] Apologists say that the American man is to blame, that he has

[13]Mrs. John Sherwood, *Manners and Social Usages* (1884), p. 45: "Care should be taken in presenting foreigners to young ladies; sometimes titles are dubious." In 1936, after years of such·imposters as Prince Michael Romanoff and Lord Ernest Desmond, the Noblemen's Club was organized in New York by Baron Suriani, to weed out the 400 authentic titles in the United States from the number of spurious ones reckoned, doubtless with exaggeration, at 8000. Applicants who pass scrutiny are given a certificate of nobility, which is said to be useful in seeking jobs and in obtaining discounts in certain shops.

not the allure and chivalry of the European lover, who knows something of music, flowers, and poetry, and can order but not pay for a complicated dinner at Foyot's. They also add that American girls possess a quality which the Duke of Windsor long ago defined by the adjective "snappy," and that this leads to the reciprocal choice. How they explain the coincidence that in the vast majority of cases threadbare nobility finds its spiritual affinity in the rich parvenu it would be too curious to inquire.

Indeed the quest for titles is and always has been essentially the mark of wealth insecure of its social footing, as novels like Mrs. Burton Harrison's *Anglomaniacs* (1890) and Abel Hermant's *Les Transatlantiques* (1905) have described it. Mrs. Harrison states that newspapers in Germany used to carry matrimonial advertisements of "The International Bureau of Private Transaction, San Francisco," offering to put impoverished *junkers* in touch with American heiresses, while *The New York Tribune* gratuitously helped by drawing up a list of American women in its opinion "entitled to a place in the nobility of Europe." About 1900 the correspondence was published between King Milan and Queen Natalie of Serbia, discussing schemes for rehabilitating the fortunes of the Obrenovich dynasty by marrying their son Alexander to some American girl; the royal pair admitted to each other that they knew none as yet, but somewhere there must be one worth millions. Equally pathetic was the plight of the present Duke of Leinster, who appeared in Bankruptcy Court in London in October, 1936, bowed under debts of more than £100,000, with the rueful testimony that in 1928 he had visited the United States on a "prospecting" trip, had been twice fooled by "possibilities," and at last had married an American, Mrs. Rafaelle Van Neck, who afforded little comfort to his creditors. Last year New York society believed that Sir Robert Throckmorton was here on a similar mission. Unluckily for these late claimants the fortune-hunter has come to be something of a joke, and rich fathers have grown wary since the days when, as Henry Cabot Lodge wrote, every pork-baron "will buy a European title, because he comprehends that the title has value as a trade-mark and a trade-mark he understands." Mr. Franklyn L. Hutton, who in Paris in 1933 used to hold press conferences at the Crillon and exhibit his daughter's bills for hats, stockings, and silk underwear to reporters, was perhaps the last great exemplar of his type.

In Quest of Coronets

Parental coercion has not infrequently played its part in titled marriages. The youngest and favorite daughter of the first John Jacob Astor, Eliza, fell in love with a Vermont dentist, Eleazar Parmly, but her father determined that she should do better. He carried her to Paris and in 1824 apparently forced her marriage to Count Vincent Rumpff, who was Minister of the German Free Cities in Paris, and later held a similar post in Washington. Astor's wife Sarah objected to the loveless match, and while it was in the making she sent word to Parmly to follow and carry off his beloved; however, he arrived too late and Mrs. Astor thoughtfully gave him $1000 to cover the expenses of his trip. Old Mr. Astor greatly enjoyed the entry into petty German courts which his new son-in-law provided; though never caring for American society he adored the pomps of his fatherland, and counted among his richest experiences presentation to Charles X and Louis Philippe, and attendance at the coronation of Ferdinand II at Naples. Eliza died after eight unhappy years.

The last quarter of the nineteenth century saw a growing passion for titles. The first important match was that of Lord Randolph Churchill to Jennie Jerome, daughter of the New York broker and sportsman Leonard Jerome, in April, 1874; the present Winston Churchill is their son. In 1876 the eighth Duke of Manchester married Consuelo Yznaga, a Cuban heiress much in New York society, who lent her name and illustrious example to her relatives by marriage to the Vanderbilts. Their son the present Duke of Manchester also chose an American bride in 1900, Helena Zimmerman of Cincinnati—a marriage ended by divorce in 1931. Miss Minnie Stevens became Lady Paget, and Miss Beckwith Lady Leigh. In 1888 the widowed eighth Duke of Marlborough married the widow of Louis Hammersley of New York, born Lilian Price, daughter of a U. S. naval officer; after the Duke's death she remarried in 1895, Lord William de la Poer Beresford, a relative of the Lord Decies who espoused Vivien Gould in 1911 and Elizabeth Drexel Lehr in 1936. The first American marriage into the Dukedom of Marlborough was a relatively simple affair, with a ceremony at the Tabernacle Baptist Church on Second Avenue; but the second, which took place on November 6, 1895 at St. Thomas's on Fifth Avenue, was the most magnificent in American social annals. This was the union of Miss Consuelo Vanderbilt, daughter of Mr. and Mrs. William Kissam Vanderbilt, to His Grace the ninth Duke.

The Saga of American Society

In the previous year at the age of seventeen Consuelo had fallen deeply in love with Winthrop Rutherfurd, a New York bachelor of thirty belonging to the Stuyvesant and Winthrop clan. But her mother, the future Mrs. O. H. P. Belmont, had already set her inflexible will upon a ducal title, and as the daughter testified before the Rota in 1926: "My mother tore me from the influence of my sweetheart. She made me leave the country. She intercepted all letters my sweetheart wrote and all of mine to him. She caused continuous scenes. She said I must obey. She said I knew very well that I had no right to choose a husband, that I must take the man she had chosen, that my refusal was ruining her health and that I might be the cause of her death." The family doctor was called in to tell Consuelo that her mother had a very bad heart, and that any grievous disappointment might prove fatal. "There was a terrible scene in which she told me that if I succeeded in escaping she would shoot my sweetheart and she would, therefore, be imprisoned and hanged and I would be responsible." Having carried her daughter to London for the summer season, Mrs. Vanderbilt met the twenty-four-year-old Duke of Marlborough, proud, crotchety, but badly in need of money, and invited him to Newport. In September, 1895, he came and stayed a fortnight at Marble House, arranged the match with his future mother-in-law, and from her estranged husband William K. Vanderbilt the Duke agreed to take 50,000 shares of the Beech Creek Railway Company, valued at $2,500,000, as a marriage settlement.[14] Consuelo's mother testified thirty years later, "When I issued an order nobody discussed it. I, therefore, did not beg, but ordered her to marry the Duke." The wedding day was fixed for the first week in November, and on the crucial day Mrs. Van-

[14]The official document, dated on the wedding day, November 6, 1895, thus begins: "Between the Most Noble Charles Richard John, Duke of Marlborough, of Blenheim Palace, in the County of Oxford, England, party of the first part, and William Kissam Vanderbilt of Oakland, in the county of Suffolk, N. Y., Esq., of the second part, Consuelo Vanderbilt, party of the third part, and the Hon. Ivor Churchill Guest of Arlington Street, in the County of Middlesex, England and Mr. Vanderbilt, their trustees, of the fourth part. Whereas, a marriage is intended between the said Duke of Marlborough and the said Consuelo Vanderbilt, and whereas pursuant to an agreement made upon the treaty for the said intended marriage, the sum of $2,500,000 in 50,000 shares of the capital stock of the Beech Creek Railway Company, on which an annual payment of 4 per cent is guaranteed by the New York Central Railroad Company, is transferred this day to the trustees. And shall during the joint lives of the said Duke of Marlborough, Consuelo Vanderbilt, pay the income of the said sum of $2,500,000 . . . unto the Duke of Marlborough for his life," etc.

Not All in the Market

FOREIGN PURCHASER: "I think I will take one of those gals in the gallery, ye know"
PROPRIETOR: "No; they are not for sale. You must take your choice from these four hundred"

C. D. Gibson in *Life* in the "early nineties"

derbilt had a guard stationed outside her daughter's room, and forbade any one to speak to or approach the girl.

Under the caption "She is Now a Duchess" *The New York Times* for November 7 gave this wedding precedence over all other news. It told of St. Thomas's decorated with "thousands of yards of smilax and holly" and at the end of every fifth pew "a huge floral torch surmounted by a feathery palm . . . intended to represent flambeaux, such as are to be found on some of the old houses in London." The church was filled two hours before the ceremony, with the ushers struggling manfully to keep order: "Many of the women insisted on taking seats in the center of the church; others absolutely refused to be seated in the pews assigned to them, either on the side aisle or in the galleries, and still others actually stood on the seats whenever some well-known woman arrived so that they might catch a better glimpse of her gown." Finally Mrs. Vanderbilt arrived and walked up the aisle with her two sons, William K., Junior, in frock coat and carrying a top-hat, and Harold in black knickerbockers and white Eton collar. The groom followed immediately thereafter. But "for fully twenty minutes" the bride failed to appear. Mrs. Vanderbilt's state of mind can be imagined. At long last the sexton at the door waved his handkerchief at Mr. Walter Damrosch, who burst into "the first crashing notes of the bridal chorus from 'Lohengrin.'" Then came the bridesmaids: Katharine Duer, Elsa Bronson, Julia Jay, Daisy Post, Marie Winthrop, Edith Morton, Evelyn Burden, and May Goelet who was to get her own Duke within eight years. And the bride herself very pale and "much troubled," as Marlborough recollected long afterward. As the pair stood before Bishop Henry Codman Potter and Bishop Littlejohn, a choir of fifty voices sang

> O! perfect love, all human thought transcending,
> Lowly we kneel in prayers before thy throne,
> That theirs may be the love that knows no ending,
> Whom thou forevermore dost join in one.

When the new Duchess came down the aisle, at last smiling bravely, "people were surprised to discover that she was fully half a head taller than the bridegroom." Nor was the superiority of stature wholly physical, for as the Duchess later bore witness of her husband, "This arrogance of his character created in me a sentiment of hostility. He seemed to despise everything that was not British and my pride was therefore hurt." But the Vanderbilts with scrupulous honesty paid the piper. Blenheim Palace —built for the soldier adventurer who had founded the Churchill fortunes—was rehabilitated, and maintained by an annual expense roll of $100,000. Sutherland House was constructed in London at the cost of $2,500,000. The marriage settlement was but the beginning; all in all the match is said to have cost the Vanderbilt estate ten million dollars, which at that time was easily afforded. F. F. Richards in *Life* drew the Duke as a ragged Columbus, with the Vanderbilts meeting him on the shore laden with wampum. Finley Peter Dunne, the wit of the clubs, said through the plebeian mouthpiece of Mr. Dooley: "The Jook iv Marlburrow is a young lad an' poor . . . I dunno how he done it, whether th' Ganderbilks asked him 'r he asked thim. Anyhow, it was arranged. 'Twas horse and horse between thim. The Ganderbilks had th' money, an' he was a jook."

In 1908 after she had borne his heirs the Duchess separated from the Duke of Marlborough, and in 1921 a civil divorce followed. Still he continued to receive his $100,000 each year under the terms of the contract. In 1926 the marriage was annulled by the Rota, with the aging Mrs. Belmont, long reconciled to her favorite child, giving evidence zealously to prove coercion; the Duke of Marlborough was then received into the Catholic Church. Meanwhile the lost Duchess, increasingly weary and wistful of face, had found happiness in marriage with an ex-army officer, a French Catholic, Jacques Balsan. Gladys Deacon, her successor as Duchess of Marlborough, was the sister of Princess Radziwill and daughter of Edward Parker Deacon of Boston—who rather melodramatically in 1892 had shot and killed a Frenchman whom, it was alleged, he had found in his wife's bedroom, and so spent a year in prison until pardoned by President Carnot. For many years Miss Deacon was rumored to be engaged successively to a half dozen British and Continental titles; finally her long friendship with the late Duke of Marlborough was ended by their marriage on June 25, 1921.

The year 1895 witnessed also the wedding of Pauline, daughter of William C. Whitney, and Sir Almeric Paget, Baron Queenborough; after her death he remarried in 1921, the daughter of William Starr Miller of New York. And in 1895 came the marriage of Jay Gould's daughter Anna to one of the most disreputable of heiress-hunters, Count Boni de

The Saga of American Society

Castellane; after his coup he built in Paris a copy of the Trianon in pink marble, with heavy chandeliers of rock crystal, and between banquets and yachts contrived to spend $5,500,000 of his wife's money before their divorce in 1906. This marriage also received Papal annulment nine years

© *Life Publishing Co.*

"Both those lords are after her, and she doesn't know which to accept"
"Isn't one as good as the other?"
"Yes, but she can't tell in advance which is the cheaper"

C. D. Gibson in *Life* in 1902

later. In 1908 Anna married the Prince de Sagan, of the house of Talley-rand-Périgord, which has been most amiable to American heiresses.[15] In

[15]The fourth Duc de Dino, of Talleyrand-Périgord, in 1867 had married Eliza-beth Curtis of Murray Hill, New York; the year following their divorce in 1886 he married Adèle Stevens, divorcée, *née* Livingston Sampson. Another Curtis daugh-ter married Prince Ruspoli.

The brother of the present Prince de Sagan, the Duc de Valençay, wedded Helen Morton, as indicated elsewhere. Their first cousin, the Duc de Montmorency, in 1917 married the late Cecilia Blumenthal, *née* Ullman, of New York.

Griswold in his recent memoirs, *The Horse and Buggy Days*, pp. 32–33, has recall-ed the scintillating social career in France of the '70's and '80's of the Duchesse de La Rochefoucauld, born Mattie Mitchell of the U. S. A. She and her inseparables of the old aristocracy, the Duchesse d'Uzès, the Duchesse de Luynes, and the Duchesse de Noailles, formed the inmost circle of the Faubourg St. Germain—which Proust has described so lovingly—as well as of the sporting society which eddied about Auteuil, Puteaux, Longchamps, and the Polo Club in the Bois.

1889 Clara, adopted daughter of Collis P. Huntington, married Prince von Hatzfeld-Wildenburg, and received a dowry of several million dollars. In 1892 Florence, daughter of John H. Davis of New York, married the second Marquis of Dufferin and Ava. In 1890 Clara Ward of Detroit, with a *dot* of $2,500,000, married the fourth Prince de Chimay et de Caraman of a Franco-Belgian house; divorced in 1897, she enjoyed a gay and scandalous career which gossips compared to that of Lola Montez. The brother of this Prince, Alexander, married the widow of Rutherfurd Stuyvesant in 1933. Without the help of a watchful father the famous Tennessee Claflin from Pittsburgh, amateur stock-broker in Wall Street, suffragette, exotic, and friend of Commodore Vanderbilt, finally moved abroad and became Lady Cook and Marchioness of Montserrat in Portugal, dying in 1923. At Newport in 1899 Julia Grant, granddaughter of President Grant, wedded Prince Michael Cantacuzene of Russia; their son Prince Michael is now in the real estate business in Chicago. In 1895, the *annus mirabilis*, Mary Leiter became the wife of the future great statesman the Marquis Curzon of Kedleston. At a precocious age Miss Leiter had resolved to make a great marriage, and in addition to her native social skill she cultivated a spiritual, rather bookish attitude like that of the London "souls" who were setting the current fashion in bluestockings. After meeting her in Washington on his round-the-world cruise Lord Curzon debated with himself as far as Japan, and then cabled a proposal which was accepted by cable. Nine years later her sister Marguerite, or "Daisy," married the bankrupt Earl of Suffolk. Six months previously a kindly American dowager had suggested that he "try one of the Leiter girls." A Vice-President of the United States, Levi P. Morton, who had begun his career as a clerk in a Vermont country store, had the satisfaction of seeing his daughter Helen married to the Duc de Valençay et de Sagan at Newport in 1901; in 1904 they were divorced. In 1903 May Goelet became Duchess of Roxburghe.

The present Marquis of Hertford when Earl of Yarmouth sought to capture Byrd Thaw, a Pittsburgh heiress, but failed. He then turned to her aunt Alice Cornelia Thaw, and was accepted. On the morning of his wedding day, 27 April, 1903, the Earl was arrested in Pittsburgh for a debt of £317 5s 2d. by writ from the High Court of Justice of the King's Bench, London. To the embarrassed constables he said cheerily, "I suppose they sent that here because they understood a settlement was to be made today." A delay of forty-five minutes in beginning the ceremony, and the absence of the bride's brother, Mr. Harry K. Thaw, who was supposed to give her away, caused much mystification among those who did not know there had been a last-minute haggle over the million-dollar settlement. At last however the ceremony was gone through, though the match did not prove a happy one and was dissolved five years later. Ava Alice Muriel Astor, sister of Vincent Astor, also found disillusion after her marriage to Prince Serge Obolensky. But the marriage in 1908 of Gladys Vanderbilt, cousin of the Duchess of Marlborough, to a Hungarian noble and future diplomat in Washington, Count László Széchényi, has proved lasting despite the handicap of a $12,000,000 portion. In 1935 their daughter Gladys married Viscount Maidstone, heir of the Earl of Winchilsea.[16]

Elinor Douglas Wise of Baltimore became the Duchesse de Richelieu in a cathedral wedding of 1913, with Cardinal Gibbons officiating. Amelie Rives of Virginia, author of the novel *The Quick and the Dead,* divorced from erratic Armstrong Chanler or Chaloner, became the wife of Prince Pierre Troubetzkoy. Baron Camoys in 1911 married Mildred, daughter of Mr. and Mrs. William Watts Sherman. During the same era two granddaughters of Alexander Macdonald, an oil millionaire, became respectively Princess Murat and Princess Rospigliosi. The latter is now hostess of the Ambassador Hotel in New York. Aimée Crocker of San Francisco came to be Princess Galitzine, while Margaret Strong, granddaughter of the senior John D. Rockefeller, married a Spanish grandee, the Marquis de Cuevas. Clara Longworth of Cincinnati became the Countess de Chambrun. Frieda Huck, daughter of a rich brewer, married Baron Komosky, while her sister Marie became the Italian Marchioness Spinola; a third sister was content with Marshall Field II, to whom she bore the present Marshall Field. In 1922 the present Earl of Carnarvon married Catharine Wendell of New York, and in 1924 Margaret Green, great-granddaughter of the philanthropist Peter Cooper,

[16]In general, however, Vanderbilts have become less keen upon titles than they were a generation ago. Richest of their heiresses today are Muriel and Consuelo, daughters of the second William K. and Virginia Graham Fair Vanderbilt, with the New York Central on the spear-side and the Comstock Lode on the distaff.. The former, now Mrs. Henry D. Phelps of Carmel, California, has chosen two American husbands. The latter, with a reputed income of a million dollars annually, married first the polo-player Earl E. T. Smith and secondly Henry Gassaway Davis, former husband of Grace Vanderbilt, and a fisherman of skill.

became the bride of Prince Viggo of Denmark, nephew of the late Queen Alexandra of England. Most dazzlingly publicized of the post-War marriages was that of the widowed Mrs. William B. Leeds to Prince Christopher of Greece; May Birkhead, expert society writer for the old *New York Herald* and today the Paris correspondent of both *New York Times* and *Chicago Tribune,* was Mrs. Leeds's house guest for a week prior to the wedding and handled the public relations with professional skill. The junior William B. Leeds was for a time the husband of Russian Princess Xenia Romanov.

Thelma Morgan, the twin of Mrs. Reginald Vanderbilt, became Lady Furness; Catharine Wolff of Philadelphia the Baroness Eugene de Rothschild; and Caroline Foster the Princess Faucigny-Lucigne—all of them members of the smart international set, and periodically selected by Paris dressmakers as among the dozen best-dressed women in the world. Estelle Manville, daughter of the asbestos king, married Count Folke Bernadotte in a notable military wedding of 1928; since their new son-in-law was nephew of the King of Sweden, Mr. and Mrs. H. E. Manville had constructed in their yacht an extra-length bed for His Majesty. Louise Astor Van Alen married in succession two of the Mdivani brothers, since deceased. Jean Banks Gimbernat, New York divorcée, married in 1931 the Earl of Lincoln and heir presumptive of the Duke of Newcastle; in 1932 Josephine Dennehy of Chicago became the wife of Prince Nicholas Galitzine; in 1934 Anita Stewart, relict of Prince Miguel de Braganza, Pretender to the Throne of Portugal, saw her sister-in-law Princess Maria-Antoinette de Braganza marry Ashley Chanler; and a year later Mrs. James B. Tailer, born Leslie Cornell, became Lady Doverdale. Katharine Kresge has married and divorced Baron Carl Wijk, keeping abreast of her Woolworth rivals; and in 1936 Helen Wardman, daughter of Harry Wardman, a self-made real-estate dealer of Washington, D. C., married Prince Naselli, "of an old Roman family" now living in Mexico. Thus continues the aspiration after European titles, though the public and its newspapers have grown more blasé since the Vanderbilt-Marlborough decade, and now nothing less than the romantic abdication of a king for an American woman can command the full resources of publicity. In recent years titles have fallen from the gold standard, and a number of American women who bear courtly names now use them prosaically enough in business—such as the Marquise de Polignac, born

The Saga of American Society

Nina Crosby of Boston, who helps promote in New York the sale of her husband's Pommery champagne, and the Baroness Rosencranz, née Vida Moore, whose Manhattan shop makes shoes for ladies of quality. It is ironic also that one of the few apparently true-love matches between an heiress and a great noble—that of the late Katherine Elkins of West Virginia coal millions and the Duke d'Abruzzi—was forbidden by the King of Italy.

The only approximation to an American court society is that of Washington, a point of tangency at which so many European alliances of the lesser sort have been made. As early as 1841 an observer in Washington reports that "some of the ladies, who are full of romance and curiosity, grow very frisky at sight of an attaché, and cannot conceal a longing they have to dance and flirt with the interesting foreigners." Forty years ago Lord Dufferin asserted: "Nearly all the attachés of the various embassies at Washington are captured, before their term of office expires, by American beauties and American heiresses," and the British journalist W. T. Stead in his *The Americanization of the World* (1902) cited such examples as Count Hatzfeld, Count von Waldensee, Baron d'Estournelles, Baron de Bildt, and the Honorable Michael Herbert. During the intervening years the foreign services of all countries have been so elaborately tissued with international mating that France, Italy, Brazil, Portugal, Chile, Turkey, Belgium, and other countries have attempted to discourage diplomatic marriages to aliens and the possibly divided loyalties they breed. In December, 1936, the United States Government took its first step in that direction, and confronted with 127 husbands of foreign-born women out of 684 married officers, and 202 out of 724 U. S. clerks, the State Department issued an order binding all such servants of this country below the rank of Ambassador or Minister to receive permission from the Secretary of State, or else resign, before taking an alien to wife.

Washington is the only city in America which has a rigid order of social precedence, again because of its official and diplomatic character. A foreign sovereign or president outranks by courtesy the President of the United States, then in the President's absence comes the Vice-President. Ambassadors in order of senior appointment, the Chief Justice, Speaker of the House, Associate Justices, Secretary of State, and so forth. The British Ambassador is traditionally the social leader of the diplomatic set. In the nineties a bitter war was waged over the deadlock of

In Quest of Coronets

Vice-President and Ambassadors, and today the rivalry of Ambassadors and Chief Justice is so debatable that discreet hostesses never ask them to the same party. Miss Helen Cannon, daughter of the late Speaker, and Mrs. Dolly Gann, half-sister of the late Vice-President Curtis, were doughty warriors for their rights. The Division of Protocol and Conferences of the State Department—itself a sort of club which favors the Boston accent and an independent income—is arbiter in such matters, but upon moot points its decrees are sometimes Delphic. So ironclad is the order of precedence that if a dinner be given for a guest of medium rank he and his wife cannot sit at the honor-places, unless those of higher rank volunteer to waive their claim, and they seldom do. After a few seasons in Washington the wife of a representative from the corn-belt or a colonel's lady from an army post in windswept Texas learns before sitting down at any table to appraise with a gleam in her eye the social situation, and to sniff the odor of battle where before she had detected only the imminence of Brussels sprouts. Prompt calls upon newcomers of higher rank, visits of digestion paid within a week, official "at home" days, and a snowstorm of calling-cards are still in evidence in Washington, however lax the rest of the country may have grown. Addison might have written of present-day Washington: "I have known my friend Sir Roger de Coverley's dinner almost cold before the company could adjust the ceremonials of precedence and be prevailed upon to sit down to table."

Every one in Washington society is expected to leave his card at the White House at least once a year, and in return he expects an invitation to at least one of the four great winter receptions, exclusive of New Year's Day: for the Diplomatic Corps, which carries by far the greatest éclat and represents what some still call "the Court Society of America," and in diminishing pomp the Judiciary, the Army and Navy, and Congress. The quality of entertaining in the White House, previously sketched from Washington to Grant, has undergone during the last two generations much fluctuation. Succeeding Julia Dent Grant as First Lady came Lucy Hayes, a staunch Methodist who refused to serve drinks, ousted the billiard-table from the White House, and to add to the horrors of the Administration purchased with an appropriation from Congress "a state dinner service, illustrating the fauna and flora of the United States." William M. Evarts, questioned about the first Hayes diplomatic reception, replied, "Altogether brilliant. Water flowed like champagne." In time the steward learned to serve oranges filled with frozen punch at state dinners, and Mrs. Hayes was never told why second and third helpings were taken. Mrs. Garfield, though no sophisticate, brought back the billiard-table and restocked the cellar. President Arthur, a widower, entrusted social affairs into the competent hands of his sister Mrs. McElroy. He was succeeded by Cleveland, whose first chatelaine was his sister Rose Elizabeth, a prim spinster schoolteacher who reported that during her brother's Inauguration she had kept her composure "by conjugating a Greek verb." Greater social grace at the close of his first term and throughout his second came after his marriage to the young and pretty Frances Folsom, daughter of his law partner in Buffalo. But she, like the late Mrs. Harding, kept social reporters at bay and was timorous of her dignity before the public, though unlike the "Duchess" of 1922 Mrs. Cleveland knew nothing about mixing rounds of highballs for poker-players.

The administrations of Benjamin Harrison and McKinley were socially mediocre, but quite different was that of Theodore Roosevelt, with a resourceful wife and a dashing, eligible daughter who was fêted by New York and Newport, toured the Orient, and climaxed her career with a gorgeous wedding in the White House. Mrs. Taft entertained lavishly though with less personality; she continued Mrs. Roosevelt's precedent of giving her dinner-lists to the press, but dropped the costume notes which her predecessor had inserted. Because of illness, death, and the onset of the Great War the Wilsons entertained little; both Wilson and Harding cancelled the Inaugural Ball on grounds of economy, the latter after sharp criticism from Senator Borah. Mrs. Coolidge, a woman of great charm, was compelled by her husband to follow stereotyped traditions; Mrs. Hoover, the perennial Girl Scout, maintained a cautious and rather Victorian social atmosphere, which for the first two years did not include even the indulgence of ash-trays. Mrs. Franklin D. Roosevelt, outspoken, spirited, affable, with her early decision to serve beer and wine, her Monday press conferences for women only, her syndications and frank sharing of her life with the public, her shrewd business sense plus the Roosevelt political flair, has broken the ice-locked Puritanism and reticence of the White House. Upon this fact, but with a different inflection, both friends and enemies agree.

Behind the changing pageant, foreign and domestic, remain the "cave-

dwellers" of northwest Washington, "the army of unalterable law."
There are the four Patten sisters, of whom only one has married; with
one generation of moderate wealth behind them, they long ago set out
to rule Washington, by giving great tea parties at which one's presence
was the sign manual of society. Their tireless energy in unearthing obscure facts raised gossip to the plane of research. The McLeans and the
Leiters now regard themselves as cave-dwellers, along with really old
families like the Beales and the Blairs. As early as the social annals of
Van Buren's day we read: "Mr. Blair gave a party, the cards of invitation
to which had long colored ribbons attached to them, streaming through
the air as they were borne along." Whether adorned with streamers or
stamps, invitations from the Montgomery Blairs and the Woodbury
Blairs are always manna to the social appetite. And there are the Larz
Andersons, socially impressive with the prestige of an Ambassadorship
to Japan in their past, who think it more genteel to come from Boston
than Cincinnati. And finally a small coterie of clever and enterprising
women, like Alice Roosevelt Longworth, who but for her irrepressible
mockery might have commanded a brilliant political career, Miss Mabel
Thorp Boardman of Cleveland, Secretary of the American Red Cross,
and Mrs. J. Borden Harriman, formerly Florence Jaffray Hurst, who
loves to dine celebrities, boasts something of a salon, and has published
her memoirs called *From Pinafores to Politics*. These women are great
friends, upon the same principle that England and France are allies.

Washington has always suffered the lack of throne and diadem. There
is so little permanent society, so conspicuous an absence of the pomp and
purple which Jay, Hamilton, Adams, and even Washington longed for
in their hearts. Thanks largely to Jeffersonian principles Americans must
cross the Atlantic in order to be presented at Court. The custom of
presentation at Court dates from the subject's traditional right to enter
the presence of his sovereign—to watch him eat and drink, revel or
mourn, and even to see him die. It was the wage for his fealty. In the
life of a queen neither the morning toilette nor childbed served to disbar
loyal subjects from her chamber; the former occasion, used for purposes
of reception by English rulers as late as Queen Anne, created the word
levée, which is still in use. There is scant evidence that any particular
qualifications or credentials were demanded in early times; cats looked
at queens, and push and cheek seem to have counted for much. During

the reign of George II (1727–60) records indicate that almost any one decently dressed could go on any evening to watch the Royal Family play ombre. Rules for the more formal introductions or "presentations" grew up long ago, stipulating that an unmarried woman could not present either a married or single woman, and according to a regulation of the Heralds' College under George II no illegitimate daughter could be presented until she was married, "however high in rank her father may be." Divorcées have never been countenanced. Under the four Georges the king kissed all the ladies at a Presentation, but the Queen kissed only earls' daughters and those of higher rank. Victoria instituted mid-afternoon "Drawing Rooms"—a term since abandoned in favor of "Courts," which are held usually in the evening—and for a time amid great unpopularity abolished food, drink, music, and men, and sent her ladies home hungry to so-called Drawing Room Teas, where friends dropped in to criticize their costumes. When the Prince and Princess of Wales began to receive in her place, without full prerogatives of a sovereign, kissing was abandoned and has never been revived. A silent bow to each of the approximately 800 who pass the Presence in an hour is now the only acknowledgment of their curtsies.

In England society is defined by tradition as those who are eligible for presentation at Court, and once a name has been inscribed upon the Royal List invitations to the Buckingham Palace Garden Parties and other large functions follow as a matter of course. This clarity of definition, of belonging beyond dispute to English society after one has bent the knee, makes many Americans eager to achieve such an honor—even though they vote the straight Republican ticket and instruct Nanny to provide fireworks for the children on the Fourth of July. In Colonial times gentlemen with well-dowered daughters, like the third Philip Ludwell of Virginia with his Hannah and Lucy, sometimes took them to London for presentation and a chance at a noble husband. Among Anglophiles the fashion continued after the Revolution, so that Harrison Gray Otis observed, "the women after presentations to the court of George III or Louis XVI transplanted into Philadelphia society the manners of the English aristocracy and the fashions of Paris." Sturdy patriots grumbled at the custom even when, as in the case of diplomats, it was a political necessity. Abigail Adams, wife of the first American Minister to England, was presented in June, 1785, while London newspapers were still

Waiting to be Presented

From a drawing by Charles Dana Gibson made at the time Mrs. Gibson was presented at Court in 1896 through the invitation of United States Ambassador Bayard

frothing against the Rebels—in a dress of white lutestring trimmed with white crêpe, a train three yards long, "ruffle cuffs for married ladies," and two white plumes in her hair. "I consider myself as complimenting the power before which I appear as much as I am complimented by being noticed by it," she wrote home, like a true Adams wife. "Nor would I ever again set my foot there if the etiquette of my country did not require it." And the Queen, she added, was stout and homely in purple-and-silver. Few Americans outside the diplomatic corps seem to have been presented during that social nadir, the early nineteenth century.[17] But with the rise of great fortunes in railroads, Western mines, coke and steel, the trophy of presentation came eagerly to be sought. The American Ambassador to the Court of St. James's, having formerly nominated to the Lord Chamberlain certain of his visiting countrywomen with distinguished names, now found himself besieged with applications. Old business connections in "the States," political pressure through Washington, impressive letters of introduction, impassioned pleas of ambitious mother-love—all were mobilized in the assault. Often the appeal was carried to the Ambassador's wife, for it is she who usually performs the nominal presentation of her compatriot to the British Crown, though that duty may be delegated to the wife of the American Chargé d'Affaires or in rare cases the Doyenne of the diplomatic corps. Since only three to

[17]Cf. Robert E. Spiller, *The American in England* (New York, 1926), Chapter VII, "A Note on Women." During this period the great majority of American men traveling in England apparently were not accompanied by wives, daughters, or sisters. Business and hasty sight-seeing had crowded out much of the leisurely social residence of Colonial days, and unlike the Izards and Manigaults of an earlier time few women seem now to have been taken to Southern Europe except for reasons of health.

Among the rare travel diaries and letters which survive, one finds that Catherine Hickling (later Mrs. William Prescott, mother of the historian) was dazzled by fashionable London, "all looked *to me* like nobility"; Abigail Adams Smith, like her mother, refused to be overawed and wrote flippant comments on royalty; while Harriet Balch had nothing but a bare glimpse of the Princesses Maria and Augusta, and wrote with a touch of spleen: "They are ugly women, more like housemaids than ladies."

One of the first American Ministers whose description of Courts survives was Mr. Rush, in 1817. Although it took him three-quarters of an hour to climb the Palace staircase in the Processional, he enjoyed the pomp with which Queen Charlotte surrounded herself. "No lady was without her plume," he wrote. "The whole was a waving field of feathers; some were blue, some tinged with red; here you saw violet and yellow, there shades of green, but most were like tufts of snow: the diamonds encircling them caught the sun and threw dazzling beams around." Percy Armytage, *By the Clock of St. James* (London, 1927).

In Quest of Coronets

five American women are presented at each of the successive Courts during the early summer, competition is keen.

For an American woman the routine may be briefly described. If she is sure of being presented, she will probably wait till late May or early June before going over, and in the meantime will have had her Court dress fitted at Farquharson & Wheelock's in New York—dressmakers who specialize in grooming American women for such occasions, and enjoy a certain amount of recognition from Buckingham Palace. Less sure of herself, the candidate may go early to London and offer her credentials at the American Embassy.[18] If she is favored by the Ambassador and sanctioned by the Comptroller of the Lord Chamberlain's office, at present Lieutenant-Colonel Nugent, she will receive a summons card about three weeks before the Court at which she is required to appear. Details with regard to dress are issued with the summons card, but if the candidate does not repose full trust in her dressmaker she will probably go to the Lord Chamberlain's office, St. James's Palace, to study the sketches of approved costumes there on display, or con the manual *Dress and Insignia Worn at His Majesty's Court* from which she will learn:

Three Small White feathers mounted as a Prince of Wales's Plume, the centre feather being a little higher than the two side ones, to be worn slightly on the left side of the head, with the tulle veil of similar colour attached to the base of the feathers.

The veil should not be longer than 45 inches.

Lace lappets may be worn.

Coloured feathers are inadmissible, but in cases of deep mourning Black feathers may be worn.

The Train, which should not exceed 2 yards in length, must not extend more than 18 inches from the heel of the wearer when standing.

There are no restrictions with regard to the colour of the dresses or gloves for either débutantes or those who have already been presented.

Gloves *must* be worn.

Bouquets and fans are optional.

Unless her husband is in the diplomatic service he is ineligible for these evening Courts, and is thus spared the parallel indignity of black silk

[18]Before the War certain British women of position were well known as willing sponsors of ambitious Americans. In 1904 Doctor Nichols stated that a presentation guaranteed by them cost $5000.

knee-breeches. As late as the reign of Edward VII American Ambassadors had traditionally spurned such garb as unrepublican, but since that time it has become good form to do as the Romans and adopt the court dress of every country to which they are are accredited. Private gentlemen from the United States may however attend one of His Majesty's noon *levées,* or be invited for a less formal presentation along with their wives under the royal tent at a garden party.

On the evening of a Court the ambitious wife is driven up to Buckingham Palace, leaves then her husband and her wraps in the motor-car, and is taken in charge by the first of three gentlemen ushers. With her gilt summons card in hand, and her train carried looped over her arm until the moment of entry into the presence, she waits patiently in the state library with a throng of similarly attired women. Since one's turn may not come for several hours, until ten-thirty or later, books, portable card-tables, and even tea-baskets with light collations are sometimes brought by the débutantes to royalty. As one approaches the throne-room the Comptroller gives full instructions, including a reminder not to talk above a whisper; hitherto lesser sounds have been drowned out by the military band playing in the west gallery.

Meanwhile "the crowning act of the royal social system," as the late Ambassador Walter Hines Page called it, is in progress. His own description, in a letter to Woodrow Wilson, 9 June, 1914, is still valid and amusing. At exactly 9:30 P.M. the orchestra begins to play "God Save the King" and Their Majesties enter, with the Gold-Stick, the Silver-Stick, and the rest of their attendants backing before them. The Royal Family take their places on a dais under a gold-embroidered canopy of crimson velvet, and, standing, receive the obeisance first of Ambassadresses and then Ambassadors. Their Majesties now sit down, with diplomatic ladies on one side of the throne and peeresses on the other. All men, and ladies of no high rank, remain standing for the next two hours. Then the presentees are herded in, while the orchestra plays softly, and Ambassadors chat in undertones with Princes and Gentlemen-in-waiting. Occasionally a lady trips, or steps on the train in front. Her card, handled by six officials, finally reaches the Lord Chamberlain, who announces her name to Their Majesties. She curtsies, often badly and usually with a frozen smile or *risus sardonicus* which is meant to be pleasing. The King bows; the Queen bows and smiles. That is all. "But every one has been

After Presentation

From a drawing made by C. D. Gibson in 1896 at the time Mrs. Gibson was presented at Court

admitted to the royal presence; that's the game, you see, and when you've done that you've won—over the 38,000,000 other persons who are not on that evening so admitted." Yet as Page freely concedes, "This show is perhaps the best managed, best mannered show in the whole world."

Then comes the Recessional to the supper-room, where quail, peaches, and champagne are waiting. "The Americans are everywhere, Americans of all sorts, from twenty-four karat to tinsel." He notes that the two American duchesses have as glaring coronets as anybody in the throng, and one heiress who is married to a high title "tells me confidentially that she's trying to marry the rich American girl that we see in front of us to the young Duke of ——. I venture to advise her to let the young lady alone: she can find a husband for herself. 'My dear compatriot,' she says to me, 'it is delicious to see how touchingly simple you yet are.' That 'yet' rather got my tag, as the old hussy meant it should."

Such is the supreme social rite to which every American woman, undivorced and of respectable antecedents, is eligible—except members of the Wetmore family of Rhode Island. Edith Keteltas Wetmore, wife of the late distinguished senator, according to tradition once offended King Edward VII, who ordered that forever after no Wetmore should set foot in Buckingham Palace. This ban has not impeached their standing among the oldest of the Old Guard in Newport, but is accepted as a pleasant distinction. Other Americans at Continental Courts have displayed various audacities—beginning perhaps with the band of squaws and twelve warriors from the Illinois wilderness who in 1720 were presented at Versailles, with the added entertainment of a deer hunt in the Bois de Boulogne and the baptism of their Princess at Notre Dame. Upon their return to the wilds of Illinois they fell upon and slaughtered Sergeant Dubois and the other whites who had induced them to be presented. And there was Mrs. Jack Gardner who was presented to the King of Italy on January 28, 1895 and six weeks later sent him a bunch of yellow roses on his birthday, remarking that she always sent flowers to gentlemen she liked and the fact of Umberto's being a king made no difference. But the King, greatly puzzled as to her intentions, sent an equerry to call. Though Mr. Gardner gravely assured the man his wife's purposes were honorable, the enigma was not cleared up until American Minister Wayne MacVeagh visited the King's secretary and explained that Mrs. Jack Gardner was a lady, but had the quaint habit of doing as she pleased. And finally there was Harry Lehr who after presentation at the Schleppen Court of Kaiser Wilhelm II in January, 1907, felt so free as to attend an Imperial Reception in a tweed suit and spotted necktie and perform, for the Emperor's pleasure, a few tricks which had formerly convulsed Mrs. Fish's dinner-table. Wilhelm II was not amused to such a degree that Ambassador Tower, responsible for the introduction, resigned soon afterwards.

CHAPTER ELEVEN

SOCIETY AND SPORT

SOME day sport will find its wide-visioned philosopher. He will show us how cricket, with its white clothes and leisured boredom, and sudden crises met with cool mastery to the ripple of applause among the teacups and cucumber sandwiches, is an epitome of the British Empire. Or the bull-fight with its scarlet cape and gold braid, its fierce pride and cruelty, and the quixotic futility of its perils, is the essence of Spain. Or that football with its rugged individualism, and baseball with its equality of opportunity, are valid American symbols, while Soviet Russia favors mass games in preference to the Olympic sports which aim at world's records and other tacit assertions of one man's superiority over another. Most of these things have been felt or hinted before, but their synthesis has never been made. Nor has any one explored Thomas Jefferson's interesting remark in a letter to Peter Carr, that "games played with a ball stamp no character on the mind," and that the horse and gun are the only instruments of true discipline.

Aristocracy and sport have always been drawn together. One demands the leisure of the other. The bodily fitness for war, the study in self-control, competition without envy or material gain, are worshipped instinctively by patricians in every age. In this régime of the six- or eight-hour day sport is far less the aristocratic prerogative, but still those games which demand expensive equipment, enormous acreage, and a staff of assistants remain marks of caste. Although old Continental nobilities had their costly diversions—fencing, feats of horsemanship in tourneys, hunting the wild boar, royal or "real" tennis—the concept of aristocratic sport known to America since Colonial times is a purely Anglo-Saxon one. Among Europeans only the upper-class Englishman really sees in sport a way of life and the cult of gentlemanliness. He may doubt some of the eternal verities, but his blood tells him that to

428

Society and Sport

gallop across the downs, to live much with dogs and horses and the smell of the earth, and to feel the salt wind against his cheek as he grips the wheel, are good things and requisite to the salvation of his class. The dictatorship of England to fashionable America is nowhere so compelling as here. Many of our great sporting families whose names and origins are quite un-English—like Belmont, Vanderbilt, Lorillard, Oelrichs, Iselin, Widener—usually began to feel this impulse in the second generation, and by the third to produce sportsmen who lived and breathed it. Although America has never followed sport so consistently around the calendar as Great Britain—where the London season is merely an interlude sandwiched between the end of spring hunting and the start of grouse shooting—the Horse Show at Madison Square Garden for many years after its beginning in 1885 marked the opening of a social period which brought the sporting gentry into town during the four months when outdoor sports were most curtailed by weather.

Though the Jockey Club in Paris, established 1833, and the English Jockey Club, dating from 1750, are among the smartest sporting groups in the world, neither vaunts the antiquity of the South Carolina Jockey Club which expired in 1900. The founding date 1734 with the honor of being the first Jockey Club in existence is claimed for this association. Noted sportsmen of the pre-Revolutionary period were John Drayton, Edward Fenwick, John Izard, Frank Huger, William Moultrie, and Doctor Daniel Ravenel. In 1754 the earlier York Course was abandoned in favor of the New Market Course, named after the celebrated English track laid out under James I. In 1792 it in turn was supplanted by the Washington Course. During the Revolution and again in the Civil War all activities of the South Carolina Jockey Club were suspended, including the brilliant gaieties of Race Week with its Wednesday Banquet and Ball on Friday. The president of the Jockey Club at its annual dinner always sang a song of innumerable stanzas called "The High-Mettled Racer," which was heard in reverence, and then applauded with the ringing of glasses. In addition to regularly scheduled races, the gentry of Charleston and Virginia often pitted their best horses against one another in impromptu rivalry—as in the noted contest between those two aristocrats John Randolph of Roanoke and Sir John Nesbit of Dean Hall, Cooper River, each riding his own horse; Randolph won.

Virginia however was the cradle of American racing, with William

The Saga of American Society

Randolph of Henrico County the first great turf enthusiast. His own county boasted no less than five race-courses, with such famous horses as Young Fire (*ca.* 1693), Smoker, and Folly (1695) setting the pace. The raffish vices of the sport were already beginning to disturb honest middle-class citizens, for in 1696 we find a group of them in Northumberland County complaining to the House of Burgesses that Saturday

Wild enthusiasm at the Horse Show, during a critical event in the ring
C. D. Gibson in *Life* in 1897

races led to Sabbath breaking—evidently because drinking-parties lasted all night. On the other hand the benediction of the sporting parson appears in the same decade in the person of the Reverend James Blair, who was one of the most popular judges to be had; a little later we begin to hear not only of horsy but of "cock-fighting parsons" also. Needless to say, they belonged to the genial communion of Canterbury. Climate, geography, occupation, and English tradition all helped foster the cult of the horse in Virginia. The Reverend Hugh Jones, professor of mathematics at William and Mary, writes of the upper class in 1724: "I have known some spend the Morning in ranging several Miles in the Woods to find and catch their Horses only to ride two or three Miles to Church, to the Court-House, or to a Horse-Race, where they generally appoint to meet upon Business; and are more certain of finding those that they want to speak or deal with, than at their Homes."[1] Following the example of South Carolina the blades of tidewater Virginia started Jockey Clubs shortly before the Revolution at Petersburg, Fredericksburg, Portsmouth, and elsewhere, though the capital Williamsburg remained the focus of both sport and society. John Tayloe, William Fitzhugh, Moore Fauntleroy, Mann Page, and Peter Presley Thornton raced horses whose breed was constantly being bettered after the importation of Bully Rock and other fine strains from England. A certain snobbery was also inevitable; it is revealed in this order of the York County Court as early as 1674: "James Bullocke, a Taylor, haveing made a race for his mare to runn w'th a horse belonging to Mr. Matthew Slader for twoe thousand pounds of tobacco and caske, it being contrary to Law for a Labourer to make a race, being a sport only for Gentlemen, is fined for the same one hundred pounds of tobacco and caske."

The Maryland Jockey Club was founded in 1745, and gave a great impetus to the maintenance of costly stables throughout that colony. There were races for three- and four-year olds, colts and fillies, over a distance varying from one to five miles, for the best two out of three heats. The Jockey Club Plate, the Town Purse, and the Free Mason's Plate were all handsome prizes, and to heighten the gala occasion "ladies' galleries" or grandstands were provided. Robert Eden, Governor of Maryland, 1769–1775, was a keen sportsman and under his régime the Annapolis turf attained its heydey of fashion. His best horse, Why Not, carried off many subscription purses. Calverts, Lloyds, Tilghmans, and Hamiltons were great racing families; while among individual sportsmen of the late eighteenth century Charles Carroll of Carrollton, Colonel John Eager Howard, and General Cadwalader were outstanding.

Quakers, Dutch, and Puritans looked upon horse-racing with suspicion,

---

[1]He adds that they "don't much admire Labor, or any manly Exercise except Horse-racing, nor diversion except Cock-fighting, in which diversion some greatly delight." Cock-fighting has always attracted some of the "fast" and high-gambling aristocrats of America, but its connotations of cruelty and chicanery have perhaps kept it from the top rank of social sports. One might note in passing that Colonel Jerome Napoleon Bonaparte, a young blood in America during the post-Civil War era, was reprimanded by the faculty of Harvard College "for having a private cock-pit in his rooms," as he boasted to the admiring Julia Newberry on board the *Lafayette* in 1870.

because it was worldly, cavalierish, expensive, and probably immoral. Least straight-laced of these were the Dutch, who witnessed their first race at Hempstead in 1665 under the sponsorship of the first English Governor, Nicolls. His successor, Colonel Francis Lovelace, a great courtier under the Merry Monarch, decreed that an annual race should be held on Long Island in May for "a crown in silver or the value thereof in wheat." In 1670 a course called New Market was laid out at the present Hyde Park, and continued to be popular for more than a century. A London racing-book of 1776 reports that contests "are held twice a year for a silver cup, to which the gentry of New England and New York resort." On the eve of the War the two chief racing stables in the colony were owned by Lewis Morris, Jr. and James De Lancey, whose "colors were seen on every course for ten years before the Revolution." A New York sporting group called the Macaroni Club offered in 1764 and perhaps in other seasons handsome purses of £100 and £50. The breed of trotting horses was improved during the closing years of the century by importation of the renowned English stallion Messenger, bought in 1793 by Henry Astor the prosperous butcher, elder brother of John Jacob. Messenger sired the even more famous Hambletonian owned by General Nathaniel Coles.

In 1802 with the city of Washington just rising from its "Serbonian bog" a Jockey Club was begun and a race-track laid out by a great sportsman from across the Potomac, John Tayloe of "Pentworth." A slightly earlier one near Philadelphia flourished under the presidency of Richard Penn, while some years later in 1821 the Long Island races were given revived social prestige by the foundation of the Union Course. Here in 1842 Philip Hone witnessed the great race between the mare Fashion and the horse Boston. He and his friends had gone down in a barouche, and with characteristic scorn of the *vulgus* he noted in his Diary: "The tens of thousands of the sovereign people who wished to see this race made their arrangements to go by the railroad from the South Ferry, but the numbers were so great that the locomotives refused to draw. They balked and would not go ahead; the mob who had provided themselves with tickets, finding it was 'no go,' became riotous, upset the cars, placed obstructions on the rails, and indulged in all sorts of violence." Thus from time to time have the rabble sought to invade the diversions of

The carriages of August Belmont and Leonard W. Jerome on the road to the race course of the Jockey Club at Jerome Park near New York City

Drawn by A. R. Waud for *Harper's Weekly* in 1866

The Saga of American Society

gentlemen.[2] Some dozen years later Fashion Park was opened on Long Island, but attracted so many flashy sports and crooked gamblers that it brought racing into local disrepute. Not until after the close of the Civil War did this sport regain favor among conservative society in the purlieus of New York City; then in 1866 William R. Travers, August Belmont, and Leonard W. Jerome founded the American Jockey Club on the British pattern, and on a site of 230 acres in Westchester County built Jerome Park, with its grandstand accommodating 8000. The sale of liquors was here banned. General Grant attended the opening races, and all the quality flocked from Murray Hill and Gramercy Park. Its success was assured, and soon the towns north of New York built a splendid drive leading to Jerome Park, so that rich sportsmen could trot their pacers across the Harlem River and up the countryside.

Meanwhile other racing clubs had sprung up wherever wealth, gaiety, and the love of hazard throve. In New Orleans, where the croupier and the duellist helped to make life recklessly competitive, the beautiful Metairie track drew throngs of spectators and probably the finest horses of ante-bellum days. The victory of Lexington, owned by Richard Ten Broeck, over Lecompte, from the stable of T. J. Wells, in their second match for a world's record, April 24, 1855, was the talk of the racing aristocracy for a generation. Ten Broeck was also the first American to take his thoroughbreds to European tracks. Even at that date the grandees of Nob Hill had already gathered to form the Pioneer Jockey Club in San Francisco. But not until after the Civil War was the Louisville Jockey Club founded by Colonel M. Lewis Clark; in 1875 the later-famous Derby was first run. Today the Kentucky Jockey Club owns the tracks at Lexington, Louisville, and Latonia, and its rules control Southern racing.

The most celebrated spa in the United States had seen its first horse-

[2]It should be noted that the great annalist of the American turf during this period was a younger son of nobility in exile, the Hon. Henry William Herbert, nephew of the second Earl of Carnarvon, but known always by his sporting pseudonym "Frank Forester." In disgrace at home apparently because he had fled debts of honor, he came to America, met up with Anson Livingston and other young sportsmen of New York, claimed to have beaten professional jockeys, drank heavily and quarreled, wrote for *The American Turf Register and Sporting Magazine* which was started in 1839, and produced two classics, *Field Sports in the United States* (1848) and *Horse and Horsemanship of the United States* (1857). Frank Forester is one of many links which unite the chronicles of British and American sport.

Prevailing styles of riding habits

From *Godey's Lady's Book*, June, 1845

The Saga of American Society

race in 1863, though not until a generation later when William C. Whitney and Richard T. Wilson bought the track from a certain Gottfried Walbaum did racing become fashionable at Saratoga, and compensate for the failing power of the waters to attract the *ton*. The history of Saratoga began in the later eighteenth century when the British General Sir William Johnson, wounded in the defense of Fort William Henry, was instructed by the Indians to drink from High Rock Spring. In 1802 Gideon Putnam built the first hotel, Union Hall, which later became the Grand Union Hotel. In 1812 Congress Hall was added and in 1824 the larger and more luxurious United States Hotel, though as Buckingham found in 1838 "the more ancient families" stayed at Congress Hall, leaving the United States Hotel in possession of "the rich mercantile class." He adds: "Hundreds who, in their own towns, could not find admittance into the circles of fashionable society there—for the rich and leading families are quite as exclusive in their coteries as the aristocracy of England—come to Saratoga, where, at Congress Hall or the United States, by the moderate payment of two dollars a day, they may be seated at the same table, and often side by side, with the first families of the country; promenade in the same piazza, lounge on the sofas in the same drawing-room, and dance in the same quadrille with the most fashionable beaux and belles of the land; and thus, for the week or month they may stay at Saratoga, they enjoy all the advantages which their position would make inaccessible to them at home." Hence Tennessee and Arkansas planters, speculators in Ohio real estate, capitalists from Boston and New York, professors from New Haven and Cambridge, could be found smoking their cigars on the shady piazzas, strolling about the square to hear the German band, or watching belles in muslin bowl or dancers "polking themselves into perspiration." There was much riding and driving in carriages between a formidable breakfast at eight and an even more devastating dinner at two. Often after supper at seven came a "hop" or a ball—the latter more staid and stuffy, but offering the inducements of champagne, ice-cream, and blanc-mange. During the second quarter of the century Mrs. DeWitt Clinton was the tyrant of the spa. In August, 1839, she heard that President Van Buren was coming to Saratoga, and as Hone tells us began "boasting of her intention to insult him." And so in the great saloon of the United States Hotel the President caught sight of her, and little knowing what was in store for him, crossed the floor and extended his hand. "In the view of the whole company, she folded her arms, gave him a scornful look, and turned off." As soon as he had gone, his great rival Henry Clay arrived in Saratoga, and since his politics were much more to Mrs. Clinton's taste she prepared a garland of roses and hyacinths with which to crown her hero as he entered the United States Hotel. Mrs. Ellet describes the scene: "Lady Westmoreland stood in the front rank of the crowd, her brow sparkling with diamonds; General Scott was leaning against a beech-tree. As Clay came near the door, the coronet descended from the window of Mrs. Clinton's room, attached to a silken cord, and touched the brow of Henry Clay. He put it aside, and it lighted on the shoulders of a gentleman from Richmond, Virginia."

Thus went the giddy round in the meridian of Saratoga Springs, which passed its prime in the fifties when under growing sectional feeling the Southern gentry seceded to White Sulphur Springs, Tryon, in North Carolina, and small watering-places along the Gulf coast of Mississippi. After the Civil War it enjoyed a brief renascence as the "cradle of fashion and intrigue, rendezvous of lacqueys and jockeys," as Bennett's *Herald* once called it. The spa itself declined as Newport rose in favor, and Saratoga would have been relegated to the attic of oblivion along with its namesake the trunk had not certain sportsmen like Whitney and Wilson, Pierre Lorillard, and the Hitchcocks come to patronize its track and organize the Saratoga Association for the Improvement of the Breed of Horses. Today the racing season in August brings to Saratoga wealthy cottage-owners like Alfred Gwynne Vanderbilt, Cornelius Vanderbilt Whitney, Marshall Field III, Mrs. Oliver Iselin, and Pierre Lorillard; some like Mrs. Dodge Sloane rent expensive houses for a few weeks, while still others lease quarters in the south wing of the United States Hotel. Tammany politicians and sporting gangsters mingle at the races with aristocrats, but it is horseflesh rather than social ambition which now draws such casuals to Saratoga. Though the course is valued at only a million dollars, as against a four-million-dollar assessment of Belmont Park on Long Island, Saratoga has a color and distinction without which American sport would be poorer.[3]

[3]In 1935 the great Saratoga Spa under the auspices of the State of New York was opened after an expenditure of $8,500,000. The sponsor of this new idea was Bernard Baruch, with the sympathy of Mr. Roosevelt as Governor and President. The controlling body, the Saratoga Springs Authority, has added a new, comfortable,

The Saga of American Society

The patronage of the turf by newly rich capitalists began with the first August Belmont, president of the Jockey Club. Commodore Vanderbilt loved smart horses, and in later years drove his curricle daily through Central Park; his son William Henry in 1878 bought the famous trotter Maude S. and kept her in de luxe stables, under her own monogrammed blankets; but not until the third generation did the Vanderbilts blossom into lavish sponsors of racing. The inherited wealth of the Lorillards was dedicated to sport in 1873 when the father of the present Pierre Lorillard bought his first racers, and began to make world-renowned his racing colors of cherry and black. He built the celebrated Rancocas Stables at Jobstown, N. J. and entered his winners at Epsom Downs and Longchamps. In 1881 with Iroquois he won the English Derby, the first time an American had captured that supreme trophy—though Lorillard had presaged his victory by winning the City and Suburban in 1879 with his brown gelding Parole, over the great Ridotto, while the British *Sporting Life* gloomed: "Overeducation, pampering, free trade, and the defeat of Ridotto are ruining the country, and the sooner we get back to truths the better." The American invasion continued, and during the next forty years other sportsmen won the Derby—William C. Whitney with Volodyovski, Richard Croker with Orby, and Herman Duryea with Durbar—though never again an American horse. Whitney, who upon his triumph in 1901 handed over his winnings to British charity, was the most noted and popular sponsor of the turf in his generation. He started the sporting tradition of the family partly out of rivalry with his Wall Street contemporary, James R. Keene, whose racing colors—white, blue spots—were flashing past so many winning-posts.[3a] Knowing

but not socially exclusive hotel, the Gideon Putnam. Somewhat ironically Saratoga used to be the most fiercely anti-Semitic of American communities, bearing on the prospectuses of its hotels the reminder "Jewish patronage not solicited" and, so it is related, more class placards "No Jews or Dogs Admitted Here"; even the distinguished patrician Moses Thompson was almost rebuffed because of his unchristian name. Today, after their disbarment from Baden-Baden and other popular German spas, American Jews with their passion for taking the cure have become Saratoga Springs's most welcome and affluent guests.

[3a]James R. Keene (1838–1913) was second only to Whitney in sporting fame. From obscure origins in Britain he and his father reached California in the rear-guard of the Forty-Niners. In Shasta County young Keene peddled milk, worked in a mill, cared for horses, taught school, studied law, and ventured into mining and freighting. By speculation in Nevada silver he soon made a fortune on the San Francisco stock exchange. There too he met "Uncle Sam" Ward, gourmet and first cousin of Ward McAllister, who remained a lifelong friend, and in exchange for tips on the stock-

438

at first nothing about horses, Whitney had the sound judgment to hire Sam Hildreth and other expert horse-trainers and give them carte blanche, and to engage at their suggestion the best jockey of that day, Tod Sloan from Kokomo, Ind. Within three years the light blue, brown cap of the Whitneys was leading every field, and Whitney's son, the late Harry Payne, received as his inheritance the best racing stud in America, and an income from traction lines and oil which enabled him to spend as much as half a million annually upon horses. The second son, Payne Whitney, was an almost equally keen horseman, and today his widow, daughter of the statesman John Hay, is the premier sportswoman of the American turf. The third generation, represented by Cornelius Vanderbilt Whitney and his cousin John Hay Whitney, maintain the Whitney flair for racing, polo, and shooting. Joseph E. Widener, who rebuilt Belmont Park and the more garish Hialeah Park at Miami, is also a mainstay of the American Jockey Club, along with A. C. Bostwick, Thomas Hitchcock, W. Averell Harriman, William Woodward, Marshall Field, Perry Belmont, and Admiral Cary T. Grayson of Washington and Virginia. This Club, sometimes called by the press with pardonable exaggeration "the most exclusive social organization in America," is restricted to fifty members, and only death or the less likely contingency of resignation offers hope to the newcomer. Its blue-lettered silver button is a proud emblem, for out of all American racing clubs it is the only one recognized by the English Jockey Club, and its rules are pontifical for racing in the

---

market and other financial favors instructed Keene in etiquette, dress, and the art of entertaining. Keene also achieved social promotion by marriage to Sara Jay Daingerfield of an old Virginia family.

In 1876, planning to go to Europe, Keene stopped in New York, innocently accepted an offer from Jay Gould to enter into partnership on a deal in Western Union stock, and was notably fleeced. This however put him on his mettle and he recouped three years later. Faring better with Havemeyers in sugar, Morgan in steel, and Hill in railroads, Keene won and lost three large fortunes by his "plunging" but died a rich man. During his early New York phase he began to buy horses, and his first great victory on the turf came in 1881 when his three-year-old Foxhall won the Grand Prix in Paris, the Cesarewitch and the Cambridgeshire Handicaps, and the following year took the Ascot Cup. Other horses—Domino, Cap-and-Bells, Sysonby—increased his total prize winnings to an estimated $2,000,000. Today James R. Keene's son Foxhall is one of America's best-known social sportsmen.

In the light of such successful aspiration as Keene's, one cannot rebuke the great jockey of his day for graduating from "Toad" Sloan—as called by his father, an Indiana barber—into "James Todhunter Sloan," as he began to sign his name when he travelled with twenty trunks. See the account of Tod Sloan in the *Dictionary of American Biography*.

United States. It has and needs no clubhouse, for most of its members belong to the Turf and Field Club, Meadow Brook, and other top sporting associations. Outside the conservative pale of society has always been a fringe of rich but less acceptable patrons of the turf—like John W. Gates, John A. Drake, and Lucky Baldwin a generation ago, and today Harry F. Sinclair, Edward R. Bradley, and John D. Hertz. Perhaps the costliest race-track in America, the newly opened Santa Anita course near Pasadena on the old estate of Lucky Baldwin himself, represents the creation of flash rather than fashion.

From 1875 to the coming of the automobile, coaching was the smartest diversion of American society. William Jay had brought back to friends at the Knickerbocker Club stories of his drives with the Duke of Beaufort, who in England in the sixties had sought amusement in reviving the pageantry and exhilaration of stage-coach days. Colonel Jay bought and shipped to New York the Old Dorking Coach which Major Peter Withington and the Marquis of Blandford, future Duke of Marlborough, had driven as a public vehicle between London and Dorking. So with the purpose of establishing four-in-hand driving in the United States the Coaching Club began in 1875, under the enthusiasm of James Gordon Bennett, Jr., Frederic Bronson, Leonard W. Jerome, De Lancey A. Kane, S. Nicholson Kane, Thomas Newbold, and A. Thorndike Rice. Its first public parade was held in April of the next year, led by its president, Colonel Jay, in bottle-green coat with gilt buttons, silk topper, yellow-striped waistcoat, and nosegay. The Club was a stickler for form: the driver's apron had to be folded, when not in use, outside out, and *de rigueur* were the artificial flowers affixed to the throat-latch of each horse. These annual Spring and Autumn Parades, which formed at Madison Square and drove up Fifth Avenue to Central Park, and returned for a dinner at the Hotel Brunswick, were the cynosure of fashion and the astonishment of the proletariat. Frank Sturgis became the most celebrated amateur whip, but Robert Livingston Gerry, F. Augustus Schermerhorn, Alfred G. Vanderbilt, C. Oliver Iselin, and Theodore Havemeyer of the great sugar capitalists, were all close rivals. Fairman Rogers, who later wrote the manual of coaching, once turned up from Philadelphia with negro grooms and there was much solemn controversy about turning him out of the Parade for his breach of British orthodoxy. James Van Alen, on the other hand, was applauded because he imported an expert from England to teach American guards how properly to wind their horns. De Lancey Kane ran a road-coach on a regular schedule from the Hotel Brunswick to the Westchester Country Club, where his passengers lunched before their return, and the name of his equipage "The Tally-ho" was popularly though incorrectly adopted for any coach and four. Today the Coaching Club officially survives under the presidency of Reginald W. Rives, who in 1935 privately printed his handsome volume *The Coaching Club,* but its parades and gay junkets to Tuxedo, Lenox, Newport, and elswhere were abandoned in the first decade of this century. That era when a Boston wit, Mrs. Joseph M. Bell, daughter of Rufus Choate, remarked to an admiring dinner-table, "The motor-car is speedily dividing the inhabitants of this country into two classes: the quick and the dead."

The National Horse Show has also suffered eclipse. For fifteen years after its beginning in 1885 it was a primary social event, with a directorate containing such names as that of the elder Thomas Hitchcock, De Lancey Kane, Newbold Morris, and several Vanderbilts. In those days the odor of tanbark conveyed as subtle a social dignity as incense from the high altar of the Church of the Heavenly Rest. Yet by 1905 Edith Wharton reported in *The House of Mirth* that the Horse Show "had ostensibly come to be classed among the spectacles disdained of the elect; but, as the feudal lord might sally forth to join in the dance on his village green, so society, unofficially and incidentally, still condescended to look in upon the scene." The Great War further dimmed its former brilliance, and although in the past five years it has shown symptoms of reviving social vigor it seems unlikely that it will ever occupy its old eminence. This does not mean of course that society has forsworn the horse—for that would be one of the signs of the Apocalypse. It is simply a change in emphasis. Sportsmen may take assurance from the fact that hunting and polo are more popular than ever before in America, and that this is the heyday of hard-riding equestriennes. During the Revolutionary War the Marquis de Chastellux was startled all through New England by the sight of "fair girls, either driving a carriage, or alone on horseback, galloping boldly, with an elegant hat on the head," which, he decided, proved "the early cultivation of their reason, the safety of the roads, and the general innocence of manners." Then came the nineteenth century, when it was believed as Donald Walker wrote in *Exer-*

cises for Ladies (1837) that riding horseback produces "unnatural consolidation of the bones of the lower part of the body, ensuring a frightful impediment to future functions which need not here be dwelt upon." The side-saddle was the answer, and a much more tame, discreet, ladylike manège, with a few sportswomen venturing to trot in

From left to right: Rawlins Cottenet, Frank Gray Griswold, James L. Kernochan,
Miss Hewitt, Stanley Mortimer, R. Livingston Beeckman

From Harry Whitney McVickers' *The Greatest Show on Earth: Society*

Central Park, their blue veils fluttering from tall silk hats. The real emancipation of women did not come until a generation and a half ago, under such pioneers as the late Mrs. Thomas Hitchcock, Mrs. Charles Cary Rumsey, and Mrs. Allen Potts, of the sporting Rives family of Virginia; it is ably sustained today by Miss Charlotte Haxall Noland, headmistress of Foxcroft, who was born an F. F. V. and has achieved an M. F. H., Mrs. Robert Winmill, of the Warrenton Hunt, Mrs. William du Pont, Jr. of the Foxcatcher Hounds, and others. By all odds the greatest woman in American sport was the late "Lulie" Eustis, granddaughter of William W. Corcoran who founded, in Washington, the Art Gallery which

The Story of the Hunt
C. D. Gibson in *Life* in 1898

bears his name. In 1891 she married Thomas Hitchcock, noted poloist and huntsman. A few years later they began to spend their winters in the then unknown South Carolina village of Aiken, where they found good quail shooting, established their winter home, attracted friends, and thus created a new colony for sporting society. A valiant and even reckless horsewoman, she coached her son Thomas and his friends Winston and Raymond Guest on the Hitchcock polo field near Westbury, L. I., and was well repaid by the international success of her protégés. As the M. F. H. of the Aiken Drag Hounds she received grave injuries when her horse fell during the Christmas hunting of 1933, and died on April 1 following.

Society has always adored both horses and dogs. The companionship of dogs in the life of the aristocracy is a pleasant and fine tradition going back to the days of neolithic hunters; the headman, the chief, the king always had his pack for protection as well as friendship and æsthetic delight. Samuel Butler wrote in his Notebooks: "The great pleasure of a dog is that you may make a fool of yourself with him and not only will he not scold you, but he will make a fool of himself too." Many a threadbare aristocrat, dissipated scion, simple extravert, or cynical man of the world has found his best comrade in a dog. Fashions may come and go—Dalmatians, Basset hounds, Russian wolfhounds, Samoyedes, blue Bedlingtons, Papillons, even Pekingese—but the essence remains. During the past winter the palmary hostess in American society has been appearing at tea- and cocktail-parties with a griffon beneath her arm, seeming more content than the animal in question. A sport then which combines both dogs and horses stirs deeply the aristocratic heart.

Foxes were hunted in Virginia in the seventeenth century, though there is no record of dogs being bred especially for this purpose, and certainly there were no organized packs. In 1742 Doctor Thomas Walker of Castle Hill in Albemarle County owned and hunted what seems to have been the first such pack; his descendants continued to hunt with the same strain of hounds up to 1912, when the multiplicity of wire fences caused Mrs. Allen Potts to abandon the sport. The oldest surviving hunt in that region is the Piedmont Fox Hounds, begun in 1840, and supported in recent years by visitors from the North—notably Whitneys, Iselins, and that most enterprising huntsman from Massachusetts, Harry

Society and Sport

Worcester Smith. In 1905 as its M. F. H., Smith took part in the famous Fox Hounds Match which showed the superiority of James Gordon Bennett's American hounds over the English breed against which they were pitted. The $2000 plate which they won, and the columns of publicity in Bennett's *Herald,* determined the future career of Harry Worcester Smith and the rehabilitation of fox-hunting in Virginia. Kindling enthusiasm at the Loudoun Hunt and the Orange County Hunt which Harrimans had founded and sponsored, Smith accomplished much by his forceful if egotistic manner. The Warrenton, begun in 1887, with a mixed Virginian and Yankee membership; the Middleburg, dating from 1906 and predominantly Northern; and the Casanova, started in 1909 and almost purely Virginian, likewise felt the revival of interest which has grown steadily during the last twenty years, greatly to the prosperity of rural Virginia. Pink coats for riding and dinner-coats with facings in hunt club colors have followed the British fashion, and at least one hunt, the Keswick, has adopted the ceremony of blessing the pack, under Episcopal auspices. Wits have always made game of customs like this—for even in England satirists of fox-hunting have been known from 1760 when Shenstone observed "The world may be divided into people that read, people that write, people that think, and fox-hunters," until the close of the last century when Oscar Wilde defined a fox-hunt as "the uneatable pursued by the unspeakable."

Maryland has been known as good hunting country since Colonial times, though there was little formal organization until 1892 when the Green Spring Valley Hunt Club began. In addition to members of the Garrett clan, the great magnifico of Green Spring Valley and its sporting life was the late General Felix Agnes, an Irish boy who had come over steerage, saved enough to buy an interest in a newspaper, risen to great affluence in business, and more because of his blarney and personal charm than increasing wealth became a favorite of Baltimore society. In Green Spring Valley he kept a vast establishment with a black boy to wait on every guest, and computed that 10,000 mint juleps were required to run it from Friday to Monday. In recent years with the Yankee invasion of the Green Spring Valley Country Club, and the florescence in Maryland of such alien groups as the Harford Hunt, begun by Foxhall Keene and his Long Island friends, the Bostwicks, conservative Baltimoreans have clung to the Elkridge Kennels as their local citadel and for hunting have begun to go to Carroll and Frederick Counties. Some nine miles out of Philadelphia at Horsehead's or Chew's Landing, fox-hunting throve in the 1790's and attracted sportsmen from the national capital, but not until many years later did the gentry of Philadel-

Headquarters of the Green Spring Valley Hunt Club
The Old Stone Tavern on the Reisterstown Turnpike, Baltimore County, Maryland
Drawn by Orson Lowell in 1895

phia organize packs for this purpose—the Rose Tree Fox-Hunting Club in 1859, the Radnor Hunt 1883, the Brandywine Hounds 1892, and the Pickering Hunt 1911. The Altemus and Clothier families have been keen huntsmen with these packs.

The introduction of fox-hunting on Long Island must be ascribed to F. Gray Griswold, scion of a shipping and tobacco fortune from whose active affairs he early retired to devote himself to hunting, polo, fishing, and other sports whose annals he has written in many volumes with reminiscent charm. Having learned to hunt at Pau, Griswold persuaded four friends to join him in 1876–77 in purchase of a pack of hounds from Ireland. Quartered on Meadow Brook farm as a subscription pack, they were the beginning of the Queens County Hunt. Horses were bought at Bull's Head, the old New York mart, and trained laboriously to jump; a few additional good hunters were imported from Montreal. Mr. Griswold found even greater difficulty in the training of friends who had never seen a hunt before, and brought to it the keen competitive sense of businessmen. He recalls two amateur sportsmen who collided violently just as the fox was killed, and fell from their horses, "one man sitting on the dead fox, and demanding the brush." In 1880 the Queens County Hunt moved to Westchester to try the hazards of a wall country, and in their absence the Meadow Brook Hunt began over their old terrain. Today the Southampton Hounds and similar groups have popularized drag-hunting—*i.e.,* the following of bait wrapped in a fox-scented gunny-sack which is dragged ahead of hounds and riders—while for the best fox-hunting one must go farther afield to Peapack, N. J.

Polo, a game of great antiquity, was first discovered by English colonials in Northern India about 1854, and reached Britain fifteen years later. A mark of its origin is the word "chukker" for period, dropped for a time but now coming back to favor. In 1876 James Gordon Bennett, Jr., brought the first polo balls and mallets to the United States. His sporting enthusiasms had already embraced yachting, coaching, fencing, and spectatorship at boxing-matches, cock-fights, dog-fights, and rat-baitings. For exercise in the late evenings it was Bennett's wont to ride a bicycle repeatedly around the block, his butler standing by on the sidewalk holding a decanter of brandy on a silver tray. With so catholic an appetite for sport, Bennett was immensely taken with polo, and started the first team at Dickel's Riding Academy during noon hours. Finding that the balls buried themselves in the tanbark, he carried the team in his coach to Jerome Park, and there on the lower field the first game of polo was played in the United States. Bennett soon found that polo matches immediately following races were popular. Lavish in ordering all the affairs of life he built a clubhouse and brought Delmonico himself from Manhattan to preside over the dinners there. The Westchester Polo Club counted among its original members F. Gray Griswold, Colonel William Jay, Fairman Rogers, S. S. Howland, Frederic Bronson, Hermann Oelrichs, and August Belmont. The rules were borrowed from Hurlingham and Ranelagh; there were no restrictions as to the number of players to a side, and six or eight instead of the present four were common. Bennett also laid out the Newport polo field, where in 1886 the first International Match was played.

The greatest sponsor of American polo was the late Harry Payne Whitney. Beginning in 1909 when he captained the "Big Four" and brought the International Cup back from England, Whitney lent the game a new scientific skill. In 1911 and again in 1913 he brilliantly defended the Cup, and came to be rated as that *ne plus ultra,* a ten-goal player. His withdrawal after 1924 and death in 1930 left polo in the hands of his protégé Devereaux Milburn, a New York lawyer with an English schooling. He and his brother-in-law, Francis Skiddy von Stade, together with Whitneys, Harrimans, and Bostwicks, have helped keep Meadow Brook the capital of American polo. Among the best-known players are four grandsons of the late Henry Phipps, Hubert and Michael Phipps, and Winston and Raymond Guest—the latter being sons of Amy Phipps' marriage to the Right Hon. Frederick E. Guest, Secretary of State for Air 1921–22 and younger brother of Lord Wimborne. The greatest living poloist, maintaining consistently the ten-goal handicap, is Thomas Hitchcock, Jr. In the present day of individual brilliance and spectacular play before large galleries, he is undoubtedly America's best asset in this the most costly of land sports.[4]

The most expensive amusement known to society—if one may ignore baccarat, and bridge at ten cents a point[5]—is yachting. The term "yacht" correctly applies less to the design and equipment of a vessel than to its

[4]One of the infrequent attempts to bring polo to the masses is the Bethpage Polo and Riding Club, started on Long Island in 1932, and later helped by WPA labor. Its large membership and middle-class ineptitude have caused it to be despised in private, or else vaguely patronized, by the experts of Meadow Brook. The polo teams of most Army posts and of the large state universities in Middle and Far West are also socially negligible. Over 70 clubs and 2700 players are registered with the U. S. Polo Association.

[5]The social ethics of card games in America remains a minor but fruitful field for the historian of manners. Chastellux reports that during the Revolution fashionable Boston agreed not to play whist for money, though this rule was sometimes violated in men's clubs: "Bostonians like high play, and perhaps it is fortunate that the War came at this time to moderate a passion whose consequences had begun to be dangerous." In Philadelphia after the War Mrs. Bingham's set gambled heavily, "tea-and-cards" being a favorite occasion; not uncommonly a man or woman lost $300 to $400 at a sitting. Of New York Rebecca Franks reports in the later eighteenth century: "By the bye, few ladies here know how to entertain company in their own

The Radnor Hunt Club of Philadelphia

The Club House near Bryn Mawr, drawn by F. S. Coburn in 1895

exclusive use as a pleasure craft. In this sense the burghers of New Amsterdam sailed the first yachts in America up and down the Hudson. But the earliest yacht of which there is specific knowledge was the *Jefferson,* a 22-ton sloop built for Captain George Crowninshield, Jr., in 1801. He came from a noted line of China traders in Salem. Though brought up, as was the custom of merchants, with a common-school education which ended at the age of eleven, plus years of practical navigation, Captain Crowninshield prospered mightily and became a great swell. Dressed in elaborate waistcoats, exquisitely tailored small-clothes, and Hessian boots he frequently drove about Salem in a yellow curricle. For service in saving lives he had received the gold medal of the Massachusetts Humane Society. A bachelor with no domestic bonds, he finally decided to build a yacht which would serve as home for the rest of his life. In 1816 he commissioned Retire Becket to model a pleasure craft on the lines of the old *America,* fastest of the Crowninshield merchant fleet. At a cost of $50,000 the sumptuous vessel was constructed, called at first *Car of Concordia* and then in a happier moment *Cleopatra's Barge.* The owner gave free rein to his eccentricities, and painted one side of her hull in horizontal stripes of every color, and the other in herringbone pattern. As a pendant to the capstan was a wooden American Indian, life-size—which his crew later convinced pious Genoans was the effigy of a New World saint, so that several kissed its feet. The saloon of *Cleopatra's Barge,* 19 x 20 feet, with its handsome First Empire furniture covered with red velvet and gold lace, cost Captain Crowninshield an added $7000. So great a curiosity was she while moored at the Salem docks, that 900 people inspected her in a single day. But after a year's cruise to the Azores and along the Mediterranean, and the presentation of 300 letters of introduction to consuls and other officials, Captain

houses, unless they introduce the card-table . . . you enter the room with a formal, set curtsy, and after the how-dos, things are finished: all's a dead calm till the cards are introduced, when you see pleasure dancing in the eyes of all the matrons, and they seem to gain new life."

After attending a party at Mrs. James Monroe's, Mary Boardman Crowninshield writes to her mother, 24 February, 1816: "We played loo and I won—I am afraid to say how much, but shall give it to the orphan asylum." The same vestige of Puritan morality lingered on in various shapes; in memoirs of his childhood in Philadelphia Joseph Hergesheimer recalls "card packs whereon fruit replaced the customary wicked symbols." On the other hand as the *Dictionary of American Biography* informs us, Elbert H. Gary refused to play cards "because he believed it below the dignity of the head of the U. S. Steel Corporation."

Crowninshield died in 1817. Sold at auction, converted into a packet-ship, and finally taken across the Pacific, *Cleopatra's Barge* ended her career before wreckage upon a reef as the royal yacht of His Majesty Kamehameha I, King of the Sandwich Islands.

During the 1830's a number of small sailing vessels for pleasure were built for Boston merchants and shippers like R. B. Forbes and John P. Cushing. But the keenest devotee of yachting during these years was John C. Stevens, son of a prosperous New Jersey lawyer who had built a mansion on Castle Point, Hoboken and experimented with steam navigation along with his friends Chancellor Livingston and Nicholas J. Roosevelt and a promising inventor named Fulton. Young Stevens spent his boyhood on the water. In his letter of farewell and resignation as first Commodore of the New York Yacht Squadron in 1855 he wrote: "I have been a yacht owner for more than half a century, commencing in 1802, as builder, captain, cook, and all hands of the celebrated yacht *Diver*—nine feet long, three feet wide, and three feet deep—and ending as commodore of a squadron whose flagship carries her pennant 150 feet above the surface of the sea." He was the prime mover in organizing the New York Yacht Club, which first met aboard his yacht *Gimcrack* July 30, 1844, and comprised Hamilton Wilkes, owner of *Spray;* William Edgar, *Cygnet*; John C. Jay, *La Coquille;* George L. Schuyler, *Dream;* James M. Waterbury, *Minna;* Louis A. Depau, *Mist;* James Rogers, *Ida;* and George B. Rollins, *Petrel.* Stevens spent his time between Livingston Manor on the Hudson, where he moved after marriage to Maria C. Livingston, and the Elysian Fields, an amusement park along the waterfront at Hoboken which he and his brother had opened in 1831. Here "a handsome Gothic cottage" was built by Stevens as the first clubhouse of the N. Y. Y. C., where high feasts were eaten with turtle as the prime favorite and a famous punch brewed by the Commodore himself. Numerous regattas were held each summer in Long Island Sound, and with growing enterprise expeditions farther afield even to Cape Hatteras.

Others outside New York were taking up pleasure-sailing during this decade. In 1848 Joseph C. Hart, U. S. consul at Santa Cruz, beguiled the hours between rum punches by writing apparently the first American book on the subject, *The Romance of Yachting.* This volume is not in itself notable, except that in the course of his musings Mr. Hart was the first to question the ascription of Shakespeare's plays to William Shakespeare—and thus blew up the Baconian tempest, which has enriched psychiatry rather more than scholarship. Meanwhile the Royal Yacht Squadron at Cowes had conferred the utmost British accolade upon this sport, and in 1851 in connection with the first World's Fair in London offered the Queen's Cup for a difficult race around the Isle of Wight. Hearing of this prize Commodore Stevens, Edwin A. Stevens, Hamilton Wilkes, George Schuyler, and J. Beekman Finley commissioned George Steers, son of a Devonshire shipwright, to design a vessel of radically new style. The celebrated yacht *America* was the result. Her sensational victory, sale to Lord de Blaquiere, years of obscurity, service as a Confederate blockade-runner, and ultimate conversion into a U. S. naval school ship, are well known. Meanwhile her former owners presented the *America's* Cup to the N. Y. Y. C. as "a perpetual challenge cup for friendly competition between foreign countries." Later events were to prove the singular irony of that phrase.

The New York Yacht Club, at its inception a small band of friends of chiefly Knickerbocker stock with the income and leisure needed for this princely sport, decreed under expansion certain social criteria. Yet it was not too snobbish to accept the popular actor W. E. Burton, who in 1855 offered a prize in a regatta from Glen Cove Harbor. The conduct of members and would-be members was perhaps more closely scrutinized than their pedigrees. Thus on the eve of the Civil War the N. Y. Y. C. expelled Captain William C. Corrie when it heard "that a cargo of upwards of 300 negroes from the coast of Africa had been landed in Georgia from the *Wanderer* . . . a traffic repugnant to humanity and the moral sense of the members of this association." In 1872 it blackballed G. H. Beling because of suspicion that he had shifted the ballast of his sloop during races; henceforth he adopted two black balls as his signal on the *Meta,* and entered her for all possible prizes. The most celebrated member of the N. Y. Y. C. who recouped himself from disgrace was James Gordon Bennett, Jr. Soon after admission he raced his sloop *Rebecca* around Long Island on June 24, 1858, and took a short cut through Plum Gut instead of through the Race. It was an arduous rather than canny stratagem, but he was disqualified chiefly because older members still loathed his father and expected the worst from the son. Undismayed, young Bennett bought the schooner *Henrietta,* and began to lay heavy bets upon her, which he won or lost with equal nonchalance. In December, 1866, he entered her in the most spectacular race in the history of American yachting—the great transatlantic contest to the Needles for a purse of $90,000 put up triply by George and Franklyn Osgood with *Fleetwing,* Pierre Lorillard, Jr. with *Vesta,* and Bennett with his winning *Henrietta.* Through the wintry seas they battled, with one serious mishap, when on December 19 the *Fleetwing,* scudding before a heavy gale, took a sea aboard which washed six of the crew out of the cock-pit to their death. Tremendous publicity attended this race, and in consequence the membership of the N. Y. Y. C. almost doubled within the year. Bennett himself was unanimously elected Vice-Commodore in 1868. In the summer of 1870 he raced the challenger for the *America's* Cup, James Ashbury's *Cambria,* all the way across the Atlantic, and though beaten through a miscalculation of distance did have the satisfaction of coming in ahead of her in the Cup race. In 1871 Ashbury again challenged, was beaten once more, and protested so vigorously that the three cups he had formerly given to the N. Y. Y. C. were curtly returned to him by Bennett, now Commodore.

A minor social crisis was precipitated in 1881 when a little club in Ontario, the Bay of Quinte Yacht Club, challenged for the *America's* Cup to gain publicity. Canadians bitterly resented the aspersions of New York journalists "that the social position of the members of the N. Y. Y. C. was, perhaps, rather more elevated than that of the members of the challenging club." After defeating these Ontario upstarts members of the N. Y. Y. C. took care, by changing the rules of competition, that they should not challenge soon again. Hermann Oelrichs, A. Cass Canfield, Ogden Goelet, and the Lorillards were among its keenest yachtsmen and prize-donors during this era. The ninth challenge in 1895 caused a painful quarrel between Lord Dunraven, whose *Valkyrie* was beaten, and C. Oliver Iselin whose crew it was alleged had sailed the *Defender* on a longer water line than the one officially measured. After a committee appointed by the N. Y. Y. C. had exonerated Iselin, Lord Dunraven's continued protests brought expulsion from honorary membership in the New York club—though he tried to forestall this by cabling his resignation. It was the most disagreeable episode in the social relations of America and England during the nineties. A day of greater good will dawned with the five challenging *Shamrocks* of Sir Thomas Lipton, who because he had started his business with a small grocery store and hence was branded as a "tradesman" for life, was blackballed for thirty years by the Royal Yacht Squadron—though warmly sponsored by King Edward VII, and long an honored member of the N. Y. Y. C. Not until the eve of his eighty-first birthday, five months before his death, did Sir Thomas cease to be "in trade" in the eyes of the old guard at Cowes— and win the privilege of flying the white ensign service flag of the British Navy. The last race in 1934 when Harold S. Vanderbilt's *Rainbow* beat T. O. M. Sopwith's *Endeavour* was not without its ruffled feelings. Rather significantly, a complimentary dinner arranged for Sopwith by the "American British Friendly Relations Society" was cancelled when guests learned that no such organization existed.

Other and less famous yacht clubs might be named, like the Southern Yacht Club founded at New Orleans in 1849 for sailing open boats on Lake Pontchartrain, the Brooklyn Yacht Club in 1857 to which the midget Tom Thumb belonged and sailed the *Maggie B.* with a crew of Bridgeport fishermen, and the Boston Yacht Club begun in 1865 which has gained glory through the *Puritan* and other famous boats. In 1867 the San Francisco Yacht Club was started, and in 1871 the well-known Seawanhaka Yacht Club—which later, to show its devotion to amateur or "Corinthian" principles, added that title to its name.[6] Blackballed in actuality by the Eastern Yacht Club and potentially by the New York Yacht Club whose dictatorship remained in the background, Jay Gould founded the American Yacht Club, which came to be patronized chiefly by owners of steam yachts like his own *Atalanta*. The steam yacht was the product of an age of luxury and fabulously rich capitalism. Its precursor had been Commodore Vanderbilt's wooden side-wheel passenger steamer *North Star* of 2000 tons, which after his family cruise of 1853 he turned over to regular passenger service. William H. Aspinwall's *Firefly*, Leonard W. Jerome's *Clarita*, William Astor's *Nourmahal*, and E. S. Stokes's *Fra Diavolo*, were later examples. The upkeep of James Gordon Bennett's *Namouna* was reported awesomely to run to $150,000 annually, while Anna Gould and her husband Boni de Castellane bought the equally grand *Valhalla* in 1897 but it was seized three years later by

[6]The list might be almost indefinitely extended. As early as 1874 a small but fairly complete register of American yachts was published in New York. In 1903 the first Lloyd's Register of American Yachts appeared, and quickly became standard. Today there are some 450 yacht clubs in North America.

Society and Sport

Castellane's creditors. The U. S. Government in 1891 temporarily impounded the *Conqueror*, bought by Frederick W. Vanderbilt in England, and six years later the Payne Bill was passed by Congress in a vain hope of protecting American shipbuilders against competition from Hull and Kiel. To many millionaires foreign-built yachts had a much smarter cachet. Today among the best-known yachts are Vincent Astor's *Nourmahal*, General Cornelius Vanderbilt's *Winchester*, William K. Vanderbilt's *Alva*, J. P. Morgan's *Corsair*, and Mrs. Joseph E. Davies's *Hussar* which like its owner lately changed its name and became the *Sea Cloud*.

In July, 1844, Hone observed "a gay, saucy-looking squadron of schooner yachts lying off the Battery," and added: "The arrival of the squadron at Newport will, of course, occasion a sensation among the company there, and serve to relieve the monotony of a tolerably dull place of sojournment." Newport, long the summer capital of society, is linked with the social pageantry of yachting as is no other American resort. It was founded by William Coddington, disciple of Anne Hutchinson, in the spring of 1639 for the professed end of attaining a more democratic government in New England. By the next century it was doing a thriving trade in rum, molasses, and negroes, attracting Sephardic merchants from Portugal and Spain, and creating an atmosphere of art, learning, and idealism. Most magnificent of the traders was Captain Godfrey Malbone, born in Virginia; according to tradition he once entertained George Washington at Newport, and in the midst of conviviality the future President broke a bowl, and paid for it on the spot with £4. Here his grandson the miniaturist Edward G. Malbone grew up, as did the elder and even greater artist Gilbert Stuart.[7] Revolutionary visitors of the French aristocracy like Lauzun and the Prince de Broglie were charmed by its hostesses, the Hunters, the Champlains, Polly Lawton the Quakeress, and wrote of "that charming place regretted by the whole army." But the British sacked the town, wealthier citizens moved to Providence, and in 1788 Brissot reported, "Newport seems to me a tomb where living skeletons quarrelled over a few herbs." Its commerce never wholly recovered, but by about 1830 Newport came to be known as a pleasant summer resort. A handful of South Carolina and Georgia aris-

[7]For an account of this little known period see William B. Weeden, "Ideal Newport in the Eighteenth Century," *Proceedings American Antiquarian Society*, vol. 18 N. S., pp. 106–117.

tocrats arrived, and William Beach Lawrence of New York built the first "cottage" on Ochre Point. In preference to Nahant a circle of New England intellectuals began spending their vacations here—Bancroft, Longfellow, the elder Agassiz, Professors Gibbs and Pumpelly, and for one summer the parents of Henry Cabot Lodge. A little later came Julia Ward Howe, Clarence King, John Singer Sargent, and Henry James who many years later recalled its all-year colony of "slightly disenchanted" cosmopolites: "Where in the world, the hard American world, they *could* have hibernated, how they could even, in the season, have bowed their economic heads and lurked, if it hadn't been for Newport . . . over their winter whist, under their private theatricals, and pending constantly their loan and their return of the *Revue des Deux Mondes.*" Today Mrs. Maude Howe Elliott, daughter of Julia Ward Howe and one of the few townspeople whom visiting Society never dared snub, is the last descendant of that generation.

But destruction of the old order had long hung imminent. In 1846 the Ocean House had been opened with a fancy-dress ball, by subscription at $10 a ticket, and henceforth each summer witnessed at least one fête for Southern and Manhattan grandees. The Civil War eliminated the former, but ushered in the régime of Ward McAllister, Mrs. August Belmont, Mrs. Archibald Gracie King, and Mrs. Astor. Real estate boomed; great palaces of stone arose; trees were at such a premium that Miss Katherine Lorillard Wolfe and others transplanted full-grown elms, and reserved the right to remove all foliage upon sale of their villas. Matrons in demi-daumonts made by Binder drove glitteringly down Bellevue Avenue. In 1880 the U. S. Navy, largely through the influence of Admiral Luce, undertook to solve Newport's perennial shortage of men by establishing here a war college and torpedo station—at least the colony complacently ascribed to it that motive.

From 1890 to 1914, when Newport loved to boast that even the best newcomer needed at least four seasons to get "in," a new social phenomenon was created in America—a clique formed not by natural propinquity, intellectual interests, common background or family tradition, but quite artificially by the repute of exclusiveness. Although the Four Hundred of New York remained its core, in the way that Palm Beach has been essentially Philadelphian, yet the rich and ambitious from a score of American cities here sought anchorage. The Pembroke Joneses

Photograph by Morris Rosenfeld
Harold Vanderbilt at the wheel of the cup winner *Enterprise*, Newport, 1930

Left: Dyson Moore, Col. William Jay, and Isaac G. Beresford.   *Right:* Elbridge T. Gerry's yacht.
Mrs. James Kernochen, center
Both photographs from the Harold Seton Collection

From a photograph by the Associated Press
The tally-ho of Mr. F. Ambrose Clark arriving at the estate of Mr. Hugh A. Murray,
Roslyn, L. I., with a group of friends for the United Hunts Meet, May 20, 1933

From the Depths

From a drawing by Wm. Balfour Ker originally published in "The Silent War," by John Ames Mitchell.

Society and Sport

from the rice-fields of North Carolina, the Berwinds with millions from Pennsylvania coal, Paul J. Rainey the Ohio coke operator and big-game hunter, and the Leedses from Indiana who had converted tin plate into gold, were representative. Other than social consciousness the only bond which drew this summer colony together was sport—which might consist of sailing around Block Island, or having cocktails upon one's steam yacht reached by motor-boat from the landing of the New York Yacht Club, or bathing at Bailey's Beach or the Gooseberry Island Club, or tennis on the Casino courts. For more than a generation the horse played little part in the milieu of Newport—which was avoided by strenuous sportsmen like Thomas Hitchcock and the Whitneys in favor of shooting-lodges in the Adirondacks or polo-fields abroad. But lately with the horse-shows and gymkhanas of the Newport Riding Academy, run by two ex-grooms from the stables of society, the horse is growing markedly popular with youth. Notwithstanding, Newport remains the most sedentary of fashionable communities, for even in respect to yachting the steam vessel has supplanted the sailing ship, and except for regattas and Cup races the true social sea-dog seldom puts into its placid harbor. Rarely in the headlines as it was forty years ago, staid, correct, formal, loyally recruited from the old swells who look askance at the Hamptons and Bar Harbor, Newport lives in richly gouty senescence. Like an aged Gargantua or an unsleeping Gulliver it smiles indulgently at the few newly-rich grocers' wives and oleomargarine makers who think it worthwhile to clamber up its sides. Though it may feign languid motions of brushing them away, it is really flattered by the nostalgia which they bring of its Golden Day. There is no better symbol of the Twilight of the Social Gods.

CHAPTER TWELVE

THE SELF-JUSTIFICATIONS
OF SOCIETY

IN WASHINGTON in February, 1936, Mr. J. P. Morgan, relaxing from the ordeal of another investigation, told reporters: "If you destroy the leisure class, you destroy civilization. . . . By the leisure class I mean the families who employ one servant, 25,000,000 or 30,000,000 families." The president of the Housewives League of America and a dozen editors immediately seized upon the blurred and magnified image which Mr. Morgan had of American domesticity—pointing out that according to the 1930 census there were less than 30,000,000 families in the whole United States, and fewer than 2,000,000 cooks and other servants to attend them all. But Mr. Morgan's cardinal belief was much more important than his statistics. The relation between leisure and civilization has fascinated a great many thinkers from Plato to Thorstein Veblen. In America it was argued with greatest heat just before the Civil War, when all the rationale of slavery seemed to hinge upon the answer; today it is inseparable from the claims of Marxism. If the mazes of that argument are too long here to trace, one can at least point out certain bonds which unite the social plutocracy to art, music, letters, learning, philanthropy, public service, and religion in America.

Opera, that rather showy hybrid, was long the special pet of American society. After elaborate dinners it offered what Henry James called "the only approach to the implication of the tiara known to the American law"; thirty years ago he termed it "the great vessel of social salvation."[1]

---

[1] In *The American Scene* with his usual felicity James described a lavish dinner-party, with ladies in tiaras and a semblance of court-trains, but—in the slang of the time—"all dressed up and nowhere to go." He wrote: "There was nothing for us to do at eleven o'clock—or for the ladies at least—but to scatter and go to bed. There was nothing, as in London or in Paris, to go 'on' to; the going 'on' is, for the New York aspiration, always the stumbling-block. A great court-function would alone have met the strain, met the terms of the case—would alone properly have crowned the hour." He adds that the opera season helps to assuage, at least in part, this republican emptiness.

The Self-Justifications of Society

In that, the first decade of the present century, grand opera achieved its most fashionable standing, and not in the United States alone but in Germany, where quite apart from the special cult of Bayreuth the opera season in Berlin assumed the aspect of a court function, and in England where it was said of the reigning monarch, Edward VII, that "he only talked freely when he went to the opera."[2] Every city developed its pet conventions. In New York for example Monday night was smarter than the rest of the week for opera-going, because in the '70's and '80's Mrs. Astor and Ward McAllister had chosen Monday evenings for Patriarchs, Assembly Balls, and Family Circle Dancing Classes. Hence on every Monday night between New Year's Day and Lent the *ton* dined, attended the opera in full regalia, and then went on to waltzes and cotillions. It was also the fashion to wait until the second intermission to go out and smoke or visit other boxes—partly because going out at the first intermission savored of vulgar impatience, and partly because one had only just arrived, coming late being also *de rigueur*. Opera-glasses were made by Lemaire, and one famous pair surmounted by a lyre encrusted with diamonds and sapphires cost $75,000.

The first performance of any opera in America seems to have been the English ballad-opera of *Flora, or Hob in the Well,* in Charleston in 1735; a little later Annapolis, Baltimore, New York, and Philadelphia sponsored others of the same kind. Although wealthy planters and merchants naturally bought the best seats, there seems to have been no seasonal subscription, no building exclusively for opera, and no company of singers beyond itinerant troupes and amateurs. Thus whatever social aureole was created about music surrounded concert societies like the St. Cecilia in Charleston and the Orpheus Club of Philadelphia, founded 1759: usually at the fashionable hour of half-past six they gave concerts vocal or instrumental before "a very polite company." Not until the rise of French and Italian opera late in the eighteenth century did society begin to lend its special patronage. The Creole aristocracy of New Orleans made that city the capital of opera in America up to the Civil War. First

[2]His Majesty probably had never read Hill's *Manual of Social and Business Forms,* published in America in 1887: "In an exaltation of sentiment that lifts the spirit almost out of the body, the ear attuned to the lingering melody hears some commonplace voice remark, 'We had puddin' for dinner yesterday.' Mrs. Stowe relates that she once attended a concert where, just as the music had sunk to a calm of sweetest melody, she heard a female voice say, 'I always cook mine in vinegar.'"

had come the Théâtre de St. Pierre with its first grand opera in 1791. It was supplanted in 1808 by the St. Philippe, built at a cost of $100,000 and containing a parquet with two tiers of boxes. Then came the Théâtre d'Orléans, with grilled loges for those in mourning, and finally in 1859 the famous French Opera House designed by James Gallier the younger. For two generations its horseshoe of boxes glittered with the jewels of Latin and American society, until before the Great War it lost caste, was badly neglected, and finally burned in 1919. In New Orleans an evening of opera began traditionally at six-thirty and lasted till eleven or midnight; in the narrow streets congestion before and after performances was so great that elbowings, treading upon ladies' toes, and supposed insults not infrequently led to the Duelling Oaks on a morning after the opening night. Also the easy accessibility of gambling dens sometimes caused the sudden disappearance of escorts.

Italian opera, closely followed by French, stood at the forefront of fashion during the nineteenth century; English companies always drew larger but much less select audiences, though seldom did English and Italian troupes wage outright war as they did in Chicago during the season 1859–60. The snob loved to sleep through the more soporific rhythms of a foreign language, while the plain man with an inherited touch of John Bull professed to deride all such folderol. During the Civil War even Emerson wrote in his journal regarding grand opera and its orchestra: "Politics, bankruptcy, frost, famine, war,—nothing concerns them but a scraping on a catgut, or tooting on a bass French horn."

Italian grand opera first reached New York as early as 1810 with a performance of Paisiello, but the first great opera troupe to establish itself there was Nathaniel De Luce's company at the Park Theatre, beginning November 29, 1825. It was sponsored by the great swell Dominick Lynch, and graced on the opening night by the presence of an ex-king, Joseph Bonaparte. *The Evening Post* said, "An assemblage of ladies so fashionable, so numerous, & so elegantly dressed, was probably never witnessed in our theatre." With such encouragement Lynch, Philip Hone, Gerard Coster, G. C. Howland, John C. Cruger, and a few others subscribed $6000 apiece for boxes in the Italian Opera House at Leonard and Church streets which was opened in November, 1833, under the direction of Rivafinole. On the exterior, as Hone noted, it was "very plain and unpretending, and the subscribers' money has not been spent to please the eyes of non-subscribers." But the interior was a different matter. The floors were all handsomely carpeted, and the ground of the front boxes was white, with medallions and octagonal panels of crimson, blue, and gold. The owners of the twenty boxes in the second tier had not only the privilege of a total of 116 free tickets for each night, all transferable, but also the right to decorate their own boxes as they pleased. One vied with another in magnificence—in rich silk ornaments, paintings in fresco, satin cushions, arm-chairs and sofas in diverse colors. Yet despite the great outlay this formidable horseshoe had undeniably what *Hudibras* would have called "an odd promiscuous tone." Hone reports that many people soon tired of their self-created magnificence, and quietly slipped back to plainer but less invidious seats at the Park Theatre, and this fact coupled with ruinous management plunged the Italian Opera House into bankruptcy after two seasons.

With scant formal patronage from society opera kept on at Niblo's Garden and the old Broadway Theatre. In 1845 an impresario named Palmo with a good orchestra and an able company tried his hand, failed utterly, and fainted away in the lobby when a deputy sheriff impounded the box-office receipts of the closing night. Then in 1847 society once more undertook the sponsorship of grand opera when 150 New Yorkers of wealth and prestige subscribed to build the Astor Place Opera House— "a species of peerage of the fashionable society of New York, containing the birth, parentage, life, occupation, and pursuit of those who have organized society in New York on a similar footing as it exists in the high circles of the great capitals of Europe," as a reporter wrote with more grandeur than lucidity. An ornate chandelier shut out a view of the stage from the uncomfortable fifty-cent seats, and further discrimination was achieved by rules of admission which required freshly-shaven faces, evening dress, white waistcoats, and kid gloves for gentlemen. Many commonplace music-lovers fell into line, for soon *The Herald* was observing: "The élite are carrying everything their own way and even the *canaille* are washing their faces, shaving themselves, and having their hair cut and pomatumed, and what is more, are actually putting on white kids and seating themselves in any and every part of the house where they can procure a seat for love or money. Boors are becoming gentlemen by the influence of sweet sounds and a congregation of beautiful faces." We also learn that the beneficent function of opera was not wholly in the direction of social settlement work, for "as a place for well dressed and genteel people to congregate in on a cold evening the opera house seems to possess great advantages."

Yet after a blaze of glory the Astor Place Opera House closed before the end of its first season, in April, 1848, with twenty performances still due its subscribers, and was taken over by Niblo and Hackett for legiti-

The Great Riot at Astor Place Opera House, May 10, 1849.
Engraved by W. N. Dunnel
New York Public Library

mate drama. Then in the following spring, May 10, 1849, the British actor Macready's feud with his American rival Forrest[3] touched off a long-explosive popular indignation against the Opera House which had

[3]Macready had added fuel to the flame by his scorn of American vulgarity. "Let me die in a ditch in England, rather than in the Fifth Avenue of New York here," he cried. In reprisal for his remarks on Cincinnati, while he was playing Hamlet in that robust city "a ruffian from the gallery threw into the middle of the stage the half of the raw carcass of a sheep." Forrest on the other hand had lately been playing such rôles as Jack Cade, Spartacus, and Metamora, in which he appeared as the champion of the masses against entrenched privilege, and in private life also shrewdly played up his defiant Americanism. Greeley's *Tribune* with its supposed "socialism" had gone beyond the traditional badinage of *The Herald* in inflaming class consciousness; after the Riot the latter commented self-righteously: "To ridicule and expose the follies . . . of certain portions of the opulent classes of society is one thing, to denounce them as robbers and tyrants another."

enforced clean faces and white waistcoats. A mob collected at the doors of the building, roaring "Tear it down! Burn the damned den of the aristocracy!" One man in the crowd cried bitterly, "You can't go in there without kid gloves on. I paid for a ticket and they wouldn't let me in because I hadn't kid gloves and a white vest, damn them!" To a protesting fop in evening clothes a Bowery boy answered blithely: "To hell with you! America rules England tonight, by Jesus!" Clubs appeared, while brick-bats and paving stones hurtled through the air, shattering windows and reverberating in the ears of the pale Macready—who got through his performance, and was smuggled through a back-door and thence out of town. Meanwhile a detachment of troops, sixty cavalry and three hundred infantry, was dispatched immediately, with another soon to follow. Their arrival was greeted with showers of brick-bats and abuse. "Under this provocation," wrote Hone, "with the sanction of the civil authorities, orders were given to fire. There or four volleys were discharged; about twenty persons were killed and a large number wounded. It is to be lamented that in the number were several innocent persons, as is always the case in such affairs . . . although the lesson has been dearly bought, it is of great value, inasmuch as the fact has been established that law and order can be maintained under a Republican form of government."

Opera first struck deep root in social New York at the Academy of Music, 14th Street and Irving Place, opened October 2, 1854. In the beginning it contained six large proscenium boxes, which belonged to stockholders. This number was too limited, and when the Academy was rebuilt after the fire of 1866 the boxes were increased to eighteen, though the three upper boxes on each side of the stage were never very fashionable. In the '70's these boxes were occupied by the families of Pierre Lorillard, William R. Travers, August Belmont, Henry G. Stebbins, Sheppard Gandy, S. L. M. Barlow, Isaac Townsend, Isaac Bell, Robert L. Cutting, and Louis Hoffman, and by Messrs. Lazarus, Coles, Heckscher, Dinsmore, Garner, and Lukemeyer. Late comers, like some of these last named, had to take less desirable ones. By the year 1880 it was seen that the number of possible box-holders had again been outgrown by ambitious wealth; crusty oligarchs refused as much as $30,000 for a box. Parvenus, led by William K. and Cornelius Vanderbilt, did the inevitable and built their own house, the Metropolitan Opera. The entry of the Vanderbilts into society on March 26, 1883, as previously explained, antedated the apportionment of boxes in the new Opera House by only two months and helped greatly to assure the social future of their project. Meanwhile other newcomers like Darius O. Mills, William Rockefeller, Collis P. Huntington, George F. Baker, and Jay Gould were proud to join forces with older families like the Roosevelts and the Astors who had taken no permanent *pied à terre* at the Academy of Music. On the opening night, October 22, *The New York Dramatic Mirror* reported: "The Goulds and the Vanderbilts and people of that ilk perfumed the air with the odor of crisp greenbacks. The tiers of boxes looked like cages in a menagerie of monopolists." There were two rows of boxes, held to be of equal social prominence, called the Golden Horseshoe by reporters, who estimated the wealth there represented at $540,000,000. After the fire of 1892 the inner circle of the Metropolitan Opera, now secure of itself with the decay of the old Academy, decided to consolidate its gains by reducing the double-horseshoe to thirty-five luxurious parterre boxes at $60,000 each, soon styled the Diamond Horseshoe. The grand tier and stall boxes at the Metropolitan, like the six upper boxes in the Academy of Music, were and are socially second-class—which in society means worse than nothing, so that if one loves prestige more than music he would do better to stay at home.

After this reduction in the number of stockholders, a parterre box at the Metropolitan—which was either hereditary or else the result of purchase from an original investor—remained up to the Great War the most luscious of social plums. In 1903 Henry T. Sloane supplied the gold and deep maroon décor which has now become traditional; the fact that he also held a box, No. 13, in the sacred circle caused *Town Topics* to remark: "In what other country could we find the society man and the upholsterer combined in the one person—the man occupying on an opera gala night a box draped with curtains made in his own shop?" The same magazine later observed that in the heyday of the Metropolitan Opera "millionaires would willingly crawl on hands and knees up the red velvet stairs to the Diamond Horseshoe and feel that the dust accumulated on their knees in the painful Odyssey was a hallmark of social progress." Today the *santa scala* has become much less alluring to the socially devout, though Opening Night can still muster a few tiaras, orchids, and ermines for flashlight photography. It is still taken with moderate seriousness by the Old Guard—Goelets, Vanderbilts, Webbs, Kanes, Shermans, Gillespies—and by sincere patrons of music like the Juilliards and Mrs. Vincent Astor. A sprinkling of the ambitious, Manvilles, Jelkes, and McCanns, have bought boxes within the past ten years to catch the aroma of a fast evaporating perfume. But today considerable financial support comes from endowment, notably the Juilliard Foundation, and from popular subscription. The Metropolitan Opera Guild, now in its fourth year under the capable presidency of Mrs. August Belmont (Eleanor Robson), has canvassed for new patrons among non-season subscribers. Though society will long cherish a sentimental feeling for the Diamond Horseshoe, as it clings to Newport and the Junior Assembly, it is unlikely that setting suns will ever rise again upon the same social horizon. Beyond deep-seated causes like the crumbling of old solidarity and leadership, three specific reasons may be assigned: the increasing practice of sub-leasing which has sold exclusiveness down the river, the greater number of performances each season, and sharp competition from other forms of musical entertainment and the theatre.[4]

If Opera as an institution has declined in society, the social position of individual singers has risen appreciably. In the nineties Eduard and Jean de Reszke, with their aristocratic manners and name, were regarded as a unique duality because they were invited to smart little suppers at Mrs. Ogden Mills's. In 1903 the fact that the late Mrs. William Osgood Field (then Lilian Sloane), daughter of Mr. and Mrs. William D. Sloane, had invited Geraldine Farrar to a social gathering at her mother's house caused a considerable amount of friendly gossip, as that was then regarded as a rather daring innovation, even though Miss Farrar was the favorite of European royalty. Today the social hostess is highly flattered to have her invitations accepted by an operatic star like Lucrezia Bori or a great actress like Katherine Cornell; distinguished artists are now in a position to snub social lights, and not infrequently do. For more than forty years, however, the favorite lecturer on music and giver of musicales in New York has been Albert Morris Bagby, who belongs to the Metropolitan Club and lives at the Waldorf—under whose sponsorship in 1892 he began his "Musical Mornings," after Julia Ward Howe had introduced him at Newport. He shortly came to be the Orpheus of the Four Hundred. His

---

[4]Irving Kolodin, *The Metropolitan Opera: 1883–1935,* New York, 1936, offers a full discussion of these reasons and on pp. 425–26 compares the personnel of the original Diamond Horseshoe with that of today.

causeries on musical appreciation gave one a sense of vicarious knowledge and comfort, like Bishop Potter's sermons on Heaven.

The theatre has never lent itself to concerted patronage in the manner of grand opera, being more irregular and individualistic. As early as 1838 Buckingham reported of Philadelphia: "There are three large theatres, one of which is closed, and the other two but occasionally opened; these are not much frequented by the more opulent and intelligent classes, but are sustained by the middle and humbler ranks. Music is more cultivated and better supported."[5] And he mentions a Musical Fund Society, which appears to have been an early type of civic symphony. In Boston, with Puritan apology for the fine arts, the traditional theatre is named the Boston Museum, while opera was long held in a vast barn, associated with dog and poultry shows, called Mechanics' Hall. The most noted sponsorship of music by Brahminism came after 1881–82 when Major Henry Lee Higginson founded the Boston Symphony; its socially elect performances were those on Friday afternoons.

In San Francisco five years after the Gold Rush the bonanza kings built an opera house with silk-curtained boxes from which their wives might learn the manège of a lorgnette—even as the miners in Central City, Colorado, in 1878 lavishly subscribed to build the Opera House with its stone walls two feet thick and classic frescoes done by a wandering artist from San Francisco, which still stands in that ghost-town and serves as the mise-en-scène for the annual festival of music and drama which during the past five years has caused incessant·quarrels and irreparable wounds among the sponsoring aristocracy of Denver. In San Francisco a new and grander Opera House arose in 1873, built by Wade, with a capacity of 4000. After many vicissitudes opera is still regarded respectfully in San Francisco; upon the Opening Night of 1936–37 the *Argonaut's* society editor reported: "Certainly the smartest party after the opening

---

[5]To avoid misconception it should be added that in modern times, and especially after informal dinners, the theatre is highly favored by Society, but that such patronage—while extremely important financially—is unorganized. It would be equally unfair to assume that music and social snobbery have ever depended upon each other to a vital degree. The passion for music easily transcends red plush and ormolu. Talleyrand found "on the banks of the Ohio River, in a house built of roughly hewn logs, a piano, adorned with really beautiful bronzes. When Monsieur de Beaumetz opened it Mr. Smith said to him, 'Don't try to play on it, because our piano-tuner, who lives a hundred miles away, didn't come this year.' " A traveller in Colorado in 1878 observed a Chickering piano in a miner's tent at Leadville.

performance of the opera was that given by Mrs. John Drum at her penthouse on the Fairmont roof. This brought together the cream which had risen on the top of the evening's social milk." In Atlanta the palmy days of opera came twenty years ago, when Caruso was hired for a series of engagements, and the Georgia gentry sat in their boxes during intermissions sipping bottled Coca-Cola through a straw.

Chicago's first Grand Opera House was destroyed by the Great Fire. To offer housing to a troupe soon due after that catastrophe, Ferdinand Peck, young social and financial leader, son of a self-made millionaire of the fifties, improvised the Michigan Central Railway Station for opera, with 1400 seats and a tier of boxes. In 1888–89 under his sponsorship the Auditorium was built for opera and other civic activities; it was designed with startling simplicity by the great architect Louis Sullivan. An impressive ceremony, with the assistance of President Benjamin Harrison, Vice-President Morton, and other dignitaries was planned for the opening. The Pecks were just erecting a magnificent town house on Michigan Avenue, and because it was still in the hands of masons and carpenters George M. Pullman let fall the suggestion that he would be host to President Harrison. When this report reached the ears of Mr. Peck he exclaimed with true American enterprise, "Does any one think that I am going to let George Pullman, who hasn't a dollar in the Auditorium, have the President, just because my house isn't finished? Not much!" And so by a miracle of energy worthy of that king who created the Hanging Gardens for his consort, Mr. Peck evoked a mansion in which his wife worthily entertained President Harrison, while the Auditorium was dedicated with Adelina Patti singing "Home, Sweet Home." For the next forty years it housed grand opera, though the official Grand Opera Company of Chicago was not organized until 1910, under the patronage of such names as Ryerson, Armour, Dawes, and Insull. The archangel of winter opera was later found in the person of Harold Fowler McCormick, who for many years generously met all deficits. In 1922 Samuel Insull—a sponsor who, like Otto Kahn in New York and Edward T. Stotesbury in Philadelphia, was not averse to enjoying the social rewards of all good Medicis—undertook to bring opera to the masses with his Civic Opera Company. With methods of high-pressure salesmanship, this aggressive Briton, whom England gave to Chicago in exchange for Gordon Selfridge, increased the list of guarantors to more than three thousand. Low-priced Sunday evening performances proved to be an excellent business scheme, and in harmony with the new democracy the rising Auditorium at 20 Wacker Drive abolished the aloof horseshoe of boxes in crimson and gold. The new boxes were half-way down, with simple décor, and offered no obstruction to anybody's view. The unwritten law of evening dress was also revoked. After a term of prosperity which later seemed less the bloom of health than a hectic flush, the Civic Opera fell like its master upon evil days. At present, under an Italian impresario who is struggling desperately with indifferent talent, opera in Chicago has ceased definitely to be fashionable.

The patronage of instrumental music and of painting in Chicago has enjoyed a much steadier and more intelligent direction. The Art Institute for example benefited by the long presidency (1882–1924) of B. P. Hutchinson, packer, banker, and grain-trader, whom friends regarded as a liberal and enemies as something of an iconoclast. In a speech he once declared: "The State has a right to demand from a man not only a part of his money, but also a tithe of his thought, his time, and his life." The Art Institute counted among its generous donors the first Mrs. Albert A. Sprague, Martin A. Ryerson, Chauncey McCormick, Mr. and Mrs. Frederick Clay Bartlett, Marshall and Henry Field, and Potter Palmer, Jr., who succeeded Hutchinson as president. In the intellectual life of social Chicago the influence of those literary sisters Margaret Ayer Barnes and Janet Ayer Fairbank should not be forgotten, nor of President Robert M. Hutchins and his artist wife born Maude Phelps McVeigh.

A significant change was wrought in Chicago society by the first Mrs. John Alden Carpenter, *née* Winterbotham, who as a girl had travelled much in Europe, knew Post-Impressionism as well as Renaissance masters, and first made art fashionable in that city. In contrast to the empty frivolity of the first Mrs. Potter Palmer, Mrs. Carpenter and her patrician composer husband created a society on fine arts and intellect. Today the presidency of the Arts Club represents a very desirable social leadership. It is now held by Mrs. Charles B. Goodspeed, who with great charm but less knowledge builds her parties about the admiring musicians like Horowitz, Milstein, and Egon Petri, and enjoys the friendship of Continental painters beginning with the great Picasso, who delight in her as "la belle sauvage Américaine." Once when all the Monte Carlo Ballet save Massine had seceded from Mrs. Goodspeed to assist at a more hysterically gay party given by her rival Betty Field, writer for Hearst newspapers, that forlorn hostess was advised by her friend Gertrude Stein: "Remember that Russians always need the knout. Never make the mistake of fraternizing with artists—*command* them!" Mrs. Walter Brewster, though failing to best Mrs. Goodspeed for the presidency of the Arts Club, is also something of an oracle on art. Not long ago she was consulted by hitherto unknown neighbors, heirs of Lady Esther cosmetics, who had sent an agent to Soviet Russia to try to buy for them a Leonardo da Vinci. Mrs. Arthur Meeker, wife of a dull but friendly broker for the packing companies, also loves the *beaux arts* and the circle which in Chicago is called "fashionable Bohemia." The term "Bohemian" has a less happy connotation in London, where it implies the seedy phase of Soho ateliers. Not long ago the Meekers gave a dinner for Lady Sibyl Colefax, greatest lion-hunter of Mayfair, who has at her beck and call the leading statesmen, painters, sculptors, poets, and novelists of the empire. As the dinner drew to a close Mr. Meeker rose with his glass of champagne and said impressively, "Let us drink a toast—to the Queen of Bohemian society!" Lady Colefax looked at him for the fraction of a second with uncomprehension. Then brightening she remarked pleasantly, "Yes, let us drink to her, wherever she may be."

Society's patronage of painting in the United States has been acquisitive rather than creative. It has consisted largely in the purchase of Old Masters painted under the more virile stimulus of Italian princes and Dutch merchants of the Renaissance, and Tudor, Stuart, or Bourbon kings. When it has followed the judgment of an expert like Bernhard Berenson, buyer for Mrs. Jack Gardner, it has usually collected works of enduring beauty—even though they may fail to rhyme with any American craft or culture. Henry Clay Frick, Henry E. Huntington, and the elder J. P. Morgan bought under the guidance of connoisseurs, and since their death the public has been given a full or partial access to their treasures. The public also holds the promissory note of Andrew W. Mellon. On the other hand William Henry Vanderbilt paid $1,500,000 for Rosa Bonheurs, Bretons, Bougereaus, and Meissoniers whose sentimental pleasantries and pomps are now seen to be almost worthless. The enormously expensive collection made by the late Senator William A. Clark, the Pennsylvania farm-boy who became the mining king of Montana and built "Clark's Folly" on Fifth Avenue, contained so many banal paintings that the Metropolitan Museum refused to absorb it *in toto,* and it ultimately found a home in Washington's Corcoran Gallery. Yet the Metropolitan did assimilate the erratic and in some respects outmoded collection of Katherine Lorillard Wolfe. Some years ago H. G. Wells told of hearing a London picture-dealer rebuff a rich American spender with the words: "If you want a Botticelli that size, Mr. Record, I can't find it; you'll have to have it made for you."

In Colonial times the art of portrait-painting was richly supported by Society, and many artists were welcomed at aristocratic tables. John Smibert from Scotland married a minor heiress in Boston in 1730, and seems to have moved in the upper circles. In South Carolina during the same period Jeremiah Theus advertised that "gentlemen and ladies may have their pictures drawn"; he also married well, and dined with Izards and Manigaults. Benjamin West, of lowly Quaker stock, gained by his art the friendship of Governor Hamilton of Pennsylvania; upon going to England he fraternized with peers and royalty, and had a pedigree manufactured for him by none less than the Marquis of Buckingham, which connected him with the ancestors of Lord Delaware. John Singleton Copley, whose widowed mother kept a tobacconist's shop in Boston, so advanced the family fortune that his son became Lord Lyndhurst, Lord Chancellor of England. Charles Willson Peale started his career in desperate poverty as apprentice to a saddler; when art brought him fame and fortune he married Elizabeth de Peyster of New York. Gilbert Stuart, son of a New England snuff-maker, gained the patronage of the Duke of Northumberland and upon returning to America spent his later days as an honored guest of John Jay and the New York smart set. Today such rapid mounting in the social world through art is less possible; a few seasonal lions are tracked by occasional *safaris* of the fashionable, but in general American society since the death of Sargent has gone abroad to the more flattering Royal Academicians like the late Sir William Orpen, or to Bernard Boutet de Monvel, for its prized portraits.

In 1808 the New York Academy of the Fine Arts was founded under the auspices of Livingstons, Cuttings, and Clintons; its first president was Robert R. Livingston, U. S. Ambassador to France. Conservative, formal, and Europeanized, it was long the pet of Knickerbocker aristocracy. In opposition in 1825, under the leadership of Samuel F. B. Morse, painter and future inventor of the telegraph, the National Academy of

The Self-Justifications of Society

Design was started in New York City. William Dunlap, a professor of historical painting but best known as the annalist of American art, in a notable speech before this Academy in 1831 denounced the patronage of painting by wealth, ending thus: "The aristocracy of Nature is composed of the nobles who are stamped such by their Maker, and are in principle and practice true democrats—lovers of their fellowmen and supporters of the equal rights of all. I trust that such aristocrats will be found in this Academy." Such was the æsthetic moral drawn in the age of Andrew Jackson. One feels that the chief fallacy of plutocratic patronage within our own century has been the belief that a great American art as well as a great American literature could be called forth if only big enough prizes, endowments, fellowships, and subsidies were offered. Certainly there has been much liberality in this direction, but less judgment. These awards often are bestowed upon works of glossy and plausible mediocrity —in forgetfulness of the fact that American genius has characteristically expressed itself through brilliant, eccentric, and cross-grained revolt. During the late depression another theory of art patronage, that of the Federal Government, has begun to take the place relinquished by the tax-ridden and nervous millionaire. Though final results must be judged later, its first-fruits do not seem greatly rewarding.

In 1845 Emerson wrote: "One would like to see Boston and Massachusetts agitated like a wave with some generosity, mad for learning, for music, for philosophy, for association, for freedom, for art; but now it goes like a peddler with its hand ever in its pocket, cautious, calculating." Yet Van Wyck Brooks has lately retold the story of a Boston merchant who, when one of his ships was overdue, passed from worry over his cargo to worry at his manifest love of lucre—and so to settle his conscience computed the value of the ship and goods, and gave that sum to charity. American philanthropy has often arisen from a kind of Puritanic malaise seeking to justify its wealth in the sight of envious man and retributive God. It is a spirit seen at its worst in the foundation of the Drew Theological Seminary by that skinflint and rogue Daniel Drew. Among other motives of questionable worth have been the love of display, of popular approval, and of social recognition. However, no other country in the modern or ancient world has shown so warm or ready a response to give its money for the public good—schools, libraries, hospitals, medical research, charity for the blind, the cripple, and the incurable. The comradeship of the frontier has never wholly died out, nor the ideal of the better life, which under prosperity expanded quickly to embrace the community. The ease with which wealth was often gained lent also to donorship the prodigality of the successful gambler when the hat was passed around.[6] Gifts like Girard College, Cooper Union, the Perkins Institute for the Blind, and the fund raised in 1847 by A. T. Stewart to relieve the Irish famine, illustrate in as many different ways the early spirit of American philanthropy. George Peabody's creation of the Peabody Trust for rehousing the British poor, Andrew Carnegie's meditations on "The Gospel of Wealth" which led him to endow libraries at home and abroad,[7] Marshall Field's gift of a Museum of Natural History to Chicago at the suggestion of friends though he himself had no interest in such things, the foundations of the University of Chicago, Vanderbilt University, Stanford University, the Drexel Institute, and the Armour Institute of Technology, were anticipations of even greater bequests to education, medicine, and public service from Harkness, Sterling, Rosenwald, and the younger John D. Rockefeller in our own time. Between the end of the World War and 1930 American philanthropy is said to have equalled twenty billion dollars.

A few families of social smartness have given generously—the Whitney support of the Cornell Medical Center to the extent of more than $40,-000,000 being a case in point—but in general the greatest generosity has come from the nobs rather than the swells. The Rockefellers for example

[6]Buckingham observed in 1838: "There is no country on earth, perhaps, where so large a portion of the wealthy are generous philanthropists as in America." In replying to John Stuart Mill's sneer that in the United States "the life of one sex is devoted to dollar hunting, and of the other to the breeding of dollar hunters," the *North American Review* wrote in October, 1848: "So well established is the custom of liberality that very wealthy people are in a manner constrained to make large bequests for public objects in their wills; and if one occasionally fails to comply with the general expectation in this respect, his memory incurs such obloquy that sometimes his heirs have been shamed into an attempt to atone for his neglect."

[7]In 1889 Carnegie first published the two essays later collected under this title; they became classics of the new philanthropy. He considered three ways in which surplus wealth might be disposed of: (1) left to found a rich name, and thus minister to human vanity, (2) surrendered at death to public uses, but often maladministered or foolishly applied, (3) given wisely under direction of the donor himself. He observed that a foundation like the Cooper Institute, or Tilden's bequest for a public library in New York, or Enoch Pratt's gift for a similar purpose in Baltimore, promoted more happiness than would the same amount scattered as a few dollars *per capita,* in those cities, and probably wasted "in the indulgence of appetite." Hence the making and wise redistribution of wealth is a public service.

have dwarfed all other donors in American history, with gifts totalling an approximate $750,000,000—divided between the Rockefeller Foundation, the Rockefeller Institute, the General Education Board, the International Education Board, the University of Chicago, Hampton and Tuskegee, the Riverside Church, Williamsburg, the Bodleian Library, Rheims and Versailles, and minor projects.[8] Few phenomena in mass opinion are so amazing as the way in which these gifts—under the wise direction of the late Ivy L. Lee, pioneer "public relations counsel" to the rich—succeeded in transforming the senior Rockefeller from a hated pirate, assailed by curses of the under-privileged from Hoboken to Hong Kong, and with hands supposedly imbrued by the so-called Ludlow Massacre, into a sagely benevolent oracle of Pocantico Hills, smiling on small children and struggling young photographers, and rounding the century-mark to the applause of a nation. That both pictures are sentimental distortions it is needless to add. But the public relations counsel himself is a symbol of immense significance—for John Jacob Astor, Commodore Vanderbilt, and their children never thought it worth while to placate opinion, or to shear more than a few hundred thousand dollars from fortunes of many millions.[9] Whether it be true, as Mr. John D. Rockefeller, Jr. has lately forecast, that the next thirty years will see the end of all great American fortunes, it is a safe assumption that the old-time arrogance and lack of social responsibility will never return.[10] In England during the recent Depression the sons

[8]The Rockefeller benefactions were moulded by the theories of John D. Rockefeller, Sr., namely (1) that no fortune is sufficient to relieve all the sufferings and needs of humanity, and hence any program of charity must be carefully selected, (2) preventive measures are better investments in happiness than the relief of already acute suffering. Hence the concentration on medical research, and the methods devised by the Rockefeller Foundation to curb pandemics like malaria and hookworm.

[9]Astor's gift of $400,000 to found a Library out of a fortune between twenty and thirty million, and Vanderbilt's building of a modest church and donation of one million dollars to Southern education from an accumulated hundred million, are typical of the former ratio.

A good example of present philanthropy is seen in the will of the late Charles Hayden, a broker whose hobby was boys' clubs. Made public in January, 1937, it left the bulk of a $50,000,000 estate for "the moral, mental, and physical well-being, uplift, and development of boys and young men."

[10]Next to William Henry Vanderbilt's dictum 'The Public be damned,' the most celebrated pronouncement of the old school was made during the Coal Strike of 1902 by George F. Baer, president of the Reading Railway, Morgan partner, and spokesman for the anthracite coal operators: "The rights and interests of the laboring man will be protected and cared for—not by the labor agitators, but by the

and daughters of wealth and nobility followed a vogue for running tea-shops, sandwich stands, flower stalls, and the like, to show that they were in touch with the masses. Whatever one may think about the economic futility of such actions, the underlying attitude is one to which the American plutocracy is increasingly alert.

Certain charities have long been fashionable in every large American city. Mrs. Alexander Hamilton found solace after her husband's death on the duelling-field by working to found the Infant School Society of New York Ladies, a pioneer in the care of orphans which attracted many women of the first quality; it later became the Orphan Asylum Society in the City of New York. During the Civil War the death of Brigadier-General Van Rensselaer from typhoid made his daughter Euphemia resolve to become a trained nurse—the first woman to embark upon this career in New York and probably in the entire country. Her sincerity in the face of opposition from pulpit and newspaper, and under conditions of squalor and ignorance, cannot be gainsaid.[11] She designed the blue and white uniform, apron, and cap of the Bellevue Training School for Nurses, established under the sponsorship of Mrs. Hamilton Fish, her sister Mrs. Griffin, the Misses Schuyler, and Mrs. William Osborn, as an outgrowth of the Sanitary Commission promoted by aristocratic ladies of the North during the Civil War. Maternity hospitals, orthopædic foundations, free sanatoria, homes for the blind and the aged, and similar good works have received the patronage of society in almost every community. They are the usual beneficiaries at subscription balls, concerts to open fashionable hotels, bazaars and the like. The annual Charity Ball in New York City thus began at the Academy of Music in 1857, but for the last forty years has been associated with the Waldorf; it has long had a representative social character.

Society's patronage of churches and religion is illustrated by a remark

Christian men to whom God in his infinite wisdom has given the control of the property interests of the country."

[11]Of her the late Mrs. John King Van Rensselaer wrote, in describing the end of a day spent in New York hospitals: "When she returned to her family's home, she entered the basement, took off her verminous clothes, and then stood on a sheet while her old nurse cleansed her body and combed her hair. Only after this purification would she permit the rest of the household to greet her." Later she entered a Catholic sisterhood. In the praise of Florence Nightingale, the name of Euphemia Van Rensselaer has been unfairly slighted.

The Self-Justifications of Society

ascribed to the late dissipated and worldly Duke of Cambridge. Week-ending at an English country house, His Highness came down to breakfast to find the family, their guests, and servants on their knees in the hall, with the host reading from the Prayer-Book. The Duke gazed for a moment, and then was heard to mutter to himself, "Family prayers! And a damn fine custom too," as he plumped goutily to his knees at the foot of the staircase. Aristocracy sees in the externals of religion a sheet-anchor of the conservatism so necessary to its own existence. Radicals are usually flagrantly irreligious, painting murals to show God and the rich man as fellow-plunderers, and delighting to quote horrid remarks about the opium of the People. The Tory prefers of course an established church, which cements into visible form the *status quo* in economics, politics, and theology, and supplies the archbishop so necessary to the coronation of a king.

With its English heritage society in America has always had a pre-eminent fondness for the Protestant Episcopal Church—to which many churchmen would still like to give a flavor of establishment by chang-ing its name to "The American Church," "The Church in America," "The American Episcopal Church," or simply "The Episcopal Church" divested of the aggressive Protestantism which has grown unfashion-able since the High Church movement. The National Cathedral in Washington, and the Cathedral of St. John the Divine in New York, erected by subscription from all creeds, represent the architectural dream of bishops ambitious to achieve a measure of nationalization. Episco-palianism has lent itself well to social purposes. It is still said that, although there may be other roads to the Celestial City, no gentleman would choose any save the Episcopal way. The good taste of its churches, the amiability and excellent manners of its clergy, its dignified ritual without unseemly manifestations of religious fervor, its worship of a highly respectable First Cause, its omission of the coarser passages in the Marriage Service, and the substitution in the Lord's Prayer of the more elegant "Our Father who" instead of "which"—these evidences of decorum address themselves to those conservative churchgoers "whose circle," as Edith Wharton once phrased it, "is so large that God is in-cluded in their visiting-list." Here the dangerous democratic innu-endoes of the New Testament are read from the lectern in so bland and inexpressive a voice that no one is apt to become frightened. **Was** it not the Right Reverend Phillips Brooks, Bishop of Massachusetts, who was described as "an Episcopalian—with leanings toward Christianity?"[12]

The Episcopal Church in America first achieved its identification with society among the tidewater planters of Virginia. In early Colonial times the Congregational was the established church in Massachusetts, New Hampshire, and Connecticut, to which all taxpayers had to contribute; throughout New England it was the faith to which Saltonstalls, Dudleys, Winthrops, and Quincys lent their favor and often the ministry of their younger sons. Not until the close of the eighteenth and the opening of the nineteenth century did it lose ground to Unitarianism among the more intellectual Brahmins—Emersons, Channings, Sedgwicks, Lowells, Eliots. The Reverend Ralph Waldo Emerson wrote in his Journal: "Boston or Brattle Street Christianity is a compound of force, or the best diagonal line that can be drawn between Jesus Christ and Abbott Lawrence"; a later analyst would describe the God of the Unitarians as "an oblong blur." In New York the Dutch Reformed Church drew the Knickerbocker aristocracy and its imitators; one of its first and greatest ministers, John Van Meklenburg or Megapolensis, was chaplain to the Van Rensselaers. In 1693 under the British flag an official effort was made to establish the Church of England, but that sect never made good its claim in the face of plodding, determined Dutch Calvinism. In New Jersey there was a similar ineffectual decree, but here and in adjoining Pennsylvania the older bourgeoisie was

[12]The British foundation from which springs this attitude may best be shown by a story current in Oxford several years ago about Mrs. Anne Besant, the noted theosophist, and her protégé Krishnamurti—then believed by the pious to be an avatar of the Eternal Vishnu. Supervising the young Hindu's education, Mrs. Besant came up to Oxford to provide for his admission to one of the colleges. She called first upon Dean White of Christ Church, and impressively told him that her candidate was no less than the Messiah. "Most interesting, Madam," he answered politely, "but I fear that would render him a bit conspicuous here at the House." She then turned her steps to the Master of Balliol, presented her request, and assured him that her young charge was no less than the incarnation of the Divine. "We've had some very extraordinary people here at Balliol," the Master told her, "but you see we *have* to draw the line somewhere." Finally Mrs. Besant approached the late Sir Herbert Warren, President of Magdalen, most grandly snobbish of all possible colleges. Again she related her story, and ended with the statement that her young protégé was none other than the Everlasting God Himself. At that Sir Herbert brightened. "By all means let us have him at Magdalen, Madam," he said cordially. "I can assure you that our undergraduates will soon come to accept him on terms of almost perfect equality."

Quaker, with new but lowly Scotch-Irish mixtures that clung to Presbyterianism, while the more cosmopolitan class was Anglican. Presbyterians were also sprinkled among the gentry of Carolina and the South;
during the Revolution their numbers were swelled by patriotic seceders
from the English Church, so that below the Mason and Dixon Line the
Presbyterian Church has always ranked highest socially among the
dissenters.

But in Colonial Virginia the Church of England flourished most conspicuously. Not, to be sure, in numbers—for a conservative estimate at
the close of the seventeenth century, cited by Sweet, places the ratio of
Episcopalians at one out of twenty citizens. On the eve of the Civil
War, in the deeper South from Charleston to Galveston, Professor Dodd
estimates the total count of Episcopalians as not over 20,000. Yet throughout the Cotton Kingdom and America in general communicants of the
Episcopal Church have represented more wealth and social standing
than any other fold. The cotton-planter, the rice-grower, the great
ship-owner, the prosperous merchant, banker, and capitalist of real
estate—these and their fashionably dressed wives were the traditional
pewholders of Anglicanism.[13] In the heyday of tidewater Virginia many
great squires followed the English mode of having their own chap-
lains; the presence of a tame man of God on the premises gave them
a sense of power such as the savage chieftain feels from the maintenance of a *shaman* or medicine-man. Landon Carter of Sabine Hall,
for example, son the great "King" Carter, kept a chaplain whom he
compelled—albeit the cleric was unwilling—to pray for rain.

Under Bishop Berkeley in the eighteenth century, wielding his influence from remote Britain, a law was passed in Virginia forbidding any
other than an Anglican clergyman to conduct religious services—and
up until about 1760, in the teeth of Scotch-Irish immigration, the struggle to maintain this amazing monopoly lasted. Not until 1786 how-

[13]The Sunday fashion revue afforded by the Lord's House is a stale subject of
American humor. But it is at least interesting to find the Abbé Robin, a French
chaplain with an eye for style and beauty, recording of American women in the late
eighteenth century: "Having no theatres or public promenades, the churches are the
only places of public resort where they can show off their new and constantly increasing luxury. They there display themselves arrayed in silk, and sometimes
shaded with superb headdresses, their hair piled up on frames in imitation of the
French fashions of some years ago." The Duc de la Rochefoucauld makes a similar
observation about the pomps of the Sabbath.

ever was the Anglican Church disestablished in Virginia, long after New York, Maryland, and other states had cut it adrift at the first shot of the Revolutionary War. Thomas Jefferson, deist and democrat, supported by Baptists and Presbyterians, finally accomplished its downfall along with primogeniture and entail. Yet the affiliation of George Washington and other Virginia patricians with the Episcopal Church, and the fact that after Inauguration he, the Vice-President, cabinet officers, and many senators and representatives repaired to St. Paul's Chapel in Broadway where Doctor Provoost invoked the blessings of God upon the Administration, lent a new semi-official character to the Church.

Samuel Seabury, first Episcopal bishop whom America possessed— consecrated by non-juring Scottish prelates in 1784 under the disapproval of Canterbury—and Samuel Provoost, first Bishop of New York, both represented the conservative, socially aristocratic strain to which the standing of the clergy owes so much. The social as well as the apostolic succession has been unbroken through such bishops of blue blood as William Ingraham Kip, Mark Antony De Wolfe Howe, and William Heathcote De Lancey. Nor is the lineage by any means extinct; for Bishop William Lawrence, descended on his mother's side from the Appletons and on his father's from Adamses and Lawrences, now retired from the see of Massachusetts to such lighter labors as the chairmanship of the board at Groton, today symbolizes admirably the social dignity of the cloth. In 1900 he observed that the charitable millionaire "is Christ's as much as was St. Paul, he is consecrated as was St. Francis of Assisi. . . . Material prosperity is helping to make the national character sweeter, more joyous, more unselfish, more Christ-like." More comfortable words could hardly be uttered. At the turn of the century another type of ecclesiastic was represented by Dean E. A. Hoffman of the General Theological Seminary, descended from an old Dutch family and owner of millions in real estate, said to be the richest clergyman in the world, who with his shooting, fishing, and active membership in the New York Riding Club conformed to the type of sporting parson. And at the same time there was Bishop Henry Codman Potter, himself the son of an Episcopal bishop; as clerk in a dry-goods store he had felt the vocation, had become rector of Grace Church in 1868, and in 1883 assistant bishop of New York and destined to succeed his uncle Bishop

The Self-Justifications of Society

Horatio Potter. It was said that he always adapted his formula for grace before meat to the social and financial standing of his host, from "all these, Thy manifold blessings" to "even the least of these, Thy mercies." He was very proud that English visitors often pronounced him to be "a typical mid-Victorian bishop," and was never happier than when officiating at the titled marriage of a Vanderbilt or a Goelet, or travelling to a church convention in the private car of J. P. Morgan. It was he who in 1892 began work on the Cathedral of St. John the Divine. His cope now rests upon the stern and somewhat angular shoulders of William Thomas Manning, more combative than unctuously social.[14]

Every large American city has its most fashionable Episcopal Church, and happy is the bride who treads its aisle. In New York for example Trinity Church, first built in 1737, was long the parish of quality. During the Revolution the Reverend Samuel Auchmuty was its rector. After its destruction by fire it was reconsecrated in 1790 by Bishop Provoost in the presence of Washington—for whose use, as President of the United States, a richly-ornamented pew covered by a baldachin was reserved. William Alexander, self-styled Earl of Stirling, Alexander Hamilton, Robert Fulton, John Slidell, Albert Gallatin, and other aristocrats lie buried in its churchyard. Today a few old families take pride in maintaining a pew in Trinity Church, but rarely go there except on special occasions like Easter. St. Mark's achieved a measure of social fame; its rector in the 1840's was the Reverend Henry Anthon, relative of the future Mrs. Stuyvesant Fish. St. George's in Stuyvesant Square used to be fashionable, and many tourists ventured in upon its Sabbath hush for the distinction of dropping a quarter into the plate passed by the first J. P. Morgan; the present Morgan church is less accessible to the

[14]The average Episcopal clergyman was thus described in 1847 on occasion of a national Episcopal convention, by Philip Hone, a devoted vestryman of Trinity: "One may know these reverend visitors in the streets by their good-looking, complacent, self-satisfied countenances, well-brushed black coats and white neck-cloths, and gentlemanly, dignified deportment. Some of them may be seen with neat little wives hanging on their arms, well dressed, each with a little satin bonnet, a little inclining to the gay; and many a wistful glance is cast at Beck's, and Seaman & Muir's and Rogers' windows, and at Stewart's palace of haberdashery, with a suppressed sigh of regret that the doctor's stipend is so small." A less pleasant type of fashionable curate was drawn as the Rev. Cream Cheese by Curtis in *The Potiphar Papers* (1853).

metropolitan tripper, being St. John's of Lattingtown in Locust Valley. St. Bartholomew's has also had its claim to fashion, but at present no church can rival St. Thomas's, which long ago followed the march of vogue up Fifth Avenue. Designed by Cram, Goodhue, and Ferguson, St. Thomas's contains two significant details inserted by a waggish young architect in Mr. Cram's employ—a dollar-sign worked into the tracery over the Bride's Door, and three money-bags initialed "J. P. M." carved above the choir-stalls.

Variable is the social standing of the Roman Catholic Church in America. In Baltimore, with the tradition of Calverts and the great Archbishop John Carroll, it is very high. St. Louis and New Orleans, with their Creole aristocracy, cause it to outrank even the Episcopal Church. In New York several very old families like the Van Rensselaers have had their converts to Rome; that clan still recalls with amusement the spectacle of Henry Van Rensselaer, S. J., leading a St. Patrick's Day parade of Knights of Columbus down Fifth Avenue. A few old French families of New York, with blue blood but no publicity, like Du Vivier and Binsse, belong to the Catholic group, as do the Iselins and even newer families like the Mackays or the late Virginia Fair Vanderbilt. The dignity and liturgical color of Catholicism, its association with the premier Duke of England and with a host of Continental nobilities, and the markedly aristocratic stamp of certain of its orders such as the Benedictine, which maintains a monastery in Austria to which only sons of titled houses are admitted, or the lay-order the Knights of Malta, which requires sixteen quarterings for membership—all help to lend it social luster. On the other hand the presence in America of fellow-communicants left by waves of Irish, South German, and Italian influx has been, from the snobbishly social point of view, deplorable. The Reverend Doctor Nichols, with somewhat unclerical candor, wrote: "The Episcopal Church and the Catholic Church are the churches of beautiful manners, and if your birth has placed you under the social ban of being a dissenter, cultivate Episcopal emotions and shuffle off the mortal coil of Presbyterianism on as short notice as possible. Ralph Waldo Emerson, in his *English Traits*, said no truer thing than 'You can tell a dissenter by his manners.' You can divine some women were not born in the Church by their smiles."

The dissenting sects, following the decline of Puritanism and Knicker-

The Self-Justifications of Society

bocker Calvinism, have never attracted the socially ambitious. In revenge perhaps they long stressed the equalitarian aspects of Christianity,
at least here below, while comforting their lowly adherents with the
assurance that they were the Chosen People hereafter. Presbyterians
and Congregationalists used to despise Methodists and Campbellites, and
they in turn snubbed Baptists. Francis Asbury, first bishop of the Methodist Church in America—who incidentally left on record his opinion
that Boston was "famous for poor religion and bad water"—wrote in
1784 from North Carolina: "Wonderfully entertained with a late publication by Silas Mercer, a Baptist preacher, in which he has anathema-
tized the whole race of kings from Saul to George III; his is republican-
ism run mad." Others have agreed with John Williams, fourth Bishop
of Connecticut, that "Baptists are the least of God's creatures." Until
Holy Rollers and Four Square Gospellers came along in the South,
Baptists, with no sect upon which to look down, were indeed in an
unenviable position. Yet even they contributed something to the Protestant Gospel of Success. This cult—primarily an economic but sec-
ondarily a social one—can be traced as early as 1701 in the sermons of
Cotton Mather. He states that salvation of the soul and success in
business are life's main ends: "A Christian at his two Callings is a man
in a boat, rowing for Heaven, the house which our Heavenly Father
hath intended for us. If he mind but one of his Callings, be it which it
will, he pulls the oar but on one side of the Boat, and will make but a
poor dispatch to the Shoar of Eternal Blessedness."[15] The expedient
deism of Benjamin Franklin, the success-novels of the Reverend Horatio Alger, Doctor Russell H. Conwell's "Acres of Diamonds," Quimby
and Mrs. Eddy and New Thought, and *Little Journeys to the Homes
of Great Business Men* by Elbert Hubbard, the Fra Diavolo of Mam-
mon-worship, are apostolic stepping-stones in its progress. "Business is
religion, and religion is business," preached the Reverend Maltbie D.
Babcock of the Brick Presbyterian Church in New York in 1900, while

[15]With great wealth of detail this subject has been treated by Mr. A. Whitney
Griswold of Yale in *The American Gospel of Success,* a dissertation submitted in
1933 and in the main still unpublished. Mr. Griswold's kindness has allowed the
present author to read and make notes upon the manuscript. R. H. Tawney, *Religion
and the Rise of Capitalism,* London, 1929, and Max Weber, *The Protestant Ethic
and the Spirit of Capitalism,* London, 1930, are valued but in some ways questionable interpretations of the subject.

the elder John D. Rockefeller was gravely testifying, "I believe the power to make money is a gift from God." Formerly Baptists and Methodists had taken a certain pride in calling theirs the poor man's church, but now they began to speak of the "sanctification of wealth" and of "consecrated power." Since the Depression they have grown a little uneasy over the new unpopularity of the rich, and many a Protestant pastor has lately begun to jazz up the old-time religion with Sidney and Beatrice Webb, John Strachey, Reinhold Niebuhr, or at least the Christian pink of Sherwood Eddy. The Gospel of Success, along with its social airs and graces, has fallen to the lot of the Reverend Frank Nathan Buchman—who, it is reported, has brought God to Newport, which it must be confessed is a somewhat easier achievement than bringing Newport to God.

In review the self-justifications of society in America are none too impressive. It has bought Old Masters, but fed few living artists. Its tastes in music and opera have been both timid and grandiose, and its patronage of literature has been negligible. Unhappily it forsook politics more than a century ago, though for reasons not wholly unselfish it longs just now to return. With generosity it has sometimes given to charity and education, though it has wasted other great sums in foolish ways. To the wisdom, goodness, and piety of mankind it has afforded at best an erratic and whimsical support. In all these ways American society has shown characteristic short-sightedness. A favored minority which nourishes well the arts and good works gives hostages for its own safety; one which slights them for selfish ends—"conspicuous waste," lavish living and dining, amusement and sport—loses its compass of idealism and invites disaster. This fact has been dimly recognized at all times, though it is a far cry from the Cæsars lulling the mob with bread and circuses to the American banker winning his way from odium to fame with schools and clinics. Lacking the English tradition of public service, or the feudal bond between lord and liege, plutocracy in America has seldom sat at ease on its pyramid of privilege. Every depression will bring more cries of "soak the rich," fresh criticism from intellectuals, and new defection of rebels from plunder on the left, in the Jeffersonian tradition. Only the rash will dare forecast the future.

As was suggested in the beginning, it is a little hard triumphantly to

The Self-Justifications of Society

vindicate society in the economy of human life. The genesis of all groups which have called themselves "Society" was described long ago by Vauvenargues: *Quelques fous se sont dit à table: Il n'y a que nous qui sont bonne compagnie, et on les croit.* Without some tincture of snobbery, society is never found; and snobbery is more amusing than admirable. Originally "snob" meant a cobbler's helper, a person of low birth and breeding, and then came to signify a person ashamed of his low birth and breeding. That snobbery and eminent rank have become linked, at least in the popular mind, is an irony due largely to the mediation of society.

The acute social awareness which society has come to typify is chiefly the result of this modern world—with its industrialism, competition, insecurity, and whirligig of quick riches today and poverty tomorrow. In this hasty exchange of identifications society is the chevron worn on the sleeve rather than the inner grace. Or, to change the metaphor, society is the flower which blooms in economic springtime upon the stout boughs of an aristocracy. It is ornamental and transitory, as well as attractive to the bees of cross-fertilization, but sustenance must be drawn through the tap-root. Many an aristocracy fallen upon wintry days has lost its social blossoms, and withdrawn quietly into that deeper life which may truly find some sort of justification. All human experience, as the biographer of Doctor Samuel Johnson long ago remarked, cries out irresistibly, *Un gentilhomme est toujours gentilhomme.* Lacking the simplicity, courage, generosity, and honor of this ideal the life of mankind would indeed be poorer.

A NOTE ON BIBLIOGRAPHY

An important source is of course *The Dictionary of American Biography*, completed in 1936 under the editorship of Dumas Malone. A. W. Calhoun, *Social History of the American Family*, 3 vols., Cleveland, 1917–19; Vernon L. Parrington, *Main Currents in American Thought*, 3 vols., New York, 1927–30; *The Chronicles of America*, in 50 volumes, under the general editorship of Allen Johnson; and volumes in the current series, *A History of American Life*, edited by Arthur M. Schlesinger and Dixon Ryan Fox, cited separately below, are basic. Popular but scholarly reviews of American life and history, like James Truslow Adams, *The Epic of America*, Boston, 1931, and Charles A. and Mary R. Beard, *The Rise of American Civilization*, new ed., New York, 1935, are valuable syntheses of material offered in greater detail by historians like Henry Adams, J. B. McMaster, Albert Bushnell Hart, and Charles McLean Andrews. The content of social history in these works must of course be winnowed from a mass of political and economic fact. Voluminous local histories yield much social information: James Grant Wilson ed., *The Memorial History of the City of New York*, 4 vols., New York, 1892; Martha J. Lamb and Mrs. Burton Harrison, *History of the City of New York*, 3 vols., New York, 1896; and the comment and pictorial matter in I. N. P. Stokes, *The Iconography of Manhattan Island*, 6 vols., New York, 1915–28, represent the metropolis, along with more chatty trivia found in *Valentine's Manual of the City of New York*, ed. Henry Collins Brown, 1916–27. Typical of other cities are J. T. Scharf and T. Westcott, *History of Philadelphia: 1609–1884*, 3 vols., Philadelphia, 1884; Justin Winsor, ed., *The Memorial History of Boston: 1630–1880*, 4 vols., Boston, 1881; Mrs. St. Julien Ravenel, *Charleston: the Place and the People*, New York and London, 1906; Grace King, *New Orleans: the Place and the People*, New York, 1895; Eliza Ripley, *Social Life in Old New Orleans*, New York, 1912; Lloyd Lewis and Henry Justin Smith, *Chicago: the History of Its Reputation*, New York, 1929, and as a more specialized work, Harvey W. Zorbaugh, *The Gold Coast and the Slum: a Sociological Study of Chicago's Near North Side*, Chicago, 1929. Useful but not uniformly trustworthy are the popular Appleton-Century books on American cities, now appearing—Will Irwin on Manhattan, Lucius Beebe on Boston, C. C. Dobie on San Francisco, Lyle Saxon on New Orleans, Henry Justin Smith on Chicago, and others. The magazine *Fortune*, whose files are of great interest to the student of American plutocracy, has published since 1930 accounts of various cities with emphasis on social and financial aspects—Boston, Philadelphia, Newport, Saratoga, Palm Beach, Charleston. The files of older magazines—*Godey's Lady's Book, Harper's Weekly, Scribner's, Life, Vanity Fair, Town Topics, The New Yorker*—are often richly rewarding. The New York *Herald, Times, Tribune, Sun*, and *World*, as well as the Boston *Evening Transcript*, Philadelphia *Public Ledger*, Baltimore *Sun*, Washington *Post*, Chicago *Tribune*, St. Louis *Post-Dispatch*, New Orleans *Times-Picayune*, Denver *Post*, San Francisco *Examiner*, and others—offer fruitful archives.

CHAPTER I

Matthew Arnold, *Civilization in the United States*, New York, 1888, applies to American life the theory of Amiel about society which is cited in the text. The nature of "noblesse" as an aristocratic ideal has been presented by Ruth Kelso, *The Doctrine of the English Gentleman in the Sixteenth Century,* Urbana, 1929; research into the cult of the gentleman in Colonial America is now being done by members of the staff of the Huntington Library, San Marino, California, under the direction of Doctor Max Farrand, to whom the author is indebted for suggestions. Henry Dwight Sedgwick, *In Praise of Gentlemen,* Boston, 1935, gracefully defends the conservative viewpoint. From the radical wing, Thorstein Veblen's *Theory of the Leisure Class* has now become a classic. Some of the underlying ideas in this chapter are discussed, with a socialist bias, by Gustavus Myers, *The History of American Idealism,* New York, 1925.

CHAPTER II

Herbert I. Priestley, *The Coming of the White Man,* New York, 1927, and T. J. Wertenbaker, *The First Americans: 1607–1690,* New York, 1927, give a residue of early social history. Wertenbaker's *Patrician and Plebeian in Virginia,* Charlottesville, 1910, and J. T. Adams, *Provincial Society: 1690–1763,* New York, 1927, stress social values. For the planter class Philip A. Bruce, *Social Life of Virginia in the Seventeenth Century,* Richmond, 1907, is excellent. R. A. Stewart's *Index to Printed Virginia Genealogies,* Richmond, 1930, is indispensable to the subject, and for genealogy and topical matters E. G. Swem's *Virginia Historical Index,* 2 vols., Roanoke, 1934. A popularly written account of some Virginia family histories is found in Moncure D. Conway, *Barons of the Potomack and Rappahannock,* New York, 1892. "The Randolph Family," by W. G. Stanard, October, 1898, pp. 122 ff. and many other valuable studies in genealogy will be found in files of the *William and Mary College Quarterly.* Burton J. Hendrick, *The Lees of Virginia,* Boston, 1935, deals ably with one of the great families. *The Writings of Colonel William Byrd,* ed. John Spencer Bassett, New York, 1901, offers excellent material. Mary N. Stanard, *Colonial Virginia, Its People and Customs,* Philadelphia, 1917; Mary Johnston, *Pioneers of the Old South,* New Haven, 1918; and Grace King, *Creole Families of New Orleans,* New York, 1921, are useful. A picture of British social life of the middle and upper classes, with some suggestion of the cosmopolitan influences transmitted to the Colonies, is found in Jay B. Botsford, *English Society in the Eighteenth Century: as Influenced from Oversea,* New York, 1924. For the strongest single bond between the British aristocracy and America see Evarts B. Greene, *The Provincial Governor in the English Colonies of North America,* Harvard Historical Studies VII. *The Commonwealth History of Massachusetts,* ed. Albert Bushnell Hart, 5 vols., New York, 1927–30; Samuel Eliot Morison, *Builders of the Bay Colony,* Boston and New York, 1930; Charles M. Andrews, *The Fathers of New England,* and *Colonial Folkways,* New Haven, 1919, and the same author's monumental *The Colonial Period of American History,* of which two volumes have been published, New Haven, 1935–36; and George F. Dow, *Every Day Life in Massachusetts Bay Colony,* Boston, 1935, all contain a mass of material on social Puritanism. For a brief anthology of Puritan writings which bear upon this subject, Elizabeth Deering Hanscom's *The Heart of the Puritan: Selections from Letters and Journals,* New York, 1917, is useful. New England is rich in local histories; Sarah E. Hughes, *History of East Haven,* New Haven, 1908, for example, gives some little-known facts about the Saltonstalls not included in a work of thumb-nail biographies like Mary Caroline Crawford, *Famous Families of Massachusetts,* 2 vols., Boston, 1930. Information about well-known families in respect to origin and ramifications may be found in biographies of their more celebrated members, such as J. T. Adams's *The Adams Family* and S. Foster Damon's *Amy Lowell,* though Lowells currently insist that the latter is not wholly accurate in its genealogy. For special

A Note on Bibliography

topics see R. N. Toppan, "The Failure to Establish an Hereditary Aristocracy in the Colonies," *Colonial Society of Massachusetts Publications,* vol. III, pp. 407–11; F. B. Dexter, "On Some Social Distinctions at Harvard and Yale," *Proceedings American Antiquarian Society,* vol. IX, p. 50; and W. G. Brooks, "The Rank of Students in Harvard College," *Proceedings Massachusetts Historical Society,* vol. IX, pp. 252–54. For Colonial Society in New York see Esther Singleton, *Social New York under the Georges, 1714–1776,* New York, 1902; Alice Morse Earle, *Colonial Days in Old New York,* New York, 1896, and the same author's *Home Life in Colonial Days,* rev. ed., New York, 1928; Maude Wilder Goodwin, *Dutch and English on the Hudson,* New Haven, 1919; and Harold G. Eberlein, *The Manors and Historic Homes of the Hudson Valley,* Philadelphia and London, 1924. Dixon Ryan Fox, *Caleb Heathcote: Gentleman Colonist. The Story of a Career in the Province of New York: 1692–1721,* New York, 1926, traces the progress of a first generation aristocracy. For Huguenot elements see Lucian J. Fosdick, *The French Blood in America,* New York, 1906. James Fenimore Cooper's novel *Satanstoe,* first published 1845, gives an excellent picture of Knickerbocker social life in the latter half of the eighteenth century. Margharita A. Hamm, *Famous Families of New York,* 2 vols., New York and London, 1902, is more adulatory than accurate. Sydney G. Fisher, *The Quaker Colonies,* New Haven, 1919, and the material on Binghams, Willings, Shippens, and others found in Rufus W. Griswold's *The Republican Court: or American Society in the Days of Washington,* New York and London, 1856, should be mentioned. Likewise for Revolutionary and post-Revolutionary times, James Schouler, *Americans of 1776,* New York, 1906; Louise B. Dunbar, "A Study of 'Monarchical' Tendencies in the United States from 1776 to 1801," *University of Illinois Studies in the Social Sciences,* vol. X, Urbana, 1922; Henry J. Ford, *Washington and His Colleagues,* New Haven, 1918; and George M. Wrong, *Washington and His Comrades in Arms,* New Haven, 1921.

For this and later periods the student is obliged to rely heavily upon the comments of travellers upon American social life. Convenient excerpts are found in Newton D. Mereness, *Travels in the American Colonies,* New York, 1916; Jane L. Mesick, *The English Traveller in America: 1785–1835,* New York, 1922; Allan Nevins, *American Social History as Recorded by British Travellers,* New York, 1923; and Charles H. Sherrill, *French Memories of Eighteenth-Century America,* New York, 1915. An exhaustive bibliography is afforded by Frank Monaghan, *French Travellers in the United States: 1765–1932,* New York, 1933.

CHAPTER III

Anne H. Wharton, *Social Life in the Early Republic,* Philadelphia and London, 1902; *The First Forty Years of Washington Society: portrayed by the family letters of Margaret Bayard Smith,* ed. Hunt, New York, 1906; and *The Diary of John Quincy Adams: 1794–1845,* ed. Nevins, New York, 1929, are very helpful. For the historical background Henry Adams, *History of the United States: 1801–1817,* has become a classic. Charles A. Beard, *Economic Origins of Jeffersonian Democracy,* New York, 1915; Allen Johnson, *Jefferson and His Colleagues,* New Haven, 1921; Claude G. Bowers, *Jefferson and Hamilton: the Struggle for Democracy in America,* Boston and New York, 1925, and *Jefferson in Power: the Death Struggle of the Federalists,* Boston, 1936, are filled with the social implications of this conflict. For the background of primogeniture see Courtney S. Kenny, *History of the Law of Primogeniture in England,* Cambridge, 1878; the rise and fall of primogeniture and entail in America apparently has never been treated at full length, but the materials are scattered throughout legal encyclopedias and monographs. Dixon Ryan Fox,

A Note on Bibliography

The Decline of Aristocracy in the Politics of New York, New York, 1919, is scholarly and detailed in showing how the aristocracy of birth was supplanted by money and gross political machination from 1800 to 1840. James Fenimore Cooper's *The American Democrat, or Hints on the Social and Civic Relations of the U. S. A.*, Cooperstown, 1838, is the meditation of a Tory. Alexis de Tocqueville, *De la démocratie en Amérique*, Paris, 1835, is essential. Biographies of Jackson and his times are legion; Frederic A. Ogg, *The Reign of Andrew Jackson*, 1919, is brief but adequate. Among studies of the frontier which begot Jacksonianism should be noted Frederick J. Turner, *The Frontier in American History*, New York, 1920, and Frederic L. Paxson, *History of the American Frontier*, Boston, 1924. Out of many travel books, three are particularly rich in social comment, Frances M. Trollope, *Domestic Manners of the Americans*, London, 1832; Harriet Martineau, *Society in America*, 3 vols., London, 1837; and James Silk Buckingham, *America: Historical, Statistic and Descriptive*, 2 vols., New York, 1841. Two excellent interpretations of American culture should be cited—Howard Mumford Jones, *America and French Culture: 1750–1848*, Chapel Hill, 1927, and Van Wyck Brooks, *The Flowering of New England: 1815–1865*, New York, 1936. Social trivia are presented by Mrs. E. F. Ellet, *The Court Circles of the Republic . . . from Washington to Grant*, Hartford, 1869, and by Abram C. Dayton, *Last Days of Knickerbocker Life in New York*, New York, 1882. The lingering of the old aristocracy in the South is treated by William E. Dodd, *The Cotton Kingdom*, New Haven, 1919; Ulrich B. Phillips, *Life and Labor in the Old South*, Boston, 1930; and Alice R. Huger Smith, *A Carolina Rice Plantation of the Fifties*, New York, 1936. Older sources are R. Q. Mallard, *Plantation Life before Emancipation*, Richmond, 1892, and Thomas Nelson Page, *Social Life in Old Virginia before the War*, New York, 1897. Extremely illuminating is Carl Russell Fish, *The Rise of the Common Man: 1830–1850*, New York, 1927.

CHAPTER IV

Gustavus Myers, *History of the Great American Fortunes*, 3 vols., Chicago, 1911, and revised for the Modern Library, 1936, contains a vast amount of useful fact, with slight inaccuracies and a strong socialist prejudice. Theodore J. Grayson, *Leaders and Periods of American Finance*, New York and London, 1932, offers short scholarly biographies of plutocrats from Robert Morris to E. H. Gary. Meade Minnigerode, *Certain Rich Men*, New York and London, 1927, and Matthew Josephson, *The Robber Barons*, New York, 1934, should be noted. Arthur D. Howden Smith has devoted himself to writing popular lives of the rich—*John Jacob Astor: Landlord of New York*, Philadelphia, 1929, is much superior to his *Commodore Vanderbilt*, New York, 1927, with its endless faked conversations; his *Men Who Run America*, Indianapolis and New York, 1936, presents sketches of important living financiers. Bessie G. du Pont, *E. I. du Pont de Nemours and Company: a History*, Boston and New York, 1920, and John K. Winkler, *The Du Pont Dynasty*, New York, 1935, should be mentioned. Kenneth W. Porter, *John Jacob Astor*, 2 vols., Cambridge, Massachusetts, 1931, is most exhaustive and scholarly. Clara Longworth de Chambrun, *The Making of Nicholas Longworth*, New York, 1933, devotes the first 114 pages to Nicholas Longworth I and early Cincinnati. Jay Gould, Jim Fisk, Andrew Carnegie, John D. Rockefeller, Andrew W. Mellon, and the Morgans have all had their popular biographers. *Fortune* has retold the story of the Astors (October, 1933), the Vanderbilts (May, 1930), and the Goulds (February, 1931), and chiefly from the viewpoint of business treated at other times Rockefellers, McCormicks, Armours, and some notably rich women of today. Henry Clews, *Fifty Years in Wall Street*, New York, 1908, is a revealing memoir. The social history of the Gold Rush is told by Soulé, *The Annals of San Francisco*, 1855, by Stewart Edward White, *The Forty-Niners*, 1919, and by A. B. Hulbert, *Forty-Niners*, 1931. Sir Philip Burne-Jones, *Dollars and Democracy*, New York, 1904, is an amusing but spiteful meditation on the worship of gold in society. Among recent books which analyze American capitalism, with incidental social content, should be mentioned Burton J. Hendrick, *The Age of Big Business*, New Haven, 1919; Frederick L. Allen, *The Lords of Creation*, New York and London, 1935; and Ida M. Tarbell, *The Nationalizing of Business*, New York, 1936. For a short but sound account of the Jew in American finance and social life see Burton J. Hendrick, *The Jews in America*, London, 1923.

CHAPTER V

An excellent bibliography for etiquette-books contemporary with Colonial America is found in John E. Mason, *Gentlefolk in the Making*, Philadelphia, 1935, which discusses primarily the rise of the self-made in England from 1531 to 1774. Titles of etiquette manuals cited in the text need not be repeated here; that of Washington, however, was edited in 1926 by Charles Moore under the name *George Washington's Rules of Civility and Decent Behaviour*. Many extracts from such manuals are given in C. J. Furness, ed., *The Genteel Female*, New York, 1931, and in Arthur Train, *Puritan's Progress*, New York, 1936. Ruth E. Finley, *The Lady of Godey's*, Philadelphia, 1931, discusses the social influence of that magazine. George M. Towle, *American Society*, 2 vols., London, 1870, attempts a description of all classes, while F. Gaillardet, *L'aristocratie en Amérique*, Paris, 1883, discusses the characteristics and manners of the upper stratum. The delightful *Diary of Julia Newberry*, ed. Barnes and Fairbank, New York, 1933, gives a precocious glimpse of post-Civil War Society in Chicago and Eastern resorts. Mark Twain's *The Gilded Age*, William Dean Howell's *The Rise of Silas Lapham*, F. Hopkinson Smith's *Colonel Carter of Cartersville*, Edith Wharton's *Age of Innocence*, are authentic social documents. Memoirs of sympathetic tourists like Fredrika Bremer or of discerning Americans like Henry Cabot Lodge greatly enrich the picture of manners and folkways in the nineteenth century. Plays like Mrs. Anna C. Mowatt's *Fashion*, Bronson Howard's *Saratoga*, and Langdon Mitchell's *The New York Idea*, are useful. Among recently published books whose horizon is the social life of the later nineteenth century might be mentioned Mabel Dodge Luhan's *Intimate Memories*, New York, 1933, chiefly for Buffalo, and Lloyd Lewis and Henry Justin Smith, *Oscar Wilde Discovers America: 1882*, New York, 1936. A crop of "period" books is very helpful: Meade Minnigerode's *The Fabulous Forties*, Branch's *The Sentimental Years*, Lewis Mumford's *The Brown Decades*, Thomas Beer's *The Mauve Decade*, Henry Canby's *The Age of Confidence*, Frederick L. Allen's *Only Yesterday*, and Mark Sullivan's series *Our Times*. Two volumes in the History of American Life are heavily saturated with material about Victorian conventions in America, Allan Nevins, *The Emergence of Modern America: 1865–1878*, New York, 1927, and Arthur M. Schlesinger, *The Rise of the City: 1878–1898*, New York, 1933.

CHAPTER VI

Austin B. Keep, *History of the New York Society Library*, Privately printed, 1908, and catalogues and bulletins issued by the Boston Athenæum, the Library Society of Charleston, the Rookwood Library, and the Library Company of Philadelphia, are useful; for the origin of the last named, Benjamin Franklin's *Autobiography* is authoritative. The New-York Historical Society has also issued pamphlets

A Note on Bibliography

of retrospect. Copies of the various social directories named in the text may be found in the New York Public Library and in the Yale University Library. For the history and policy of the Social Register see Norman S. Hall, "The 'Ins' and 'Outs' of American Society," *Liberty*, February 13, 1926, pp. 7 ff., and much more satisfactory, "The Social Register," *Fortune*, March, 1933, pp. 40 ff. Philip Hone's *Diary*, ed. Nevins, *passim*, gives valuable information about Dominick Lynch, while G. W. Curtis, *The Potiphar Papers*, first published 1853, sketches an amusing picture of social ambition in the Fifties. Life among the exquisites is portrayed by C. Astor Bristed, *The Upper Ten Thousand: Sketches of American Society*, New York, 1852, and by the ephemera of Nathaniel P. Willis, *People I Have Met; or, Pictures of Society and People of Mark*, New York, 1850, *Hurry-graphs; or, Sketches of Scenery, Celebrities and Society*, New York, 1851, *Life, Here and There;* or, *Sketches of Society and Adventure*, Auburn and Rochester, 1853, *Famous Persons and Places*, New York, 1854, and *The Rag-Bag*, New York, 1855. Ward McAllister, *Society as I Have Found It*, New York, 1890, and Moran Tudury, "Ward McAllister," *American Mercury*, June, 1926, pp. 138–143, should be noted. For the social background in New York, 1850–1880, Edith Wharton's novelettes *The Old Maid, New Year's Day, False Dawn,* and *The Spark,* are excellent, and for the first decade of the twentieth century *The House of Mirth,* together with the novels and *The American Scene,* 1907, of her master Henry James. Helpful though somewhat too dependent on an antiquarian's memory are the books of Henry Collins Brown, such as *The Story of Old New York,* New York, 1934, *Fifth Avenue Old and New,* New York, 1924, *In the Golden Nineties,* Hastings-on-Hudson, 1928, and *Brownstone Fronts and Saratoga Trunks,* New York, 1935. Among the gossipy but often helpful pictures of modern society, chiefly in the metropolitan area, should be noted Mrs. John King Van Rensselaer and Frederic Van de Water, *The Social Ladder,* New York, 1924; Elizabeth Drexel Lehr, *'King Lehr' and the Gilded Age,* Philadelphia and London, 1935; and Helen Worden, *Society Circus,* New York, 1936. Juliana Cutting's series in *The Saturday Evening Post* should also be noted: "From Cotillion to Jazz," April 1, 1933, "Society Today and Yesterday," May 6, and "The Stag Line," June 24.

CHAPTER VII

For the background of English clubs J. Timbs, *Clubs and Club Life,* London, 1866, is useful. Most elaborate is *A History of the Schuylkill Fishing Company: 1732–1888* and *1888–1932,* 2 vols., Philadelphia, 1889 and 1932. Owen Wister has written the centenary volume of the Philadelphia Club, and Reginald T. Townsend that of the Union Club, New York. Year-books of the Knickerbocker, Brook, Metropolitan, Racquet, Somerset, and other clubs are available; the Tavern Club of Boston has printed a book of its songs. The Index to the files of *Fortune* serves as a guide to articles treating in whole or in part the Union, the Somerset, the Philadelphia Club, the clubs of Washington, D. C., and others. Jerome A. Hart, *In Our Second Century,* San Francisco, 1935, treats extensively the Bohemian Club of San Francisco. The Tuxedo Club issued an historical brochure on its fiftieth birthday in 1936; and other country clubs mentioned in the text have their year-books. Oliver Wendell Holmes, *Over the Teacups,* Boston, 1890, discusses fraternal orders. The psychology of college societies is sympathetically analyzed by Thomas Arkle Clark, *The Fraternity and the College,* Menasha, 1916. The Porcellian and several other secret college clubs have printed periodic lists of members, and in histories of their respective universities they are discussed with discretion and brevity; but in general information about them must be gathered orally. *A History of the Ivy Club* was privately printed at Princeton in 1929, and a full account of President Wilson's

A Note on Bibliography

campaign against the eating clubs will be found in Ray Stannard Baker, *Woodrow Wilson, Life and Letters: Princeton, 1890–1910,* New York, 1927. For college fraternities *Baird's Manual,* now in its 13th edition, is essential. The club-like aspect of the American luxury hotel is best represented by James Remington McCarthy, *Peacock Alley: the Romance of the Waldorf-Astoria,* New York and London, 1931.

CHAPTER VIII

Emily James Putnam, *The Lady,* New York and London, 1910, is a wise and skilful analysis; Mary Sumner Benson, *Women in Eighteenth Century America,* New York, 1935, deals in a scholarly way with all classes. For the early background of feminism and society see Anne H. Wharton, *Salons Colonial and Republican,* Philadelphia and London, 1900, and *Colonial Days and Dames,* Philadelphia, 1908. Mrs. E. F. Ellet, *The Queens of American Society,* New York, 1867, and Lydia L. Gordon, *From Lady Washington to Mrs. Cleveland,* Boston, 1889, are light but informative. For the new consciousness of woman's place, Margaret Fuller Ossoli, *Woman in the Nineteenth Century,* Boston, 1855, and M. J. McIntosh, *Women in America,* New York, 1850, should be consulted though neither is narrowly social in its approach. Only a distant vista of smart society is glimpsed in Abba Goold Woolson, *Woman in American Society,* Boston, 1873, with an Introduction by John Greenleaf Whittier. Meade Minnigerode, *Some American Ladies,* New York and London, 1926, gives vignettes of Martha Washington, Abigail Adams, Dolly Madison, Elizabeth Monroe, Louisa Adams, Rachel Jackson, and Peggy Eaton. H. Addington Bruce, *Woman in the Making of America,* rev. ed., Boston, 1933; Mary R. Beard, ed., *America through Women's Eyes,* New York, 1933; Inez Haynes Irwin, *Angels and Amazons: a Hundred Years of American Women,* New York, 1933; and Sophonisba P. Breckenridge, *Women in the Twentieth Century,* New York and London, 1933, all deal with women in various rôles, with however some implication of the social. For Victorian psychology, Doctor C. Willett Cunnington, *Feminine Attitudes in the Nineteenth Century,* New York, 1936, about the British lady, should be compared with Furness's anthology *The Genteel Female,* from American letters and magazines, previously cited. The feminine viewpoint on dress and style is wittily discussed by Robert Cortes Holliday, *Unmentionables,* New York, 1933. Mrs. Burton Harrison's *Recollections Grave and Gay,* New York, 1911, is probably the best memoir left by a smart American hostess. Mrs. J. C. Croly, *The History of the Woman's Club Movement in America,* New York, 1898, presents in its 1184 pages a surplus of detail. The Year Book of the Colony Club, a memoir of the Acorn Club printed by that organization, information supplied by the secretaries of the Vincent and the Chilton Club, the Year Book for 1936–37 of the Association of Junior Leagues of America, Inc., articles in the *Junior League Magazine,* and information sent by the Executive Secretary of the Association of Junior Leagues, all afforded much help.

CHAPTER IX

Lucy M. Salmon, *The Newspaper and Authority,* New York, 1923, is a fine analysis of the press as a creator of values, social and otherwise. W. D. Bowman, *The Story of "The Times,"* New York, 1931, gives the history of the great London newspaper which has established the "court circular" style in social reporting. *Bohemian Days in Fleet-Street,* by "A Journalist," London, 1913, presents a memoir of society journalism as begun by the smart West End weeklies. For American journalism Frederic Hudson, *Journalism in the United States,* New York, 1873, gives much scattered information up to that date; recent historians of journalism,

A Note on Bibliography

such as James Melvin Lee, *History of American Journalism,* Boston and New York, 1923, offer surprisingly little about the society page. Some details may be gleaned from Allan Nevins, *The Evening Post: a Century of Journalism,* New York, 1922, and Don C. Seitz, *The James Gordon Bennetts: Father and Son,* Indianapolis, 1928. James L. Ford, *The Literary Shop and Other Tales,* New York, 1895, writes pleasantly of journalistic conventions, foibles, and pruderies in the United States. The hard-boiled cynicism of metropolitan journalism, with some social overtones and various inaccuracies, is shown in Stanley Walker, *City Editor,* New York, 1934, and *Mrs. Astor's Horse,* New York, 1936. The sole attempt carefully to present the feminine society editor and her place in current journalism is Ishbel Ross's *Ladies of the Press,* New York and London, 1936. The files of *Town Topics* and of *Collier's* for 1905–6 are indispensable to the history of that celebrated case; Robert R. Rowe, "Mann of *Town Topics*," *American Mercury,* July, 1926, pp. 271–280, is an amusing résumé.

CHAPTER X

W. P. Trent, "English Culture in Virginia," *Johns Hopkins Studies in History and Political Science,* 7th Series, V–VI, Baltimore, 1889, and H. M. Jones, *America and French Culture,* previously cited, are noteworthy studies of transatlantic social influence. R. E. Spiller, *The American in England,* New York, 1926, presents for the early nineteenth century the obverse of this subject. The genealogical works of Bolton, Browning, Crozier, and their amateur followers are mentioned in the text; the genealogical societies here named have all issued their brochures or prospectuses, upon which the author has drawn for information. J. D. Champlin, Jr., "The Manufacture of Ancestors," *Forum,* vol. X, pp. 565–72, contains instructive details. Grace King, *Mount Vernon on the Potomac: History of the Mount Vernon Ladies' Association,* New York, 1929, gives a full account of that organization. N. A. Woods, *The Prince of Wales in Canada and the United States,* London, 1861, and newspaper files for the year 1924 in regard to the visit of his grandson, are illuminating. The career of America's only self-created nobleman is told with vivacity by J. P. Marquand, *Lord Timothy Dexter of Newburyport,* New York, 1925. W. T. Stead, *The Americanization of the World,* New York and London, 1902, discusses the titled marriage of American heiresses; in verifying the records of such matches, the files of the New York *Times* so conveniently indexed since 1912, as well as *Burke's Peerage* and the *Almanach de Gotha,* proved useful. Price Collier, *England and the English from an American Point of View,* New York, 1909, offers a good deal of social commentary. For presentation at Court, the *Letters of Walter H. Page,* 2 vols., New York, 1922; Percy Armytage, *By the Clock of St. James's,* London, 1927; the Court Manual; information from the Royal Librarian at Windsor Castle, Mr. O. F. Morshead; and details supplied by Mr. Arthur Train on authority of Mr. Angus Fletcher, British Library of Information, New York City, were all of great help.

CHAPTER XI

John Allen Krout, "Annals of American Sport," *The Pageant of America,* vol. 15, New Haven, 1929, offers some good factual and pictorial matter. More detailed in its account of hunting, polo, coaching, and yachting, written by devotees of each sport, is *The Book of Sport,* ed. William Patten, New York, 1901. Francis B. Culver, *Blooded Horses of Colonial Days,* Baltimore, 1922; anon., *The South Carolina Jockey Club,* Charleston, 1857; and Fairfax Harrison, *The St. John's Island Stud: 1750–1788,* Richmond, 1931, are contributions to the early history of horse-racing. Frank Forester, *Horse and Horsemanship of the United States,* 2 vols., New

A Note on Bibliography

York, 1857, is notable; the facts about the author given in the text are drawn from W. S. Hunt, *Frank Forester: a Tragedy in Exile,* Newark, 1933. Copious are the writings of amateurs on hunting. Frank Sherman Peer, *Cross Country with Horse and Hound,* New York, 1902, and Anole Hunter (pseud.), *Let's Ride to Hounds,* New York, 1929, are representative; the latter, though not too accurate in detail, contains some interesting information on the various American hunts. F. Gray Griswold has devoted years to writing the memoirs of a sportsman's life, privately printed for the most part; his most recent volumes are *After Thoughts,* New York and London, 1936, and *The Horse and Buggy Days,* New York, 1936. Reginald W. Rives, *The Coaching Club,* New York, 1935, supplements the earlier *Manual of Coaching* by Fairman Rogers. For yachting, the first section of Charles A. Peverelly, *The Book of American Pastimes,* 2nd ed., New York, 1868, is useful; also Frederick S. Cozzens, *Yachts and Yachting,* New York, 1887, and W. P. Stephens, *American Yachting,* New York, 1904. For the first noted American pleasure craft see Francis B. Crowninshield, *The Story of George Crowninshield's Yacht "Cleopatra's Barge,"* Boston, 1913. For Newport see the monograph of W. B. Weeden on Colonial backgrounds, cited in the text; Hiram Fuller, *Belle Brittan on a Tour at Newport,* New York, 1858; Mrs. John King Van Rensselaer, *Newport, Our Social Capital,* Philadelphia, 1905; Henry James, "The Sense of Newport," *The American Scene,* New York, 1907; and "Newport, Rhode Island," *Fortune,* September, 1933, pp. 56 ff.

CHAPTER XII

O. G. Sonneck, *Early Opera in America,* New York, 1915; Julius Mattfeld, *A Hundred Years of Grand Opera in New York: 1825–1925,* New York, 1927; and Irving Kolodin, *The Metropolitan Opera: 1883–1935,* New York, 1936, are works of accuracy. Books previously cited on the history of Boston, Chicago, New Orleans, and San Francisco have information regarding the rise of grand opera in those cities. Eola Willis, *The Charleston Stage in the Eighteenth Century with Social Settings of the Time,* New York, 1924, gives a glimpse of social patronage in the early theatre. The sponsorship of painting by Society in former days may be seen in William Dunlap, *A History of . . . the Arts of Design in the United States* (first published 1834), revised by Bayley and Goodspeed, 3 vols., Boston, 1918. An account of the most famous and picturesque connoisseur in American society will be found in Morris Carter, *Isabella Stewart Gardner and Fenway Court,* Boston and New York, 1925. William S. Perry, *The History of the American Episcopal Church: 1587–1883,* 2 vols., Boston, 1885, is a standard source-book; see also Charles C. Tiffany, *A History of the Protestant Episcopal Church in the United States,* New York, 1895; W. W. Manross, *A History of the American Episcopal Church,* New York and Milwaukee, 1935; and E. L. Goodwin, *The Colonial Church in Virginia,* Milwaukee, 1927. For other denominations, M. L. Edwards, "Religious Forces in the United States, 1815–1830," *Mississippi Historical Review,* vol. V, pp. 434–449; W. W. Sweet, *The Story of Religions in America,* New York and London, 1930; and articles in the Schaff-Herzog *Encyclopedia of Religious Knowledge* and *The Catholic Encyclopedia.* Some of the problems in the first serious questioning of capitalism and its *raison d'être* are discussed by Harold Underwood Faulkner, *The Quest for Social Justice: 1898–1914,* New York, 1931; its present ramifications in book and magazine literature are almost endless.

INDEX

495

Index

496

Index

Index

Index

Hergesheimer, Joseph, 450
Hertz, John D., 440
Hewitt, Peter Cooper, 273
Heyward, Du Bose, 154; Edward, 154
Higginson, Major Henry Lee, 2, 268, 466
Hill, Mrs. Crawford, 344, 348, 349; Nathaniel P., 348
Hill, James J., 136
Hitchcock, Center, 270, 370; Thomas, 274, 439, 444; Mrs. Thomas, 442; Thomas, Jr., 444, 448, 457
Hoffman, Dean E. A., 478
Hoffman, Louis, 463
Hoffman, Ogden, 261
Hollywood, 151
Holmes, Oliver Wendell, 5, 9, 10, 278; Oliver Wendell, Jr., 10, 278
Hone, Catherine, 358; (family), 357; Mary, 358; Philip, 114, 118, 169, 170, 172, 208, 209, 261, 262, 358, 460; Robert S., 264
Hooper, Hooper, 227
Hooper, Mrs. Robert, 248
Hoover, Mrs. Theodore J., 397
Hopkins, Governor Stephen, 150
Hosack, Dr. David, 205
Hotel St. Charles (New Orleans), 288
Houston, Mrs. George H., 396
How to Behave, 168
Howard, Thomas, 228
Howe, Julia Ward, 89, 184, 324, 333, 456, 465; Maude, 89, 456
Howe, Bishop Mark Antony de Wolfe, 268, 478
Howells, William Dean, 268
Howland, G. C., 460
Howland, S. S., 447; Mrs. S. S., 338
Hoyt, H. S., 265
Huck, Frieda (Baroness Komosky), 414; Marie (Marchioness Spinola), 414
Huger (family), 232
Hummel, Abraham H., 375
Humphrey, John, 38; Lady Susan, 38
Huneker, James G., 187
Hunt (fox), Brandywine, 446; Casanova, 445; Green Spring Valley, 445; Harford, 445; Keswick, 445; Loudun, 445; Middleburg, 445; Orange County, 445; Pickering, 446; Queens County, 447; Radnor, 446; Rose Tree Fox Hunting Club, 446; Warrentown, 445
Hunt, Richard, 254
Huntington, Collis P., 129, 198, 376, 378, 413, 464; Clara (Princess von Hatzfeld-Wildenburg), 413
Huntington, Henry E., 469
Hutchins, Maude Phelps McVeigh, 468; Robert M., 468
Hutchinson, Anne, 298
Hutchinson, B. P., 297, 468
Hutton, Barbara, 2, 151, 190; Edward F., 5; Franklyn L., 406
Hyde, James Hazen, 227, 371, 374, 375

I

I. C. Sorosis (Pi Beta Phi), 287
Ingraham, Phoenix, 228
Institute Society (Harvard), 277
Insull, Samuel, 235, 467
International Polo Matches, 274
Irish Club, 255
Irving, Washington, 112
Iselin, Adrian, 121, Mrs. Adrian, 121; Adrian II, 121, 384; C. Oliver, 440, 453; Eleanor Jay, 121; (family), 120, 121, 263, 429, 480; Georgine, 121; Isaac, 121; Mrs. Oliver, 437; William Jay, 121
Italian Opera House, 460, 461
Ivy Club (Princeton), 283, 284, 285
Izard, Ralph, 231, 308, 309; Mrs. Ralph, 308, 309

J

Jackson, Andrew, 76, 91–95, 296, 297; Mrs. Andrew, 91
Jacobs, Henry Barton, 270; Mrs. Henry Barton, 230
James, Henry, 456, 458
Jay (family), 51, 197, 230; John, 56, 213, 256, 305; Mrs. John, 199, 204, 305, 309, 312; Colonel William, 174, 440, 447

Jay, John C., 451
Jay, Julia, 410
Jefferson, Thomas, 72, 76, 82, 84–89, 300, 304
Jelke (family), 465; Frazier, 147
Jerome, Leonard, 407, 440, 454
Jerome Park, 154
Jerome, William Travers, 378
Jews (wealth), 152–156
Jockey Club, the, 360; (American), 154, 434, 439, 440; (Kentucky), 434; (Louisville), 434; (Maryland), 431; (Pioneer, San Francisco), 434; (South Carolina), 32, 429; (Virginia), 431; (Washington), 432
Johnson, Andrew, 100, 106
Johnson, Lady Arbella, 38, 298
Johnston, Lt.-General Sir Henry, 153; Rebecca Franks, 153
Jones, David B., 285
Jones, E. Clarence, 375
Jones, Pembroke, 142, 152, 456, 457
Jones, Ruth E., 363, 364
Jones, Samuel, 262
Joy, Sally, 363
Juilliard (family), 465; Foundation, 465
Jumel, Madame Stephen, 163
Junior League, the, 327, 328, 329

K

Kahn, Otto H., 155, 464, 467
Kane, De Lancey, 174; Mrs. De Lancey, 121; De Lancey A., 440, 441; (family), 212, 464; Grenville, 273; S. Nicholson, 440
Kappa Alpha, 286
Kappa Alpha Theta, 287
Kappa Kappa Gamma, 287
Kaufman, Louis G., 235
Keene, Foxhall, 439, 445; James R., 375, 378, 438, 439; Sara Jay Daingerfield, 439
Keller, Charles M., 232; Louis, 232, 233, 234, 372
"Keller's Baltrusol and Pacific," 233, 234
Kent, A. Atwater, 67
Keteltas (family), 59, 197
King, Archibald Gracie, 183, 214; Mrs. Archibald Gracie, 456
King, Charles, 357
King, Clarence, 456
King, Edward, 269
King, Frederick Gore, 198, 229; James Gore, 205, 401; Mrs. James Gore, 229
King, Governor John Alsop, 262; Rufus, 68, 262
Kip (family), 59; Leonard, 60
Kip, Bishop William Ingraham, 478
Kirkland, Caroline, 360
Kissam (family), 295
Kitten Club, 264
Kiwanis Club, 287
Knickerbocker Club, 10, 209, 254, 263–265
Knights of Pythias, 276
Knox, Henry, 304; Mrs. Henry, 304
Knudsen (family), 147
Kountz (family), 150
Kresge, Katharine, 415
Krishnamurti, 476

L

Labouchère, Henry, 363
Ladies' Association of Mount Vernon, 397
Ladies Library Society, 324
Lamont, Corliss, 90
Lamont, Thomas, 34
La Montagne, Edward, 265
Land (family), 119
Lawrence, Prescott, 270
Lawrence, Bishop William, 478
Lawrence, William Beach, 269, 456
Lawson, Thomas W., 375
Lazarus (family), 153, 463
"Lebanon," the (tavern), 257
Ledger, the (Philadelphia), 365
Lee, Blair, 283
Lee (family), 35, 104, 105
Lee, Colonel Henry, 268
Lee, Ivy L., 473
Lee, Colonel Richard, 19
Lee, General Robert E., 19, 153
Leeds (family), 457
Leeds, William B., 340; Mrs. William B., 415; William B., Jr., 415

499

Index

Index

Index

Index

Index